MARKETING *the core*

FOURTH CANADIAN EDITION

ROGER A. KERIN
Southern Methodist University

STEVEN W. HARTLEY
University of Denver

WILLIAM RUDELIUS
University of Minnesota

CHRISTINA CLEMENTS
Humber College Institute of Technology & Advanced Learning

HARVEY SKOLNICK
Sheridan Institute of Technology and Advanced Learning

ARSENIO BONIFACIO
Sheridan Institute of Technology and Advanced Learning

 McGraw-Hill Ryerson

MARKETING: THE CORE
Fourth Canadian Edition

The Internet addresses listed in the text were accurate at the time of publication. The inclusion of a Web site does not indicate an endorsement by the authors or McGraw-Hill Ryerson, and McGraw-Hill Ryerson does not guarantee the accuracy of the information presented at these sites.

ISBN-13: 978-1-25-903-070-3
ISBN-10: 1-25-903070-9

2 3 4 5 6 7 8 9 10 CTPS 1 9 8 7 6 5

Printed and bound in China.

Care has been taken to trace ownership of copyright material contained in this text; however, the publisher will welcome any information that enables them to rectify any reference or credit for subsequent editions.

Director of Product Management: Rhondda McNabb
Senior Product Manager: Karen Fozard
Executive Marketing Manager: Joy Armitage Taylor
Product Developer: Amy Rydzanicz
Senior Product Team Associate: Marina Seguin
Supervising Editor: Stephanie Gay
Photo/Permissions Editor: Tracy Leonard
Copy Editor: Michael Kelly
Plant Production Coordinator: Sheryl MacAdam
Manufacturing Production Coordinator: Emily Hickey
Cover and Interior Design: Dave Murphy
Cover Image: HEAD Canada
Page Layout: Miriam Brant/ArtPlus Limited
Printer: China Translation & Printing Services Limited

Library and Archives Canada Cataloguing in Publication

Kerin, Roger A., author Marketing : the core / Roger A. Kerin, Southern Methodist University, Steven W. Hartley, University of Denver, William Rudelius, University of Minnesota, Christina Clements, Humber College Institute of Technology and Advanced Learning, Harvey Skolnick, Sheridan College Institute of Technology and Advanced Learning, Arsenio Bonifacio, Sheridan College Institute of Technology and Advanced Learning.
—Fourth Canadian edition.

Includes bibliographical references and index.

ISBN 978-1-25-903070-3 (pbk.)

   1. Marketing--Textbooks. I. Rudelius, William, author II. Skolnick, Harvey, 1948-, author III. Hartley, Steven William, author IV. Clements, Christina, author V. Bonifacio, Arsenio, author VI. Title.

HF5415.M374 2015   658.8   C2014-905548-X

Author Profiles

Roger A. Kerin is the Harold C. Simmons Distinguished Professor of Marketing at the Edwin L. Cox School of Business, Southern Methodist University, in Dallas, Texas. Professor Kerin holds a B.A. (magna cum laude), M.B.A., and Ph.D. from the University of Minnesota. His teaching and research interests lie in marketing planning and strategy, product management, financial aspects of marketing, and marketing research. Professor Kerin is a frequent participant in executive development programs and is also an active consultant on matters of marketing planning and strategy. Professor Kerin has published and authored several texts and many articles on marketing. He also serves on numerous journal editorial review boards and is currently a member of the Board of Governors of the Academy of Marketing Science.

Steven W. Hartley is professor of marketing in the Daniels College of Business at the University of Denver. He holds bachelor of mechanical engineering, M.B.A., and Ph.D. degrees from the University of Minnesota. Dr. Hartley was formerly the chair of the Department of Marketing at the University of Denver, and he has taught at the University of Colorado, the University of Minnesota, and in several executive development programs. His teaching interests include principles of marketing, marketing research, and marketing planning. Dr. Hartley's research has appeared in many leading marketing publications. He is an active consultant to several prominent U.S. corporations and is active in many professional organizations, including the American Marketing Association, the Academy of Marketing Science, and the Marketing Educators' Association.

William Rudelius holds the Endowed Chair in Global Marketing at the Graduate School of Business of the University of St. Thomas in Minnesota. He holds a B.S. degree in mechanical engineering from the University of Wisconsin and an M.B.A. in marketing and Ph.D. in applied economics from the Wharton School of the University of Pennsylvania. Professor Rudelius has co-authored other marketing textbooks. His articles have appeared in leading academic journals. During the past 10 years, he has taught extensively in Europe. He serves on the board of directors for several business and not-for-profit organizations.

Christina Clements is an award-winning professor from the Business School at Humber College Institute of Technology & Advanced Learning in Ontario. She is renowned for the creativity and knowledge she brings to the field of marketing education. She is a recipient of the Leadership in Faculty Teaching Award, honouring Ontario's best university and college faculty, from the Ministry of Training, Colleges and Universities, and the Distinguished Faculty award from the Humber Institute of Technology and Advanced Learning. She holds an M.B.A. from the Bradford University Management Centre in the U.K. and a master certificate in Internet marketing from the University of San Francisco. She has a wealth of experience in marketing and advertising—from both client and agency perspectives—in consumer packaged goods, cosmetics, food service, and personal care. She now channels her practical experience, knowledge, and creativity into the field of education, by teaching, managing social media sites, and developing written materials, online resources, and educational tools. Her passion lies in teaching marketing communications and Internet marketing courses. She is frequently called upon to mentor others in the field of education.

Harvey Skolnick has recently retired as a marketing professor in the School of Business at the Sheridan Institute of Technology and Advanced Learning. He is the author of many articles that have appeared in Marketing magazine and other business publications. He holds an M.B.A. from the University of Toronto, specializing in marketing, and a B.Sc. from McGill University, specializing in psychology. Professor Skolnick's teaching interests include principles of marketing, consumer behaviour, integrated marketing communications, and marketing management. He has also previously taught at York University and the University of Toronto.

Arsenio Bonifacio teaches in the Faculty of Business of Sheridan Institute of Technology and Advanced Learning. He facilitates marketing and financial planning courses, applying his experience as a marketing executive in the investment industry to the classroom. Arsenio holds an M.B.A. from Wilfrid Laurier University and a B.Sc. from McMaster University. His career in marketing has involved leading teams and initiatives in Canada, the United States, and the United Kingdom. Arsenio gained practical experience in sales, advertising, public relations, direct marketing, market research, and recruitment marketing. Aside from his teaching, Arsenio is a member of the executive leadership team for one of the largest credit unions in Ontario and is responsible for deepening member relationships within the organization.

Brief Contents

Contents

Part 4 Focusing on New and Evolving Areas

Part 5 Putting It All Together

Preface

Welcome to the exciting and dynamic field of marketing! Boosted by technological change, this fast-paced environment quickly evolves and today challenges marketers to stay informed and knowledgeable on new marketing approaches, regulations, and ideas. New digital approaches have surfaced in social media marketing, mobile marketing, and customer relationship management programs, as well as in other Internet marketing pathways that may be integrated into offline or online marketing practices.

We now see real-time marketing and content marketing approaches used in increasingly creative ways to reach consumers, businesses, and organizations. We also see conventional marketing approaches used to reach target markets and new regulations put in place to ensure a smooth transition into this new marketing reality. In all instances, marketing messages now compete in a sea of information that floods people's daily lives, which challenges marketing programs to be noticed, to be relevant, and to be engaging. This is the new marketing reality that uses metrics to monitor and measure marketing performance and analytics to reveal insights and areas of improvement.

The fourth Canadian edition of *Marketing: The Core* reflects this new marketing reality with its standard features as well as new elements and content that are designed to engage. A new chapter, "Mobile Marketing and Social Media Marketing," focuses on these new marketing approaches, and a revised research chapter, renamed "Market Research, Metrics, and Analytics," includes a significant overlay of easily understood metrics and analytics. There is also a focus on financial fluency that has been integrated into the chapters on pricing and strategic planning in a way that students can understand. Each chapter is boosted by new content, examples, and features to ensure the text reflects the very latest online and offline marketing approaches in Canada.

The fourth Canadian edition of *Marketing: The Core* returns with its popular magazine-style format that engages with its visual appeal, direct writing style, sound pedagogical features, and fresh new content. New features include *Chapter Features* and *Chapter Outlines* that open each chapter and that flag interesting topics and help students navigate chapter content.

New pedagogical elements include *infographics* and *video integration,* which identifies when a video exists in the text's companion Connect website, as well as newly introduced critical-thinking *end-of-chapter* features that help apply and bring the material to life. These elements are in addition to the highly rated opening chapter vignettes, Marketing NewsFlash boxes, and Focus on Ethics boxes that are all new and interspersed throughout each chapter.

The fourth Canadian edition of *Marketing: The Core* is designed so that students learn and enjoy learning about marketing. It is current. It is real. It reflects marketing in Canada.

Text Organization and Content

Marketing: The Core, Fourth Canadian Edition, is divided into five parts:

Part 1, "Understanding Marketing," looks first at what marketing is and how it creates customer value and customer relationships (Chapter 1). Chapter 2 analyzes the major environmental factors in our changing marketing environment.

Part 2, "Understanding Markets and Their Behaviour," first describes, in Chapter 3, how individual consumers reach buying decisions. Chapter 4 examines the marketing research function, metrics and analytics, and how information about prospective consumers is linked to marketing strategy and decisions. Chapter 5 looks at industrial and organizational buyers and how they make purchase decisions. The process of segmenting and targeting markets and positioning products appears in Chapter 6.

Part 3, "Designing Marketing Strategies and Marketing Mix Elements," covers the four Ps of marketing: product, price, place, and promotion. The product element is divided into two chapters. Chapter 7 looks at the way existing products, services, and brands are managed. Chapter 8 discusses the development of new products and the product life cycle. Pricing is discussed, focusing on the way organizations set prices (Chapter 9). Two chapters address the place aspects of marketing: "Marketing Channels and Supply Chain" (Chapter 10) and "Retailing and Wholesaling" (Chapter 11). Chapter 12 discusses marketing communications from an online and offline perspective, including integrated approaches.

Part 4, "Focusing on New and Evolving Areas," includes a new Chapter 13, "Mobile Marketing and Social Media Marketing," as well as Chapter 14, "Customer Relationship Management," which takes a deeper look into customer relationship management.

Part 5, "Putting It All Together," provides an overview of the strategic marketing planning process that occurs in an organization and includes a new marketing plan example as an appendix on **connect**.

What's New? *Marketing: The Core*

The fourth Canadian edition of *Marketing: The Core* builds on the strengths of the previous editions, adding new and exciting elements that make the material even more interactive and engaging. Our authors go to extreme lengths to interview respected Canadian marketers so that content is fresh and accurately reflects current marketing practices. The authors also turn to the teaching environment so that each chapter includes solid pedagogical features that help students learn and faculty teach. The freshness of this new edition is reflected in the following:

- *Enhanced magazine-style format.* The popular magazine-style format returns with its fresh visual appeal, direct writing style, and active-learning techniques that challenge students to understand and enjoy learning about marketing. New features have been added to this edition to enhance learning, as noted below.
- *New chapter features and outlines.* New to this edition are chapter roadmaps that start each chapter with a splash page that highlights newsy features within the chapter and creates a path that guides readers through the chapter and its content.
- *New infographics.* Each chapter now includes a vibrant infographic that visually provides perspective and metrics on a topic. These infographics help students focus on the importance of data gathering and analysis for marketers and help them become familiar with this increasingly popular way that marketers visually portray metrics.
- *New video integration.* The fourth Canadian edition integrates videos within the text, using video icons to designate when an appropriate video exists

within the companion Connect website to enhance learning. These video icons may accompany an opening chapter vignette, a Marketing NewsFlash box, or a separate discussion within the text. Video cases also accompany these videos and reside within the Instructors' Manual and within the **connect** website. These cases may revisit an opening chapter vignette or a Marketing NewsFlash, or include enhanced content that accompanies the text narrative. Videos focus on interesting iconic brands such as Tim Hortons and Google. Others reveal census information from Statistics Canada, provide insights into social media practices from the Canadian Marketing Association, and use Salesforce to explain the importance of mobile marketing approaches. Successful Canadian digital agency Rich Media discusses digital marketing techniques, while Leo Burnett gives us a taste of non-profit marketing with its Raising the Roof campaigns that focus on homelessness awareness in Canada. Students will also be interested in the ICA Next Generation Day video that focuses on working in the ad agency world, as well as the burrito-eating contest created by Mucho Burrito to reach its fans and the TACKLA video that explains an innovative new hockey skate, just to name a few. Video icons are hot-linked within the eBook.

- All videos are also conveniently packaged together on a DVD for faculty and accessible for faculty and students through the online **connect** website, the book's online learning centre.
- *New opening chapter vignettes.* The popular opening chapter vignettes return with all-new content that provides a glimpse into real marketing situations, with advice from senior business professionals in Canada. The discussions centre on many exciting brands that will be familiar to students, such as Mucho Burrito, Molson Canadian, Telus, HEAD, President's Choice, and TACKLA as well as many other stellar brands and companies.
- *New Marketing NewsFlash and Focus on Ethics boxes.* These popular features return with all-new content, meticulously researched to provide perspective on the latest marketing approaches. Examples are the Dove Real Beauty sketches, the Bell Let's Talk campaign, the Raising the Roof non-profit organization, and Tim Hortons coffee.
- *New end-of-chapter critical thinking features.* New to the fourth Canadian edition are end-of-chapter "Video Clip Questions" and "Infographic Data Analysis" assignments that complement the hands-on assignments to help students interact with a topic and provide material for in-class or home assignments.

- *New chapter on mobile marketing and social media marketing.* To ensure that students are up to date on the latest marketing approaches, a new chapter on mobile marketing and social media marketing has been created to explain the intricacies of this fast-moving area. Employers expect students to understand this area, and this chapter provides students with a solid knowledge base.
- *New sections on metrics, analytics, and big data.* Marketing requires students to understand the metrics and analytics used by the industry. Entirely new sections have been created on this topic in a newly titled chapter, "Market Research, Metrics, and Analytics," which explains this topic and discusses the issues surrounding big data.
- *Updated sections on forecasting, budgeting, financial analysis, and profit-and-loss statements.* Marketers are involved in forecasting and budgeting, and use financial analyses and profit-and-loss statements to evaluate programs and brand success. These areas are enhanced in the fourth Canadian edition through discussions in the pricing chapter and the strategic planning chapter.
- *New marketing plan appendix.* A brand new marketing plan example and template has been built into the **connect** online learning centre. This example was developed in collaboration with marketing consultant Glenn Cressman, from Share of Marketing, to ensure that it reflects current marketing planning approaches.
- *Updated Instructors' Manual.* The highly rated Instructor's Manual returns with updated chapter summaries, answers to questions from the book, and additional questions that can be used with students in the classroom. The popular "Bring It to Life" section contains new worksheets and handouts for video cases, Marketing NewsFlash boxes, as well as in-class activities and metrics assignments.

Chapter-Specific Additions

In addition to an updated narrative for each chapter and all-new opening vignettes, Markeing NewsFlash and Focus on Ethics boxes, databoxes, and infographics, the following new topics have been added:

Chapter 1: Marketing Fundamentals
- Business sustainability
- Greenwashing
- Real-time marketing
- Content marketing

- Mobile marketing
- Social media marketing
- Metrics and analytics
- Marketing regulations and ethical considerations

Chapter 2: The Marketing Environment
- New Statistics Canada demographic data from the latest census
- Social media monitoring tools
- New media-viewing trends
- Canadians' use of technology
- The Canadian Anti-Fraud Centre
- The Canadian Wireless Telecommunications Association (CWTA)
- The Mobile Marketing Association (MMA)
- The Wireless Code
- Common short code guidelines
- The *Privacy Act*
- Canada's anti-spam legislation (CASL)
- Online behavioural advertising (OBA)
- Digital Advertising Alliance of Canada (DAAC)
- Steps in a marketing environment scan

Chapter 3: Consumer Behaviour
- The impact of online technology on consumer purchase behaviour
- The impact of mobile technology on consumer purchase behaviour
- Prizm C2 clusters, courtesy of Environics Analytics
- Expanded content on Canadian subcultures

Chapter 4: Market Research, Metrics, and Analytics
- Metrics
- Analytics
- Dashboards
- Market share
- Brand development index (BDI)
- Web analytics
- Social media analytics
- Predictive analytics
- Big data
- Recency, frequency, and monetary value analysis (RFM)
- Data mining
- Data: structured data, unstructured data, semi-structured data, and legacy data

Chapter 5: B2B Marketing
- Cross-border strategic partnerships

- Content marketing
- Sustainability considerations in B2B marketing
- Top global exporters
- Largest global companies

Chapter 6: Segmentation, Targeting, and Positioning

- Revised definitions for segmentation strategies: mass, segment, niche, and individualized strategies
- Enhanced figure on target market profiles
- Personas
- Segmentation analytics—Pitney Bowes Psyte HD, Environics Prizm C2, and SuperDemographics
- Recency, frequency, and monetary value (RFM) analysis

Chapter 7: Products and Brands

- Customer service Consumerology report
- The role of websites for online brands
- New product mix and product depth
- Ipsos' *Most Influential Brands* study
- Brand influence factors
- Sub-brands

Chapter 8: New Product Development

- Drivers of new product success
- Enhanced sections on product life cycle stages

Chapter 9: Pricing

- Enhanced examples of pricing strategies in practice
- Enhanced sections on forecasting and financials
- Enhanced sections on legal and ethical considerations, including price fixing

Chapter 10: Marketing Channels and Supply Chain

- Enhanced examples of supply chain in practice
- Omni-channel marketing
- QR codes
- Impact of the Canadian restaurant industry on the economy

Chapter 11: Retailing and Wholesaling

- The impact of mobile technology on retailing
- Sustainability in retailing
- Top online shopping sites

Chapter 12: Marketing Communications

- Connected consumers
- Real-time marketing
- Content marketing

- Social media marketing
- Mobile marketing
- The Canadian Wireless Telecommunications Association (CWTA)
- CWTA short code guidelines

Chapter 13: Mobile Marketing and Social Media Marketing

- Mobile marketing
- Social media marketing
- Mobile devices and mobile usage
- Mobile marketing tools: mobile web, mobile apps, mobile advertising
- Mobile sales promotional tools: text messaging, e-mail, voice messaging, and 2D barcodes
- Proximity marketing: Bluetooth. near field communications (NFC), radio frequency identification (RFID) tags, augmented reality (AR), mobile check-in, and mobile discovery
- Mobile marketing regulations: the Wireless Code and common short code guidelines
- The Mobile Marketing Association's (MMA) Code of Conduct
- Mobile marketing best practices
- Characteristics of social media
- Social media networks in Canada: Facebook, YouTube, Google+, LinkedIn, Instagram, Twitter, Tumblr, and Pinterest
- Planning social media marketing
- Measuring social media marketing
- Best practices in social media marketing

Chapter 14: Customer Relationship Management

- Enhanced examples of customer relationship management (CRM) in practice
- Customer satisfaction
- Customer experience management (CEM)
- Loyalty program participation

Chapter 15: Strategic Marketing Planning

This chapter on strategic marketing planning has been placed at the end of the text so that students can gain a greater understanding of marketing before embarking on this more complex topic. The following new content has been included:

- Strategy defined for business versus marketing plans
- Corporate social responsibility
- Canada's most profitable companies
- Marketing budgets and financials

A Student's Guide to *Marketing: The Core*

Marketing: The Core offers an array of features to help readers learn and apply marketing concepts.

Each chapter opens with a **vignette** on a Canadian marketing situation or program. No revamp of an article here—only current facts, real approaches, and tangible examples from one-on-one interviews with marketers in Canada. New **Chapter Features** and **Chapter Outlines** give an overview of the key features and provide an outline of each chapter. Clear and precise **Learning Objectives** help students preview chapter content and study effectively. **Reality Check** questions appear at the end of each vignette.

Chapter 2

the marketing environment

LEARNING OBJECTIVES

LO¹ Understand the importance of a marketing environment scan and how it is used to improve marketing programs

LO² Describe the elements of a marketing environment scan and summarize the trends affecting each area

LO³ Outline the current demographic and socio-cultural influences that affect marketing approaches

LO⁴ Explain how changes in the economic environment influence consumer purchase behaviour

LO⁵ Discuss the technological developments shaping current marketing practices

LO⁶ Describe the different forms of competition and the regulatory forces that shape the marketing industry

LO⁷ List the steps in a marketing environment scan

We start by looking at a new iPhone app for touring Ontario wine country, GrapeTrail, created by marketer and entrepreneur Mohammed Asaduallah and his development team Mark Gage and Kirisanth Subramanian. Asaduallah takes us inside this business, providing a glimpse into how elements in the marketing environment were considered when creating this product. GrapeTrail is a free wine tour app developed by Canadian start-up GrapeTrail Inc., a company that develops mobile marketing solutions for the wine industry. Products in its suite have to be simple and easy-to-use and create meaningful experiences. Once the app is downloaded, users can quickly discover local wineries by region, create a personal itinerary, and have GrapeTrail guide them through the local wine country with its intuitive in-app navigation system. All of this takes place within the app, an important feature since users today demand a seamless experience, and most competitive apps in the market require users to step outside the app and use Google Maps for functionality.

"Australia is where it started," explains Asaduallah. "While living in Australia, I noticed local wineries had little presence on mobile devices—apps were expensive and the mobile web was daunting. Wineries lacked digital expertise and funds to hire a professional." In Canada, Mohammed noticed similar circumstances and flipped this into an opportunity to create a wine tour app—no easy task and one that required a thorough review of the market.

Asaduallah evaluated demographic and socio-cultural trends, looked at the economic environment, reviewed consumers' use of technology, thoroughly analyzed competitive apps, and examined regulations—all the elements in a marketing environment scan that we discuss in this chapter. GrapeTrail analyzed these factors to ensure it considered the latest trends, concerns, and opportunities, and addressed potential issues.

Let's look at the factors Asaduallah reviewed to develop the app and to make it successful. Specifically, the following were noted:

- **Demographic factors:** The Canadian population is aging and is well educated and knowledgeable. The aging baby boomers are active, relatively affluent, and interested in travel and new experiences. Young couples are having children later in life, which frees up leisure time to enjoy local and international tourist

Chapter Features

GrapeTrail App in Action
Marketing environment scan helps create wine country app.

Statistics Canada— Census Update
Canada characterized by more centenarians, an evolving family structure, and a multitude of languages.

Understanding Millennials
Jobs and debt are top concerns. Social networking is key for communications.

Baby Boomers—Technophobes?
Ipsos Inter@ctive Reid Report concludes baby boomers keep pace with technology.

Media Habits in Flux
Binge viewing, social TV surfaces. Device usage is platform agnostic.

New Marketing Regulations Clamp Down on Spam
Online behavioural advertising guidelines and anti-spam laws introduced.

Ethics—You've Been Hacked!
Canadian Anti-Fraud Centre cracks down on scareware scams.

Visit your favourite Ontario wineries with GrapeTrail
Now available on the App Store

Chapter Outline:
GrapeTrail app → Marketing environment → Demographic and socio-cultural forces → Economic and technology forces → Competitive and regulatory forces → Steps in marketing environment scan

reality CHECK ✓

As you read Chapter 1, refer back to the Mucho Burrito vignette to answer the following questions:

- Is Mucho Burrito a good, a service, or an idea?
- Who is the target market for Mucho Burrito?
- What marketing tools does Mucho Burrito use to create relationships with its consumers?

Infographics are used to draw attention to metrics that relate to a topic within the chapter and to help students become familiar with this visual approach to presenting marketing information.

Real metrics are used to emphasize points within the text through standalone data boxes that bring attention to the importance of metrics in marketing. **Data boxes** present tangible facts and numerical examples of elements discussed in the text, and serve as important examples of how metrics are used by the industry.

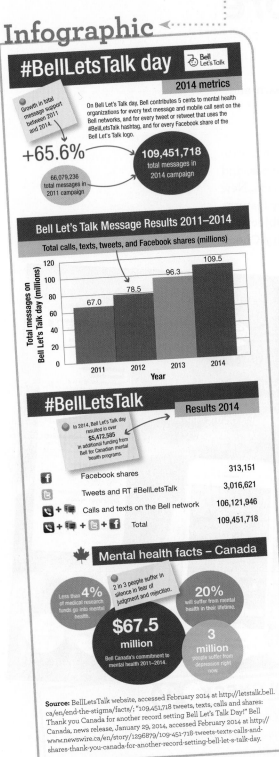

Infographic

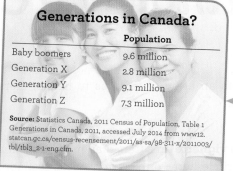

Generations in Canada?

	Population
Baby boomers	9.6 million
Generation X	2.8 million
Generation Y	9.1 million
Generation Z	7.3 million

Source: Statistics Canada, 2011 Census of Population, Table 1 Generations in Canada, 2011, accessed July 2014 from www12. statcan.gc.ca/census-recensement/2011/as-sa/98-311-x/2011003/tbl/tbl3_2-1-eng.cfm.

Marketing Tips showcase valuable thoughts from real-world marketers that are relevant to the topics discussed in each chapter.

Marketing Tip

"Brands need to be nurtured and respond to evolving consumer needs and competitive challenges while remaining true to their core DNA."

—Ian Gordon, senior vice president, Loblaw Companies Ltd.

The Street House installation was a success. Over a two-day period, 2,200 people visited the house and over 100,000 people acted to help the homelessness issue.

▶ Video Raising the Roof

Video integration icons point to areas within the text where a video from the companion Connect website can be used to illustrate a point.

Ask Yourself checkpoints, found near the end of major sections in each chapter, allow students to test their comprehension of the chapter material before moving on.

ask yourself

1. *What is the difference between a consumer's disposable and discretionary income?*

2. *What is the most common form of competition?*

3. *What are the indirect competitors to a bag of Doritos chips?*

Marketing NewsFlash boxes provide exciting, current examples of marketing in action, making the material relevant and memorable. **Focus on Ethics boxes** focus on current topics of ethical and social concern. Discussion questions at the end of each box encourage students to apply marketing concepts and critically assess marketing situations.

focus on *Ethics*

You've Been Hacked!

Did your computer just freeze and a pop-up message from the RCMP announce that your computer is locked as it is linked to child pornography? The logo looks authentic and a fine needs to be settled to pay for the offence. The Canadian Anti-Fraud Centre warns that this is a *scareware* scam, designed to frighten users into immediately paying the purported $100 fine (or more) through the visible online payment button. This scam is cleverly designed, understanding that some recipients may prefer to pay the fine, rather than report it to police and incur additional hassles. Nonetheless, over 1,500 people in Canada logged complaints with the Canadian Anti-Fraud Centre on this very issue, which also surfaced in the U.K. Th

computer of the malware that immobilized the device, not pay the fraudsters, and report the incident to the Canadian Anti-Fraud Centre at **www.antifraudcentre.ca**.

Scareware scams infect computers through malware that comes from infected links, attachments, or downloads often associated with spam messages or pop-up ads. Canadian law enforcement recently cooperated with the FBI and other authorities in Sweden, Denmark, the U.K., France, Germany, Romania, Lithuania, Latvia, Ukraine, the Netherlands, and Cyprus to help foil another scareware scam where pop-up ads sold fake anti-virus software for $129 per download. Over 950,000 unsuspecting victims were defrauded of over $71 million. Eventually, one of the European perpetrators was extradited to the U.S.

Scams should be reported to the Canadian Anti-Fraud Centre.

and sentenced to four years in jail and fined $650,000.

The Canadian Anti-Fraud Centre advises us to turn on pop-up blockers and to never open spam e-mail or unknown attachments. In addition, consumers should not click on spam pop-up images to download anti-viral programs and always use up-to-date, trusted, anti-virus software. If you are the recipient of a scareware scam, you are asked to contact your local police department and the Canadian Anti-Fraud Centre.[66]

Question

1. Do you t
Why or

2. Many c
of the c

marketing *NewsFlash*

Logos Influence Behaviour

Marketers know that a logo encapsulates consumers' feelings about the company that are formed over time. The sentimental brand association of a logo can be so powerful that it inspires consumers to take actions they might not have otherwise intended to take. According to a University of Toronto study, even a glimpse of a fast-food logo can make a person more impatient and impulsive with money. "The logo activates associations with the brand," explains study co-author Chen-Bo Zhong, professor of organizational behaviour and human resource management at the university.

In one part of the study, the fast-food group saw logos of McDonald's and KFC; the control group instead viewed pictures of two generic low-priced dinners. Afterward, they were all asked if they would like to receive a higher amount of money in one week or a lower amount of money

immediately. Those exposed to the fast-food logos were much more likely to want the money immediately. "Fast food seemed to have made people impatient in a manner that could put their economic interest at risk," the study concludes.

A 2008 Duke University study found people who looked at the Apple logo scored higher on a creativity test than those who had looked at an IBM logo—presumably because they were reflecting the differing brand traits they associated with those logos. The stronger the brand "personality," the stronger the association, Mr. Zhong said. In the case of fast food, logos from popular chains such as McDonald's promote associations with fast food, namely relating to immediate gratification and saving time.

Recent research from the University of Michigan found children

as young as three can recognize brand logos and products. Children viewed logos of 50 brands across 16 product categories, including fast food, toys, electronics, and apparel, and were asked questions about the brands. The results showed that a majority of the children recognized logos of fast-food restaurants.[15]

Questions

1. When you think of the four companies discussed in this example, what associations come to mind?

2. Give some examples of logos that elicit positive associations and those that elicit negative associations.

AdAlyze features give students the opportunity to critically evaluate and dissect the message of an actual print advertisement, helping them understand real-world application.

At the end of each chapter, the **Summary** and list of **Key Terms** help students review the chapter's most important concepts. **Hands On...Apply Your Knowledge** assignments direct students back to the beginning of the chapter to solve a practical marketing scenario related to the opening vignette. **Chapter Vignette... Reminder** features point students back to the opening vignette to answer its Reality Check questions, which test their understanding of chapter topics. New **Video Clip...Questions** sections highlight a relevant video that resides within the online ▤ **CONNECT** website and ask students to answer questions. New **Infographic... Data Analysis** features focus students on relevant metrics and asks them to complete an exercise such as updating the data and analyzing changes. Video cases, quizzes, comprehension and discussion questions, and additional resources are available within ▤ **CONNECT**.

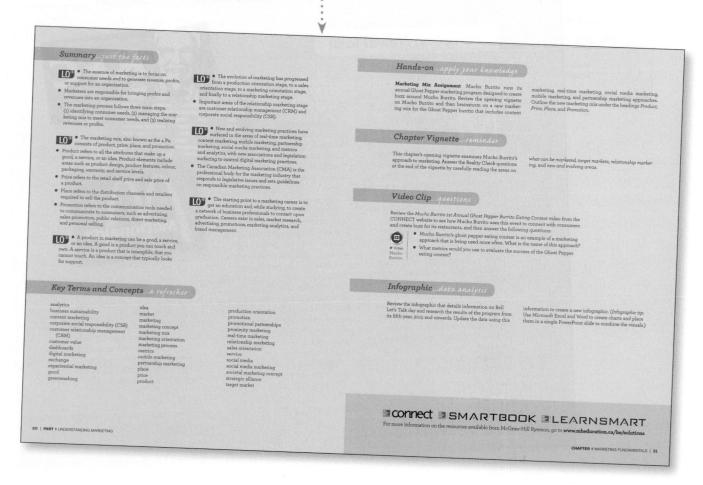

Supplements Guide to *Marketing: The Core*

To help instructors and students meet today's teaching and learning challenges, *Marketing: The Core*, Fourth Canadian Edition, offers a complete, integrated supplements package.

For Instructors

McGraw-Hill connect

McGraw-Hill **connect**™ is a web-based assignment and assessment platform that gives students the means to better connect with their coursework, with their instructors, and with the important concepts that they will need to know for success now and in the future. With **connect**, instructors can deliver assignments, quizzes, and tests easily online. Students can practise important skills at their own pace and on their own schedule. With **connect**, students also get 24/7 online access to an eBook—an online edition of the text—to aid them in successfully completing their work, wherever and whenever they choose. The **connect** Instructor Library provides all the critical resources instructors will need to build their courses including:

- *A Test Bank:* More than 1,400 multiple-choice, true-false, and short answer questions, each categorized according to learning objective, topic, level of difficulty, level of Bloom's taxonomy, text page reference, and correct answer.

- *An Instructors' Manual:* The highly rated Instructors' Manual returns with lecture notes, video cases, supplementary in-class activities, worksheets, handouts, teaching suggestions, online assignments, metrics assignments, as well as answers to questions that are embedded within each chapter. Answers are provided for questions on opening vignettes, Marketing NewsFlash boxes, Focus on Ethics boxes, Ask Yourself checkpoints, adAlyze features, and video clips.

- *PowerPoint® Presentations:* Two versions of ready-made presentations are available: lecture style, which are heavier on text than visuals, and magazine style, which incorporate high-quality images, including figure slides, product shots, and advertisements. As an aid for instructors who wish to create their own presentations, an **Image Library** containing all visual elements from the text is also available.

- *Video Case Studies:* A unique series of 21 contemporary marketing video cases is available. Each video corresponds to chapter-specific topics that are highlighted within the text as either Marketing NewsFlash boxes, opening chapter vignettes, or in-text examples. Each video is closed-captioned, and is accompanied by a written case, questions and answers, handouts, and teaching suggestions that are in the Instructors' Manual. This series is also available on DVD.

- *Alternate Cases:* Marketing Advisor cases and Marketing Metrics cases provide even more opportunities to bring course content to life for students. Cases are accompanied by teaching notes, teaching suggestions, and answers.

- *Brief Video Discussion Clips:* This new resource provides short video clips and companion discussion questions that instructors may wish to use to prompt in-class discussions.

- *Author Blog:* These frequently updated blog posts help provide instructors with innovative teaching resources to improve student learning, offer timely marketing examples, and help make class preparation time easier.

By choosing **connect**, instructors are providing their students with a powerful tool for improving academic performance and truly mastering course material. **connect** allows students to practise important skills at their own pace and on their own schedule. Importantly, students' assessment results and instructors' feedback are all saved online so that students can continually review their progress and plot their course to success.

connect also provides 24/7 online access to an eBook—an online edition of the text—to aid them in successfully completing their work, wherever and whenever they choose.

For Students

connect

McGraw-Hill **connect** allows students to practise important skills at their own pace and on their own schedule. Importantly, students' assessment results and instructors' feedback are all saved online so that students can continually review their progress and plot their course to success. **connect** also provides 24/7 online access to an eBook to aid students in successfully completing their work, wherever and whenever they choose.

connect offers practice quizzes as well as other study tools and resources including:

- *Applying Marketing Concepts and Perspectives* questions that allow you to assess your comprehension of chapter material.

- *Discussion Forum* questions that present a thought-provoking scenario for you to discuss with other students.

- *Internet Exercises* that ask you to think critically about a topic —helping you apply your knowledge of key chapter concepts and terms.

- *Video Case Studies* that provide an up-close look at an example—reinforcing the chapter content, while bringing the material to life.

- The *Creating a Successful Marketing Plan* appendix that can be used in a number of ways, throughout your use of this text and beyond. This guide to planning, researching, and writing a winning marketing plan incorporates marketing plan rationale, detailed plan contents, and effective design and execution of the plan, as well as checklists for implementing and evaluating the marketing plan.

LEARNSMART

No two students are alike. Why should their learning paths be? LearnSmart uses revolutionary adaptive technology to build a learning experience unique to each student's individual needs. It starts by identifying the topics a student knows and does not know. As the student progresses, LearnSmart adapts and adjusts the content based on his or her individual strengths, weaknesses, and confidence, ensuring that every minute spent studying with LearnSmart is the most efficient and productive study time possible.

SMARTBOOK™

As the first and only adaptive reading experience, SmartBook is changing the way students read and learn. SmartBook creates a personalized reading experience by highlighting the most important concepts a student needs to learn at that moment. As a student engages with SmartBook, the reading experience continuously adapts by highlighting content based on what each student knows and doesn't know. This ensures that he or she is focused on the content needed to close specific knowledge gaps, while it simultaneously promotes long-term learning.

Superior Learning Solutions and Support

The McGraw-Hill Ryerson team is ready to help you assess and integrate any of our products, technology, and services into your course for optimal teaching and learning performance. Whether it's helping your students improve their grades, or putting your entire course online, the McGraw-Hill Ryerson team is here to help you do it. Contact your Learning Solutions Consultant today to learn how to maximize all of McGraw-Hill Ryerson's resources!

For more information on the latest technology and Learning Solutions offered by McGraw-Hill Ryerson and its partners, please visit us online at **www.mcgrawhill.ca/he/solutions.**

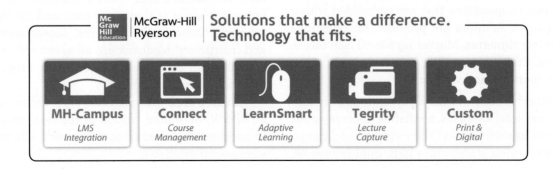

Acknowledgements

We appreciate the time and effort spent by individual marketers who shared their expertise, knowledge, examples, and videos to make this book real, practical, and a true reflection of marketing in Canada today. This content is spread across opening chapter vignettes, Marketing NewsFlash boxes, videos, and chapter content. It brings the content alive and makes a difference to marketing education in Canada. We specifically thank the following people for their contributions:

Chantelle Anderson, *North Strategic*
Mohammed Asaduallah, *GrapeTrail Inc.*
David Bigioni, *Molson Coors Canada*
Lucy Brun, *Agnew Peckham and Associates*
Constantine Campaniaris, *George Brown College*
Rosanne Caron, *Out-of-Home Marketing Association of Canada*
Ed Cartwright, *Canadian Marketing Association (CMA)*
Pat Cawley, *Agnew Peckham and Associates*
Karen Charness, *ZenithOptimedia*
Louisa Clements, *LivingLou.com*
Glenn Cressman, *Share of Marketing*
Joycelyn David, *Western Union Canada*
Alan Flint, *Canadian Marketing Association (CMA)*
Gardenia Flores, *Institute of Communication Agencies (ICA)*
Nicolas Gaudreau, *Yellow Pages Group*
Gillian Graham, *Institute of Communication Agencies (ICA)*
Ian Gordon, *Loblaw Companies*
Mike Jackson, *webTactics*
Ruth Klostermann, *ZenithOptimedia*
Marci Maddox, *OpenText*
Lenny Malley, *AMJ Campbell*
Morgan Matthews, *Impact Machine Design Inc.*
Sharon Metz, *Rovi Corporation*
Renny Monaghan, *Salesforce*
Ian Morell, *HEAD Canada*
Rob Morash, *HEAD Canada*
Paul Paquette, *AMJ Campbell*
Norm Pickering, *Extreme Brandz*
Tina Quelch, *Calador Communications*
Jake Rich, *Rich Media*
Jennifer Roberts, *Sklar, Wilton and Associates*
Bernie D. Schmidt, *Weeneebayko Area Health Authority*
Luke Sklar, *Sklar, Wilton and Associates*
Shannon Sloan, *Rich Media*
Zac Stanley, *Rich Media*
Aaron Surkis, *TELUS*
Mike Welling, *dougeserge+partners*
Hilary Zaharko, *H&R Block Canada*

To all the companies who have provided us with images to include in the book, we thank you.

In addition, we extend our appreciation to the reviewers who helped steer the development of this new edition with their comments, feedback, and suggestions:

Denton Anthony, *St. Francis Xavier University*
Mark Boivin, *University of Calgary*
Ingrid Brand, *Durham College*
Marc Ford, *Durham College*
Kim Galvin, *Nova Scotia Community College*
Richard Hill, *Capilano University*
Navjote Khara, *Niagara College*
James Li, *Assiniboine College*
Jack Michienzi, *Fanshawe College*
Beth Pett, *Niagara College*
Tim Richardson, *Seneca College*
Nicole Rourke, *St. Clair College*
Mike Sullivan, *Centennial College*
Wendy Tarrel, *Nova Scotia Community College*
Mark Valvasori, *Mohawk College*

We also extend our gratitude to the people at McGraw-Hill Ryerson for their professionalism, namely Karen Fozard (Senior Product Manager), Amy Rydzanicz (Product Developer), Stephanie Gay (Supervising Editor), Tracy Leonard (Permissions Editor), and Mike Kelly (copy editor), who were invaluable in their attention to detail and moving the process forward. Thank you also to Leanna MacLean, who helped guide the initial stages of this book with the development of new features that are central to its refreshed elements. And thanks also to designer Dave Murphy and the composition team at ArtPlus.

Finally, we would like to thank our families for their enthusiasm and patient support.

Christina Clements and Arsenio Bonifacio

Chapter 1

marketing fundamentals

LEARNING OBJECTIVES

LO 1 Understand the essence of marketing and explain the marketing process

LO 2 Define and analyze elements of the marketing mix

LO 3 Differentiate between goods, services, and ideas

LO 4 Describe the evolution of different business philosophies

LO 5 Discuss the latest marketing approaches

LO 6 Summarize careers that exist in marketing

Marketing in the fast-paced business world centres on understanding consumers—how they think, what drives purchases, and what does not. Marketers have to be aware of these facts, be knowledgeable about the technological changes that impact the path-to-purchase, and understand what new communication options are surfacing. They also need to have insights into the new trends and the ways consumers interact with each other, with brands, and with companies.

Technological advances are resulting in new and evolving marketing approaches, which we discuss in this book to give students a clear understanding of current marketing practices in Canada. We look at how marketers use time-tested off-line marketing strategies, often adding layers of mobile marketing, social media marketing, and database marketing approaches to better reach consumers. A new Chapter 13 about mobile marketing and social media marketing puts a spotlight on these topics.

This marketing book also highlights the importance of big data, metrics, and analytics to the marketing world with an embellished Chapter 4, re-titled "Market Research, Metrics, and Analytics" to reflect this important new content. Digital technology now provides marketers with a wealth of data, often in real time, to help improve marketing programs. This data also allows marketers to gain insights into consumer behaviour so that marketing approaches can be tweaked to achieve better results. Big data, metrics, and analytics are the building blocks of many marketing strategies, products, and programs.

Marketers also need to be financially savvy, be able to create realistic forecasts, dissect a profit and loss statement, and discuss return on investment (ROI) strategies. These important elements have been added into the pricing chapter as well as the chapter about marketing and strategic planning.

We start here with Chapter 1 to introduce students to the fundamentals of marketing and to explain the building blocks and concepts used by marketers to reach consumers. It also touches on evolving areas to ensure new approaches are top of mind with readers. We start by looking at Canadian fast-casual restaurant Mucho Burrito and talk to its marketers, who provide us with a glimpse inside the world of fast-food marketing and how it uses new and traditional marketing approaches to reach consumers.

Chapter Outline:

- Mucho Burrito manages the marketing mix
- The marketing process
- The evolution of business philosophies
- New and evolving marketing practices
- Marketing careers

Mucho Burrito, created in 2006 by Canadian entrepreneurs Mark Rechichi, Alex Rechichi, and Sean Black, was a fast-food opportunity that capitalized on healthier and tastier food trends. "Mexican food was underdeveloped at that time and what most Canadians experienced as 'Mexican' was not delicious, authentic Mexican cuisine," states Norm Pickering, director of marketing, North America, for Mucho Burrito. He explains that in 2006, other than Taco Bell and a few independent restaurants, Canadian consumers had little choice when it came to Mexican food. Mucho Burrito gave Canadians a new alternative: reasonably priced, good-quality Mexican food in a fast-casual restaurant. Its mission from inception was to provide customers with unmatched Mexican flavour with the freshest and best-quality burritos—made right in front of their eyes. By 2015, Mucho Burrito had grown to over 115 franchise locations in Canada with additional locations in the U.S.

The fast-food market is fiercely competitive, and today, Mexican food is one of the hottest food trends in Canada. Taco Bell is a mainstay with its inexpensive, lower-quality "Tex-Mex" food, but there are new U.S. competitors in Canada, such as Chipotle Mexican Grill and Qboda, focusing on higher-quality, fast-casual Mexican fare. Various popular, local, independent establishments also exist, such as Big Fat Burrito, Burrito Boyz, and Fat Bastards. Quick-service restaurants also litter the market with short-term promotional Mexican-type products such as McDonald's Fiesta Signature McWrap.

Mucho Burrito manages the marketing mix (product, price, place, and promotion) for its restaurants to ensure it meets customer expectations and remains a leader in the Mexican fast-food category. Let's look at its marketing mix in more detail:

Product Mucho Burrito, fresh Mexican grill, is a fast-casual Mexican restaurant with higher-quality food than your regular Mexican fast-food outlet. Items are made-to-order with fresh, healthy ingredients. Its name reflects its signature item, a large gourmet burrito with "Mucho food and Mucho quality." Fast-casual dining is a step above regular quick-service fast food in that it provides quickly made-to-order food with fresh ingredients in an atmosphere that encourages customers to pull up a chair and enjoy. At Mucho Burrito, upbeat Mexican music plays in the background while green, brown, and orange tones in the decor reflect its Mexican fare. Many Mucho Burrito restaurants, targeted to the 19-to-34 age group, are also licensed to serve alcoholic beverages.

Mucho Burrito offers fresh, high-quality hand-rolled burritos, hard and soft tacos, quesadillas, salad bowls, and soups with carefully seasoned beef, pork, chicken, fish, or shrimp. Barbacoa (shredded beef) and carnitas (shredded pork) are slowly cooked for about eight hours, and Mexican salsa and guacamole are freshly made each day. Consumers choose menu items, contents, and toppings at the front food counter and watch while their meal is assembled on rectangular metal trays lined with craft paper with logos. The meal is then purchased and eaten within the restaurant or as take-out food.

Periodically, Mucho Burrito introduces short-term, limited-time promotional products to reward loyal customers and to increase awareness and trial with new fans. All promotions are Mexican themed to reinforce Mucho Burrito's authentic Mexican positioning. Its recent "La Taqueria Trio" promotion, for example, introduced a trio of soft tortillas featuring mango steak, fiery chicken chorizo, or guacamole pineapple carnitas.

Price In line with its higher-quality positioning and good-quality food, a meal at Mucho Burrito is priced at approximately $8 to $13 per meal (including taxes), a few dollars higher than the $7 to $8 price point at quick-service restaurants such as McDonald's or Wendy's, and slightly lower than the Mexican food sold at Chipotle.

Place More than 115 Mucho Burrito franchises are located across Canada, with additional locations in the U.S. market. Mucho Burrito offers stand-alone restaurants as well as food-court locations. Restaurants are situated in outdoor neighbourhood malls, shopping centres, universities, airports, and downtown city centres. Locations are selected on the basis of anticipated retail traffic, the existence of residential and business establishments, and the presence of other eateries.

Promotion "Promotional support is essential to driving business for Mucho Burrito with new and loyal users," explains Mike Welling, partner at Mucho Burrito's brand communications agency, dougserge+partners. "It establishes a distinctive voice for Mucho Burrito so it stands out in the fiercely competitive fast-food market. After years of consistently weaving Mexican authenticity through humour and heavily accented Mexican-English into radio and billboard campaigns, people now associate Mucho Burrito with good-quality Mexican food and fun."

The first campaign from dougserge+partners used radio and billboard ads to establish Mucho Burrito as a fun, Mexican-style fast-casual restaurant. Radio ads used heavily accented Mexican-English to introduce a mythical Mexican character, Johnny Mucho, to highlight the Mexican aspect of the food. Eye-catching billboards (reminiscent of hand-painted signs seen in Mexico) used artistic graphics, images of appetizing burritos, over-sized logos, and headlines that could not be ignored, such as "Ponchos don't have buttons for a reason!" to reach consumers. This distinctive Mexican tone still permeates Mucho Burrito campaigns today.

On an annual basis, Mucho Burrito supports its business with quarterly promotions and offers. The emphasis is on the spring, back-to-school, and fall seasons. Many promotions tie into popular Mexican holidays such as Cinco de Mayo, when Mucho Burrito offers $5 burritos on May 5, or the Ghost Pepper Burrito (made with the second-hottest pepper in the world, the ghost pepper), which is featured around the November Mexican holiday, Day of the Dead. The first "Ghost Pepper" promotion used window posters that showed a fire-monster engulfing a burrito in a stylized illustrative approach very familiar to Mexicans, while local radio ads challenged the "manhood of the gringos" by focusing on the product's extreme heat and limited-time offer. The poster, created by the British design firm ilovedust, with art direction from Raj Gupta at dougserge+partners, was very popular with Mucho Burrito customers; the ad can be seen in the adAlyze feature at the end of this chapter.

The "Ghost Pepper" promotion also used Facebook, Twitter, and YouTube to create buzz. A YouTube video, created by a film student, showed Mexican gangsters eating Ghost Pepper Burritos, while social media contests asked people to post their most creative photos of a person eating a Ghost Pepper Burrito. In addition, Mucho Burrito launched its first annual Ghost Pepper Burrito eating contest, giving $2,500 to the person who ate the most Ghost Pepper Burritos in eight minutes. "In its first year, the 'Ghost Pepper' promotion was a huge success. It boosted traffic by 20 percent and increased same store sales by 15 percent," states Welling.

On an ongoing basis, Mucho Burrito uses social media and mobile marketing programs to reach consumers. Social media includes ongoing updates on Facebook and Twitter, with its most recent programs including a blogger outreach through its Mucho Ambassador Club where 56 brand advocates, profiled on the Mucho Burrito website, advise on new products and help spread the word on blogs and social networks. Mucho Burrito's mobile marketing approaches include text message alerts, e-mail reminders, and smartphone apps to engage consumers. On occasion, Mucho Burrito places banner ads on third-party mobile apps such as the UFC app (Ultimate Fighting Championship) and the Urban Spoon local restaurant review app. New Mucho Burrito restaurant openings always receive special attention with low introductory prices and offers.

Mucho Burrito's website is an important part of its marketing mix. Designed by the team at dougserge+partners, it highlights the brand's authentic Mexican positioning and provides information on menu choices, nutritional content, and restaurant locations. It allows loyal consumers to register for e-mail updates, log in for gift card balances, and link to Facebook and Twitter pages. Investors can also turn to the Mucho Burrito website for information on franchise opportunities.

"Mucho Burrito is a super example of a Canadian marketing success story," explains Welling. "Starting with its brand name, it uses its entire marketing mix to consistently deliver on its promise of good-quality, Mexican-inspired food. Its name, logo, restaurant design, products, and communication tools all shout that Mucho Burrito is a fun place to eat good-quality Mexican food at affordable prices." You can see more about Mucho Burrito by navigating to its website at **www.muchoburrito.com**.[1]

▶ Video
Mucho
Burrito

reality CHECK ✓

As you read Chapter 1, refer back to the Mucho Burrito vignette to answer the following questions:

- Is Mucho Burrito a good, a service, or an idea?
- Who is the target market for Mucho Burrito?
- What marketing tools does Mucho Burrito use to create relationships with its consumers?

▶ *"Building a brand that has a distinctive, but authentic, image is important for success in the short term and the long term."*

— *Mike Welling, partner at dougserge+partners*

The Essence of Marketing

 The Mucho Burrito vignette demonstrates the marketing reality that ties long-term business success to carefully designed product, pricing, distribution, and promotional strategies that meet current consumer needs, trends and expectations. Brands need to stand out, and marketers are challenged to stay current to ensure marketing approaches resonate.

Often, students believe marketing revolves around slick commercials and fancy promotions. In fact, marketers' ultimate objectives are to drive profits for a company, or if working in the non-profit sector, to generate revenue and support to fund programs and run operations. Only one aspect of marketing revolves around promotion, with all other elements required to drive profitability or revenue generation.

This chapter works to explain the fundamental principles that guide marketing, dispelling the myth that promotion and marketing are one and the same. In this introductory chapter, we emphasize the basic marketing principles of meeting customer needs and providing customer value, while also providing background on the evolution of business approaches. We explain the marketing process, the concept of target markets, and the importance of integrating each element of the marketing mix into marketing programs that focus on consumer needs. We also review new and evolving marketing approaches such as real-time marketing, content marketing, mobile marketing, social media marketing, partnership marketing, metrics and analytics, and evolving marketing regulations and ethical considerations. Finally, we lead students into a discussion on careers in the marketing industry.

Focusing on Customer Needs

The essence of successful marketing is focusing on customer needs and developing programs that delight consumers and encourage customer loyalty. Frequently, the challenge is to clearly determine these needs and to understand how they can best be met. Marketers often turn to research to provide clarity; however, consumers do not always know what they want and may not want (or be able) to articulate feelings and opinions. In certain categories, such as fragrances or luxury cars, choices are not entirely rational, but partly based on self-image and emotional attachment to a brand, which are difficult to articulate. In other situations where children or professionals are involved, a child may be unable to express ideas while professionals may not have the time to participate in research. Sometimes, marketers may not be asking the right questions.

The digital world adds another level of complexity to market research. On the one hand, it facilitates the online gathering of information, while on the other hand, it introduces new communication platforms that challenge marketers to understand the biases that may exist in this new environment.

There are some general insights about how consumers navigate the online environment that marketers need to consider when developing marketing programs. First, the initial point of contact for consumers with a brand is often online on a corporate website, on a promotional microsite, on a company blog, on one of its social media sites, perhaps on a product review site, or even on a Wikipedia page. Marketers must therefore understand the role of the online environment in the consumer path-to-purchase and the need to have a solid presence on all these online destinations with information that engages, informs, and motivates. Second, consumers must be able to quickly find a company's online site through search engines such as Google or Bing. Websites must therefore be written so that they are highly ranked by the search engines and consumers can find them quickly during online searches. Third, consumers are impatient in the online environment—websites must therefore load quickly within a few short seconds and have simple and pleasing designs that deliver content within two to three clicks.

The travel industry is an example of where marketers spent time to understand consumers' online needs and developed new approaches to remain relevant in

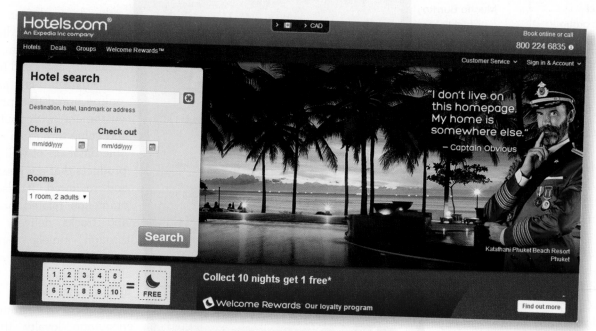

The Hotels.com website uses a simple design to facilitate online search.

the online environment. Consider a person booking a trip to Banff, Alberta: The first point of contact is no longer a travel agent and a brochure, but instead an online travel website such as **www.itravel2000.com**, where travel options, hotel prices, and flight information are easily accessible. The second point of contact may be **www.tripadvisor.com**, a social media product review site, to read customer reviews on hotels and vacations. Finally, the traveller may navigate to a hotel comparison website such as **www.hotels.com** to locate the best deals. At some point in this process, the traveller may turn to social media to gather more information and to reach out on social networks for advice from friends and followers. In this online environment, there is no need to visit a travel agent, speak to an airline, or make inquiries at a hotel.

Travel websites, hotels, and airlines now all consider the online needs and expectations of travellers, including how they search online to gather information and use customer-review websites for product ratings and price comparisons. Travel websites, recognizing these needs, often provide these tools within their websites.

> " *The essence of marketing is focusing on the consumer.* "

Creating Customer Value

Harnessing customer loyalty to secure ongoing customer support is encouraging firms to provide value to its customers in two ways. First, companies create products that provide goods and services with added value versus competitive offerings. Second, they reward customers for their loyalty through marketing programs that focus on repeat purchases and incentives that encourage future purchases. For our purposes, **customer value** is the unique combination of benefits received by targeted consumers that includes quality, price, convenience, delivery, and both before-sale and after-sale service. Marketers work diligently to deliver this value by carefully managing each element of the marketing mix (product, price, place, and promotion) so that this value is evident to consumers who in turn purchase or use the products. Ongoing marketing programs then come into play, encouraging these consumers to become long-term loyal customers and spread the word to others.

Creating products with added value is often achieved through a combination of (1) product design, (2) pricing strategies, and (3) service elements. Retailers such as Walmart focus on the lowest price; Mountain Equipment Co-op claims to provide the best products; Mucho Burrito highlights its all natural ingredients and fresh products; and companies such as Pizza Pizza

customer value
The unique combination of benefits received by targeted buyers that includes quality, price, convenience, delivery, and both before-sale and after-sale service

Mucho Burrito highlights customer benefits in this in-store poster.

(with its award-winning app for mobile ordering) highlight its fast purchase and delivery service as added-value elements for its consumers. Let's examine two online brands to find out how they balance product design, pricing, and service levels to create meaningful products with added value.

Google is an online brand designed to deliver highly accurate data with a product that is easy to use and fast, and that provides exceptional value. The product is provided free to users and has become the gold standard in the search industry with a market share in Canada of 89.1 percent, followed by Bing at 7 percent, and Yahoo at 3 percent.[2] Its branded platform has been extended into other areas such as Google Maps, Gmail, and Google Analytics, all providing the same value proposition that balances product design, pricing, and service to deliver value. Google encourages customer loyalty by keeping customers informed on its latest products and providing incentives to use its related products that may not be free of charge, such as Google AdWords, an online advertising platform. In a recent promotion, Google used direct mail to provide added value to its customers by sending them $100 gift cards to try its paid AdWords product.

Google adds exceptional value to the world on another level, through its humanitarian efforts. For example, during the 2013 Typhoon Haiyan in the Philippines, Google immediately launched its online Person Finder application to help locate displaced persons with a searchable database where people and humanitarian organizations could post queries and updates about missing persons in real time. It also launched an online disaster relief map that provided updates on shelters, command centres, and the communication hubs that helped with the disaster relief efforts. Google Person Finder was first launched in 2010 to help the earthquake disaster relief efforts in Haiti, and has been used by the Google Crisis Response team to help with

other humanitarian efforts after the natural disasters in Chile, Pakistan, New Zealand, Japan, and India.[3]

Amazon is another online brand that presents customers with outstanding value through a searchable database of well-priced products that are peer rated and reviewed. It also recommends related products and tracks delivery dates through timely e-mails—design, price, and service all rolled into one. E-mail updates may be sent out to its database of customers to encourage loyalty through special offers, featured gifts, and the announcement of new releases. Amazon's consistent value proposition continues to result in strong business metrics—it dominates online retailing and had a global annual growth rate of 30.4 percent in 2012. In 2013, Amazon added further value to its brand in Canada by introducing its Amazon Prime service, which for an annual $79 fee provides members with free shipping on hundreds of items. This same service in the U.S. also comes with free access to over 40,000 movies and TV shows, and free borrowing from the Kindle Owners' Lending Library, signalling potential future services for the Canadian market.[4]

Appealing to Target Markets

In a competitive marketplace, companies cannot satisfy everyone's needs with a single product, and so products are designed to appeal to specific groups of consumers. Marketing follows the principle that, with limited funds, it is better to channel resources toward consumers who are most interested in purchasing a product, rather than target everyone and squander funds on those who have little interest. This approach results in marketers tailoring products to meet the specific needs of different target markets. A **target market** can be formally defined as the specific group of existing and potential consumers to which marketers direct their marketing efforts. Marketing efforts are geared to appeal to a product's specific target market, ensuring that each element of the marketing mix appeals to the characteristics of the target group.

Coordinating the Marketing Mix

LO² The elements of the **marketing mix**—known as the 4 Ps: product, price, place, and promotion—need to be carefully managed by marketers to ensure that they are well coordinated and that each appeals to the distinct characteristics of the target market. There is no point in having an amazing product if consumers cannot find it at the retail stores they frequent or online through a search. If the product is priced too high for the target market, it will be unaffordable; if it's priced too low, it will simply portray the wrong image. If marketers promote a product on TV but the target market rarely watches TV, instead spending time online, then the message will not be received. In all instances, marketers need to understand what makes their consumers tick: what delights them, what does not, and how to best send communications. This information is often clarified by market research and metrics on consumer behaviour to help determine how marketing efforts can be designed or modified to meet consumer needs and deliver profits or support for a company. Marketers use this information to improve marketing programs and coordinate each element of the marketing mix to meet specific target market needs. These elements are all included in a brand's annual marketing plan where details for each element of the marketing mix are outlined, together with the required budgets and profit and loss statements for the brand. Chapter 15 provides more details on this area.

The elements of the marketing mix in either an online or offline environment can be simply described as follows:

1. **Product:** All the attributes that make up a good, a service, or an idea, including product design, features, colour, packaging, warranty, and service levels.

2. **Price:** The expected regular retail or sale price for a product.

3. **Place:** The distribution channels, retail formats, and merchandising used to sell a product.

4. **Promotion:** The communication tools needed to inform consumers about a product, including advertising, public relations, sales promotion, direct response, event marketing and sponsorship, and personal selling.

We look at two Nestlé products, Smarties and After Eight Straws, to review how marketers at this company carefully craft each element

> *"Marketers need to understand what makes their consumers tick: what delights them, what does not."*

of the marketing mix to appeal to two distinct target groups. Smarties, targeting youth aged 13 to 17, are brightly coloured, candy-coated chocolates that come in bright blue packages. The product comes in round bite-sized pieces that are fun, colourful, and easy to share. It is relatively inexpensive, selling for approximately $1.09 for 50 grams, making it an affordable treat. It is merchandised at retail in supermarkets, convenience stores, and drug stores, often close to cash registers to stand as a visual reminder of this treat and to prompt impulse purchases. The product continues its appeal to youth with both online and offline marketing campaigns. Today, promotional efforts focus on the imaginative ways Smarties can be enjoyed by creating fun treats for family occasions. Previous campaigns revolved around the reintroduction of its blue-coloured Smarties. Promotional elements included TV spots airing during youth programming such as the MuchMusic Video Awards (MMVAs), integration with the MMVAs through sponsored blue

Nestlé encourages families to enjoy Smarties in fun creative ways.

marketing mix
The 4 Ps—product, price, place, and promotion

product
Attributes that make up a good, a service, or an idea, including product design, features, colour, packaging, warranty, and service levels

price
Expected regular retail or sale price for a product

place
Distribution channels, retail formats, and merchandising used to sell a product

promotion
Communication tools needed to inform consumers about a product, including advertising, public relations, sales promotion, direct response, event marketing and sponsorship, and personal selling

marketing process
The process of
(1) identifying
consumer needs,
(2) managing the
marketing mix to
meet these needs,
and (3) realizing
profits

rooms for celebrities, a promotional microsite at **www.smarties.ca** with details of a contest to win an Apple computer, and social media involvement with a Facebook page.

On the other hand, After Eight Straws, targeting adults, are dark-chocolate mints designed to be sleek, stylish, and classy. The product comes in an upscale dark-green cylinder that contains 20 thin After Eight Straws that are filled with a delicate mint-cream filling. The product combines bitter, dark chocolate with a minty flavour that appeals to adults. The product is sold at a premium price of approximately $3.99 for a 90-gram package, reflecting its high-quality image and adult target market. Typically, this product is not merchandised at cash registers, but instead on the shelves of many grocery stores and drug retailers. It enjoys more-prominent seasonal displays during the winter holidays when the product is popular for entertaining. Over the years, After Eight Straws have been promoted as a stylish accompaniment for dinner parties and have been promoted at the Toronto Symphony Orchestra as a product for adult entertaining.

In both instances, Nestlé moulded each element of the marketing mix to appeal to its specific target group. Neither product is geared to appeal to everyone. Instead, Smarties targets youth, and After Eight Straws targets adults. It is important to note that, over time, marketers gather extensive information on their target markets, being able to identify purchase motivation that goes beyond age and gender into behavioural and psychological motivation, which is an important determinant in many purchases. In this way, marketers define their target markets in more-complex terms, including elements such as likes, dislikes, motivation, interests, and concerns.

The digital reality has prompted many new marketing approaches that make the marketing mix more complex. Marketers realize that each element now has many layers that need to be managed, no easy task in

the online environment. A product, for example, now has many faces: offline in stores and online on corporate websites, on blogs, on promotional microsites, on apps, and on social media sites where marketers carefully monitor and join conversations to engage consumers. This is made even more complex by the different technical requirements needed for websites to render appropriately on different mobile devices.

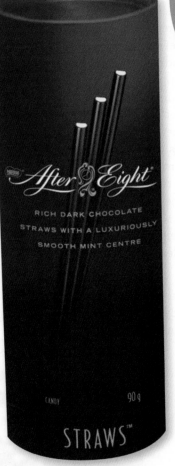

After Eight Straws
targets adults.

ask yourself

1. *What is the essence of marketing?*

2. *What is a target market?*

3. *What is the marketing mix?*

The Marketing Process

The marketing process is a continuous one that requires marketers to pay attention to detail and apply strategic, analytical, and creative-thinking skills. In short, the **marketing process** involves (1) identifying consumer needs, (2) managing the marketing mix to meet these needs, and (3) realizing profits, or in the case of non-profits, securing revenue support or providing services to those in need (see Figure 1–1). Throughout the cycle, marketers constantly evaluate program success, implementing and recommending future changes to strengthen efforts. We look to the non-profit Google product mentioned earlier, its Google Person Finder, to see how this works.

Google.org created Google Person Finder as a non-profit crisis response service in 2010 to assist in disaster relief efforts in Haiti and has subsequently used it to assist with other disasters such as earthquakes in Chile, Japan, New Zealand, and China. When Typhoon Haiyan hit the Philippines in 2012, Google recognized a need to help find missing persons and put its Google Person Finder service into action with

Figure 1–1
The marketing process

| Identify consumer needs | Manage the marketing mix to meet consumer needs | Realize profits for a company (or objectives for non-profit organizations) |

A logical process that focuses on consumer needs.

the marketing mix to make this happen. The *product* was its online searchable database, easily accessed by individuals and disaster relief organizations, that could post information on missing persons or search for updates. The *price* was free to ensure maximum utility. The *place* was online to maximize global reach and to circumvent traditional telecommunications services that were not accessible. *Promotion* was through the news media, directly to disaster relief organizations, and through the Google website. In terms of *profit*, Google was not looking to make a profit with this product; the service was managed through its Google Crisis Response humanitarian arm, which facilitates critical information dissemination during times of crisis.

It is imperative to understand that marketers are ultimately responsible for generating company profits (or revenues and support for non-profit organizations), and that marketing programs are designed with this end in mind. On occasion, students have the misconception that marketing is all about advertising or selling, when in fact it is about managing *all* the elements of the marketing mix and using research to help generate profits or revenues and support for an organization. Formally, **marketing** is described as the process of planning and managing goods, services, or ideas to meet consumer needs and organizational objectives. It includes the conception of these products, and the pricing, promotion, and distribution programs designed to make a profit and generate revenue or support for an organization.[5] The objectives of both buyers and sellers must be met for exchanges to occur and for profits to be realized.

Exchange is the trade of things of value between buyers and sellers so that each benefits. In simple terms, the trade is money for a product or service. However, there is more to exchange than just money—customers may provide referrals to a tutoring service or to a fitness club in return for discounts or additional services. A consumer may volunteer time with a non-profit organization such as the Heart and Stroke Foundation, which in return may satisfy the consumer's need to support the cause. In the online environment, exchange is often more complex. In many instances, websites may not be selling a product at all but instead providing free information or a service that drives traffic to their website where advertising is served to help pay for the service. The numbers of page views to the website and data on its demographics is used to sell this advertising space and generate revenue for the website. Many news websites, such as **www.ctv.ca**, **www.theglobeandmail.com**, and **www.macleans.ca**, and web portals, such as Yahoo! Canada and **Canada.com**, fall into this category.

What Can Be Marketed?

LO 3 In marketing, the term **product** encompasses goods, services, and ideas. These can all be marketed to encourage people to buy something or, as in the case of ideas, to encourage support.

A **good** is a product you can touch and own. Examples are a pair of Adidas

---

marketing
The process of planning and managing goods, services, or ideas to meet consumer needs and organizational objectives. It includes the conception of these products and the pricing, promotion, and distribution programs designed to make a profit and generate revenue or support for an organization

exchange
The trade of things of value between buyers and sellers so that each benefits

product
A good, service, or idea

good
A product you can touch and own

The marketing process is a continuous one that requires marketers to pay attention to detail and apply strategic, analytical, and creative-thinking skills.

running shoes or a can of Red Bull energy drink. Red Bull energy drink is a tangible product that is marketed in different varieties, sold at a premium price, merchandised in-store, promoted with humorous ads and social media, and publicized through the sponsorship of extreme sporting events. Red Bull streams highlights from its action, motor sports, and music events online on its Web TV channel, designed to appeal to its target market that engages with online content.

A **service** is an intangible product you cannot touch. It does not result in something you take home. A physiotherapy session, a holiday, or going to a movie are examples of services. When you watch a movie at Cineplex Entertainment, marketers have worked to ensure the experience encourages you to return. Movie selection, theatre layout, seating, loyalty programs, and concession items have all been carefully selected and designed with the comfort and needs of the target market in mind. The Cineplex-Scotiabank SCENE loyalty rewards program has been created with rewards that encourage customers to return to Cineplex Entertainment theatres time after time to collect points and receive benefits such as discounted concession items, free movies, or discounted DVDs.[7]

Ideas can also be marketed. An **idea** is a concept that typically looks for support. An example is the Bell Let's Talk campaign that asks people to support mental health programs by helping to remove the stigma that often accompanies the illness. This campaign has been tremendously successful and will run for at least five years with an annual awareness day that asks people to share the message. On Bell Let's Talk day, Bell contributes five cents to mental health for every text message and call sent on the Bell network, and also (regardless of carrier) for every tweet or retweet that uses the #BellLetsTalk hashtag, and for every Facebook share of the Bell Let's Talk logo. As part of this campaign, Bell also announced a $50 million donation to mental health, in addition to the funds it will pledge from its Bell Let's Talk day program, which have already reached over $17 million. This program is widely applauded, although a few naysayers consider it a public relations program with questionable ethics. (See the Focus on Ethics box, "Marketing Ideas: #BellLetsTalk Puts Mental Health on the Map.")

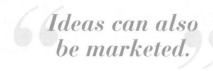

"Ideas can also be marketed."

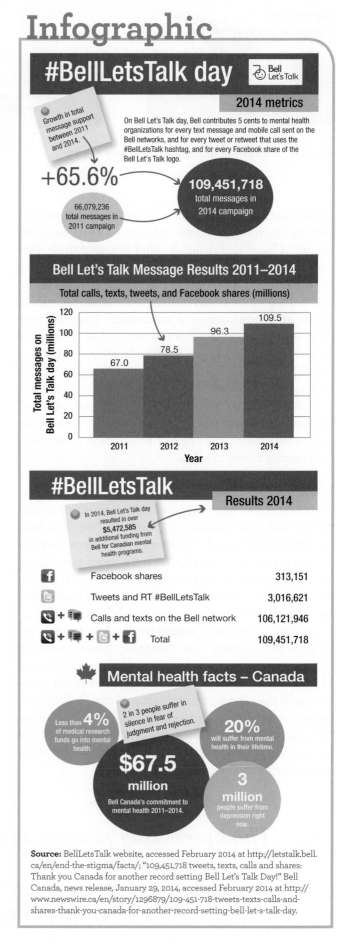

Infographic

#BellLetsTalk day — Bell Let's Talk

2014 metrics

Growth in total message support between 2011 and 2014.

+65.6%

66,079,236 total messages in 2011 campaign

109,451,718 total messages in 2014 campaign

On Bell Let's Talk day, Bell contributes 5 cents to mental health organizations for every text message and mobile call sent on the Bell networks, and for every tweet or retweet that uses the #BellLetsTalk hashtag, and for every Facebook share of the Bell Let's Talk logo.

Bell Let's Talk Message Results 2011–2014

Total calls, texts, tweets, and Facebook shares (millions)

Total messages on Bell Let's Talk day (millions)

Year	Value
2011	67.0
2012	78.5
2013	96.3
2014	109.5

#BellLetsTalk — Results 2014

In 2014, Bell Let's Talk day resulted in over $5,472,585 in additional funding from Bell for Canadian mental health programs.

Facebook shares		313,151
Tweets and RT #BellLetsTalk		3,016,621
Calls and texts on the Bell network		106,121,946
Total		109,451,718

Mental health facts – Canada

Less than **4%** of medical research funds go into mental health.

2 in 3 people suffer in silence in fear of judgment and rejection.

20% will suffer from mental health in their lifetime.

$67.5 million Bell Canada's commitment to mental health 2011–2014.

3 million people suffer from depression right now.

Source: BellLetsTalk website, accessed February 2014 at http://letstalk.bell.ca/en/end-the-stigma/facts/; "109,451,718 tweets, texts, calls and shares: Thank you Canada for another record setting Bell Let's Talk Day!" Bell Canada, news release, January 29, 2014, accessed February 2014 at http://www.newswire.ca/en/story/1296879/109-451-718-tweets-texts-calls-and-shares-thank-you-canada-for-another-record-setting-bell-let-s-talk-day.

Marketing Ideas: #BellLetsTalk Puts Mental Health on the Map

On February 12 the more you text the more you help

Bell Let's Talk

Marketing ideas can encourage people to support causes.

Did you retweet the #BellLetsTalk hashtag on Twitter in January 2014, share its logo on Facebook, or send a text message on the Bell network on Bell Let's Talk day? The odds are that maybe you did as #BellLetsTalk raised nearly $5.5 million for mental health on January 29, 2014, with a grand total of 109,451,718 tweets, texts, calls, and Facebook shares, making it the top trending Twitter topic in Canada and third worldwide. The tweets, texts, calls, and shares for Bell Let's Talk day increased 14 percent over 2013 levels, with wide-ranging support from individuals and families, as well as business leaders, government officials, hospitals, educational institutions, the armed forces, sports teams, and athletes and entertainers that embraced this worthy cause. There were tweets ranging from Prime Minister Stephen Harper, to comedian Rick Mercer and astronaut Chris Hadfield, to athlete Milos Raonic and sports teams such as the Ottawa Senators, the Toronto Raptors, the Toronto Blue Jays, the Toronto Maple Leafs, and the Winnipeg Blue Bombers (just to mention a few), as well as from everyday people who lent their support to the cause.

Bell Let's Talk day is a five-year annual marketing campaign designed by Bell Canada to reduce the stigma of mental illness in our society through greater awareness, increased funding, research, treatments, and understanding of mental health. Rather than just donate funds, Bell uses its marketing clout and the power of celebrity spokespeople such as Olympic athlete Clara Hughes as a springboard to encourage others to spread the word and to ignite conversations to help change attitudes and behaviours toward mental health.

On Bell Let's Talk day, Bell contributes five cents to mental health organizations for every text message and call sent on the Bell network, and also (regardless of carrier) for every tweet or retweet that uses the #BellLetsTalk hashtag, and for every Facebook share of the Bell Let's Talk logo. As part of this initiative, Bell created the Bell Let's Talk Community Fund, which provides $5,000 to $50,000 grants to grassroots, registered not-for-profit organizations, charities, hospitals, and social service agencies that apply and want to improve access to mental health in their communities. More than 150 local mental health organizations have already received funds.

Since 2011 when the campaign first started, Bell Canada has committed $67 million toward mental health programs, starting with a $50 million initial announcement and the subsequent annual additions from its Bell Let's Talk day. Already, $10 million has been donated to the Centre for Addiction and Mental Health Foundation (CAMH), $1 million to the Royal Ottawa Hospital for telepsychiatry, $1 million to Sunnybrook Hospital for research into adolescent mood and anxiety disorders, and more to many other organizations.

Bell is a longtime supporter of mental health programs in Canada; 25 years ago, it became a founding partner of Kids Help Phone so that children in distress can call a phone number to speak to a trained counsellor. It most recently donated $2.5 million to help Kids Help Phone expand into online live chat services, web postings, mobile web, and mobile apps.

Despite the outpouring of support for Bell and its Bell Let's Talk program, a few people negatively criticize Bell for using mental health as a prop to market its brand. In general, the media positively covers the event but also notes that Bell benefits from the high levels of publicity that surround this event, pointing out that Bell has its name front and centre in the campaign with its hashtag and logo #BellLetsTalk. Others openly suggest that Bell should just have made a donation to mental health instead of profiting from what critics term a publicity stunt, missing the fact that Bell's approach serves as a catalyst in bringing mental health to the forefront and that its name and leadership add credibility to the cause.

At the end of the day, the data shows that people support Bell Let's Talk day in droves and are happy to lend their voice to Bell's philanthropic effort, which is helping to break down the stigma of mental illness so that society can be a healthier and more welcoming place.[6]

Questions

1. What idea is being marketed by Bell Let's Talk day?

2. What are the benefits of Bell Let's Talk day to society?

3. How do you respond to the critics that claim Bell Let's Talk day is a publicity stunt for Bell?

market
Potential consumers with both the willingness and ability to buy

production orientation
Focusing organizational efforts on the manufacture of goods

sales orientation
Focusing organizational efforts on selling as many products as possible

marketing concept
The idea that an organization should strive to satisfy the needs of consumers while also trying to achieve organizational goals

marketing orientation
Focusing organizational efforts to collect and use information about customers' needs to create customer value

Many successful marketers today launch products with layers of goods, services, and ideas to connect with consumers. For example, Smart cars, a division of Mercedes-Benz, staggered the launch of its new electric vehicle, Smart fortwo Electric Drive, over the 2010 to 2012 period, as a zero-emissions car (*product*) that can run 135 km on a single battery charge. During the testing phase, Smart Canada worked with Toronto Hydro to provide battery charging stations in testers' garages. Smart Canada also provided auxiliary services such as winter tire packages and 24-hour roadside assistance (*services*). Promotional programs such as the Smart Electric Lounge at the 2011 International Auto Show also pointed to the importance of using electric power to support the environment (*idea*).

ask yourself

1. *What steps are involved in the marketing process?*

2. *What are the differences between goods, services, and ideas?*

3. *Are credit cards goods, services, or ideas?*

What Is a Market?

The term **market** is used in marketing to describe potential consumers who have both the *willingness* and *ability* to buy a product. Importantly, just being willing to buy a product does not constitute a market. For example, Fisher Price's iXL learning tablet is an interactive hand-held gadget for children 3 to 7 years old. Kids can interactively read, draw, look at pictures, and play video games using the product's six programs, which are accessed through touchscreen technology. Programs include a story book, game player, notebook,

photo album, art studio, and music player—learning and fun all rolled into one. Although the product is designed for young children, these children are not considered the market because they do not have the money or the physical means to buy the product. The market consists of parents with young children aged 3 to 7 years.

This product touches on an interesting marketing issue: Sometimes the market, target market, and consumers are different groups of people, and marketers need to decide on a balance of who should be targeted with their programs. While the *market* for Fisher Price's iXL is parents with children 3 to 7 years old, the marketing also needs to focus on the children, who may exert some influence over their parents. Therefore, we see the *target market* for the product includes both children and parents. Finally, the *consumers* of the product, in this case the users, are the children, not the parents, and marketers need to ensure that the product is designed with their abilities and interests in mind, without overlooking the parents who are the main decision-makers in the purchase process.

The Evolution of Business Philosophies

LO 4 Marketing was not always the driving force in business philosophy. Up until the 1930s, businesses were in the **production orientation** stage. This stage focused on manufacturing, which until the industrial revolution was not a widespread phenomenon. Manufactured goods tended to sell, regardless of their quality, because they were in short supply. Consumer needs were not a priority. The second stage, from the 1930s to the 1960s, was the **sales orientation** stage. This stage focused on selling as many products as possible. The market had become more competitive, production had become more efficient, and products were in abundance. Companies started to hard-sell to make a profit, and consumer needs were still not a major consideration. As the marketplace became more competitive, businesses developed more-sophisticated approaches, and the basic marketing stage evolved in the 1960s. At this point, consumer needs became paramount, and the marketing concept became the focus of businesses. The **marketing concept** stage focuses on the idea that an organization should strive to satisfy the needs of consumers while also trying to achieve an organization's goals. The **marketing orientation** stage follows this idea. An organization that has a marketing orientation focuses its efforts on continuously collecting information about customers' needs, sharing this information across departments, and using it to create customer value.[8]

In the last decade, marketing has evolved from a discipline with a short-term focus on transactions to one that now also focuses on building long-term customer relationships. This relationship marketing stage sees organizations considering the lifetime value of their customers and striving to offer better services, higher-quality products, and meaningful long-term relationships. Over the last few years, relationship marketing has included a greater use of social media, and an increased focus on customer relationship management and corporate social responsibility to create meaningful relationships. These approaches emphasize customer retention and ongoing customer satisfaction rather than short-term transactions. It carefully uses information on customer interests to develop relationships with customers and retain their loyalty. Businesses recognize that improved customer relationships can result in increased customer loyalty, improved customer retention levels, and greater profits for an organization. Formally, the concept of **relationship marketing** is when organizations create long-term links with their customers, employees, suppliers, and other partners to increase loyalty and customer retention. (Figure 1–2 summarizes this evolution of business philosophies.)

It is important to understand that relationship marketing involves a personal, ongoing relationship between an organization and its customers that often starts before a sale occurs and lasts well beyond the point when a sale has concluded. The automobile industry has used this approach for many years, seeing the value of a satisfied customer play out in future purchases. It is common practice for car dealerships to regularly phone customers with invitations to events, send out mailings with car maintenance information, and even distribute branded magazines for customers to enjoy. Car manufacturers also develop online relationship marketing tools. For example, Smart Canada has created online opportunities to make connections with its consumers and build lasting customer relationships. Owners of Smart cars can join an online club (**www.clubsmartcar.ca**) to access forums, post articles, and view updates. Consumers can also access the Smart Canada website to view product information and subscribe to newsletters, while the Smart Canada Facebook page posts promotional offers and timely responses to questions.

Internet technology is fuelling the growth of relationship marketing as a business approach. Social media, database technology, and the increased importance of corporate social responsibility are all pointing toward creating meaningful relationships with customers to drive business success. Let's look at these three elements of relationship marketing in more detail.

First, social media, with its ability to interact with consumers, often in real time, through social networks such as Facebook, YouTube, Google+, Twitter, LinkedIn, Instagram, Tumblr, Pinterest, and blogs, has added a new dimension to relationship marketing, making it more immediate and interactive. Social media provides consumers with the ability to interact with marketing messages by posting comments that are visible to all. This open environment encourages companies to be more transparent and interactive in their communications. **Social media** is formally defined as a form of online media that allows members to create their own network of friends and contacts to share comments, articles, opinions, videos, and images as a form of self-expression.

Social media can be used by marketers in various ways, with the following four approaches seeing positive results. First, marketers use social media to engage and connect with consumers. Special offers such as coupons may be sent out through Twitter or Facebook, and interesting images can be shared on all social media sites but particularly on Pinterest and Instagram. YouTube can be used to share how-to videos or entertaining and informative brand-related videos, while promotional microsites can provide further details on all promotional elements and link to social media. Second, marketers use social media to provide customer service. Social media monitoring tools can be purchased from analytics companies to monitor social media engagement and flag comments that

relationship marketing
When organizations create long-term links with customers, employees, suppliers, and other partners to increase loyalty and customer retention

social media
A form of online media that allows members to create their own network of friends and contacts to share comments, articles, opinions, videos, and images as a form of self-expression

Figure 1–2
The evolution of business philosophies

Production orientation — 1930s — Sales orientation — 1960s — Marketing orientation — 1990s — Relationship marketing orientation

Social media is used by marketers to interact with target audiences.

require responses. This allows marketers to quickly respond to customer queries in real time and to resolve potential issues. Third, marketers use social media analytics platforms to monitor real-time consumer engagement and brand buzz so that social media programs can be measured and evaluated. Fourth, marketers can use social media to identify brand advocates that can spread positive messages about a brand. Typically, marketers seek brand fans with influential social networks and send them brand updates and information they may find useful, sometimes appointing brand ambassadors that are paid a small sum to support the brand with positive messaging. Social media is discussed at length in Chapter 13.

Second, database technology has surfaced as a tool that facilitates relationship marketing by putting a focus on **customer relationship management (CRM)** for the marketing industry. This approach is rooted in the knowledge that it is less expensive to service and maintain current customers than to obtain new ones. CRM identifies a firm's most-valued customers and builds loyalty programs to appeal to their needs. It systematically identifies what leads to customer satisfaction and profitable brand loyalty. It is often facilitated by CRM software. Formally, CRM is defined as the overall process of building and maintaining profitable customer relationships by delivering superior customer value and satisfaction.[9]

We look to the Canadian retail industry to better understand CRM and to find out how it is applied. In its

customer relationship management (CRM)
The overall process of building and maintaining profitable customer relationships by delivering superior customer value and satisfaction

corporate social responsibility (CSR)
When organizations voluntarily consider the well-being of society by taking responsibility for how their businesses impact consumers, customers, suppliers, employees, shareholders, communities, the environment, and society in general

simplest form, CRM involves the occasional customer phone call about upcoming events such as an open house. In a more advanced state, it includes sophisticated customer loyalty programs that reward continued purchases and usage. Air Miles is an example of a widely recognized and sophisticated CRM program that partners with brands to provide members with travel rewards.

Retailers use CRM loyalty programs to help secure a greater *share-of-wallet* (dollars purchased) from their customers. They use loyalty cards to track individual purchases and then correlate the data with offers and incentives to determine what works best. Offers are then customized to meet the purchase habits of people with similar buying preferences. Hudson's Bay with its rewards card and Shoppers Drug Mart with its Optimum Card are pioneers of CRM in Canada.

Advanced CRM considers the value of specific customers over their lifetime and what offers are most suited to their stage in life. Let's look at a simple example. If a pregnant woman buys prenatal vitamins at a store that uses CRM tracking software, such as through its loyalty cards, in time she may start receiving coupons for diapers, baby food, and tips on infant nutrition; her prenatal purchase has triggered sophisticated computer programs to recognize her eventual need for baby products. As this woman's needs evolve, and as the children get older, the offers may change to include over-the-counter medications for toddlers or school supplies for youths. This is one of the ways that companies can use CRM to encourage customer loyalty.

Another simple example of how CRM can be applied at retail is in the area of store design. Retailers can use customer purchase data to analyze departmental purchases to improve store design and maximize profitability. If, for instance, CRM identifies organic foods as a highly purchased product for a store's catchment area, when the store is refurbished, the section for these products may be expanded and given more prominence. CRM is covered in more detail in Chapter 14.

Finally, **corporate social responsibility (CSR)** has become an important part of the relationship marketing stage with companies realizing that consumers want to be associated with companies that share their values and interests. CSR is a concept where organizations voluntarily consider the well-being of society and the environment by taking responsibility for how their businesses impact consumers, customers, suppliers, employees, shareholders, communities, the environment, and society in general. In this manner, CSR programs become part of a brand's fabric and help to build long-term relationships and solidify brand

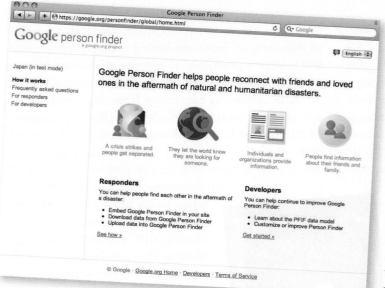

The Google Person Finder is an example of corporate social responsibility (CSR).

Google and the Google logo are registered trademarks of Google Inc., used with permission.

connections with consumers. Three robust examples of companies that follow CSR approaches are the BMO Financial Group (Bank of Montreal) and Tim Hortons, as well as the Google Person Finder initiative mentioned earlier.

The BMO Financial Group provides a good example of CSR through a variety of projects. These projects include, among others, an annual volunteer day where bank employees participate in one of 6,000 volunteer activities organized by the bank to improve the lives of people that work in the communities in which they work. It also supports children's literacy by partnering with First Books Canada to distribute over 60,000 new books to 20,000 young children, and raises funds to help Kids Help Phone ($600,000 in 2013). In addition, it has a wide range of sustainability initiatives to help the environment by reducing energy usage in its branches including programs that have successfully reduced its greenhouse gas emissions by 5 percent over three years.[10]

Tim Hortons is another example of a company with leading-edge CSR programs. Its green

Sustainability is an important cornerstone for Tim Hortons' restaurants.

restaurant-building program is Forest Stewardship Council (FSC) certified. Its recycling and waste management programs have resulted in over 80 percent of its corporate operation's waste being diverted from landfills (excluding restaurant waste). The Tim Horton Children's Foundation was established in 1974 to honour Tim Horton's love for children and his desire to help those less fortunate. The foundation is a non-profit, charitable organization committed to providing a fun-filled camp environment for children from economically disadvantaged homes. Annually on Camp Day®, Tim Hortons® restaurant owners donate 100 percent of their proceeds from coffee sales to the Tim Horton Children's Foundation, raising over $11 million to help send more than 17,000 children to camp in 2013. Tim Hortons also sponsors local children's house leagues for hockey, soccer, lacrosse, T-ball, and baseball with over 337,000 children involved in the Timbits® Minor Sports programs in 2013, and its Smile Cookie program raises several million dollars a year, donating the proceeds to local charities. And, the Tim Hortons Coffee Partnership helps small-scale coffee farmers and their communities by supporting them in key economic, social, and environmental areas that will improve their coffee business and their lives. You can read about these and other Tim Hortons' CSR initiatives by navigating to its website at **www.timhortons.com**.[11]

Many organizations now include CSR components in their business plans, issuing annual CSR reports and CSR plans to ensure they live up to their directives. Over the last five years, *Maclean's* magazine has partnered with Sustainalytics, a leading organization in sustainability analytics, to determine Canada's top 50 socially responsible companies by reviewing their environmental, social, and governance approaches to business. Its latest report points out that best-in-class organizations perceive CSR as fundamental to the fabric of their organizations. Organizations that rank highly on the *Maclean's Top 50 Social Responsible*

business sustainability
The long-term viability of a business related to its financial results, social performance, and environmental impact

greenwashing
The deceptive use of marketing practices to give the impression that a good, service, or organization is environmentally friendly

societal marketing concept
Marketing programs that focus on the consumer *and* the well-being of society

Companies 2013 are BMO in the banking sector, noted earlier for its CSR programs; Cenovus Energy in the energy sector for its low energy usage; Danone in the food industry for linking departmental manager compensation to energy footprint reduction; and 3M in the industrial sector for its pollution prevention strategies that have reduced volatile organic air emission by 95 percent since 1990.[12]

Business sustainability is a term linked to CSR programs. It refers to the long-term viability of a business based on its financial results, its social performance, and its impact on the environment. The three pillars of a sustainable business are healthy profits, healthy people, and a healthy planet. Sustainable businesses do not compromise the future of society and the environment to meet short-term financial gain.[13]

Unfortunately, a few companies have taken advantage of the environmental movement by deceptively positioning products as being *green*, when in fact they do little to help the environment. This has given rise to the term greenwashing. **Greenwashing** refers to the deceptive use of marketing practices to imply that a good, service, or organization is environmentally friendly. The

The Cadbury brand has sent over 23,000 bicycles to Ghana.

Canadian Marketing Association provides a number of resources on green marketing to help reduce unethical business practices. Its website at **www.the-cma.org** includes green tips and information on best practices.

CSR initiatives can range from the simple to the complex, and typically include one of three approaches. In its simplest forms, CSR can involve (1) the sponsorship and/or spearheading of community programs, and (2) the sponsorship and/or involvement in fundraising initiatives for charitable organizations. In its most advanced form, CSR is used (3) as a business philosophy that permeates an organization that implements socially responsible business practices to positively impact the community at large. At its most sophisticated level, executive compensation is linked in part to CSR results.

The marketing community is also putting an increased focus on the well-being of society and the environment in its marketing programs. It is commonplace to now see charitable components in marketing initiatives, an approach described as the **societal marketing concept**. An example is the Cadbury Bicycle Factory project where annually from April to June, Cadbury asks consumers to go to its microsite to enter UPC codes from chocolate and confectionary products in an effort to collect bicycles for Ghana. Each UPC code corresponds to a piece of a bicycle, with the goal of collecting enough UPC codes to send 5,000 bicycles to Ghana. Since 2009, Cadbury has sent over 23,000 bicycles to Ghana, where bicycles are considered a luxury and are an important mode of transportation for running family errands and taking children to school.[14]

New and Evolving Marketing Practices

LO 5 Marketing today focuses on meeting short-term consumer needs and generating immediate company profits as well as on the long-term viability and sustainability of its business through the transparent connections it makes with its business partners and by creating meaningful

Tim Hortons' Community Contributions in 2013

Camp fundraising day	$11.8 million
Local community programs	$16 million
Smile Cookie fundraiser	$5.1 million
Timbits Minor Sports program	337,000 participants
Kids sent to camps	17,700 children

Source: "Tim Hortons Sustainability and Responsibility 2013 Summary Report," accessed July 2014 at http://sustainabilityreport.timhortons.com/pdf/2013_summary_report_28pages.pdf.

customer relationships and community initiatives. Many new tools are now available for marketers to communicate organizational approaches and product benefits. In this section, we review some of the latest new and evolving marketing practices.

Some of the most recent marketing approaches include customer relationship management programs and corporate social responsibility (as already discussed), with newly evolving areas including (1) real-time marketing, (2) content marketing, (3) mobile marketing, (4) social media marketing, (5) partnership marketing, (6) metrics and analytics, and (7) new marketing regulations and ethical considerations.

The backdrop to new and evolving marketing approaches is the rapid adoption of Internet technology by our society, with consumers and businesses having access to lower-priced computers, multiple mobile devices, high-speed Internet connections, and cloud computing. In addition, many free online services are available, such as e-mail, online search, cloud file storage, and social media platforms.

Digital technology has changed consumer behaviour, with many people using smartphones and tablets to stay connected with friends, family, and work throughout the day and to get media updates on their areas of interest. In 2013, there were over 28 million subscribers to mobile devices in Canada,[15] with smartphone penetration reaching 62 percent.[16] People in Canada are the most connected in the world, spending over 34 hours per month online. Online video viewing is particularly high, with Canadians logging an average of 25 hours per month watching online videos. Social networking is also very popular, with people increasingly accessing social networks on mobile devices.[17]

The widespread use of digital technology in Canada is the most important trend impacting how marketers go to business. Digital technology has changed the path-to-purchase and drives how consumers gather information, connect with each other and businesses, and purchase products. The amount of time consumers spend on the Internet has changed significantly over the last few years, prompting marketers to increasingly use digital marketing approaches to reach consumers. Specifically, 18- to 34-year-olds spend an average of 30 hours per week on the Internet, 35- to 49-year-olds are online 20.1 hours per week, and people over 50 years of age access the Internet 12.7 hours per week.[18] **Digital marketing** is an approach that uses electronic means to reach consumers, whether this be through computers, gaming devices, out-of-home electronic screens, or mobile devices such as smartphones, tablets, MP3 players, and e-readers.

Digital marketing includes many stellar online tools, such as display advertising, affiliate marketing, search engine marketing, search engine optimization, pay-per-click advertising, mobile marketing, e-mail marketing, and social media marketing. An example of digital marketing can be seen with the online retailer **www.amazon.ca**, which created Kindle tablets and e-readers to appeal to digital-savvy consumers as well as a companion app store that services these devices. It also provides affiliates with display ads to place on their websites, sends e-mail alerts with special offers to its database of customers, uses pay-per-click advertising when various book terms are entered into a search engine, and carefully manages its website for optimization so that search queries render its

Internet Usage—Rankings by Country

Average monthly data per visitor

Rank	Country	Website Visits/ Month	Hours per Visitor/ Month
1.	Canada	88	34.6
2.	U.S.	82	36.2
3.	U.K.	81	36.0
4.	France	76	30.4
5.	Brazil	73	32.5
6.	Russia	65	32.6

Source: comScore, "2014 Canada Digital Future in Focus," April 2014, accessed at http://www.comscore.com/Insights/Presentations_and_Whitepapers/2014/2014_Canada_Digital_Future_in_Focus.

Digital marketing provides many online communication tools.

digital marketing
Using digital technology to reach consumers through computers, gaming devices, out-of-home electronic screens, or mobile devices such as smartphones, tablets, MP3 players, and e-readers

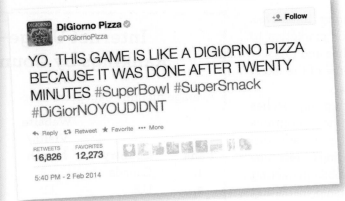

real-time marketing
A planned tactical approach where brands make themselves relevant online during events or newsworthy occurrences by diving into conversations as they occur with aligned short-term messaging that takes advantage of the current buzz

content marketing
Creating and sharing expertise, information, or branded content that is designed to inform and engage with tools such as research papers, e-books, infographics, how-to videos, blogs, webinars, e-newsletters, case studies, and events that can readily be found with search engines

Twitter is often used in real-time marketing programs.

website at the top of search results. In 2013, it increased its presence on social media by purchasing the book-lover's social network Goodreads, which allows users to share their passion for books by posting reviews, rating books, joining discussions, starting book clubs, contacting an author, or writing their own works.

Let's examine some of the new and evolving areas in marketing today: real-time marketing, content marketing, mobile marketing, social media marketing, partnership marketing, metrics and analytics, and new marketing regulations and ethical considerations.

Real-Time Marketing

Real-time marketing is when brands make themselves relevant online during events or newsworthy occurrences by creating or joining conversations as they occur to create buzz that is shared by others on social media. Sophisticated approaches use large-scale media events such as the Super Bowl, the Olympic Games, or the Academy Awards as pivotal points, and real-time marketing experts creatively engage in online conversations related to the event to take advantage of the buzz and reach a wide audience. Real-time marketing is planned with teams of real-time marketing experts ready during the selected events to create and post engaging marketing messages. The teams often include brand specialists and advertising experts, as well as senior executives and lawyers that may be needed to approve messaging. On a smaller scale, real-time marketing is used by many companies on a daily basis through empowered front-line social media managers who continuously monitor social media conversations and respond to issues, questions, and conversations as they occur.[19]

Some interesting examples of real-time marketing relate to the use of Twitter during the Super Bowl. In 2013, during a game-time power outage, Oreo cookies (marketed as "delicious dunked in a glass of milk") tweeted an image of a darkened room with a dimly lit Oreo cookie and the tag line, "You can still dunk in the dark." This image and the quick-thinking tweet, "Power out? No problem." was retweeted over 15,000 times and was a media focus for many days, securing considerable free publicity for Oreo cookies. In 2014, reacting to a boring and uncompetitive Super Bowl, DiGiorno Pizza tweeted, "YO, THIS GAME IS LIKE A DIGIORNO PIZZA BECAUSE IT WAS DONE AFTER TWENTY MINUTES." Again, quick-thinking humour successfully promoted the brand, with the tweet "favourited" by at least 12,273 people and shared through at least 16,826 retweets.[20]

Content Marketing

Content marketing is when brands or companies reach out by creating and sharing expertise and/or brand information that is designed to inform and engage with tools such as research papers, e-books, infographics, how-to videos, blogs, webinars, e-newsletters, case studies, and events. This information can be readily found with search engines.[21] Many business-to-business marketers use this approach to attract new customers by providing valuable tools and expertise to help companies manage their businesses. HubSpot is a top-rated marketing services provider that follows this approach. HubSpot is a marketing software company that helps clients monitor, measure, and manage their marketing efforts. It provides an online platform that helps manage company blogs, e-mail efforts, social media outreach, and search engine optimization with automated approaches and easy-to-use analytics. Its content marketing approaches include the creation of free e-books on how to use social media for marketing purposes, search engine optimization tips, online advertising approaches, free online webinars on marketing practices, and case studies with best-in-class examples. HubSpot uses social media, search engine optimization, and e-mail marketing to disseminate its content marketing to current, new, and prospective clients.

Mobile marketing reaches people on their personal devices.

Mobile Marketing

Mobile marketing is when marketers communicate with audiences through a mobile device or network using elements such as cellphones, tablets, e-readers, handheld gaming devices, or portable MP3 players. Mobile marketing uses specific marketing tools that render appropriately on mobile devices; these tools include mobile web, apps, mobile advertising, and various mobile sales promotional tools that we discuss in detail in Chapter 13.[22]

Marketers understand the popularity of mobile devices in Canada and increasingly use mobile marketing approaches to reach consumers both in and out of the home or work environment. Common approaches include short-code messaging to donate to charities or texting to vote for winners of TV reality shows such as *American Idol*. Mobile apps are also created to facilitate interactions, such as the Pizza Pizza app that allows for easy ordering on a mobile device and the Weather Network app for weather updates. A more complex app worth noting is the CBC Sochi 2014 mobile app that provided push notifications about medal winners, real-time event stats, schedules, videos, and live-streamed events of the Winter Olympic Games.

Mobile marketing may also include branded games that can be played on mobile devices to encourage brand loyalty. The Scarecrow game by Chipotle Mexican Grill is such an example that was created to connect users with the brand and to allow game winners to receive discount coupons off its products. Other mobile marketing tools include e-mail marketing approaches that

render correctly on mobile devices; 2D barcodes, such as QR codes that can be scanned by a mobile device for further information; and local **proximity marketing** approaches that allow consumers to opt in to receiving marketing information in a restricted geo-location, such as a shopping mall, local business district, or event.

Social Media Marketing

Social media marketing is when brands reach out to consumers online through social networks where people connect with friends and contacts to share comments, articles, opinions, videos, and images as a form of self-expression. Brands can take various approaches with social media. A brand can place ads on social networks that accept advertising to increase awareness and can hire social media community managers to deploy social media programs and to monitor, measure, and respond to questions, comments, and inquiries. While the popularity of social networks can rapidly change due to the ease with which consumers gravitate to other platforms, the most popular social networks in Canada today are Facebook, YouTube, Google+, Twitter, LinkedIn, Instagram, Tumblr, and Pinterest, with numerous other niche social networks. Niche social networks focus on consumer interests and passions such as music (Last.fm), fashion (Kaboodle), creativity (Behance), food (Allrecipes), and philanthropy (Care2), just to mention a few.

Red Bull has mastered social media marketing to boost its brand equity. It regularly posts updates on social media each day but shies away from posting product images. Instead, it uses stunning photography and videos of its extreme sporting events and sponsored athletes to engage fans. Its brand, associated with extreme sports and thrill-seeking stunts, also uses images of its cool athletes to get traction. Red Bull has a combined social media audience of 42 million users that are engaged on Facebook, Twitter, YouTube, Google+, or Instagram; specifically, for Red Bull, Facebook has over 37 million fans, YouTube over 2 million subscribers, and Instagram over 600,000 followers. Instagram, although its platform has the lowest social media following, is the most engaged for Red Bull

experiential marketing
Creating opportunities for consumers to directly interact face-to-face with brands

partnership marketing
The creation of formal associations between brands that will result in incremental business for both brands that could not have been achieved separately

promotional partnerships
Simple short-term promotional offers between brands

strategic alliance
Long-term arrangement between companies with similar values and marketing objectives that extend beyond short-term promotional offers into long-term formal business agreements

with the most interactions per post due to the quality and substance in its posted images. YouTube is Red Bull's fastest-growing channel due to its professional video content, while Twitter stands as its most active channel due to its ability to quickly post newsworthy text, videos, and images.[23]

Marketers often embed experiential marketing approaches within their social media marketing programs to create buzz and a focal point for social media programs. **Experiential marketing** is an approach where marketers create opportunities for consumers to directly interact face-to-face with a brand. Instead of relying on mass media, a brand may create an occasion for a few consumers to interact personally with it and then spread the word to others, often through social media. This approach can build awareness and generate word-of-mouth buzz and other forms of publicity for the brand. The brand goes from being passive to actively interacting with the target market. A brand can follow a number of approaches with experiential marketing, often using a combination of public relations, event marketing, and promotions to break through the clutter of competing marketing messages.

A recent example of experiential marketing in Canada is "The Street House," a campaign run by the Raising the Roof organization and its pro-bono advertising agency Leo Burnett to bring attention to the homelessness issue in Canada. The campaign included the creation of an installation and the use of public relations and social media. The installation came in the form of the Street House, a house made of cardboard and placed in an alleyway in a highly trafficked street in Toronto to increase visibility and draw attention to homelessness. Within the house, large cardboard walls spoke to the realities of homelessness with facts and questions that made people stop and think. The installation coincided with the Open Doors festival in the city, which invites people to tour grand heritage buildings that are generally not open to the public, and so served as a stark contrast. You can read more about this experiential marketing campaign in the Marketing NewsFlash, "Cardboard House Raises Homelessness Awareness."

Social networking not only is a consumer marketing approach but also has recently morphed into a platform that is used by organizations to connect internally with employees and suppliers. Closed-access company social platforms are used to more quickly connect employees together on projects and for organizations to more quickly and directly interact with and update employees. Instead of relying on e-mail updates and meetings that are time-consuming to write and attend, closed-access social networks with interfaces similar to Facebook are now used by companies to provide timely and quick notifications. The company Salesforce, a leader in CRM management and analytics, provides these closed-access social interfaces for its clients under its Chatter platform with excellent results for companies such as the fashion house Burberry and the vacation destination firm G Adventures. (See the Marketing NewsFlash, "Chatter Takes Social to a New Level.")

Partnership Marketing

Partnership marketing has gained momentum over the last few years with companies providing customers with added value through complementary promotional offers. The intent of **partnership marketing** is to create formal associations between brands that will result in incremental business for both brands that could not have been achieved separately. The purpose of partnership marketing is to drive incremental business and a strong return on investment (ROI). It is rooted in the idea that brands with similar customers but different distribution channels can combine marketing expertise and use each other's strengths to build brand awareness and incremental revenue streams. The challenge lies in finding appropriate partners, setting realistic goals, tracking results, and aligning partnership goals with business objectives.[26]

Examples of companies that practise partnership marketing are Shoppers Drug Mart, Yahoo!, Sears, Coca-Cola, and the Ontario Science Centre. When Shoppers Drug Mart selects a certain day to provide customers with $20 Esso gift cards for in-store purchases over $75, this is an example of partnership marketing. Shoppers Drug Mart and Esso teamed up to drive increased distribution to their retail outlets and provide exceptional customer value.

Partnership marketing takes many forms, permeates different platforms, and exists online or offline. Partnerships can be simple **promotional partnerships** and involve short-term offers between brands such as Shoppers Drug Mart and Esso, as noted above.

Another form of partnership marketing, with a longer-term focus, is the **strategic alliance**. This

Cardboard House Raises Homelessness Awareness

If you think homeless people choose to live the way they do, spend one night sleeping on the street. See how that changes your perspective. — Where would you rest your head?

Raising the Roof is a non-profit organization that works with partners at the grassroots level to reduce homelessness in Canada. It encourages businesses, community groups, schools, and individuals to get involved to help reduce homelessness and looks for long-term solutions so that all people can have access to safe and stable homes and the support needed to thrive.

Since its beginnings in 1996, Raising the Roof has channelled over $3.5 million at the community level to help reduce homelessness, and starting in 2010, it has worked with advertising agency Leo Burnett to raise homelessness awareness. Leo Burnett provides its services pro bono (free) to Raising the Roof and works to secure support from other companies so that media time, media space, and other services are provided at no cost.

In 2012, Leo Burnett created an experiential marketing campaign, "The Street House," in the form of an installation that made emotional connections with people in the city and caught the eye of the media—elements that helped raise awareness about the realities of homeless people. The intention was to dispel the myth that homeless people are lazy, troublemakers, or drug addicts who choose to live this way. There are over 200,000 homeless people in Canada.

The campaign included the installation itself, a provocative cardboard house, as well as an outreach to the media through press releases and personal direct media contacts to provide facts about homelessness in Canada and an invitation to visit the Street House.

The Street House was a mock-house that was made entirely of cardboard, a point that emphasized the fragility of life on the streets, and the fact the homeless people often use pieces of cardboard to protect themselves from the elements. The house was located on a highly trafficked street, lodged in a small alleyway, and open to the public to tour for two days. The installation coincided with the Doors Open festival that annually occurs in Ontario, Newfoundland, and Alberta, with a focus on Toronto that weekend. Doors Open is a heritage event that invites people to visit, tour, and discover beautiful heritage buildings, many of which are not generally open to the public. These grand homes and buildings were in stark contrast to the cardboard Street House, which invited people to come in and tour a living space that lacked many of life's basic necessities. It was a tour of homelessness.

In appearance, the facade of the Street House seemed to show a small bungalow, complete with a roof and chimney. However, upon entering the house, visitors realized that it was made entirely of cardboard and that the building actually had no roof or chimney. Instead, the house was a series of unsettling open rooms with startling information about living life on the streets. The rooms told narratives on large cardboard walls about the realities of homelessness that included facts and questions that made people stop and think. The narrative pointed to why people may end up homeless, the difficulties that they face on a daily basis, and the harsh realities of living

The Street House used experiential marketing to draw attention to homelessness and immersed visitors in the homeless experience.

life on the streets. Some rooms asked questions about how homeless people can get money for dinner or how they can find a place to sleep. Other rooms put people in the shoes of the homeless by discovering how people their age face homelessness.

The final room changed the tone of the experience by relaying positive personal stories about individuals who were once homeless and turned their lives around. It also explained the role and purpose of the Raising the Roof organization and how it helps homelessness. Finally, people were encouraged to help reduce homelessness by donating to the cause, volunteering their time, or spreading the word by talking to others or through Twitter, Instagram, and other social media networks using the hashtag #StreetHse. People could also show empathy by signing a cardboard wall of support.

The Street House installation was a success. Over a two-day period, 2,200 people visited the house and over 100,000 people acted to help the homelessness issue. Many more were exposed to this issue through social media postings as well as through conventional media channels that covered the installation in print and broadcast media. Many people were moved by the experience and commented that the house had touched their lives.[24]

▶ Video
Raising the Roof

Questions

1. What new and evolving marketing practices were used in "The Street House" campaign?

2. What role did partnership marketing play in this marketing campaign?

Chatter Takes Social to a New Level

If you thought social just referred to consumers' use of social networks as well as companies' use of social media to reach consumers, think again! Salesforce has created Chatter, a secure, customizable social intranet platform that companies purchase to enhance business communications within an organization, often inviting suppliers to join for relevant updates.

Similar to Facebook, Chatter is based in the cloud and updates happen in real time. On Chatter, employees can collaborate by asking questions and posting comments or uploading images, videos, and documents. On Chatter, people share information, brainstorm on ideas, follow topics and company experts, and receive real-time business updates in their newsfeed. In this way, collaboration is easier, issues are resolved quickly, and important information is shared easily with others. Unlike Facebook, Chatter is completely secure, and access is restricted to people within the company. Chatter is not for posting personal information but instead

for collaborating and communicating on business-related topics.

In Canada and internationally, this social business platform is becoming widespread. Canadian companies such as the Duha Group (a large international manufacturer of paint chips) use Chatter to provide better service—

Salesforce Chatter takes social to a new level.

customers are given access to their Chatter platform to get real-time updates on orders, while employees use it to communicate on business topics. G Adventures is another Canadian organization (international adventure travel company) that uses Chatter. It uses a Chatter app to allow its in-field tour organizers to access company updates on mobile devices, whether this be new marketing materials, customer records, pending

approvals, or asking and responding to questions, just to name a few uses.

Internationally, Salesforce Chatter is used by clients such as Burberry, which uses Burberry Chat for internal communications. Burberry's CEO and creative director post weekly video updates to the company, while employees use it to collaborate on business developments and to share and access information.

Companies that use Salesforce Chatter find e-mail clutter is reduced, meetings are less necessary, and people can more easily access project updates. Now every morning, employees can turn to their Chatter newsfeed and scroll down to get important updates, rather than spend countless hours sifting through e-mails, many of which are distracting and irrelevant.

Chatter makes collaboration more enjoyable, solves problems more effectively, and provides all employees with a voice that can be heard. To read more about Chatter, visit **www.salesforce.com/chatter**.[25]

Questions

1. What benefits do organizations accrue by using social media platforms such as Salesforce Chatter?

2. What benefits do employees recognize by using social media platforms such as Chatter for business purposes?

involves long-term arrangements between companies with similar values and objectives that extend beyond short-term promotional offers into long-term business agreements. An example of a strategic alliance exists with the SCENE loyalty movie rewards program where Cineplex Entertainment and Scotiabank formed a long-term arrangement to benefit both companies. SCENE members collect points when purchasing Cineplex Entertainment tickets or concession items. Points can

be redeemed for free movies or discounted DVDs. Scotiabank Visa credit card holders earn additional points when paying with their Scotiabank Visa card. In its first 14 months, the SCENE loyalty program built a database of a million customers, with Scotiabank adding 100,000 new bank accounts, many from the 18-to-34 demographic it was targeting with this program.[27]

Partnership marketing does not just involve the use of loyalty cards. The Ontario Science Centre uses

A strategic alliance between Scotiabank and Cineplex Entertainment created the SCENE loyalty card.

partnership marketing to add value to its educational programs and to offset costs. It looks for partners with similar marketing objectives and parallel values. One of its valued partners, Telus, shares similar interests in education, youth, science, and technology. This resulted in a 15-year partnership that saw the creation of the Teluscape outdoor learning space as well as the Telus Rain Forest exhibit. Annually, Telus and the Ontario Science Centre review joint promotional opportunities that can benefit each organization.[28]

Metrics and Analytics

The Canadian business world is a performance-based culture that uses metrics and analytics to improve programs and deliver better results. Digital marketing results in a deluge of data that challenges marketers to interpret and manage, a process that is assisted by analytics companies and easy-to-use software that gathers the data, sorts it into actionable areas for increased focus and analysis, and flags elements that require immediate attention. Robust paid analytics platforms can be provided by companies such as IBM and Salesforce with their analytics platforms, or through free metrics platforms such as Google Analytics and Social Mention.

Digital technology is prompting an influx of data due to its ability to measure interactions on the Internet. For example, metrics and analytics software can measure and track online sales and drill down into the origin of each sale. It can also measure website interactions such as unique visitors, time on site, page views, returning visitors, newsletter signups, and digital downloads. It can measure the effectiveness of e-mail blasts and online advertising campaigns, as well as the impact of social media programs. In the social media sphere, for example, analytics platforms can collect data that measure online buzz, identify positive and negative sentiment, and point to online brand advocates. It can flag online conversations about your brand, keep an eye on competitor sentiment, and track topics of interest, whether they be on blogs, social networks, video-sharing sites, photo-sharing sites, or on the websites of mainstream media. Importantly, this data can be meshed with a marketer's costing information so that financial insights can determine metrics such as costs per click, costs per conversion, costs per interaction, and the ROI of specific programs.

In the offline marketing world, metrics and analytics are also important, again pointing to performance. Routine metrics are measured against marketing plan targets and look at elements such as sales, market share, profit margins, and profit levels. Program-specific metrics analyze specific marketing programs and measure performance against benchmarks and targets. Theses metrics can include elements such as return on investment (ROI), awareness levels, ad recall, sales conversions, coupon redemption rates, contest entries, or media mentions, depending on the task at hand.

Metrics refers to numeric data that is collected and grouped to track performance. It is often presented in spreadsheets and dashboards, so it is easy to understand and interpret. **Dashboards** visualize data using graphs, charts, and numbers so that the data is easy to use and understand. **Analytics** refers to the process of taking metrics data and applying smart thinking and technology to gain actionable insights that can help make better business decisions. An analytics platform helps answer questions and provides customer insights, and predicts patterns that can improve marketing performance. Analytics can help segment customers, plan and forecast, manage risk, and take corrective action.

Marketers are challenged to use metrics and analytics to better understand how to build better customer relationships. Metrics, analytics, and types of data are covered in more detail in Chapter 4.

Marketing Regulations and Ethical Considerations

The latest marketing practices see companies and marketers focus more and more on the well-being of society and the environment, realizing that they can make a difference. However, not all organizations and marketers are interested in CSR or the societal marketing concept. This orientation requires a long-term financial investment from an organization and a genuine commitment from its employees. In Canada, regulations are put in place to safeguard people, communities, and the environment from businesses that

may not have their well-being in mind. These regulations can take many forms, such as pollution-emission thresholds, water safety guidelines, food and safety regulations, advertising standards, competitive guidelines, and telemarketing regulations, just to name a few. In some instances, consumer groups exert pressure on government bodies to protect society. This was seen in 2010 when Toyota's ethics came into question regarding its delayed response to necessary product recalls. This prompted consumer advocates to demand stricter government regulations, which expedited a federal bill that now allows the government to directly recall dangerous products, rather than rely on voluntary manufacturer recalls.[29]

The changes in marketing practices over the last few years due to digital technology has forced marketing associations and government bodies to revise and update legislation and implement new guidelines. New laws now protect consumers' rights to privacy and provide strict guidelines that marketers need to follow. New anti-spam legislation has also been put in place to regulate e-mail marketing practices, while do-not-track policies have been created for online behavioural advertisers to use. In addition, new industry associations and regulatory bodies have surfaced to control the wireless industry in Canada so that its marketing practices are ethical, legal, and transparent. Chapter 2 reviews in more detail the regulations that govern marketing in Canada.

In addition to government regulations, many companies, industries, and professional associations have guidelines and codes of ethics that provide direction to employees and members on areas that are considered unacceptable. The Canadian Marketing Association (CMA) is the professional body for the marketing industry, and its guidelines, codes of ethics, and educational programs help shape the future of marketing in Canada. It responds and provides input on legislative issues such as Canada's anti-spam legislation (CASL) and digital advertising do-not-track guidelines. The CMA has dealt with policy issues concerning telemarketing fraud, electronic commerce, and consumers' right to privacy. It has over 800 corporate members from major financial institutions, insurance companies, manufacturers,

The Canadian Marketing Association provides excellent resources for marketers.

publishers, retailers, charitable organizations, agencies, relationship marketers, and those involved in e-business and Internet marketing.

The CMA has a code of ethics by which all members must comply. Its purpose is to encourage high marketing standards that are honest, truthful, accurate, fair, and professional. Marketing programs are expected to be both ethical and legal and give consumers, businesses, and the government confidence in the industry. The code of ethics covers topics such as accurate representations, truthfulness in marketing communications, price claims, fulfilment practices, privacy, marketing to children, and marketing to teenagers. It also provides direction on direct marketing practices, sales promotion, public relations, and media usage. Navigate to the CMA code of ethics on its website at **www.the-cma.org** to review the details in this important document.

The CMA website also contains a wealth of information for marketers with practical guides, best practices, white papers, case studies, news releases, job postings, and information on its educational courses and conferences. CMA student memberships are available at significantly discounted prices for students that are enrolled full-time in Canadian postsecondary education. CMA membership gives students timely updates on marketing developments, bulletins on key marketing issues, access to research papers, practical guides, and webinars, as well as discounted tickets to CMA events such as conferences, awards, roundtables, and workshops.

> *The CMA website also contains a wealth of information for marketers.*

Marketing Careers

LO 6 Many students wonder whether there are jobs in the marketing field. As in any business, it is somewhat dependent on the strength of the economy, and entry-level jobs exist for college and university graduates. The starting point is to get an education and, while studying, to create a network of business professionals to contact upon graduation. Creating this network can be done through summer jobs and volunteering in areas that might be of interest. Networking with guest speakers who may visit your institution is also an important avenue to pursue. These strategies are a wonderful way to gain exposure to the marketing discipline. Be sure to also bookmark Canadian marketing job-search websites and to track job postings. Examples of sites that have job postings include **www.iabcanada.com**, **www.marketingmag.ca**, **www.strategymag.com**, **www.the-cma.org**, and **www.mediajobsearchcanada.com**.

Entry-level positions exist in sales, marketing, and promotions in a variety of fields. Job titles vary from company to company, but typical jobs include marketing coordinators, marketing analysts, marketing assistants, sales representatives, and account coordinators. These entry-level jobs usually include on-the-job training, the creation of analytical reports, liaison with other departments within the company, exposure to marketing program development, and the potential to move up within the organization. Areas of growth are in promotions and digital marketing services. Opportunities exist in creating your own business, as well as working in small, medium, and large organizations in the private sector, in the non-profit sector, or in the government. In the private sector, marketers are required in consumer marketing and in the business-to-business market. For students who have the advantage of fluency in a foreign language, this language can be leveraged with companies dealing in foreign markets, or in Canada with multicultural target groups. Companies are often looking for employees with language skills.

Students wanting to get into the marketing field need to be analytical, be able to work with others, be capable of working in teams, and have strong communication skills in both written and verbal contexts. They must be competent with technology, be able to problem-solve, and not hesitate to drill down into data analysis. As a marketer, you need to keep your

ask yourself

1. *What are the stages in the evolution of business philosophies?*

2. *What is involved in a relationship marketing orientation?*

3. *In your own words, explain mobile marketing?*

4. *What is CSR?*

finger on the pulse of the consumer. This requires you to stay current, to be intellectually curious, and to be involved in the conversation of life. Marketers need to read online web portals, blogs, newspapers, and magazines; follow social media sites; attend conferences and webinars; surf the Internet, watch TV, and listen to the radio; and absorb the trends that are evolving in society and around the world. Publications such as *Marketing* magazine, *Strategy* magazine, *Canadian Business*, and *Maclean's* magazine are highly recommended, as well as subscribing to the *Mashable* blog and *eMarketer* online newsletter.

Marketers can enjoy varied careers in marketing-related fields ranging from sales, market research, advertising, marketing analytics, or mainstream marketing roles. We look to a recent marketing graduate, Zac Stanley, to get a glimpse into the types of jobs available in the marketing field. Zac Stanley entered the marketing arena while still completing his full-time studies, working part-time as a social media coordinator and occasionally coordinating experiential marketing programs to gain experience. Upon graduation, Zac focused on the growing digital marketing space and immersed himself as a digital account manager at the digital agency Rich Media, which focuses on website, microsite, video, mobile, print, and interactive display development. "My job is insanely busy and each day is different," explains Zac. "Energy, creativity, strategic thinking, attention to detail, and the ability to work with others and sell your ideas is what is needed."

Zac manages projects for clients such as Scotiabank and Samsung and works closely with technical experts, animators, videographers, writers, and designers to bring together websites, videos, mobile tools, and apps that build business. He has worked on projects such as the Scotiabank Dream Home Finder and Samsung's in-store Home Appliance Feature Discovery Tool that helps consumers decide on appliances based on key features.

Zac Stanley enjoys the fact that his job allows him to be on the leading edge of new marketing developments

MARKETING
July 4, 2011

p 8 THE 2011 MARKETING AWARDS WINNERS | p 12 PAYOFFS AND PERILS OF AGING CONSUMERS | p 29 THE BRC 2011 FALL TV PREVIEW

GREAT TIMING since 1908

'Don't call it an obit'

OMD Canada president Lorraine Hughes leaves at the top of her game. Next stop, cottage country

Page 16

$5.95

Marketing is a Canadian magazine that focuses on marketing developments in Canada.

and that it combines creative and strategic thinking with tangible results that demonstrate success. "My advice to students is to absorb information from sales, strategy, planning, database, Internet marketing, and marketing communications courses and to be relentless in pursuit of internships and part-time jobs—these will build your resume and give you a network and a taste of what is out there so you can understand what may be a good fit." He explains that if you can build your marketing experience while still studying, you can hit the ground running upon graduation and apply for jobs that require some experience. "Find a job that fits your personality. Showcase who you are in your cover letter, sell yourself in the interview, and make sure your soft skills come through."

Zac Stanley also cautions students to be wary of poorly defined job specs as these may materialize into something entirely different than what is expected and to dive into the marketing field with the energy and motivation that it requires. "Not everything I do is fun—often, the hours are long and sometimes technology can get in the way—but I love the diversity of the marketing field and the challenges and the new learning it presents. Are you smart, a creative thinker, and willing to work hard? If so, then marketing may be the career for you."

As for what it takes to work in marketing, Stanley emphasizes the importance of having a passion for what you do, thriving in a fast-paced environment, having strong communications skills, and being analytical, creative, and hard-working. Zac Stanley also believes in the value of volunteering and frequently volunteers his time speaking to marketing graduates about the field of digital marketing.

Marketing is an exciting area where change is the norm and being able to rise to the challenge is imperative. Learn the fundamentals through education and apply your knowledge by working in the industry. Thank you, Zac Stanley!

adAlyze

LO¹ ● The essence of marketing is to focus on consumer needs and to generate revenue, profits, or support for an organization.

● Marketers are responsible for bringing profits and revenues into an organization.

● The marketing process follows three main steps: (1) identifying consumer needs, (2) managing the marketing mix to meet consumer needs, and (3) realizing revenues or profits.

LO² ● The marketing mix, also known as the 4 Ps, consists of product, price, place, and promotion.

● Product refers to all the attributes that make up a good, a service, or an idea. Product elements include areas such as product design, product features, colour, packaging, warranty, and service levels.

● Price refers to the retail shelf price and sale price of a product.

● Place refers to the distribution channels and retailers required to sell the product.

● Promotion refers to the communication tools needed to communicate to consumers, such as advertising, sales promotion, public relations, direct marketing, and personal selling.

LO³ ● A product in marketing can be a good, a service, or an idea. A good is a product you can touch and own. A service is a product that is intangible, that you cannot touch. An idea is a concept that typically looks for support.

LO⁴ ● The evolution of marketing has progressed from a production orientation stage, to a sales orientation stage, to a marketing orientation stage, and finally to a relationship marketing stage.

● Important areas of the relationship marketing stage are customer relationship management (CRM) and corporate social responsibility (CSR).

LO⁵ ● New and evolving marketing practices have surfaced in the areas of real-time marketing, content marketing, mobile marketing, partnership marketing, social media marketing, and metrics and analytics, with new associations and legislation surfacing to control digital marketing practices.

● The Canadian Marketing Association (CMA) is the professional body for the marketing industry that responds to legislative issues and sets guidelines on responsible marketing practices.

LO⁶ ● The starting point to a marketing career is to get an education and, while studying, to create a network of business professionals to contact upon graduation. Careers exist in sales, market research, advertising, promotions, marketing analytics, and brand management.

Key Terms and Concepts...a refresher

analytics
business sustainability
content marketing
corporate social responsibility (CSR)
customer relationship management (CRM)
customer value
dashboards
digital marketing
exchange
experiential marketing
good
greenwashing

idea
market
marketing
marketing concept
marketing mix
marketing orientation
marketing process
metrics
mobile marketing
partnership marketing
place
price
product

production orientation
promotion
promotional partnerships
proximity marketing
real-time marketing
relationship marketing
sales orientation
service
social media
social media marketing
societal marketing concept
strategic alliance
target market

Hands-on...*apply your knowledge*

Marketing Mix Assignment Mucho Burrito runs its annual Ghost Pepper marketing program designed to create buzz around Mucho Burrito. Review the opening vignette on Mucho Burrito and then brainstorm on a new marketing mix for the Ghost Pepper burrito that includes content marketing, real-time marketing, social media marketing, mobile marketing, and partnership marketing approaches. Outline the new marketing mix under the headings *Product*, *Price*, *Place*, and *Promotion*.

Chapter Vignette...*reminder*

This chapter's opening vignette examines Mucho Burrito's approach to marketing. Answer the Reality Check questions at the end of the vignette by carefully reading the areas on *what can be marketed, target markets, relationship marketing,* and *new and evolving areas.*

Video Clip...*questions*

Review the *Mucho Burrito 1st Annual Ghost Pepper Burrito Eating Contest* video from the CONNECT website to see how Mucho Burrito uses this event to connect with consumers and create buzz for its restaurants, and then answer the following questions:

▶ Video
Mucho
Burrito

- Mucho Burrito's ghost pepper eating contest is an example of a marketing approach that is being used more often. What is the name of this approach?
- What metrics would you use to evaluate the success of the Ghost Pepper eating contest?

Infographic...*data analysis*

Review the infographic that details information on Bell Let's Talk day and research the results of the program from its fifth year, 2015 and onwards. Update the data using this information to create a new infographic. (*Infographic tip:* Use Microsoft Excel and Word to create charts and place them in a single PowerPoint slide to combine the visuals.)

the marketing environment

We start by looking at a new iPhone app for touring Ontario wine country, GrapeTrail, created by marketer and entrepreneur Mohammed Asaduallah and his development team Mark Gage and Kirisanth Subramanian. Asaduallah takes us inside this business, providing a glimpse into how elements in the marketing environment were considered when creating this product. GrapeTrail is a free wine tour app developed by Canadian start-up GrapeTrail Inc., a company that develops mobile marketing solutions for the wine industry. Products in its suite have to be simple and easy-to-use and create meaningful experiences. Once the app is downloaded, users can quickly discover local wineries by region, create a personal itinerary, and have GrapeTrail guide them through the local wine country with its intuitive in-app navigation system. All of this takes place within the app, an important feature since users today demand a seamless experience, and most competitive apps in the market require users to step outside the app and use Google Maps for functionality.

"Australia is where it started," explains Asaduallah. "While living in Australia, I noticed local wineries had little presence on mobile devices—apps were expensive and the mobile web was daunting. Wineries lacked digital expertise and funds to hire a professional." In Canada, Mohammed noticed similar circumstances and flipped this into an opportunity to create a wine tour app—no easy task and one that required a thorough review of the market.

Asaduallah evaluated demographic and socio-cultural trends, looked at the economic environment, reviewed consumers' use of technology, thoroughly analyzed competitive apps, and examined regulations—all the elements in a marketing environment scan that we discuss in this chapter. GrapeTrail analyzed these factors to ensure it considered the latest trends, concerns, and opportunities, and addressed potential issues.

Let's look at the factors Asaduallah reviewed to develop the app and to make it successful. Specifically, the following were noted:

- **Demographic factors:** The Canadian population is aging and is well educated and knowledgeable. The aging baby boomers are active, relatively affluent, and interested in travel and new experiences. Young couples are having children later in life, which frees up leisure time to enjoy local and international tourist

Visit your favourite Ontario wineries with GrapeTrail

Now available on the App Store

Sandbanks Estates Winery
PRINCE EDWARD COUNTY
$ VQA
♡ 91% from 102 ratings

We are a family owned winery along the picturesque shores of Lake Ontario. Our summer season is packed with vineyard tours, complimentary tastings,

READ ALL

TYPES OF WINES PRODUCED

RED   WHITE   ROSE   SPARKLING

+ 2 MORE

ADD TO ITINERARY

destinations. These demographic trends were seen as a good fit for a local wine tour app.

- **Socio-cultural factors:** GrapeTrail noted that wine is becoming increasingly popular in Canada. In fact, wine consumption is growing at an average of 4.5 percent a year, with forecasted growth rates of over 14 percent between 2012 and 2016. In addition, a strong foodie trend exists with more and more people enthusiastically learning about different cuisines, ingredients, cooking techniques, and associated beverages. This trend is spilling into the travel and tourism business in North America, where wine tours and culinary tours are increasingly popular.

  In addition, GrapeTrail noted the delight Canadians have with social media, incorporating it into their daily routines and using it to get updates. Facebook Login was used as one of the options to log in to GrapeTrail, which provides users with the ability to personalize their in-app experiences. Through this integration, users can check in at local wineries within GrapeTrail and keep a personal log of all the wineries they visit.

- **Economic factors:** A review of economic factors revealed that although the Canadian economy is robust, the Euro crisis and continued U.S. economic uncertainty is making Canadians cautious in their spending, saving money to pay down debt. This presented a vulnerability, but also an opportunity to tap into local tourism, a growing alternative to expensive overseas' travel.

- **Technological factors:** GrapeTrail noted that smartphone and tablet usage in Canada is strong and that these devices are woven into the fabric of our daily lives, enabling people to easily access content and communicate on the go. Apps are widely downloaded on these devices and used to make tasks easier and more enjoyable. However, noting the popularity of three mobile platforms in Canada—iOS (Apple), Android, and BlackBerry—Asaduallah recognized the need to develop his app for more than one platform. He decided to start with an iPhone app, knowing that its users tend to be more affluent, a similarity shared with GrapeTrail's target market.

- **Competitive factors:** A competitive review of similar apps revealed a lack of well-designed, highly functional apps. In addition, local wine country associations were reluctant to spend $30,000 or more to develop their own apps, and lacked the digital expertise to maintain them. A few competitive wine tour apps existed, such as the free Winery Passport app and the more expensive Ontario Wineries Guide app. The latter was priced at $2.99 and provided an alphabetical listing of wineries, including details on each winery and its associated wines, tours, and tastings, but it had no search or navigation within the app. Uncork Ontario is a similar app, with a free download, that provided limited info but again without the ability to create itineraries or navigation within the app. This analysis highlighted the importance of focusing on user needs and the overall in-app experience. The app needed to be easy to use, contain all the functionality within the app, have intuitive navigation, have a stunningly beautiful interface, have social media integration, and be free to download. GrapeTrail wondered if an opportunity existed to develop an app for local wine country associations that lacked technical expertise and funds.

- **Regulatory factors:** A review of regulatory factors flagged two important areas: (1) People must be over 19 years of age to drink alcohol legally in most of Canada, and so the app required age restrictions; and (2) iPhone apps need to pass Apple's strict approval process, which includes a $99 annual iOS Developer Program fee, strong functionality, no viruses, stringent content policies such as no nudity or pornography, no illegal payment methods, and an approval process that can take up to two weeks. In addition, 30 percent of all revenue generated through the app, including paid downloads, in-app purchases, and iAds, is payable to Apple.

GrapeTrail looked at all these marketing elements and saw substantial business upside in a highly functional wine tour app. An opportunity existed for a free, technically robust app with an intuitive interface, built-in navigation, social media integration, and the ability to easily explore all aspects of a wine country. GrapeTrail was created with all this functionality as a free iPhone app and made available to Ontario wineries without having to incur any upfront costs or requiring technical expertise to maintain it.

Asaduallah explains, "It took a lot of hard work, constant revisions, and the need to recognize and respond to market needs. What started off as an idea for individual consumers, turned into an innovative product that provides added value to the overall wine country experience. Without the analyses, we wouldn't have uncovered this opportunity, which has become very successful for us." GrapeTrail continues to be downloaded regularly from the App Store with more and more wineries signing up to be part of its mobile marketing solution. Thank you and good luck, Mohammed Asaduallah! To see more about the marketing of GrapeTrail, visit its blog at **http://grapetrail.ca**.[1]

┌─────────────────────────────────┐
reality CHECK ✓

As you read Chapter 2, refer back to the GrapeTrail vignette to answer the following questions:
- Which generations are targeted by GrapeTrail?
- What new features do you think GrapeTrail should incorporate into its app to appeal to its target market and meet upcoming trends?
└─────────────────────────────────┘

The GrapeTrail app was created after analyzing factors in the marketing environment.

The Marketing Environment

LO¹ Chapter 2 focuses on understanding the marketing environment and how it provides marketers with direction on marketing new and current products. Marketers and consumers do not function in a vacuum and marketers understand that successful marketing programs must reach out and address changes and new opportunities in the marketplace. In the GrapeTrail example noted in this chapter's opening vignette, the developer recognized an opportunity to create a more robust app for wine country tours that had better functionality than the competition and meshed with consumers' use of mobile technology. It also met industry regulations and privacy restrictions, and considered the economic realities of the market. This resulted in the creation of a successful new app.

Marketers take similar approaches and scan the elements of the marketing environment to identify business risks and opportunities. After conducting further analysis and research, marketers integrate sound business ideas into marketing plans that provide direction for the business.

Marketers constantly monitor the marketing environment with a view to capitalizing on new opportunities and curtailing potential threats that may challenge their businesses. In short, marketers scan the marketing environment and review six key areas: (1) demographic forces, (2) socio-cultural forces, (3) economic forces, (4) technological forces, (5) competitive forces, and (6) regulatory forces. This chapter looks at developments in these areas, providing a variety of examples that demonstrate how noting and responding to these changes can result in more-effective marketing programs.

A Marketing Environment Scan

LO² A **marketing environment scan** is the process of continually acquiring information on events occurring outside an

marketing environment scan
The process of continually acquiring information on events occurring outside an organization to identify trends, opportunities, and threats to a business

> *Successful marketing programs must reach out and address changes and new opportunities in the marketplace.*

organization to identify trends and pinpoint opportunities and threats to a business. Marketers use this knowledge to ensure that goods, services, and ideas are relevant and meaningful, often using a marketing environment scan as a stepping stone to conducting a more extensive SWOT analysis. A **SWOT analysis** (**S**trengths, **W**eaknesses, **O**pportunities, and **T**hreats) is discussed in more detail in Chapters 6 and 15, but in simple terms, it involves assessing how well a company is servicing its businesses and/or consumers by assessing an organization's internal strengths and weaknesses, as well as its external opportunities and threats. It looks at this in relation to the industry, its competitors, and to marketplace trends that are identified in a marketing environment scan. This information is then used to set the future direction for a business and to lay the groundwork for competitive marketing programs that can bring revenue into an organization. A marketing environment scan looks at six key areas, namely demographic forces, socio-cultural forces, economic forces, technological forces, competitive forces, and regulatory forces.

Demographic Forces

LO 3 The statistical study of populations is referred to as **demographics**. It looks at characteristics of a group of people, such as gender, age, ethnicity, income, education, and occupation. Marketers can access demographic information through Statistics Canada and through their own

Generations in Canada?

	Population
Baby boomers	9.6 million
Generation X	2.8 million
Generation Y	9.1 million
Generation Z	7.3 million

Source: Statistics Canada, 2011 Census of Population, Table 1 Generations in Canada, 2011, accessed July 2014 from www12.statcan.gc.ca/census-recensement/2011/as-sa/98-311-x/2011003/tbl/tbl3_2-1-eng.cfm.

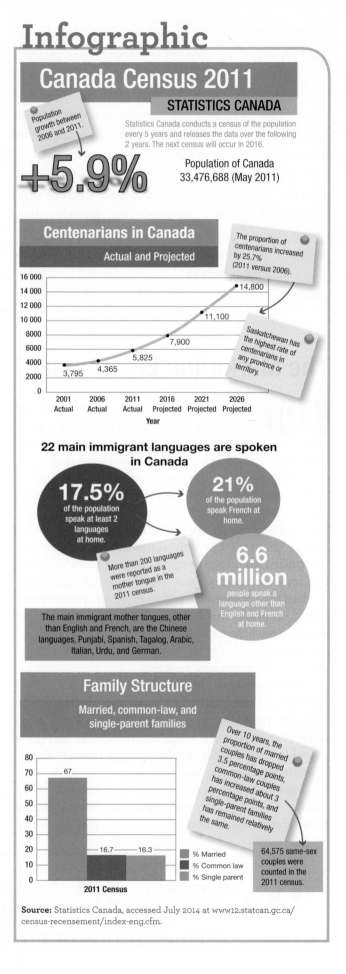

Infographic

Canada Census 2011

STATISTICS CANADA

Population growth between 2006 and 2011.

+5.9%

Statistics Canada conducts a census of the population every 5 years and releases the data over the following 2 years. The next census will occur in 2016.

Population of Canada
33,476,688 (May 2011)

Centenarians in Canada
Actual and Projected

The proportion of centenarians increased by 25.7% (2011 versus 2006).

Saskatchewan has the highest rate of centenarians in any province or territory.

- 2001 Actual: 3,795
- 2006 Actual: 4,365
- 2011 Actual: 5,825
- 2016 Projected: 7,900
- 2021 Projected: 11,100
- 2026 Projected: 14,800

Year

22 main immigrant languages are spoken in Canada

17.5% of the population speak at least 2 languages at home.

21% of the population speak French at home.

6.6 million people speak a language other than English and French at home.

More than 200 languages were reported as a mother tongue in the 2011 census.

The main immigrant mother tongues, other than English and French, are the Chinese languages, Punjabi, Spanish, Tagalog, Arabic, Italian, Urdu, and German.

Family Structure

Married, common-law, and single-parent families

Over 10 years, the proportion of married couples has dropped 3.5 percentage points, common-law couples has increased about 3 percentage points, and single-parent families has remained relatively the same.

- % Married: 67
- % Common law: 16.7
- % Single parent: 16.3

2011 Census

64,575 same-sex couples were counted in the 2011 census.

Source: Statistics Canada, accessed July 2014 at www12.statcan.gc.ca/census-recensement/index-eng.cfm.

surveys and databases of information. It is important for marketers to clearly understand changes that are occurring in the demographic arena to ensure that marketing efforts are well placed and opportunities are not overlooked.

Statistics Canada provides demographic data through its census information, which is collected every five years. The latest census of Canada occurred in 2011 and shows that the Canadian population is aging, contains diverse generations, is settling in large cities, is ethnically mixed, and is increasingly settling in Western Canada. People are also more frequently living in non-traditional families.[2] We look at these trends and identify their impact on marketing efforts.

An Aging Population The 2011 Census of Canada shows that Canada is populated by approximately 33.5 million people. The fastest growth rate is in the 60-to-64 age range with an increase of 29 percent versus the previous census. In addition, 5 million people are over the age of 65, an increase of 14.1 percent over the 2006 Census, setting seniors at 14.8 percent of the population.[3] Although this representation of seniors is high, it is in fact among the lowest in the G8 countries; for example, Italy, Germany, and Japan all have senior populations that account for over 20 percent of their country's population (see Figure 2–1). The G8 countries are the world's most industrialized nations and consist of Canada, France, Germany, Italy, Japan, Russia, the United Kingdom, and the United States.

Interestingly, among centenarians in Canada (people over 100 years old), the rate of population growth increased 25.7 percent over the 2006 Census. By 2031, more than 17,000 centenarians are projected to be living in Canada,[4] mainly due to a combination of good living conditions and strong health care services that exist in a politically and geographically stable society. For people born in 2008, the life expectancy of women is expected to be 105 years and for men 97 years.[5] An anomaly in this aging population trend is the increased growth of children under 5 years of age by 11 percent, due to more women of child-bearing age and a slight increase in fertility levels (see Figure 2–2).

Government agencies and marketers are taking note of these demographic changes and determining the needs of a greying market. Hospitals, for example, are reviewing the need for more orthopedic surgeons to conduct joint replacement surgeries; the health care industry is reviewing its home-care policies; manufacturers of bathroom equipment are designing safer alternatives for seniors; and the marketers of personal care items are creating more products for an older population, such as face creams that reduce the signs of aging, hair dye that covers grey, and medicines such as Tylenol Arthritis Pain to relieve painful joints.

▶ Video
Statistics
Canada

Diverse Generations Marketers note four main generational groups of consumers: baby boomers, generation X, generation Y, and generation Z. The definitions of these generations vary somewhat by publication and researcher since they differ on when generations start and end. For consistency purposes, we refer to Statistics Canada's parameters for the main generations and Abacus Data's Canadian Millennial Research Practice for information on the millennials.

Baby boomers are the main reason for the greying of North America. During the baby boom years

Figure 2–1
Percentage of people over 65 years, G8 countries

The aging population is a trend shared by many countries.

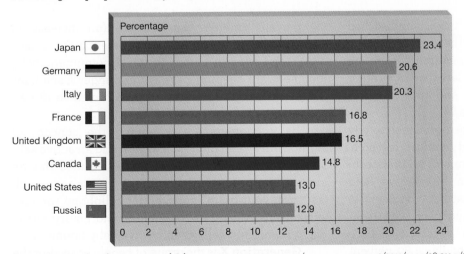

Source: Statistics Canada, 2011, accessed July 2014 at www12.statcan.gc.ca/census-recensement/2011/as-sa/98-311-x/2011001/fig/fig3-eng.cfm.

Figure 2–2
Canada's aging population

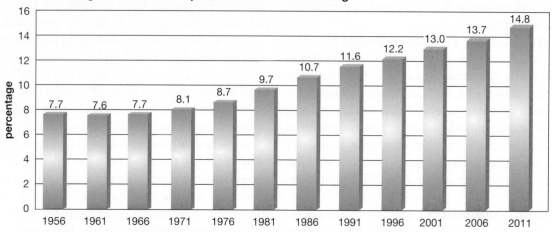

Percentage of Canada's Population over 65 Years of Age

1956: 7.7
1961: 7.6
1966: 7.7
1971: 8.1
1976: 8.7
1981: 9.7
1986: 10.7
1991: 11.6
1996: 12.2
2001: 13.0
2006: 13.7
2011: 14.8

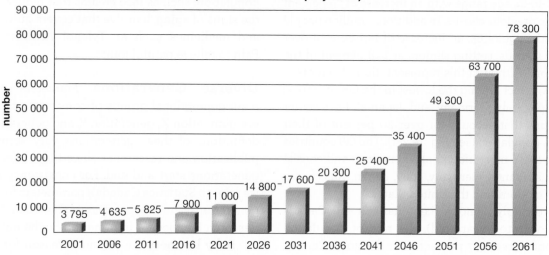

Centenarians in Canada (2011 actual – 2061 projected)

2001: 3 795
2006: 4 635
2011: 5 825
2016: 7 900
2021: 11 000
2026: 14 800
2031: 17 600
2036: 20 300
2041: 25 400
2046: 35 400
2051: 49 300
2056: 63 700
2061: 78 300

Sources: Figure 2–2a: "2011 Census Age and Sex," Statistics Canada, www.statcan.gc.ca/daily-quotidien/120529/dq120529a-eng.htm; and Statistics Canada, 2006 Census, accessed at www12.statcan.ca/census-recensement/2006/as-sa/97-551/figures/c2-eng.cfm. Figure 2–2b: "Centenarians in Canada," Statistics Canada, www12.statcan.gc.ca/census-recensement/2011/as-sa/98-311-x/2011003/fig/fig3_1-1-eng.cfm.

(people born between 1946 and 1965), families had an average of 4 children, versus the current average of 1.9, creating a surge in the population.[6] There are 9.6 million baby boomers in Canada, accounting for 29 percent of the population[7] and approximately 70 percent of the wealth in Canada.[8]

Baby boomers increasingly use digital technology to communicate with others and conduct research. While initially not at the forefront of digital technology, the 2012 Ipsos Canadian Inter@ctive Reid Report concludes that baby boomers in Canada are keeping pace with technology, although at a slower pace than younger Canadians: 89 percent of baby boomers use the Internet,

29 percent embrace smartphones (an increase in smartphone usage of 11 percentage points versus 2011), and when it comes to tablet computers, baby boomers are keeping pace with younger Canadians with ownership running at 16 percent versus 18 percent for younger consumers.[9]

Baby boomers are redefining the concept of aging with a keen interest in health and an active self-image. Marketers have noted these attitudes and are developing products that address these needs, such as "train your brain" apps, larger cellphone screens, educational vacations for seniors, and luxury retirement homes for well-off and active baby boomers.

Generation X is the group of people born after the baby boomers, between 1966 and 1971. In Canada, this

Generation X
People born between 1966 and 1971

Main Concerns of Millennials

Quality jobs	43%
Debt (student and personal)	32%
Cost of food, gas, and consumer goods	27%
Cost of education	24%
Affordable housing	20%
Pollution and environmental protection	20%
Access to quality health care	11%
Retirement security	8%
Bullying	7%
Internet regulations and online privacy	5%

The millennials are born between 1980 and 2000 and are a subset of generation Y and generation Z.

Source: Huffington Post Canada and Abacus Data from the Canadian Millennial Survey, 2012. Cited in "Generation Y in Canada: Highlights of National Poll of Millennials," accessed July 2014 at www.huffingtonpost.ca/2012/11/20/generation-y-in-canada-survey-2012_n_2151488.html#slide=1772352.

generation numbers 2.8 million, accounting for 8 percent of the population.[10] These consumers differ from baby boomers in that they are not as brand loyal and tend to be more self-reliant, entrepreneurial, and better educated. They are less prone to materialism and extravagance than the baby boomers. Generation X is becoming a key influence in the market.[11]

Generation Y is the group of people born between 1972 and 1992. These are mostly children of baby boomers. They number 9.1 million and account for 27 percent of the Canadian population.[12] Music, video games, sports, and computer purchases are key products developed to meet the needs of this demographic group. In time, this generation is expected to become as influential as their baby-boom parents. Generation Y is often casually referred to as the millennials. However, the **millennials** are the core group of people born between 1980 and 2000, a subset of generation Y and generation Z who became or are becoming adults during the Internet age. The millennials are highly influenced by Internet technology and are moulding society with their effortless integration of digital technology in all aspects of their lives.[13]

Generation Z is the group of people born in 1993 and beyond. They have grown up with the Internet, and as pioneers of social media are considered the most disruptive of the generations. Otherwise known as the *Net Generation,* they are avid users of social media, very objective in their purchases, and not very brand loyal. They are discoverers and creators of content that they readily critique and share with others. They number 7.3 million and account for 22 percent of the population.[14]

Each of these four generations has very different tastes, consumption patterns, and attitudes. For each generation, marketers need to develop distinct marketing programs, products, and services. For example, each of these generations uses the media quite differently, and marketers have to carefully select which communication tools should be used. GrapeTrail, discussed earlier in this chapter's opening vignette, decided that a wine country tour app was the best way to communicate with millennials due to their high usage of smartphones, adventurous spirit, and interest in wine.

Big City Growth Looking at the 2011 census data, a population growth rate of 5.9 percent sets Canada as the fastest-growing country in the G8, followed by the U.S. at 4.4 percent, the U.K. at 3.5 percent, and Italy at 3.2 percent. Each province and territory experienced growth, with Saskatchewan leading the way at 6.7 percent. Boosted by immigration, big cities continue to grow faster than rural areas, with the cities in Western Canada growing more rapidly. Calgary grew by 12.6 percent, Edmonton increased 12.1 percent, and Saskatoon and Kelowna saw growth rates of 11.4 percent and 10.8, respectively. Seven in 10 Canadians live in one of Canada's 33 large cities, with 35 percent of the population living in Toronto, Montreal, and Vancouver.[15]

Ethnic Diversity Canada prides itself on being a multicultural country. The latest census shows that two-thirds of the nation's growth between 2006 and 2011 was due to immigration.[16] When we look at the immigration category of permanent residents, we see that 47 percent are from Asia and Pacific, 25 percent are from Africa and the Middle East, 14 percent are from Europe, 11 percent are from South and Central America, and 5 percent are from the U.S.[17]

▶ Video Statistics Canada

Canada is linguistically diverse with over 200 languages reported by the 2011 census as either a home language or mother tongue. Twenty-two languages are spoken by more than 100,000 people in Canada, with the main immigrant languages (other than English, French, and the Aboriginal languages) being the Chinese languages, Punjabi, Spanish, Tagalog, Arabic, Italian. Urdu, and German.[18]

This multicultural mix creates an interesting array of opportunities for

Generation Y
People born between 1972 and 1992

Millennials
People born between 1980 and 2000, a subset of generation Y and generation Z

Generation Z
People born in 1993 and beyond

Millennials—Facebook Addicts?

Instagram is popular with youth.

The millennials are coming of age in a wired world and seamlessly integrate technology into their lives. While researchers do not necessarily agree on the exact boundaries of this generation, it generally covers those born between 1980 and 2000 and focuses on people between the ages of 18 and 30. The millennials are fearless users of software and digital devices. Many do not have landline phones, they frequently use the Internet to watch TV, and they keep smartphones constantly within reach. Avid users of apps, millennials use Facebook and Instagram to stay connected and often consider gaming a fun pastime.

The millennials live at home longer than previous generations. They are interested in social causes, are focused on finding quality jobs, and are concerned about paying for the retiring baby boomer generation. They see personal debt as a challenge and view marriage and children as relevant. They value service and respectability more than money and status. Millennials are not proficient in face-to-face networking.

Marketers need to know how to connect with this generation, so here are some facts to consider:

Social media

Millennials are social media addicts—90 percent use Facebook and 80 percent of users check it daily. Facebook is their top communication tool to share noteworthy events with friends, followed by text messaging. While e-mail is the least likely form of communication with friends, it is used regularly for work, school, and communicating with parents. The millennials are the most likely of all generations to share information online.

Branding

The millennials are price conscious, assessing product value before purchasing. Loyalty programs are very important to them, with 78 percent more likely to purchase a brand that has a rewards program. Rewards programs are seen as a good reason to share personal information with marketers. Millennials expect rewards to accumulate quickly and to receive their first reward within three months.

Shopping

The millennial generation accesses copious amounts of online information before making a purchase. Many read product reviews, get advice from social networks, and check prices on mobile devices while in store. This has coined the term **showrooming**, the practice of using mobile devices in store to check competitive online product reviews and prices and to then purchase the cheaper product online. Daily-deal and location-based offers do not strongly resonate with the millennial generation.

Marketers keep these facts in mind when targeting the millennials.[19]

Questions

1. How can stores best deal with the practice of showrooming?

2. Why do you think Instagram and Facebook are so popular with the millennials?

---

marketers. Specific ethnic groups have their own particular interests and habits, which can be addressed in unique ways. Companies such as Rogers Communications have risen to this challenge, offering a diverse list of foreign-based TV stations to people in Canada—a person can watch Greek TV stations, Korean TV programs, and movies from India, just to mention a few.

World Markets The world's population has reached over 7 billion people, with Africa and Asia accounting for over 75 percent of the population. China is home to almost 1.4 billion people, 19.2 percent of the world's population. India is home to 1.3 billion people, or 17.8 percent of the population.[20] These areas represent future opportunities for companies that wish to expand into foreign markets. The sheer size of these countries presents an enormous opportunity for growth.

showrooming
Using mobile devices in store to check online competitive product reviews and prices, which results in the online purchase of a cheaper product

"Canada prides itself on being a multicultural country."

Non-Traditional Families In Canada, the traditional nuclear family of two parents and two children has changed over time. Family size has decreased with families now having one or two children versus three or four (or more) in previous generations. While traditional married couples are the dominant family structure, there is an increase in the number of common-law relationships, single-parent families, blended families, and same-sex couples.[21]

Socio-Cultural Forces

Socio-cultural trends are more difficult to pinpoint than demographic changes. It is not easy to identify societal and cultural shifts in attitudes, or to track newly evolving trends. Socio-cultural changes tend to be gradual, over a prolonged period of time, and are sometimes very subtle. Statistical data is not as readily available in these areas, but marketers observe changes in society and conduct research to identify evolving trends and opportunities. Sometimes, identifying these trends involves consumer research; other times, it involves a keen eye and good intuition.

When we discuss **socio-cultural forces**, we are referring to cultural values, ideas, and attitudes that are learned and shared among a group of people. It also includes society's morals and beliefs that are demonstrated through behaviour common among a socio-cultural group. Canadians are known to be trustworthy, family oriented, worldly, organized, reliable, socially conscious, and conservative. Canadian society is tolerant of different cultural beliefs and religions; welcomes new ideas and perspectives; and values honesty, integrity, fairness, and hard work. Marketers

Five Largest Countries (population in millions)

China	1,353.6
India	1,258.4
United States	315.8
Indonesia	244.8
Brazil	198.4

Source: European Commission, Eurostat Information, November 2012 data, accessed July 2014 at http://epp.eurostat.ec.europa.eu/statistics_explained/index.php/European_population_compared_with_world_population.

monitor changes in these areas in order to capitalize on new opportunities with their marketing programs. Most recently, marketers are responding to socio-cultural changes as they relate to communications and the media, food, health and fitness, shopping, entertainment, the environment, and the modification of gender roles in society.

Media

EVOLVING MEDIA HABITS Marketers note that consumers have taken the reins of the communication channel, choosing if, how, and when to listen to marketing messages. The media landscape is blurring, making marketing communications more complex and challenging. Marketers find that consumers are

socio-cultural forces
Cultural values, ideas, and attitudes, as well as society's morals and beliefs

The 680News radio station meets consumer needs with its mobile app.

spread across multiple devices (tablets, smartphones, laptops, and TVs) and various media outlets that use websites, blogs, mobile apps, YouTube channels, Facebook pages, Twitter feeds, Pinterest boards, and Instagram accounts to communicate with audiences. Marketers integrate marketing communications approaches across these platforms to engage target markets across different devices and platforms.

The extent to which media channels have changed can be seen by looking at the Toronto radio station 680News. 680News provides news, traffic, and weather information 24 hours a day. Where once a listener could catch a live radio broadcast only at home or in the car, the station is now streamed online at **www.680news.com**, and its information can be accessed through text message alerts, e-mail alerts, and RSS feeds. In addition, news articles can be read on its website and blog, and content can be accessed on mobile devices through its 680News mobile app. This app provides four simple tabs: (1) news, (2) weather, (3) traffic, and (4) listen. 680News updates can also be accessed on Twitter and Facebook at @680News and **www.facebook.com/680News**, where the station has over 96,000 followers and 40,000 likes, respectively.

MULTIPLE DEVICES Consumers' widespread use of the Internet, and their ability and desire to access it numerous times throughout the day and on multiple devices, is changing the way marketers relate and communicate with consumers, and how people communicate and interact with each other—impacting socio-cultural norms within our society. In Canada today, we find a society that increasingly relies on electronic communication rather than face-to-face interaction, and one that is more sedentary than in previous generations.

Salesforce Marketing Cloud Radian6 is a social media monitoring tool.

Research from Internet analytics company comScore reveals that electronic devices play different roles throughout the day: A typical consumer starts the day at home checking e-mails on a smartphone, uses a desktop or laptop computer at work for business purposes, and returns home in the evening where relaxation often occurs in front of a TV, with a tablet and smartphone close at hand to respond to text messages, surf the Internet, and use interest-specific apps to get the latest information. The most popular free apps fall into six categories: social media, games, weather, messaging, music, and video. At all times throughout the day, a smartphone is close at hand for personal communication.[22]

SOCIAL MEDIA People's delight with social media to stay in touch with friends and loved ones challenges marketers to use this communication hub to speak to consumers in their online destination of choice. It is now commonplace for brands to have Facebook pages, Twitter accounts, Pinterest boards, and YouTube channels. Facebook engages consumers with offers, Twitter connects with newsworthy updates and by responding to customer queries, Pinterest is used for inspirational images and contests, and YouTube is used for storytelling, how-to content, and engaging videos.

Numerous **social media monitoring** tools have surfaced to help marketers measure success in this new environment. These tools use software to identify online brand mentions and monitor consumer sentiment, buzz, and engagement. They help marketers respond in real time to customer questions and complaints, and often identify brand advocates with strong influence scores that can amplify and spread positive brand messages.

Salesforce Marketing Cloud Radian6 is an example of a paid social media monitoring tool that monitors 150 million Internet sources ranging from blogs to social networks to the mainstream media. It listens to and sifts through online conversations, allowing users to

> *Social media monitoring tools help marketers measure social media chatter.*

drill down into the comments by source, sentiment, and amplification, responding as needed. Summary dashboards routinely identify key metrics such as the number of conversations, demographic data, top influencers, trending topics, media sources, sentiment, and share of voice. Free social media monitoring tools also exist from other companies such as Social Mention or Meltwater IceRocket. Meltwater IceRocket, for example, monitors online conversations about the topic of your choice on blogs, Twitter, and Facebook.

TV AND VIDEO VIEWING Canadians are highly engaged with TV and video viewing. While this data is changing rapidly, when it comes to TV, Canadians currently spend 80 percent of their TV viewing time watching regular TV programming on a TV console.[23] However, increasingly popular online streaming services such as Netflix are changing consumer TV viewing habits.

When it comes to online video, Canadians rank second in the world in time spent and videos watched (the U.K. ranking #1). On average, Canadians spend 24.8 hours each month watching videos online, equating on average to 291 videos. Eighty percent of Canadians turn to YouTube to watch these videos, making it the online video destination of choice; 15 million Canadians access it daily. YouTube's popularity lies in its ability to entertain as well as educate and inform with how-to videos and tutorials.[24]

Increasingly, online videos are watched on large screens (19 percent) rather than smartphones, a trend that is expected to increase with Internet-enabled TVs and well-priced viewing platforms such as Netflix. Canadian Netflix subscriptions have now reached over 1 million. Netflix's ability to provide entire seasons for viewing on demand is promoting a new form of viewing, **binge viewing** (popular among the 18- to 34-year-old demographic). This is where consumers watch episodes of complete or partial seasons over

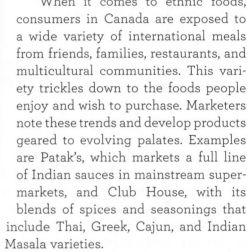

Cultural diversity stimulates the creation of new products.

a few days. The **social TV** trend is also surfacing, an industry term that refers to viewers watching live TV while adding comments on social networks—a practice enjoyed by 27 percent of online Canadians, mainly females between the ages of 12 and 49.[25]

Food Consumption The government study *Canadian Food Trends to 2020* outlines food-consumption trends over the next few years, highlighting that people will continue to demand high-quality foods that balance good taste with nutrition and convenience.[26] Consumers will also demand fresh and nutritious foods that offer good value and choice. Ethnic foods will continue to infiltrate the Canadian palate, with Asian and South American influences giving rise to blended cuisines, new dishes, novel ingredients, and unexpected food presentations.

When it comes to ethnic foods, consumers in Canada are exposed to a wide variety of international meals from friends, families, restaurants, and multicultural communities. This variety trickles down to the foods people enjoy and wish to purchase. Marketers note these trends and develop products geared to evolving palates. Examples are Patak's, which markets a full line of Indian sauces in mainstream supermarkets, and Club House, with its blends of spices and seasonings that include Thai, Greek, Cajun, and Indian Masala varieties.

Canada's aging population, shrinking household size, and high incidence of dual-income parents that balance work and family are impacting food-consumption patterns. People are shifting food expenditures away from raw ingredients toward pre-prepared foods that are purchased at supermarkets or food-service establishments. People are also replacing traditional mealtimes with snacking occasions and consuming more and more meals on the go. As the millennials become a more influential force within society, their food-consumption patterns will become more mainstream. The millennials want cheap, convenient food, but they also desire fresh, healthy offerings with recognizable ingredients, as well as sourcing information. While the baby boomers are loyal grocery store shoppers, the millennials will go to great lengths to

binge viewing
Watching complete or partial seasons of TV shows over a few days

social TV
Watching TV programming while adding comments on social networks

find ingredients and unusual foods by visiting super-markets and then going online, and visiting farmers' markets and specialty stores to purchase organic, local, ethnic, or specialty products.[27]

These shopping and eating trends are prompting innovative marketing practices. We see convenient shopping sites surfacing, such as mySupermarket (available online in the U.S. and U.K.) where a shopper registers on the site, selects products of interest, and then receives information on where they can be most affordably purchased.[28] In Canada, SupperWorks presents an interesting retail food concept by pro-viding consumers with the convenience of preparing home-cooked meals out of the house, without the fuss and bother of purchasing and preparing ingredients. There is no cleanup required at SupperWorks where recipe ingredients are already prepared, washed, chopped, and measured for patrons to include in featured recipes. Consumers come to SupperWorks to assemble ingredients into meals that are then taken home and frozen for easy thawing and cooking at a later date.[29]

A growing trend also lies with meatless meals, gluten-free prod-ucts, organic offerings, local pro-duce, and small indulgent gourmet brands that are expected to exhibit slight increases over the next few years. Food safety and health-related food issues are expected to pepper the media from time to time, focusing consumers on this all-important area. The study, *Canadian Food Trends to 2020*, points food marketers toward a continued interest in no trans fats, low-sodium/sugar products, healthy carbohydrates, high-fibre offerings, allergy identification, and foods that help prevent disease.

Health and Fitness

There is an increased focus on healthy living, with Canadian government agencies, the medical profession, the media, and educational institutions all encouraging people to be active and fit and to make healthier choices in their lives. Statistics Canada advises that since 1970, Canadian children are increasingly overweight and obese, a condition linked to insulin resistance, type 2 diabetes, hypertension, poor emotional health, diminished social well-being, and ultimately poor adult health. Its data show 31.5 per-cent of children between the ages of 5 and 17 are over-weight or obese, with 15.1 percent of boys being obese and 8 percent of girls. This stems from a variety of issues including poor eating habits, low physical activ-ity, social influence, and biological factors. In addition,

> *"There is an increased focus on healthy living."*

Statistics Canada highlights that 34 percent of people over 65 years of age who live in private households are at a high nutritional risk as they frequently skip meals (15 percent of seniors every day) and eat less than two servings of fruit and vegetables daily (18 percent).[30]

Companies recognize this shift in the socio-cultural environment and are responding with healthier products and new ideas that address concerns related to health, nutrition, obesity, and associated medical conditions. This interest in healthy living extends into a variety of sectors such as technology, food, pharmaceuticals, fit-ness, entertainment, toys, and schools. These sectors are developing products and applications that address these trends. Numerous examples exist, such as Jawbone's Up, a wrist band and iPhone app that tracks moving, eating, and sleeping patterns, vibrating after excessive inactive periods. For people with high blood pressure, Withings has developed a blood pressure monitor that plugs into an iPhone, iPad, or iPod Touch to record blood pressure levels. Its Withings Pulse O_2 device monitors sleep levels and daytime activity to give users an overall anal-ysis, including a sleep analysis, step-counter analysis, running analysis, heart-rate measurement, and blood oxygen level review. In countries where malaria is an issue, Lifelens is creating an iPhone app that diagno-ses malaria by magnifying a blood droplet to identify malarial parasites. The Apple App Store alone has 13,000 health apps with thousands also available on Android devices, resulting in a dilemma for doctors who are asked by patients to recommend apps to improve health.[31]

One of the most significant changes stemming from the socio-cultural interest in health, fitness, and nutrition is the Canadian Children's Food and Beverage Advertising Initiative (CAI). Introduced in 2007, this

Withings Pulse O_2 creates software and devices to help maintain health.

directive was voluntarily created by 16 of Canada's largest food and beverage companies to restrict children's advertising messages to healthy choices. Today, CAI consists of 19 members that promote healthier dietary choices for children under 12 years of age by shifting advertising dollars away from unhealthy products and toward more nutritious choices that meet governmental nutrition guidelines. This includes traditional TV and print advertising as well as word-of-mouth promotions, company websites, video/computer games, DVDs, smartphones, and those placed in elementary schools. Burger King, Campbell's, General Mills, Kellogg's, Kraft, McDonald's, Nestlé, Parmalat, Post, and Weston Bakeries all focus on more nutritious choices while Cadbury Adams, Coca-Cola, Ferrero, Hershey, Janes Family Foods, Mars, McCain, PepsiCo, and Unilever have committed to not advertising their products to children under 12 years.

This initiative is monitored by Advertising Standards Canada, which publishes an annual compliance report that reviews the advertising of these companies and any relevant product reformulations. The initiative shows some surprising results. Since the start of the initiative, all members have been compliant with the initiative, and many have reformulated products to be healthier. Since 2007, Campbell Soup has reduced sodium levels in its soups by 26 percent, McDonald's has reduced the sodium content of its Grilled Chicken Snack Wrap by 32 percent, Parmalat has reduced sodium in its Funcheez cheese string product by 25 percent, and General Mills has added whole grains to all its cereals and reduced sugar levels in its children's cereals by 20 percent.[32]

Environmental Awareness Global warming has received enormous attention in the press, rallying Canadians around the cause to reduce pollution and save the environment. Canadians show a keen interest in being less wasteful, recycling, and making choices that do not negatively impact the environment. However, with over 200 environmental certifications and numerous products making green claims, Canadians are confused and skeptical at point of purchase. Many companies rally around the cause and carefully manage business practices to reduce waste and provide customers with environmentally friendly products with trustworthy claims.[33] Others are accused of *greenwashing,* a term that refers to products making inaccurate environmentally friendly claims or minimal green improvements to mislead consumers and increase sales. Oil companies and a number of product manufacturers have been tarred with this greenwashing brush, while others such as Canadian Tire have been lauded for its approaches that positively impact the environment. Canadian Tire has its own green certification program that rates products on five criteria: (1) waste reducing, (2) energy conserving, (3) water conserving, (4) non-toxic, and (5) rapidly renewable. It channels considerable resources into supporting the environment, such as revamping its own packaging to reduce waste and designing new stores to be 75 percent more energy efficient. It has also created its own line of Blue Planet eco-friendly products such as cleaning products and light bulbs.[34]

From a consumer perspective, attitudes about green products waver over time and can vary from being highly engaged to being moderately interested. While people may support actions against global warming, paying extra for products that are green is not always the outcome. Recent research shows that Canadians are making changes to positively impact the environment by drinking less bottled water at home, using low-flow shower heads, installing low-volume toilets, programming thermostats to conserve energy, and using energy-efficient light bulbs. Canadians rate tops in the world for recycling, with 88 percent of people recycling waste at home.[35]

In order to avoid the green product confusion that currently exists, the industry is being advised to collaborate and standardize the claims being made. For companies without their own green certification program, UL Environment's ECOLOGO is a reputable multi-attribute certification program for green products with a certification mark that can be placed on certified products to assure consumers of authenticity.

Evolving Gender Roles Over the past 30 years, one of the most notable socio-cultural changes in Canada is the evolving role of women and men in society. Increasingly, there is a convergence of roles, with more women working outside the home and more men involved in household duties and child care. This results in dual-income families that are time-starved. Marketers identify opportunities to address this issue with more convenience products and better services to help busy families. Increasingly, we see companies offering flexible hours for employees and the continued growth of the home office. Public schools have responded to these trends with daycare centres and before- and after-school programs to assist working parents. Many restaurants

ECOLOGO provides a North American certification program for green products.

also address these needs by delivering food to help time-starved families.

Supermarkets cater to these same socio-cultural changes by offering more and more prepared foods and keeping a keen eye on shopping trends. A recent NPD Group research study notes a marked increase in the number of male primary grocery shoppers, up from 20 percent in 2006 to 25 percent in recent times. Nielsen research notes that when it comes to grocery shopping, one size does not fit all, and data show that women are more inclined to shop around for deals and balance price against taste, nutrition, convenience, and what is in the fridge. On the other hand, male grocery shoppers are on a mission, do not use shopping lists, are inclined to pay higher prices, move faster through a store, are reluctant to ask where products are located, and are more-compulsive shoppers. These studies also show that men are more apt to compare prices on mobile devices.

Grocery stores are noting these gender differences and trends and are rising to the occasion by merchandizing more male-oriented products at checkout counters—you may now see razors and batteries alongside magazines and chocolate. Grocers are also trying to slow down the male shopper with "try before you buy," displays of products grouped together to mark occasions such as barbecuing. Easy-to-read signs and maps are also surfacing to help shoppers find products, and in some male-dominated shopping areas, wide-screen TVs, comfy chairs, and bars selling wine and beer entice male shoppers to catch sports' highlights and linger longer in the stores. Smartphone apps are also available that beep when products on shopping lists are in close proximity.[36]

Not everyone fits the mould, and the challenge to retailers is to stay abreast of purchasing trends and to balance how stores can appeal to both men and women without alienating either gender.

Economic Forces

LO 4 The **economy** is another area in a marketing environment scan that marketers need to note. The economic ability of a consumer to purchase a product is what interests marketers, and with the world's economic engine being interconnected, this area has become more difficult for businesses to forecast. When the economy experiences a significant downward turn, consumer confidence wanes, resulting in delayed and cancelled purchases of unnecessary or higher-priced items. An economic downturn can also result in lower household income, again negatively impacting consumers' ability and desire to purchase. If people become unemployed, for example, they will likely defer the purchase of a new car and concentrate purchases on life's necessities. Conversely, an upswing in the economy can result in greater confidence and an increase in spending power.

In Canada, the 2009 recession officially ended in June 2009, and with annual growth rates projected at over 2 percent per year over the next five years, one would expect consumers to be spending freely. However, with Europe still not fully recovered from the recession, Canadians have become more cautious in their spending, adjusting purchases to save money and pay down debt. Between 50 and 60 percent of Canadians now plan to spend less on clothing, food, gas, and electricity, and to reduce spending on out-of-home entertainment and take-away meals.[37]

New Spending Habits in Canada

Areas where people will spend less money, shown in percentages of people

Spend less on new clothes	60%
Try to save on gas and electricity	57%
Cut down on out-of-home entertainment	56%
Cut down on take-away meals	55%
Switch to cheaper grocery brands	51%

Source: Nielsen, "Consumer Confidence: A Canadian Perspective – Q4 2012," accessed April 2013 at www.nielsen.com/content/dam/nielsen/en_ca/documents/pdf/reports/Consumer-Confidence%20-%20A-Canadian-Perspective-Q4-2012.pdf.

Infographic

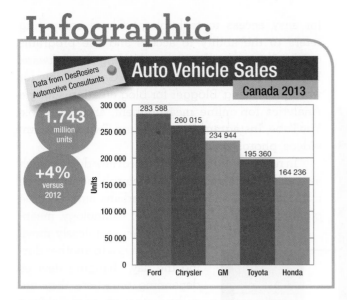

Data from DesRosiers Automotive Consultants

Auto Vehicle Sales
Canada 2013

1.743 million units

+4% versus 2012

Auto Vehicle Sales (Units):
- Ford: 283 588
- Chrysler: 260 015
- GM: 234 944
- Toyota: 195 360
- Honda: 164 236

Source: Scott Deveau, "'Year of the truck' pushes Canadian auto sales to record in 2013," *National Post*, January 4, 2014, accessed at http://business.financialpost.com/2014/01/03/chrysler-december-auto-sales/

In an economic downturn, the automotive sector is one of the first industries to suffer. The recession of 2009 saw total light-vehicle car sales in Canada fall by 22 percent versus the previous year, with light-vehicle car sales rebounding 15 percent in 2010. The most recent data show 2013 car sales in Canada increased 4 percent over 2012 levels.[38]

Marketers need to recognize how the economy affects the purchase behaviour of their target markets. Some products, such as flour, do better in a poor economy, with consumers making their own cookies and muffins rather than spending the extra money to buy more expensive ready-to-eat items. However, as noted earlier, the purchase of automobiles tends to suffer in a worsening economy.

The economy consists of macroeconomic forces and microeconomic forces. **Macroeconomic forces** refer to the state of a country's economy as a whole. Indicators of strength and weakness should be on a marketer's radar screen so that they can react quickly to changes that affect their consumers. A country's key economic indicators are its inflation rate, its unemployment rate, and its economic growth rate. Consumer confidence is also an important indicator of the economy's health, showing how people feel about their long-term economic prospects.

A key economic indicator is **inflation**, a period when the cost to produce and buy products and services gets higher as prices rise. From a marketing standpoint, if prices rise faster than consumer income, consumer purchasing power decreases.

A **recession** is a time of slow economic activity with two consecutive periods of negative growth.

During recessions, production levels decline, unemployment levels rise, and many consumers have less money to spend. At these times, consumers tend to focus their spending on life's necessities.

A country's business cycle fluctuates between different levels of growth depending on the state of the economy, international economic factors, and global pressures. Canada's growth is described by the Organisation for Economic Co-operation and Development (OECD) as relatively strong and its economy is expected to grow at a steady pace, leading the G8 over the next 50 years.[39] This strength is rooted in Canada's well-educated labour force, continued immigration, and natural resources, as well as technological advances and a well-regulated banking sector.

Marketers keep apprised of a country's key economic indicators—inflation rate, unemployment rate, and economic growth rate—to understand whether to expect a downturn or upswing in the economy. Marketers then couple this information with anticipated business performance during the expected economic climate and adjust marketing programs to maximize business results—no easy task given the uncertainty of economic forecasts and the unpredictability of consumer reactions.

Microeconomic forces directly refer to the supply and demand of goods and services and how this is impacted by individual, household, and company decisions to purchase. A marketer needs to be alerted as to how these areas affect consumer buying power. Here are some terms you need to know (see Figure 2–3):

- **Gross income:** This is the total amount of money made in one year by a person, household, or family unit, including taxes.

- **Disposable income:** This is the after-tax income that consumers have left for spending and savings. Typical purchases are for rent, clothing, and transportation. If taxes rise at a faster rate than income, consumers have less disposable income with which to pay the bills.

macroeconomic forces
The state of a country's economy as a whole as indicated by its growth rate, inflation rate, unemployment rate, and consumer confidence indexes

inflation
A period when the cost to produce and buy products and services gets higher as prices rise

recession
A time of slow economic activity with two consecutive periods of negative growth

microeconomic forces
The supply and demand of goods and services and how this is impacted by individual, household, and company decisions to purchase

gross income
Total amount of money made in one year by a person, household, or family unit, including taxes

disposable income
Balance of income left after paying taxes; income that is used for spending and savings

Figure 2–3
Three levels of consumer income

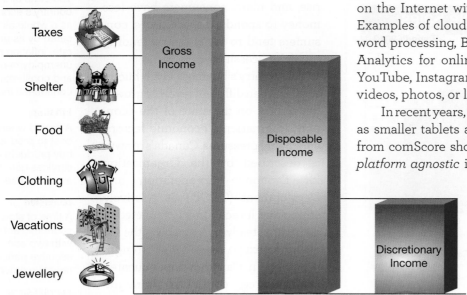

- **Discretionary income:** This is the after-tax income a consumer has left after paying for necessities such as food, shelter, and clothing. This income is used for discretionary purchases that are not deemed a necessity. Examples include going to a movie, eating at a restaurant, or going on vacation.

Technological Forces

LO 5 Changes in how consumers use technology must be understood by marketers. This is another area in a marketing environment scan that must be noted, or the results can be problematic. Marketers need to know not only what new inventions are coming on the scene but also how consumers are integrating technology into their lives.

Technological forces refer to inventions or innovations that stem from scientific or engineering research. Each new wave of technology can replace existing products, and companies need to be aware of technological changes to ensure that products do not become obsolete. Marketers must understand how consumers use technology. Research finds that Canadians are comfortable with communications technology and view computers as essential tools.[40] It is worth noting that people in Canada are captivated by mobile devices and increasingly use smartphones, tablets, and e-readers. They also readily interact through social networks and use cloud computing

discretionary income
Money that consumers have left after paying taxes and buying necessities

technological forces
Inventions from science or engineering research

for easy access to technology. Cloud computing refers to the ability to access and use programs on the Internet without downloading the software. Examples of cloud computing are Google Drive for word processing, Blogger for blog creation, Google Analytics for online measurement, and Facebook, YouTube, Instagram, Pinterest, and Twitter to share videos, photos, or links.

In recent years, with the influx of new devices such as smaller tablets and larger smartphones, research from comScore shows that Canadians have become *platform agnostic* in their use of technology, meaning that they seamlessly move from one device to another during the day, changing devices depending on where they are and what they need.[41] Many marketers recognize this and now create content that can be accessed across all devices. The trend is to use responsive web-design platforms that automatically resize website content across devices and operating systems. The result is that desktop devices see large images and animations, while smaller devices such as smartphones have simplified app-style drop-down menus and less content.[42]

Let's look at some of the latest data on Canadians' use of technology that marketers need to note:

- **Internet access:** Internet usage is high in Canada, with 86 percent of Canadians having Internet access. This number rises to 95 percent for people under 55 years of age.[43]

- **E-commerce:** As a proportion of the Canadian retail industry, e-commerce continues to be low, at about 2 percent of the industry, hampered by the low number of online Canadian retailers, poor product assortment, and high shipping costs. However, online consumer purchases continue to grow in Canada, with more and more people purchasing at least one product online. Just over 60 percent of Internet users have bought a product online, and in 2014 and 2015, annual online spending is expected to grow between 11 and 13 percent.[44]

- **Privacy:** Canadians are concerned about privacy, with 44 percent unhappy with the level of privacy in social networks.[45]

- **Music:** In Canada, the illegal downloading of music is on the decline, with 76 percent of Canadian teens paying to download music, compared to 52 percent in 2009. Increasingly, teens are using free music apps such as Songza, which legally allow them to stream music online.[46]

> *"It's important to have a clear vision and understand what's important to the user—including a cool feature is meaningless unless it adds value to the user's experience."*
>
> – Mohammed Asaduallah, co-founder and CEO, GrapeTrail Inc.

- **Tuned-out Canadians:** The number of "tuned out" Canadians (those who do not subscribe to conventional cable or satellite TV) has doubled in recent years and now represents 8 percent of the population and is expected to rise.[47]

- **PVRs and TV viewing:** When it comes to TV viewing, Canadians prefer to catch missed episodes on PVRs (personal video recorders) rather than through on-demand programming or TV websites. Most Canadians, 98 percent, watch a missed TV episode within 24 hours of the scheduled airing.[48]

- **Online video:** Canadians increasingly watch online video, with YouTube accessed daily by 15 million online Canadians. Eighty percent of online Canadians watch YouTube every month, which is now seen as a credible source of entertainment and information. YouTube is a popular destination for pre-purchase information, with 29 percent watching a YouTube video prior to a purchase.[49]

- **Computers:** Despite the increased usage of new devices (smartphones and tablets), computers are considered the screen of choice for creating content and adding data. Traditional PCs and laptops account for over 80 percent of Internet traffic, with 90 percent of young people considering their laptops as their most important device.[50]

- **Smartphones:** Ownership of smartphones is rapidly increasing in Canada, where smartphone penetration has reached over 62 percent and continues to climb. Smartphones are used for everything on the go, with usage including taking photos, texting, e-mailing, searching, checking social networks, playing online games, and using apps.[51]

- **Tablets:** These are quickly becoming popular and are used by over 21 percent of Canadians.[52] They are used mainly for *me time* during the most relaxing times at home. People use them while watching TV (50 percent), to research topics, to shop online, to check social networks, to watch videos, and to read digital magazines, books, and newspapers.[53]

The last two decades have seen disruptive technological change that is altering our lives. Search engines and e-books are slowly replacing libraries and traditional books; music downloads are quickly replacing CDs; e-mail and text messaging options are replacing traditional mail delivery; e-commerce sites are changing how and where we shop; websites, apps, and tablets are altering the way we consume news and entertainment; and social media and mobile devices are changing how we connect to friends, families, and places of work.

> *Marketers must understand how consumers use technology.*

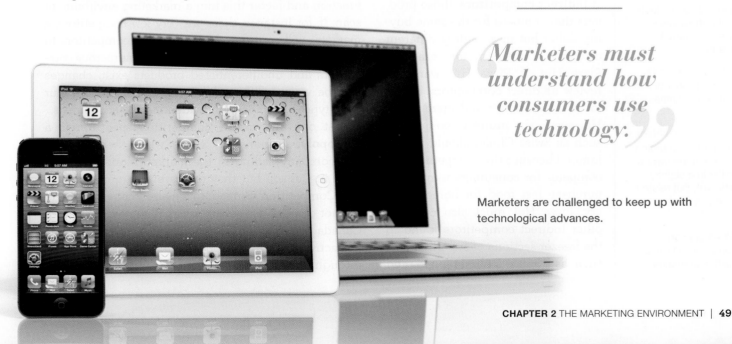

Marketers are challenged to keep up with technological advances.

Competitive Forces

LO⁶ Another important element in a marketing environment scan is the competition. This puts a focus on **competitive forces** that consumers can examine to satisfy a need. There are various types of competition, and each company must consider its present and potential competitors when designing its marketing strategy. Determining a product's main competitors can be done in a number of ways, and this varies depending upon the product and category, and whether the product exists online, offline, or in both environments. Large organizations often purchase research data from companies such as the Nielsen Company or comScore to obtain competitive market share data and to identify general industry trends and market growth patterns. Smaller companies may prefer to reduce their expenditures in this area, instead relying on competitive information gleaned from salespeople, suppliers, retailers, and available public research. Gathering consumer insights on new competitive products is also a useful tool to add to the mix.

One of a marketer's primary concerns is to monitor the competitive activity of products that compete head-to-head with its brands. Any changes made by a major competitor in areas of product, price, place, and promotion are routinely noted and detailed analyses are conducted to determine the impact on business results. These head-to-head competitors are called **direct competitors** and refer to very similar products sold in the same category. An example is Coke versus Pepsi in the cola category.

Marketers also understand that consumers do not function in a vacuum and often make choices between products that do not directly compete in the same category. Marketers therefore also look (a little less intently) at **indirect competitors**, those products that compete for the same buying dollar but in a slightly different category. Consider, for example, Pizza Hut. If Pizza Hut wants to review its direct competitors, it may focus on Domino's and Pizza Pizza. However, an indirect competitor such as Swiss Chalet should not be ignored because this competitor also competes for consumers wanting to purchase fast food for home delivery. Pizza Hut must also consider other indirect competitors found in the freezer sections of supermarkets, such as Kraft's Delissio pizza and

Direct and indirect competitors must be considered in the pizza category.

the many varieties of McCain frozen pizzas. When it comes to pizza, a consumer can order a pizza for home delivery by using a website, telephone service, or in many cases a smartphone app. A consumer can also go to a pizza parlour, take one out of the freezer, make one from scratch, or buy something altogether different. All these variables need to be considered.

Marketers need to be intimately familiar with competitive products and try to anticipate competitive moves in the marketplace. This will help avoid the pitfalls that can surface from underestimating the competition. When analyzing the competitive environment, a marketer needs to review all major competitors, taking its direction from the choices consumers make between brands and products in the category. More attention is given to those that can directly impact a marketer's business.

Apart from understanding direct and indirect competitors, marketers need to have a clear understanding of the competitive nature of the industry in which they function and factor this into a marketing environment scan. If, for instance, there are very few competitors, a marketer will consider changes among competitors to be significant, while in a situation where numerous competitors and undifferentiated products exist, changes may be viewed differently. Figure 2–4 shows the four basic types of competition as identified by economists.

At one end of the competition spectrum is a **monopoly**. A monopoly exists when there is only one company selling in the market. Monopolies are legal in Canada but they are carefully monitored by the Competition Bureau to ensure that consumers are not charged excessive prices. The government of Canada does not like to see unregulated monopolies and actively seeks to reduce their control of the market through regulations and by encouraging competition.

competitive forces
Alternative products that can satisfy a specific market's needs

direct competitors
Similar products sold in the same category

indirect competitors
Products competing for the same buying dollar in a slightly different, but related category

monopoly
When only one company sells in a particular market

Figure 2–4
Types of competitions

Monopoly
One firm
Example: regional electricity companies

Oligopoly
Few firms
Example: airlines

Monopolistic Competition
Many firms, similar products
Example: running shoes

Perfect Competition
Many firms, identical products
Example: apple farmers

oligopoly
Type of competition that occurs when a few companies control a market

monopolistic competition
Type of competition where a large number of sellers compete with each other, offering customers similar or substitute products

perfect competition
Type of competition where there are many sellers with nearly identical products and little differentiation

Examples of monopolies in Canada are regional electricity companies.

The second point in the continuum is an **oligopoly**, which occurs when a few companies control a market. In Canada, this situation exists with oil companies that control the gasoline industry. Companies such as Shell, Petro-Canada, Husky, and Esso dominate the market. Because there is limited competition, these companies can easily control prices and are often criticized for price collusion (fixing prices among competitors).

What type of competition typifies the running shoe market—monopoly, oligopoly, monopolistic competition, or perfect competition?

This has yet to be proven in the oil industry. Marketers who function in an oligopoly need to be acutely aware of competitive moves and particularly changes in price. An unnecessary price cut that is followed by the entire industry may result in profits being taken out of the category for everyone.

The third type of competition is **monopolistic competition**. This is when a large number of sellers compete with each other, offering customers similar or substitute products. Marketers need to know that in this instance branding plays an important role, as does product differentiation and added-value activities to draw consumers to the product. Being in touch with consumer needs and adjusting the marketing mix to meet those needs is crucial for long-term survival. The market for running shoes is a good example. This market is dominated by major brands such as Nike, Adidas, New Balance, Reebok, Saucony, Puma, and Asics, as well as many less-popular brands. The result is that when it comes to buying running shoes, consumers are presented with a wide array of styles and performance and pricing options. There are basic running shoes at low price points, a spectrum of medium-priced products, and premium-priced products such as the Nike+ running shoe that contains sensors that connect to iPhones for setting goals, monitoring performance, and listening to workout music. Marketers in this category need to keep the competitive nature of this market top-of-mind when marketing products.

The fourth type of competition is **perfect competition**, when there are many sellers with nearly identical products and little differentiation. Companies that deal in commodities—that is, products such as grains, vegetables, or coal—often function in an environment where perfect competition exists. In this instance, marketers need to know that pricing plays a key role in securing business, and that the focus will be on cost reduction in every element of the business.

ask yourself

1. **What is the difference between a consumer's disposable and discretionary income?**

2. **What is the most common form of competition?**

3. **What are the indirect competitors to a bag of Doritos chips?**

Regulatory Forces

The final area involved in a marketing environment scan relates to **regulations**, which are restrictions placed on marketing practices by different levels of government and industry associations. These regulations are put in place to protect consumers from unscrupulous business practices, to set acceptable standards of practice, and to encourage fair competition. Marketers need to clearly understand all the legal and ethical guidelines that affect their business practices and to retain legal guidance as needed to ensure that their practices are legal. Ethical business practices should also be followed to avoid consumer backlash and negative publicity.

Below we review the key regulatory groups and regulations that steer marketing practices in Canada. It is worth noting that regulations are updated and changed by these groups as needed to meet changing business practices. Marketers are strongly advised to check these associations regularly for updates and changes, and to consult with a marketing lawyer to ensure practices are both legal and ethical.

The key groups that regulate marketing practices in Canada are the Competition Bureau, Advertising Standards Canada (ASC), the Canadian Radio-television and Telecommunications Commission (CRTC), and the Canadian Marketing Association (CMA). In addition to these general regulatory bodies, the Canadian Wireless Telecommunications Association (CWTA) and the Mobile Marketing Association (MMA) provide specific guidance on mobile marketing practices, and Health Canada has jurisdiction over the *Consumer Product Safety Act*. Marketers also need to review other regulatory bodies and associations specific to their industry, as well as those that have jurisdiction in other countries, provinces, or states where they conduct business.

The **Competition Bureau** is an independent law-enforcement agency tasked to ensure that the market in Canada is competitive and innovative. It is responsible for the administration and enforcement of the *Competition Act,* the *Consumer Packaging and Labelling Act,* the *Textile Labelling Act,* and the *Precious Metals Marking Act,* just to name a few areas of responsibility. The bureau's role is to promote and maintain fair competition and to curtail false and misleading representations to sell products. In this manner, people in Canada can benefit from lower prices, increased product choice, high-quality services, and a reduction in fraudulent business practices.

The Competition Bureau is part of the Canadian Anti-Fraud Centre that is managed jointly by the RCMP, the Ontario Provincial Police (OPP), and the Competition Bureau to reduce marketing fraud. The centre notes more than 25,000 victims per year and maintains a website, **www.antifraudcentre.ca**, with up-to-date data on fraudulent marketing schemes and an area for consumers to report scams. These scams use various communication tools such as mail, e-mail, fax, the Internet, and the telephone to take advantage of unsuspecting people. The centre advises people to never respond to spam e-mail, spam fax, or spam telephone inquiries, and to never provide personal or financial information to secure a prize or job. In 2012, the Competition Bureau released its first edition of *The Little Black Book of Scams*, which highlights the wide range of scams that exist, such as lottery scams, money transfer scams, dating scams, job scams, charity scams, medical scams, mobile phone scams, and Internet scams. The book can be downloaded from the Competition Bureau website at **www.competitionbureau.gc.ca**.

The Competition Bureau also reviews mergers and acquisitions and prohibits deceptive business practices that include, among others, price fixing among competitors, predatory pricing by large competitors to run small companies out of business, and bid rigging among competitors to inflate prices on government contracts. Prohibited pricing practices to lure consumers

The Competition Bureau can levy hefty fines.

include bait-and-switch advertising, fraudulent advertising claims, and misleading pricing practices such as double ticketing. Bait-and-switch advertising refers to the practice of advertising a low-priced product (bait) to lure consumers into a store and then, because the product is not made available in large quantities, selling these consumers higher-priced products (switch). In 2014, the *Competition Act* was revised to include new areas that relate to Canada's new anti-spam legislation making it an offence to include false or misleading information in electronic messages, whether this be the sender, subject line, or content.[54]

Failure to abide by Competition Bureau rules can result in fines and jail time. False and/or misleading representations to sell products can result in orders by the Competition Bureau for companies to publish corrective notices, stop the prohibited practice, pay administrative costs, and pay restitution to purchasers. In addition, the Competition Bureau has the legal clout to levy hefty fines on individuals and/or companies. Guidelines for fines reach as high as $1 million for individuals and $15 million for corporations. An example of a 2012 Competition Bureau ruling relates to a fraudulent international scam based in the U.K. and Spain that reached into Australia, New Zealand, the U.K., Austria, the U.S., and Canada. A network of companies intentionally misrepresented themselves as marketers of Yellow Pages directories, using similar trademarks and names. Using faxes, thousands of businesses were contacted to confirm their existing company information in the Yellow Pages Group directory. Once confirmed, invoices for $2,856 were sent to the companies. However, these invoices were not in fact for the Yellow Pages, and the Competition Bureau fined the fraudulent companies $8 million and slapped a $500,000 penalty on the companies' two principals. In addition, the companies had to publish corrective notices on their websites, send letters to their victims, and pay full restitution. During this investigation, the Competition Bureau collaborated with agencies in the U.S., the U.K., and Australia that were conducting similar investigations.[55] To find out more about the Competition Bureau, and to see a complete list of its regulations and recent rulings, visit its website at **www.competitionbureau.gc.ca**.

Advertising Standards Canada (ASC) is a self-regulatory non-government association run by advertising, media, and marketing professionals with the purpose of setting and regulating standards of professional practice in the advertising industry. The industry has agreed to abide by its leadership, code, process, and rulings. Advertising Standards Canada sets and regulates advertising guidelines, monitored through a consumer complaint process. A single complaint will trigger a review of advertising placed in the Canadian media, with the eventual withdrawal of the ad if changes are required and not made. The ASC also provides advice and pre-clearance services for advertisers.

ASC's jurisdiction does not carry over into the legal arena. It does not levy fines or engage in legal proceedings. Instead, it relies on industry compliance to ensure that ads contravening its guidelines, the *Canadian Code of Advertising Standards* (or the *Code*), cease to air. Deceptive and fraudulent advertising, although covered under the *Code,* is also scrutinized by the Competition Bureau, which can levy fines and take legal action if necessary.

Navigate to **adstandards.com** to review guidelines and reports on advertising in Canada.

An example of a controversial complaint reviewed by Advertising Standards Canada was for a Virgin Radio bus shelter and billboard campaign that received eight complaints and a petition with 100 signatures. This ad focused on teenagers and their love of popular music and its celebrities and used their text messaging terminology to get attention. The ad placed hip-hop artist Usher front and centre in its ad with the headline, "Shirt on: OMG Shirt off: OMFG." The ASC ruled that although the campaign used terms that were commonly used by the targeted demographic, its very public display on billboards and bus shelters was offensive to those outside the demographic as it reached people of all ages, religions, and sensitivities. Despite an appeal, the ASC

ruled that the ad contravened standards of public decency and needed to be revised or taken down. The ad was replaced with others in the campaign.[56]

The *Code* has a strict set of guidelines designed to encourage truthful, fair, and accurate marketing communications. It covers 14 areas, as shown in Figure 2–5, that address issues such as comparative advertising, accuracy, safety, decency, and advertising to children. These guidelines are updated as required with a detailed list of guidelines available at **www.adstandards.com**.

The **Canadian Radio-television and Tele-communications Commission (CRTC)** is another government agency that sets guidelines and enforces a clear set of regulations on Canadian businesses. It administers a number of areas, with those most relevant to marketers rooted in the *Broadcasting Act*, the *Telecommunications Act*, the Wireless Code, the Do Not Call List, and particular areas of Canada' anti-spam policy.

The *Broadcasting Act* and the *Telecommunications Act* set guidelines for broadcast standards, and in 2013, the CRTC created the Wireless Code, a mandatory code of conduct for all wireless service providers.

The CRTC adjudicates on the cross-media ownership of media companies to ensure that a single media organization or conglomerate does not overpower local markets. It also approves broadcast licences for TV and radio stations and sets guidelines on the broadcast of Canadian content. In addition, the CRTC sets limits on the number of minutes of advertising permitted hourly on TV. While it does not directly regulate the content of ads, primarily an ASC concern, it does oversee the advertising of alcohol beverages and works with the ASC on issues related to advertising to children.

In terms of the amount of advertising that can be broadcast, the CRTC currently restricts TV advertising to the following:[57]

- Twelve minutes per hour on specialty channels

- No advertising on pay-television and pay-per-view services

- No limits on AM and FM radio stations

- No limits on regular TV stations

- No advertising on CBC radio networks except for programs that are available only on a sponsored basis

Figure 2–5
Advertising Standards Canada—The *Code*

Advertising Standards Canada (ASC) encourages truth in advertising through a *Code* that provides guidelines under these areas:

- Accuracy and clarity
- Disguised advertising techniques
- Price claims
- Bait and switch
- Guarantees
- Comparative advertising
- Testimonials
- Professional or scientific claims
- Imitation
- Safety
- Superstition and fears
- Advertising to children
- Advertising to minors
- Unacceptable depictions and portrayal

Details can be found on the ASC website at www.adstandards.com.

In all instances, advertising messages need to be legal and ethical and abide by industry guidelines. It is wise to *always* obtain legal counsel before launching a campaign to ensure that it is ethical and does not contravene any laws, including criminal ones that may not be mentioned above.

The CRTC also has jurisdiction over the telemarketing national **Do Not Call List (DNCL)**. The DNCL gives consumers the ability to elect to not receive telemarketing calls on cellphones, landline phones, and fax machines by registering their phone and fax numbers. Registration keeps these numbers in the DNCL for five years, after which consumers must re-register. Telemarketers are required by law to subscribe to the DNCL and to not call the numbers in its database.

There are five exemptions to the DNCL: registered charities, newspaper subscriptions, political parties/candidates, market research companies, and companies where business has been conducted in the last 18 months. Failure to comply with the DNCL can result in fines of up to $1,500 for an individual and up to $15,000 for a corporation for each violation. In December 2010, Bell Canada was fined $1.3 million for violating the DNCL through third-party independent telemarketers who contacted people on the DNCL to promote Bell Canada's TV, telephone, wireless, and Internet services. In March 2013, Comwave Telenetworks Inc. was similarly fined $100,000 for not complying with DNCL regulations; the fine is substantially lower than that levied on Bell Canada due to the smaller incidence of phone calls.[58]

In 2013, the CRTC introduced the Wireless Code as a mandatory code of conduct for all wireless service providers. It sets industry standards for wireless contracts, cancellation fees, the unlocking of mobile devices, the notification of roaming charges, and ceilings for overages in data plans and roaming fees. It allows Canadians to cancel contracts at no cost after two years and makes it easier for customers to understand mobile contracts, know their rights, and lodge complaints.[59] Complaints can be tabled at the Commissioner for Complaints for Telecommunications Services (CCTS) at **www.ccts-cprst.ca**.[60]

You can read more about the CRTC at **www.crtc.gc.ca**.

The **Canadian Wireless Telecommunications Association (CWTA)** provides resources on the wireless industry in Canada. It deals with the government on issues related to cellular phones, personal communication devices, text messaging, and wireless and mobile satellite carriers, and represents companies working in that space. Its website provides useful statistics on the industry as well as regulations that control the sector.[61] The CWTA introduced *common short code (CSC) guidelines* to regulate the industry's use of text messaging. This includes pricing and text messaging protocols such as the mandatory use of keywords (STOP/ARRET to stop participation, HELP/AIDE to access information on terms of use and privacy policies, and INFO to retrieve company and customer service information). To read more about mobile marketing regulations, go to Chapter 13, "Mobile Marketing and Social Media Marketing." Updates on CSC regulations can be found at **www.cwta.ca** and **www.txt.ca**.[62]

The **Mobile Marketing Association (MMA)**, headquartered in the U.S., is a global association that sets standards and guidelines, and shares best practices on mobile marketing. The MMA has over 700 members and is represented in over 20 countries. It has a resource centre for marketers; publishes a code of conduct, a best practices guide, and privacy policy templates; and sets standards for mobile messaging, mobile advertising, and mobile promotions.[63] You can read more about the MMA in Chapter 13 and on the MMA website at **www.mmaglobal.com**.[64]

The **Canadian Marketing Association (CMA)** is the backbone of the marketing industry in Canada. It provides guidelines for its members through its *Code of Ethics and Standards of Practice*. It is mandatory for all members to abide by these policies, which are clearly outlined on the CMA website at **www.the-cma.org**. This website provides marketers with numerous practical guides on topics such as mobile marketing, telemarketing, e-mail marketing, social media marketing, privacy compliance, promotional contests, fundraising, database marketing, and marketing to children and teenagers. Its latest focus pertains to legislation and regulations on privacy, spam, online behavioural advertising, and contests, which we review below.

> *"The Canadian Marketing Association (CMA) is the backbone of the marketing industry."*

You've Been Hacked!

Did your computer just freeze and a pop-up message from the RCMP announce that your computer is locked as it is linked to child pornography? The logo looks authentic and a fine needs to be settled to pay for the offence. The Canadian Anti-Fraud Centre warns that this is a *scareware* scam, designed to frighten users into immediately paying the purported $100 fine (or more) through the visible online payment button. This scam is cleverly designed, understanding that some recipients may prefer to pay the fine, rather than report it to police and incur additional hassles. Nonetheless, over 1,500 people in Canada logged complaints with the Canadian Anti-Fraud Centre on this very issue, which also surfaced in the U.K. The solution is to rid your computer of the malware that immobilized the device, not pay the fraudsters, and report the incident to the Canadian Anti-Fraud Centre at **www.antifraudcentre.ca**.

Scareware scams infect computers through malware that comes from infected links, attachments, or downloads often associated with spam messages or pop-up ads. Canadian law enforcement recently cooperated with the FBI and other authorities in Sweden, Denmark, the U.K., France, Germany, Romania, Lithuania, Latvia, Ukraine, the Netherlands, and Cyprus to help foil another scareware scam where pop-up ads sold fake anti-virus software for $129 per download. Over 950,000 unsuspecting victims were defrauded of over $71 million. Eventually, one of the European perpetrators was extradited to the U.S.

Scams should be reported to the Canadian Anti-Fraud Centre.

and sentenced to four years in jail and fined $650,000.

The Canadian Anti-Fraud Centre advises us to turn on pop-up blockers and to never open spam e-mail or unknown attachments. In addition, consumers should not click on spam pop-up images to download anti-viral programs and always use up-to-date, trusted, anti-virus software. If you are the recipient of a scareware scam, you are asked to contact your local police department and the Canadian Anti-Fraud Centre.[65]

Questions

1. Do you think the Canadian Anti-Fraud Centre will reduce the amount of Internet crime that exists in Canada? Why or why not?

2. Many consumers are unaware of the Canadian Anti-Fraud Centre. How can social media help increase awareness of the centre and encourage consumers to report fraud?

Privacy Two federal laws protect individuals' rights to privacy in Canada. The *Privacy Act* relates to the government collection of personal information, while the *Personal Information Protection and Electronic Documents Act* (PIPEDA) refers to the private-sector collection of personal data. Personal information includes age, name, social status, ID numbers, income, ethnicity, opinions, comments, evaluations, purchase habits and disputes, credit records, loans, medical information, employee files, and disciplinary actions. It does not include employee information such as name, title, address and telephone number. These acts are periodically updated, and guidelines and reports can be found on the Office of the Privacy Commissioner of Canada's website at **www.priv.gc.ca**.

The *Privacy Act* for government agencies limits federal government departments and agencies from collecting personal information unless it relates directly to the task at hand and discloses the purpose of this collection; exemptions exist for legal and police issues. Personal information cannot be shared without consent, and individuals have the right to access this information and request corrections to the data. This act is periodically updated.

Federal legislation for the private sector falls under PIPEDA and is reviewed by the government every five years to ensure that it remains current and actionable in the light of new technologies. Many provinces and territories have their own privacy legislation similar to PIPEDA and have specific requirements pertaining to health care as well as the banking and credit sectors.[66]

PIPEDA provides organizations with guidelines on data privacy, taking into consideration an organization's legitimate need to collect data with an individual's right to privacy; some exceptions exist for legal and policing situations. PIPEDA requires organizations to obtain consent from individuals for the collection, use, and disclosure of information, including video surveillance. It also stipulates that information must be safely stored and security breaches must be communicated to consumers.

PIPEDA and the Canadian Marketing Association require businesses to regularly review their privacy policies, to appoint a privacy policy officer, and to collect only necessary information. In the online environment, privacy policies must be clearly posted on all websites and detail the type of personal information that is collected, how it is collected, how it is used and protected, whether information is disclosed to outside parties, and whether the company complies with Canadian privacy legislation and anti-spam laws. A privacy policy needs to be honest, clear, and regularly reviewed. It must also be actively managed by companies so that employees are knowledgeable on privacy practices and trained to properly handle and safeguard personal information.

Individuals can table complaints on privacy issues directly to an organization's privacy officer as well as to the Office of the Privacy Commissioner of Canada. If the Office of the Privacy Commissioner of Canada finds an individual or organization knowingly contravened PIPEDA, this can be processed through the courts and result in penalties of up to $10,000 and liabilities of up to $100,000. Due to the rapid changes in digital marketing practices, PIPEDA is under constant pressure to update its legislation, and therefore, marketers are strongly advised to be well versed in the latest privacy regulations and fines, and to check the website of the Office of the Privacy Commissioner of Canada at **www.priv.gc.ca**, and the Canadian Marketing Association website at **www.the-cma.org**, for updates and guidelines. Legal counsel should also be obtained to ensure compliance in this area.[67] The most recent updates prohibit the use of automated computer programs in the unauthorized collection of e-mail addresses to comply with Canada's anti-spam policy. PIPEDA is constantly under pressure to include amendments that relate to evolving digital marketing practices.

Spam Canada's anti-spam legislation (CASL) came into effect in July 2014 to protect consumers and businesses from unwanted commercial electronic messages (CEMs) whether this be through e-mail, instant messaging, text messaging, social media, telephone, or other such communication approaches. Additional CASL elements related to computerized spam approaches will come into effect in 2015. In 2016, the Private Right to Action for individuals and businesses to take legal action against spammers will be put in place. **Spam** refers to the dissemination of unsolicited electronic messages to recipients.

The intent of CASL is to make online business interactions and e-commerce more secure. CASL comes under the jurisdiction of Industry Canada and is enforced by the CRTC, the Competition Bureau, and the Office of the Privacy Commissioner of Canada. Contravening CASL can be costly. Administrative monetary penalties for businesses reach as high as $10 million per violation, with fines of up to $1 million per violation for individuals. In addition, statutory damages can be levied of up to $1 million a day. Starting on July 1, 2016, consumers and businesses can also turn to the courts to file proceedings and recover damages. An online spam reporting centre is available at **fightspam.gc.ca** for businesses, organizations, and consumers to file complaints on unsolicited CEMs and those containing false and misleading information.

CASL includes the following guidelines:

- Businesses must have opt-in consent to send electronic messages.
- CEMs must include accurate sender information, subject line information, and content.
- CEMs must not be altered and sent to another destination without consent.
- Every electronic message must include an unsubscribe mechanism.

Canada's anti-spam legislation is enforced by the CRTC, the Competition Bureau, and the Office of the Privacy Commissioner of Canada.

spam
The dissemination of unsolicited electronic messages to recipients

- Online promotions must not be false or misleading.
- Automated computer programs should not harvest the unauthorized collection of e-mail addresses.
- Computer software cannot be installed on an electronic device without explicit consent.
- Personal information cannot be collected by unlawfully accessing a computer.

Nonetheless, various exemptions exist, such as those for registered charities that are conducting fundraising, political parties, immediate family members, and legitimate interactions between organizations and its employees. Exemptions also exist for legitimate business inquiries, quotes, applications, complaints, warrantees, recalls, and safety or security issues. Since this legislation is new and its legal interpretation is still evolving, marketers are strongly advised to become compliant with the anti-spam legislation, to obtain legal advice on their use of CEMs, and to check the CMA website for updates. The CMA advises marketers to obtain expressed opt-in consent from all business relationships so that they are in compliance with the new CASL law.[68]

Online Behavioural Advertising
Online behavioural advertising (OBA) refers to the use of web-based programs that track consumers' online browsing activities in order to serve online ads that correspond to their browsing interests.[69] OBA works by storing a text file (called a *cookie*) in a computer's web browser to track which websites are visited by the browser. It then predicts interests and serves ads that meet these interests.

The Digital Advertising Alliance of Canada (DAAC) was formed to ensure that consumers were aware of OBA and could opt in or out of having cookies placed on their machines. In 2013, the DAAC announced its AdChoices program, a self-regulatory framework that guides online behavioural advertising in Canada, making it consistent with practices in Europe, Australia,

and the U.S. Its guidelines are compliant with the Office of the Privacy Commissioner of Canada. AdChoices asks behavioural advertisers to request that consumers opt in to receive behavioural advertising messages. This is done by placing a standardized triangular blue OBA icon next to the OBA ads, which asks viewers to click on the icon to learn more and to either opt in or opt out to having cookies placed on their machines. Advertising Standards Canada is monitoring compliance.[70]

Contests
Promotional contests are widely used in Canada to encourage consumers to purchase products. They are governed by laws that protect consumers from unscrupulous marketing practices. Marketers obtain legal advice and often use professional contest administrators when conducting contests to ensure that they comply with the law. These laws fall under the Criminal Code, the *Competition Act,* the common law of contracts, and Quebec's act respecting lotteries, alcohol, publicity contests, and amusement machines.

Specifically, the following highlights important areas that need to be noted, with further details available in the *Canadian Marketing Association Guide to Promotional Contests,* which can be found on its website at **www.the-cma.org**.[71]

- Quebec's *Consumer Protection Act* prohibits advertising to children under the age of 13 in Quebec, other than on in-store displays, on packaging, or in child-specific magazines.
- The Criminal Code states that "illegal lotteries," where the winnings are based purely on chance, are prohibited unless for a government lottery or conducted under a charitable gaming licence.
- Contests that require a mix of chance and skill are legal, as well as pure skill-based contests.
- Penalties for contests contravening the *Criminal Code* include imprisonment for up to two years and a fine of up to $25,000.
- The *Competition Act* prohibits lotteries, contests, and games of chance unless there is adequate and fair disclosure of the rules, prizes, odds of winning, and allocation of prizes. All contest terms and conditions must be clear, visible, easy to read, easy to find, and easy to understand. They must include details on how to enter, age restrictions, contest entry limitations, contact information, geographic prize allocation, the odds of winning, the value and number of each prize, prize description, contest closing date, and clarification that no purchase is necessary.

This AdChoices logo is used by online behavioural advertisers that are compliant with the DAAC.

- The online environment complicates the administration of contests with the need to abide by privacy laws, security issues, and the possibility of technical glitches. Contests directed at children must adhere to further restrictions that are detailed in the *CMA Guide to Promotional Contests*.

ask yourself

1. *What role does the Canadian Radio-television and Telecommunications Commission (CRTC) play in Canadian marketing regulations?*

2. *What government body oversees privacy issues in Canada?*

3. *Does self-regulation work? Why or why not?*

Steps in a Marketing Environment Scan

LO 7 Marketing environment scans are conducted routinely by marketers to ensure that products and marketing approaches stay relevant, are engaging, and resonate with consumers. The purpose of a marketing environment scan is to gather facts, to determine trends, and to allow marketers to brainstorm on new ideas that can be implemented to build the business. A marketing environment scan will often be conducted annually as part of the marketing planning process, and also periodically during the year when new ideas and approaches are needed to boost business. At all times, marketers should be aware of changes and developments in each area of a marketing environment scan so that it is easier to determine where and when further analyses are needed. The previous sections highlighted some of the latest developments that marketers need to consider in a marketing environment scan.

In many instances, students do not know where to start with a marketing environment scan. Here is a quick checklist and a step-by-step guide:

Step 1: Collect the facts and identify trends.

 Gather data and information.

The starting point is to gather accurate and relevant information on all areas of a marketing environment scan. Many free online resources exist, such as Statistics Canada for demographic and economic data, Ipsos for research studies, and the Consumerology report for information on socio-cultural changes, technology usage, and spending patterns. Regulatory changes can be found on websites for organizations such as the Canadian Marketing Association, Advertising Standards Canada, the Canadian Radio-television and Telecommunications Commission, the Competition Bureau, and the Office of the Privacy Commissioner. Legal firms also provide excellent updates, which can be found on the Gowlings and Deloitte websites. Competitive and market updates can be followed by reading *Marketing* magazine, eMarketer newsletters, comScore reports, Nielsen updates, and special reports from WARC, the World Advertising Research Centre.

 Conduct competitive reviews.

Delve deeper into the competition and conduct a rigorous review of the marketplace and competitors to determine competitive practices and new approaches in each area of the marketing mix (product, price, place, and promotion). Understand consumer triggers and their connectivity to a brand by putting on your consumer's hat and visiting stores to review competitive products and to speak to sales representatives. Read product reviews and industry research reports.

 Cluster information into facts and trends.

Gather and sort the information you have gathered into facts and trends for each area of the marketing environment scan. Capture this information in a simple table that can be easily understood, as shown in Figure 2–6.

Note: Some information may fall into more than one area in a marketing environment scan. The information should be repeated as necessary to ensure adequate focus.

Step 2: Brainstorm on marketing ideas to build the business.

 Brainstorm.

Determine business objectives and then conduct a brainstorming session to prompt new ideas that address the facts, trends, and business objectives.

Figure 2–6
Marketing Environment Scan—GrapeTrail

	STEP 1 Facts and Trends Collect the facts and identify trends in each area	STEP 2 Brainstorming Ideas Brainstorm on marketing ideas that may build the business	STEP 3 Ideas for Implementation Assess and evaluate the ideas. Implement those that can build the business
FACTORS IN MARKETING ENVIRONMENT SCAN			

Demographic factors	• A well-educated aging population exists in Canada.
	• Baby boomers are active, relatively affluent, and interested in travel and new experiences.
	• Young couples are having children later in life, freeing up leisure time to enjoy local and international tourist destinations.
		• Create apps that allow users to more easily explore local travel destinations.
		• Create apps that allow baby boomers to explore eco-tourism and edu-tourism interests.
		• Include good-quality information in the apps to appeal to well-educated baby boomers.
		• Create apps for wine country tours for millennials.
		• Create apps for culinary food tours for millennials.
			• Develop local wine tour apps.
			• Ensure wine tour apps have better features and more functionality than the competition. Include the following:
			  – Local wine regions, including emerging regions
			  – Winery information such as trading hours, contact details, and types of wines produced
			  – Options for users to create their own personal itineraries
			  – Navigation within the app
			  – Social media login
			• Visit local wineries and get their feedback to improve the app.

Socio-cultural factors	• Wine is becoming increasingly popular in Canada. • In Canada, there is an emerging foodie culture. • Social media is part of the day for most Canadians.	• Create an app for exploring local wine country regions. • Create an app for culinary food tours. • Create an app for eco-tourism tours. • Integrate social media in the apps.	• Create an app for local wine tours. • Integrate social media in the apps so that users can share their experiences. • Allow users to sign up and log in to the app using Facebook.
Economic factors	• Consumers are concerned about the economy. • People have become more prudent in their spending habits.	• Provide free apps that help Canadians explore local tourist destinations and what they have to offer. • Consider accepting ads in the apps to make them financially viable. • Consider licensing the apps to local tourist associations. • Partner with wineries to encourage users to download the app.	• Provide app as a free download. • Partner with wineries to encourage users to download the app. • Provide wineries with marketing materials to raise awareness of the app.
Technological factors	• Smartphone and tablet usage is strong in Canada. • Apps are widely downloaded on Apple iOS, Google Android, and BlackBerry devices.	• Consider making apps for Apple iOS, Google Android, and BlackBerry devices.	• Develop the wine tour app for Apple iOS devices first. • Expand the app to other platforms at a later date.
Competitive factors	• An overwhelming number of apps exist. • Only a few worthy eco-tourism and edu-tourism apps exist. • Most wine-related apps need to be purchased for a fee. • Wine tour apps do not provide GPS navigation within the app.	• Create free, highly functional edu-tourism and eco-tourism apps. • Integrate social media in the apps. • Ensure GPS navigation exists within the app. • Provide the app for free with zero in-app purchases.	• Start with a highly functional, free wine tour app with built-in GPS navigation and social media integration. • Ensure the user interface of the app is supported for all iPhone screen sizes.
Regulatory factors	• Canadians must be 19 years of age or older to legally drink alcohol. • The app must pass the iOS strict approval process. • Developer must pay an annual fee and portions of all earnings through the app to Apple.	• Ensure the app complies with Apple's App Store Review Guidelines.	• Ensure the app is listed with an App Store rating of 17+. • Create responsible drinking messages within the app.

All reasonable ideas should be considered at this point as they will be screened down to a few actionable elements in the subsequent step.

Step 3: Assess, evaluate, and implement ideas.

 Assess ideas.

Review the ideas captured from the brainstorming session and assess which ones can realistically achieve the business objectives in the expected time horizon.

 Evaluate alternatives.

Evaluate the realistic alternatives against the business objectives and select those that are worthwhile and can be implemented.

For greater clarification, review the marketing environment scan (Figure 2–6) conducted by Mohammed Asaduallah for his wine tour app, GrapeTrail, that was discussed in this chapter's opening vignette. After gathering data and information on the market and competition, Asaduallah identified potential opportunities and determined the approach he wanted to take. What started off as a simple idea for wineries to have better online presence, turned into an app for wine country tours. Note how he distilled the data down to a few relevant points that were used as springboards for creativity and further analysis.[72]

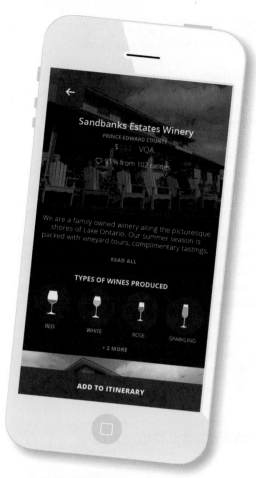

GrapeTrail scanned the marketing environment to finesse its app.

Summary...just the facts

LO¹ ● A marketing environment scan is the process of continually acquiring information on events outside an organization to identify trends, opportunities, and threats.

LO² ● Elements in a marketing environment scan include demographic factors, socio-cultural factors, economic factors, technological factors, competitive factors, and regulatory factors.

LO³ ● Demographics are the statistical study of populations, looking at characteristics such as gender, age, ethnicity, income, education, and occupation.

● Socio-cultural forces look at cultural values, ideas, and attitudes as they relate to society's trends and beliefs.

LO⁴ ● Economic forces are important in terms of a target market's disposable income and the general health of the economy, including consumer confidence.

LO⁵ ● Technological forces relate to scientific inventions and innovations that may impact the running of a business and influence consumer behaviour and interactions.

LO⁶ ● Competitive forces refer to direct and indirect competitors as well as the competitive nature of the market in which they function.

● Regulatory forces are the restrictions placed on businesses, products, or services by the government or industry associations.

LO⁷ ● Steps in a marketing environment scan involve (1) collecting the facts and identifying trends, (2) brainstorming on marketing ideas to build the business, and (3) assessing, evaluating, and implementing ideas.

Key Terms and Concepts...a refresher

baby boomers
binge viewing
competitive forces
demographics
direct competitors
discretionary income
disposable income
Do Not Call List (DNCL)
economy
Generation X
Generation Y

Generation Z
gross income
indirect competitors
inflation
macroeconomic forces
marketing environment scan
microeconomic forces
millennials
monopolistic competition
monopoly
oligopoly

online behavioural advertising (OBA)
perfect competition
recession
regulations
showrooming
socio-cultural forces
social media monitoring
social TV
spam
SWOT analysis
technological forces

Hands-on...apply your knowledge

Marketing Environment Scan Assignment Assume GrapeTrail is expanding its business to create an app for foodies. Review this chapter's opening vignette on GrapeTrail and the steps required to conduct a marketing environment scan at the end of this chapter. Create a new marketing environment scan to determine what ideas and opportunities exist for targeting food enthusiasts. Follow the steps in a marketing environment scan and outline your work in the format outlined in Figure 2–6.

Chapter Vignette...*reminder*

This chapter's opening vignette examines how a wine country tour app was created using the elements in a marketing environment scan. Answer the Reality Check questions at the end of the vignette by carefully reading the Marketing NewsFlash "Millennials—Facebook Addicts?" the data box "Main Concerns of Millennials," and the "Demographic Forces" section.

Video Clip...*questions*

Review the two Statistics Canada videos on CONNECT and answer the following questions:

▶ Video
Statistics
Canada

- What are the top three immigrant languages in Canada?
- How many aboriginal languages are spoken in Canada?
- What percentage of the population is bilingual in English and French?
- What percentage of the population is between 15 and 64 years of age?
- What is the growth rate of the 0- to 4-year-old age segment?
- What is the fastest-growing age group and what is its growth rate?

Infographic...*data analysis*

Review the infographic on auto sales in Canada and update the chart using the latest data from Canadian newspaper articles from the *Toronto Star,* the *National Post,* and the *Globe and Mail,* as well as other reputable business sources such as *Canadian Business, Maclean's,* and the DesRosiers website, which specializes in the car industry. Create your own infographic and write a short analysis of industry changes that occurred over the last year. (*Infographic tip:* Use Microsoft Excel and Word to create charts and place them in a single PowerPoint slide to combine the visuals.)

For more information on the resources available from McGraw-Hill Ryerson, go to **www.mheducation.ca/he/solutions**.

consumer behaviour

Understanding how prospective customers think and anticipating their actions is a key element to business success. In Chapter 3, we describe this as the purchase decision process—the stages a consumer passes through when choosing products and services. Prior to making a purchase, Canadians identify a need and then seek information. They use that information to determine and evaluate alternatives to addressing their need. Once they have made a decision on how to address the need, they proceed with their purchase and then reflect on that purchase.

The length of time it takes a consumer to go through this purchase decision process depends on the magnitude of the decision. Deciding on what toothpaste to purchase takes less time and research than choosing a new laptop or mobile device. It is the role of marketers to help facilitate consumer decisions by providing support and guidance through all stages of the purchase decision process.

To see how marketers do this, let's consider an organization whose services act as a catalyst to consumer decision-making. Yellow Media, a leading digital media and marketing solutions company, owns and operates a network of properties, including Yellow Pages Group (its flagship company), **RedFlagDeals.com**, **Canada411.ca**, Wall2Wall Media, and Canpages. This corporate behemoth has had to adapt to the changing needs of consumers over the past 100 years. Understanding how the company's strategy changed helps understand how consumer behaviour has changed.

"Once upon a time, it was easier for consumers to find local business information," Nick Gaudreau, chief marketing officer of Yellow Pages Group, reflects. "It was the Yellow Pages directory—a physical publication delivered to each household."

When Canadians recognized that they had a need, they would use the directory to find an answer to that need. The company's logo stems from an old company slogan, "Let Your Fingers Do the Walking through the Yellow Pages."

Although the digital revolution seems to have begun suddenly, Nick remembers the change to be more gradual. "The digital revolution began in the late 1990s, and in 2008, the print business at Yellow Pages Group was still relatively stable. Our company was delving into online media, but the paper business was still going strong." The management at Yellow Pages Group observed that consumers were behaving differently and adjusted their solutions and businesses accordingly.

TM

Chapter Outline:

Adapting to consumers → Consumer purchase decision process → Situational influences on consumer decisions → Psychological influences on consumer behaviour → Socio-cultural influences on consumer behaviour

"All of sudden, consumer behaviour changed," recounts Nick. "The smartphone meant you always had the opportunity to be connected." Fingers were now walking on screens rather than through paper directories. "The process to find information was easier with smartphone technology, and consumers were getting used to instant gratification from their searches."

With his background in traditional and digital marketing as well as product development, Nick was able to witness the change in consumer behaviour first-hand. The digital transformation of consumers may be perceived as a threat to many businesses, but Nick sees this change as opportunities for many businesses and has established a track record in digital transformation.

"Who would have thought 10 years ago that one-third of all local searches was going to be done on smartphones?" Nick asks. What used to be straightforward for businesses has now become more complex and strategic, and a thriving business for Yellow Pages Group. "It is no longer just about ensuring your name is in the directory. You have to be certain that your name is present when the right customer needs to see it."

"Traditionally, consumers made decisions through awareness, consideration, evaluation, and purchase," Nick continues. "Today, consumers are still subject to awareness, but by the time they reach the evaluation and purchase stages, they may have been in contact with 14 touch points of research. There is a lot more information to access and process for a decision than ever before. And it is easier to get."

The fact that the consumer decision-making process evolved required Yellow Pages Group to embark on one of the largest corporate transformations ever attempted. With 100 percent of its revenues coming from print in 2008, Yellow Pages Group has embraced the digital revolution and now generates close to 50 percent of its revenue from digital sources.

Nick believes that small and medium-size businesses can receive a great deal of value from the services offered by Yellow Pages Group. "Business owners want to focus on what they do best—their business operations. We support them through their advertising strategy. Every day, there is something changing with respect to technology, and small business can be completely overwhelmed with trying to keep up."

Yellow Pages Group helps businesses build websites and offers digital media services to help businesses keep up with the fast-paced evolution of technology. Since developing a local digital advertising approach can be complex, Yellow Pages Group sees small and medium-size businesses as an underserved market. Nick summarizes his company's value proposition as "you take care of your clients and we will run your marketing for you."

Although the evolution of consumer behaviour may have negatively impacted some companies, Yellow Pages Group has embraced the change and provides product solutions for small to medium-size businesses to reach consumers. For example, through its different digital properties, Yellow Pages Group reaches almost one-third of Canada's online population every month. The company's Yellow Pages™ 3600 Solution product portfolio includes website creation, commercial video filming and production, search engine marketing and optimization, online and mobile advertising, and advertising performance reporting tools. This solution provides Canada's small and medium-size businesses with the ability to reach more customers by placing them directly in the path of online consumer traffic.

"There is a huge opportunity in local advertising," explains Nick. "It is potentially a $10 billion market." The vision over the next five years is for Yellow Pages Group to capitalize on this opportunity with more marketing and media solutions for its ever-changing consumers.[1]

▶ Video
Yellow Pages Group

Since an organization's resources are limited, deciding where to allocate them is an important decision. By understanding the habits of potential customers, organizations can direct their resources in the appropriate manner. The Yellow Pages Group videos describe how Yellow Pages Group helps businesses build a brand and reach target consumers. The market segmentation process relies on **consumer behaviour**—the actions a person takes in purchasing and using products and services—and insight to group buyers that have common needs and similar habits.

---

reality CHECK ✓

As you read Chapter 3, refer back to the Yellow Pages Group vignette to answer the following questions:

- When have you used online or mobile technology to find the information you were searching for to help you make your purchase decision?
- How have advances in technology affected the consumer purchase decision process?

Consumer Purchase Decision Process

LO¹ Whether you are purchasing toothpaste or a new laptop for school, behind the visible act of making a purchase lies an important decision process. The stages that a consumer passes through when making choices about which products and services to buy is the **purchase decision process**. This process has five stages, as shown in Figure 3–1: problem recognition, information search, evaluation of alternatives, purchase decision, and post-purchase behaviour. Although technology has not changed the core elements of the process, the introduction of online and mobile technology has allowed consumers to make faster and more informed decisions.

A consumer's involvement in the purchase decision process varies based on the complexity of the decision. The time spent in each stage will depend on various factors, including what is being purchased. Access to information makes decision making a lot easier for Canadians, and access to credit makes purchasing items easier as well. This has put Canadians in a challenging situation where they are now laden with debt due to purchasing items they have no room to store.[2]

Furthermore, businesses make decisions that follow a similar purchase decision process when considering products and services from suppliers. Chapter 5 looks at marketing to organizations in detail, including the different approaches required due to the magnitude of the decisions needed.

Problem Recognition: Perceiving a Need

Problem recognition, the initial step in the purchase decision, occurs when a person realizes that the difference between what he or she has and what he or she would like to have is big enough to actually do something about it.[3] The process may be triggered by a situation as simple as finding no milk in the refrigerator. It could be more tenuous for a college or university student realizing his wardrobe is not in style with his classmates. Furthermore, problem recognition can be as complex as realizing that you need to purchase a new laptop computer. In marketing, advertisements, salespeople, or peers activate the consumer purchase decision process by highlighting the shortcomings of a consumer's cellphone compared to the latest smartphone. Consider smartphone advertisements that have been stimulating your problem recognition by emphasizing "maximum use from one device."

Information Search: Seeking Value

After recognizing a problem, consumers begin to search for information about what product or service might satisfy the newly discovered need. First, they may scan their memory for knowledge of or previous experiences with products or brands.[4] This action is called *internal search*. For frequently purchased products such as shampoo and conditioner, an internal search may be all a consumer needs. If the decision is more complex, however, a consumer may undertake an *external search* for information.[5] An external search is beneficial when a consumer lacks experience with or knowledge about a product, the risk of making a bad decision is high, and the cost of gathering information is low. The primary sources of external information are *personal sources*, such as relatives and friends who the consumer trusts; *public sources*, including various product-rating organizations such as *Consumer Reports* or government agencies; and *marketer-dominated sources*, such as information from sellers that includes advertising, company websites, salespeople, and point-of-purchase displays in stores. The Infographic, "The New Multi-Screen World," helps us understand how consumers use multiple platforms to access information when making purchase decisions.

Figure 3–1
Purchase decision process

Problem recognition: Perceiving a need → Information search: Seeking value → Evaluation of alternatives: Assessing value → Purchase decision: Buying value → Post-purchase behaviour: Value in consumption or use

Infographic

The New Multi-Screen World
Understanding Cross-Platform Consumer Behaviour

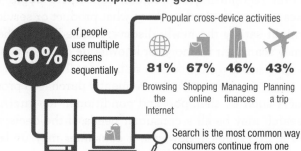

■ **Majority of media consumption is screen-based**

90% of all media interactions are screen-based

38% of our daily media interactions are on smartphones

■ **Consumers move between multiple devices to accomplish their goals**

90% of people use multiple screens sequentially

Popular cross-device activities

81% Browsing the Internet

67% Shopping online

46% Managing finances

43% Planning a trip

Search is the most common way consumers continue from one device to another

■ **Television no longer commands our full attention**

77% of the times that viewers watch TV, it is with another device

49% with a smartphone

34% with a PC/laptop

■ **Online shopping is a multi-screen activity**

Smartphones' accessibility enables spur-of-the-moment shopping

67% of people have used multiple devices sequentially to shop online

19% Planned

81% Spontaneous

Source: Google/Ipsos/Sterling, 2012.

When purchasing a smartphone, your information search may include friends and relatives, advertisements for smartphones, brand and company websites, and stores carrying smartphones (for demonstrations). You might also study comparable evaluations of various smartphones as found in *Consumer Reports,* either published in hard copy or found online.

Once you have your smartphone, you will experience how mobile technology has added new behaviours to the consumer purchase decision process. **Showrooming** is an example of how all organizations, not just retailers, must integrate online mechanisms to optimize the overall

CORE ONLINE MARKETING

Companies such as Core Online Marketing help businesses develop marketing strategies that incorporate online tools and technologies.

customer experience. Since consumers can now review products and prices online, organizations that do not seamlessly incorporate online tools and technologies into their marketing, sales, and customer service efforts will be at a distinct competitive disadvantage. These behaviours have made online marketing critical to small and medium-size businesses and created opportunities for companies such as Core Online Marketing to assist them. According to some studies, up to 50 percent of purchases are influenced by online research, and this trend is not going to reverse; it will only get more pronounced. Organizations must embrace the fact that more and more people are going online to perform research, and thus creatively leverage online tools to make it easier for prospects to make informed purchasing decisions.[6]

showrooming
Using mobile devices in-store to check online competitive product reviews and prices, resulting in the online purchase of a cheaper product.

Evaluation of Alternatives: Assessing Value

The information-search stage clarifies the problem for the consumer by suggesting criteria, or points to consider, for the purchase; providing brand names that might meet the criteria; and developing consumer value perceptions. What selection criteria would you use in buying a smartphone? Would you use price, features, or some other combination?

Think about all the factors you may consider when evaluating smartphones. These factors are a consumer's *evaluative criteria,* which represent both the objective attributes of a brand (such as the number of applications available on the iPhone versus the Samsung Galaxy) and the subjective ones (such as the status of a business executive owning a iPhone) you use to compare different products and brands.[7] Firms try to identify and make the most of both types of evaluative criteria to create the best value for consumers. These criteria are often emphasized in advertisements.

For a product like a smartphone, the information search process would probably involve visiting wireless providers such as Rogers and Telus, checking out these providers' websites, and talking to friends who own smartphones. Consumers often have several criteria for comparing products. For example, among the evaluative criteria you might think of, suppose that you focus on two that are crucial for you, namely pixel density and screen size. These criteria determine the brands in

Samsung continues to be a strong competitor in the smartphone market with offerings like the Galaxy S5.

your *evoked set*—the group of brands that a consumer would consider acceptable from among all the brands in the product class of which he or she is aware.[8] In this example, your two evaluative criteria may result in an evoked set of two brands (Samsung Galaxy and iPhone).

Purchase Decision: Buying Value

Having examined the alternatives in the evoked set, you are almost ready to make a purchase decision. Three choices remain: the chosen brand, from whom to buy, and when to buy. The choice of which wireless provider to buy from will depend on such considerations as the provider's location, your past experience buying from the provider, and the return policy.

Deciding when to buy is frequently determined by a number of factors. For instance, you might buy sooner if one of your preferred brands is on sale or its manufacturer offers a rebate. Other factors such as the store atmosphere, pleasantness of the shopping experience, salesperson persuasiveness, time pressure, and financial circumstances could also affect whether a purchase decision is made or postponed. If your decision is the latest Samsung Galaxy, you may decide to buy it from Telus because it offers unlimited local calling for six months as an added incentive.

Technology has enabled the process of gathering information, evaluating alternatives, and making buying decisions. The addition of this technological dimension to the consumer purchase decision process can accelerate the process because it puts information at consumers' fingertips.

Effects of Mobile Technology on Purchase Behaviour Mobile devices are not only popular consumer purchases, they are enablers of the consumer purchase decision. Mobile devices have allowed the

Smartphones have become an integral part of our society and the consumer purchase decision process.

purchase decision to evolve by making the information-search and purchase-decision stages easier. The younger and future consumer is expecting an online presence from companies and uses technology to research products, voice opinions, and express needs.[9]

Mobile devices have empowered consumers a great deal and caused companies to take notice. In 2012, Target reached out to its suppliers asking them to offer special products for their stores that would address its showrooming consumers.[10] For routine decisions like choosing a movie at the theatre, tickets can be purchased online at your home computer, at the box office, or at a kiosk onsite. For example, Cineplex Entertainment's Print Skip Scan offers an easy-to-use service for moviegoers to purchase tickets online.

NEXT TIME PRINT SKIP SCAN

Available at CINEPLEX.COM

By using kiosks or purchasing tickets online, moviegoers can avoid the traditional lineups at the theatre.

Post-Purchase Behaviour: Value in Consumption or Use

After buying a product, the consumer compares it with his or her expectations and is either satisfied or dissatisfied. A company's sensitivity to a customer's consumption experience strongly affects the value a customer perceives after the purchase. Studies show that satisfaction or dissatisfaction affects consumer communications and repeat-purchase behaviour. Satisfied buyers tell three other people about their experience. Dissatisfied buyers complain to nine people![11] The Internet has allowed buyers to complain and be heard by potentially thousands of people.

Some companies are hiring employees to exclusively monitor sites such as Twitter and interact with

unsatisfied customers right on the site. They are beginning to realize that the voice of the consumer on the Web is very powerful. Consumers who are not finding satisfaction when a problem occurs may take matters into their own hands online. If a company were to Google its name followed by the word "sucks," it will find a large number of hits that consist of negative stories about consumers' experiences with their products. Other consumers are venting their frustrations on Twitter and Facebook. Progressive companies use this feedback as an opportunity to link up with these disgruntled customers and resolve the problems.

Often, a consumer is faced with two or more highly attractive alternatives, such as choosing between an iPhone and a Samsung Galaxy. If you choose the Samsung Galaxy, you may think, "Should I have purchased the iPhone?" This feeling of post-purchase psychological tension or anxiety is called *cognitive dissonance*. To alleviate it, consumers often attempt to applaud themselves for making the right choice. So, after purchase, you may seek information to confirm your choice by asking friends questions like, "What do you think of my new smartphone?" or by reading ads of the brand you chose. You might even look for negative features about the brand you didn't buy. Firms often use ads or follow-up calls from salespeople in this post-purchase stage to assure buyers that they made the right decision. It is important for firms to address consumer feelings of dissonance as it impacts their satisfaction and loyalty levels.[12]

Involvement and Problem-Solving Variations

LO² Sometimes, consumers don't engage in the five-step purchase decision process. Instead, they skip or minimize one or more steps depending on the level of involvement. The level of **involvement** that a consumer has in a particular purchase depends on the personal, social, and economic consequences of that purchase to the consumer.[13] Items such as soft drinks or toothpaste may have such a low level of involvement for consumers that they may skip or minimize one or more steps in the process. But they may do just the opposite for a high-involvement purchase like a computer or an automobile.

High-involvement purchase occasions typically have at least one of three characteristics: The item to

Millions Shipped in the First Quarter of 2013

iPhone	47.8 million
iPad	22.9 million

Source: "Apple Reports Record Results," press release, Apple (Canada), January 23, 2013, accessed July 2014 at www.apple.com/ca/pr/library/2013/01/23Apple-Reports-Record-Results.html.

Logos Influence Behaviour

Marketers know that a logo encapsulates consumers' feelings about the company that are formed over time. The sentimental brand association of a logo can be so powerful that it inspires consumers to take actions they might not have otherwise intended to take. According to a University of Toronto study, even a glimpse of a fast-food logo can make a person more impatient and impulsive with money. "The logo activates associations with the brand," explains study co-author Chen-Bo Zhong, professor of organizational behaviour and human resource management at the university.

In one part of the study, the fast-food group saw logos of McDonald's and KFC; the control group instead viewed pictures of two generic low-priced dinners. Afterward, they were all asked if they would like to receive a higher amount of money in one week or a lower amount of money immediately. Those exposed to the fast-food logos were much more likely to want the money immediately. "Fast food seemed to have made people impatient in a manner that could put their economic interest at risk," the study concludes.

A 2008 Duke University study found people who looked at the Apple logo scored higher on a creativity test than those who had looked at an IBM logo—presumably because they were reflecting the differing brand traits they associated with those logos. The stronger the brand "personality," the stronger the association, Mr. Zhong said. In the case of fast food, logos from popular chains such as McDonald's promote associations with fast food, namely relating to immediate gratification and saving time.

Recent research from the University of Michigan found children as young as three can recognize brand logos and products. Children viewed logos of 50 brands across 16 product categories, including fast food, toys, electronics, and apparel, and were asked questions about the brands. The results showed that a majority of the children recognized logos of fast-food restaurants.[15]

Questions

1. When you think of the four companies discussed in this example, what associations come to mind?

2. Give some examples of logos that elicit positive associations and those that elicit negative associations.

---

be purchased is expensive; it is bought infrequently; or it could reflect on one's social image. For these occasions, consumers engage in extensive information search, consider many product attributes and brands, form attitudes, and participate in word-of-mouth communication. Marketers who sell high-involvement products such as cars, homes, and computers must understand the information-gathering and evaluation process of consumers. Researchers have identified three general variations in the consumer purchase process based on consumer involvement and product knowledge. Figure 3–2 summarizes some of the important differences between the three problem-solving variations.[14]

Routine Problem-Solving For products such as table salt and milk, consumers recognize a problem, make a decision, and spend little effort seeking external information and evaluating alternatives. The purchase process for such items is virtually a habit and typifies low-involvement decision-making. Routine problem-solving is typically the case for low-priced, frequently purchased products. An example is a consumer who stops by Tim Hortons on his way to work and purchases a coffee and a bagel. He doesn't ponder the potential benefits of going to a Second Cup or Starbucks even though they are all on his way to work. Marketers strive to attract and maintain habitual buying behaviour by creating strong brand relationships with the consumer.

Figure 3–2
Comparison of problem-solving variations

CHARACTERISTICS OF PURCHASE DECISION PROCESS	LOW ◀ CONSUMER INVOLVEMENT ▶ HIGH		
	ROUTINE PROBLEM SOLVING	LIMITED PROBLEM SOLVING	EXTENDED PROBLEM SOLVING
Number of brands examined	One	Several	Many
Number of sellers considered	Few	Several	Many
Number of product attributes evaluated	One	Moderate	Many
Number of external information sources used	None	Few	Many
Time spent searching	Minimal	Little	Considerable

Limited Problem-Solving Limited problem-solving is characterized by low consumer involvement but significant perceived differences among brands. For example, a consumer loves Activia yogourt but switches to BioBest yogourt, not out of dissatisfaction but just out of a desire to try something new. The consumer may have spent a moderate amount of time evaluating the available brands in the store before selecting BioBest. With limited problem-solving behaviour, consumers rely on past experience more than external information but they may pay attention to new varieties shown in advertising and point-of-purchase displays. Marketers of leading brands should focus on getting consumers to shift to routine problem-solving behaviour by dominating shelf space and running advertisements that remind consumers of the benefits of their brands. Consumers might use limited problem-solving when choosing a pair of jeans, deciding on a restaurant for dinner, and making other purchase situations in which they have little time or effort to spend researching options.

Extended Problem-Solving In extended problem-solving, each of the five stages of the consumer purchase decision process is used in the purchase, including considerable time and effort on external information search and identifying and evaluating alternatives. Several brands are in the evoked set, and these are evaluated on many attributes. Extended problem-solving exists in high-involvement purchase situations for items such as automobiles, houses, and financial investments.

Figure 3–3 shows the many influences that affect the consumer purchase decision process. The decision to buy a product also involves important situational, psychological, and socio-cultural influences, the topics discussed throughout the remainder of this chapter.

Consumers might use limited problem-solving when choosing a restaurant for dinner.

Situational Influences on Consumer Decisions

LO 3 Often, the purchase situation will affect the purchase decision process. Five *situational influences* have an impact on your purchase decision process: the purchase task, social surroundings, physical surroundings, temporal effects, and antecedent states.[16]

ask yourself

1. *What is the first stage in the consumer purchase decision process?*
2. *What is the name of the grouping of brands that a consumer considers buying out of the set of brands in a product class?*
3. *What is the term for post-purchase anxiety?*

Figure 3–3
Influences on the consumer purchase decision process

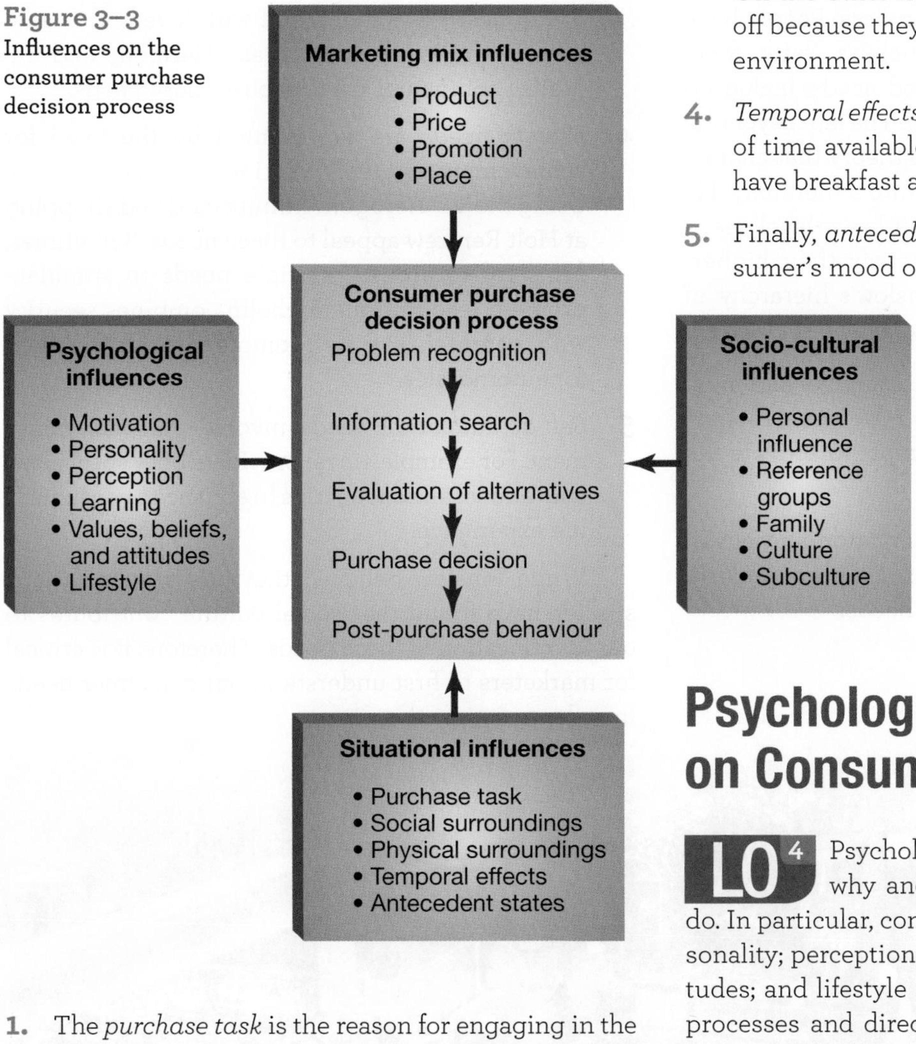

1. The *purchase task* is the reason for engaging in the decision in the first place. Information searching and evaluating alternatives may differ depending on whether the purchase is a gift, which often involves social visibility, or for the buyer's own use. For example, some consumers may be frugal shoppers when it comes to purchasing products for themselves, but may spend lavishly if the product is a gift for a friend.
2. *Social surroundings,* including the other people present when a purchase decision is made, may also affect what is purchased. For example, Paco Underhill, a behavioural research consultant, has shown that when two women shop together, they spend more time in the store shopping than they would if they were alone.[17]
3. *Physical surroundings* such as decor, music, and crowding in retail stores may alter how purchase decisions are made. Crowding, for example, is a two-edged sword. When consumers see a throng of people in the Apple Store, they may be eager to enter the store to be part of the experience. On the other hand, some people may be turned off because they don't like shopping in a crowded environment.
4. *Temporal effects,* such as time of day or the amount of time available, will influence where consumers have breakfast and lunch and what is ordered.
5. Finally, *antecedent states,* which include the consumer's mood or the amount of cash on hand, can influence purchase behaviour and choice. For example, a consumer who procrastinates buying a gift may choose one in a hurried state but may regret the purchase. If that consumer did not wait to the last moment, a more satisfying product may have been purchased instead.

Psychological Influences on Consumer Behaviour

LO 4 Psychology helps marketers understand why and how consumers behave as they do. In particular, concepts such as motivation and personality; perception; learning; values, beliefs, and attitudes; and lifestyle are useful for interpreting buying processes and directing marketing efforts. Although every consumer is a unique individual, common factors can cause similar behaviours.

Figure 3–4
Maslow's hierarchy of needs

Self-actualization needs:
Fulfillment of ambitions and hopes

Esteem needs:
Status, respect, prestige

Social needs:
Friendship, belonging, love

Safety needs:
Freedom from harm, financial security

Physiological needs:
Food, water, shelter

Motivation and Personality

Motivation and personality are two familiar psychological concepts that have specific meanings and marketing implications. They are both used frequently to describe why people do some things and not others.

Motivation **Motivation** is the energizing force that stimulates behaviour to satisfy a need. Because consumer needs are the focus of the marketing concept, marketers try to arouse these needs.

An individual's needs are boundless. People have physiological needs for basics such as water, food, and shelter. They also have learned needs, including esteem, achievement, and affection. The late psychologist Abraham Maslow developed a theory that characterized needs and arranged them into a hierarchy. He argued that people take care of their lower-level needs first and then are motivated to satisfy their higher-level needs. Figure 3–4 shows Maslow's hierarchy of needs, which contains the following five need classes:[18]

1. *Physiological needs* are basic to survival and must be satisfied first. A fast-food advertisement featuring a juicy hamburger attempts to activate the need for food.

2. *Safety needs* involve self-preservation and physical well-being. Smoke detector and burglar alarm manufacturers focus on these needs.

3. *Social needs* are concerned with love and friendship. Dating services such as eHarmony and fragrance companies try to arouse these needs.

4. *Esteem needs* are represented by the need for achievement, status, prestige, and self-respect. Using the TD Aerogold Infinite card and shopping at Holt Renfrew appeal to these needs. Sometimes, firms try to arouse multiple needs to stimulate problem recognition. Michelin combines security with parental love to promote tire replacement for automobiles.

5. *Self-actualization needs* involve personal fulfillment. For example, travel providers offer specialized educational and exotic trips to enhance a consumer's life experience.

While Maslow believed that needs were innate, studies have found that social culture contributes to our identification of these needs. Therefore, it is critical for marketers to first understand our consumer needs in order to satisfy them.[19]

Shopping malls like the Toronto Eaton Centre host various consumers with different purchase decision motivations.

motivation
Energizing force that stimulates behaviour to satisfy a need

Personality **Personality** refers to a person's character traits that influence behavioural responses. Although numerous personality theories exist, most identify key traits such as assertiveness, extraversion, compliance, dominance, and aggression, among others. Research suggests that compliant people prefer known brand names and use more mouthwash and toilet soaps. In contrast, aggressive types use razors, not electric shavers; apply more cologne and after-shave lotions; and purchase signature goods such as Gucci, Yves St. Laurent, and Donna Karan as an indicator of status.[20]

Personality characteristics are often revealed in a person's *self-concept,* which is the way people see themselves and the way they believe others see them. Marketers recognize that people have an actual self-concept and an ideal self-concept. The actual self refers to how people actually see themselves. The ideal self describes how people would like to see themselves. Marketers appeal to these two self-images in the products and brands a person buys, including automobiles, home appliances and furnishings, magazines, clothing, grooming products, and leisure products, and in the stores where a person shops. The use of attractive models in ads for grooming products appeals to a person's ideal self-concept. Men are becoming more concerned about their self-concept when it comes to body image and grooming. Unilever has responded to this trend by introducing a line of grooming products for men called Dove Men+Care.

Perception

One person sees a Porsche as a mark of achievement; another sees it as showing off. This is the result of **perception**—the process by which an individual selects, organizes, and interprets information to create a meaningful picture of the world.

Selective Perception   The average consumer operates in a complex, information-rich environment. The human brain organizes and interprets all this information with a process called *selective perception,* which filters the information so that only some of it is understood or remembered or even available to the conscious mind. *Selective exposure* occurs when people pay attention to messages that are consistent with their attitudes and beliefs and ignore messages that are inconsistent. Selective exposure often occurs in the post-purchase stage of the consumer decision process, when consumers read advertisements for the brand they just bought. It also occurs when a need exists—you are more likely to "see" a McDonald's advertisement when you are hungry rather than after you have eaten a pizza.

Selective comprehension involves interpreting information so that it is consistent with your attitudes and beliefs. A marketer's failure to understand this can have disastrous results. For example, Toro introduced a small, lightweight snow-blower called the Snow Pup. Even though the product worked, sales failed to meet expectations. Why? Toro later found out that consumers perceived the name to mean that Snow Pup was a toy or too light to do any serious snow removal. When the product was renamed Snow Master, sales increased sharply.[21]

Selective retention means that consumers do not remember all the information they see, read, or hear, even minutes after exposure to it. This affects the internal and external information-search stage of the purchase

> *Research suggests that compliant people prefer known brand names and use more mouthwash and toilet soaps.*

Dove Men+Care products appeal to the trend of men concerned about body image and grooming.

decision process. This is why furniture and automobile retailers often give consumers product brochures to take home after they leave the showroom.

Perceived Risk Consumers' beliefs about the potential negative consequences of a product or service strongly affect their purchasing decisions. **Perceived risk** represents the anxieties felt because the consumer cannot anticipate the outcomes of a purchase but believes that there may be negative consequences. Examples of possible negative consequences concerning snowboarding are the price of the product (Can I afford $400 for a snowboard?) and the risk of physical harm (Is snowboarding more dangerous than alpine skiing?). Some products such as hair colouring lend themselves to perceived risk. There is always the fear that the hair colouring may not turn out to the consumer's satisfaction. Perceived risk affects the information-search step of the purchase decision process: The greater the perceived risk, the more extensive the external search is likely to be.

Recognizing the importance of perceived risk, smart marketers develop strategies to make consumers feel more at ease about their purchases. Strategies and examples of firms using them include the following:

- **Obtaining seals of approval:** The Good Housekeeping seal that appears on many brands.
- **Securing endorsements from influential people:** Reebok's products endorsed by Sidney Crosby.
- **Providing free trials of the product:** Samples of perfume offered at Hudson's Bay.
- **Providing illustrations:** Photos of different colours and hairstyles on Clairol Canada's website.

In 2010, Sidney Crosby signed a multi-million dollar endorsement deal with Reebok.

- **Providing warranties and guarantees:** BMW's four-year, 80,000-kilometre warranty.[22]

Learning

Why do consumers behave in the marketplace as they do? Over consumers' lifetimes, they learn behaviours and they also learn responses to those behaviours—this learning is a continual process. Consumers learn which sources to use for information about products and services, which evaluative criteria to use when assessing alternatives, and how to make purchase decisions. **Learning** refers to those behaviours that result from repeated experience and reasoning.

Behavioural Learning *Behavioural learning* is the process of developing automatic responses to a type of situation built up through repeated exposure to it. Four variables are central to how one learns from repeated experience: drive, cue, response, and reinforcement. A *drive* is a need, such as hunger, that moves an individual to action. A *cue* is a stimulus or symbol that one perceives. A *response* is the action taken to satisfy the drive, and a *reinforcement* is the reward. Being hungry (a drive), a consumer sees a cue (a billboard), takes action (buys a hamburger), and receives a reward (it tastes great!). If what the consumer experiences upon responding to a stimulus is not pleasant (I feel sick now!), then *negative reinforcement* has occurred. Behavioural learning plays a major role in consumer decision-making—in this case, causing the consumer to avoid the behavioural response rather than repeat it.

perceived risk
Anxiety felt when a consumer cannot anticipate possible negative outcomes of a purchase

learning
Behaviours that result from repeated experience or reasoning

New BMW vehicles like this one have a four-year, 80,000-kilometre warranty.

> *Consumers familiar with one product will often transfer their feelings to others that seem similar—whether the similarity is in a brand name or in the shape and colour of the packaging.*

Marketers use two concepts from behavioural learning theory. *Stimulus generalization* occurs when a response brought about by one stimulus (cue) is generalized to another stimulus. Using the same brand name to launch new products is one common application of this concept, as when the makers of Tylenol followed up their original pain reliever with Tylenol Cold, Tylenol Flu, Tylenol Sinus, and others. Consumers familiar with one product will often transfer their feelings to others that seem similar—whether the similarity is in a brand name or in the shape and colour of the packaging. Are you familiar with President's Choice Cola or Costco's Simply Soda? They use red cans, similar in colour to Coca-Cola cans—this is stimulus generalization in action!

Stimulus discrimination refers to one's ability to perceive differences among similar products. Consumers may do this easily with some groups of products, such as automobiles. But in many cases, such as low-involvement purchases, advertisers work to point out the differences. For example, consumers' tendency to perceive all light beers as being alike led to Budweiser Light commercials that distinguished between many types of lights and Bud Light.

President's Choice Cola has a red can similar to other competitive cola brands.

Cognitive Learning Consumers also learn without direct experience—through thinking, reasoning, and mental problem solving. This type of learning, called *cognitive learning,* involves making connections between two or more ideas or simply observing the outcomes of others' behaviours and adjusting your own accordingly. Firms also influence this type of learning. Through repetition in advertising, messages such as "Advil is a headache remedy" attempt to link a brand (Advil) and an idea (headache remedy) by showing someone using the brand and finding relief.

Brand Loyalty Learning is also important to marketers because it relates to habit formation. Developing habits means that a consumer is solving problems (such as what to do when she's hungry) routinely and consistently, without much thought. Not surprisingly, there is a close link between habits and **brand loyalty**, which is a favourable attitude toward and consistent purchase of a single brand over time.

Brand loyalty results from positive reinforcement. If a consumer is satisfied with a product, he reduces his risk and saves time by consistently purchasing that same brand.

Values, Beliefs, and Attitudes

Values, beliefs, and attitudes play a central role in consumer decision-making.

Attitude Formation An **attitude** is a "learned predisposition to respond to an object or class of objects in a consistently favourable or unfavourable way."[23] Attitudes are shaped by our values and beliefs, which we develop in the process of growing up. For example, we speak of core values, including material well-being and humanitarianism. We also have personal values, such as thriftiness and ambition. Marketers are concerned with both, but focus mostly on personal values. Personal values affect attitudes by influencing the importance assigned to specific product attributes, or features. Suppose thriftiness is one of your personal values. When you evaluate cars, fuel economy (a product attribute) becomes important. If you believe a specific car has this attribute, you are likely to have a favourable attitude toward it.

brand loyalty
Favourable attitude toward and consistent purchase of a single brand over time

attitude
Tendency to respond to something in a consistently favourable or unfavourable way

Beliefs also play a part in attitude formation. In consumer terms, **beliefs** are one's perception of how a product or brand performs on different attributes. Beliefs are based on personal experience, advertising, and discussions with other people. Beliefs about product attributes are important because, along with personal values, they create the favourable or unfavourable attitude the consumer has toward certain products and services.

Attitude Change

Marketers use three approaches to try to change consumer attitudes toward products and brands, as shown in the following examples:[24]

1. *Changing beliefs about the extent to which a brand has certain attributes.* To reduce consumer concern that Aspirin use causes an upset stomach, Bayer Corporation successfully promoted the gentleness of its Extra Strength Bayer Plus Aspirin.

2. *Changing the perceived importance of attributes.* Consumers up to now were divided on the number of hours of sleep required for good health. Recent articles in the media are changing consumers' perceived importance of required hours. The Mayo Clinic, for example, recommends seven to nine hours of sleep for adults.[25] Sleep Country Canada emphasizes in its commercials the importance of getting a good night's rest and how Sleep Country can help the situation by providing a mattress that can improve the quality of sleep.

3. *Adding new attributes to the product.* Colgate-Palmolive included a new antibacterial ingredient, tricloson, in its Colgate Total Toothpaste and spent $100 million marketing the brand. The result? Colgate Total Toothpaste is now a billion-dollar-plus global brand.

Lifestyle

Lifestyle is a way of living that is identified by how people spend their time and resources (activities), what they consider important in their environment (interests), and what they think of themselves and the world around them (opinions). The analysis of consumer lifestyles, called *psychographics,* has produced many insights into consumer behaviour. For example, lifestyle analysis has proven useful in segmenting and targeting consumers for new and existing products and services. One of the most psychographic systems is the VALS system from Strategic Business Insights.[26] The VALS system identifies eight interconnected categories of adult lifestyles based on a person's self-orientation and resources. Self-orientation describes the patterns of attitudes and activities that help a person reinforce his or her social self-image. Three patterns have been uncovered, which are oriented toward principles, status, and action. A person's resources range from minimal to abundant and include income, education, self-confidence, health, eagerness to buy, intelligence, and energy level. Each of these categories exhibits different buying behaviour and media preferences.

VALS is an American-based system, and the psychographics of Americans differ significantly from those of Canadians. When some market researchers have tried to use American values and lifestyles to describe Canadians, they have not succeeded. For Canadian insights, marketers can turn to one of the leading firms in marketing and analytical services: Environics Analytics. Environics Analytics has segmented the Canadian population by demographics, lifestyles, and values. Figure 3–5 provides an example of clusters in the Canadian population that enjoy basketball. Although these clusters have unique characteristics, there are similar traits among them that create a larger target market for products and services related to basketball.

Figure 3–5
Prizm C2 clusters that like basketball

Source: © 2013 Environics Analytics. Used with permission.

Environics Analytics provides exceptional insight into 66 clusters of the Canadian population. For example, it describes a specific segment of the population as Grads & Pads—number 31 on the 66-rung socio-economic ladder. These individuals are described as young, well-educated individuals living near post-secondary education institutions who like to stay active skiing and working out at health clubs. While this generalized description may not describe every individual in the cluster, it provides an overall theme of the expected consumer behaviour of the individuals living in postal codes associated with that cluster.[27]

Environics Analytics is a leader in consumer segmentations. The sample clusters described earlier fall into much broader socio-economic categories, and life-stage groups continue to change with every new Canadian Census. Figure 3–6 provides examples of the broader socio-economic categories of the Prizm C2 segmentation system from 2008. By using the key drivers of demographics, lifestyles, and values, Environics Analytics creates added-value tools for marketers to understand consumer behaviour and markets anywhere in Canada.

Socio-Cultural Influences on Consumer Behaviour

LO⁵ Socio-cultural influences, which evolve from a consumer's formal and informal relationships with other people, also have an impact on consumer behaviour. These include personal influence, reference groups, family, culture, and subculture.

Personal Influence

A consumer's purchases are often influenced by the views, opinions, or behaviours of others. Two aspects of personal influence are important to marketing: opinion leadership and word-of-mouth activity.

ask yourself

1. The problem with the Toro Snow Pup was an example of selective _____.

2. What three attitude-change approaches are most common?

3. What does the concept of lifestyle mean?

Figure 3–6
Examples of Prizm C2 cluster categories

Segment Code	Cluster Category	Brief Description
U1	Urban Elite	The highest-ranking individuals in income, home value, and educational achievement. Big consumers of expensive clothes, luxury cars, financial products, and travel services.
S1	Suburban Elite	Young and middle-aged families living in recently built homes. Indulge in family-friendly products and activities aimed at families, including consumer electronics and video games.
E1	Exurban Elite	Tend to be married, middle-aged couples and families who live in comfortable homes and hold white-collar and service-sector jobs. Tied to cars and purchase $30,000 SUVs and sporty luxury cars for commuting to work and chauffeuring the kids.
U2	Urban Upscale Ethnic	An educated mix of older and middle-aged couples and large families with children in their late teens and twenties. Activities include attending the theatre and opera.
S2	Suburban Upscale Ethnic	Predominantly upper-middle class with white-collar and service-sector jobs. Have children of varying ages and own lots of consumer electronics and computer gear.
E2	Exurban Midscale	Living in older towns and cities across Canada, these young to middle-aged parents work at blue-collar and service-sector jobs. There is a strong market for family-style restaurants.
U3	Urban Young	Canada's youngest residents are university-educated singles and couples in progressive lifestyles. Typically, night owls who frequent bars and health clubs.

Source: © 2013 Environics Analytics Group Ltd.

Opinion Leadership Individuals who have social influence over others are called **opinion leaders**. Opinion leaders are more likely to be important for products that provide a form of self-expression. Automobiles, clothing, and club memberships are products affected by opinion leaders, but appliances usually are not.[28]

A small percentage of adults—from influential community leaders and business executives to movie stars—are opinion leaders. Identifying, reaching, and influencing opinion leaders is a major challenge for companies. Some firms use sports figures or celebrities as spokespersons to represent their products, such as actor Leonardo DiCaprio and tennis player Maria Sharapova for TAG Heuer watches. See, for example, the discussion about Beyoncé and Pepsi in the Marketing NewsFlash, "Beyoncé Criticized for Pepsi Partnership," later in this chapter.

Companies like TAG Heuer use celebrities as spokespeople to represent its products and influence consumer decision-making.

Word of Mouth People influencing each other during conversations is called **word of mouth**. Word of mouth is perhaps the most powerful information source for consumers, because it typically involves friends or family who are viewed as trustworthy.

The power of personal influence has prompted firms to make efforts to increase positive and decrease negative word of mouth.[29] For instance, "teaser" advertising campaigns are run in advance of new-product introductions to stimulate conversations. Other techniques such as advertising slogans, music, and humour also heighten positive word of mouth. On the other hand, rumours about McDonald's (worms in hamburgers) and Corona Extra beer (contaminated beer) have resulted in negative word of mouth, none of which was based on fact. Overcoming negative word of mouth is difficult and costly. Firms have found that supplying factual information, providing toll-free numbers for consumers to call the company, and giving appropriate product demonstrations also have been helpful.

The term *buzz marketing* refers to a brand becoming popular as a result of people talking about it to friends and neighbours. Another way that a company can create buzz is by hiring an outside agency. Word-of-mouth agencies such as Matchstick

> *"Product seeding consists of hiring people to talk up a brand to others."*

specialize in product-seeding programs. Product seeding consists of hiring people to talk up a brand to others. The Word of Mouth Marketing Association (WOMMA) has issued ethical guidelines on product seeding, including the guideline that brand representatives must always disclose their relationship to the brand when promoting it to others (see the Focus on Ethics box, "The Power of Word of Mouth).

The power of word of mouth has been magnified through online marketing. The online version of word of mouth is called *viral marketing*. This includes the use of messages that consumers pass along to others through online forums, social networks such as Facebook and Twitter, chat rooms, bulletin boards, blogs, and e-mails. These messages can be positive or negative. Companies are now recognizing the value of social media platforms such as Twitter and Facebook, and are monitoring messages so that they can respond to consumers quickly.

opinion leaders
Individuals who have social influence over others

word of mouth
People influencing each other in personal conversations

Reference Groups

A **reference group** is a group of people who influence a person's attitudes, values, and behaviours. For example, you might consider your family or the other students in your school as a reference group. Other examples of reference groups are movie stars and sports celebrities. Reference groups affect consumer purchases because they influence the information, attitudes, and aspiration levels that help set a consumer's standards. Reference groups have an important influence on the purchase of luxury products but not of necessities—reference groups exert a strong influence on the brand chosen when its use or consumption is highly visible to others.[30]

Consumers have many reference groups, but three groups have clear marketing implications:

- **Membership group:** One to which a person actually belongs, including fraternities and sororities, social clubs, and family. Such groups are easily identifiable and are targeted by firms selling insurance, insignia products, and vacation packages.

- **Aspiration group:** One that a person wishes to be a member of or wishes to be identified with. An example is a person whose dream it is to play in the NHL. Brands such as Gatorade and Nike frequently rely on spokespeople or settings associated with their target market's aspiration group in their advertising.

- **Dissociative group:** One that a person wishes to maintain a distance from because of differences in values or behaviours.

Family Influence

Family influences on consumer behaviour result from three sources: consumer socialization, passage through the family life cycle, and decision making within the family or household.

Consumer Socialization The process by which people acquire the skills, knowledge, and attitudes necessary to function as consumers is *consumer socialization*.[31] Children learn how to purchase by interacting with adults in purchase situations and through their own purchasing and product usage experiences. Research demonstrates that children show signs of brand preferences as early as age 2, and these preferences often last a lifetime. This knowledge prompted Time Inc. to launch *Sports Illustrated for Kids*. The brand of toothpaste, laundry detergent, or soft drink used in your home will very likely influence your brand choice when you purchase these items for yourself.

Family Life Cycle Consumers act and purchase differently as they go through life. The **family life cycle** concept describes the distinct phases that a family progresses through from formation to retirement, each phase bringing with it identifiable purchasing behaviours.[32] Today, the traditional family—married couples with children—constitute just over 26 percent of all Canadian households. Nearly 30 percent are households without children.[33]

The late Steve Jobs co-founded Apple, built it into the world's leading tech company, and led a mobile computing revolution with wildly popular devices such as the iPod, iPhone, and iPad that connected different generations of a family.

> *Even though women are often the grocery decision makers, they are not necessarily the purchaser. Husbands do about one-half of food shopping.*

Young single consumers' buying preferences are for nondurable items, including prepared foods, clothing, personal care products, and entertainment. They represent a significant target market for recreational travel, automobile, and consumer electronics firms. Young married couples without children are typically more affluent than young singles because usually both spouses are employed. These couples exhibit preferences for furniture, housewares, and gift items for each other. Young marrieds with children are driven by the needs of their children. These families make up a sizable market for life insurance, various children's products, and home furnishings. Single parents with children are the least financially secure type of households. Their buying preferences are usually affected by a limited economic status and tend toward convenience foods, child care services, and personal care items.

Middle-aged married couples with children are typically better off financially than their younger counterparts. They are a significant market for leisure products and home improvement items. Middle-aged couples without children typically have a large amount of discretionary income. These couples buy better home furnishings, status automobiles, and financial services. Persons in the last two phases—older married and older unmarried—make up a sizable market for prescription drugs, medical services, vacation trips, and gifts for younger relatives.

Family Decision-Making A third family-based influence on consumer decision-making occurs in the context of the relationship dynamics of the household. Two decision-making styles exist: spouse-dominant and joint decision-making. With a joint decision-making style, most decisions are made by both husband and wife. Spouse-dominant decisions are those for which either the husband or the wife has more influence in the purchase decision. Research indicates that wives tend to have the most say when purchasing groceries, children's toys, clothing, and

medicines. Husbands tend to be more influential in home and car maintenance purchases. Joint decision-making is common for cars, vacations, houses, home appliances and electronics, medical care, and long-distance telephone services. As a rule, joint decision-making increases with the education of the spouses.[34]

Roles of individual family members in the purchase process are another element of family decision-making. Five roles exist: information gatherer, influencer, decision maker, purchaser, and user. Family members assume different roles for different products and services.[35] For example, 89 percent of wives either influence or make outright purchases of men's clothing. Knowing this, Haggar Clothing, a menswear marketer, advertises in women's magazines such as *Chatelaine* and *Redbook*. Even though women are often the grocery decision makers, they are not necessarily the purchaser. Husbands do about one-half of food shopping. Increasingly, preteens and teenagers are the information gatherers, influencers, decision makers, and purchasers of products and services items for the family, given the prevalence of working parents and single-parent households. Children and teenagers directly influence billions of dollars in annual family

The Haggar Clothing Co. recognizes the important role women play in the choice of men's clothing. The company directs a large portion of its advertising toward women because they influence and purchase men's clothing.

In the **female** the ability to match colors comes at an early age. In the **male** it comes when he marries a female.

HAGGAR

The City Casuals three-button, crepe jacket, 100% cotton, French-spun shirt, Bedford cord pants, and a touch of color.

The Power of Word of Mouth

One of the most powerful forms of marketing is the result of one of the most natural activities: talking. Word-of-mouth marketing is an extraordinary tool for marketers to use as they spread their brands, as it is the most effective form of marketing available—and the simplest. The Word of Mouth Marketing Association (WOMMA) is the official trade association for word-of-mouth marketers and is a coalition composed of top marketers who are interested in learning how to encourage and utilize word of mouth while respecting and protecting its integrity.

WOMMA aids its members with the implementation of word of mouth using training, best practices, standards and metrics, and mainstreaming. WOMMA provides outreach and education, aids marketers in creating sustainable word-of-mouth programs, creates accountability for practices, and works at bringing word of mouth into the centre of the marketing world. WOMMA's mission is to improve word-of-mouth marketing by "promoting 'best practices' to ensure more-effective marketing; protecting consumers and the industry with strong ethical guidelines; evangelizing word of mouth as an effective marketing tool; and setting standards to encourage its use."

Recently, WOMMA developed a code of ethics for word-of-mouth marketing. These guidelines are meant to protect the consumer during the use of and participation in word-of-mouth marketing. The code focuses on openness between consumers,

The Word of Mouth Marketing Association (WOMMA) is the official trade association of word-of-mouth marketers.

advocates, and marketers; advocates are encouraged to be open with consumers about their relationship with marketers. Advocates are also encouraged to be honest with their opinions about the products that they are marketing and to disclose their identity to the consumers. WOMMA created a code of ethics in order to help marketers see what practices they should be supporting and to allow the word-of-mouth industry to set clear standards for itself.[38] ●

Questions

1. Assume you are being paid by an agency to promote one of Molson's brands. On your day off, you go to a restaurant and order the beverage you are promoting. A customer at another table asks how you like the drink. According to WOMMA's code of ethics, what should you do?

2. When you consider buying a large ticket item, how much do you rely on word of mouth from family, friends, etc., versus doing research yourself on the product that you want to buy?

---

purchases. These figures help explain why, for example, Johnson & Johnson, Apple, Kellogg, P&G, Sony, and Oscar Mayer, among countless other companies, spend billions annually in media that reach preteens and teens.[36]

Culture and Subculture

LO 6 **Culture** refers to the set of values, ideas, and attitudes that are learned and shared among the members of a group. Thus, we often refer to Canadian culture, American culture, or Japanese culture. Describing Canadian culture may be difficult due to the diversity in the nation, but many could agree that Canadians are individuals who are polite and fair. Canadians value politeness and feel uncomfortable in situations of conflict. It is a balance of pride and humility. This generalization does not stem to all Canadians, and inaccurate perceptions of Canada were addressed by Molson through its "rant ad" beer commercials in 2000.[37]

Subgroups within the larger, or national, culture with unique values, ideas, and attitudes are referred to as **subcultures**. Subcultures can be defined by regions, by demographic groups, or by values. The

culture
A set of values, ideas, and attitudes that are learned and shared among the members of a group

subcultures
Subgroups within a larger culture that have unique values, ideas, and attitudes

most prominent types of subcultures are racial and ethnic, and many of these exist within the Canadian mosaic of people. French, German, Italian, Chinese, and Ukrainian subcultures are the ones we see most in Canada, and they make up nearly 40 percent of the Canadian population. Each one exhibits unique buying patterns and socio-cultural behaviours.

Canada's outlook on ethnicity is that cultural and ethnic groups are welcome to continue with their traditions, languages, and values. Canada is a nation of many faces, and people have been immigrating here continually over many decades. A person may regard herself as Italian, yet never have been to Italy—her grandparents may have immigrated here many years ago. If Italian customs have been maintained by the family, she may behave much like a recently arrived Italian. Some countries encourage immigrants to join the mainstream national culture, while diversity is encouraged in Canada.

Our ethnic composition, and the philosophy that we take toward it, has led to the creation of many ethnic neighbourhoods in our cities. As our population becomes more diverse, people immigrating here bring foods from their native lands. Canadians do not have a lot of native food and preparation styles, so the country has been particularly welcoming of cuisine from around the world. Immigration has had a major influence on Canada's food market, both in the many restaurants and in food items available from all corners of the globe. Not only food consumption is affected by immigration but also many cultural events have become mainstream, and many local happenings are the result of a tradition or celebration brought here by some new Canadians.

Examples of Canadian Subcultures   There are almost 10 million French-speaking Canadians in this country, about 30 percent of the population.[39] By far, the largest majority of them live in the province of Quebec. Research shows that French-speaking Quebecers do exhibit different consumption behaviour than the rest of Canada.[40] For example, when asked what is important to them, Quebecers are more likely than other Canadians to say "enjoying life" and "seeking happiness." French Canadians, more so than English Canadians, are more likely to believe that everybody should be free to do their own thing. Quebecers are also more willing to pay higher prices for convenience and premium brands. Some people feel that French Quebec can be characterized by a set of values that are traditional, consistent, and relatively static, but changes are evident. While values are still strong regarding family life and having children in a marriage, the use of birth control is rising, and the marriage rate is below the national average.

French Quebecers are members of a Canadian subculture who are cautious about new products and often postpone trying something new until they see that the product has proven itself. They exhibit brand loyalty, but they will switch brands if offered a special. French Quebecers are less likely to buy grocery items on impulse, and are increasingly calculating in their food purchases. Some grocery chains have responded to this characteristic by offering more discount coupons, weekly specials, and money-saving tips. Quebecers like things that please the senses. For example, they like fine restaurants and fine wines. Quebecois women are also very fashion-conscious, and upscale brands such as Prada and Lancome sell well in Quebec. This desire for beauty helps explain why campaigns for anti-wrinkle products are even more successful in Quebec than in the rest of Canada.[41]

While the province of Quebec has the highest percentage of alcohol drinkers and the most-relaxed drinking laws in Canada, it also has the lowest percentage of excessive drinkers and the fewest alcohol-related problems. French Quebecers are big buyers of lottery tickets and more likely to subscribe to book clubs, but they make fewer long-distance phone calls. They travel less, whether for business or pleasure. More French Quebec adults hold life insurance policies, but they are less likely to have a credit card. They also tend to use the services of credit unions (*caisses populaires*) rather than banks. Marketers must realize that certain products and other elements of the marketing mix may have to be modified in order to be successful in French Quebec. In addition to cultural differences, there are other issues that marketers must address. Commercial advertising to children is prohibited, and greater restrictions exist for alcohol advertising. Provincial regulations also require that labels and packages must be both English

Canada's Diverse Consumers

British descent	28%
French descent	23%
Other European descent	15%
Native descent	2%
Other	6%
Mixed descent	26%

Source: "Canada," Central Intelligence Agency, The World Factbook website, accessed July 2014 at https://www.cia.gov/library/publications/the-world-factbook/geos/ca.html.

Chinese New Year celebrations take place in Vancouver each year and have become an integral part of the city's cultural fabric.

and French, while storefront signage must be in French, not English. Good investigation and analysis of this market is a requirement for all companies wishing to do business in this province.

Another Canadian subculture and one of the largest and fastest-growing visible minorities in Canada's population is Chinese, with 40 percent residing in Toronto and 31 percent in Vancouver. The average Chinese household spends $63,500 each year, slightly higher than the Canadian average of $58,500. In general, these consumers are relatively young, educated, and affluent. They tend to spend their money on home furnishings, automobiles, kids' education, high-tech gadgets, travelling, and gifts. They like to do business within their own communities and prefer media in their own languages. They have strong allegiance to brands and are very family-oriented. Because they live in close-knit communities, word of mouth is very important to them.[42]

Chinese-Canadians have a preference for luxury vehicles, and many car dealerships see them as good potential customers for new cars. In general, they tend to eat out at restaurants more than the average

Canadian, and there has been significant growth in the number of Chinese restaurants in Canada, and particularly in Vancouver and Toronto, over the past 10 years. For these, and a number of other factors, many marketers cater to the Chinese market as they see them as being good prospective customers.

Global Cultural Diversity

Canada has become increasingly multi-ethnic and multicultural, making it one of the most diverse countries in the world. Different countries take different approaches to admitting immigrants and integrating them into society. Canada's approach is often referred to as a mosaic, meaning that people who come to the country from another are welcome to maintain their cultural identities and customs—the belief is that this will create a situation where all Canadians can learn from the rich variety of over 200 cultures that make up the citizenry of the country. This environment works to increase Canadian companies' sensitivity and orientation toward other cultures, so the transition to global activities and relationships is facilitated.

Just as marketers must be sensitive to subcultures in Canada, they must appreciate the cultural differences of people in other countries if they want to market products and services to them. A necessary step in this process is **cross-cultural analysis**, which involves the study of similarities and differences among consumers in two or more nations or societies.[43] A thorough cross-cultural analysis involves an understanding of and an appreciation for the values, customs, symbols, and language of other societies.

Values   A society's **values** represent socially preferable modes of conduct or states of existence that tend to persist over time. Understanding and working with these aspects of a society are important factors in global marketing. For example, consider the following:[45]

- McDonald's does not sell hamburgers in its restaurants in India because the cow is considered sacred by almost 85 percent of the population. Instead, McDonald's sells the McMaharajah: two all-mutton patties, special sauce, lettuce, cheese, pickles, onions on a sesame-seed bun.

- Germans have not been overly receptive to the use of credit cards such as Visa or MasterCard, nor to the idea of borrowing to purchase goods and services. The German word for "debt," *Schuld,* is the same as the German word for "guilt."

Beyoncé Criticized for Pepsi Partnership

Over the years, Pepsi has had many advertising spokespersons. These celebrities have been paid to promote Pepsi's products.

In 2013, Beyoncé announced her role as global brand ambassador for Pepsi. The process to create a global advertising campaign that met her image's needs and the image needs of Pepsi was arduous. It involved a great deal of collaboration between the pop singer and the soft drink company, but eventually their collaboration paid off.

Once announced, however, news of this partnership drew criticism to both Beyoncé and Pepsi as the sugary drinks, if consumed excessively, could be detrimental to long-term health. In fact, some critics went so far to state that she was a hypocrite in being part of a national fitness campaign prior to signing her deal with Pepsi. When asked to give her perspective on the conflict, Beyoncé addressed the question below:

Some were critical at your participating in a Pepsi campaign after you moved your body for childhood obesity. Where is the balance between your career objectives and your philanthropy?

"Pepsi is a brand I've grown up seeing my heroes collaborate with. The company respects musicians and artistry. I wouldn't encourage any person, especially a child, to live life without balance."[44]

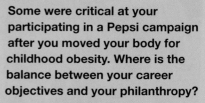

As Pepsi's global brand ambassador, Beyoncé advocates for choice and balance.

Questions

1. Describe how opinion leadership affects consumer decisions?

2. How has reading this Marketing NewsFlash affected your opinion of Beyoncé and Pepsi?

Customs **Customs** are what is considered normal and expected about the way people do things in a specific country or culture. Clearly, customs can vary significantly from country to country. Some customs may seem unusual to Canadians. Consider, for example, that in France, men wear more than twice the number of cosmetics that women do, and that the Japanese consider slurping their food to be a sign of approval and appreciation to the chef.

The custom of giving token business gifts is popular in many countries where they are expected and accepted. However, bribes, kickbacks, and payoffs offered to entice someone to commit an illegal or improper act on behalf of the giver for economic gain is considered corrupt in most cultures. The widespread use of bribery in global marketing has led to an

customs
Norms and expectations about the way people do things in a specific country or culture

Coca-Cola executives learned valuable lessons when they used the Eiffel Tower and the Parthenon in global advertising campaigns.

agreement among the world's major exporting nations to make bribery of foreign government officials a criminal offence.

The Organisation for Economic Co-operation and Development (OECD) is an international body whose goal is to foster democratic government and a market-driven economy. With its global reach, OECD addresses issues of general interest to its members and affiliates. Corruption has become an issue of major importance in the past decade, and the OECD has taken action to set guidelines and procedures for preventing international bribery and corruption. Canada has adopted the OECD's anti-corruption convention and has made bribery of foreign public officials a criminal offence.[46]

Bribery paid to foreign companies is another matter. In France and Greece, bribes paid to foreign companies are a tax-deductible expense!

Cultural Symbols

Cultural symbols are objects, ideas, or processes that represent a particular group of people or society. Symbols and symbolism play an important role in cross-cultural analysis because different cultures attach different meanings to things. By cleverly using cultural symbols, global marketers can tie positive symbolism to their products and services to enhance their attractiveness to consumers. However, improper use of symbols can spell disaster. A culturally sensitive global marketer will know the following:[47]

- North Americans are superstitious about the number 13, and Japanese feel the same way about the number 4. *Shi*, the Japanese word for "four," is also the word for "death." Knowing this, Tiffany & Company sells its fine glassware and china in sets of five, not four, in Japan.

- "Thumbs-up" is a positive sign in Canada. However, in Russia and Poland, this gesture has an offensive meaning when the palm of the hand is shown, as AT&T learned. The company reversed the gesture depicted in ads, showing the back of the hand, not the palm.

Cultural symbols stir up deep feelings. Consider how executives at Coca-Cola's Italian office learned this lesson. In a series of advertisements directed at Italian vacationers, the Eiffel Tower, Empire State Building, and the Tower of Pisa were turned into the familiar Coca-Cola bottle. However, when the white marble columns in the Parthenon that crown Athens's Acropolis were turned into Coca-Cola bottles, the Greeks were outraged. Greeks refer to the Acropolis as the "holy rock," and a government official said the Parthenon is an "international symbol of excellence" and that "whoever insults the Parthenon insults international culture." Coca-Cola apologized for the ad.[48]

of brand names and messages have ranged from the absurd to the obscene, as in the following examples:

● When the advertising agency responsible for launching Procter & Gamble's successful Pert shampoo in Canada realized that the name means "lost" in French, it substituted the brand name Pret, which means "ready."

● The Vicks brand name common in North America is German slang for sexual intimacy; therefore, Vicks is called Wicks in Germany.

Experienced global marketers use **back translation**, where a translated word or phrase is retranslated back into the original language by a different interpreter to catch errors.[50] IBM's first Japanese translation of its "Solution for a small planet" advertising message yielded "Answers that make people smaller." The error was caught by back translation and corrected. Sometimes, unintended translations can produce favourable results. Consider Kit Kat bars marketed by Nestlé worldwide. Kit Kat is pronounced "kitto katsu" in Japanese, which roughly translates to "I will win." Japanese teens eat Kit Kat bars for good luck, particularly when taking crucial school exams.[51]

Successful marketers understand the differences and similarities in consumers. They draw together commonalities and segment their audience into groups that will find their products and services appealing. By keeping current with the changing trends in consumer values and attitudes, marketers can stay in sync with their audiences.

Language Global marketers should know not only the basics of the native tongues of countries in which they market their products and services but also the subtleties and unique expressions of the language. For example, Pepsi found that Spanish-speaking people in Argentina tend to pronounce the soft drink as Pecsi rather than Pepsi. Pepsi responded by launching a successful marketing campaign that temporarily used the spelling Pecsi rather than Pepsi on billboards in Argentina. The brand name Pepsi was never really legally changed, but humorously altered for the period of the campaign.[49]

About 100 official languages exist in the world, but anthropologists estimate that at least 3,000 different languages are actually spoken. There are 11 official languages spoken in the European Union, and Canada has two official languages (English and French). Seventeen major languages are spoken in India alone.

English, French, and Spanish are the principal languages used in global diplomacy and commerce. However, the best language with which to communicate with consumers is their own, as any seasoned global marketer will agree. Language usage and translation can present challenges. Unintended meanings

TOMÁS

PECSI

AHORRÁS.

TOMÁS PEPSI, TAMBIÉN.

Pepsi, in a humorous marketing campaign in Argentina, had billboards refer to Pepsi as Pecsi.

back translation
Retranslating a word or phrase back into the original language by a different interpreter to catch errors

The Nestlé Kit Kat bar influences teens in Japan through its translated meaning.

ad**A**lyze

Summary...*just the facts*

LO¹ • The first stage of the purchase decision process is problem recognition where the consumer perceives a need.

• The second stage is the information search where the consumer seeks value in the potential purchase options.

• The third stage is the evaluation of alternatives where the consumer assesses the value of each option.

• In the fourth stage, the consumer executes the purchase decision.

• In the fifth stage, the consumer determines the value of the purchase in post-purchase behaviour.

LO² • Consumer purchase decisions range in complexity. This creates three variations of the consumer purchase decisions.

• Routine problem-solving, such as purchasing tissues when you have a cold, requires little effort.

• Limited problem-solving may occur when consumers compare and decide upon different brands, such as for refreshments.

• Extended problem-solving routinely involves time and consideration in each of the five distinct stages of the consumer purchase decision process. Purchasing electronics usually requires extended problem-solving.

LO³ • There are five situational influences that impact the consumer purchase decision process.

• The reason for engaging in the decision in the first place is called the purchase task. Why you are making the purchase may determine how much you plan on spending.

• Social surroundings, including who else is present in the process, also have an impact on the decision process.

• Another situational influence is the physical surroundings during the process. A store that is busy may have a positive or negative effect on the consumer.

• When the purchase is being made is a temporal effect, and the momentary mood or antecedent state of the consumer also affects the process.

LO⁴ • The main psychological influences affecting consumer behaviour are motivation and personality, perception, learning, values, beliefs and attitudes, and lifestyle.

• Motivation is the energizing force that causes consumers to satisfy a need, while personality and character traits influence behavioural responses.

• Perception is important to marketers because of the selectivity of what a consumer sees or hears, comprehends, and retains.

• Consumers learn from repeated experience, and brand loyalty is a result of learning.

• The values and beliefs of a consumer create their learned predisposition or attitudes toward a product.

• The consumers' lifestyle identifies how they plan to spend their time and resources.

LO⁵ • The consumer purchase decision process can be affected by personal influence, reference groups, and family influences.

• Personal influence can be seen in opinion leadership and word-of-mouth activity. These are normally created by individuals with social influence. Personal influence can also take the form of reference groups.

• Family influences on consumer behaviour include where the family is in its family life cycle and how decisions are made within the household.

LO⁶ • Culture is the set of values, ideas, and attitudes that are learned and shared among the members of a group.

• There are subgroups within larger cultures that have unique values, ideas, and attitudes. These subgroups are called subcultures.

• Both culture and subculture influence consumer behaviour as these values permeate through situational, psychological, and socio-cultural influences.

Key Terms and Concepts...*a refresher*

attitude
back translation
beliefs
brand loyalty
consumer behaviour
cross-cultural analysis
cultural symbols
culture

customs
family life cycle
involvement
learning
motivation
opinion leaders
perceived risk
perception

personality
purchase decision process
reference group
showrooming
subcultures
values
word of mouth

Hands-on...*apply your knowledge*

Changing Technology and Consumer Purchase Behaviour Assignment Yellow Pages Group helps organizations venture into the world of digital marketing. Yellow Pages Group adapted as the needs of consumers have adapted over the years. Reflecting on how technology has evolved in your lifetime and on new technology products on the rise, provide a prediction of how consumers will be searching for information in the next 5, 10, and 15 years.

Chapter Vignette...*reminder*

The vignette at the beginning of the chapter stresses the importance of understanding consumers, especially as their media habits have moved online. There are various factors affecting whether a consumer purchases a particular product. The questions at the end of the vignette can be answered by thoroughly reviewing the consumer purchase decision process as well as the various influences that consumers are exposed to.

Video Clip...*questions*

Review the Yellow Pages Group videos on CONNECT and answer the following questions:

▶ Video
Yellow Pages
Group

- Where are the majority of consumers searching for information before they make purchases?
- What percentage of consumers prefer ads that are locally relevant?
- What is Smart Digital Display?
- How have the Yellow Pages Group advertisements explained the change in how consumers search for information?

Infographic...*data analysis*

The Infographic entitled "The New Multi-Screen World" discusses the integrated access to information that consumers use to make purchase decisions. Reviewing recent articles in the *Toronto Star,* the *Globe and Mail,* and other reputable business sources, add one more section to the Infographic specifically about purchasing a laptop.

market research, metrics, and analytics

Market research, metrics, and analytics are tools used by marketers to gather data and glean insights that make fact-based decisions easier and more accurate. Today, forward-thinking organizations use these tools and foster a culture of measurement, analytics, and continuous improvement by investing in technology, partnerships, and people. The goal is to manage data and to discern patterns, correlations, and insights that are actionable and provide a competitive edge. This chapter focuses on these tools—market research, metrics, and analytics—explaining their purpose and intricacies, and how they are used in this era of big data.

We first turn to Luke Sklar, partner and founder of the market research company Sklar Wilton & Associates (SW+A), to give us clarity on the market research industry today. "Research that confirms or denies smart thinking still stands as the basic building block of market research," explains Sklar, elaborating that while many new research tools provide precise data, and lots of it, the principles of good market research are as robust as ever. "If you cannot provide clients with clarity, a vision on how to grow the business, and insights into how to solve a problem, then the data is useless—all of it, big or small." He explains that smart market researchers follow these principles and involve clients to help provide perspective and to create real hypotheses.

SW+A is a top market research firm that provides marketing clarity and strategic direction to Canada's most respected organizations, such as Mars, Cara, J.M. Smuckers, Molson, and Rogers. Its strength lies in cutting through research results and sifting through data to recommend smart strategies that build business and make a difference. Sklar points to consistently strong business results of longstanding clients Heinz Canada and Mars Canada as to how SW+A helps clients, noting that more recent clients such as Molson, Shoppers Drug Mart, and Canadian Tire work with SW+A to help elevate their brands. SW+A's philosophy is that research needs to tell simple, credible, fact-based stories that can energize and move people to action. It combines art and science with passion and objectivity to prompt innovative thinking.

SW+A has seen numerous changes in the market research industry, fuelled by computing power and the Internet. This creates an overwhelming amount of data that floods marketers' desks, making the role of market researchers more crucial and complex. In this era of *big data,* defined as high-volume, high-velocity, and high-variety information,[1] market researchers must now consider all sources of data, not just surveys. "Our clients are drowning in data and thirsty for clarity and insight. They need an integrated, single, and concise view of the facts to make decisions,"

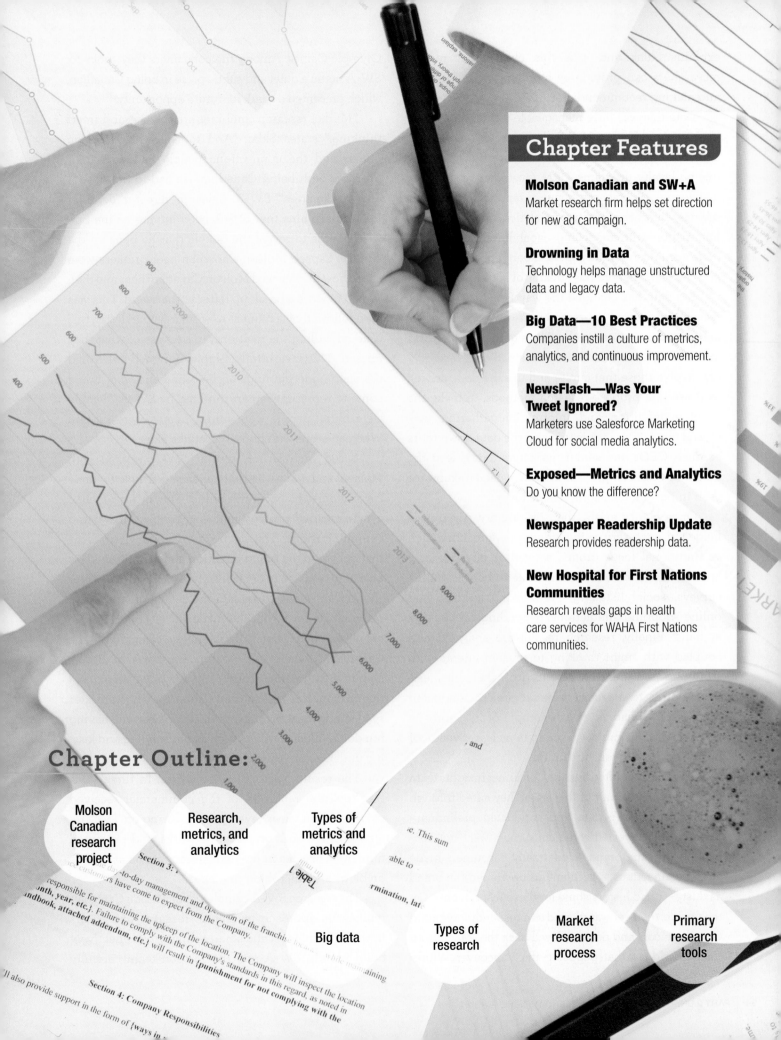

Chapter Outline:

Molson Canadian research project

Research, metrics, and analytics

Types of metrics and analytics

Big data

Types of research

Market research process

Primary research tools

explains Sklar, and it is this clarity that market researchers can provide by stepping back, focusing, and making recommendations.

Data that was once manageable resided in marketing, sales, and finance. Now with the explosion of digital and social media, it comes from all directions, whether this be loyalty programs, CRM (customer relationship management) databases, financial reports, social media metrics, Internet marketing analytics, or data mining information with modelling capabilities. In addition, there are industry white papers, expert reports, seminars, and webinars that provide streams of additional data.

Big data has changed the way SW+A approaches research projects. Its researchers now start earlier and spend more time with clients gathering, herding, and culling data that already exists. SW+A researchers involve those that curate and use the data, as well as those that propose research methods, to make the problem-definition and information-gathering task crystal clear. "Our task is to distill the data down to its essence. CEOs and senior marketers today need the fact-based *elevator pitch* of what they need to know for their important decisions," states Sklar.

Once clarity exists, then proprietary research is fielded, if necessary, using standard approaches such as traditional focus groups as well as effective new approaches found with online bulletin boards, online surveys, social listening, eye-tracking studies, and online shopping simulations, depending on the task at hand. Finally, research results are analyzed and coupled with smart thinking to present clients with strategies and ideas on how to grow their business. Sklar points to a recent research project conducted for Molson Canadian as an example of its approach to research. This project resulted in a clearer vision of how and where to take the brand.

SW+A is integrated into the Consumer Insights team at Molson, and as part of this team, they sifted through Molson Canadian's data and conducted preliminary research that revealed some consumers were not connecting with the brand. While many consumers made strong connections, a dormant group viewed the brand as dusty—it had lost its shine for these respondents. On the upside, the beer was viewed as a resoundingly proud Canadian icon, and people played back the "Made from Canada" slogan that peppered the Vancouver Winter Olympic Games. Among the consumers they spoke to, SW+A noted a quiet and subtle pride in being Canadian, which presented a spark for future opportunity.

"Market research combines art, science, and smart thinking," states Sklar. "And to really help Molson understand the connections people had with their beer and with being Canadian, we had to dig deeper and be smarter." SW+A research director Jennifer Roberts explains that SW+A used private online bulletin boards to reveal the beliefs that lie beneath the surface. Lapsed Molson Canadian beer drinkers were asked how they viewed Molson Canadian beer and then tasked to write a break-up letter to the brand. This was then followed by a request to write a second letter, this time rekindling the relationship because of what they missed! This insightfully simple approach unearthed the deep underpinnings of the brand and what it had come to represent—smart thinking by SW+A. "People were blunt, people were funny, people were serious. Who can argue with honesty?" states Sklar.

Based on research results, SW+A worked with Molson and its advertising agency Rethink to finalize strategies to boost the brand. This in turn fuelled a new creative strategy and energized its marketing communications. The agency worked on new ideas that delivered the brand direction and sent these ideas back into research to get feedback. The creative director shot a short video to explain the campaign and asked respondents for feedback on specific alternatives. The result was a top-notch, high-energy campaign, "The Canadians," where hip, young characters in Berlin, Dublin, South Africa, Tokyo, and Australia shared stories on crazy and free-spirited Canadians who were later seen letting loose at concerts, drinking beer, and having fun doing unusual things such as mud-sliding and kissing under water—patriotism with a twist!

The results speak for themselves. In three days, the YouTube rendition of the commercial received over a million views (even prior to airing on TV), created positive buzz on social networks, and prompted numerous articles in the mainstream media as well as on blogs and microblogging sites.[2]

The research SW+A completed for Molson Canadian typifies its approach to market research and shows how insightful tools and smart thinking can effectively build brands. SW+A and the Molson team carefully analyzed data, conducted focused market research studies, and used smart thinking to pinpoint how the brand could be energized in the market. It used succinct, credible, fact-based information that was precise, persuasive, and engaging.

Sklar cites this example to showcase how the world of market research is dynamic, exciting, and relevant. He encourages students who are inquisitive, intellectually curious, and creative to explore the research field as it is an exciting career choice. You can learn more about SW+A at **www.sklarwilton.com**.[3]

reality CHECK ✓

As you read through Chapter 4, refer back to this opening vignette on SW+A and answer the following questions:

- What metrics could Molson Canadian use to measure the success of its new advertising campaign?
- What insights about Molson Canadian beer drinkers were captured in the ad campaign "The Canadians"?

Market Research, Metrics, and Analytics

LO¹ An organization constantly requires data to evaluate its performance and to analyze its customers, competitors, products, and services. It needs to collect this information in the form of metrics and to analyze and interpret the data using analytics. In addition, it may need to conduct further market research studies to investigate the insights it has gathered in order to strengthen its business and improve its return on investment (ROI). In the opening chapter vignette, SW+A explained how Molson Canadian required additional market research studies to gather insights into how its brand was perceived by consumers. **Market research** is formally defined as the process of planning, collecting, and analyzing information in order to recommend actions to improve marketing activities.[4] Although market research is not perfect at explaining consumer behaviour, it can reduce the risk and uncertainty of making poor business choices. It provides managers with insights to help make sound decisions. Solid marketing assessments are often the result of managers using vision, knowledge, and experience, together with clear market research insights.

Many companies have a **marketing information system (MIS)**, a set of procedures and processes for collecting, sorting, analyzing, and summarizing marketing information on an ongoing basis to help manage the data. This data can become an important competitive advantage and a key marketing input for program development and assessment. It can help marketers understand how elements impact its business, anticipate competitive moves, and predict consumer behaviour and preferences.

Metrics

LO² **Metrics** refers to numeric data that is collected and grouped to track performance. It is often presented in spreadsheets and dashboards to make it easy to understand and interpret. **Dashboards** visualize data and key performance indicators (KPIs) using graphs, charts, and numbers so that numerical information tells a story that is insightful, easy to use, and understand. Metrics data can come from a variety of sources, such as tracking data from websites, social media pages, call centre interactions, online ads, app downloads, webinars, downloads, and subscribers, as well as sales, costs, profits, and competitive and market growth data. It can measure elements such as revenue, market share, profit margins, buzz, sentiment, amplification, engagement, response rates, sales lift, awareness levels, brand loyalty, retention rates, and brand development index. It can point to ROI, customer lifetime value, brand advocates, and sales conversion rates.

Figure 4–1 identifies a snapshot of key metrics that marketers often use to analyze performance. Importantly, companies frequently identify their specific metrics requirements and routinely identify key performance indicators to track and evaluate

market research
The process of planning, collecting, and analyzing information in order to recommend actions to improve marketing activities

marketing information system (MIS)
A set of procedures and processes for collecting, sorting, analyzing, and summarizing marketing information on an ongoing basis

metrics
Numeric data that is collected and grouped to track performance, often presented in spreadsheets and dashboards

dashboards
The visualization of data and key performance indicators using graphs, charts, and numbers so that numerical information tells a story that is insightful, easy to use, and understand

business results. Metrics are selected based on company protocols, program KPIs, and any issues and opportunities that require analysis. Marketers are often advised to use no more than five to seven key metrics for a task to make the data focused, clear, and actionable.

Let's look at brand health metrics as an example of how metrics are used. The key metrics for this task are sales, market growth rates, market share percentages, brand awareness levels, brand loyalty data, brand trial rates, repeat purchase rates, brand development indexes, category development indexes, profitability trends, and return on investment. Two key drivers are market share and brand development index. **Market share** is the percentage of sales volume for a product, relative to the entire sales volume of the category in which it competes. A car brand, for example, may have a market share of 17 percent, meaning that 17 percent of car sales in the market are attributed to this brand. This is a useful metric when tracked over time and compared to competitive market share levels. **Brand development index (BDI)** shows how well a brand's sales are developed in a region relative to the region's population size. This is a useful metric when trying to determine regional growth opportunities for a brand.

Figure 4–1
Key marketing metrics

Website	E-commerce	Online Ad Campaigns	Social Media	E-mail Programs
Visits	Purchases	Reach	Demographics	Sent and delivery
Unique visitors	Purchase frequency	Impressions	Followers	rates
Page views	Returns	Engagement	Views	Open rates
Time on site	Complaints	Dwell levels	Comments	Forward rates
Traffic sources	Customer satisfaction	Lift in site visits	Likes	Click-through rates
Referrals	Acquisition costs	Search/display overlap	Shares	Bounce rates
Bounce rate	Conversion rates	Conversions	Sentiment	Subscribe rates
Return on investment	Customer lifetime	Cost per click (CPC)	Engagement	Unsubscribe rates
(ROI)	value	Cost per thousand	Conversions	Complaints
	Return on investment	views (CPM)	Churn rate	E-mail revenue
	(ROI)	Click-through rates	Return on investment	Return on investment
		(CTR)	(ROI)	(ROI)
		Cost per conversion		
		(CPC)		
		Keywords		
		Return on investment		
		(ROI)		

Brand Health	Financial	Customer Relationship Management (CRM)	Offline Ad Campaigns	Public Relations
Sales	Sales	Prospects and leads	Awareness	Interviews
Growth rates	Revenue	Conversion rates	Recall (aided and	Press releases
Market share	Cost of goods sold	Retention rates	unaided)	Events and
Awareness levels	Gross margins	Churn rate	Share of voice	conferences
Brand loyalty	Profit margins	Engagement	Likes	Share of voice
Brand trial rates	Marketing	Cost per acquisition	Dislikes	Impressions
Repeat purchase rates	expenditures	(CPA)	Clarity of	Audience
Brand development	Earnings before	Cost per interaction	communication	Mentions
index (BDI)	income and taxes	Share of wallet	Memorable elements	Advertising value
Category development	(EBITA)	Customer lifetime	Reach	equivalency (AVE)
index (CDI)	Return on investment	value	Frequency	Return on investment
Profitability trends	(ROI)	Return on investment	Gross rating points	(ROI)
Return on investment		(ROI)	Impressions	
(ROI)			Cost per impression	
			(CPI)	
			Cost per thousand	
			views (CPM)	
			Return on investment	
			(ROI)	

> *"A robust analytics system processes a steady stream of real-time data to make faster and better decisions."*

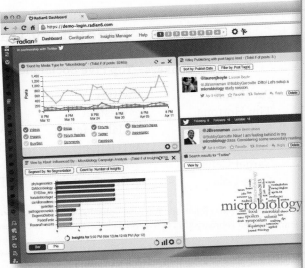

Salesforce Marketing Cloud analytics uses dashboards to visualize data.

Analytics

LO 2 **Analytics** refers to the process of taking metrics data and applying smart thinking and technology to gain actionable insights that can help make better business decisions. An analytics platform helps answer questions, provides customer insights, and predicts patterns that can improve marketing performance. Analytics can help segment customers, plan and forecast, manage risk, and take corrective action. A robust analytics system processes a steady stream of real-time data to make faster and better decisions. It may start by mining data, analyzing and scoring the information, modelling the data to predict outcomes, and visualizing data with dashboards that appear in reports. Best practices use analytics platforms that are customer focused, uncomplicated, easy to access, and in real time. The platforms need to be reliable, accurate, private, and secure, and be able to manage multiple channels at scale. Organizations use analytics in varying degrees of sophistication. Some organizations, for example, use very basic analytics platforms to manage social media, while others use complex analytics tools to model data and predict outcomes.

Let's look at three types of analytics in more detail: web analytics, social media analytics, and predictive analytics. Specifically, **web analytics** is the measurement and analysis of website data, looking at elements such as page views, time on site, bounce rate, new visitors, returning visitors, and referral traffic. Google Analytics is an example of an excellent, free web-analytics tool. **Social media analytics** uses social listening platforms to pay attention to real-time public conversations on social networks to discover trends as well as common themes, attitudes, topics, areas of interest, and how marketing programs are performing on social platforms. Social media analytics can measure social media campaign performance, assess message resonation and amplification, determine a brand's buzz level, and gauge sentiment toward a brand. It can identify key influencers, brand advocates, and opinion leaders, and it can interact in real time with consumers.

There are many free and paid social media analytics tools. A few examples are Salesforce Marketing Cloud, which is a robust, paid social media analytics platform; Hootsuite, which provides a basic, free social media analytics tool as well as a more vigorous paid platform for small businesses and larger organizations; and Socialbakers, which provides free social media statistics on social network usage and a paid social media analytics platform. Visit **www.salesforce.com/marketingcloud**, **www.hootsuite.com**, and **www.socialbakers.com** to see details on these services, and watch the CMA video *Customer Service in the Digital Age—Segment 3* to understand how marketers for Air Canada, the *Globe and Mail,* and Rogers Communications use metrics to help guide their social media customer service programs.

▶ Video
CMA

Predictive analytics combines data from varied sources to reveal patterns that are modelled to predict outcomes. For example, data can be combined from CRM databases, social media analytics, marketing program metrics, customer service databases, and purchase data to reveal groupings of customers with common attitudes and purchase patterns. This information can then be used to predict future consumer behaviour and to customize offers for specific groupings. IBM provides leading-edge predictive analytics platforms for businesses. Visit **www.IBM.com/smarterplanet** to see its suite of analytics products.

analytics
The process of taking metrics data and applying smart thinking and technology to gain actionable insights that can help make better business decisions

web analytics
The measurement and analysis of website data, looking at elements such as page views, time on site, bounce rate, new visitors, returning visitors, and referral traffic

social media analytics
The real-time measurement, interaction, and analysis of social media to assess social media campaign performance, message resonation and amplification, consumer sentiment, and common themes

predictive analytics
The combination of data from varied sources to reveal consumer behaviour patterns that are modelled to customize offers and predict business outcomes

Secondary Data

Socialbakers—Top Five Social Media Brands in Canada

Ranking	Facebook	Twitter	YouTube	Google+
1.	Tim Hortons	@WestJet	NCIX.com	G Adventures
2.	Subway Canada	@Halo_Health	McDonald's Canada	Dove
3.	Skittles	@Telehop	BMW Canada	Air Canada
4.	Target Canada	@AirCanada	Mazda Canada	Bell Canada
5.	Coca-Cola	@Eye_Doctors	Telus	Belairdirect

Source: Facebook local fans, Twitter followers, YouTube uploaded video views, Google+ followers, as measured by socialbakers.com, accessed February 2014 at www.socialbakers.com/all-social-media-stats/facebook/country/canada/.

ask yourself

1. What is the difference between metrics and analytics?

2. What tools would you use to measure a Twitter campaign?

Big Data

LO 3 **Big data** refers to the massive amounts of data that is high in volume, velocity, and variety. We refer to this as the three Vs—*volume, velocity,* and *variety.*[5] Big data can come from a variety of sources such as promotions, social media interactions, e-mail programs, customer service communications, mobile downloads, e-commerce purchases, and website metrics that measure elements such as unique visitors, time on site, page views, and traffic source, just to name a few elements. This huge volume of data is constantly changing, often in real time, making it difficult for marketers to manage and use.

> *Today, there is an explosion on the data front.*

big data
Massive amounts of data characterized as high-volume, high-velocity, and high-variety information

Today, there is an explosion on the data front, with customers increasingly interacting with companies through social media, e-mail, and other online points of contact, resulting in an exponential growth in data. The Conference Board of Canada tells us that consumers now create over 75 percent of today's data and that "marketers are like digital anthropologists that interpret these footprints." It emphasizes that consumers in Canada expect marketers to use this data to personalize offers that better meet individual needs. Consider that Facebook has over 1.1 billion active users, Twitter is home to over 140 million tweets per day, and YouTube has over 490 million users. We are currently in the era of big data with over 1.8 zettabytes (1.8 trillion gigabytes) of digital information created annually in the world.[6]

Marketers and information technology professionals are flooded with a deluge of big data, and challenged to determine which information is reliable, accurate, and relevant. People are drowning in data, and many companies, unprepared for the onslaught of big data, find it difficult to determine actionable insights and data oversight. Technology, that in many ways helps purge irrelevant data and focus marketers on useful insights, can also provide increased granulation that is overwhelming and confusing.

Data is now seen as one of an organization's most valuable assets, showing how customers behave on the path-to-purchase. Combining data sources can reveal new insights that allow marketers to ask important questions, discover opportunities, segment the market, review program performance, and make recommendations that improve return on investment. Marketers establish key performance indicators (KPIs) and then

Big data presents marketers with many challenges.

RFM analysis
The rating of customers on the basis of how recently products were purchased (recency), how often products were purchased (frequency), and the dollar value of the transactions (monetary value)

data mining
The processing of large amounts of data using sophisticated software to find insightful correlations and patterns that lead to better business decisions

structured data
Data that can be easily tagged, stored, and searched in a database using consistently identifiable terms that are systematically organized into columns, rows, and tables

analyze data using data analytics software to help provide insights. Big data analytics software can deliver automated visual dashboards of graphs and key metrics that flag important issues and opportunities for marketers. These insights can be used in various ways such as improving loyalty programs, finding cross-promotional partners, identifying profitable customers, recognizing product advocates, measuring program performance, and improving return on investment.

▶ Video IBM

Various companies provide data management and analytics services. Salesforce.com and IBM are examples, providing top-quality services that help transform data into actionable insights. Salesforce.com uses cloud-based platforms to help companies manage and use data from e-mail, mobile, social media, customer service, and sales and CRM interactions (see the Marketing NewsFlash, "Was Your Tweet Ignored?"). Salesforce's clients range from small businesses that require help with e-mail analytics and social networking insights, to large multinationals such as Toyota, Facebook, Avon, Bayer, Canon, L'Oreal, and Thomson Reuters. IBM has Business Intelligence products that allow users to collaborate, analyze, model, plan, and create reports. It has Predictive Analytics products that use statistical algorithms and data-mining techniques to predict outcomes, and it has Performance Management products that create integrated systems to increase performance. Leading-edge data management and analytics companies deal with these areas to help improve an organization's performance.[7]

An example of how big data analytics is used can be seen with **RFM analysis** (recency, frequency, and monetary value). This approach can use automated software to rate customers on the basis of how *recently* products were purchased (recency), how *often* products were purchased (frequency), and the *dollar value* of the transactions (monetary value). Customers are scored using these RFM approaches and then automatically ranked so that organizations can segment the market and tailor offers to different categories of consumers. Non-profit organizations often use RFM analyses to target people most likely to make donations. CRM loyalty programs use these analyses to segment customers. Loyalty programs such as those from Shoppers Drug Mart and Loblaw use loyalty cards to collect ongoing customer purchase data, and then use data-mining techniques to customize offers based on past purchases. **Data mining** refers to the processing of large amounts of data using software to find insightful correlations and patterns that lead to better business decisions.

> *Many organizations struggle with how to plan for big data.*

Best Practices in Big Data

While companies organize for big data in different ways, there are various best practices that help ensure that big data is carefully managed. Forward-thinking organizations implement the best practices identified in Figure 4–2. It is important to remember that regardless of data collection practices and approaches, big data will not automatically deliver results and is not a substitute for creative ideas and smart thinking. Managing big data takes time and perseverance, and it is the insights that count.

Types of Data

LO 4 Various types of data add to the complexity of big data. There is **structured data** that can be easily tagged, stored, and searched in a database using consistently identifiable terms that can be systematically organized into columns, rows, and tables. Examples are numbers, statistics, and dates related to purchase data, inventory levels, financial information, age, fixed survey responses, and website analytics. It is estimated that 20 to 25 percent of a company's data is structured. The remaining data is mostly unstructured data, with a hybrid of semi-structured data

Was Your Tweet Ignored?

Have you ever tweeted a question to a company and never received a response, not even an acknowledgement? If so, the company was probably not using the top-rated Salesforce Marketing Cloud platform to monitor, measure, and respond to social media comments and questions.

Salesforce Marketing Cloud is a cloud-based platform that allows community managers to listen, publish, and advertise on social platforms such as Facebook, Twitter, and YouTube. Real-time data is presented in dashboards that visualize demographics, highlight share of voice, pinpoint engagement levels, identify positive and negative sentiment, and show how social campaigns perform. The data can be sliced by social media channel, allowing the user to drill down into the source and respond in real time to leads, issues, and opportunities—and to identify advocates and detractors by location, channel, and topic. Social media campaigns for Facebook and Twitter can be scheduled, monitored, and

analyzed from one location and automated so that best-performing ads run more frequently.

Air Canada, TD, Brock University, and Montreal Children's Hospital, as well as a host of other Canadian companies and leading organizations around the world, turn to Salesforce Marketing Cloud to give customers the attention they deserve and to collect data that provides insights for fact-based decisions. Salesforce Marketing Cloud is used by many of the world's largest advertisers and Fortune 500 companies.

Air Canada effectively uses Salesforce Marketing Cloud to communicate with stranded customers during snowstorms that shut down airports across regions. Its call centres, backed up at these critical times by inquiries, have historically been criticized for poor customer service. Now, Air Canada supplements its call centre responses with Twitter communications that improve customer service. Social community managers communicate with stranded passengers using Salesforce Marketing Cloud to monitor questions

and comments, and to post real-time weather updates, flight cancellations, and revised schedules.

Brock University uses Salesforce Marketing Cloud to efficiently respond to social media questions from prospective, new, and current students as well as alumni and people associated with the university. The social media team assigns keywords related to the university and then listens and monitors the questions and comments that surface on social sites. Salesforce Marketing Cloud allows the team to tag, classify, and prioritize each social media inquiry or comment, and route it to the appropriate university department with notes and recommended approaches. In this manner, an international Twitter query for a last-minute accommodation request may be routed as a high priority to the housing department, while a positive alumni comment may be sent to alumni relations.[8]

You can find out more about Salesforce Marketing Cloud at **www.salesforcemarketingcloud.com**. ●

Questions

1. What are the benefits of using a social media analytics platform?

2. Should companies set standards for social media response times for their social media community managers?

<blockquote>
Organizations are challenged to manage unstructured and structured data in real time.
</blockquote>

Figure 4–2
Ten best practices for managing big data

Ten best practices for managing big data

1. Ingrain a culture of collaboration, measurement, analytics, and continuous improvement.
2. Invest in people, technology, training, and partnerships, and hire analytically inclined individuals.
3. Encourage a culture of analytics and experimentation.
4. Create data governance policies that set standards, procedures, rules, calculation guidelines, and universal terminology.
5. Formalize consistent rules on data collection, data hygiene, analyses, and reporting formats.
6. Set universal privacy policies for data collection and usage.
7. Assign responsibility and accountability for analytics.
8. Insist that key metrics are built into all programs and recommendations.
9. Measure things that matter, not those that are just easy to measure.
10. Share best practices.

ask yourself

1. *What are the challenges of big data?*
2. *What is an RFM analysis and how can it improve ROI?*

unstructured data
Data that comes from word-processed documents, presentations, audio files, images, video, and e-mail or social media messages that cannot be easily categorized and tagged in a database using fixed terms and definitions

semi-structured data
A hybrid data format that consists of structured and unstructured data

legacy data
Data that is difficult to use as it has been collected and stored in an obsolete format or system that is no longer compatible with current computer systems and databases

also surfacing. **Unstructured data** comes from word-processed documents, presentations, audio files, images, video, and e-mail or social media messages that cannot be easily categorized and tagged in a database using fixed terms and definitions. **Semi-structured data** is a hybrid data format that consists of structured and unstructured data, typically containing data that can be captured in a database as well as information that is free flowing and more difficult to categorize.

Today, organizations are challenged to manage unstructured and structured data in real time so that it is easily accessible and actionable. This has led to an increased demand for data scientists and analysts who are well versed in computer programming and statistics and use mathematical modelling and visualizations to analyze structured and unstructured data. These specialists also help companies deal with legacy data and convert it into meaningful and useful formats. **Legacy data** is data that is difficult to use as it has been collected and stored in an obsolete format or in a system that is no longer compatible with current computer systems and databases.

Types of Market Research

LO5 Companies often require proprietary research studies to answer questions that cannot be answered through regular metrics and analytics. They turn to market research studies and field market research projects to gather accurate and reliable information that helps answer these questions. Market research studies and projects provide marketers with various types of information. For example, they can help identify consumer trends, assess future business opportunities, evaluate new product

Market research helps provide clarity on marketing issues and opportunities.

"Market research is not an easy undertaking."

ideas, and determine purchase intent. Market research can also assess marketing practices and troubleshoot problems. A methodical approach is followed to expedite the process and to help ensure accuracy and contain costs.

Market research is not an easy undertaking, as gleaning accurate information from consumers can be difficult. If a researcher asks the wrong questions, or fails to investigate an important insight, the research will be inaccurate. For example, sometimes, the topic being researched is personal, which can result in reluctant respondents and untruthful responses; other times, a market researcher may ask respondents about pricing options, and inevitably, respondents will suggest a lower price; in other situations, respondents may be asked about new product concepts they have never seen, and they will find it difficult to respond.

The task of a market researcher is to overcome these challenges and to reveal actionable and accurate insights for marketers. Methodical approaches are used to plan the research, and marketers and researchers work together to carefully plan areas of inquiry and to script questions. This all occurs within mathematical frameworks to certify that the data is accurate and reliable.

Market research can be classified into three basic areas: (1) exploratory research, (2) descriptive research, and (3) causal research. Each area serves a different function and uses different techniques.

Exploratory Research

Preliminary research that clarifies the scope and nature of a marketing problem or opportunity is referred to as **exploratory research**. It generally provides researchers

The Dairy Farmers of Canada used market research to discover insights on milk consumption.

with a better understanding of the dimensions of the marketing problem or opportunity before focusing on areas that require further research. Marketers who are well versed in their businesses may be quick to assume general conclusions about their research needs and prone to avoiding the exploratory research step. However, exploratory research provides research projects with direction and identifies where business problems and opportunities may lie. Marketers understand that avoiding exploratory research comes with the risk of heading down the wrong path and missing potential opportunities or issues.

Exploratory research is often conducted with the expectation that subsequent and more-conclusive research will follow. For example, the Dairy Farmers of Canada, an association representing dairy producers in the country, wanted to discover why milk consumption was declining in Canada. They conducted a search of existing literature on milk consumption, talked to experts in the field, and even conducted preliminary interviews with consumers about why they were drinking less milk. This exploratory research helped the association crystallize the issues and identified areas that required more detailed follow-up.

Descriptive Research

Research designed to describe the basic characteristics of a given population or to clarify its usage and attitudes is known as **descriptive research**. Unlike exploratory research, with descriptive research the researcher has a general understanding of the marketing problem and is seeking more-conclusive data that answers particular questions. Examples of descriptive research include providing more-detailed profiles of product purchasers (e.g., the characteristics of the Canadian health food shopper), describing the size and characteristics of markets (e.g., the types of products sold in Canadian pizza restaurants), detailing product usage patterns (e.g., how frequently people use bank machines), or outlining consumer attitudes toward particular brands (e.g., Canadian attitudes toward store brands). Magazines, radio stations, and television stations almost always conduct descriptive research to identify the characteristics of their audiences in order to present it to prospective advertisers. As a follow-up to its exploratory research, the Dairy Farmers of Canada conducted descriptive research to determine the demographic characteristics of milk consumers, their current usage patterns, and their attitudes toward milk consumption.

Causal Research

Research designed to identify cause-and-effect relationships among variables is termed **causal research**. In general, exploratory and descriptive research precede causal research. With causal research, there is usually an expectation about the relationship to be explained, such as predicting the influence of a price change on product demand.

Typical causal research studies examine elements such as the effect of advertising on sales, the relationship between price and perceived product quality, and the impact of package design on sales. When the Dairy Farmers of Canada conducted their descriptive research on milk consumers, they discovered that many people believed milk was fattening and high in cholesterol. The association felt that these beliefs factored in to the decline of milk consumption. To test this assumption, it conducted causal research that included running a TV campaign stating that milk was healthy and essential to a healthy diet. The causal research found that the TV campaign changed consumer attitudes toward milk and helped improve milk consumption.

Procter & Gamble (P&G) is a company that believes in using causal market research to improve business results. Specifically, it often uses causal research to assess the effectiveness of its advertising campaigns. When creating new ads, P&G routinely looks to the advertising research it has conducted over the years. It also tests its new creative ideas to ensure that they are clear and compelling. For example, recent ads for the Tide brand typically cite market research data to support claims. This data is then used visually to portray its products as superior. Over the years, P&G's advertising research indicates that this advertising approach yields results. It is worth noting at this point that P&G could not make these competitive advertising claims unless its claims were accurate and the facts supported by data.

The Six-Step Market Research Approach

LO⁶ Effective market research is not left to chance. A systematic approach ensures that market research is done thoroughly, all elements are considered, and results are accurate. Agnew

Peckham and Associates, a group of health care facility planners, gives us insight into the market research process it followed to determine hospital and health care facility needs for six remote Northern Ontario First Nations communities. It followed a rigorous market research process that encompassed experts, community members, and First Nations Chiefs and Councils. It started with a review of available secondary research from areas such as Statistics Canada and other official data sources, followed by primary qualitative research to determine the scope and needs of the research project. This then resulted in quantitative research surveys to ensure that individuals in the community were involved, and culminated in a research report that highlighted findings, next steps, and recommendations. You can read more about this research project in the Marketing NewsFlash, "Research Flags Hospital Needs in First Nations Communities," which demonstrates market research in practice.

Let's look at the basic six-step approach outlined below that is commonly used to conduct market research studies. It is worth noting that not all research projects require qualitative and quantitative studies (steps 3 and 4). In many instances, qualitative research can suffice, while in others, quantitative studies are required for greater certainty.

1. Define the problem/issue/opportunity.

2. Design the research plan.

3. Conduct exploratory and qualitative research.

4. Collect quantitative primary research.

5. Compile, analyze, and interpret data.

6. Generate reports and recommendations.

Figure 4–3 shows this sequence of steps, and in the next few pages, we will discuss these steps in detail.

causal research
Research designed to identify cause-and-effect relationships among variables

ask yourself

1. *What are the three research classifications?*

2. *What steps are included in the six-step market research process?*

Research Flags Hospital Needs in First Nations Communities

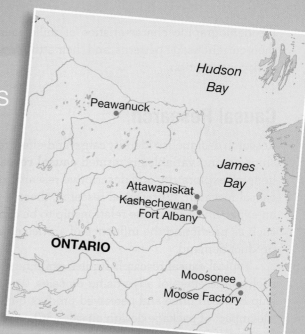

After months of fact-based research in six remote Northern Ontario First Nations communities, health care and facility planners Agnew Peckham recommended that a new district hospital be developed to replace the old wooden structure in Moose Factory and a new acute care health facility be developed in one of the isolated coastal communities. This was in addition to the provision of birthing/midwifery, dialysis, and long-term elder care facilities in four of the communities, as well as improved dentistry, rehabilitation, mental health, and telemedicine services. No longer would women in remote communities have to leave their families and travel to the Moose Factory hospital to give birth to their children, or elders have to leave their communities when unable to live independently, just to name a few changes.

Let's look at the research process undertaken by Agnew Peckham to determine the health care facility requirements in the WAHA (Weeneebayko Area Health Authority) region. First, working with leaders from WAHA, Agnew Peckham learned that for the research to be accurate, it had to involve local health care providers, residents in each community, and the respective First Nations Chiefs and Councils. Cultural sensitivities had to be front and centre, Cree translation was imperative, and the research process would pause during the hunting season, the spring ice breakup, and any special events in the communities.

The following process was followed:

Step 1: Secondary research

The first step analyzed already published secondary data. This included Statistics Canada census information that was unfortunately unreliable due to inconsistent numeration in the area, as well as reports from Aboriginal Affairs and Northern Development's on-reserve data and the Registered Indian Population Growth Scenario for Canada, 2004–2029. The data and population growth assumptions were cross-checked with local community leaders and health care providers to ensure accuracy.

Available strategic plans were also reviewed from WAHA, the North East Local Health Integration Network, Aboriginal Affairs and Northern Development, and Indian and Northern Affairs Canada to help understand underlying health care concerns and opportunities.

Step 2: Primary qualitative research

The second step used focus groups and discussion forums in each community to gather insights from health care staff, educators, community representatives, and Chiefs and Councils. Discussions focused on health care service concerns, unmet health care needs, and health care facility expansion requirements. In-depth consultations focused on traditional healing programs, elder care, midwifery, diabetes, and mental health. The findings were returned to the communities for further comment, and additional input was made possible online.

Step 3: Primary quantitative research

The third step fielded a quantitative survey to people in the communities, ensuring that individuals had the opportunity to comment on local health care requirements, as well as to suggest changes, additions, and improvements to health care services.

All in all, the research process spanned 18 months and became the building block of a successful new health care service plan for WAHA and the James Bay coastal communities, including Peawanuck, Attawapiskat, Kashechewan, Fort Albany, Moosonee, and Moose Factory. The goal of developing a new district hospital and an acute care health care facility and substantially improving health care services in these communities is being pursued, and discussions are underway with the provincial Ministry of Health.[9] ●

Questions

1. What cultural elements did Agnew Peckham and Associates consider in its research process?

2. What difficulties were faced in the initial secondary research stage?

Figure 4–3
The basic market research process

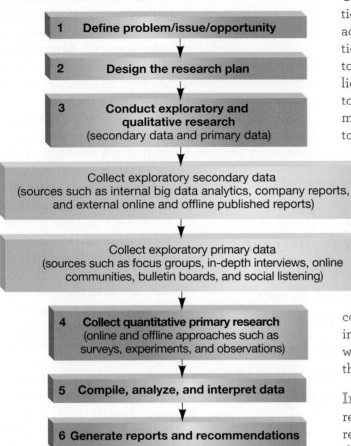

1. **Define problem/issue/opportunity**

2. **Design the research plan**

3. **Conduct exploratory and qualitative research**
   (secondary data and primary data)

Collect exploratory secondary data
(sources such as internal big data analytics, company reports, and external online and offline published reports)

Collect exploratory primary data
(sources such as focus groups, in-depth interviews, online communities, bulletin boards, and social listening)

4. **Collect quantitative primary research**
   (online and offline approaches such as surveys, experiments, and observations)

5. **Compile, analyze, and interpret data**

6. **Generate reports and recommendations**

Step 1: Define the Problem/Issue/Opportunity

The first step in the market research process is to clearly define the problem, issue, or opportunity, and to clarify the objectives. This is often posed as a question that needs to be answered. Most market researchers would agree with the saying that "a problem well-defined is half-solved," but defining a problem is a difficult task. Most market research issues stem from poorly defined problems and objectives that are vague and unclear: If objectives are too broad, the problem may not be tangible; if the objectives are too narrow, the value of the research may be questionable. Market researchers spend considerable time precisely defining marketing problems and clarifying research objectives in formal proposals that clearly describe the research task and its approach. **Objectives** are specific, measurable goals that the decision maker seeks to achieve. Common research objectives are to discover consumer needs and wants, and to determine why a product is not selling.

Let's look at the Insurance Corporation of British Columbia (ICBC) as an example. This Crown corporation is responsible for providing auto insurance and administering driver licensing and vehicle registration for drivers in British Columbia. It is committed to reducing injuries and fatalities, and has spent millions on advertising to encourage British Columbians to drive more safely. Looking at the large amount of money spent on advertising, ICBC realized it needed to know whether its anti-speeding ads were working. Did the ads change the speeders' behaviour? This was the basis of the problem and its research objectives.

Step 2: Design the Research Plan

The second step in the market research process is to identify which approach will be taken to complete the project. This includes identifying what information is needed, how it will be collected, and whether a sampling plan is needed. Let's look at these three areas.

Information Requirements Often, market research studies collect data that is interesting but not relevant to the task at hand. Marketers need to avoid this situation because it is time-consuming, confusing, and costly. In ICBC's situation, the researchers may have been curious about which cars were most likely to speed, but this information was not relevant to the research objectives—understanding whether anti-speeding advertisements worked. One of the research study's first tasks was to determine how to best collect this information affordably. Clearly, speeders could tell the ICBC what it needed to know, but how are speeders defined and how can they be contacted? Is a speeder a driver who has received a speeding ticket in the past two years, or is it a driver with three or more speeding tickets in the past twelve months? Perhaps the research study should consider drivers who had never received a speeding ticket but nonetheless drive over the speed limit? ICBC had to determine its approach.

Collection Methods In order to collect data in an organized fashion, it is important to have a data collection plan. There are mathematical considerations and operational issues that the researcher must consider. Determining *how* to collect the data is often as important as actually collecting the data. Researchers can purchase data from a pre-existing

objectives
Specific, measurable goals

study, or conduct their own research using a variety of data-collection methods such as in-depth personal interviews, focus groups, telephone surveys, central location surveys, personal questionnaires, or mail surveys. The Internet also provides numerous online tools that facilitate the gathering of information. Surveys can be easily completed online, and online communities and online bulletin boards can also be used to provide additional data.

To ensure that accurate answers are obtained, researchers carefully select research methodologies that encourage honesty. The method chosen is critical to obtaining accurate results. In the case of the ICBC, it may be more helpful to conduct focus groups or personal interviews, rather than telephone interviews or online surveys where the responses may be questionable and not easily probed.

Canadian market researchers rely on their training, expertise, and judgment to make appropriate methodology decisions. They can also turn to their professional association, the Professional Marketing Research Society, for resources and training.

Sampling
Sampling is another important factor in research design. A researcher's sampling plan identifies who is to be sampled, how large the sample should be, and how the sample will be selected. Rarely does a research project involve a complete census of every person in the research population because this is time-consuming and costly. Therefore, market researchers use smaller samples that are representative of the population being surveyed. **Sampling** is the process of gathering data from a subset of the total population, rather than from all members of that particular group.

A properly selected sample should be representative of the population being researched; however, sampling errors can occur, and thus the reliability of the data is sometimes an issue. Savvy researchers know that the first and most-critical sampling question for researchers is: *Who is to be sampled?* Another key question concerns sample size: *How big should the sample be?* The final question relates to selection: *How should the sample be selected?*

Currently, a number of market researchers are debating the validity of online market research studies, questioning whether online samples are valid because they exclude respondents who are not online. Luke Sklar from SW&A advises us to consider the reality that each methodology has its limitations and that while online market research may overlook certain respondents, it is not unlike telephone or mail surveys, which also exclude certain groups. Market researchers always need to understand the limitations of the methodology they select.

> *Rarely does a research project involve a complete census of every person in the research population, because it is time-consuming and costly.*

How do you research hazardous driving?

Obtaining truthful responses is always a top consideration in market research.

sampling
The process of gathering data from a subset of the total population rather than from all members of that particular group

There are two basic sampling techniques: probability and non-probability sampling. **Probability sampling** involves precise rules to select the sample so that each element of the population has a specific known chance of being selected. For example, if your university wants to know how last year's 1,000 graduates are doing, it can put their names into a bowl and randomly select 100 names to contact. The chance of being selected (100 out of 1,000, or 1 in 10) is known in advance, and all graduates have an equal chance of being contacted. This procedure helps to select a sample (100 graduates) that should be representative of the entire population (the 1,000 graduates), and allows conclusions to be drawn about the population being researched.

Non-probability sampling involves the use of arbitrary judgment by the market researcher to select a sample so that the chance of selecting a particular element of the population is either unknown or zero. If your university decided to talk to 100 of last year's graduates, but only selected those who lived closest, many graduates would be excluded. This would introduce a bias, tainting the representativeness of the sample and its ability to draw accurate conclusions.

It is worth noting at this point that the researcher may decide to follow this non-probability sampling approach in the interest of time and to maintain costs. In fact, non-probability samples are often used when time and budgets are limited, or for exploratory research purposes when conclusions are mostly directional and may require further research. In general, market researchers use data from such non-probability samples with caution. The data can provide valuable information, but the results need to be viewed carefully as they may not accurately represent the population being researched.

ask yourself

1. *How do research objectives relate to marketing actions?*

2. *What different methods can be used to conduct market research?*

3. *What are the differences between probability and non-probability samples?*

Step 3: Conduct Exploratory and Qualitative Research

Exploratory research is preliminary research conducted to clarify the scope and nature of a marketing problem. It is done to ensure that researchers have not overlooked key insights that are important to the study. Exploratory research is often conducted with the expectation that subsequent and more-conclusive quantitative research may follow.

If researchers decide to conduct exploratory research, they have two avenues from which to glean data. The first avenue is to collect exploratory *secondary data,* which is already available through big data analytics, company reports, or external online and offline published reports. A second avenue involves researchers creating their own data, exploratory *primary data,* through options such as focus groups, in-depth interviews, online communities, online bulletin boards, and social listening research. Let's look at these approaches in more detail.

Focus group research, in-depth interviews, online communities, online bulletin boards, and social listening are forms of research called **qualitative research**. This research provides insightful and directional information to the researcher, with the understanding that although the data is not gleaned from a large consumer base, it provides useful direction to the research study and may in fact thoroughly answer the questions at hand. In this manner, it may allow marketers to avoid costly quantitative research studies. In other instances, qualitative research may not be enough to draw firm conclusions and will be used instead to provide insights and direction for a more detailed quantitative research study.

Quantitative research, discussed later in this chapter, is statistically reliable information that uses observational techniques and/or questioning methods such as surveys or experiments to deliver statistically significant results.

Let's take a hypothetical example to demonstrate this point. The marketing manager for cranberry juice at Ocean Spray is considering an opportunity to export cranberry juice to Asian markets. He needs to determine whether this is a viable opportunity but is concerned that these consumers may not be

probability sampling
Selecting a sample so that each element of a population has a specific known chance of being selected

non-probability sampling
Selecting a sample so that the chance of selecting a particular element of a population is either unknown or zero

qualitative research
A form of research that uses approaches such as focus groups, in-depth interviews, online communities, online bulletin boards, and social listening to provide insightful and directional information

What form of research is a focus group?

interested in cranberries because they are virtually unknown in Asia. This may, however, present an opportunity to sell something unique in the market. One of the major stumbling blocks is that the word "cranberry" does not exist in any of the Asian languages. Exploratory research would be advisable in this situation, starting with secondary research to find out whether any information is available on beverage consumption in Asia. This may be followed up by focus groups or research with online communities and bulletin boards to probe attitudes and opportunities in this area.

Cultural differences can be revealed through market research.

Secondary Data Exploratory research can include the gathering of **secondary data**. This data comes in two forms: external data and internal data. *Internal data* exists within a company and can include data derived from big data analytics, or simpler approaches that review basic sales reports, profitability data, and costing information. *External data* comes from published sources outside the organization, which can track what consumers watch on television, on mobile devices, or online, as well as what they buy from online or offline retailers.

As a form of self-promotion, many research companies, service experts, and media companies now publish top-line research data on their websites free for public viewing, with full report access requiring either a subscription or payment. Such companies include,

secondary data
Facts and figures that have already been recorded by a third party

among others, Leger, The Research Intelligence Group; Ipsos Canada; Nielsen; Solutions Research Group; comScore; Forrester Research; and the Interactive Advertising Bureau of Canada (IAB Canada). Leger posts research data on demographic trends and voting intentions; Ipsos Canada posts research highlights on economic, social, lifestyle, and political studies; Nielsen posts research updates on Canadian consumer insights; Solutions Research Group focuses on digital consumer behaviour; comScore provides updates on digital marketing trends; Forrester Research specializes in business and technology; and IAB Canada routinely publishes reliable research reports on digital marketing.

The GFK Group is another example of a reputable research company that provides an international perspective of various research topics with a focus on local markets. A recent study, *The Consumer Journey to 2020: Five Trends Driving the Future of Brands,*[10] annually measures more than 37,000 consumers over the age of 15 from over 25 countries. This includes consumers from Canada and the U.S. as well as Asia, Latin America, Western Europe, China, the Middle East, and Africa. Its data shows that when compared to the global average, Canadians value experiences more than possessions, and place more importance on leisure time. Canadians have adjusted to the fast pace of change in their lives, see advertising as a source of information, and increasingly use their smartphones to access online product reviews, websites,

Infographic

The Consumer Journey to 2020
FIVE TRENDS DRIVING THE FUTURE OF BRANDS

- Secondary data
- Research report

GFK Roper conducts an annual worldwide quantitative research study on consumer trends.

37,000+ people

25+ countries

49% of Canadians agree that experiences are more important than possessions.

78% of Canadians find that things are changing faster than ever

People are becoming more comfortable with the rapid pace of change.

64% of Canadians are disappointed in the lack of meaningful change today.

There is increased pessimism in the quality of change.

Mobile Phone Usage

Activity of mobile phone users in last 30 days (ages 15+)

Mobile phones are increasingly used for multiple activities.

Most common use is downloading apps and social networking.

Activity	Percentage
making a small purchase using a code or smart reader	7
geo-location check-in	8
access coupons, offers	5
scan barcodes	9
download music, games, audio	14
navigation	20
video	16
social network	21
download apps	24

Percentage (0, 5, 10, 15, 20, 25, 30)

Source: Kathy Sheenan, *The Consumer Journey to 2020: Five Trends Driving the Future of Brands,* GFK Roper Webinar for CMA, July 30, 2013.

Secondary Research Identifies Reasons for Brand Loyalty Decline

Percentage of people who state they are less brand loyal due to:

Word of mouth; people like to try recommended brands	67%
Deals; people buy whatever is on sale or with coupons	58%
Variety; people like to try new and different things	45%
No wow factor; people can't find a really satisfactory brand	42%

Source: Kathy Sheenan, *The Consumer Journey to 2020: Five Trends Driving the Future of Brands,* GFK Roper Webinar for CMA, July 30, 2013.

and recommendations from friends. They have also become platform agnostic in their use of technology, using smartphones, PCs, laptops, and tablets interchangeably depending on the time, place, and circumstance. Consumers are also more brand agnostic, readily switching between brands at purchase time.

Statistics Canada, the federal government's statistical agency, publishes a wide variety of useful reports, such as census data that includes information on the number of people per household and their age, gender, ethnic background, income, occupation, and education. Statistics Canada also publishes a wide range of other statistical reports that are used by businesses across the country. These reports include information on the following:

- Economic indicators
- International trade
- Culture and leisure
- Agriculture
- Tourism and travel
- Manufacturing
- Government
- Environment
- Justice and crime
- Health

The $78 Billion* Question

What's in your basket?

Nielsen has the solutions to help you understand what's in your shopper's basket - so you can influence their behaviour.

In order to grow, you need to know.

www.nielsen.com

*Nielsen Total Retail Sales, Canada All Channels 52 Weeks to March 13, 2010

Just ask
nielsen

Secondary data on retail purchases can be purchased from companies such as Nielsen.

A list of online secondary research sources is detailed in Figure 4–4, and an overview of information sources can be seen in Figure 4–5. These sources are often posted online. Marketers can read interesting articles, view snapshots of research projects, download full reports, or read synopses of research studies. Examples include third-party organizations that audit magazine and newspaper circulation or the popularity of TV shows. Often, a portion of this information is provided at no charge, with full report coverage provided for a price. Similarly, competitive market-share data is available for marketers to purchase to help track competitive activity. Check our list of top online resources that are used by marketers in Canada and visit their websites to gain an understanding of the available information.

 **Primary Data** In a research project, a general rule is to first obtain secondary data followed by detailed, proprietary primary data. **Primary data** is data that is original and specifically collected for the project at hand. This sequencing is because secondary data is lower in cost and easier to obtain than primary data. Secondary data can also help illuminate further data requirements. These advantages of secondary data must be weighed against its disadvantages, namely that (1) the secondary data may be out of date, (2) the definitions or categories may not be right for the project, and (3) the data may not be accurate or specific enough for the study. Let's review the primary sources of information.

FOCUS GROUPS A popular exploratory research technique is the focus group. A **focus group** is an informal interview session in which six to ten people are brought together in a room with a moderator to discuss topics surrounding the market research problem. The moderator poses questions and encourages individuals to discuss the issues. Often, focus-group sessions are watched by observers and are videotaped. Participants are

Figure 4–4
A selection of market research sources for online secondary data

Alliance for Audited Media	www.auditedmedia.com
Numeris	www.numeris.ca
Bensimon Byrne Consumerology Report	http://consumerology.ca
Canadian Marketing Association	www.the-cma.org
Communispace	www.communispace.com
comScore	www.comscore.com
Forrester Research	www.forrester.com
GFK Group	www.gfk.com
Government of Canada	www.canada.gc.ca
Industry Canada	www.ic.gc.ca
Interactive Advertising Bureau of Canada	www.iabcanada.com
Ipsos Canada	www.ipsos.ca
Leger, The Research Intelligence Group	www.legermarketing.com
Media Digest	www.cmdc.ca
Newspaper Audience Databank	www.nadbank.com
Nielsen Canada	www.ca.nielsen.com
Print Measurement Bureau	www.pmb.ca
SEDAR	www.sedar.com
Solutions Research Group	www.srgnet.com
Statistics Canada	www.statcan.gc.ca
Television Bureau of Canada	www.tvb.ca

Worth Noting

Your library may have access to various online databases that can assist with research projects. Examples of these databases are Business Source Complete, CBCA Business, Canadian Newsstand, Statistics Canada, LexisNexis Academic, Scott's Directories, and Warc (World Advertising Research Centre).

Figure 4–5
Information sources

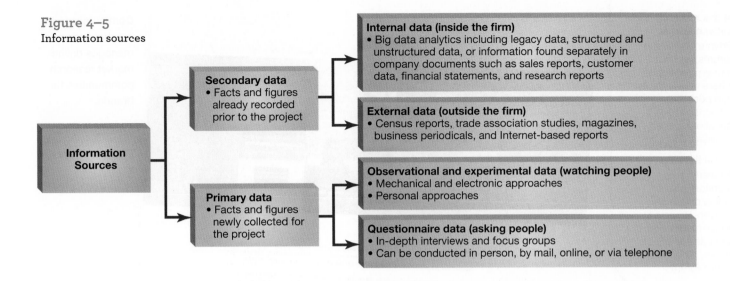

Information Sources

Secondary data
• Facts and figures already recorded prior to the project

Internal data (inside the firm)
• Big data analytics including legacy data, structured and unstructured data, or information found separately in company documents such as sales reports, customer data, financial statements, and research reports

External data (outside the firm)
• Census reports, trade association studies, magazines, business periodicals, and Internet-based reports

Primary data
• Facts and figures newly collected for the project

Observational and experimental data (watching people)
• Mechanical and electronic approaches
• Personal approaches

Questionnaire data (asking people)
• In-depth interviews and focus groups
• Can be conducted in person, by mail, online, or via telephone

> *A popular exploratory research technique is the focus group.*

always informed that they are being observed and/or taped and asked for permission to do so.

The ICBC research study discussed earlier in this chapter included focus groups where participants were shown anti-speeding ads and probed on their attitudes and responses to these messages. The focus groups suggested an association between personality and speeding. This exploratory research stage was followed up by quantitative research with a larger number of people to confirm the personality/speeding linkage and to further understand the effectiveness of the ICBC advertising campaign.

IN-DEPTH INTERVIEWS Another exploratory research technique used to obtain primary data involves the use of in-depth interviews. **In-depth interviews** are detailed individual interviews where a researcher discusses topics with an individual at length in a free-flowing conversation in order to discover information that may help solve a marketing problem. Sometimes, these interviews can take a few hours, and they are often recorded with respondents' consent.

ONLINE RESEARCH COMMUNITIES A relatively new qualitative research tool used by marketers to gain feedback on marketing approaches is the online research community. **Online research communities** involve the use of consumer groups, brought together privately in an online environment, to answer questions, respond to ideas, and collaborate with researchers in real time. This approach uses vocal consumers, often in high-involvement categories such as sports and entertainment, or other areas where consumers are passionate about their products, such as chocolate and baby food. These consumers provide feedback to researchers in a private online environment

---

PMB Research Data— Top Three Saturday Newspapers

The Print Measurement Bureau (PMB) provides online secondary data on the readership and circulation of newspapers and magazines in Canada.

Newspaper	Circulation
1. *Toronto Star*	474,000
2. *The Globe and Mail*	319,000
3. *National Post*	138,000

Source: "PMB 2014 Spring Topline Report," Canadian Print Measurement Bureau, accessed at www.pmb.ca/public/e/pmb2014_spring/release/pmb2014spring_topline.pdf.

---

in-depth interviews
Detailed interviews where a researcher questions an individual at length in a free-flowing conversational style in order to discover information that may help solve a marketing problem

online research communities
The use of consumer groups, brought together privately in an online environment, to answer questions, respond to ideas, and collaborate with researchers in real time

Communispace creates and manages online market research communities for brands.

where only the marketers, researchers, and respondents are privy to the conversations. Typically, this approach invites consumers to join an online community on a specific topic in return for interesting and lively debate, thought-provoking ideas, and a small stipend for their time. An online community is managed by a research company to ensure that the community is engaged and continues to be interested in the topic. Participants can be gathered from a variety of sources such as website visitors, consumer lists, or company databases. The community usually exists for one year, involves regular two-way communication visible to all within the community, is managed by a researcher, and can involve 200 to 300 people depending on the need. Multinational brands often maintain large global communities to help answer their marketing questions.

A research company considered best-in-class for online community research is Communispace, known as the consumer collaboration agency, which can be found online at **www.communispace.com**. This company is used by many companies around the world and by top researchers in Canada such as SW&A to help provide real-time feedback for its clients. It has over 600 online communities with members in more than 96 countries.

ONLINE RESEARCH BULLETIN BOARDS Another new research tool available to researchers is the online research bulletin board. **Online research bulletin boards** are private online forums where respondents can post their responses to questions. Unlike online communities, online research bulletin boards do not engage respondents through dialogue. Instead, they are static website locations where questions

are posted online, and respondents are asked to comment on ideas. Only those with access to the bulletin board are privy to the posted questions and responses. While online bulletin boards may not provide researchers with the depth of information available through an online community, they are easier to manage and administer.

ask yourself

1. *Why do researchers use exploratory research?*

2. *What are some of the online tools available to market researchers?*

3. *What are the advantages and disadvantages of secondary data?*

SOCIAL LISTENING The growth in social media and its ability to influence consumers has given rise to a new exploratory research technique, **social listening**, which monitors public online consumer conversations on social media sites such as social networks, blogs, and public forums. The metrics derived from social listening can measure positive and negative sentiments, popularity scores, and message reach, as well as the levels of conversation and buzz. Social listening research can take the form of qualitative or quantitative information depending on the parameters of the study. Well-respected research companies such as Forrester Research and Nielsen both emphasize that the benefits of social listening research extend beyond measuring brand mentions and into gaining insights that can lead to new ideas and opportunities.

Nielsen notes Kraft as an example of a food company that used social listening to better understand product trends and consumer profiles. Kraft used social listening to determine market segmentation profiles for people who eat hamburgers at home and how sliders (mini-hamburgers) are viewed. The research helped identify the following four distinct segments for at-home hamburger eaters:

Aficionados: People who create gourmet hamburgers for their spouses, friends, and sometimes children. This group is found online on personal blogs and foodie community websites.

Dieters: People who purchase pre-made hamburgers, turkey burgers, and veggie burgers and cook them on an electric grill or in the microwave. These people are found online on personal blogs and on weight-loss community websites.

Moms and household chefs: People who cook basic hamburgers or turkey burgers for family dinners and weekend cookouts with their spouses and children. This target market can be found online on personal blogs, recipe-sharing websites, and mom websites.

Entertainers: People who cook hamburgers or turkey burgers on an outdoor grill in a fun casual atmosphere on weekends and holidays and during warm-weather days, with friends and extended family.

Listening to the conversations around mini-hamburgers also helped Kraft understand the popularity of sliders. Social conversations pointed out

Social listening raises an important ethical issue.

Kraft used social listening to better understand hamburger consumption.

that sliders are flexible items that can be served as appetizers, as snacks, or as main meals for different target groups. They are often available at adult social functions, can be served as a fun treat for kids, and are used as late night snacks by students.[11]

Social listening raises an important ethical issue: While participants in social networks realize many of their comments are publicly posted, they may not be aware that their conversations may be monitored and used for research purposes. Social networks are required to have privacy policies that protect consumer data from being kept and misused by third parties, and marketers need to abide by these laws.

A term worth noting at this point is *netnography*. This academic term refers to the online market research tools previously mentioned.

Step 4: Collect Quantitative Primary Research

LO7 Further research can be conducted using quantitative research through observational and/or questioning techniques. The main advantage of **quantitative research** is that it is designed to be statistically accurate and it is less open to interpretation. The main disadvantage of quantitative research is that it is far more costly and time-consuming to collect than exploratory research. The primary quantitative research techniques include (1) observations, (2) surveys, and (3) experiments (see Figure 4–6).

Observational Research

Observational research is obtained by watching how people behave, either in person or by using a machine to record events. National TV ratings, such as those provided by Numeris Nielsen Media Research Inc., is an example of electronic observational data collected by a Portable People Meter (PPM). The PPM is a pager-like device worn by

quantitative research
Statistically reliable information that uses observational and/or questioning techniques such as observations, surveys, and experiments

observational research
Obtained by watching how people behave, in person or by using a machine to record events

Figure 4–6
Quantitative research: Comparing techniques

Technique	Examples	Advantages	Disadvantages
Observations	• Portable People Meters • Google Analytics • Personal observations of consumer interactions • Social listening • Store scanner information	• Reflect actual behaviour • Highly accurate when collected by machines • Mechanical observations reduce interviewer bias • Appropriate when respondents cannot clearly articulate opinions	• Do not indicate why consumers behave as they do • Do not provide data on attitudes and opinions • Different researchers may interpret behaviour differently • May require further explanation • Ethical questions exist around privacy issues
Surveys	• Personal interviews • Central location interviews such as mall-intercepts • Mail questionnaires • Telephone interviews • Internet surveys	• Can ask numerous questions • Questions are standardized • Interviewers can often probe for in-depth answers • Questions can be administered via e-mail, mail, telephone, the Internet, or in person	• Results can be biased by the methodology • Results can be influenced by the interviewer • Can be expensive and time-consuming
Experiments	• Test markets • Simulated test markets • Lab experiments	• Researchers can change key variables and measure results in a controlled setting • Can avoid costly failures by allowing marketers to modify marketing programs prior to full launch • Can provide a more accurate reflection and predictor of consumer behaviour than other forms of research	• Can be expensive and time-consuming • Results can be difficult to interpret • Actual test markets may be visible to the competition • Difficult to find a representative sample

> " *Market researchers have to make important tradeoffs to balance costs against the expected quality of information.* "

participants to monitor their TV-viewing and radio-listening habits. The device automatically detects and logs audio signals into a database, which is then uploaded to a central site together with information from other participants. It can detect signals from TV, radio, movie theatres, and in-store media.[12] Other examples of observational research can be in the form of store scanner information, which captures data on consumer purchases; the social listening research mentioned earlier; and web-tracking software such as Google Analytics, which measures website traffic, unique visitors, page views, time on site, and referring sites. Observational research can also be done in person, with researchers observing elements such as children's play patterns to determine the potential for new toys.

Observational research tools are both useful and flexible, but they can be costly and unreliable when dependent upon human observation, which can at times report different conclusions after watching the same event.

Surveys Surveys are also used to gather quantitative information. Survey questions can be standardized in the form of a **questionnaire** and asked to a large representative sample to obtain accurate data. These surveys can be conducted in person, through the mail, on the telephone, or through the Internet, with each method having limitations.

In choosing from these alternatives, market researchers have to make important tradeoffs to

questionnaire
Obtaining information by posing standardized questions through surveys that can be conducted in person, through the mail, on the telephone, or through the Internet

balance costs against the expected quality of information. Personal interviews have the major advantage of enabling interviewers to ask probing questions and get reactions to visual materials. However, this approach is very costly. Mail surveys are less costly but have low response rates and are usually biased because those most likely to respond have had positive or negative experiences. Telephone interviews allow respondents to be probed but they are increasingly difficult to complete due to call-display features and respondents' reluctance to participate. Internet surveys are restricted to respondents that have the technology, but this approach is becoming an increasingly popular method of gathering information. Figure 4–7 summarizes the advantages and disadvantages of different survey approaches.

Researchers can reduce the costs of proprietary questionnaires by joining established syndicated studies that are conducted by well-respected research conglomerates. **Syndicated studies** are a hybrid of primary and secondary research conducted by a research company, spreading the cost across many clients to reduce the price. These studies are routinely conducted with extensive panels of consumers to determine trends. TNS Canadian Facts conducts individual

panel surveys and *omnibus* surveys on topics such as financial products and services, health care practices, family opinions, and teenage attitudes. Depending on the panel, questions are administered online, through the mail, or on the telephone.

syndicated studies
A hybrid of primary and secondary research whereby the cost of a research study is shared among clients and made available at a price to interested parties

Surveys can gather data from a large number of consumers.

Figure 4–7
Advantages and disadvantages of survey techniques

Survey Technique	Advantages	Disadvantages
Personal interview	• Can probe for detailed responses • Can demonstrate marketing programs • Can result in high levels of accuracy	• Time-consuming • Expensive • Interviewers can bias responses
Telephone survey	• Can be conducted quickly and cheaply • Computerized techniques allow for randomized calling • Appropriate when data is needed quickly	• People are reluctant to participate • Low response rates • Call-display features screen-out calls • Increasing number of people with no home phone • Interviews are limited to 5–10 minutes • Interviewers can bias responses • Questionable representativeness of samples
Mail survey	• No interviewer bias • Useful for national surveys • If using a panel, can track changes over time • Can be affordable if part of a syndicated or omnibus survey	• Lengthy time-lag for data collection • Low response rates • Questionable data accuracy • Inability to probe respondents
Internet survey	• No interviewer bias • Can be conducted quickly and cheaply • Efficient for electronic data collection • High Internet penetration can lead to good sampling • Can easily target customer databases • Useful for national surveys • If using a panel, can track changes over time • Can be affordable if part of a syndicated or omnibus survey	• Difficult to verify respondents' identity • Questionable data accuracy due to anonymity • Inability to probe respondents • Difficult to provide incentives for completion • Some debate over sample representativeness

Formally, a survey **panel** includes a large sample of respondents that voluntarily complete questionnaires on a regular basis so that researchers can assess changes in behaviour and attitudes. An **omnibus survey** also includes the voluntary participation of respondents in routine surveys, allowing individual marketers to add a small number of questions to an existing survey to receive cost-effective data on their questions.

Experiments Experiments are the third quantitative research approach used in market research. It involves measuring changes in consumer behaviour over time to determine reactions to new-product introductions or new promotional offers. A marketing **experiment** involves changing a variable involved in a purchase to find out what happens. Ideally, the researcher changes just one element, usually one of the factors in the marketing mix, and keeps the other variables constant.

Experiments can be conducted either in contrived environments that mimic real-life situations, known as *simulated* test markets, or *in-market* through real-time in-field tests where the product/promotion is actually sold in a limited location and monitored for success during a specific time period. Contrived, simulated experiments use computer simulations to predict consumer behaviour. Marketers typically input marketing mix variables and rely on complex forecasting programs to determine potential success levels. Formally, a **test market** is an in-market localized regional approach, or short-term

online destination, used to test the success of promotional offers, new services, or new-product launches.

Test markets can provide a more realistic evaluation of product or promotional success than other research options. However, test markets are time-consuming, costly, and visible to the competition. In terms of promotional offers, Internet marketers routinely test pay-per-click advertising campaigns, alternative online consumer offers, and the design of various website landing pages. For new products, large companies often use test markets to determine whether consumers will buy new products or brands, or shop at a new store concept. The fast-food industry is a well-known user of test markets. In the U.S., McDonald's recently tested chicken wings as a new menu item in Chicago restaurants to help determine future plans.

Step 5: Compile, Analyze, and Interpret Data

After data has been collected, it has to be compiled, analyzed, and summarized so that it can be turned into actionable information. The researcher must know how to analyze the data and what tools to use. There are many statistical packages that can make this task easier. Market researchers face the challenge of synthesizing and simplifying pages of data into dashboards as well as individual charts with relevant observations and conclusions that can help marketers address business problems, challenges, and opportunities.

Step 6: Generate Reports and Recommendations

Once the data has been analyzed, the researcher will discuss the results with a marketing manager and prepare a report to communicate the research findings. The report will include recommendations that address the marketing problem and research objectives. It is

panel
A large sample of respondents that voluntarily complete questionnaires on a regular basis so that researchers can assess changes in behaviour and attitudes

omnibus survey
The voluntary participation of respondents in routine research surveys that allow marketers to add a small number of questions to an existing survey to receive cost-effective data

experiment
In marketing, changing a variable involved in a customer purchase to find out what happens

test market
An in-market localized regional approach, or short-term online destination, used to test the success of promotional offers, new services, or new-product launches

> *The future of market research sees a continued growth in online market research approaches as well as the increased use of analytics platforms to help manage big data and glean insights.*

important to understand that marketing data and information have little value unless translated into findings and recommendations that lead to marketing action. Managers generally prefer clear, concise reports where key findings are highlighted within dashboards and individual charts, graphs, and tables of data.

In our example of the ICBC, the corporation's final research report pointed out that the people who like speeding resisted the ads. The research told the ICBC that its advertising dollars were not well spent and recommended changes.[13]

ask yourself

1. *Which survey approach provides the greatest flexibility for asking probing questions: mail, telephone, Internet, or personal interview?*

2. *In the field of research, what is the difference between an online bulletin board and an online community?*

The Future of Market Research

In today's world of big data, marketers have extensive information on consumers, the competition, and the market. This information can come from secondary sources or primary sources and is used to help marketers make fact-based decisions. Technology is facilitating the gathering and sifting of this information, using analytics platforms to flag issues and highlight opportunities for marketers. Market research projects are sometimes needed to reveal further insights, and these projects increasingly use the Internet to discern attitudes and opinions. Leger, The Research Intelligence Group, tells us that 20 percent of research surveys in Canada are already online,[14] and we learned from Luke Sklar at SW+A that online market research is the way of the future.

The future of market research sees a continued growth in online market research approaches as well as the increased use of analytics platforms to help manage big data and glean insights. Organizations are expected to increasingly invest in technology and training programs that will help marketers separate unreliable and useless information from critical and actionable facts. Organizations will come to realize that actionable data and data-savvy employees are among their most valuable assets and will invest in these areas as business-building opportunities.

Ethically and legally, marketers and market research practitioners will need to keep consumers' privacy top-of-mind. Privacy laws in Canada require businesses to comply with the *Personal Information Protection and Electronic Documents Act* (PIPEDA) as well as Canada's anti-spam legislation (CASL). You can read more about these areas in Chapter 2 where marketing regulations are discussed in detail. Marketers are well advised to check the latest privacy legislation and anti-spam laws in Canada at the Canadian Marketing Association's (CMA) website at **www.the-cma.org**, the CASL website at **http://fightspam.gc.ca**, and the Office of the Privacy Commissioner of Canada at **www.priv.gc.ca**. Legal marketing experts should be consulted to ensure that market research practices are legal.

Market researchers are also well advised to visit the website of the Marketing Research and Intelligence Association (MRIA) of Canada at **http://mria-arim.ca**, a not-for-profit association that represents all aspects of the market-intelligence and survey-research industry, including social research, competitive intelligence, data mining, insight, and knowledge management. It provides education for market researchers, publishes a market research magazine, and provides a wealth of information to its members.

LO¹ • Market research, metrics, and analytics are used by marketers to help gather data and glean insights. Metrics use numeric data to track performance. Analytics applies smart thinking and technology to metrics data to gain actionable insights.

• Market research is the process of defining a marketing problem or opportunity, systematically collecting and analyzing information, and recommending actions to improve an organization's marketing activities.

LO² • Some of the main uses of metrics are for measuring and monitoring website traffic, e-commerce interactions, ad campaigns, brand health, financial performance, and public relations activities.

• There are numerous types of analytics. Common types are web analytics, social media analytics, and predictive analytics.

LO³ • Big data is the massive amounts of data characterized as high-volume, high-velocity, and high-variety information. The challenge is to gain valuable insight. The opportunity lies in better understanding consumers' path to purchase.

• Big data best practices measure things that matter, not just those that are easy to measure, and ingrain a culture of collaboration, measurement, analytics, and continuous improvement into organizations.

LO⁴ • Data can be categorized as structured data, unstructured data, semi-structured data, and legacy data.

• Structured data can be easily tagged, stored, and searched in a database.

• Unstructured data cannot be easily tagged and categorized in a database and comes from word-processed documents, presentations, audio files, images, video, and e-mail or social media interactions.

• Semi-structured data is a hybrid data format that consists of structured and unstructured data.

• Legacy data is difficult to use as it has been collected and stored in an obsolete format or system that is no longer compatible with current systems.

LO⁵ • Market research can be classified as exploratory, descriptive, or causal research.

• Exploratory research is preliminary research that clarifies the scope and nature of a marketing problem. Descriptive research clarifies usage and attitudes toward a product or theme.

• Causal research identifies cause-and-effect relationships.

LO⁶ • The market research process follows six steps: (1) describe the problem, issue, or opportunity and establish the research objectives; (2) design the research plan and identify the methodology required to gather the information; (3) conduct exploratory and qualitative research; (4) collect quantitative research; (5) analyze and interpret the data; and (6) create research reports and recommendations.

LO⁷ • Primary research data consists of qualitative or quantitative studies.

• Qualitative studies include focus groups, in-depth interviews, online communities/bulletin boards, and social listening.

• Quantitative studies include surveys, observations, and experiments.

Key Terms and Concepts...*a refresher*

analytics
big data
brand development index (BDI)
causal research
dashboards
data mining
descriptive research
experiment
exploratory research
focus group
in-depth interview
legacy data
marketing information system (MIS)
market research

market share
metrics
non-probability sampling
objectives
observational research
omnibus survey
online research bulletin boards
online research communities
panel
predictive analytics
primary data
probability sampling
qualitative research

quantitative research
questionnaire
RFM analysis
sampling
secondary data
semi-structured data
social listening
social media analytics
structured data
syndicated studies
test market
unstructured data
web analytics

Hands-on...*apply your knowledge*

Market Research Assignment   The course you are completing may require you to submit a report on the marketing of a product. Navigate your way to the online research sources identified in Figure 4-4 to review and collect secondary data on your product or its target market. Summarize and source your findings with bullet points for future reference.

Chapter Vignette...*reminder*

This chapter's opening vignette examines how research firm SW+A views and manages its research projects and provides an example with Molson Canadian. Answer the Reality Check questions at the end of the vignette by carefully reading this chapter's sections on metrics and reviewing Figure 4-1 on key marketing metrics. Also conduct a search on YouTube to locate and view the Molson Canadian ad, "Molson Canadian—The Canadians."

Video Clip...*questions*

Review the Canadian Marketing Association video *CMA: Customer Service in the Digital Age* from the CONNECT website and answer the following questions:

▶ Video
CMA

- What are some of the metrics used to measure digital customer service?
- Has social customer service complicated how companies respond to consumers?
- How can senior management make social customer service easier?

Infographic...*data analysis*

Review the Infographic on the GFK Roper trend report, *The Consumer Journey to 2020: Five Trends Driving the Future of Brands*. Create a new infographic and write a short analysis of a recent secondary data report that you can find from Ipsos Canada at **www.ipsos.ca** or from comScore at **www.comscore.com**. Be sure to select a study that contains Canadian data. (*Infographic tip:* Use Microsoft Excel and Word to create charts and place them in a single PowerPoint slide to combine the visuals.)

b2b marketing

LEARNING OBJECTIVES

LO¹ Identify the distinguishing characteristics of industrial, reseller, government, and non-profit markets and how they are measured

LO² Describe the importance of content marketing to B2B marketers

LO³ Explain which key characteristics of organizational buying make the process different from consumer buying

LO⁴ Describe how buying centres and buying situations influence organizational purchasing

LO⁵ Outline the process of business segmentation

LO⁶ Explain the growing importance of and the approaches to online buying for industrial, reseller, and government markets

Technology has enabled businesses to develop efficiencies. These efficiencies make items available for purchase by consumers that would have been unimaginable in the past. As end users, consumers usually do not realize the extent of the marketing that businesses do with one another to ensure the best products available to them. The businesses in Canada's industrial markets, reseller markets, governments, and non-profit organizations have a number of companies they can choose from to partner with. Although the purchase decision process is similar to that of consumers, the scope and size of purchase decisions are magnified. This in turn magnifies the number of people involved in the process as well as the time it takes to complete the purchase. When a business partnership makes sense, incredible synergies arise. Although the benefits are clear when the details are finalized and contracts are signed, the process for getting to that stage can take years.

As consumers, we sometimes take for granted the work that needs to be done in the background to offer end-user services. We are familiar with companies such as Apple and Best Buy and amazed by their offerings. What we may not realize is that these companies turn to others for the ability to enhance their products and services for consumers. Rovi Music provides the back-end support to online stores and social networking sites. This service, which adds artist biographies and reviews to sites, is offered by Rovi Corporation to companies such as Apple and Best Buy, enhancing the end-user experience.

Business-to-business marketing is conducted with multi-billion dollar companies, but also with small to medium-size companies. In 2013, Cogeco Cable Inc. and Rovi Corporation launched two new interactive applications. Cogeco Remote Cable powered by Rovi TV Listings, and TotalGuide xD allowed Canadian subscribers to find television shows and schedule recordings from their tablets. The partnership was a win for consumers and the two businesses. Upon the announcement, executives from both companies shared the excitement of the purchase decision and what it meant for customers.

Ron Perotta, vice president and strategic planning at Cogeco Cable, said, "Our subscribers are going to appreciate the convenience of using their portable tablets and enjoy the new sleek, graphically rich design of the Cogeco Cable portal as they

rovi guide

Chapter Outline:

engage in a fuller and more satisfying entertainment experience." His counterpart, Bob Shallow, senior vice president of sales and marketing worldwide at Rovi, shared, "We're proud to be working with Cogeco Cable to launch a brand new service to their subscribers that will provide [consumers] with even greater access to Cogeco Cable's industry-leading digital entertainment products and services." Rovi Corporation needed to market its services to Cogeco Cable in order to provide this incredible entertainment experience to the end consumer.

Partnerships similar to the Rovi example arise in other industries. Automobile companies purchase from parts manufacturers to ensure their final product meets the needs of Canadian drivers. Hospitals make strategic purchase decisions from medical equipment manufacturers to enhance patient care. Large grocery store retailers go through a detailed process to ensure your favourite potato chips are stocked on their shelves. Business decisions like this take more time than a consumer purchase, as the size of the order and number of people involved may be significantly greater.

Although there are clearly benefits to partnerships between companies, developing these partnerships takes time. Because of the magnitude of the impact of a business purchase decision, business-to-business marketing may be considered more complex than marketing involving the consumer purchase decision process. "To ensure we execute on these business collaborations effectively, we invest a lot of time," says Sharon Metz, vice president of marketing at Rovi. "In B2B marketing, there may be numerous departments and people involved. When you are working with so many people, and trying to ensure all needs (especially, the consumers' needs) are met, it can take years to get the solution just right." Due to the impact and extent of the purchase being made, business marketing normally involves decisions by committee rather than by individual.

Similar to strategies that draw in consumers to make purchases, marketing to businesses requires a strong digital footprint and social media presence. Companies look to partner with companies that are innovative and have growing markets. This is extremely important as technology has enabled more marketing opportunities on a global scale.[1]

The Nature and Size of Organizational Markets

business marketing
Marketing to firms, governments, or non-profit organizations

organizational buyers
Manufacturers, wholesalers, retailers, and government agencies that buy goods and services for their own use or for resale

LO 1 Effective marketers have a clear understanding of buying behaviour. Effective business marketers also have an understanding of organizational markets. Also referred to as business-to-business (B2B) marketing, **business marketing** is the marketing of products to companies, governments, or non-profit organizations for use in the creation of goods and services that they then produce and market to others.[2] Many firms engage in business marketing, so it is important to understand the buying behaviour of organizational buyers, as they differ from consumer buying behaviour. Marketing plans are important as road maps for firms selling industrial products, just as they are for companies that sell consumer products. Chapter 15 describes marketing plans in greater detail.

Organizational buyers are those manufacturers, wholesalers, retailers, and government agencies that buy goods and services for their own use or for resale. For example, these organizations buy computers and smartphones such as the BlackBerry for their own use. Manufacturers buy raw materials and parts that they reprocess into the finished goods they sell, and wholesalers and retailers resell the goods they buy without reprocessing them. Organizational buyers include all

Marketing Tip

▶ *"In B2B marketing, there may be numerous departments and people involved. When you are working with so many people, and trying to ensure all needs (especially, the consumers' needs) are met, it can take years to get the solution just right."*

—*Sharon Metz, vice president, vertical marketing at Rovi Corporation*

buyers in a nation except ultimate consumers. These organizational buyers purchase and lease large volumes of equipment, raw materials, manufactured parts, supplies, and business services. They often buy raw materials and parts, process them, and sell them. This upgraded product may pass through several different organizations (as it is bought and resold by different levels of manufacturers, distributors, wholesalers, and retailers) before it is purchased by the final organizational buyer or final consumer. So the total purchases of organizational buyers in a year are far greater than those of ultimate consumers.

According to Industry Canada, there are a variety of industries that a business can sell to, including construction, manufacturing, wholesale trade, retail trade, and public administration. Organizational buyers are divided into three different markets: industrial, reseller, and government markets.[3]

Industrial Markets

Industry Canada also notes there are over 2.4 million business locations in Canada. These *industrial firms* in some way reprocess a product or service they buy before selling it again to the next buyer. For example, there are many suppliers that sell to car companies. Although the consumer purchases one consumer product (i.e., the car), the automobile company

Organizational buyers make purchases on a larger scale than consumers.

purchases parts from many suppliers just to make that one car. There are suppliers for such parts as steering wheels, brakes, doors, tires, seats, etc. The business market involves more purchases and dollars than the consumer market.

The importance of services in Canada today is emphasized by the composition of the industrial markets. Primary industries (agriculture, fishing, mining, and forestry), utilities, manufacturers, and construction firms sell physical products. The service market sells diverse services such as legal advice, auto repair, and dry cleaning, and includes organizations such as finance, insurance, and real estate businesses; transportation, communication, and public utility firms; and non-profit associations. Furthermore, there are over 1 million small businesses in Canada. Small businesses are defined as having fewer than 100 employees.[4]

Reseller Markets

Wholesalers and retailers that buy physical products and sell them again without any reprocessing are *resellers*. In Canada, there are over 200,000 retailers and over 65,000 wholesalers. Some of the largest Canadian-owned retailers in Canada include Loblaw, Alimentation Couche-Tard, Empire Company Limited (Sobeys), Metro, Shoppers Drug Mart, and Canadian Tire. This chapter focuses on how resellers act as organizational buyers and make decisions on which products they choose to carry.

Government Markets

Government units are the federal, provincial, regional, and municipal agencies that buy goods and services for the constituents that they serve. With a spending budget of over $280 billion in 2013, the federal government is a major customer, possibly the largest in Canada. To hold itself accountable, it created an online database to explain where taxpayer dollars are going.[5]

North American Industry Classification System (NAICS)
Provides common industry definitions for Canada, Mexico, and the United States

Car manufacturers are part of the industrial market.

In addition to specialized purchases for the military, government agencies also buy almost everything that regular consumers buy, from toilet paper to chewing gum to cars for federal prisons, hospitals, and schools. At the federal government level, the bulk of the purchasing is done by Public Works and Government Services Canada. Provincial and municipal governments typically have government departments that do the buying for them. In addition, hundreds of government departments, agencies, and Crown corporations (owned by the government on behalf of the people of Canada) such as CBC, VIA Rail, and the Royal Canadian Mint purchase supplies and services to operate. An example of a very successful Canadian company is Bombardier. Over the years, it has produced regional aircraft, business jets, mass transportation equipment such as subways and passenger rail vehicles, and recreational equipment. Many of its sales are to governments.

Non-Profit Organizations

Organizations that operate without having financial profit as a goal, and which seek to provide goods and services for the good of society, are called *non-profit organizations*. They are also known as charitable organizations, and some 83,000 of them are registered with the Canada Revenue Agency.[6] Tax advantages make it beneficial for this type of organization to register with the federal government.

You are probably familiar with many non-profit organizations. Were you a member of the Boy Scouts or Girl Guides? Have you participated in a Canadian Cancer Society run or marathon? Have you been asked for a donation to the United Way? Hospitals, arts organizations, cultural groups, and some research institutes can be classified as non-profit organizations.

The Big 12

Canada is the 12th largest exporter.

1. China	7. Republic of Korea
2. United States	8. Russian Federation
3. Germany	9. Italy
4. Japan	10. Hong Kong, China
5. The Netherlands	11. United Kingdom
6. France	12. Canada

Source: "Trade to remain subdued in 2013 after sluggish growth in 2012 as European economies continue to struggle," World Trade Organization, press release, April 10, 2013. Retrieved February 2014 from www.wto.org/english/news_e/pres13_e/pr688_e.htm.

In your school, you may have a foundation office that raises money for student awards and aid; this too is a non-profit organization. In the past, marketing in these organizations has been limited, but increasingly they are adopting the same types of marketing techniques that other business firms employ, and with good success. As purchasers, this sector of business buys a wide array of goods and services to conduct their operations.

Measuring Industrial, Reseller, Government, and Non-Profit Markets

The measurement of industrial, reseller, government, and non-profit markets is an important first step for a firm interested in determining the size of one, two, or all of these markets in Canada and around the world. This task has been made easier with the **North American Industry Classification System (NAICS)**.[7] The

The North American Industry Classification System (NAICS) provides common industry definitions for Canada, Mexico, and the United States.

NAICS provides common industry definitions for Canada, Mexico, and the United States, which facilitate the measurement of economic activity in the three member countries of the North American Free Trade Agreement (NAFTA). The NAICS replaced the Standard Industrial Classification (SIC) system, a version of which had been in place for more than 50 years in the three NAFTA member countries. The SIC neither permitted comparability across countries nor accurately measured new or emerging industries. Furthermore, the NAICS is consistent with the *International Standard Industrial Classification of All Economic Activities,* published by the United Nations, to help measure global economic activity.

The NAICS groups economic activity to permit studies of market share, demand for goods and services, competition from imports in domestic markets, and similar studies. The NAICS designates industries with a numerical code in a defined structure. A six-digit coding system is used. The first two digits designate a sector of the economy, the third digit designates a subsector, and the fourth digit represents an industry group. The fifth digit designates a specific industry and is the most detailed level at which comparable data is available for Canada, Mexico, and the United States. The sixth digit designates individual country-level national industries. Figure 5–1 presents an abbreviated breakdown within the Arts, Entertainment, and Recreation sector (code 71) to illustrate the classification scheme.

Content Marketing

LO² Because of the lengthly process for making decisions, as well as the extensive research required by businesses before decisions are made, companies like Rovi Corporation in the opening vignette need to adopt effective content marketing strategies. Content marketing keeps potential customers engaged by ensuring that relevant and valuable content is available at various touch points.

Although content marketing has been a part of marketing strategy for hundreds of years, as technology has evolved, the importance of content marketing has increased. In fact, nine out of ten B2B marketers use content marketing tactics; that is, they will choose various ways to reach their target audience, including social media, eNewsletters, videos, and research reports, as discussed in the Marketing NewsFlash, "Copy This Content Marketing Strategy." B2B marketers can engage audiences to act by implementing an effective content marketing strategy, so companies may now spend approximately a quarter of their marketing budgets on getting content marketing right for their audience. Since technology and talent are now readily available to most organizations, there is tremendous value to a company to get its message right and keep it relevant.

Not only has technology allowed businesses to reach other businesses through a variety of channels, it has provided the opportunity for regular feedback. By tracking usage and views, B2B marketers can adjust content accordingly to make information for clients more and more relevant.[8]

Figure 5–1
NAICS breakdown for the Arts, Entertainment, and Recreation sector: NAICS code 71 (abbreviated)

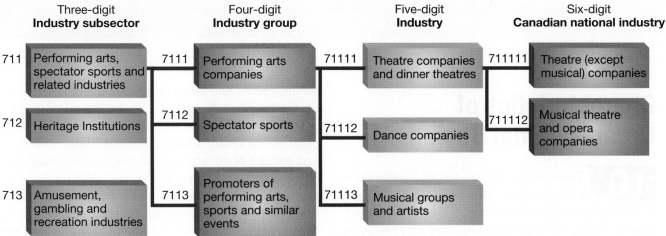

Source: Statistics Canada.

marketing *NewsFlash*

Copy This Content Marketing Strategy

Web communities have emerged as business enablers for B2B marketing. By creating interactive and collaborative environments, social media has become the go-to resource for B2B customers, both to share feedback about companies they are doing business with as well as to monitor discussions about products and services they are considering. The control of a B2B company's brand is rapidly changing from corporate marketing departments to the customer-to-customer conversations taking place on social media networks. Just as shared positive experiences can drive new prospects to a business, unmanaged negative comments can spread like wildfire, incinerating the organization's hard-earned reputation. Not surprisingly, customers recognize their growing influence and realize the impact of their praise or, more importantly, their criticism on a company.

Businesses of all sizes are learning the importance of listening, rather than preaching, in order to acquire

and retain their customers. Customers using social media are not interested in vague and impersonalized advertising and sales pitches. They are socially savvy and know how to connect with one another (more than half of active Twitter users follow at least one company, brand, or product) and possess little desire to maintain loyalty for a company that does not care for and accommodate their needs.

Social media such as Twitter can help level the playing field for B2B marketers.

This new environment creates big challenges but also incredible opportunities for B2B sales. Sales professionals can no longer completely rely on traditional e-mail and cold-calling campaigns. The good news is that social media is levelling the playing field for selling to customers. Sales

professionals can now gain timely and relevant insights about their customers as well as engage at a very deep and personal level—two huge boons to the B2B sales process. Thanks to social media monitoring and conversation, individuals within the organization have the ability to champion the identity of their corporate brand.

Social media is just one tactic in content marketing. In 2013, Xerox was recognized for its content marketing thought leadership as it expanded into the health care industry. The HealthBiz Decoded website was launched by Xerox and filled with articles from Xerox subject matter experts and other freelance journalists. The end result is a digital magazine that hosts videos and infographics to enhance the content. It is a subtle, but effective strategy for Xerox to show it is not just a copier company; it is a company that is an effective service provider.[9]

Questions

1. If you are a new, small B2B company with limited resources, how could content marketing (including social media) enable your business?

2. How has content marketing levelled the playing field between business marketers and their customers?

Characteristics of Organizational Buying

LO³ The business card is a key tool to introduce a company to consumers or businesses. The Infographic "One Card Says So Much" shares best practices using business cards. Organizations are different from individuals in the way they purchase goods and

services, so buying for an organization is different from buying for yourself and your family. In both cases, the objective in making the purchase is to solve the buyer's problem—to satisfy a need or want. Unique objectives and policies of an organization put special constraints on how it makes buying decisions. Understanding the characteristics of organizational buying is essential in designing effective marketing programs to reach these buyers. Key characteristics of organizational buying are listed in Figure 5–2 and discussed next.[10]

Infographic

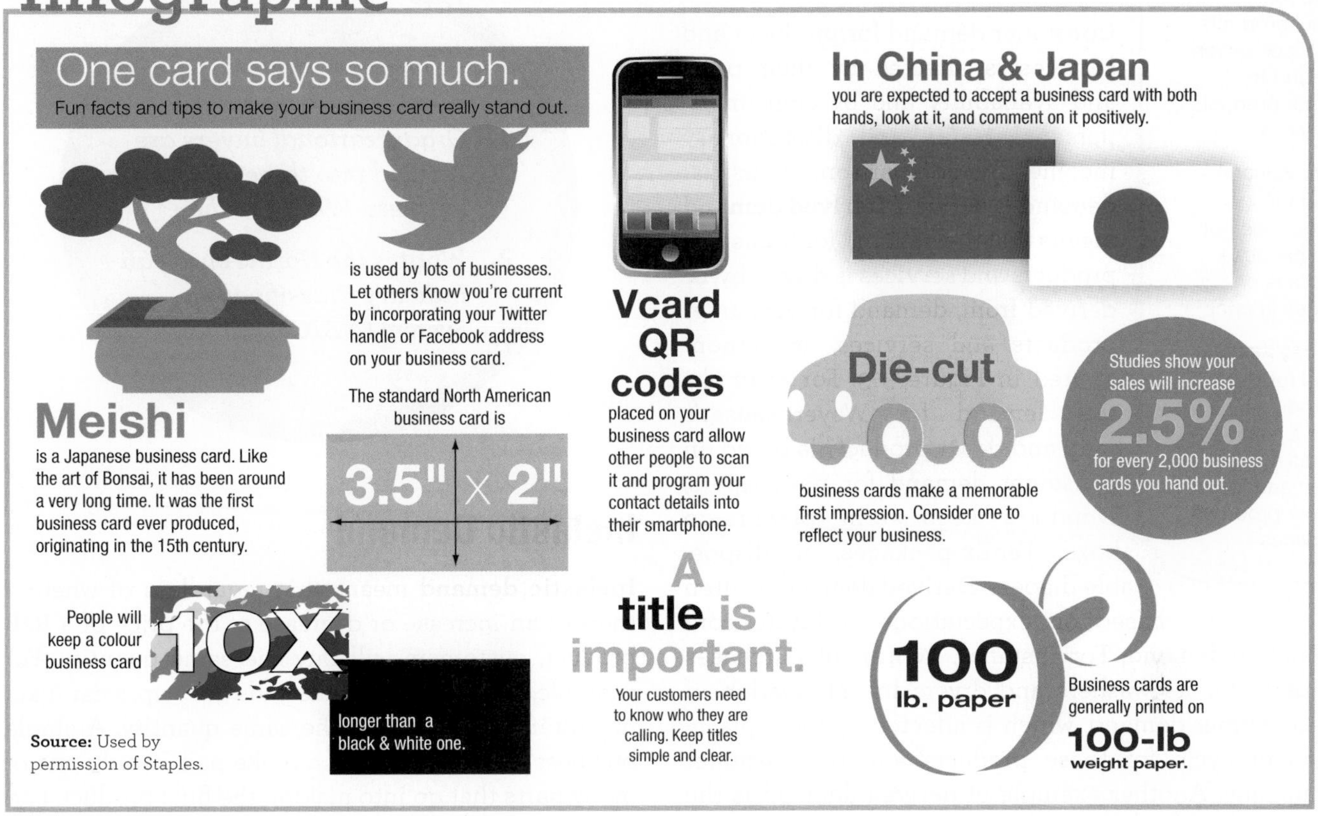

One card says so much.
Fun facts and tips to make your business card really stand out.

Meishi
is a Japanese business card. Like the art of Bonsai, it has been around a very long time. It was the first business card ever produced, originating in the 15th century.

People will keep a colour business card

10X

longer than a black & white one.

Source: Used by permission of Staples.

is used by lots of businesses. Let others know you're current by incorporating your Twitter handle or Facebook address on your business card.

The standard North American business card is

3.5" × 2"

Vcard QR codes
placed on your business card allow other people to scan it and program your contact details into their smartphone.

A title is important.
Your customers need to know who they are calling. Keep titles simple and clear.

In China & Japan
you are expected to accept a business card with both hands, look at it, and comment on it positively.

Die-cut
business cards make a memorable first impression. Consider one to reflect your business.

Studies show your sales will increase

2.5%

for every 2,000 business cards you hand out.

100 lb. paper

Business cards are generally printed on

100-lb weight paper.

Figure 5–2
Key characteristics of organizational buying behaviour

CHARACTERISTICS	DIMENSIONS
Market characteristics	• Demand for industrial products and services is derived. • The number of business customers is typically small, and their purchase orders are typically large.
Product or service characteristics	• Products or services are technical in nature and purchased on the basis of specifications. • Many goods purchased are raw or semi-finished. • Heavy emphasis is placed on delivery time, technical assistance, and postsale service.
Buying process characteristics	• Technically qualified and professional buyers follow established purchasing policies and procedures. • Buying objectives and criteria are typically spelled out, as are procedures for evaluating sellers and their products or services. • There are multiple buying influences, and multiple parties participate in purchase decisions. • There are reciprocal arrangements, and negotiation between buyers and sellers is commonplace. • Online buying over the Internet is widespread.
Marketing mix characteristics	• Personal selling to organizational buyers is used extensively, and distribution is very important. • Advertising and other forms of promotion are technical in nature. • Price is often negotiated, evaluated as part of broader seller and product or service qualities, and frequently affected by quantity discounts.

derived demand
Demand for industrial products and services driven by demand for consumer products and services

inelastic demand
Demand for products does not change because of increases or decreases in price

fluctuating demand
Demand for business products and services fluctuates more than demand for consumer products and services

Derived Demand

Consumer demand for products and services is affected by their price and availability and by consumers' personal tastes and discretionary income. By comparison, industrial demand is derived. **Derived demand** means that the demand for industrial products and services is driven by, or derived from, demand for consumer products and services, as demonstrated in Figure 5–3. For example, the demand for Weyerhaeuser's pulp and paper products is based on consumer demand for newspapers, Domino's "keep warm" pizza-to-go boxes, FedEx packages, and disposable diapers. Derived demand is often based on expectations of future consumer demand. For instance, Whirlpool purchases parts for its washers and dryers in anticipation of consumer demand, which is affected by the replacement cycle for these products and by consumer income. Another example of derived demand is the car industry. Demand for auto parts is driven by new car sales. Magna International Inc., a Canadian company based in Aurora, Ontario, is Canada's largest automobile parts manufacturer, and one of the country's largest companies.

Figure 5–3
Direct versus derived demand

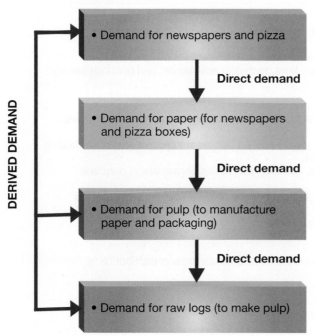

ask yourself

1. *Organizational buyers are divided into three different markets. What are they?*

2. *What is the North American Industry Classification System (NAICS)?*

Inelastic Demand

Inelastic demand means that regardless of whether there is an increase or decrease of the price of a B2B product, customers will buy the same quantity. For example, if the price of brake pads goes up, a car manufacturer will still order the same quantity. A single business product, such as a brake pad, is only one of many parts that go into making the final product, and is only a minor portion of the price of the car.

Fluctuating Demand

Small changes in demand for consumer products can result in large increases or decreases in demand for the facilities and equipment needed to make the consumer product. This is referred to as **fluctuating demand**. A product's life expectancy also has a bearing on this type of demand. For example, business products

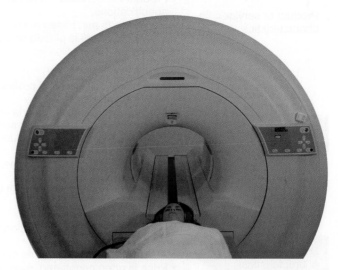

The number of potential buyers of computerized axial tomography (CAT) scanners is limited.

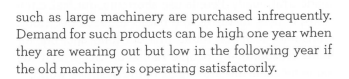

Bombardier markets to organizational buyers such as the Toronto Transit Commission (TTC).

In 2010, Bombardier sold 186 new subway cars to the Toronto Transit Commission (TTC) for a value of $390 million.

such as large machinery are purchased infrequently. Demand for such products can be high one year when they are wearing out but low in the following year if the old machinery is operating satisfactorily.

Size of the Order or Purchase

The size of the purchase involved in organizational buying is typically much larger than that in consumer buying. The dollar value of a single purchase made by an organization often runs into the millions of dollars. For example, in 2009, the Toronto Transit Commission (TTC) received approval to spend $1.2 billion to purchase 204 new streetcars from Bombardier. The following year, Bombardier sold 186 new subway cars to the Toronto Transit Commission (TTC) for a value of $390 million.[11]

With so much money at stake, most organizations place constraints on their buyers in the form of purchasing policies or procedures. Buyers must often get competitive bids from at least three prospective suppliers when the order is above a specific amount, such as $5,000. When the order is above an even higher amount, such as $50,000, it may require the review and approval of a vice president or even the president of the company. Knowing how the size of the order affects buying practices is important in determining who participates in the purchase decision and makes the final decision, as well as the length of time required to arrive at a purchase agreement.

Number of Potential Buyers

Firms selling consumer products or services often try to reach thousands or millions of individuals or households. For example, your local supermarket or bank probably serves thousands of people, and Kellogg tries to reach millions of Canadian households with its breakfast cereals and probably succeeds in selling to a third or half of these in any given year. In contrast, firms selling to organizations are often restricted to far fewer buyers. Bombardier Aerospace can sell its Challenger business jets to a few thousand organizations throughout the world, and B. F. Goodrich sells its original equipment tires to fewer than 10 car manufacturers.

Organizational Buying Objectives

Organizations buy products and services for one main reason: to help them achieve their objectives. For business firms, the buying objective is usually to increase profits through reducing costs or increasing sales. 7-Eleven buys automated inventory systems to increase the number of products that can be sold through its convenience stores and to keep those products fresh. Nissan Motor Company switched its advertising agency because it expects the new agency to devise a more effective ad campaign to help it sell more cars and increase sales. To improve executive decision-making, many firms buy advanced computer systems to process data.

The objectives of non-profit firms and government agencies are usually to meet the needs of the groups they serve. Thus, a hospital buys a high-technology diagnostic device to serve its patients better. Understanding buying objectives is a necessary first step in marketing to organizations.

Organizational Buying Criteria

Consumers use criteria when purchasing a product. Businesses also use criteria in their purchasing: They specify *organizational buying criteria,* which are detailed specifications for the products and services they want to buy and the characteristics of the suppliers that will supply them. When suppliers are selected, their products and their firm's characteristics are evaluated using these criteria. The following lists some of the most commonly used criteria:

- Price
- Ability to meet the quality specifications required
- Ability to meet the required delivery schedules
- Technical capability
- Warranties and claims policies
- Past performance on previous contracts
- Production facilities and capacity

Many organizational buyers today are transforming their buying criteria into specific requirements that are communicated to suppliers. This practice, called *reverse marketing,* means that organizational buyers are attempting to work with suppliers to make their products, services, and capabilities fit the buyer's needs. Working closely and collaboratively like this with suppliers also helps build buyer–seller relationships and leads to supply partnerships. Companies such as Tim Hortons will work with external partners to build stores and host events.

▶ Video
Tim
Hortons

Fear in Organizational Buying Behaviour

It's important at this point to examine the role of emotion in the organizational buying process. Emotions drive human behaviour and are the engines that propel people forward to reach their goals.

According to one author, B2B buying decisions are usually driven by one emotion—fear. Specifically, B2B buying is all about minimizing fear by eliminating risk. There are two distinct types of risk. There is organizational risk, typically formalized and dealt with in the buying process, and then there is personal risk, which is unstated but remains a huge influencing factor in organizational buying. For example, a buyer who chooses to deal with the same trusted supplier for many years is minimizing fear by eliminating organizational risk. Personal risk is explained by the buyer who chooses not to work with a new supplier even if that potential supplier's products offer better value. The buyer may fear that the latter may not produce a quality product, for example, and the buyer fears being reprimanded and thus may fear working with new suppliers to avert any risk. Humans do not always make rational decisions. In fact, some decisions are made irrationally. People use shortcuts, gut feel, emotions, beliefs, instincts, and habits to reach decisions. Consumer research found this out long ago, but for some reason, many people refuse to accept that the same mechanisms are at play in the business world.[12]

Buyer–Seller Relationships and Supply Partnerships

Another distinction between organizational and consumer buying behaviour lies in the nature of the relationship between organizational buyers and suppliers. Specifically, organizational buying is more likely to involve complex and lengthy negotiations concerning delivery schedules, price, technical specifications, warranties, and claims policies. These negotiations can last for more than a year.

Reciprocal arrangements also exist in organizational buying. Reciprocity is an industrial buying

Fear may cause organizational buyers to make irrational decisions they will regret.

The Value of Innovation and Emotions

In 2010, RIM (Research in Motion), the maker of the BlackBerry, scored well in many aspects of the Reputation Institute's study on corporate brands. The Reputation Institute measures both the emotional appeal of a brand along with a handful of so-called rational attributes, such as how consumers perceive the quality of products and services offered by a company. Canadian consumers ranked RIM as the most innovative company in the study, and rated it first in terms of its work environment, leadership qualities, and financial performance. As an example of RIM's work environment, employees of RIM were loaded onto a bus for a very special evening. The Waterloo-based tech giant had rented out the Rogers Centre in Toronto and brought in U2 to play a private concert for its employees.

RIM lagged in one key area relative to its high marks elsewhere: emotional appeal. Canadians know in their heads that RIM is a well-run company, but it does not set their hearts atwitter. Tim Hortons, on the other hand, came first as having the best corporate reputation

in the country because of a high score received for its emotional appeal.

Referring to RIM, Rob Jekielek, a principal consultant with the Reputation Institute, says, "You really get the feeling that if they were able to create the right emotional appeal in addition to all the things they do well rationally, they could improve their reputation even more. The attitude Canadians have toward RIM illustrates a fundamental truth about consumers in this country. Like others around the world, they are primarily emotional beings. That means a corporation will find it difficult to build a good reputation if it fails to connect on an emotional level."[13]

This strategy for emotional appeal may be in play as RIM made a strategic decision in 2013. Faced with market challenges, RIM officially changed its name to BlackBerry, allowing the company to associate itself better with the product it produces. The BlackBerry name change

BlackBerry product launches appeal to consumer emotions.

was approved by shareholders, but its full impact among consumers and business customers remains to be seen. Its next step is to get back to basics, focus on fewer products, and cut costs, as well as continue to stay true to its signature keypad.[14] ●

Questions

1. Why do you think that RIM (now known as BlackBerry) scores lower on emotional appeal than Tim Hortons?

2. What other Canadian company do you think should score high in emotional appeal? Why?

---

practice in which two organizations agree to purchase each other's products and services. Governments frown on reciprocal buying because it restricts the normal operation of the free market. However, the practice exists and can limit the flexibility of organizational buyers in choosing alternative suppliers.

Because of the need to ensure that both buyer and seller perspectives are understood and addressed, buyer–seller relationships develop into supply partnerships in some cases. These partnerships are long-term

relationships built on transparency and understanding.[15] A **supply partnership** exists when a buyer and its supplier adopt mutually beneficial objectives, policies, and procedures for the purpose of lowering the cost or increasing the value of products and services delivered to the ultimate consumer. For example, Rovi Corporation, featured in the opening vignette, partners with companies

supply partnership
Relationship between a buyer and supplier that adopt mutually beneficial objectives, policies, and procedures

that are market leaders in entertainment to enhance its offering. Just as computer companies have the "Intel Inside" logo prominently displayed on each computer, Rovi Corporation ensures that the end user is aware that Rovi powers the consumer-facing technology.

ask yourself

1. *What is derived demand?*

2. *A supply partnership exists when _____.*

The Organizational Buying Process and the Buying Centre

LO 4 Organizational buyers, like consumers, engage in a decision process when selecting products and services. **Organizational buying behaviour** is the decision-making process that organizations use (1) to establish the need for products and services, and (2) to identify, evaluate, and choose among alternative brands and suppliers. There are important similarities and differences between the two decision-making processes. To better understand the nature of organizational buying behaviour, we first compare it with consumer buying behaviour. We then describe a unique feature of organizational buying: the buying centre.

Stages in the Organizational Buying Process

As shown in Figure 5–4, the five stages that a student might use in buying a smartphone also apply to organizational purchases. However, comparing the two right-hand columns in Figure 5–4 reveals some key

differences. For example, when a smartphone manufacturer buys digital cameras for its smartphones, more individuals are involved, supplier capability becomes more important, and the post-purchase evaluation behaviour is more formal. The buying decision process of an organization purchasing cameras for smartphones is typical of the steps made by organizational buyers.

The Buying Centre: A Cross-Functional Group

For routine purchases with a small dollar value, a single buyer or purchasing manager often makes the purchase decision alone. In many instances, however, several people in the organization participate in the buying process. The individuals in this group, called a **buying centre**, share common goals, risks, and knowledge important to purchase decisions. For most large multistore chain resellers, such as 7-Eleven convenience stores or Safeway, the buying centre is very formal and is called a *buying committee*. However, most industrial firms or government units use informal groups of people or call meetings to arrive at buying decisions.

A firm marketing to industrial firms and government units must understand the structure, technical, and business functions represented, and the behaviour of the buying centre. One researcher has suggested four questions to provide guidance in understanding the buying centre in these organizations:[16]

- Which individuals are in the buying centre for the product or service?
- What is the relative influence of each member of the group?

Formal presentations to buying centres are part of the organizational buying process.

Figure 5–4
Comparing the stages in a consumer and organizational purchase decision process reveals subtle differences

STAGE IN THE BUYING DECISION PROCESS	CONSUMER PURCHASE: SMARTPHONE FOR A STUDENT	ORGANIZATIONAL PURCHASE: CAMERA FOR A SMARTPHONE
Problem recognition	Student doesn't like the features of the cellphone now owned as compared to the features of a smartphone and desires to purchase one.	Marketing research and sales departments observe that competitors are improving the quality of cameras that are contained in a smartphone. The firm decides to improve the cameras on their new models, which will be purchased from an outside supplier.
Information search	Student uses past experience, that of friends, ads, the Internet, and magazines to collect information and uncover alternatives.	Design and production engineers draft specifications for the camera. The purchasing department identifies suppliers of cameras.
Evaluation of alternatives	Alternative smartphones are evaluated on the basis of important attributes desired in a smartphone, and several stores are visited.	Purchasing and engineering personnel visit with suppliers and assess facilities, capacity, quality control, and financial status. They drop any suppliers not satisfactory on these factors.
Purchase decision	A specific brand of smartphone is selected, the price is paid, and the student leaves the store.	They use quality, price, delivery, and technical capability as key buying criteria to select a supplier. Then they negotiate terms and award a contract.
Post-purchase behaviour	Student re-evaluates the purchase decision, and may return the smartphone to the store if it is unsatisfactory.	They evaluate the supplier using a formal vendor rating system and notify the supplier if camera does not meet their quality standard. If the problem is not corrected, they drop the firm as a future supplier.

- What are the buying criteria of each member?
- How does each member of the group perceive the potential supplier, its products and services, and its salespeople?

People in the Buying Centre Who makes up the buying centre in a given organization depends on the specific item being bought. Although a buyer or purchasing manager is almost always a member of the buying centre, individuals from other functional areas are included, depending on what is to be purchased.[17]

In buying a million-dollar machine tool, the president (because of the size of the purchase) and the production vice president would probably be members. For key components to be included in a final manufactured product, a cross-functional group of individuals from research and development (R&D), engineering, and quality control are likely to be

> *A major question in understanding the buying centre is finding and reaching the people who will initiate, influence, and actually make the buying decision.*

added. For new word-processing software, experienced office staff who will use the equipment would be members. Still, a major question in understanding the buying centre is finding and reaching the people who will initiate, influence, and actually make the buying decision.

Roles in the Buying Centre

Researchers have identified five specific roles that an individual in a buying centre can play (see Figure 5–5).[18] In some purchases, the same person may perform two or more of these roles.

- *Users* are the people in the organization who actually use the product or service, such as office staff who will use new word-processing software.

- *Influencers* affect the buying decision, usually by helping define the specifications for what is bought. They usually have specialized knowledge. The information systems manager would be a key influencer in the purchase of a new computer network.

- *Buyers* have formal authority and responsibility to select the supplier and negotiate the terms of the contract. The purchasing manager probably would perform this role in the purchase of a computer network.

- *Deciders* have the formal or informal power to select or approve the supplier that receives the contract. Whereas in routine orders the decider is usually the buyer or purchasing manager, in important technical purchases it is more likely to be someone from R&D, engineering, or quality control. The decider for a key component being included in a final manufactured product might be any of these three people.

- *Gatekeepers* control the flow of information in the buying centre. Purchasing personnel, technical experts, and office staff can all help or prevent salespeople (or information) from reaching people performing the other four roles.

Buying Situations and the Buying Centre

The number of people in the buying centre largely depends on the specific buying situation. Researchers who have studied organizational buying identify three types of buying situations, called **buy classes**. These buy classes vary from the routine reorder, or *straight rebuy*, to the completely new purchase, termed *new buy*. In between these extremes is the *modified rebuy*.[19]

- **Straight rebuy:** Here the buyer or purchasing manager reorders an existing product or service from the list of acceptable suppliers, probably without even checking with users or influencers from the engineering, production, or quality control departments. Office supplies and maintenance services are usually obtained as straight rebuys.

- **Modified rebuy:** In this buying situation, the company is purchasing a product that it has experience purchasing, such as new laptops for salespeople, but it wants to change the product specifications, price, delivery schedule, or supplier. The changes usually mean involving users, influencers, and/or deciders in the buying decision—more input than would be necessary for a straight rebuy.

Figure 5–5
Roles in the buying centre

Gatekeeper: President's Assistant
Does the President really need to talk to this salesperson?

Decider: President
Can we afford to spend $500,000 on this equipment?

Buyer: Purchasing Manager
I have to make sure that the services the firm promises are all completed, such as setting up all the computers and loading basic software.

Influencer: Director of Computer Systems
These computers seem to be the latest in technology, and the firm seems committed to providing updates on software and maintenance support.

User: Faculty member
I need to make sure that the computers are what the students need, as well as what will work well for us in the classrooms.

- **New buy:** In this situation, the company is buying the product or service for the first time. This purchase involves greater potential risk and is more complex than other buying situations. The buying centre is larger, comprising people representing those parts of the organization having a stake in the new buy. In 2013, the Government of Canada awarded a $15 million contract to ARUP Canada Inc. for a new St. Lawrence Bridge in Montreal. ARUP Canada Inc. will provide engineering and coordination services for the new bridge.[20]

Figure 5-6 summarizes how buy classes affect buying centre tendencies in different ways.[21]

B2B Market Segmentation

LO 5 Chapter 6, "Segmentation, Targeting, and Positioning," focuses primarily on the consumer market. Here we focus on the business market. Consumer market segmentation groups consumers into groups that have common needs and respond similarly to marketing programs. The process of segmenting business markets divides markets based on type of customer, size, buying situation, customer location, and benefits sought. By applying market segmentation concepts to groups of business customers, a marketer can develop a strategy that best suits a particular segment's needs.

Type of Customer

The NAICS codes discussed earlier provide a useful tool for identifying business target markets. For example, Steelcase, a major producer of office furniture, segments its customers into 10 industries, including banking, higher education, hospitality, and health care.

Size of Customer

Many B2B marketers divide their potential market into large and small accounts, using separate distribution channels to reach each segment. For example, marketers may develop one strategy to reach Fortune 500 corporations, which have complex purchasing procedures, and another strategy for small firms where decisions are made by one or two people. American Express provides information and assistance for small business owners with its Small Business Services unit, which is dedicated exclusively to the success of small business owners and their companies.

ask yourself

1. *What one department is almost always represented by a person in the buying centre?*

2. *What are the three types of buying situations or buy classes?*

Type of Buying Situation

B2B marketers can divide their potential market by the three types of buy classes: new buy, modified rebuy, and straight rebuy. We recognized in that discussion above that a new buy is significantly different

Figure 5–6
How the buying situation affects buying centre behaviour

Buying Centre Dimension	BUY-CLASS SITUATION		
	Straight Rebuy	Modified Rebuy	New Buy
People involved	1	2–3	Many
Decision time	Short	Short	Long
Problem definition	Well-defined	Minor modifications	Uncertain
Buying objective	Low-priced supplier	Low-priced supplier	Good solution
Suppliers considered	Present	Present	New/present
Buying influence	Purchasing agent	Purchasing agent and others	Technical/operating personnel

from a straight rebuy in several important respects. Consequently, a business seller might well segment its market into the three buy-class categories.

Customer Location

The product manager might segment on the basis of region or actual location of the potential customer. Firms located in a metropolitan area might receive a personal sales call, whereas those outside this area might be contacted by telephone.

Benefits Sought

The market may also be segmented on the basis of benefits sought. Xerox may decide to focus on firms looking for quality products and good customer service as opposed to those looking simply for lower prices.

Online Buying in Organizational Markets

LO 6 Organizational buying behaviour and business marketing continue to change with the use of the Internet and e-commerce. Due to the rising competition, organizations are learning from their successes and adapting to their failures. Scale allows organizations to vastly outnumber consumers in terms of both online transactions made and purchase volume.[22] In fact, organizational buyers account for about 80 percent of the total worldwide dollar value of all online transactions. Online organizational buyers around the world purchased between $8 and $10 trillion worth of products in 2010. Organizational buyers in North America will account for about 60 percent of these purchases.

Prominence of Online Buying in Organizational Markets

Online buying in organizational markets is prominent for three major reasons.[23] First, organizational buyers depend heavily on timely supplier information that describes product availability, technical specifications, application uses, price, and delivery schedules. This information can be conveyed quickly online. The Internet has altered one aspect of B2B purchasing: Buyers have much more knowledge at their fingertips about the seller's product than in the past. Second, web-based technology has been shown to substantially reduce buyer order-processing costs. At General Electric, online buying has cut the cost of a transaction from $50 to $100 per purchase to about $5. Third, business marketers have found that web-based technology can reduce marketing costs, particularly sales and advertising expenses, and broaden their potential customer base for many types of products and services. For these reasons, online buying is popular in all three kinds of organizational markets. For example, airlines order over $400 million in spare parts from the Boeing Company website each year.

Online buying can assume many forms. Organizational buyers can purchase directly from suppliers. For instance, a buyer might acquire a dozen desktop photocopiers from **Xerox.ca**. This same buyer might purchase office furniture and supplies online through a reseller, such as Staples at **staples.ca**. Increasingly, organizational buyers and business marketers are using e-marketplaces and online auctions to purchase and sell products and services.

> *At General Electric, online buying has cut the cost of a transaction from $50 to $100 per purchase to about $5.*

E-Marketplaces: Virtual Organizational Markets

A significant development in organizational buying has been the creation and growth of online trading communities, called **e-marketplaces**, that bring together buyers and supplier organizations.[24] These online communities go by a variety of names, including portals, exchanges, and e-hubs, and make possible the real-time exchange of information, money, products, and services. Globally, the number of e-marketplaces for businesses is extensive.

E-marketplaces can be independent trading communities or private exchanges. Independent e-marketplaces typically focus on a specific product or service, or serve a particular industry. They act as a neutral third party and provide an online trading platform and a centralized market that enable exchanges between buyers and sellers. Independent e-marketplaces charge a fee for their services and exist in settings that have one or more of the following features:

- Thousands of geographically dispersed buyers and sellers
- Frequently changing prices caused by demand and supply fluctuations
- Time sensitivity due to perishable offerings and changing technologies
- Easily comparable offerings between a variety of suppliers

Well-known independent e-marketplaces include PaperExchange (paper products), PlasticsNet (plastics), Altra Energy (electricity, natural gas, and crude oil), and **XSAg.com** (agricultural products). Small business buyers and sellers, in particular, benefit from independent e-marketplaces. These e-marketplaces offer suppliers an economical way to expand their customer base and reduce the cost of purchased products and services.

Large companies tend to favour private exchanges that link them with their network of qualified suppliers and customers. Private exchanges focus on streamlining a company's purchase transactions with its suppliers and customers. Like independent e-marketplaces, they provide a technology trading platform and central market for buyer–seller interactions.

Large firms such as IBM, General Motors, and Toyota have formed private exchanges. Some, such as IBM and GE, have mandated that their suppliers must deal with them primarily through online exchanges.

These private exchanges provide tremendous cost savings through the elimination of periodic negotiations and routine paperwork.

Ariba is an e-marketplace that connects one million businesses. Ariba's global membership includes buyers and suppliers from a variety of industries. It

Figure 5–7

How buyer and seller participants and price behaviour differ by type of online auction

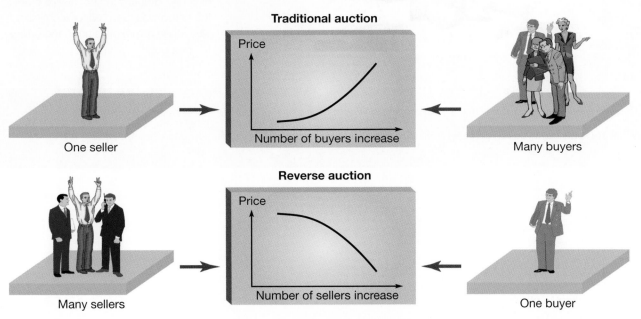

Marketing Mishaps in the Global Economy

There is a heightened sense of formality in Japanese interaction. When doing business in Japan, your suitability with respect to conducting business will be assessed during a first meeting. It is important to maintain a sense of professionalism and be aware of the host country's customs. Offending a professional from another country could affect your business relationship.

In Japanese society, the bow is used when meeting, when getting attention, to show gratitude, to express sympathy, or as an apology. When doing business in Japan as a Westerner, you would not be expected to bow. You will most likely be greeted with a handshake combined with a slight nod of the head. Introduce yourself with your full name followed by your company name. It is important to use proper titles when addressing someone, so always establish the position of the other person.

The exchanging of business cards when doing business in Japan involves a degree of ceremony. The card is seen to represent the individual, so it should be treated with respect. Before travelling to Japan, ensure you have ample cards and have one side translated into Japanese. Include your position within the company on it. Invest in a carry case to store cards and keep this in an easy-to-access location. When exchanging cards, offer your card with both hands with the Japanese side up. Ensure that there is no barrier between you and the recipient, such as a table, chair, or plant. When accepting a card, always use two hands as this shows deference. For Japanese people, as elsewhere in the Asia-Pacific region, exchanging cards is like shaking hands. If you are in a formal situation, it is proper to place the card face up on the table in front of you and refer to it when necessary.

The Japanese like dealing with quiet, sincere, and compromising individuals. Extroverts are seen as brash and arrogant. Early on in negotiations, remain humble, indirect, and non-threatening. Silence is considered a virtue. If things go quiet when doing business in a meeting, don't panic. Reflection is taking place. Silence may be also be accompanied by the closing of the eyes. Never interrupt or break the silence.[25]

Some marketing mistakes that have happened in the past include Nike's release of women's leggings in New Zealand that had a pattern that resembled a Samoan tattoo. The international company did not realize that the tattoo was reserved for men. Nike was made aware of its error and pulled the product.[26] ●

Presenting business cards with two hands is normal business practice in Japan.

Questions

1. Can you think of other customs that a businessperson should be aware of in doing business in other countries?

2. What are some ways you can prepare for meetings or discussions with business people from other countries?

was originally set up as a one-stop solution to specifically meet the e-procurement needs of the natural resource industry."[27]

Online Auctions in Organizational Markets

Online auctions have grown in popularity among organizational buyers and business marketers. Many e-marketplaces offer this service. Two general types of auctions are common: a traditional auction and a reverse auction.[28] Figure 5–7 shows how buyer and seller participants and price behaviour differ by type of auction. Let's look at each auction type more closely to understand the implications of each for buyers and sellers.

In a **traditional auction**, a seller puts an item up for sale and would-be buyers are invited to bid in competition with each other. As more would-be buyers become involved, there is an upward pressure on bid prices. Why? Bidding is sequential—that is, bidders bid in order, one at a time. Prospective buyers observe the bids of others and decide whether to increase the bid price. The auction ends when a single bidder remains and "wins" the item with its highest price. Traditional auctions are frequently used to dispose of excess merchandise. For example, Dell Computer sells surplus, refurbished, or closeout computer merchandise at its **dellauction.com** website.

A reverse auction works in the opposite direction from a traditional auction. In a **reverse auction**, a buyer communicates a need for a product or service and would-be suppliers are invited to bid in competition with each other. As more would-be suppliers become involved, there is a downward pressure on bid prices for the buyer's business. Why? Like traditional auctions, bidding is sequential and prospective suppliers observe the bids of others and decide whether to decrease the bid price. The auction ends when a single bidder remains and "wins" the business with its lowest price. Reverse auctions benefit organizational buyers by reducing the cost of their purchases. As an example, General Electric, one of the world's largest companies, has its own Global eXchange Services unit, which runs online reverse auctions for the company. It claims that it saved $780 million on the purchase of $6 billion worth of products and services.[29]

Clearly, buyers welcome the lower prices generated by reverse auctions. Some suppliers also favour the reverse auction process because it gives them a chance to capture business that they might not have otherwise had because of a long-standing purchase relationship between the buyer and another supplier. On the other hand, suppliers argue that reverse auctions put too much emphasis on prices, discourage consideration of other important buying criteria, and threaten supply partnership opportunities.[30]

traditional auction
Occurs when a seller puts an item up for sale and would-be buyers bid in competition with each other

reverse auction
Occurs when a buyer communicates a need for something and would-be suppliers bid in competition with each other

ask yourself

1. What are e-marketplaces?

2. How do traditional auctions and reverse auctions affect bid prices?

LO¹ ● Organizational buyers are divided into four different markets:
- Industrial firms reprocess a product or service and then sell it.
- Resellers buy physical products and sell them without reprocessing them.
- Government units at the federal, provincial, regional, and municipal levels purchase goods and services to help serve their constituents.
- Non-profit organizations purchase products and services to help their organizations serve the good of society as opposed to a financial goal.

● The North American Industry Classification System (NAICS) is a convenient starting point to begin the process of measuring business markets.

LO² ● Content marketing keeps potential customers engaged by ensuring that relevant and valuable content is available at various touch points.

LO³ ● Key differences between the business and consumer buying processes include demand characteristics, number of potential buyers, buying objectives, buying criteria, size of the order or purchase, buyer–seller relationships and partnerships, and multiple buying influences within companies.

LO⁴ ● The buying centre is a group of people in an organization that participate in the buying process.

● The buying centre usually includes a person from the purchasing department and possibly representatives from R&D, engineering, and production, depending on what is being purchased. These people can play one or more of five roles in a purchase decision: user, influencer, buyer, decider, or gatekeeper.

● The organizational purchasing process is influenced by the extent of the buying situation:
- A straight rebuy is a routine purchase that may not involve any users or influencers.
- A modified rebuy would involve users and influencers since there is a change to the specifications of the original purchase.
- A new buy will be more complex and involve more people in the buying centre.

LO⁵ ● The process of segmenting business markets divides markets based on type of customer, size, buying situation, customer location, and benefits sought.

● By applying market segmentation concepts to groups of business customers, a marketer can develop a strategy that best suits a particular segment's needs.

LO⁶ ● Online buying is prevalent in industrial, reseller, and government markets.

● Globally, the number of e-marketplaces for businesses is extensive, and online auctions are commonly used by organizational buyers and business marketers.

Key Terms and Concepts...a refresher

business marketing
buy classes
buying centre
derived demand
e-marketplaces

fluctuating demand
inelastic demand
North American Industry
    Classification System (NAICS)
organizational buyers

organizational buying behaviour
reverse auction
supply partnership
traditional auction

Hands-on...apply your knowledge

B2B Marketing Differences In the opening vignette, Sharon Metz of Rovi Corporation reflects on some of the challenges of marketing to medium-to-large organization. In particular, for larger purchases and key partnerships, decisions need to be made by a committee as opposed to an individual. Review the opening vignette and identify other differences in the organizational buying purchase decision process that need to be considered in B2B marketing.

Chapter Vignette ...reminder

Strategic partnerships are critical to the success of many businesses. This chapter's opening vignette describes how B2B marketing helped build a partnership between Canadian company Cogeco Cable and U.S. company Rovi Corporation.

At the end of the vignette, consider the question about the numerous individuals involved in a decision like this partnership. Relate this to the concept of the buying centre and the different roles of individuals outlined in this chapter.

Video Clip ...questions

To celebrate its 50th anniversary, Tim Hortons "updated" its first store to a 1964 look. There are a number of other businesses that Tim Hortons works with to make this opportunity a reality. Watch the CONNECT video, *Tim Travels Back to 1964*, and answer the following questions:

▶ Video
Tim
Hortons

- Name some of the strategic partners that Tim Hortons worked with to make its anniversary event special.
- What process do you think Tim Hortons went through to select the different companies needed to produce the components of the 1964 store?
- How do you think the 1964 clothing was acquired?

Infographic ...data analysis

Consider the B2B marketing tips regarding social media and doing business in foreign countries when reviewing the Infographic entitled "One Card Says So Much."

Reviewing recent articles and reflecting on your knowledge of Canada and other countries, add another fact to this Infographic.

segmentation, targeting, and positioning

Target markets, market segmentation, and product positioning are the foundations of marketing practices. These elements work together to craft approaches and create products that meet consumer need and help build marketing success. We turn to Rob Morash, general manager of HEAD Canada, to learn how these concepts are applied in the world of sports marketing, and then we explore these elements in detail within the chapter.

Have you heard of Kaya Turski, world-renowned Canadian freestyle skier from Montreal, winner of numerous X Games competitions, and member of the daredevil Canadian Olympic team for slopestyle skiing, a new freestyle skiing event at the 2014 Olympic Winter Games in Sochi, Russia? The marketing team at HEAD Canada certainly had, and they recommended that HEAD sign her to a three-year sponsorship deal, adding its name to Red Bull, Oakley, and Nike as major sponsors of this winning world-class athlete. In slopestyle skiing, athletes navigate a half-kilometre course, completing exciting aerial jumps and skiing down rails and over ramps with skill and expertise.

Turski is part of the HEAD international freestyle skiing team for 2012 to 2015 and was a major part of its plans for the high-profile 2014 Olympic Winter Games. "Athlete sponsorship is a major component of our freestyle skiing plans," explains Rob Morash, expert sport marketer with experience at Nike, Atomic skis, and now HEAD Canada. "Our target market for freestyle skiing is young, busy, and elusive. Communicating with them is no easy task, but we understand their passion for the sport and share their excitement when watching top athletes compete."

The target market for freestyle skiing is young, free-spirited, and fearless. It consists of teenagers and young adults who get an adrenaline rush doing backflips and spins in terrain parks, thrills from skiing down half-pipes and over jumps, and enjoyment from skiing down rails. Watching their favourite skiers compete in world-class events is an important part of their lives, and they turn to social media and the Internet for information, updates, and entertainment. The question is how to communicate with these risk-takers who never read a hard-copy newspaper, rarely pick up magazines, and spend very little time watching TV? HEAD's answer is multi-faceted and includes elements of product placement, advertising, social media, merchandising, and sponsorship. Sponsorship tops the list, so let's look at this in more detail:

- In freestyle skiing, HEAD sponsors world-class athletes such as slopestyle skier Kaya Turski. HEAD provides her with funding and the top-quality skis and

Chapter Features

HEAD Signs Top Canadian Skier
Slopestyle skiing becomes a focus for HEAD in the 2014 Olympic Winter Games.

Niche Marketing Thrives Online
Companies use strategies to target consumers with niche offerings.

Kellogg's Segments the Market
New and traditional cereals are used to appeal to different target groups.

Personas Visualize Target Consumers
Marketers use personas to visualize and better understand consumers.

Social Media Segmentation
AIMIA research reveals five distinct social media segments.

Burberry's Flagship Store Creates Buzz
Burberry reinvents its brand as cool, vintage, and British.

Segmentation Analytics Data Revealed
Environics Prizm C2, SuperDemographics, and Pitney Bowes Psyte HD provide granular segmentation data.

Chapter Outline:

- HEAD segments the ski market
- Market segmentation
- Segmentation strategies
- Target markets and personas
- Segmentation analytics
- Product positioning
- Steps in market segmentation

boots that appear front and centre during major sporting events. Many of these events are streamed online on sites such as Red Bull TV and other online destinations of choice for this elusive target market. TV sports stations also include a selection of these events in their winter sports coverage and sports' apps, such as *theScore: Sports & Scores,* that keep fans up to date on mobile devices.

- Sponsored athletes attend press conferences that are covered in detail on sports programs with clips and sound bites uploaded to YouTube.

- Sponsored athletes are profiled on company websites with their images front and centre on home pages, within articles, and in advertising campaigns.
- Sponsored athletes attend retail store openings to garner support from the trade, and attend company sales meetings to provide excitement.

"Sponsorship is not the only tool used to reach this target market," explains Morash. "We also use online advertising, product placement, and social media with Facebook and YouTube to engage fans."

- Product placement in ski films is an important part of the mix. Ski films are immensely popular with this target market, and fans attend private screenings and watch ski films online for entertainment. HEAD donates ski equipment and provides travel allowances and promotional funds to assist in the production of 10 to 12 ski films per year with companies such as Red Bull Productions and Matchstick Productions. Trailers to these films are uploaded to HEAD's YouTube channel where athletes, competitions, and ski films are profiled.
- Online ads are also part of the marketing mix for HEAD Canada, with ads placed on Internet ski sites and e-commerce sport sites to profile the brand. Morash also reminds us that the in-store retail environment is crucial to the marketing of skis. Posters, in-store signage, and merchandisers are created and placed in sporting goods stores to add luster to the product.

Let's look at how HEAD segments the ski and ski boot business for the ski market in Canada. Overall, the ski market in Canada is in decline, impacted by the aging population and increasingly high travel costs—and, some would argue, global warming. It is very competitive, and the major companies—Atomic, Rossignol, Volkl, and Solomon—carefully segment the market to strengthen their brands and to carve out profitable businesses.

HEAD Canada segments the ski market into clusters with common lifestyle and demographic characteristics as well as product needs. Three main segments are (1) freestyle skiers, (2) racers, and (3) recreational skiers. For each segment, HEAD develops specific products and marketing programs that meet the needs and expectations of the target group. The high-profile freestyle skiing segment garners high media exposure and is used to boost the entire HEAD brand. Morash explains, "The freestyle skiing segment is growing at 20 to 25 percent each year, and as an exciting sport that gets attention, we use it to help boost our overall brand relevance in North America." Let's look at these segments in more detail:

Freestyle skiers: This growing market segment, outlined earlier, accounts for about 15 percent of the market and consists of teenagers and young adults. These skiers like to live life on the edge, enjoy taking risks, and are passionate about freestyle skiing, music, and sports. They are interested in fashion and are brand loyal. Sponsorship is the main marketing tool used by HEAD to market to this segment, along with the secondary tools of product placement, social media, online advertising campaigns, and in-store merchandising.

The product itself plays a major role in the marketing mix. This target group is very knowledgeable about skis, and looks for skis that are affordable and that not only perform but also have graphics that align with their free-spirited image. Kaya Turski skis with the HEAD Caddy ski, which has bright, funky graphics and energetic colours that appeal to this segment. Freestyle skis are sold at specialty dealers and ski shops such as Comor in Vancouver and resort shops at Whistler and Mont Tremblant.

Racers: This small declining segment of 5- to 35-year-old downhill skiers accounts for about 10 percent of the market and includes higher-income young families whose children enjoy ski racing. It also includes high-performance athletes who compete at the elite level in the racing category. These skiers are competitive and conservative and look for reliable, technically advanced equipment that delivers results. They are very brand loyal and see technical design as more important than graphic design.

HEAD markets to this segment with high-performance skis that carve and go fast. Promotional spending focuses on athlete sponsorship programs, particularly of World Cup racers such as Canadian Ben Thomsen or U.S. superstar Lindsey Vonn. Racing skis are sold at specialty ski shops such as Sign of the Skier in Toronto and Ski Cellar in Calgary.

Recreational skiers: This segment accounts for about 75 percent of the market and is characterized by 5- to 55-year-old casual skiers who ski for pleasure. They are conservative, higher-income young families and active teenagers and adults. They purchase skis primarily based on price and appearance rather than performance. Graphic design is the main purchase trigger and preferences lie in safe, somewhat conservative graphics. These consumers are moderately brand loyal.

HEAD markets to this segment with lower-tech skis with limited features that aim to enhance the "skiability" of the product. Promotion is limited to in-store merchandising, trade shows, and retail employee incentives, as well as venue marketing at ski resorts where demo-tents and posters draw attention to brands. Recreational skis are sold at sporting goods stores such as SportChek and specialty ski shops throughout Canada.

"The business of sports marketing is dynamic and exciting, but as a declining business, the ski market has its own set of challenges and opportunities," states Morash. He sees the freestyle skiing segment as one that can boost business by encouraging young people to try the sport. "Yes, sports marketing is fun," explains Morash. "But at the end of the day, a plan of carefully designed products that are priced to appeal to a market segment and are promoted to maximize visibility and engagement must deliver results." Morash explains that revenues must turn into profits, which at the end of the day is what marketing programs are designed to achieve.[1]

You can see more about HEAD skis and Kaya Turski on its social media ski accounts: Twitter at **@HEAD_WS**; Facebook at **www.facebook.com/headski**; and YouTube at **www.youtube.com/headski**. HEAD's products and athletes are profiled on **www.head.com**. Thank you, Rob Morash, and good luck, Kaya Turski.

reality CHECK ✔

As you read Chapter 6, refer back to the HEAD skis vignette to answer the following questions:

- What market segmentation strategy is HEAD using: mass marketing, segment marketing, niche marketing, or individualized marketing?
- What is the demographic profile of HEAD's freestyle skier segment?
- What is the psychographic profile of HEAD's freestyle skier segment?
- What is the behavioural profile of HEAD's freestyle skier segment?

Segmentation, Targeting, and Positioning

Segmentation, targeting, and positioning are fundamental concepts that are central to how marketers run their businesses and market their products. These concepts are intertwined and work together to create and reinforce a product's image to its consumers and to the market in general.

When creating annual marketing plans and developing new marketing ideas to strengthen a product, marketers immediately look to how a product is positioned in the market, consult with its positioning statement to understand how it is perceived in the marketplace, and use its target market profile to gather consumer insights that can be used to ensure new marketing ideas will ring true to its target market needs, interests, and values.

In marketing, consistently reinforcing a product's image helps to solidify what it represent to consumers. Marketers are careful to consistently reinforce a product's image by ensuring all elements of the marketing mix are well-coordinated to reflect the product's positioning and target market expectations. Portraying an inconsistent image will result in consumers being unclear of the product's benefits, which will result in a product losing consumers to a better defined competitive offering.

Market segmentation helps marketers place their product offerings in the context of a competitive market. It allows them to see the bigger picture from a consumer perspective, and to focus on how competitors are servicing consumer needs. A market segmentation analysis also allows marketers to identify which segments should be a focus, and where gaps in the market exist and where future opportunities may lie.

Marketers such as Rob Morash at HEAD Canada use these approaches to ensure that their product offerings and marketing programs are fresh, relevant, and focused. This approach helps maintain a competitive edge in the market and helps marketers to stay in touch with the latest trends.

Market segmentation, targeting, and positioning are key factors in the world of marketing.

Market Segmentation

LO 1 The essence of market segmentation, target markets, and product positioning is based on three important facts. First, consumers have diverse needs, and a single product cannot satisfy everyone. Second, companies have finite amounts of money, and it needs to be spent efficiently and effectively on consumers who are most likely to purchase the product. Third, as demonstrated in the vignette on HEAD Canada, marketers need to have clear consumer insights on their target markets in terms of product needs, price expectations, purchase habits, and the communication tools used to gather information, stay informed, and be entertained.

> *In simple terms, a market segment means a piece of the market.*

In simple terms, a market segment means a piece of the market. In the marketing world, there are two main market segments: the consumer market and the business market. The **consumer market** consists of goods, services, and ideas that a person can purchase or support for his or her own personal use. The **business market** involves products that are purchased either to run a business or to be used as a component in another good or service. How a product is classified depends on its usage. Let's look at an example to clarify this point. A person buys an iPad in order to connect on social networks, surf the Internet, stream music, upload photos, and watch movies for entertainment. A company buys its salespeople iPads so that they can make better customer presentations and more easily access head-office files. The products are exactly the same. In the first instance, the iPad is a consumer product for personal use; in the second instance, the iPad is a business product for assisting salespeople. There are many other similar examples, but it is important to understand that many products are tailored specifically for one market or the other, and not necessarily both. Heavy machinery used for landscaping is not a consumer product, and a comic book is not a business product.

Formally, **market segmentation** involves aggregating prospective buyers into groups that have common needs and respond similarly to marketing programs. These groups are relatively homogeneous

consumer market
Products, ideas, and services that a person can purchase, use, or support for personal use

business market
Products that are purchased either to run a business or to be used as a component in another product or service

market segmentation
The aggregation of prospective buyers into groups that have common needs and respond similarly to marketing programs

and consist of people who are fairly similar in terms of their consumption behaviour, attitudes, and target market profiles.

There is normally more than one firm vying for the attention of prospective buyers in a market. This results in marketers following a strategy of **product differentiation** to position their products apart from the competition in the eyes of consumers so that they appear distinct from competitive offerings. It is important to note that product differentiation does not mean a product has to be better than the competition. Marketers position their products as best they can to meet the needs of their target consumers. Sometimes, this may mean adding a unique feature; other times, it may mean minimizing all costs to provide a cheaper alternative to the market.

Forms of Market Segmentation

LO 2 There are a number of different approaches companies can take to segment the market. Whether a company is in the business-to-business market or the consumer market, it can follow one of these four strategies: a mass marketing strategy, a segment marketing strategy, a niche marketing strategy, or an individualized marketing strategy.

Mass Marketing Strategy This approach exists in a limited capacity today due to the competitiveness of the market and the need for marketers to specifically address consumer needs with their offerings. A **mass marketing** strategy is when a product with broad appeal is widely marketed to the entire market with no product or marketing differentiation at all. Examples can be found in the utilities area, with items such as tap water or natural gas being marketed to all consumer groups with no variation from either

a product or marketing perspective. Other examples can be found in the fruits and vegetables market with products such as broccoli, radishes, and spring onions also being sold indiscriminately to all target groups.

Segment Marketing Strategy

This form of market segmentation is the most common form of segmentation followed by large companies such as HEAD Canada, discussed in this chapter's opening vignette. **Segment marketing** involves the marketing of a wide range of different products and brands to specifically meet the needs of an organization's varied target markets. Examples of this approach can be seen in competitive industries that are dominated by large organizations, such as the food business, car industry, and cellphone market, just to name a few. For example, in the car industry, companies such as Toyota market cars, trucks, sport utility vehicles, crossovers, and minivans under a wide range of brands and models. Well-known Toyota brands include Scion, Yaris, Corolla, Camry, RAV4, Avalon, and Prius, as well as its premium Lexus brand for its luxury vehicles. These brands are created and marketed with a wide range of models to appeal to different market segments in the automobile market—all owned and marketed by Toyota.

The Yaris, for example, is a small two-door or four-door hatchback that has modern styling, is reliable and comfortable, and is designed for individuals or young couples who need a small, affordable, stylish car that is fuel-efficient, easy to park, and comfortable for driving to work and on weekends. Another Toyota brand, the Prius, is designed for a different market segment, one that focuses on green, high-tech living, and making a statement for supporting the environment. The Prius is a fuel-efficient, high-tech hybrid that comes in various models, such the Prius C, a four-door hatchback for singles or young couples living in the city, or the Prius V, a larger vehicle, a crossover, designed with greater space for family usage. The Prius brand, appealing to the high-tech needs of this market segment, includes keyless ignition, Bluetooth connectivity, and a touch-screen electronics interface. Higher-end models also include a rearview camera, voice controls, a navigation system, HD radio, and Toyota's Entune app capability with real-time updates on traffic, weather,

What segmentation strategy is used to market these products?

sports, stocks, fuel prices, and streamed music from sites such as Pandora and iHeartRadio.

Let's look at the breakfast cereal category for additional clarity and examine the Kellogg's brand approach to market segmentation. If we look at the cereal market in general, there are products that appeal to different demographic and psychographic groups. For example, there are adult-oriented, healthy cereals; fun, pre-sweetened children's cereals; and wholesome family cereals that are neither too healthy nor too sweet. In 1906, Kellogg's started the cereal business as the Battle Creek Toasted Corn Flake Company with only one product, Kellogg's Corn Flakes. This product was marketed to everyone, and Kellogg's followed a mass-marketing approach. Now, generations later, Kellogg's is a company with multiple cereal products and brands that appeal to different market segments. It now follows a segment marketing approach, using different products and brands to meet the needs of different target groups. For example, for the mainstream health-oriented adult, Kellogg's has All Bran, Special K, Vector, and Müslix. For families who demand fun, pre-sweetened cereals, Kellogg's offers Froot Loops, Mini-Wheats, Corn Pops, Frosted Flakes, and Krave, a chocolate flavoured cereal. For wholesome family goodness, consumers can turn to Rice Krispies, Corn Flakes, or Just Right.

Each product not only caters to the specific product needs of distinct target markets but also has its own marketing program to ensure that each target group's needs are properly met. If you look at the packages for these products, they reflect different target market interests and needs. Mini-Wheats, for example, has a fun package that uses bright colours and a cartoon character to appeal to young families, while Müslix, with a focus on health and nutrition, uses more subdued graphics and warmer colours, and focuses on natural grains, fruits, and nuts to portray a wholesome cereal. Similarly, each product's promotional programs are designed to speak to each target group in a different manner. Mini-Wheats, targeting young families, uses catchy TV ads with jingles and fun graphics placed around family-oriented programming. Müslix, designed as an adult-focused healthy cereal, concentrates on the product's nutrition and delicious taste in its marketing communications.

A segment marketing strategy is also followed by companies in the business-to-business market. An example can be seen in the food-service industry where suppliers are asked to create specific products to meet the needs of their accounts. A pickle manufacturer such as Bick's may create customized products for its large food-service accounts and, in this way, secure contracts for its business. For example, a large fast-food chain may request a customized pickle to go on its hamburgers. The product would have to meet the chain's specifications, such as size, slicing, flavouring, and packaging. The same pickle manufacturer may also create a customized pickle product for another key account. This time, the product may be customized for a large retail food chain and be packed in small glass jars, with a particular spice, and labelled under the retailer's brand name. In both of these business-to-business instances, customized products are being created for the company's key accounts. The business-to-business market is often segmented by the needs of key accounts.

> "A segment marketing strategy is also followed by companies in the business-to-business market."

Kellogg's follows a segment marketing strategy with its cereals.

> ### "Products are carefully designed to appeal to market segments and must deliver revenues that turn into profits."
> —*Rob Morash, managing director, Head Canada*

Niche Marketing Strategy The market segmentation strategy where a company restricts its efforts to marketing a limited product line to a narrow but profitable segment of the market that is of marginal interest to major competitors is called **niche marketing**.[2] Staying within the car industry and the cereal market, we look at the Tesla Motors car brand and the Kashi cereal brand to see niche marketing approaches. Tesla Motors is an independent car company centred in California that only manufactures and markets electric vehicles. Its first car, a Roadster, was launched in 2008, and today, it also markets a Model S sedan and a Model X sport utility vehicle that compete with high-end car manufacturers such as BMW and Mercedes, but it restricts its offerings to only the niche electric vehicle category. Tesla products are not sold through dealerships, but instead through a small number of exclusive Tesla stores located in upscale shopping malls.

Kashi cereal is an example of a product that started using a niche marketing approach. The cereal was initially launched in 1984 by a small independent company that concentrated its efforts only on cereals with all-natural ingredients. The Kashi brand did not try to sell to all market segments, but instead sold a line of cereals limited to the healthy market segment. Interestingly, Kashi's successful niche-marketing approach prompted its eventual acquisition by The Kellogg Company, which now carefully markets the Kashi brand separately from its Kellogg's brand as a more wholesome brand.[3]

In the online digital world, there are many examples of niche marketing approaches with products that fly somewhat under the radar in small but profitable market segments. The Mashable blog is an example of a product that follows a niche market segmentation approach, focusing on all things digital with its daily news blog posts, Facebook entries, and Twitter updates. It enjoys over 20 million monthly unique visitors and over 6 million social media followers by dedicating its coverage to news on digital innovation, technology, digital culture, and social media.[4] Mashable is monetized through the placement of advertising on its blog.

New or smaller firms often adopt niche marketing approaches to compete with large corporations that dominate categories. This can be seen with successful Quebec-based Canadian food company Maison le Grand, with its inroads into the competitive pre-made sauce market. It successfully holds its own against established brands from Kraft and Campbell's, as well as popular store brands such as President's Choice. Its line of uncooked premium gourmet sauces contains only the highest-quality fresh ingredients and sophisticated flavours. The products' upscale packaging stands out with its appealing photography, colourful graphics, and unique pour-spout for the pesto line. The company limits its products to five pesto sauces, three rosée sauces, and a Greek tzatziki yogourt-garlic sauce. The line is sold across Quebec and Ontario in the refrigerated sections of retailers such as Loblaw's Maxi and Provigo, and is making inroads into Western Canada. The line also sells in various U.S. markets through specialty retailers such as Whole Foods.[5]

What segmentation marketing strategy is used by Maison le Grand with its sauces?

niche marketing
Marketing a limited product line to a narrow but profitable segment of the market that is of marginal interest to major competitors

In the business-to-business market, a niche marketing approach is followed by companies such as the Stitt Feld Handy Group, which provides services in training, negotiation, mediation, arbitration, and dispute resolution to corporations, government bodies, and their agencies. Stitt Feld Handy provides specialized services that assist in dispute resolution and conflict management. Its marketing efforts, directed specifically at this group, include targeted e-mail and mail campaigns, radio ads on 680 NEWS in Toronto, and newspaper ads in publications such as the *Toronto Star*. It also markets through specialized publications, association newsletters, and events. From an online perspective, it uses Facebook, YouTube, and pay-per-click advertising, and ensures that its website at **www.sfhgroup.com** is optimized for search engines.

Individualized Marketing Strategy

New technology has boosted individualized marketing as a segmentation option for marketers. The Internet allows marketers to use database technology to track consumer purchases and predict interests and future purchases. This enables marketers to customize offers and, in some cases, products to fit individual needs. **Individualized marketing** can also be called personalized marketing or one-to-one marketing and it involves customizing offers and, in some cases, products to fit individual needs.

Stitt Feld Handy targets the B2B market

Marketers are rediscovering today what previous generations knew running a general store a century ago. Every customer is unique, has particular wants and needs, and requires special care from the seller. Efficiencies in manufacturing and marketing during the past century made mass-produced goods so affordable that most customers were willing to compromise their individual tastes and settle for standardized products. Today's Internet ordering and flexible manufacturing and database marketing techniques have facilitated individualized market segmentation by making it easier to tailor goods and services to suit individual customer needs.

Burberry is an upscale fashion design house and retailer that includes an individualized marketing approach in its mix of other segmentation strategies. A consumer can hop online at its **Burberry.com** website to purchase standard items or navigate to its BESPOKE (meaning: made to order, custom made) section of trench coats to customize a Burberry raincoat with a wide choice of fabrics, colours, linings, buttons, lengths, collars, sleeves, buttons, and belts. The price for this individualized marketing is not cheap as a Burberry customized trench coat may set you back $1,800!

A simpler and more affordable example of individualized marketing can be seen with the chocolate manufacturer Hershey and its Hershey Kisses product. A consumer can go online to its website at **www.hersheys.com/kisses** and navigate to its "Experience" section to customize a virtual electronic image of a Hershey Kiss that can be e-mailed to a friend. Consumers can customize the plume at the top of the chocolate with a special message, change the colour of the foil wrapper, and include a personal message—simple, free, and engaging.[6]

Internet marketing analytics companies now provide digital marketers with metrics that can help marketers customize offers to better meet customer needs. Database marketing approaches can track individual purchases and

ask yourself

1. *What are the advantages of a segment marketing approach to market segmentation?*

2. *Does Kashi still follow a niche market segmentation approach?*

3. *What are the disadvantages of individualized market segmentation?*

Would you be interested in customizing a Hershey Kiss?

send offers that meet personal preferences. If you use the same travel website, visit the same restaurant, or use a loyalty card to purchase groceries, over time these companies will recognize and predict your needs, sending you information, offers, or special services tailored to you. For example, if you purchase vintage DVDs from **Amazon.ca**, the site may start sending you product alerts when similar products enter their portfolio. If you use their loyalty cards when shopping at Shoppers Drug Mart or Loblaws, these companies will start sending you offers directly related to your past purchases.

The key to successful product differentiation and market segmentation strategies lies in finding the ideal balance between satisfying a customer's individual wants and being able to do this profitably.

Target Market Profiles and Personas

Target Market Profiles

LO³ Marketers need to have a clear understanding of what drives their consumers, what delights them, and what does not. This helps marketers develop meaningful products, design programs that meet their target market needs, and communicate to their target markets in the manner in which they are accustomed. A **target market** is the specific group of existing and potential consumers to which marketers direct their marketing efforts.

Developing an accurate target market profile is crucial to the success of all marketing initiatives as it drives decisions about the product's marketing mix and the product's positioning in the market. This **target market profile** contains specific information about the target group in four areas: (1) geographics, (2) demographics, (3) psychographics, and (4) behaviouristics. It is updated periodically as new information surfaces and is included in key strategic documents such as annual marketing plans. Figure 6–1 clearly outlines these four variables.

Often, students wonder why it is important to identify all these variables when describing a target market. If consumers are buying chewing gum, what is the relevance of their income level or where they live? In fact, usually only a few elements in a target market profile are the main determinants in why a consumer purchases a product—we generally find these in the behaviouristics area. Nonetheless, all variables need to be included in the target market profile as this profile is used in other marketing areas. If elements are missing, crucial errors can be made. For example, a target market profile is used extensively when creating advertising programs. The consumer insights are used to help develop campaigns that speak to the target group, and media is bought against the specific target market data such as age, income, location, interests, and media habits.

Geographics A **geographics** descriptor of a target market looks at where a target market lives, using variables such as country, region, province, city size, and type of location, such as urban, suburban, or rural. Marketers often find that Canadians differ in terms of needs or preferences based on where they live. An example is found in the flour industry: Consumers in Western Canada tend to buy larger packages of flour than those in Ontario and Quebec due to a greater incidence of baking. Another example is a product such as the Smart car, which is small and compact and geared toward urban dwellers. The target market for this car mainly resides in city centres. Its car2go car-sharing business in Canada has an

target market
The specific group of existing and potential consumers to which marketers direct their marketing efforts

target market profile
A description of the target market that contains specific information about the target group in four areas: geographics, demographics, psychographics, and behaviouristics

geographics
Where a target market lives, using variables such as country, region, province, city size, and type of location, such as urban, suburban, or rural

Who is the target market for the car2go?

even more focused target market. In Canada, car2go currently operates only in the city centres of Vancouver, Toronto, and Calgary, where its cars, located at numerous local city parking lots, can be located through a smartphone app and accessed with free membership cards that allow members to rent cars by the minute, the hour, or the day. The car drop-off is at any of its parking lot locations and does not require the user to return the car to its original pick-up spot. Car2go has over 900 vehicles in its Canadian car-sharing service.[7]

Figure 6–1
Examples of typical target market variables in Canadian consumer markets

TARGET MARKET PROFILES		
Categories	**Variables**	**Typical Breakdowns**
Geographics (Where does the target market live and work?)	Region	Atlantic; Quebec; Ontario; Prairies; British Columbia
	City or census metropolitan area (CMA) size	Under 5,000; 5,000–19,999; 20,000–49,000; 50,000–99,999; 100,000–249,000; 250,000–499,999; 500,000–999,000; 1,000,000–3,999,999; 4,000,000+
	Density	Urban; suburban; rural
Demographics (What is the basic factual census-type information on the target market as a whole?)	Age and family composition	Infant; under 6; 6–11; 12–17; 18–24; 25–34; 35–49; 50–64; 65+
	Gender	Male; female
	Marital status	Single or equivalent; married or equivalent
	Income	Under $24,999; $25,000–$34,999; $35,000–$49,999; $50,000–$74,999; $75,000–$99,999; $100,000–$149,999; $150,000+
	Occupation	Professional; managerial; clerical; sales; blue collar; white collar; student; retired; housewife; unemployed
	Education	Some high school; high school graduate; completed college or university; completed post-graduate studies
	Ethnic background	Country of origin
	Home ownership	Own home; rent home
Psychographics (What are the prevailing attitudes, values, interests, habits, opinions, and approaches to life that this target market shares?)	Personality traits	Social; compulsive; extroverted; introverted; intuitive; analytical; judgmental
	Lifestyle values and approaches	Rigid; disciplined; discontented; fearful; confident; positive; optimistic; energetic; resentful; dependent; negative; caring; materialistic; conformist; adventurous; independent; sharing
	Leisure activities, hobbies, and interests	Politics; music; sports; the arts; entertaining; fashion; gaming; health and fitness; travel; food; gardening; cars; movies; arts and crafts; the environment
	Media habits	Internet; newspaper; magazine; TV; radio; out-of-home
	Technology usage	Desktop computer; laptop; tablet; e-reader; smartphone; TV
Behaviouristics (How does this target market use and interact with the product?)	Main occasion for product use	Leisure; recreation and socializing with friends; professional and work situations; medical and personal care, home care, family care, etc.
	Main product benefit sought	Entertainment; self-improvement; fashion; fun; personal status; performance; specific product features such as taste, nutritional value, speed, etc.
	Primary and secondary product usage	Specific main usage and secondary usage of the product. (For example, the main usage of a cereal may be as a nutritious start to the day, but its secondary usage may be as a baking ingredient.)
	Frequency of use	Multiple times throughout the day; daily; weekly; monthly; every few months; biannually; annually
	Frequency of purchase	Daily; weekly; monthly; every few months; biannually; annually
	Product usage rate	Light user; medium user; heavy user
	Product usage status	Non-user; ex-user; prospect; first-time user; regular user
	Product loyalty status	None; some; medium; strong

Vitamins are often formulated for specific age groups.

Demographic Profile:
Maclean's **Magazine**

Gender	Men/women	53%/47%
Age	Average	47 years
Income	Average annual household income	$92,233

Source: *Maclean's Media Kit 2013,* accessed July 2014 at www.rogersconnect.com/files/Macleans_MediaKit.pdf.

Demographics   One of the easiest factors to determine is the **demographics** profile of a target market. This includes identifying ranges for age, gender, family composition, income, occupation, education, ethnic background, and home ownership for the main target market. This information can be identified through a company's market research information and other secondary data sources, such as Statistics Canada. An example of where demographics plays a leading role in a target market profile is with the Centrum vitamin brand. Centrum formulates and markets many of its products based on age and gender requirements. Centrum Select 50+ is formulated for adults over 50 years of age; Centrum for Women is formulated for female nutritional needs; Centrum for Men includes supplements for males; and Centrum Junior is geared to children between the ages of 2 and 12.

Other examples of demographic descriptors can be seen with *Maclean's* magazine. *Maclean's,* with a circulation of 321,275 and a readership of 2,474,000 readers per week, identifies its demographic profile as male and female, slightly skewed toward the male demographic (54 percent male), averaging 47 years, with an average household income of $77,000.[8]

Psychographics   **Psychographics** is one of the most difficult variables to identify for marketers. It involves understanding consumers' attitudes to life, values, personalities, general interests, opinions, media usage, technology preferences, and activities. This information is generally based on the primary research that marketers conduct to gather insights on their consumers. Psychographic variables are central to understanding the delight points of consumers and what gives them that extra spark. Image-based products gear much of their marketing

efforts around these psychographic variables. The fragrance industry, for example, relies heavily on psychographics, as do many soft drink companies. Reflect for a minute on Coca-Cola, positioned as a traditional, refreshing soft drink rooted in old-fashioned Americana. Now think of Pepsi-Cola, marketed as the energetic cola for those with a youthful attitude to life. The products may vary only slightly in taste, but their target markets differ considerably in attitudes, interests, and opinions. Coca-Cola and Pepsi-Cola use psychographics as main variables in their marketing efforts.

Behaviouristics   **Behaviouristics** directly refers to how and why consumers buy and use products. It is one of the most important target market variables as it directs the product's positioning in the market and drives the main marketing communication messages of the brand, as well as promotional ideas and areas for new product development.

How do the target markets for Coca-Cola and Pepsi-Cola differ?

demographics
Ranges for age, gender, family composition, income, occupation, education, ethnic background, and home ownership

psychographics
Understanding consumers' attitudes to life, values, personalities, general interests, opinions, and activities

behaviouristics
How and why consumers buy and use a product, including the desired product benefits, how often it is purchased, how frequently it is used, and whether consumers are brand loyal in their purchase behaviour

Behaviouristics looks at why consumers buy a product, the expected product benefits, how a product is used, how often it is purchased, how frequently it is used, and whether consumers are brand loyal in their purchase behaviour. Database marketing analytics can collect data on consumer purchases and over time identify what triggers consumer purchases: Is it a coupon? Is it a points program? Is it a contest? Is it a free information download? This data can be used not only to drive promotional programs but also to uncover insights into what drives these consumers. Often, this data is used in individualized marketing approaches that can encourage greater brand loyalty.

Brand loyalty refers to the favourable attitudes that a consumer has over time toward a brand that results in varying levels of purchase insistence and commitment to the brand. Brand loyalty varies by product and from person to person. Marketers strive toward having highly committed, brand-loyal consumers as this helps insulate their brands from competitive marketing practices.

In reality, consumer brand loyalty will range from very little to consumers that insist on your product in all circumstances. Fickle consumers with low levels of brand loyalty will frequently switch between brands, while those with moderate levels of brand loyalty will often lean toward their preferred brand choices. Marketers often use analytics to measure the varying degrees of brand loyalty and may use a rating system to help guide interactions with these different user groups.

On a more strategic level, companies such as those in the cellphone carrier industry often use behaviouristics to market to different customer groups with completely separate companies and brands. Telus, for example, owns Koodo, which is used to market cheaper plans with no contracts to younger consumers who want basic talk, text, and social media access. Bell, in turn, owns Virgin Mobile, again to market to a hip, younger, more budget-conscious crowd, while Rogers owns Fido, targeting a more youthful demographic. How and why these consumers use their phones and the benefits they desire are the key drivers in these marketing efforts.

Personas

Personas are character descriptions of a brand's typical customers. Personas started in online marketing to help marketers consistently focus on target market needs, and are now widely used in other areas of marketing. Personas bring target market data alive by creating fictional character narratives, complete with images, in one-page descriptions or snapshots that capture the personalities, values, attitudes, beliefs, demographics, and expected interactions of a typical user with a brand. Personas take target market research data and simplify and synthesize it, adding a few fictional details, such as name and image, so that human traits and characteristics become memorable for marketers.

Well-defined personas usually include information on gender, age, interests, hobbies, education, goals, jobs, influencers, media usage, technology preferences, fears, concerns, drivers, and delights and interactions with a brand. They may capture a "day in the life of" a typical user. A branded product may have more than one persona: a primary persona on the typical main consumer, and a secondary persona that captures the profile of other, less important groups who should not be overlooked.

An example of personas can be seen with one of the top-ranking Canadian food blogs, LivingLou.com, which shared its marketing insights with us. Youthful, energetic, and focused on simple healthy eating, this blog has two main target groups that are captured by two personas—Phoebe and Keisha. Phoebe is the primary persona and tends to be older, married, and focused on her children. Keisha is younger, single, and exploring life through varied interests. During a recent website redesign, these personas helped focus on what was important to the target market.

ask yourself

1. *What elements are included in demographics?*

2. *What is the difference between psychographics and behaviouristics?*

3. *In what ways are personas useful to marketers?*

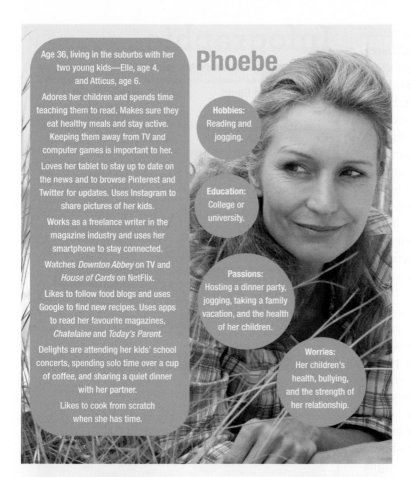

Phoebe

Age 36, living in the suburbs with her two young kids—Elle, age 4, and Atticus, age 6.

Adores her children and spends time teaching them to read. Makes sure they eat healthy meals and stay active. Keeping them away from TV and computer games is important to her.

Loves her tablet to stay up to date on the news and to browse Pinterest and Twitter for updates. Uses Instagram to share pictures of her kids.

Works as a freelance writer in the magazine industry and uses her smartphone to stay connected.

Watches *Downton Abbey* on TV and *House of Cards* on NetFlix.

Likes to follow food blogs and uses Google to find new recipes. Uses apps to read her favourite magazines, *Chatelaine* and *Today's Parent*.

Delights are attending her kids' school concerts, spending solo time over a cup of coffee, and sharing a quiet dinner with her partner.

Likes to cook from scratch when she has time.

Hobbies: Reading and jogging.

Education: College or university.

Passions: Hosting a dinner party, jogging, taking a family vacation, and the health of her children.

Worries: Her children's health, bullying, and the strength of her relationship.

Keisha

Age 26, living in the city, loves learning, Apple products, and her communications job.

Stays connected though her iPhone and never misses a message. Uses her iPad at home for Facebook and Twitter, watching movies on NetFlix, and listening to Songza playlists.

Watches CNN and The Food Network on TV.

Special treats are attending concerts, discovering a local restaurant, and meeting up with friends.

Health conscious and interested in staying fit. Likes to cook when she has time.

Education: College or university.

Worries: Not having a job that she loves, and meeting that special someone.

Passions: Movies directed by Sofia Coppola, vintage films with Audrey Hepburn, quirky music by Mumford and Sons, sushi, and having a beer at BBQs with friends.

Hobbies: Yoga, movies, and cooking.

Personas for **LivingLou.com**.

Segmentation Analytics

LO⁴ Marketers need to be aware that research companies can provide general data on the size and growth of markets to assist in segmentation analysis. Data can be purchased from companies such as Nielsen or Euromonitor that shows trends, market size, competitive products, market share, and future prospects for industries. Euromonitor, for example, provides data on 28 industries, 84 countries, 850 cities, and 300 companies on elements ranging from alcoholic beverages, apparel, and automotive, to appliances, packaged foods, pet care, and travel and tourism, just to mention a few.[9] Marketing service companies also conduct specific, confidential research projects for its clients that provide useful data on its market segments. Separately, these companies may conduct segmentation studies for public consumption as a way to showcase its expertise. AIMIA is such an example. This highly reputable Canadian loyalty-management company recently released an insightful segmentation study on social network users. The study revealed five clearly defined segments based on social media behaviouristics. Details on this study are outlined in the Marketing NewsFlash, "AIMIA Announces Social Media Segmentation."

Other segmentation analytics companies provide segmentation data on a more granular basis to pinpoint information on population clusters that assists marketers. These companies, such as Environics, Pitney Bowes, and SuperDemographics, analyze populations and create market segments and detailed data to help marketers target specific groups with high levels of accuracy. Environics Analytics has its Prizm C2 cluster analysis that provides a lifestyle analysis by postal code; Pitney Bowes has its Psyte HD clusters that detail demographic, psychographic, and behavioural data by postal code; and SuperDemographics has a trade reporting tool that provides purchase data in minutely defined shopping locations. Let's look at these tools in more detail.

Environics Analytics is a highly acclaimed global market research company based in Canada that provides insights into the shared demographic, lifestyle, and behavioural traits of the Canadian population. Its Prizm C2 segmentation system slices the Canadian population into 66 lifestyle clusters, such as Cosmopolitan Elite, Electric Avenues, Les Chics, and Lunch at Tim's, based on common demographics, lifestyles, interests, and values. Its data synthesizes information from the latest census with Environics' demographic projections, as well as its research on social values and consumer behaviour. This data gives users the ability to review information on what consumers are purchasing, what they enjoy doing, and their attitudes to life. When marketers combine Prizm C2 data with their own databases, they can determine their most profitable segments and where similar target groups exist within the country.

Prizm C2 also provides detailed data on each cluster's media usage, such as favourite TV programs, radio stations, magazines, newspaper sections, and websites. Data funnels down to the granular postal code level where a breakdown of the population for a single postal walk is available. This is particularly useful for database marketing campaigns where postal code information triggers a host of data that assists companies in their targeting and segmentation efforts. This information helps guide marketing campaigns and media strategies.[10]

Pitney Bowes Psyte HD also provides granular segmentation data through its segmentation system, which results in 59 rich lifestyle clusters. Postal code detail helps marketers discover untapped markets, finesse the targeting of their marketing campaigns, launch new products in appropriate markets, design cost-effective mailing and sampling programs, streamline retail offerings, and select the most profitable locations for new stores, restaurants, and retail developments.

Let's look at a Psyte HD cluster to demonstrate the data that is available. The Mussels and Malbec cluster #42 is young (under 25 years), is single with no kids, and lives an independent, fast-paced lifestyle. This cluster is well-educated, has an average annual household income of $58,000, likes to experiment with exotic foods, and works mainly in the information, arts, or entertainment industry. This cluster is found in the urban core of Ontario and Western Canadian cities. It reads the *Globe and Mail,* blogs, and entertainment/celebrity magazines. It listens to jazz and classical music, watches TVtropolis and CBC's *The National,* and belongs to local fitness clubs. Interests include jogging, yoga, movies, cooking, nightclubs, and travel. It shops at food chains and drugstores and up-market clothing retailers such as Harry Rosen and Holt Renfrew, as well as Banana Republic and Club Monaco.[11]

Infographic

Comparing Two Psyte Clusters

Europa Blend
Cluster #26

Culturally diverse neighbourhoods that exist in and around Ontario cities with some representation in Western Canada and Quebec. People who live here are from a wide range of countries from Eastern Europe, Western Europe, and Asia. Multiple languages can be heard in the streets. The area is typified by semi-detached housing and high-rise apartments.

Metro Singles
Cluster #21

Metropolitan core urban neighbourhoods with mainly single young people of diverse attitudes and cultures. They live busy lives and walk or ride bicycles to work or school and live in older apartments or new condo rentals. They are well-educated with a post-secondary education or are completing a college or university education.

$79,000	Average Household Income	$85,000

Mainly high school and trade and apprenticeship programs	Education	Mainly university or college

Media Usage

TORONTO SUN JAZZ	TV TENNIS PODCASTS
TV BRAVO URBAN MUSIC	REPORT ON BUSINESS
FASHION MAGAZINE	ONLINE NEWSPAPERS
TORONTO STAR	INDEPENDENT FILM CHANNEL
ETHNIC RADIO TV SOCCER	GLOBE AND MAIL BBC
TV TELELATINO	CLASSICAL MUSIC JAZZ

Leisure

Aerobics, swimming, walking, hiking, gourmet cooking, entertaining at home, photography, dancing, live theatre, all-inclusive resorts, travel to Europe	Fitness clubs, jogging, gourmet cooking, museums, galleries, night clubs, live theatre, foreign movies, travel within Canada, travel to Asia, travel to Europe

Shopping

Holt Renfrew	Mastermind
Harry Rosen	Sporting Life
Banana Republic	Grand and Toy
Indigo	National Sports Centres
The Bay	Indigo
Mastermind	Club Monaco
Talbots	Pet Valu
Mountain Equipment Co-op	International Clothiers
H&M	PJ's Pets
The Gap	Town Shoes

Source: Pitney Bowes Software Canada, Psyte HD, accessed September 2013 at http://www.utahbluemedia.com/pbbi/psyte/psyteCanada.html.

SuperDemographics from Manifold Data Mining is another reputable service provider in the segmentation analytics area. It too provides data down to the postal code level. It uses census data as well as statistics from Citizenship and Immigration Canada, Health Canada, Canada Post Corporation, and its Manifold proprietary databases.[12]

AIMIA Announces Social Media Segmentation

Canadian loyalty-management leader AIMIA, operating in over 20 countries around the world and owner of Aeroplan, announced the results of a segmentation study that analyzed people in the social media space. The study's purpose, to determine and understand the motivation and purchase behaviours behind social media interactions, points to how marketers can engage customers on social networks and focus on what adds value to consumers, rather than just count likes, followers, and interactions. It buckets social media users into five different market segments and creates engaging personas to help marketers focus on their target market needs.

Although the study uses U.S. data, its emotional parameters are common to the Canadian social network user, which makes the segments useful for Canadian marketers. The research looks at the level of *trust* people have with their social media as well as how much *control* they feel they have over the information they share. In brief, the more trust and control that people have over their social networking activity, the greater their engagement and participation.

Five distinct market segments surfaced:

- **Passive single-network users:** Those who reluctantly join a social network so as to not feel left out, they have little trust and limited involvement with social networks.

- **Passive multi-network users:** Those who like to use social networks to gather information but rarely share personal information due to a lack of trust in social networks.

- **Active single network users:** Those who limit their social network of friends and share information only with the most trusted friends.

- **Active multi-network users:** Those who freely share personal information and create content that they readily share across social networks.

- **Non-users:** Those who have never used a social network or have not used one in the last month.[13]

Questions

1. Which social network segments apply to you and your family? Review the social media behaviour of three family members and determine which segments apply.

2. How can this information on the segmentation of social networks help marketers?

Target Market Data—Active Multi-Network Segment (AIMIA)

Demographics: Female; 24 years; income $80,000; in grad school; lives with partner

Psychographics: Creative, engaging, and social; digitally savvy; comfortable buying products online; watches online videos; active on social networks; uses an iPhone, iPad, and laptop computer

Behaviouristics: Heavy user of social media as a form of self-expression; always connecting on social networks; 1,000+ connections across multiple networks; frequently engages with brands on social networks; writes online reviews; participates in online forums; publishes blog posts; concerned about online privacy; user of Facebook, Twitter, and blogs; creates her own content for sharing on social networks; enthusiastic brand ambassador

Source: Mona Askalani, "Staring at the Sun. Identifying, Understanding, and Influencing Social Media Users. Research Brief, The leading Edge of Consumer Insight," Aimia, 2012, accessed at www.aimia.com/files/doc_downloads/Aimia_SocialMedia_Whitepaper.pdf; "New Aimia study reveals six social media personas," Examiner.com, June 12, 2012, accessed at www.examiner.com/article/new-aimia-study-reveals-six-social-media-personas; Pam Dyer, "The 6 Types of Social Media Users," *Social Media Today*, June 25, 2012, accessed at http://socialmediatoday.com/pamdyer/564409/6-types-social-media-users.

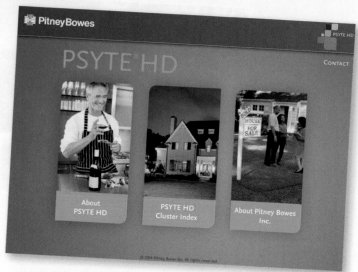

Pitney Bowes Psyte HD
provides segmentation analytics data.

Students are advised to visit the websites of these three companies to review samples of the rich data that is available for marketers. While Internet sites can change, currently, the following websites will provide you with a solid understanding of what data is available from these companies:

- Navigate to the Prizm Lifestyle Lookup section of the Environics website at **www.environicsanalytics.ca/prizm-c2-cluster-lookup** and enter a postal code to see an overview of the cluster information.

- Navigate to the Psyte HD Cluster Index at **www.utahbluemedia.com/pbbi/psyte/psyteCanada.html** and enter a postal code to view a cluster overview as well as a detailed breakdown of the cluster's demographics, geographics, media habits, leisure activities, and shopping activities.

- Navigate to the SuperDemographics website at **www.superdemographics.com** and try its free trade report area. Follow the steps and fill in the postal code to view the clusters within the area and its demographic breakdown.

Product Positioning

LO 5 One of the central elements in marketing is product positioning. Marketers position products in the market to appeal to certain target groups and to present a particular impression relative to the competition. **Product positioning** refers to the impression of the branded product you want to establish in consumers' minds relative to their needs and also in contrast to the competition. Companies generally use a combination of factors to position their products, always leading with the elements that are real; to differentiate the product; and to create long-term, memorable impressions with consumers. In this way, there are three basic factors, or combinations of factors, that tend to surface in product positioning:

1. *Image:* Products are often positioned as leaders, contenders, or rebels in the market, also taking on characteristics such as trusted, prestigious, or thrifty. Google, for instance, positions itself as an innovative and trusted leader in the market and a company that provides services that make people's lives easier and better in some meaningful way. All the products that it creates meet this positioning of the brand, whether this is Google search, Google maps, Google Chrome, or any other Google platform. In 2012 and 2013, Google was rated as the most influential brand in Canada by Ipsos' *Most Influential Brands* study.

▶ Video
Google

2. *Product attribute:* Products with features that differentiate them from the competition are often positioned on this platform, bringing product claims to the forefront. The retailer Danier, for example, positions itself as the premier leather retailer in Canada, providing quality leather and suede for men and women. Its brand is synonymous with luxury, style, and value—a positioning that combines image, product attribute, and price. Danier uses its stylish, contemporary designs and collections to support this positioning.

3. *Price:* Products with brand parity and little product differentiation may position themselves on a price platform. Retailers such as Walmart position themselves as offering the lowest retail prices to support its image in the market.

Marketers create positioning statements to clearly and simply outline the positioning of a product in the market. These statements are used to crystallize the image for marketers so that they can design a marketing mix that aligns with the product's positioning. This is very important; otherwise, the product may present a confusing image to consumers who will refrain from buying it. A **positioning statement** is a formalized statement that identifies the image a branded product represents in the market and what sets it apart from the competition. A positioning statement is generally included in a brand's annual marketing plan and its relevant strategic documents.

Positioning statements are simple, clear, and focused. They identify the main reasons a target market buys the branded product and what sets it apart in the market. It is important to understand that a branded product's positioning is reflected in all areas of its marketing mix, and one needs to look at each element of the marketing mix to accurately determine its positioning in the market. Positioning statements identify two key areas: (1) how the branded product meets consumer needs, and (2) how the branded product is differentiated in the market versus the competition.

Students were asked to identify a positioning statement for the Smart car2go product discussed earlier. Their starting point was to research the product and determine its target group by reading business articles, visiting the company's website, and seeing the cars in parking lots and around the city. In terms of an overview of its target market, students noted that the product is most likely geared to well-educated, single young adults, males and females, of varied occupations, living and working in city centres, earning a moderate income, and needing a car for short trips in the downtown core for running errands, for meeting work requirements, or for social occasions.

Students created the following positioning statement to clearly and simply express the possible positioning of this branded product: *"Smart car2go is positioned in the car-share market as a flexible and affordable alternative to purchasing or renting a car, and as an extension of public transportation in city centres."* For the product's competitive stance, the students mentioned that, *"Unlike other options, this car can be picked up and dropped off at different locations across the city that are easily located with an app or on its website. The car can be rented by the minute, hour, or day."*

Positioning statements are simple, clear, and focused. They average a short paragraph and identify four elements: (1) the branded product name, (2) the category in which the product competes, (3) one or two main reasons why the target market buys the branded product (product benefits), and (4) what sets the product apart from the competition.

> *Positioning statements are simple, clear, and focused.*

How is car2go positioned in the car-share market?

Repositioning

Companies rarely change a product's positioning but do so when long-term changes in consumer attitudes or opinions of the brand require a shift in the brand's image to more accurately meet consumer needs and to reflect how it fits their lifestyle and needs. **Repositioning** is often implemented in stages over time with a refresh of a brand and the elements of its marketing mix. Burberry and McDonald's provide us with recent examples.

Burberry, a luxury British clothing manufacturer had lost its lustre due to counterfeit products in the market and its own discounting. Its image was becoming old and dusty, rather than vintage and hip. A revamp of the brand brought it back to its roots and revitalized it as a successful luxury brand. The Marketing NewsFlash, "Burberry Cements Its Positioning with Flagship Store," provides details on how this repositioning occurred and points to how digital and retail innovation helped this transformation.

McDonald's is a recent example of a repositioning effort that started in 2007 and continued into 2012 and 2013 with the rollout of its premium McCafé beverages. McDonald's repositioning started in 2007 with its restaurant redesigns that included free Wi-Fi and comfortable seating nooks for the coffee-loving crowd, complete with fireplaces, leather chairs, and large-screen TVs—in addition to fast-moving areas to grab a quick burger

McDonald's new McCafé products and healthier Happy Meals help reposition McDonald's.

repositioning
A revamping of a branded product and its marketing mix to more accurately meet consumer needs

Burberry Cements Its Positioning with Flagship Store

Do you remember Burberry knock-offs—cheap imitations of the expensive camel, black, red, and white checkered brand that typifies Burberry clothing and accessories? So did Burberry, and took note that illegal knock-offs, promotional discounts, and inconsistent licensing agreements around the world cheapened and weakened the brand.

Over the next few years, from 2006 to 2013, Burberry etched a path to reclaim its brand as a luxury celebration of British design. It pulled on its U.K. heritage, which dates back to 1856, and appointed brand champion Christopher Bailey, chief creative officer, to ensure consistent imagery for all things Burberry, and to help reinvent the brand to embody digital hipness and cool, vintage British style.

The brand reduced its discounting, purged and evolved its product lines, embraced the digital web, connected on social media, and trained its salespeople to be better informed on the Burberry brand. It used its iconic and uniquely Burberry trench coat to showcase Burberry's heritage and to present a consistent and uniquely Burberry image to the fashion industry. Its edgy advertising campaigns featured only hip young British actors and models such as Eddie Redmayne (*Les Misérables* and *My Week with Marilyn*), Romeo Beckham (10-year-old son of soccer star David Beckham), and supermodel Cara Delevingne. It reduced its reliance on licensing and strategically opened new stores in high-end international luxury markets, including upscale locations in Canada.

The Burberry brand evolved beyond stores and runways into the digital space with an e-commerce website at **Burberry.com** that reached millions of consumers. It also used a social media program that connected with consumers on Facebook, Twitter, YouTube, Pinterest, and Instagram. Burberry is the leading luxury fashion brand on social media, with vast followings on Facebook (+15 million fans), Twitter (+2 million followers), YouTube (+24 million lifetime views), Pinterest (+56 thousand followers), and Instagram (+1 million followers). **Burberry.com** contains breathtaking images and video, and an extensive product line that dwarfs its in-store merchandise. It allows visitors to select standard items, made-to-order runway products, and customized trench coats. Up-and-coming unsigned British music artists and celebrity advertising images grace the website to add a cool lustre to the brand.

In order to cement its revitalization, in September 2012, Burberry launched a 44,000-square-foot, four-storey, global flagship store on Regent Street in London, England, as a tangible and digital representation of the reinvented Burberry brand. It fused the digital website experience with breathtaking retail design, allowing people to experience the brand as they do online and in person. By entering the store, visitors enter a physical representation of the website, complete with the digital ability to customize trench coats, order engraved name plates, or select Runway Made to Order items from Burberry fashion shows. In the store, visitors live within the brand, admiring

Burberry successfully revitalized its luxury brand image.

displays of vintage trench coats that date back to the early 1900s and browsing current merchandise.

The Burberry flagship store features over 500 speakers, 100 digital screens, and a 22-foot movie-theatre backdrop. When chip-enabled Burberry products are shown in the store in front of full-length mirrors, the mirrors transform into digital screens that play runway footage of the product or show video on how the product was made. At synchronized times during the day, the entire store momentarily morphs into a virtual raincloud with beautiful rain shower footage playing on every screen and heard on every speaker, emphasizing the importance of the Burberry trench coat to the Burberry brand. The store is home to exclusive, invitation-only music events of unsigned British bands and live screening events of Burberry runway shows. In support of the Burberry Foundation, 1 percent of Regent Street store purchases support the Burberry Foundation, which invests in charities that support needy and creative young people.

Around the world, Burberry now speaks with one voice and owns its positioning as an iconic, cool, vintage British luxury brand. Its vision is to protect, explore, and inspire.[15]

Questions

1. What two elements do you think most helped to reposition the Burberry brand and why?

2. Navigate to the BESPOKE section of the Burberry website to research the customization of the Burberry trench coat. What elements can be customized and what is the price tag of a customized Burberry trench coat?

on-the-go. This repositioning flowed into McDonald's menu choices where healthier food items were slowly added, such as oatmeal, apple slices, yogourt, and veggie wraps, with other products reformulated to contain less sodium and no trans fats. From 2010 to 2013, McDonald's rolled out its McCafé brand with high-quality teas, coffees, and fruit smoothies, competing with other coffee establishments such as Starbucks and Tim Hortons and fitting with its new restaurant redesigns.

McDonald's is repositioning itself as a more engaging fast-food restaurant, offering not only healthier food choices but also a place where consumers can enjoy a high-quality casual beverage while reading a newspaper, chatting with friends, or browsing the Internet. McDonald's goal is to be Canada's favourite place to eat and drink. It is working to gain a greater share of the food-service beverage market.[14]

Positioning Maps

Positioning maps, also known as perceptual maps, are visual representations of how products or product groups are positioned within a category to consumers/customers. Positioning maps can visually represent categories within a market, or more specifically, product and brand offerings within a segment. Positioning maps are useful tools for marketers as they can reveal gaps in the market where consumers may be underserved, while also highlighting the competitive nature of the category.

Positioning maps need to clearly identify the two most important attributes that drive purchases in a category, whether this is in the business-to-business or the consumer market. One must be able to assess these attributes objectively from a consumer perspective. One might rush to immediately identify price as a key variable, but often, this is a less important feature, evaluated by consumers once a short list of attributes on which they initially evaluate a purchase are identified. Let's make this clear with two examples. First, in the cereal market, nutrition and sweetness might be key attributes used by parents of young children to evaluate product offerings. (Price would come into play later in the purchase decision.) These factors of nutrition and sweetness can be used objectively to evaluate products in the category and identify how one product is positioned against another. In a second example, looking at the fast-food business, speed of service and nutritional offerings may be two of the parameters used to create a positioning map. In each instance, the variables in the positioning map should be objective and reflect the most important purchase variables to a specific target group in this category.

Figure 6–2 provides an example of a positioning map for store-bought beverages. It plots milk, tea, sports drinks, fruit juices, and soft drinks relative to each based on nutritional value and whether they are appropriate for adults or children. For these key elements, we can see diet drinks are geared to adults, while milkshakes appeal to teenagers.

positioning maps
Visual representations of how products are positioned in a category to consumers

Figure 6–2

A positioning map to suggest a strategy for positioning beverages

High nutritional value

Orange juice · ★ Organic milk

Regular milk ·

Chocolate milk ·

Milk shakes ·

· Sports drinks · Tea

· Nutritionally designed diet drinks

Children — **Adults**

Mineral water

· Fruit-flavoured drinks

· Flavoured teas and coffees

· Coffee

· Sugared soft drinks

Low nutritional value

Figure 6–3
The 10-step process for segmenting a market

Steps in Market Segmentation

1. Review strategic company objectives.
2. Identify specific business unit objectives.
3. Identify consumer/customer needs and common characteristics in the market.
4. Cluster common consumer/customer variables to create meaningful market segments.
5. Conduct SWOT analyses on the segments to determine strengths, weaknesses, opportunities, and threats.
6. Identify the segment that best meets strategic company objectives.
7. Identify marketing programs and budget requirements needed for this segment.
8. Create a sales forecast for this segment.
9. Conduct a profit-and-loss financial analysis for this segment.
10. Check financial forecasts against specific business unit objectives.

Steps in Market Segmentation

LO 6 Segmenting a market requires a number of skills. A marketer needs to combine strong analytical skills, sound strategic thinking, an understanding of the consumer, a vision on where the market is heading, and how this all fits with the company's direction. The process of segmenting a market for both the consumer market and business-to-business market is divided into 10 steps, which can be seen in Figure 6–3.

1. *Review strategic company objectives.* Objectives need to be clear and quantifiable. They should include sales, revenue, and profit targets, but also qualitative elements such as corporate social responsibility initiatives and new business direction for its divisions.

2. *Identify specific business unit objectives.* These objectives need to be in line with a company's strategic direction and outline the specific sales, market share, and profit targets for the business unit.

3. *Identify consumer/customer needs and common characteristics in the market.* This should be done from a consumer/customer perspective, looking at what drives the category and what future trends are evolving. Marketers should be able to easily identify common interests and evolving trends by analyzing what products currently exist in the category, which areas of the market are expanding and shrinking, and where consumer/customer interests

lie. Looking to other countries sometimes provides interesting ideas on where potential future interests may lie. At this point, marketers will turn to market research studies and analytics data to see what the facts reveal. Database analyses may reveal some interesting facts about purchase patterns and point to finite segments that had not been considered. Sometimes, marketers may need to conduct further market research to clarify questions.

4. *Cluster common consumer/customer variables to create meaningful market segments.* A marketer needs to stand back from the market and look for clusters of products and gaps in the market that point to common consumer/customer interests, usage patterns, and prevailing attitudes. New areas of interest should not be overlooked as these may point to evolving segments. These clusters will identify the segments that exist in the market. Sometimes, there is overlap between segments, and other times, the segments are not well-defined, but this is generally a reflection of the consumers/customers, who can be fickle and non-committal.

Segmentation analytics companies, as noted earlier, can provide marketers with data on market clusters, which combined with marketing analytics can help reveal profitable new approaches and opportunities. Companies may use its own data from CRM (customer relationship management) databases that group consumers by purchase behaviour and monetary value to a company. Software can run an **RFM analysis** (recency, frequency, and monetary value) to rate customers on how *recently* products were purchased (recency), how *often* products were purchased (frequency), and the *dollar value* of the transactions (monetary value). Customers are then scored and rated to create segments that organi-

zations use to tailor offers and marketing messages. Non-profit organizations frequently use RFM analyses to target those most likely to make donations, while CRM loyalty programs use loyalty cards to collect customer purchase data to then customize offers.

It is very important during this step to review the market from a consumer/customer perspective and not from a product perspective. For example, if we continue to review the cereal market, we may group products into those that contain whole grains and establish this as a segment. However, if we look at this category from a consumer perspective, we would see whole-grain products as only one of many appealing to health-conscious adult consumers. The segment is in fact better defined, and more meaningful to marketers, when identified as appealing to health-conscious adults.

Groups of students were asked to review the cold-cereal market, to cluster consumer needs into possible market segments, and to give product examples for each segment. They came up with four main clusters that addressed the market's needs for health, taste, and nutrition, which are shown in Figure 6–4.

5. *Conduct SWOT analyses on the segments to determine strengths, weaknesses, opportunities, and threats.* A **SWOT analysis** can be conducted on

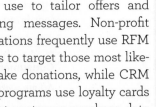

RFM analysis
The rating of customers on the basis of how recently products were purchased (recency), how often products were purchased (frequency), and the dollar value of the transactions (monetary value)

SWOT analysis
The assessment of how well an organization or brand is servicing its businesses and target markets by evaluating its internal strengths and weaknesses, and its external opportunities and threats

Marketers segment the market to more effectively and more efficiently reach their target markets.

Figure 6–4
Identifying consumer clusters

CONSUMER CLUSTERS EXAMPLE: COLD CEREALS		
Consumer Cluster	**Cluster Attitudes**	**Product Examples**
Adults with dietary needs	Feeling healthy Taste is secondary	All Bran Fibre First
Adults focused on taste and nutrition	Nutrition is key Taste is important Not health fanatics	Oatmeal Crisp Müslix
Families looking for fun and taste	Family-oriented Want kids to eat breakfast Taste is important Nutrition is not as important as taste	Froot Loops Nesquik
Families focused on wholesome goodness	Taste and nutrition are both important Good family health is key	Cheerios Rice Krispies

> *SWOT stands for strengths, weaknesses, opportunities, and threats.*

many different areas in marketing. It is very useful when analyzing a market as it can identify opportunities and whether a company has the strength to compete in a segment that may already be well-served by the competition. SWOT stands for *strengths, weaknesses, opportunities,* and *threats.* The strengths and weaknesses refer to the internal areas of a company or a product/brand. Examples may be the product image, its quality, or a lack of advertising spending. The opportunities and threats look to areas outside the company, product, or brand, such as the competition, consumer trends, or technology. It is important to involve a number of people when conducting a SWOT analysis so that different perspectives and ideas are captured. A SWOT analysis is discussed more fully in Chapter 15.

6. *Identify the segment that best meets strategic company objectives.* At this point in the process, a marketer sifts through the facts and ideas that have surfaced during the SWOT analysis and generally assesses the opportunities and threats in relation to a company's strategic direction. A market segment may surface as particularly interesting at this point.

7. *Identify marketing programs and budget requirements needed for this segment.* If a particular segment has surfaced as an area of interest, it will require further investigation. This will include a full financial evaluation of the opportunity to assess the costs of doing business and identify what programs are required to support an initiative. It also highlights what resources are needed to adequately compete in this segment.

8. *Create a sales forecast for this segment.* Once a thorough market assessment has been conducted, a marketer is tasked with forecasting the sales potential for this segment, which should also consider anticipated competitive reactions. Sales forecasting techniques are discussed in Chapter 9.

9. *Conduct a profit-and-loss financial analysis for this segment.* The marketing programs, budget requirements, and sales forecasts are put together with projected costs to determine what level of profits can be achieved in this market segment. A projected profit-and-loss statement is created to assess the financial viability of doing business in this market segment. Marketers often work with financial analysts to determine these costs. Chapter 9 reviews budgeting and profit-and-loss statements.

10. *Check financial forecasts against specific business unit objectives.* Once the financial analysis is complete, marketers have the information needed to objectively assess whether they can achieve their business unit objectives for this segment. Specific data on projected sales, market share, and profit targets are analyzed against targets and evaluated in terms of meeting the company's overall strategic direction.

> *A market segmentation analysis also allows a marketer to identify gaps in the market and determine where future opportunities may lie.*

adAlyze

What demographic data can you determine about the target market from this ad?

What psychographic interests can you determine about the target market from this ad?

What behavioural insight can you determine about the target market from this ad?

LAUNCH PAD

«My Caddy skis and boots are better than anything I have ever used. With HEAD, traveling 20+ feet out of the pipe feels normal.»

SCAN THIS QR CODE FOR A CHANCE TO WIN THIS SKI.

Competition will start the 1/10/2012 and end the 31/03/2013

THE CADDY

THE CADDY

head.com
facebook.com/headski
youtube.com/headski
Follow us on twitter: head_ws

Athlete: Simon Dumont
Photographer: Marcel Lämmerhirt

cool earth
coolearth.org

Summary...just the facts

LO¹ ● Market segmentation involves aggregating prospective buyers into groups that have common needs and respond similarly to marketing programs.

● In the marketing world, there are two main market segments: (1) the consumer market and (2) the business market.

LO² ● There are four different market segmentation strategies: mass marketing, segment marketing, niche marketing, and individualized marketing.

LO³ ● Marketers define their target markets by looking at four main variables: (1) geographics, (2) demographics, (3) psychographics, and (4) behaviouristics.

● Geographics looks at where a target market lives, such as a country, region, province, city size, and type of location, such as urban, suburban, or rural.

● Demographics includes identifying ranges for age, gender, family composition, income, occupation, education, ethnic background, and home ownership.

● Psychographics involves understanding consumer attitudes to life, values, personalities, general interests, opinions, and activities.

● Behaviouristics looks at why consumers buy a product, the product benefit, how and when the product is used, and whether consumers are brand loyal in their purchase behaviour. Usage rate also plays a role in this information.

● Personas are character descriptions of a product's typical customers in the form of fictional character narratives, complete with images that capture the personalities, values, attitudes, beliefs, demographics, and expected interactions of a typical user with a brand.

LO⁴ ● Segmentation analytics analyzes market segments and provides data to help target specific groups with high levels of accuracy.

● Segmentation analytics data clusters consumers into lifestyle segments and provides information that details geographics, demographics, psychographic, and behaviouristic data by postal code, defined shopping areas, or neighbourhood.

LO⁵ ● Product positioning refers to the image of a branded product relative to the competition.

● Marketers create positioning statements to clearly and simply outline the positioning of a product.

● Repositioning includes a shifting of the product image and adjusting its marketing mix to more accurately meet consumer needs.

● Positioning maps are otherwise known as perceptual maps. They visually represent how products or product groups are positioned within a category to consumers.

LO⁶ ● Segmenting the market involves 10 steps that require analytical skills, strategic thinking, an understanding of the consumer, a vision of where the market is heading, and how this fits with company objectives.

● The 10 market segmentation steps start with a review of company and business unit objectives and continues by clustering consumer needs, conducting a SWOT analysis, and finally identifying the segment and product potential by analyzing its forecasted sales, and pinpointing marketing budgets and profit projections.

Key Terms and Concepts...a refresher

behaviouristics
brand loyalty
business market
consumer market
demographics
geographics
individualized marketing
market segmentation

mass marketing
niche marketing
personas
positioning maps
positioning statement
product differentiation
product positioning

psychographics
repositioning
RFM analysis
segment marketing
SWOT analysis
target market
target market profile

Hands-on...*apply your knowledge*

Positioning Assignment   HEAD targets its ski products to three distinct market segments: freestyle skiers, recreational skiers, and racers. Carefully read the sections on product positioning and positioning maps, as well as the chapter's opening vignette about HEAD Canada, and take note of the interests of the target markets. Determine which variables you think should be used for the two axes in a positioning map for the ski market and create a positioning map for the ski market that plots these categories.

Chapter Vignette...*reminder*

This chapter's opening vignette examines how HEAD Canada segments the ski market. Answer the Reality Check questions at the end of the vignette by carefully reading the section in this chapter on the forms of market segmentation.

Video Clip...*questions*

Review the video *Most Influential Brands Study—Google* from the CONNECT website to understand how Google focuses on behaviouristic and psychographic information to build its businesses. Answer the following questions:

▶ Video
Google

- What overriding benefit does Google, as a company, attempt to provide its users?
- What element does Google foster to increase brand loyalty?
- What psychographic changes has Google noted about consumers in Canada?
- What challenge is Google facing with its business partners?

Infographic...*data analysis*

Review the Infographic that compares two clusters from the Pitney Bowes Psyte HD segmentation analytics. Navigate to its website at **www.utahbluemedia.com/pbbi/psyte/psyteCanada.html** and compare two other clusters to create a new infographic. Write a short analysis of the differences that exist between the two new clusters that you have selected. (*Infographic tip:* Use Microsoft Excel and Word to create charts and place them in a single PowerPoint slide to combine the visuals.)

Mc Graw Hill Education connect   **Mc Graw Hill Education SMARTBOOK**   **Mc Graw Hill Education LEARNSMART**

For more information on the resources available from McGraw-Hill Ryerson, go to **www.mheducation.ca/he/solutions**.

products and brands

Managing the marketing mix is no easy task, and this chapter explores the areas that marketers consider when managing products and brands. We speak with Ian Gordon, senior vice president at Loblaw Companies Ltd., who manages product innovation for President's Choice (PC), to better understand these elements. He takes us inside their new sub-brand, the PC black label collection, and explains how exceptional quality is the backbone of this successful new line that strengthens one of Canada's best-known premium brands, President's Choice.

Launched in the mid-1980s, the President's Choice brand brought energy to a dull private-label grocery business. The new PC brand was exciting; it was fun, unique, delicious, and premium. Cleverly showcased in the *PC Insider's Report*, people now tried new multicultural foods and unexpected flavour combinations. PC products were reasonably priced—higher than *no name* items, but below expensive branded products from companies such as Kraft, Procter & Gamble, and Unilever—premium, yet affordable.

"People love the PC brand," states Gordon, "and we've added a new dimension that makes it even stronger—our PC black label collection." He explains that Loblaw noted a trend with *foodies*—food enthusiasts, inspired by TV food shows, celebrity chefs, food writers, and cookbooks—who bought regular fare at supermarkets, but shopped at high-end gourmet stores such as Whole Foods and Pusateri's for high-quality specialty items. Gordon tells us, "These people are on the leading edge of food—it's important to their lives. They enjoy new flavours, experiment with ingredients, try new cooking techniques, and enthusiastically talk about food. PC black label was created to satisfy their inner foodie."

The PC black label line launched in late 2011 with a number of challenges for Gordon, a veteran food marketer with experience managing new product innovation at Loblaw, as well as marketing at Frito-Lay, Unilever, and Robin Hood Multifoods. The overriding issue was how to launch a line of exceptional specialty products without cannibalizing the flagship President's Choice brand, which stands for quality and discovery. The products needed to stand alone and also strengthen the overall equity of the President's Choice brand.

Chapter Outline:

Let's look at the details to see how experts successfully launched and continue to manage this sub-brand today:

Branding PC black label is positioned as a line of gourmet food products that inspires foodies with culinary choices that excite taste buds without paying specialty-store prices. Every item in the line has an exceptional *wow* factor, as in "Wow, I have never tasted anything like that!" or "Wow, this is the best I have ever tasted!" Its positioning is captured by its slogan, "Satisfy your inner foodie."

The new line was created under the trusted, high-quality President's Choice brand name, known for food exploration and discovery. However, PC black label also needed to differentiate itself and so the sub-brand PC black label collection was crafted and precautions were taken to ensure all products in the line were of *exceptional* quality—a step beyond the *premium* quality of President's Choice. In this way, the point of difference was clear.

Packaging An eye-catching package was designed to carry the brand. It was sleek and elegant and included outstanding photography from top Canadian photographer Michael Mahovlich, commissioned to create authentic images from a product's place of origin. Products from the south of Italy, for example, have authentic images on their packaging from that location, as do products from other countries such as Switzerland, France, and Scotland. The black packaging stands out in the store environment and makes a clear statement of exceptional quality.

Product line Products in the PC black label line were inspired by food trends, specialty-store products, and items discovered at European and North American fancy food shows. Suppliers were challenged to submit ideas that met the line's positioning, and eventually a line of exceptional products evolved. These were capped at 400 items to ensure adequate in-store presence while presenting an air of exclusivity.

The line consists of exceptional products such as unusual oils and vinegars, as well as exotic spice blends and exquisite sauces and marinades, not to mention aged cheeses, fancy mustards, and regionally renowned jams. There is a harissa spice blend for Moroccan dishes, a jalapeño and passion fruit salsa for snacking, and a bacon marmalade to accompany aged cheddar. There are also exceptional pastas and crackers that encourage less adventurous consumers to explore the collection.

Price PC black label products are priced to compete with specialty-store products, ranging from $1.99 to $24.99, depending on the item. Consistent with PC's image as a high-quality/good-value proposition, items are pegged at approximately 20 percent below comparative specialty-store products.

PC black label products are never discounted but instead are promoted to increase awareness and trial. Products are seasonally grouped and merchandized at retail with oversized placards that use striking photography to send consumers to the PC black label website for recipes and inspiration.

Place The PC black label line is sold across Canada at all Loblaw Companies' stores, with the exception of No Frills, which has limited foodie appeal. Loblaw stores include Loblaws, Fortinos, IGA, No Frills, Extra Foods, Real Canadian Superstore, Zehrs, Atlantic Superstore, Save Easy, valu-mart, Dominion, Maxi, and Provigo.

Promotion Foodies enjoy new food experiences and like to entertain and cook while seeking to understand the scope of unusual ingredients. Trial and awareness programs were created around these insights and a launch program was designed to create connections with top influencers.

A kickoff dining event invited 50 to 60 movers and shakers in Canada's food community to a culinary extravaganza. Famous chefs, food writers, and celebrities arrived at an upscale art gallery to admire a photography exhibit of Michael Mahovlich's stunning black and white images that also adorned PC black label packaging. Meanwhile, Canada's best-known chefs (commissioned to create a tasting menu based on the products) plated a four-course menu that showcased the PC black label line. Word-of-mouth buzz was immediately created and numerous articles appeared in the media.

In-store awareness was an additional focus, with centrally located freestanding displays situated at retail to attract attention. On-shelf merchandising units were also designed to group complementary PC black label products together and to make a splash of colour that could not be missed. End-aisle displays were also scheduled to provide focal points where people expected them. Finally, a top-quality PC black label recipe book was merchandized near displays and sold at $9.99 to help consumers explore the PC black label collection through delicious recipes such as bacon and apple cheese bites, truffled mushroom tartine, and pistachio and honey brittle.

Digital support was central to PC black label's success. Oversized in-store signage pointed consumers to an online destination for PC black label at **www.presidentschoice.ca**, where product information, beautiful food photography, recipes, tips, and videos invited consumers to explore and discover the brand.

"It's a winner," states Gordon. "There's intrigue and the products are moving. People love them but we need to boost trial, as some consumers are unsure how to use the products—once they know, they keep coming back—people are even having black label parties!" PC black label is now increasing trial and awareness with an advertising campaign that airs on the Food Network and with an outreach to food bloggers that profiles the collection.

As a parting thought, Gordon emphasizes that what he likes about PC black label is that it demonstrates the creation of a sub-brand and how each element of the marketing mix differentiates and uniquely positions the line so that it simultaneously borrows from the parent brand while also giving back to make it even stronger. You can see more about President's Choice products online at **www. presidentschoice.ca**. Thank you, Ian Gordon.[1]

reality CHECK ✓

As you read Chapter 7, refer back to this vignette on PC black label to answer the following questions:

- What type of brand is PC black label: a manufacturer's brand, a private label brand, or a generic brand?
- Review the elements of a good brand name and discuss the strength of the PC black label brand name in the food industry.

Types of Products

LO 1 The essence of marketing lies in managing and developing products and brands such as PC black label that meet the needs of their target markets. In marketing, a **product** is a good, a service, or an idea, consisting of a bundle of tangible and intangible attributes. Tangible attributes include physical characteristics such as colour or sweetness, and intangible attributes include those aspects of a product that can't be "touched," such as how cooking with a PC black label product may make you feel.

Products can include a variety of things in either the online or offline environment. In the offline environment, examples of products are breakfast cereals, cars, or the emergency services provided by a hospital. In the online world, examples are search engines such as Google, micro-blogging sites such as Twitter, online gaming websites from Microsoft, and software websites such as McAfee, which sells downloadable software to protect computers from viruses and spyware. It is important to realize that with the widespread use of the Internet today, even offline products develop a strong web presence, realizing that the first point of contact for consumers with a brand is often online at a company website or on its Facebook page. The PC black label collection creates synergy between its offline and online retail presence with a distinct area on the President's Choice website, complete with inspiring photography, recipes, videos, and product information.

Products are divided into three main categories: (1) non-durable goods, (2) durable goods, and (3) services. A **non-durable good** is an item that does not last and that is consumed only once, or for a limited number of times. Examples of non-durable goods are food products and fuel. A **durable good** is a product that lasts for an extended period of time and encompasses items such as appliances, automobiles, and stereo equipment. A **service** is an intangible activity, benefit, or satisfaction, such as banking, conducting an online search, using cloud-based software to create websites or blogs, using online analytics platforms such as Google Analytics, visiting a doctor, taking a vacation, going to a movie, or taking a course. Canada has a strong service-based economy with services accounting for approximately 72 to 75 percent of its gross domestic product (GDP).[2]

In the service industry, it is useful to distinguish between a company's primary service and its supplementary services. A bank's primary service may be providing bank accounts,

product
A good, a service, or an idea consisting of tangible and intangible features

non-durable good
An item that does not last and is consumed only once, or for a limited number of times

durable good
An item that lasts over an extended number of uses

service
An intangible activity, benefit, or satisfaction

but it also offers supplementary services such as parking, ABMs, foreign exchange transactions, and monthly statements. Supplementary services often allow products to differentiate their offerings from the competition while also adding value to consumers. Common supplementary services for products can include product updates, free delivery, and payment terms as well as complimentary consultations, order-taking, and sales assistance. Companies also offer free trials, online support services, complimentary webinars, and elements such as free subscriptions as added-value services to its customers. PC black label collection's supplementary services include free online recipes.

It is important to note that consumers rate customer service levels as highly relevant to their purchases. A Consumerology report on customer service highlighted that Canadians consider customer service as an important consideration when purchasing a product. Topping the list is product quality, followed by value, durability, necessity, and convenience. Customer service then kicks in, rated sixth and considered more important than brand name, environmental factors, ethical approaches, and being made in Canada. Specifically, the report notes that 56 percent of Canadians stopped using a product or brand due to poor customer service, with almost two-thirds of these unhappy customers sharing this experience with others. Importantly, the research reveals that 49 percent of Canadians will avoid a product or store that they have never tried due to the poor customer service experience of a friend or family member.[3]

Many products cannot be defined as "pure goods" or "pure services" but are in fact hybrids—a combination of goods and services to offer a more competitive product to consumers. Many goods are augmented with intangible services such as warranties, websites, and online support. Services also use goods to ensure a more complete offering to consumers. A college or university, for example, provides educational services, but it also provides graduates with hard-copy diplomas and transcripts. Importantly, the online environment is giving rise to new **virtual services** that exist *only* online and have no form of physical person-to-person

interaction or tangible component. Social media sites, online gaming sites, and online analytics are examples of virtual services.

As companies look at what they bring to market, there is a range from the tangible to the intangible, or goods-dominant to service-dominant. This is defined as the **service continuum** and is demonstrated in Figure 7–1 where the services continuum for a number of products is shown. Online analytics, nursing, and going to the theatre are examples of intangible, service-dominant activities, while salt, neckties, and dog food are goods-dominant. Fast-food restaurants are in the middle of the service continuum, offering a combination of both tangible and intangible goods and services; the food is the tangible good, while the courtesy, cleanliness, speed, and convenience are the intangible services threy provide.

The Uniqueness of Services

There are four unique elements to services: intangibility, inconsistency, inseparability, and inventory. These four elements are referred to as the *four Is of services*.

Intangibility Services are intangible; that is, for the most part, they cannot be held, touched, or seen before a purchase. In contrast, before purchasing a physical good, a consumer can touch a box of laundry detergent, kick a car tire, or sample a new beverage. Services tend to be more performance-oriented and, as experiences, cannot generally be tried before

Figure 7–1
The service continuum

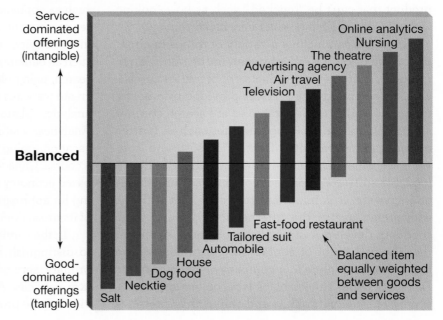

Infographic

Customer Service Report
Bensimon Byrne

Consumerology 17: Customer Service

The Consumerology Report is a quarterly survey focused on Canadian concerns, interests, and trends.

Bensimon Byrne is a Canadian advertising agency founded in 1993. It commissions the Consumerology Report from the Gandalf Group every quarter.

56% of Canadians have stopped using a product/brand due to poor customer service.

Bensimon
on what this study means to marketers.

Get it wrong, and it's a brand killer. But get it right, and the upside—and potential for business growth—is huge.

The average consumer has the power to influence the brand preference and purchase decisions of everyone in his/her network and beyond.

Source: Press release, "Consumerology: Customer service has the power to make or break a brand," Bensimon Byrne, September 6, 2012.

The fine print

49% avoid a product or store they have never tried due to the poor customer service experience of a friend or family member.

Only **31%** of unhappy customers will tell the service provider of their sub-par experience.

58% of unhappy customers will share their bad customer experience with other consumers.

Friendly and polite associates (online and in person) are considered the most important customer service factor.

Source: Bensimon Byrne, "The Bensimon Byrne Consumerology Report: Consumerology 17: Customer service," August 2012, accessed at http://consumerology.ca/assets/Consumerology_August_2012/Customer_Service_August_2012_RevisedSEPT27.pdf.

What type of product is being marketed by the Royal Ontario Museum?

purchase. Free trials are often provided to overcome this drawback. To help consumers assess and compare services, it is important for marketers to demonstrate the benefits of using the service. Techniques that are frequently used are online video testimonials or demonstrations that show the quality of a service. Online services often provide potential customers with free limited online trials or time-sensitive downloads as a means of testing out the service. A successful approach that is prompting consumers to try new services (and goods) are the local "deal-of-the-day" e-mail campaigns from e-mail discount marketers such as Groupon, LivingSocial, or **Dealicious.ca**.

Inconsistency Developing, pricing, promoting, and delivering services is challenging because the quality of a service is dependent on the people who provide it, and it can therefore differ in consistency. Quality can vary with each person's capabilities, experience, motivation, and even personality. One day, the Toronto Blue Jays baseball team may have a great game, and then the next day, it may have a very disappointing showing. Similarly, you may have a very successful stay at one location of a Travelodge hotel, but then have a terrible experience at another due to the varying standards of the staff at its locations. Companies try to overcome the inconsistent delivery of services by training employees on how to deliver a consistent quality experience.

Online products are often able to overcome issues of inconsistency through standardized software, consistent website interfaces, and reliable Internet servers that limit service disruptions. However, when new online services are launched, they often cannot keep up with demand and therefore provide subpar services to users. This was the case with the micro-blogging site Twitter, which was often overcapacity during its early days.

Inseparability A third difference between services and goods, and related to problems of consistency, is inseparability. In most cases, the consumer cannot (and does not) separate the deliverer of the service from the service itself. For example, in the non-profit industry, the quality of an educational institution may be high, but if a student has difficulty interacting with certain instructors, the student may not be satisfied with the educational experience. Similarly, if a surgeon has a poor bedside manner, this immediately reflects poorly on the hospital, which may in fact be excellent.

Inventory In many instances, the inventory of services is more complex than that of goods due to the nature of services. Inventory problems exist because services cannot necessarily be stored and accessed when in demand. This is complicated by the fact that sales forecasts may be inaccurate, warehousing of related items can be expensive, and some services may be perishable. **Perishability** arises when products cannot be stored for long periods of time for use at a later date, as in the instance of concerts where unsold tickets become lost revenue forever. As with goods, not all services are perishable. Online services can often be stored and accessed at a later date, as evident with online virus scans that can be run as needed. Similarly, online movies are often configured to be conveniently viewed on demand to suit viewers.

> *In today's marketplace, firms often combine goods and services to offer a more competitive product to consumers.*

In the service industry, issues arise due to fluctuating demand throughout the day and the difficulty in assessing the requirements needed to service customers at peak times. Idle production capacity is expensive and arises when a service is available when there is little demand. **Idle production capacity** is formally defined as a situation when the supply of a service exceeds its demand. To deal with this issue, the service industry often uses part-time employees who are paid an hourly wage and are scheduled to work shifts. This is clearly demonstrated in a grocery store setting where the number of cashiers varies depending on the time of day and day of the week. The number of cashiers at 2.30 p.m. during the week will be far fewer than the number of cashiers available at noon on a Saturday due to the number of people shopping at these times. Similarly, online customer service centres reduce the number of employees responding to inquiries during off-peak times and will often close during non-business hours and post the times when inquiries will be answered.

Product Elements

The Total Product Concept

LO² Marketers view products as having three different layers: the core product layer, the actual product layer, and the augmented product layer. The more complex and expensive the product, the more intricate the layers used to differentiate the product from the competition. Figure 7–2 shows how these layers work together.

The *core product* refers to the fundamental benefit that a consumer derives from having the product. In the case of a bicycle, the core benefit may be the transportation it provides, or the pleasure of participating in a leisurely sport. For a service such as a massage, the core benefit may be the relaxation it provides.

The *actual product* is the physical good or the service that a consumer purchases when buying a product. It includes the product's branding, design, and features. With a bicycle, a consumer purchases a piece of equipment, directly associated with a brand name, design, and features. With a massage, the actual

perishability
When products cannot be stored for long periods of time to use at a later date

idle production capacity
When the supply of a service exceeds its demand

product is the massage itself and the time spent having a trained and expert massage therapist relax a client's muscles. In this instance, one may think that branding has no role to play. On the contrary, in the case of a massage, the brand becomes either the name of the massage therapist or the organization providing massage-therapy services.

Finally, the *augmented product* refers to the additional features and attributes that accompany a product, such as a warranty, a service contract, delivery options, installation assistance, or a website used to distinguish the product from competitive offerings. For a bicycle, this may be a warranty, while for a massage there may in fact be no augmented product layer. Generally, augmented product layers exist for more expensive purchases such as cars, computers, or TVs, and are not part of a simple purchase such as a chocolate bar or a newspaper.

It is important to note that for online products it is more difficult to differentiate the core, actual, and augmented components of the product. Take, for example, the social network Facebook: What are the components of its core, actual, and augmented product? Refer to Figure 7–2 and determine these elements.

Packaging can differentiate a brand.

Packaging and Labelling

Marketers need to pay close attention to a product's packaging and labelling, as well as the logos and websites it uses to communicate its brand positioning to consumers. For many products, the packaging and labels are an integral part of the product, and for other products (such as online products), there may in fact be no packaging at all, and their websites become a form of packaging, central to communicating the brand elements to consumers.

Packages and labels also provide many functional benefits, such as protection or facilitating product usage. In addition, they serve as platforms from which to communicate brand imagery, establish brand logos, and provide detailed product information and offers. Take, for example, Grolsch beer, which intentionally uses a traditional swing-top bottle cap to differentiate the beer from competing products. This bottle cap also provides a reliable seal to the beer bottle. The beer bottle is also purposefully made from thick, antiquated green glass with the brand name moulded into the glass to give it that authentic old-fashioned feel and to communicate its heritage and brand positioning.

Figure 7–2
The total product concept applied to a bicycle

THE TOTAL PRODUCT CONCEPT		
Layer	**Description**	**Example (Bicycle)**
Core product	What the product does for the customer—the benefits derived from using the product	Provides transportation and leisure activity
Actual product	The physical good or service, including the branding, design, and features that the consumer receives	A branded product, with a metal frame, two wheels, and a seat
Augmented product	Additional features or benefits that accompany the product, such as a warranty, a service contract, delivery options, installation, or a website	Warranty or repair contract

Packaging and labelling decisions are of paramount importance to a product's success, and marketers work hard to ensure that designs clearly reflect a product's positioning, its brand equity, and its image, which have all been nurtured over time. Changes to existing packaging and label designs need to be approached with caution to ensure that consumers are not confused and do not feel that their favourite brands have been altered. Let's look at the recent redesign of the logo for the clothing retailer Gap that appears on its store signage, shopping bags, and labels to demonstrate this point. In 2010, Gap decided to redesign its logo to give it a more contemporary look and feel. However, the unveiling of the new logo prompted a barrage of negative comments on the Internet and in the media. Within a week, Gap swiftly changed its decision and reverted back to the old logo that people had come to love and respect.[4]

Many products only exist online, such as many online publications, online software, and cloud-based services. For these products, their websites become a form of packaging and are used to provide functionality and to communicate the brand's positioning and relevance. Similar to packaging, marketers must work to ensure websites are always up-to-date, appeal to their consumers, and contain the latest product and company information. In this manner, website designs are refreshed every few years to ensure that they are current, reflect the brand's positioning, and take advantage of the latest technology and design trends.

Brand names, logos, and packaging reflect a brand's image.

We look to **LivingLou.com**, one of Canada's top food blogs, to see how an online brand can successfully evolve and be refreshed to meet changes in online design. For **LivingLou.com**, its website is a form of packaging, an initial interface that communicates with consumers. The importance of this interface is heightened in the online world where the decision to stay on a website is made in three to five seconds.

LivingLou.com is positioned as a youthful and authentic online source of simple, delicious, mouth-watering recipes. It differs from other food blogs in its youthful appeal and stunning photography. Its success is echoed by public relations firm Hill+Knowlton, which rates it as one of Canada's top 10 food blogs, and by the Institute of the Psychology of Eating, which ranked it internationally as one of the top 100 food blogs for 2012 and 2013.

Although **LivingLou.com** was a popular destination for foodies and people looking for original recipes, the brand wanted to refresh its image in line with website design trends and to boost traffic. In addition, **LivingLou.com** needed to differentiate its brand from other food websites by emphasizing its beautiful photography, which reflected its high-quality, delicious recipes. It noted the impact of Pinterest on website design and saw newly designed websites giving more prominence to visual interfaces and images. This was an opportunity to showcase its photography.

BEFORE

AFTER

A refreshed logo and website redesign boosted website traffic and engagement for **LivingLou.com**.

The LivingLou logo was its starting point. The logo was refreshed to include the brand's colour palette of pale greens and purples and to incorporate a tag line to emphasize its authenticity. The result was a more modern logo with a polished feel that did not lose sight of its original roots.

The LivingLou website was then redesigned to include the new logo, the new colour palette, and a highly visual interface. The website was finessed by replacing text-based lists with visual categories that pulled from the website's photography. Instead of seeing one image on the home page, two stunning photographs pointed to the latest posts, while thumbnail images encouraged website visitors to browse the site and read more. Social media buttons that linked to Twitter, Pinterest, Instagram, and Google+ were given a more prominent position in the redesign, and an image of the website author was included to emphasize its authenticity. The result was a decidedly more appealing website that saw significant increases in traffic and website engagement.

Similar to **LivingLou.com**, companies are constantly reviewing the competitive landscape and making adjustments to ensure that their connections with consumers remain strong. The Bay, a fixture on the Canadian retail scene since 1670, changed its logo and store signs in 2013 to more clearly reflect its repositioning as a high-end retailer and to strengthen its Canadian heritage as the Hudson's Bay Company—all in view of U.S. retail giants Target and Nordstrom entering the Canadian marketplace. Details are captured in the Marketing NewsFlash, "Refresh—Hudson's Bay."

Product Lines and Product Mixes

LO 3 Marketers often manage groups of products that are closely related under an umbrella product line and brand name. A **product line** is a group of similar products with the same product and brand name. It is directed to the same general target market and is marketed together as one line to retailers and consumers. A product line can be identified through its common product name, brand name, and package design. Examples of a product line can be seen by examining Gatorade's G Series that was launched in Canada in 2011. The G Series consists of three related product lines: the Gatorade Prime line, designed for athletes prior to exercise; the Gatorade Perform line for consumption during exercise; and the Gatorade Recover line, which helps athletes recover after exercise. All three lines are marketed under the G Series flagship brand name. They are differentiated by the benefit of the specific line as well as its name and packaging. The Prime line comes in two flavours, orange and fruit punch, which are formulated to be used 15 minutes before an exercise session. The Perform line comes in several flavours and is designed to deliver hydration during exercise. The Recover line is created for use within 30 minutes after completing exercise and comes in mixed berry and lemon-lime orange flavours. These three product lines are clearly differentiated by their benefits and packaging.

Looking to the service industry, online and offline products in this sector can also be grouped into product lines. The services offered by the Hospital for Sick Children, for example, can be grouped into three main

Gatorade's G-Series consists of three product lines that come in a variety of flavours.

product line
A group of similar products with the same product and brand name that is directed at the same general target market and is marketed together

Refresh—Hudson's Bay

I f your brand was a household name and part of Canadian history since 1670, what would you do if U.S. retail giants Target and Nordstrom set up shop in your neighbourhood? Would you strengthen your brand, pull on its heritage, spruce up your stores, and strengthen your offering? That is exactly what Hudson's Bay did.

In March 2013, the same week Target opened its doors in Canada, Hudson's Bay revealed its new logo, a stylish and classy coat of arms with the words HUDSON'S BAY front and centre, replacing the dated and less elegant THE BAY logo that was introduced in 1965. Gone was the dusty, stylized yellow font, pushed aside by its heritage to represent the more upscale Hudson's Bay.

Over the last few years, Hudson's Bay had become a destination where fashionable, high-quality brands could be found, allowing consumers to easily browse and find the latest quality styles in branded nooks of high-quality merchandise. Hudson's Bay had become a house of brands, almost a mall within a mall, and was slated for nationwide renovations to reflect its positioning and to effectively compete in the new retail landscape. Flagship stores in Vancouver, Montreal, and Toronto undertook major facelifts with the inclusion or renovation of The Room, an in-store destination for exclusive up-and-coming Canadian and international designers. Areas were also set aside to flaunt Olympic branded merchandise and the Hudson's Bay Signature Collection of its trademarked blue, yellow, red, green, and white striped products, including its well-known blankets, as well as coats, T-shirts, teddy bears, bags, and umbrellas, just to name a few. Other stores refreshed their decor and ambience to reflect this high-quality, fashionable, and classy Canadian icon.

Project Adventure was launched in the summer of 2013 to cement Hudson's Bay branding with consumers and to pull on its Canadian heritage. A Hudson's Bay–branded RV was home to four 20-something men, decked out in Hudson's Bay Signature Collection clothes (often wrapped in Hudson's Bay blankets), who crossed Canada in a 49-city tour. They documented their adventures travelling from the East Coast to the West Coast through online videos, Facebook posts, Twitter updates, Vine snippets, Instagram photos, and Pinterest images of beautiful Canadian landscapes, towns, and cities.

All the while, Hudson's Bay strengthened its business through a revamped e-commerce site, competitive retail promotions, and the announcement that it was purchasing U.S. retailer Saks Inc. and bringing it to Canada![5]

BEFORE

A rebranding for The Bay repositioned the brand as a traditional high-quality Canadian icon.

AFTER

HUDSON'S BAY

INCORPORATED 2 MAY 1670

Questions

1. Review Hudson's Bay new logo and identify its strength and weakness in light of its retail positioning?

2. Visit a Hudson's Bay store and its website at **www.thebay.com** to experience the brand and discuss what elements are used to reflect the brand's positioning.

product lines based on usage: in-patient hospital care, outpatient physician services, and medical research. Looking to the digital arena, the product lines for a digital brand such as Google can also be grouped into product lines based on usage. For example, one of Google's product lines consists of advertising services for businesses that wish to reach consumers through online ads. This product line currently includes products bucketed together under the Google brand name, including Google AdWords, Google AdSense, and Google Analytics.

Product lines are part of a company's product mix. **Product mix** refers to the array of product lines marketed by a company. While one can slice and analyze a company's product line in many different ways depending on the depth of analysis required, it is often helpful to drill down into the product mix by looking at the product categories and product lines within these categories. An example can be seen in Figure 7–3, where a snapshot of the Kellogg's brand product mix shows that Kellogg's is not just a breakfast cereal but a brand that now extends into new areas such as morning beverages, chips, crisps, and breakfast sandwiches.

The product mix for Kellogg's is captured by aggregating its products into six main categories: (1) beverages; (2) cereals; (3) crackers and chips; (4) snack bars and crisps; (5) breakfast pastries, waffles, and sandwiches; and (6) cooking ingredients. A more in-depth analysis can then be conducted to pinpoint the specific products within each line, such as the five different varieties of Kellogg's All-Bran bars or the three different Kellogg's Special K Flatbread morning sandwiches.

Figure 7–3 also shows Kellogg's **product width** and **product depth**. The *width* of a company's product mix refers to the number of different categories offered by the company. The *depth* of a company's product mix refers to the variety of product lines and products sold within its product categories, groups, and lines.

Procter & Gamble uses this same concept of multiple product lines to market a wide selection of products to consumers. In the laundry and fabric care category, for instance, Procter & Gamble markets at least six different product lines: Tide, Ivory, Gain, Era, Dreft, and Cheer. Each product line carries many different product sizes, varieties, and formats. The Tide website at **www.tide.com** illustrates the wide range of products offered under the umbrella Tide brand and the extensive product depth within most categories. Visit the Procter & Gamble website at **www.pg.com** and examine its product mix, product width, and product depth.

ask yourself

1. *Explain the difference between non-durable goods, durable goods, and services.*

2. *What elements make services unique?*

3. *What is included in the total product concept?*

The product mix for Kellogg's products consists of Kellogg's morning beverages, cereals, chips, crisps, pastries, waffles, breakfast sandwiches, and cooking ingredients.

Figure 7–3
Reviewing the Kellogg's brand product mix

PRODUCT MIX AND PRODUCT DEPTH FOR KELLOGG'S

← Width of Product Mix →

↕ Depth of Product Mix

KELLOGG'S PRODUCT MIX					
Beverages	**Cereals**	**Crackers and Chips**	**Snack Bars and Crisps**	**Breakfast Pastries, Waffles, and Sandwiches**	**Cooking Ingredients**
• Special K Morning Shake (3)	• All-Bran (5) • Corn Flakes (1) • Corn Pops (2) • Crispix (1) • Froot Loops (2) • Frosted Flakes (1) • Just Right (1) • Krave (2) • Mini-Wheats (9) • Müslix (5) • Rice Krispies (3) • Special K (8) • Two Scoops Raisin Bran (1) • Vector (1)	• Special K Cracker Chips (5) • Special K Popcorn Chips (2)	• All-Bran Bars (5) • Nutri-Grain Bars (9) • Rice Krispies Squares (3) • Rice Krispies Granola Bars (1) • Special K Bars (3) • Special K Granola Bars (5) • Special K Fruit Crisps (4) • Vector Energy Bars (4)	• Eggo Pancakes (2) • Eggo Waffles (9) • Pop-Tarts Toaster Pastries (8) • Special K Flatbread Morning Sandwiches (3)	• Corn Flake Crumbs (1)

The number of flavour varieties is noted in brackets.

Consumer and Business Products

consumer products Products purchased for their personal use by the ultimate consumer

business products Products that are purchased either to run a business or to be used as a component in another product or service

convenience products Items purchased frequently that are inexpensive and require minimum risk and shopping effort

shopping products Items that require comparison-shopping between different brands and an investment of shopping time

LO 4 Products are classified as either consumer or business products depending on their usage. **Consumer products** are purchased by the ultimate consumer for their personal use while **business products** (also called *industrial goods* or *organizational products*) are purchased either to run a business or to be used as a component in another product or service. In many instances, the differences are obvious: Oil of Olay face moisturizer and the Ontario Science Centre are examples of consumer products, while a cement mixing truck is primarily a business product. Some products, however, are both consumer and business products depending on their usage. A Canon printer can be classified as a consumer product when purchased as a final product for personal use, or it can be classified as a business product when purchased by an organization to help run a business. Consumer and business products consist of numerous types of products, as explained below.

Consumer Products

Convenience, shopping, specialty, and unsought products are the four different types of consumer products that exist in the market. These items differ in terms of the amount of effort that a consumer puts into making a purchase, and how often the items are purchased.

Convenience products are inexpensive items that a consumer purchases frequently with minimal shopping effort. If the product does not meet expectations, there is little risk because the product is inexpensive and easy to purchase. Examples of convenience products are bread, newspapers, or items purchased from a vending machine. **Shopping products** are items for which the consumer comparison-shops, assessing the attributes and prices of different products and brands. These types of products require a greater investment of shopping time, are more expensive than convenience products, and require a greater assurance of purchase satisfaction. Examples are jeans, books, and items such as TVs.

Rolex watches are specialty products.

Specialty products are items that require considerable time and effort to purchase. They tend to be more-expensive branded products in a category that are needed for special occasions. They include specialty brands and require high purchase satisfaction. Examples of specialty products include a Rolex watch, taking a cruise with Norwegian Cruise Lines, or buying specialty one-of-a-kind cupcakes from the Cupcake Shoppe for Valentine's Day. **Unsought products** are items that the consumer either does not know about or is not interested in purchasing. Examples of unsought products may be diapers for a person who does not have a baby or epilepsy medication for a person who does not suffer seizures.

The manner in which a consumer product is classified depends on the individual. One person may view a camera as a shopping product and quickly visit a couple of stores before deciding on a brand to purchase. A friend, however, may view a camera as a specialty product, looking for a high-end camera for her photography hobby. This may result in extensive shopping at high-end camera shops for a specific type of camera. It is important to understand that although many products are clearly separated into one category or another, people in varying stages of life will classify products differently. Figure 7–4 generally compares the different types of consumer products and how their marketing mixes may vary depending on the type of product.

Business Products

A major characteristic of business products is that their sales are often directly related to the sales of products with which they are associated. For example, if consumers' demand for Ford cars increases, the company's demand for industrial-grade paint and car stereo equipment, both business products, will also increase. Business products may be classified as production goods and services, or support goods and services.

Production Goods and Services Items used in the manufacturing process that become part of the final product are production goods and services. These can include raw materials, such as grain or lumber, or component parts, such as door hinges used by Ford in its car doors.

Support Goods and Services The second class of business products is support goods and services, which are items used to assist in producing other goods and services. Support goods and services can include installations, accessory equipment, supplies, and the provision of services such as the delivery of component parts or the provision of training programs for new component parts.

- *Installations* consist of buildings and fixed equipment. Industrial buyers purchase these assets through sales representatives who often submit competitive bids.

The Cupcake Shoppe sells an assortment of specialty products, including cupcakes and cakes, for a treat or special occasion.

Figure 7–4
Classification of consumer products

TYPE OF CONSUMER PRODUCT

	CONVENIENCE	SHOPPING	SPECIALTY	UNSOUGHT
Purchase behaviour of consumers	• Frequent purchases • Little time and effort spent shopping	• Occasional purchases • Needs to comparison-shop	• Infrequent purchases • Needs extensive time to search and purchase	• Very infrequent purchases • Some comparison shopping
Brand loyalty of consumers	• Aware of brand, but will accept substitutes	• Prefers specific brands, but will accept substitutes	• Very brand loyal • Will not accept substitutes	• Will accept substitutes
Product examples	• Newspapers, chocolate bars, soft drinks, and bread	• Cameras, TVs, briefcases, and clothing	• Wedding dresses, luxury items such as Rolex watches	• Insurance products, such as life and disability insurance
Price	• Inexpensive	• Fairly expensive	• Usually very expensive	• Varies
Place (distribution)	• Widespread; many outlets	• Large number of outlets	• Very limited distribution	• Often limited distribution
Promotion (communication)	• Emphasis on price, availability, and awareness	• Emphasis on differentiation from competitors	• Emphasis on uniqueness of brand and status	• Emphasis on awareness

- *Accessory equipment* includes tools and office equipment and is usually purchased in small-order sizes by buyers. As a result, sellers of industrial accessories use distributors to contact and deal directly with a large number of buyers.

- *Supplies* are the business equivalent of consumer convenience goods and consist of products that are used continually, such as stationery, paper clips, and brooms. These are purchased with little effort, as price and delivery are the key considerations.

- *Services* are intangible activities needed to assist a business in its operations and in producing its goods and services. This category can include transportation services, maintenance and repair services, and advisory services such as tax or legal counsel. This may also include online analytics to monitor website traffic, the creation of a website to support a business, or the use of an e-mail database to send out newsletters.

ask yourself

1. *What is the difference between consumer products and business products?*

2. *What are the four main types of consumer products?*

3. *What are the classifications of business products?*

Branding

LO⁵ A **brand** is a name or phrase uniquely given by a company to identify its product(s) and to distinguish the product(s) from the competition. These names are often created in tandem with associated brand-marks or logos, designed to visually represent the brand to consumers and to build brand recognition. Over the long term, the support that goes into marketing a brand results in strong brand associations for the brand and a certain degree of consumer loyalty to the product. This creates **brand equity**, which is formally described as the value of a brand that results from the favourable exposure, interactions, associations, and experiences that consumers have with a brand over time.

Developing and nurturing a brand is an important factor in the marketing of a product. This involves creating a new brand name or selecting a name that already exists in a company's arsenal. A brand also needs to be supported with marketing activity, starting with creating its logo as well as designing its packaging (if relevant) and website, and developing new products and promotions to engage users and bring revenues and profits into the company. Research needs to be conducted periodically to help determine trends and requirements, while metrics and analytics are needed to determine success and areas of improvement.

Starting in 2012, Ipsos Reid annually conducts its *Most Influential Brands* study, which looks at five key variables that "define, determine and ultimately drive brand influence. In order of importance, these dimensions are: Trustworthy, Engagement, Leading Edge, Corporate Citizenship, and Presence."[6] Ipsos conducts its own research and, with input from advertising agencies and associations as well as consumers, determines this annual influential brand study and rankings.

Let's look at these brand elements in more detail:

- **Trustworthiness.** This is considered the most important element for a brand. It encompasses the consistently dependable image that consumers have for a brand and fosters their ongoing confidence in recommending it to others.

- **Engagement.** Brands that engage consumers encourage brand loyalty by creating interactions, so consumers can learn more about a brand and ultimately share it with others.

- **Leading edge.** Brands that stand out are often unique, innovative, and forward thinking. Their approach tends to be edgy and somewhat different and stands as a benchmark for other brands.

- **Corporate citizenship.** Brands that are caring have the ability to connect with consumers by instilling pride. These brands are involved in community initiatives that focus on the environment and the social well-being of society.

- **Presence.** Brands need to have a high profile with consumers and stand out from the crowd. Through their marketing, they are often top-of-mind with consumers and are used regularly in consumers' daily lives. These brands make a statement about themselves and the people that use them.

The top 10 most influential brands in Canada in 2013 were as follows:

1. Google
2. Facebook
3. Microsoft
4. Apple
5. Visa
6. Tim Hortons
7. YouTube
8. President's Choice
9. Walmart
10. MasterCard

> *Brand equity is the result of considerable marketing investment and needs to be protected.*

Eight of these brands are U.S.-born brands that have become international successes, with Google topping the list for two consecutive years. Ipsos tells us that Google is considered an innovative brand that has transformed the way we look for information. It has become a highly trusted source for reliable online information and entertainment. Its products are leading edge and innovative and include (among others) Google Search, Google Chrome, Gmail, Google+, Google Earth, and Google Analytics. In this way, Google has become a highly relevant brand for consumers and is integrated into their daily lives. Google is a brand that is uncomplicated, intuitive, easy to use, and, in most instances, free.

Tim Hortons topped the list of Canadian brands in Ipsos' *Most Influential Brands* study. Ipsos tells us that Tim Hortons is a highly trusted brand that people find relatable. It instills people with a sense of Canadian pride that consumers find inspiring. Trust, authenticity,

brand
A name or phrase uniquely given by a company to a product to distinguish it from the competition

brand equity
The value of a brand that results from the favourable exposure, interactions, associations, and experiences that consumers have with a brand over time

▶ *"Brands need to be nurtured and respond to evolving consumer needs and competitive challenges while remaining true to their core DNA."*

—Ian Gordon, senior vice president, Loblaw Companies Ltd.

▶ Video
Tim
Hortons

and good corporate citizenship also set Tim Hortons apart, with many consumers aware of its Tim Horton Children's Foundation and other community programs. Tim Hortons tells us that its customers have functional and emotional connections with the brand. Functionally, Tim Hortons provides consumers with a trusted level of freshness, quality, and service, while emotionally, consumers relate to Tim Hortons through its communication programs that make emotional connections with consumers and set it apart as a neighbourhood brand that consistently lives up to its promise.

Brands are classified as either individual brands or family brands, depending on whether the name has been extended to cover more than one product category. An **individual brand** is when a company uses a brand name solely for a specific product category. Two examples are the Yop brand name, used by Ultima Foods Inc. only for this milk-based beverage, and Twitter, used solely for the micro-blogging social networking site.

A **family brand** is when a company uses a brand name to cover a number of different product categories. The brand name Crest, although initially used only for toothpaste, is now used by Procter & Gamble for toothpaste, dental floss, mouthwash, and teeth-whitening products. Crest extended the use of the brand name and used it to market other products; we call this a **brand extension**. President's Choice is another family brand that was introduced by Loblaw for its premium store-branded items ranging from soups and sauces, to toiletries and small kitchen appliances, just to name a few. Over the years, the President's Choice (PC) brand has been extended into a number of sub-brands, such as PC Blue Menu for healthier products, PC Organics

for organic products, PC Green for environmentally friendly items, and the PC black label collection for upscale, gourmet specialty-food items. A **sub-brand** uses the family brand name as well as its own brand name and identity so that it can take on the strengths of the parent brand but also differentiate itself.

The advantage of using an established family brand name for new goods or services is that brand equity is quickly transferred from the flagship brand to the new product, thus saving the company the marketing funds needed to build up this brand equity from scratch. A disadvantage of using a family branding approach is that if the new product does not live up to the image of the flagship brand, or does not share in its values, then the brand equity built up over time can be eroded for all products under this family brand name.

individual brand
When a company uses a brand name solely for a specific product category

family brand
When a company uses a brand name to cover a number of different product categories

brand extension
When new goods or services are introduced under an existing flagship brand name

sub-brand
A brand that uses the family brand name as well as its own brand name and identity so that it can take on the strengths of the parent brand but also differentiate itself

A family branding approach from Crest.

Protecting Brands—Patents, Trademarks, and Copyright

Brand equity is the result of considerable marketing investment and needs to be protected. Patents, copyrights, and trademarks are used to protect products, brands, and processes from unethical infringement and illegal use. **Patents** are used to legally protect new technologies, unique processes, or specific formulations from other companies that may wish to benefit from their use. A patent is a right, granted by government, to exclude others from making, using, or selling an invention.[7] In Canada, patents currently protect owners for a period of 20 years after the patent was filed, providing that maintenance fees are paid during this time. After 20 years, this patent then becomes available to the market.

Copyrights are used to legally protect the written word, a sound-recording, or a form of communication from being copied by others. It covers music, literature, and performances, and can include slogans.

Trademarks are used by people or organizations to protect brand images, names, and designs from usage by others.[8] Trademarks are limited to a period of 15 years from the date of registration, but can be renewed by their owners to maintain their investment. A trademark legally protects a brand name and its related logo, colours, fonts, and various combinations that exist for use in a particular category and in a part of the world. If trademarks are to be used in foreign countries, the owner is wise to register an international application. Companies hold separate trademarks for each version of a brand name and its associated graphics and logo. For a brand to be trademarked, a company first conducts a trademark search to ensure that the trademark is not already owned by another company. If the trademark is available and not challenged, then the brand and its associated design and logos can be legally registered in the company name. Care must be taken to renew these trademarks as required to ensure that they do not expire. Information on trademarks in Canada can be found at the Canadian Intellectual Property Office website at **www.cipo.ic.gc.ca**. Here you can easily conduct a search of the trademark database and its registered trademarks. The Canadian Intellectual Property Office provides information on which trademarks are registered, when they were registered, and who owns the trademark.

Scrabble protected its trademark from online knock-offs.

One of the best examples of trademark infringement in the digital age relates to Scrabble and the online game Scrabulous created illegally as a knock-off of the popular board game Scrabble. Scrabble was trademarked in 1948 with trademark ownership residing with Hasbro in Canada and the U.S. and with Mattel elsewhere. It is sold in 29 different languages. Scrabulous, created by Rajat and Jayant Agarwalla and their software development company J Software, was made available in 2007 as a Facebook application with no prior discussions with the Scrabble owners. Enjoying over 500,000 online players per day, the game became one of Facebook's most popular applications.

Hasbro and Mattel soon sent cease-and-desist letters to Facebook and the Agarwalla brothers for copyright and trademark infringement of their Scrabble name and game. Facebook, staying neutral in the controversy, passed correspondence over to the developers of Scrabulous, who insisted Scrabulous did not infringe on the Scrabble® trademarks or copyrights. They claimed that Scrabble had become a generic term for word games and that the Scrabble board, rules, and design were not protected under copyright protection law.

Unable to easily resolve the issue, Hasbro eventually launched its own Scrabble Facebook application and then filed a lawsuit against the two brothers and the J Software company. A few months later, facing the probable loss of the pending lawsuit, the Agarwalla brothers took down the Scrabulous application in Canada and the U.S., which caused an uproar among fans of the online game. Meanwhile, legally, the courts in Delhi, India, found the term Scrabulous was too close to the original Scrabble trademark, and the brothers were told to cease using the Scrabulous name.[9]

patents
Used to legally protect new technologies, unique processes, or formulations from usage by other companies

copyrights
Used to legally protect the written word, a sound-recording, or a form of communication from being copied by others

trademarks
Used to legally protect brand images, names, and designs from usage by others

> "*The degree of attachment that consumers have to a particular brand tells a marketer about their brand loyalty.*"

Loyalty runs deep

BMO ♠ Financial Group

PROUD SPONSOR AND LOYAL FAN OF TORONTO FC

In sports marketing, brand loyalty is a primary marketing objective.

Another good example of a trademark issue can be seen with the Apple iPad name. The iPad, launched by Apple in 2010, ran into various issues when attempting to trademark the international rights to the brand name iPad. Trademark searches showed that trademark applications for the iPad existed from 2003 and 2009 for Japanese tech company Fijitsu, which sold a product under this name in the U.S. In addition, Chinese company Proview had owned the trademark for China since 2000. The Focus on Ethics box "iPad Trademark Issues" explains how these issues were resolved.

Brand Loyalty

Just how much do consumers like and insist on a particular brand? Will they choose another if their first choice is not available, or will they insist on finding their brand? These are brand loyalty decisions. The degree of attachment that consumers have to a particular brand tells a marketer about their brand loyalty. **Brand loyalty** refers to the favourable attitudes that a consumer has over time toward a brand that results in varying levels of purchase insistence and commitment to the brand. Brand loyalty varies by product and from person to person. Marketers strive to have highly committed, brand-loyal consumers as this helps insulate their brand from competitive marketing practices.

Consumers that readily switch brands depending on price generally have very little brand loyalty. Consumers with a stronger brand attachment may have some brand loyalty but may easily brand-switch if the brand is not available. A brand's most loyal consumers will insist on purchasing their brand of choice and will postpone a purchase if the brand is not available. Most people have different degrees of brand loyalty depending on the product, brand, or category. Consider the products you purchase, and determine where you have strong brand loyalty and where you have very little.

Many large, well-entrenched brands are often marketed around the world and have become **global brands**. Global brands tend to enjoy strong brand equity due to their hefty marketing budgets and well-recognized trademarks. Starting in 2000, Interbrand has conducted an annual study on global brands with publicly available financial records. To be included

Interbrand's Top 10 Global Brands

Ranking	Brand	Brand Value ($ millions)
1	Apple	98,316
2	Google	93,291
3	Coca-Cola	79,213
4	IBM	78,808
5	Microsoft	59,546
6	GE	46,947
7	McDonald's	41,992
8	Samsung	39,610
9	Intel	37,257
10	Toyota	35,346

Source: "Best Global Brands 2013," Interbrand, accessed October 2013, at http://www.interbrand.com/en/best-global-brands/2013/top-100-list-view.aspx.

iPad Trademark Issues

The launch of the Apple iPad seemed smooth sailing in April 2010, but behind the scenes, lawyers, court cases, and trademark requests punctuated the buzz. Trademarks and patents are often disputed in the tech world, and this high-profile new product from Apple was no exception.

Prior to launch, as close as March 2010, Japanese tech company Fijitsu claimed ownership of the iPad trademark with its Fujitsu iPad, a Wi-Fi- and Bluetooth-enabled handheld mobile device sold mainly in the U.S. for $2,000. The device was used by retailers at the shelf level to check prices and inventory on-the-go. The company had pending trademark applications for the Fijitsu iPad dating back to 2003 and 2009 and challenged Apple on ownership of

the iPad name. Negotiations resulted in Fujitsu officially assigning the iPad trademark to Apple on March 17, 2010, just a few short weeks before the Apple iPad went on sale; monetary transactions were not disclosed.

Fast forward to 2012 when Apple settled an iPad trademark dispute with Chinese company Proview Technology, which initially had owned the iPad trademark name in China since 2000. In 2009, Apple (under a different company name) had proactively purchased the iPad trademark from Proview Technology for $55,000 but according to Proview had not purchased the trademark from all of Proview's subsidiaries. This resulted

in the disputed ownership of the iPad trademark in China. In July 2012, a Chinese court mediated an out-of-court $60 million settlement to be paid by Apple to Proview Technology to resolve the trademark issue and to turn the iPad trademark in China over to Apple.[10]

The Apple iPad had to overcome trademark disputes.

Questions

1. Was it ethical for Apple to purchase the Proview iPad trademark under the guise of another company? Why do you think Apple followed this approach?

2. Was it ethical for Proview to initially sign its trademark rights to the iPad name over to Apple when it did not involve all its subsidiaries?

---

in this brand study, a brand needs to meet certain criteria: 30 percent of its revenues need to be from outside its home region; it must be present in three continents and in emerging markets; it must have publicly available financial records; it must have future profit growth expectations; and it must have a public profile and awareness levels outside its own marketplace. Interbrand's *Best Global Brands 2013* identified Apple, Google, Coca-Coca, IBM, and Microsoft as the top five global brands in the world. Its ratings look specifically at a brand's competitive strength, the role it plays in the purchase decision, and its financial performance.[11]

Brand Personality

Marketers recognize that brands offer more than product recognition and identification. Successful brands take on a **brand personality** of their own—a set of human characteristics associated with the brand.[12] Research shows that consumers often associate particular personality traits with certain brands and prefer those whose personalities are most appealing. For example, Pepsi-Cola is seen as being youthful in spirit and exciting, while Dr Pepper is viewed as being unique and non-conformist. Through marketing practices, and

brand personality
A set of human characteristics associated with a brand

particularly advertising campaigns, marketers work to associate brands with specific personality traits and to help consumers make emotional connections with their brands. Often, marketers of highly recognized brands, realizing that consumers screen out advertising messages, turn to product placement agencies to help integrate products and brands into movies and TV shows with similar associations.

Brand Names

When we say Xbox, iPad, Virgin Mobile, Porsche, Pepsi, or Adidas, we typically do not think about how companies determined these brand names. Selecting a successful brand name can be an arduous and sometimes expensive process. Companies can spend thousands of dollars developing and testing a new brand name. Intel, for example, spent US$60,000 developing the Pentium brand name for its microchips.[13] Here are some key points to consider when determining a good brand name:

- **The name should suggest the product benefits.** This is demonstrated by brand names such as Easy-Off (oven cleaner) and *American Idol* (TV show), both of which clearly describe the product's benefits. Care should be taken to review how the brand name translates into other languages to avoid future pitfalls. The 7Up brand name, for example, roughly translates into "death through drinking" in a local dialect in Shanghai, China, which clearly does not positively influence sales in this region.[14]

- **The name should be memorable, distinctive, and positive.** A number of new brands have been introduced over the last few years with distinctive brand names such as iPad, Xbox, Twitter, and Google. All these names are very distinctive and were entirely unique and unknown when first introduced. Today, these brand names have high awareness in Canada and enjoy very strong brand recognition.

- **The name should fit the company or product image.** The brand names iPad, Xbox, Twitter, and Google all reflect the products they portray. iPad suggests something high-tech and flat; Xbox is a strong, crisp brand name associated with a video console (box) and the forbidden nature of something new and on the edge (X); Twitter expresses the short conversations (twittering) that can occur on this platform of 140 characters; and Google is a fun, casual word associated with creativity (doodle). Google is actually derived from the intentional misspelling of the word "googol," which refers to the

digit "1" followed by 100 zeros, a representation of the amount of data the search engine manages.[15]

- **The name should have the ability to be legally protected.** A brand name must be "trademarkable" to protect a company's investment. If the brand name is too generic, or the trademark is owned by another company, the proposed brand name cannot be trademarked. For example, you cannot trademark the name "Bottled Water," as it is not unique enough to warrant a trademark. Increasingly, brand names also need a corresponding website address, which can complicate name selection. An interesting example existed for a teenager in Victoria, British Columbia, named Mike Rowe who set up the website **www. MikeRoweSoft.com** to promote his web-design business. The software giant Microsoft demanded that Mike give up the domain name because it violated the Microsoft trademark. This generated negative publicity for Microsoft, which backed down and reached a settlement with Mike Rowe, who renamed his site **www.MikeRoweForums.com**.[16]

- **The name should be simple.** The brand names iPad, Xbox, Twitter, and Google are all simple names to spell and remember. This makes them more memorable and helps build brand equity.

ask yourself

1. *In what instances are patents, copyrights, and trademarks used?*

2. *Explain the concepts of brand equity and brand loyalty.*

3. *What are the components of a good brand name?*

Types of Brands

LO 6 There are three types of brands: (1) manufacturer's brands, (2) private label brands, and (3) generic brands. This is easily understood by looking at the pharmaceutical industry and over-the counter pain medications.

A **manufacturer's brand** is one that is owned and produced by the manufacturer. Tylenol is the manufacturer's brand created by Johnson & Johnson and sold to drugstores throughout Canada. In turn, drugstores display the product on their shelves and sell it at retail to consumers. Johnson & Johnson invested considerable time and effort into researching, creating, and marketing this brand. When initially launched, this product was protected by a patent, but as mentioned earlier, a patent is restricted to a limited number of years, currently 20 years in Canada. Once a patent expires—and this patent has—other manufacturers can produce a similar product. Regular Strength Tylenol is currently sold at drugstores at a cost of approximately $13.99 for 100 tablets.

A **private label brand**, otherwise known as a store brand, is owned by a retailer that contracts its manufacturing out to major suppliers and then sells the product at its own retail stores, under its own store-brand name. Private label products are very popular in Canada, with 84 percent of consumers agreeing that private label products have mainstream appeal.[17] A private label brand provides a retailer with the opportunity to offer its customers a less expensive alternative to a manufacturer's brand. Private label products are generally sold at lower prices than manufacturers' brands because these store brands do not have to pay high listing fees and they have lower marketing costs.

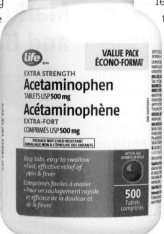

What type of brand is "Life"?

An example of a private label product in the over-the-counter pain reliever category is Shoppers Drug Mart's Life Brand Acetaminophen. Life Brand is one of Shoppers Drug Mart's private label brands used to compete directly with other over-the-counter pharmaceutical products. In this instance, Life Brand Acetaminophen competes directly with Tylenol, whose main ingredient is also acetaminophen. The current retail price for 100 tablets of Life Brand Regular Strength Acetaminophen is approximately $9.99 for 100 tablets, considerably less than the comparable Tylenol product priced at $13.99.

A **generic brand** has no branding at all and is sometimes produced as a cheap alternative to a manufacturer's brand and to a private label branded product. A generic brand typically highlights the main product ingredient as a means of selling the product, with its main point of difference being price. Although a less expensive alternative to other branded products, a generic product lacks the brand equity and product recognition that is enjoyed by both a manufacturer's brand and branded

private label brand
Otherwise known as a store brand, a brand owned by a retailer that contracts its manufacturing out to major suppliers, and then sells the product at its own retail stores, under its own store-brand name

generic brand
A product that has no branding and is produced as a cheap alternative to a manufacturer's brand and to branded private label products

Canadian Fast Facts—Private Label Products

Annual sales	$11.6 billion
Shopping trips where private label is purchased	41%
Shopping basket: # of private label items	9.1 items on average
Private label consumer profile	Smaller, older, higher-income households
Average household $ spent on private label	$833 per year
Average price differential	28% below regular-priced national brands 19% below sale prices of national brands
Retail sector importance	23.5% of grocery $ sales 16.7% of drugstore $ sales

Source: Report "Canadian private label: The value alternative 2011," Nielsen, accessed October 2013 at www.nielsen.com/us/en/reports/2012/private-label-outlook--us-and-canada.html and www.nielsen.com/content/dam/corporate/us/en/reports-downloads/2012-Reports/Canadian-Private-Label-White-Paper.pdf.

private label products. In the pharmaceutical industry, many generic versions of prescription medications whose patents have expired are created and sold to pharmacies by generic drug manufacturer Apotex Inc., Canada's largest generic drug manufacturer, which exports to 115 countries around the world and has approximately 5,000 employees in Canada. When a prescription is filled, often these cheaper generic versions manufactured by Apotex are substituted by pharmacists for the branded medicines prescribed. This saves governments, insurance companies, and consumers substantial sums of money.

In 2010, Apotex, which follows a socially responsible approach to business, contributed close to $2 million in earthquake relief medications to people in Haiti. It also recently addressed the ethical dilemma of third-world countries being unable to afford life-saving HIV/AIDS drugs. Apotex applied through the Canadian Access to Medicines Regime (CAMR) to sell cheaper generic versions of patented HIV/AIDS drugs to Rwanda. Apotex was awarded the contract and now sells Apo-TriAvir at cost to Rwanda where the medication is priced at 19.5 cents (US) per pill versus a comparable patented drug regime at $6.[18]

Outside of the pharmaceutical area, generic products can often be found at various retail outlets such as dollar stores where select products with no associated brand names are sold. Dollarama stores, for instance, sell plastic clogs for $2 per pair that are direct knockoffs of Crocs but have absolutely no branding at all.

A Practical Look at Marketing Products and Brands

LO 7 So how are products and brands actually managed by marketers? A marketer is responsible for marketing products and brands in order to bring revenues or profits into an organization. To do this, marketers create annual marketing plans for the upcoming year to formally identify marketing activities and to establish funding requirements and budgets that will help generate profits and revenue streams for the company. These marketing plans review each element of the marketing mix and itemize when marketing programs will be in place, as well as their expected impact on sales, revenues, and profits. Any changes that relate to the product, its branding, and its product positioning will be clearly identified in the marketing plan, including elements such as new product launches, package changes, website redesigns, new sizes, and market research requirements.

Despite the existence of a marketing plan, the world of marketing is dynamic and ever-changing, and therefore, throughout the year, marketers constantly evaluate and assess product needs in light of competitive and market changes and against marketing plan expectations. Marketers then recommend changes that are needed to help reach planned revenue and profit targets.

Managing a product requires a marketer to wear many hats. On an ongoing basis, a marketer needs to analyze daily sales numbers, be up-to-speed on marketing analytics, review profit targets, be alerted to changes in product costs, be in contact with the salesforce, and understand changes in the

ask yourself

1. What are the advantages and disadvantages of using a family brand rather than an individual brand to launch a new product?

2. Explain the difference between a private label and a manufacturer's brand.

3. What type of price differences would you expect to see for a manufacturer's brand, a private label brand, and a generic brand for products within the same category?

selling environment. A marketer must also be aware of market research insights, understand consumer interests, and work with a team to create meaningful marketing programs. Examples of how a marketer practically manages products are as follows: If a food-product marketer plans to introduce a new plastic container, but realizes that there is a consumer movement away from plastic due to health concerns, this marketer would most likely recommend against this planned program. Similarly, a marketer of an SUV may decide to delay the introduction of a new model due to the high price of gasoline and consumers' movement toward more fuel-efficient vehicles. In addition, if a product's profits are under pressure due to a sudden increase in the cost of manufacturing, then an expensive advertising campaign may be delayed or modified to reduce expenditures in an attempt to reach short-term profit targets. If a competitor unexpectedly reduces prices, then marketers will need to determine whether their product pricing needs to be adjusted and how this may impact profits.

In addition to managing these types of issues that arise as the year unfolds, a marketer must look to the future of the brand to ensure its relevancy to consumers. Product marketers manage the current competitive environment while also working on future programs and products for the upcoming years. In marketing, nothing remains static, and currently three main categories of interest are surfacing as areas where marketers need to be involved.

First, we see marketers in Canada and around the world investing in sustainable and environmentally friendly initiatives that meet company goals and consumer expectations in these areas. A second category of interest for Canadian marketers is the increasingly multicultural composition of our society. Marketers look to ensure that their products are relevant to these cultural groups and constantly examine the need to communicate their programs in a variety of languages. A third area of interest for marketers in Canada is the impact of digital technology on consumer interactions and how this is changing the path-to-purchase. Marketers conduct research in this area and create new marketing programs that reach consumers on digital platforms.

In practical terms, the managing of a product requires marketers to intimately understand the dynamics of the marketplace and to quickly assess the financial impact of recommendations that are needed to boost the business. Marketers must quickly react to market situations and recommend necessary changes to planned programs. Managing a product is not a static event but a process that is constantly changing and requires marketers to use their analytical skills, creativity, and strategic thinking to keep the business moving forward. In all instances, being true to a product's positioning, meeting consumer needs, and implementing competitive marketing programs helps ensure that products and brands are well-managed and have longevity.

> *A marketer is responsible for marketing products and brands to bring revenue into an organization.*

Summary...just the facts

LO 1 ● A product is a term used in marketing to designate non-durable goods, durable goods, and services that are marketed. Some products are a combination of both goods and services.

● There are four unique elements to services: intangibility, inconsistency, inseparability, and inventory. These four elements are referred to as the four Is of services.

LO 2 ● The total product concept includes the core product, the actual product, and the augmented product.

LO 3 ● Product mix is the combination of product lines managed by a company. The width of the product mix refers to the number of different categories offered by the company. The depth of the product mix refers to the number of product groups and product lines offered by a company within each category.

LO 4 ● Consumer products are classified into convenience products, shopping products, specialty products, and unsought products.

● Business products are classified into production or support goods. Production goods include raw materials and components parts, while support goods include installations, accessory equipment, supplies, and services.

LO 5 ● A brand is a name or phrase used to identify a product and to distinguish it from the competition. Brand equity is the result of the positive experiences consumers have with the brand over time and results in brand loyalty.

● Trademarks are used to legally protect brands, patents are used to protect unique processes, and copyrights are used to protect the written or spoken word.

LO 6 ● Brands are categorized as manufacturer's brands, private label brands, and generic brands.

● Companies may restrict a brand name for use with a single product line, thus using an individual brand, or may extend a brand name to encompass a number of different product categories, resulting in the creation of a family brand and, in some instances, sub-brands.

LO 7 ● A marketer is responsible for marketing products and brands in order to bring revenues or profits into an organization.

● Marketers create annual marketing plans to formally identify marketing programs, budget requirements, and forecasted revenues and profits for the brands and products they manage.

● Throughout the year, marketers constantly evaluate and assess product and brand performance against marketing plan benchmarks and recommend changes to programs that may be needed to help reach targets.

Key Terms and Concepts...a refresher

brand
brand equity
brand extension
brand loyalty
brand personality
business products
consumer products
convenience products
copyrights
durable good
family brand

generic brand
global brands
idle production capacity
individual brand
manufacturer's brand
non-durable good
patents
perishability
private label brand
product
product depth

product line
product mix
product width
service
service continuum
shopping products
specialty products
sub-brand
trademarks
unsought products
virtual services

Hands-on...apply your knowledge

Branding Assignment President's Choice extended its brand to encompass the black label collection of products. Carefully review the opening vignette on the PC black label collection, and gather additional information by visiting a Loblaws grocery store and navigating to its website at **www.presidentschoice.ca**. Outline the advantages and disadvantages of extending the President's Choice brand name into the black label collection and determine the strengths and weaknesses of the PC black label sub-brand, including its name, logo, packaging, and website.

Chapter Vignette...reminder

This chapter's opening vignette reviews how Loblaw Companies Ltd. launched a line of exceptional specialty products under the President's Choice brand, which strengthened the overall PC brand without cannibalizing its sales. Answer the Reality Check questions at the end of the vignette by carefully reading the chapter sections on brand names and types of brands.

Video Clip...questions

Review the video *Most Influential Brands Study—Tim Hortons* from the CONNECT website to get an insight into the Tim Hortons brand and how it has evolved over time. Answer the following questions:

▶ Video Tim Hortons

- What is the brand promise that Tim Hortons makes to consumers?
- Why are Tim Hortons' customers brand loyal?
- What changes is the brand facing as it moves forward?
- What are the five drivers of brand influence noted in the video?

Infographic...data analysis

Review the infographic that details the customer service report from *Consumerology #17: Customer Service*. Navigate to its website at **http://consumerology.ca**, select a Consumerology report from the current year, and create a new infographic to summarize its findings. Write a short analysis of your findings. (*Infographic tip:* Use Microsoft Excel and Word to create charts and place them in a single PowerPoint slide to combine the visuals.)

connect | **SMARTBOOK** | **LEARNSMART**

For more information on the resources available from McGraw-Hill Ryerson, go to **www.mheducation.ca/he/solutions**.

Chapter 8

new product development

This chapter looks at new products and how they are developed, launched, and managed over time. Morgan Matthews, owner and senior partner at the Canadian product design firm Impact Machine, provides insight into this important area and takes us inside the development of the innovative TACKLA QuikBlade Shift251 hockey skate, showing us how the road to product development is not easy, but dynamic and takes many twist and turns.

Impact Machine is a seasoned product design company that provides clients with intricate services for new product development. It focuses on sports products and promotional items, and takes a product from its initial research stage through to concept development and engineering. It also provides consulting services for production and supply chain management and develops sales and marketing strategies. Specifically, Impact Machine conceptualizes and engineers products and designs packaging, retail displays, trade exhibits, and promotional items. It also provides outsource relationship management services to assist with factory and material sourcing, supply chain management, and factory and buyer relations. Products in its roster include, among others, promotional items for Labatt Breweries and Alliance Films, the Roberto Alomar Baseball Pro Series Baseball Glove, a line of hockey equipment for Winnwell Clean Hockey, protective hockey gear for the Forzani Group/Canadian Tire VIC hockey line, Sonic Shield items for DR Hockey, the Vault anti-concussion hockey helmet, and the TACKLA QuikBlade Shift251 hockey skate.

Impact Machine emphasizes that new products succeed only if they sell and make a profit. "We start at the end and work backwards, creating a 360-degree view of the product to foresee hiccups," explains Matthews. "We look at consumers and what they want in a product. We analyze competitive offerings to understand the dynamics of the market. We focus on retail realities, such as how a product is displayed, to avoid problems, and we look at the business side to make sure costs are in line with the market." In this manner, Impact Machine looks at price points and profit margins to ensure that products are profitable at each stage in the supply chain, and considers the realities of manufacturing, all before detailed concepts are developed.

Impact Machine launched the TACKLA QuikBlade Shift251 hockey skate with Canadian Tire in August 2012 as the first of its kind on the market. The TACKLA QuikBlade Shift251 is an innovative hockey skate that comes with a set of replaceable

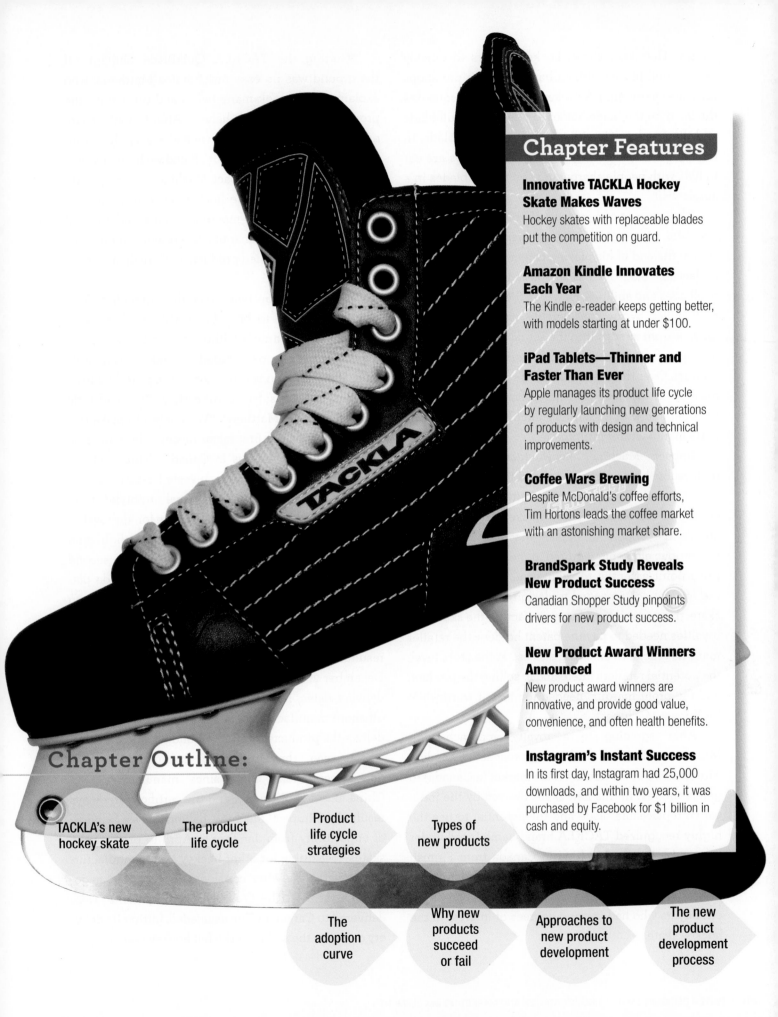

Chapter Features

Innovative TACKLA Hockey Skate Makes Waves
Hockey skates with replaceable blades put the competition on guard.

Amazon Kindle Innovates Each Year
The Kindle e-reader keeps getting better, with models starting at under $100.

iPad Tablets—Thinner and Faster Than Ever
Apple manages its product life cycle by regularly launching new generations of products with design and technical improvements.

Coffee Wars Brewing
Despite McDonald's coffee efforts, Tim Hortons leads the coffee market with an astonishing market share.

BrandSpark Study Reveals New Product Success
Canadian Shopper Study pinpoints drivers for new product success.

New Product Award Winners Announced
New product award winners are innovative, and provide good value, convenience, and often health benefits.

Instagram's Instant Success
In its first day, Instagram had 25,000 downloads, and within two years, it was purchased by Facebook for $1 billion in cash and equity.

Chapter Outline:

- TACKLA's new hockey skate
- The product life cycle
- Product life cycle strategies
- Types of new products
- The adoption curve
- Why new products succeed or fail
- Approaches to new product development
- The new product development process

blades. The skate allows hockey players to quickly replace dull blades without having to visit pro shops for skate sharpening. A hockey player merely squeezes the latch on the blade holder to release the dull blade and then replaces it with an alternate sharp blade. In this manner, visits to skate sharpening shops are cut in half, with people sharpening two sets of blades in a single visit.

The concept of a replaceable blade started in the late '70s with ex-NHL defenceman Rick Hampton, who at the end of his playing career came up with the replaceable blade idea as an option for hockey players of all ages and abilities. However, the idea did not take root, stalled by the considerable expertise needed to move it from an idea into the actual design, engineering, manufacturing, and selling stages of a marketable product. Over the years, Hampton's business dealings resulted in ownership of the replaceable blade (trigger operated with a rotational latch) residing with car parts manufacturer Multimatic.

Impact Machine, knowledgeable about the replaceable blade concept, entered the picture in 2011 and approached and negotiated with the patent holders to use the blade in a new hockey skate. Using its 360-degree approach, Impact Machine determined the various elements required in the project: the retail price point essential to selling the skate in Canada; the upfront costs needed to design and engineer the skate; the costs required to manufacture the skate; the royalties needed to pay the patent holders; the retailer margins crucial to ensuring success at the store level; the potential retailers interested in selling the product; and the profit margins needed to make it worthwhile for Impact Machine.

After agreeing to a royalty approach with Multimatic, Impact Machine approached Canadian Tire (leaders in the hockey skate market in Canada) to gauge interest in this new skate. Swayed by the innovative replaceable blade and the potential to use the highly recognized TACKLA brand name (used under licence by Impact Machine in Canada from Finnish company TACKLA), Canadian Tire signed on, but only after considerable back and forth between different buyers who had varying degrees of interest in the hockey skate.

"Getting the TACKLA QuikBlade Shift251 off the ground was no easy task," states Matthews, who explains that it took many twists and turns until the product finally hit retail shelves. "After Canadian Tire announced it was on board, we had a very short window of a few months to pull it off and we hit many hurdles along the way." Impact Machine had to quickly design and engineer the hockey skate in seven different sizes, determine manufacturing standards and specs for each, source manufacturers and components, and deliver the finished products to Canadian Tire on time and on budget!

The first major twist was that Canadian Tire needed the skate to be safety-certified. There were no business guarantees without the certification, and Impact Machine now needed to sink considerable time, effort, and money into conducting product tests to obtain official safety certifications. "We had little choice," explains Matthews. "We wanted to make this work but we hit our first major hiccup—there were no certification labs for this in Canada." Three months later, after Impact Machine invested resources into building a testing lab in China, final prototypes were certified and shipped to Canadian Tire for approval.

Canadian Tire gave them the green light and things were ready to move ahead. Here the second twist surfaced. This time, Multimatic, the blade patent holder, decided to put the product through its own testing procedures, a standard practice in the car parts industry where it conducted most of its business. This resulted in further delays until finally, at the end of December 2011, four months before required product delivery dates, Impact Machine was ready to secure off-shore manufacturing in China that could reliably deliver the products on spec, on budget, and on time.

However, the window for manufacturing was now exceptionally short since manufacturing in China closes in February, and the certification delays resulted in Impact Machine having only a window of opportunity from January to April to produce the skates—peak time for other hockey skate manufacturers. Nonetheless, after considerable work and negotiations, the TACKLA QuikBlade Shift251 skates were delivered to Canadian Tire as needed, hitting its delivery dates for the sell-in of the fall hockey season.

In its first year, the TACKLA QuickBlade Shift251 hockey skate disrupted the market with its innovative hockey skate. However, in 2013, a competitive replaceable-blade hockey skate was introduced to the market, adding to the continuous twists and turns that exist in the road to new product development.

▶ Video
TACKLA

You can read more about Impact Machine and its approach to product development on its website at **www.impactmachine.com**. Be sure to follow the future success of the TACKLA skate in the business press and stay apprised of any further twists and turns that may evolve. Thank you, Morgan Matthews.[1]

reality CHECK ✓

As you read Chapter 8, refer back to the TACKLA QuikBlade Shift251 opening vignette to answer the following questions:

- What type of innovation is the TACKLA QuikBlade Shift251: a minor innovation, a continuous innovation, or a radical innovation?
- What stage in the product life cycle is the TACKLA QuikBlade Shift251: introductory, growth, maturity, or decline?
- Considering the adoption curve (Figure 8–6), which group of consumers is TACKLA targeting with its new hockey skate: (1) innovators, (2) the early majority, (3) the late majority, or (4) laggards?

> *The length of each stage in the product life cycle depends on the product, the category, and how it is being marketed.*

The Product Life Cycle

LO 1 The concept of the **product life cycle** describes the stages that a new product goes through, starting with its initial introduction into the marketplace and moving through to stages of growth, maturity, and decline. The concept of the product life cycle is used by many marketers to help manage a product from its initial launch through to its eventual decline. Marketers try to manage products so that they do not reach the decline stage. Instead, products are revamped, retooled, and repositioned to meet evolving consumer needs and competitive challenges.

Products in the online environment follow this same product life cycle approach, often experiencing shorter cycles that require frequent boosts to stay competitive. We see this frequently with social media sites such as Facebook, Pinterest, and Twitter that frequently add new features for its users, as well as new tools for marketers. Twitter, for example, was launched in 2006 and has updated its homepage interface every year since 2008. Its logo has been refreshed three times, and new features periodically added. For example, hashtags were added in 2007, promoted tweets and accounts were added in 2010, official mobile apps and geo-location features were added in 2011, and video snips through Vine were added in 2013, all to keep it relevant and to help monetize the business. In November 2013, Twitter became a publicly traded company with a valuation of $24.9 billion and over 200 million active users.[2] As this brand continues to grow and evolve, we can expect continued updates and new features to keep it relevant.

Figure 8–1 traces the curve of a product life cycle by plotting a product's sales and profits over time. The curves change in response to the competitive environment and to consumers' demand for the innovation.

Initially, during the introduction stage, a product enjoys minimal sales, profits, and competition, but then over time, propelled by marketing programs and product demand, a product moves into a period of rapid growth and profit increases. As the competition becomes more severe, consumers are presented with competitive products, which cause a product's sales and profits to flatten out and eventually, if not addressed by a marketer, decline. The length of each stage in the product life cycle

> **product life cycle**
> The stages that a new product goes through, starting with introduction and evolving into growth, maturity, and decline

Figure 8–1
Product life cycle

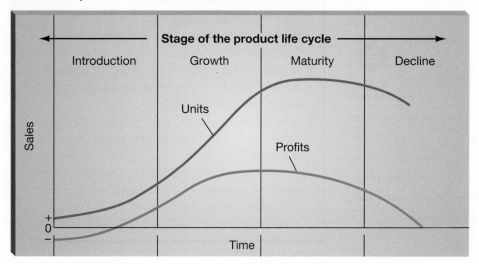

Stage of the product life cycle

| Introduction | Growth | Maturity | Decline |

Sales

Units

Profits

+
0
−

Time

depends on the product, the category, and how it is being marketed.

We look to the music player business of Sony to see an example of how marketers use the product life cycle to innovate and stay relevant to the market. As a pioneer of new technology, in the '80s, Sony partnered with Philips to be first to market with the digital CDs and CD players that replaced audio tapes and vinyl records. At that point, its innovation plan looked five years into the future, mapping the sequential introduction of CD players for automobiles, CD technology for jukeboxes, and the portable CD Walkman player for people on the go.[3] Today, Sony uses this same approach to managing its product life cycles, adjusting technology and innovating with gadgets and software that are better suited to changing listening habits. Portable CD players have long gone, replaced by MP3 players that are now in the decline stage. The Walkman brand has now morphed into the Walkman app that allows users to access music and uses social media integration for sharing favourite tunes with others. Sony has also developed its Music Unlimited and Video Unlimited apps that allow users to easily access its content in the music and entertainment industry on mobile devices. Sony also integrates its music capabilities into its smartphones, smart watches, smart TVs, and tablets.[4]

A more detailed example of how products are marketed through their life cycles can be seen in the e-reader category. Amazon launched its e-reader, the Kindle, in 2007, and it has changed the product's features, pricing, and marketing over time to stay relevant and competitive against new category entries such as the iPad, the Nook, and the Kobo (see Figure 8–2). In 2007, the first-generation Kindle hit the market at a price of $399, with a six-inch screen, and a capacity for 200 non-illustrated books. As the market became more competitive and with the popularity of tablets, Kindle was challenged to continuously innovate. Upgraded Kindles that are faster and thinner, and have greater storage capacity have been introduced each year since 2009. In 2013, the sixth-generation Kindle was introduced. It now comes in seven different models, has Wi-Fi or 3G capability, can access thousands of books, and is priced from $69 to $89 for its basic model and up to $399 for the Kindle Fire, an 8.9-inch colour tablet.[5]

Mass advertising for the Kindle was unheard of during its introductory stage in 2007. At this introductory point, specifically online ads generated demand on the Amazon website and popularity spread through word of mouth. During the Kindle's 2010–2011 growth phase, the Kindle modified its approach and started to advertise on TV networks such as CNN to reach a wider audience of interested consumers. Competitive TV spots showed how the screen had no glare (unlike tablets) and emphasized its low price of $139. During the Kindle's maturity stage (2011–2013 and beyond),

Amazon's Kindle introduces new features and models to keep it relevant and competitive.

Figure 8–2
Kindle product life cycle

AMAZON.COM'S KINDLE—MANAGING THE PRODUCT LIFE CYCLE (PLC)			
Product	**Product Description**	**Stage in PLC**	**Price (US$)**
2007: 1st Generation • Kindle	• 1 model • 6-inch screen • Capacity up to 200 books	Introduction	• Kindle, $399
2009: 2nd Generation • Kindle 2 • Kindle DX	• 2 models • 6- or 9.7-inch screen (model dependent) • Capacity up to 1,500 books	Introduction, entering growth	• Kindle 2, $259 • Kindle DX, $489

2010: 3rd Generation
• Kindle 3 Keyboard
  Wi-Fi/3G
• Kindle DX Graphite
	• 3 models
	• Wi-Fi or 3G (model dependent)
	• 6-, 7-, or 9.7-inch screen (model dependent)
	• Slightly smaller device
	• Text-to-speech audio options
	• Includes MP3 player
	• Capacity up to 3,500 books
		Growth,
		entering maturity
			• Kindle 3,
			  $139–$189
			• Kindle DX, $379

2011: 4th Generation • Kindle 4 Keyboard Wi-Fi • Kindle Touch Wi-Fi/3G • Kindle Fire	• 4 models • Wi-Fi or 3G (model dependent) • Slightly smaller and lighter • Touch interface (model dependent) • 6- or 7-inch screen (model dependent) • Colour interface for Kindle Fire • Capacity up to 6,000 books (model dependent) • Can borrow books from libraries	Early maturity	• Kindle 4, $79–$109 • Kindle Touch, $99–$189 • Kindle Fire, $199

2012: 5th Generation
• Kindle 5
• Kindle Paperwhite Wi-Fi/3G
• Kindle Fire HD 7-inch
  Wi-Fi/3G
• Kindle Fire HD 8.9-inch
  Wi-Fi/3G
	• 7 models
	• Wi-Fi or 3G (model dependent)
	• 6-, 7-, or 8.9-inch screen (model dependent)
	• Faster and lighter
	• Built-in light (model dependent)
	• Capacity up to 6,000 books (model dependent)
		Maturity	• Kindle 5, $69–$89
			• Kindle Paperwhite,
			  $119–$199
			• Kindle Fire HD,
			  $199–$299

2013: 6th Generation
• Kindle 6
• Kindle Paperwhite 2013
  Wi-Fi/3G
• Kindle Fire HDX 7-inch
  Wi-Fi/3G
• Kindle Fire HDX 8.9-inch
  Wi-Fi/3G
	• 7 models
	• Faster
	• Improved lighting
	• Kindle Fire includes HD cameras
	• Wi-Fi or 3G (model dependent)
	• 6-, 7-, or 8.9-inch screen (model dependent)
	• Capacity up to 6,000 books (model dependent)
		Maturity	• Kindle 6, $69–$89
			• Kindle Paperwhite
			  2013, $119–$209
			• Kindle Fire HDX,
			  $154–$399

Source: Kindle 3rd generation product information accessed from the Amazon.com Kindle Store, January 2011, at www.amazon.com/dp/B002Y27P3M/?tag=gocous-20&hvadid=5729120357&ref=pd_sl_cazfqv6ny_b; Kindle 4th generation product information accessed from Amazon.com, October 2011, at www.amazon.com/gp/product/B0051QVESA; Kindle 6th generation product information accessed from Amazon.com, November 2013, at www.amazon.com/dp/B00CTUKFNQ.

new product launches used public relations to gain traction with the media, complementing this with information and videos placed on the Amazon website to clearly communicate product benefits. It also used its affiliate marketing programs to spread the word through its database of associates.

In the following sections, we look at each stage of the product life cycle in more detail to appreciate how marketers use this concept to manage their products profitably (see Figure 8–3). It is important to understand that this concept is widely used by marketers in many different ways. It is most often used to help manage

products, but it can also be used to manage brands and, in some instances, to analyze an industry in general.

Introduction Stage

The introduction stage of the product life cycle occurs when a product is first introduced to its intended target market. During this period, sales grow slowly, and profits are minimal. Low profit levels are typically the result of three things: (1) slow sales growth, (2) high research and development costs to bring the product to market, and (3) high levels of marketing spending needed to launch the new product. The marketing objective during this stage is to create consumer awareness and to stimulate trial for the new product.

This stage is characterized by little competition and a lack of consumer awareness about the product. Radical new categories or technological innovations also come with the added challenge of having to educate consumers on the existence and relevancy of the category itself. During this stage, companies often spend heavily on advertising and use other promotional tools to build awareness and trial among consumers. The other elements of the marketing mix are also carefully crafted to ensure that they are in step with the product launch and its consumers.

During the introduction stage, pricing is typically high, but there are instances when a low pricing approach is used to encourage rapid acceptance of the product. A high initial price is called a *price skimming strategy* and is used by companies to help recover research and development costs. This approach takes advantage of the price insensitivity of innovators and early adopters. If a company uses a low price to enter the market, this is referred to as a *penetration pricing strategy* and is used to encourage rapid acceptance of an innovation or to combat a competitive threat.

Distribution can often be a challenge during the introduction stage of the product life cycle because channel members may be hesitant to carry a new

> "*Distribution can often be a challenge during the introduction stage of the product life cycle because channel members may be hesitant to carry a new product that is unproven.*"

Figure 8–3
Managing the stages of the product life cycle

STAGE IN PRODUCT LIFE CYCLE	INTRODUCTION	GROWTH	MATURITY	DECLINE
Competition	Few competitors exist	More competitors enter the market	Many competitors in the market	Reduced competition, with some competitors leaving the market
General marketing objective	Awareness	Product differentiation	Brand loyalty	Product rationalization
Product	Focus on a new product or brand	Introduce more features	Ensure full product line is available and innovate with new ideas	Retain only best sellers or discontinue
Price	Use a skimming or penetration strategy	Prices are slowly reduced	Price discounts are used frequently	Very low prices
Place (distribution)	Limited distribution	Distribution is increased	Full distribution is achieved	Distribution is reduced
Promotion (communication)	Focus on building awareness with advertising	Emphasize points of difference versus the competition	Focus on pricing and sales promotion	Only minimal promotion, if any
Profit	Minimal profits, if any	Increased profits that reach their maximum	Maximized profits that level off	Decreasing and minimal profits

product that is unproven. Listing fees may also present themselves as an expensive proposition for marketers, who often experience retailers charging to recover the costs and risks of listing, shelving, and merchandising a new product in stores.

Looking at the Kindle product mentioned earlier, during its introductory stage, it underwent a continuous trickle of innovative product updates and price changes to stay relevant to its users and to build on market momentum.

Growth Stage

The growth stage of the product life cycle sees an increase in competition and a rapid rise in sales and profits. The market is flooded with competing brands that thrust a category and its products into the forefront. This results in new consumers being enticed into the category and a resultant increase in sales and profits.

In this competitive arena, marketers focus their programs on differentiating products from competitive offerings. New features are added to original designs, and product proliferation often occurs. Pricing levels are generally lowered to become more competitive and distribution increases. Promotion at this stage becomes more product-specific, with advertising playing a key role in focusing consumers toward particular brands.

We look at the Apple iPad as an example of a product that quickly leapt into the growth stage of its product life cycle, limiting its introductory stage to months rather than years. The iPad was announced to the world in a press conference in January 2010 and first sold only in the U.S. starting in April of that year. Using the hype created by its press conference that showcased the product, and by allowing people to pre-order the product, over 300,000 iPads were sold on its first day, reaching over 1 million units in its first month. Units were initially available only through the Apple retail store or its website.[6] Meanwhile, a carefully staged rollout released the iPad internationally: May 2010 saw the product roll out into Australia, Canada, France, Germany, Italy, Japan, Spain, Switzerland, and the U.K.; July 2010 saw the iPad launched in Austria, Belgium, Hong Kong, Ireland, Luxembourg, Mexico, the Netherlands, New Zealand, and Singapore; and by the end of 2010, it was also available in China and Malaysia.

In its first year, the iPad successfully launched its first-generation Wi-Fi and 3G versions, and hinted at the iPad 2, which was launched a year later in early 2011. This created further hype and momentum for the product and, no surprise, by the time the iPad 2 arrived on store shelves, the tablet market was now in its growth stage and flooded with competing gadgets such as tablet computers from HP, LG, Acer, Samsung, and more.

The iPad 2 is an example of a product that pushed itself into the growth stage of the product life cycle by creating hype for the category and satisfying pent-up product demand by including highly anticipated new features, such as video chat. To stay competitive in this growth market, the iPad refocused its advertising to be more feature-driven, and increased product availability through electronic retailers. Apple also continued to innovate and in 2012 added the iPad Mini to the line, a smaller and lighter iPad tablet with improved display and camera capabilities. In 2013, in a very competitive tablet market, Apple launched the iPad Air, a thinner and lighter tablet with greater capacity and improved features as an eventual replacement to the iPad 2. The tablet market was continuing to grow, and to fend off the looming maturity stage, Apple continued to innovate and grow the market.

> "The maturity stage of the product life cycle is characterized by a slowdown of growth."

Maturity Stage

The maturity stage of the product life cycle is characterized by a slowdown of growth in both the sales and profit areas. Competitors are well-established and fewer new consumers enter the market. Marketing focuses on gaining market share and uses pricing as a key promotional tool. This results in decreased profits for the market as a whole and also for individual products.

The maturity stage is generally the longest stage in the product life cycle, with marketers focusing efforts to ensure that the product does not go into decline. Marketers use short-term promotional tactics such as consumer promotions to encourage consumers to purchase the product. Product innovation can also become a priority as marketers try to reposition products in the market and revamp product lines to be more competitive and relevant to consumers' needs. The purpose of this renewed focus on innovation is to try to take the product back into the growth or early maturity stages of the product life cycle, as we have seen with products such as the Kindle e-reader and the Apple iPad.

Numerous well-established products are in the maturity stage of their product life cycles; examples include Heinz Ketchup, Hellmann's Mayonnaise, and Kraft Dinner. What do marketers of these products do to maintain product relevancy in these categories and to stop them from going into decline? Packaging changes, product modifications, and extended-usage approaches are often used to keep them relevant.

Let's look at some less conventional products and examine how they manage their product life cycles. Television networks and individual TV shows are also products that need to be managed. Unlike products in the food industry, these services have relatively short product life cycles and go into decline when they no longer draw large audiences. At this point, a network typically replaces the show with a new program. The risk of managing these products is relatively high, with many new shows not making it past the pilot stage and others not lasting more than a single season. This requires TV networks to constantly monitor program and station ratings and look to new products to add life to the network. TSN is an example of a successful Canadian specialty network that continually brings new programming to its viewers. TSN periodically upgrades its studios, brings in new announcers, and adds new programming from around the world to keep its product fresh and

current. Examples are the addition of Major League Soccer programming and Tour de France cycling broadcasts in 2011, the inclusion of English Premier League soccer in 2013, and supplementary broadcasts of the Olympic Winter Games in 2014.

Decline Stage

The decline stage of the product life cycle occurs when sales and profits steadily decline over time. Frequently, a product enters this stage when products become obsolete due to technological innovation or changes in consumer needs. The word-processing capability of personal computers pushed typewriters into decline, CDs replaced vinyl records in the music industry, downloadable music files are replacing CDs, DVDs replaced VHS tapes, and video-on-demand services such as Netflix and Rogers on Demand are threatening the existence of DVDs. In the TV broadcast industry, shows in the decline stage are generally discontinued, as seen with programs such as *Ugly Betty* and *Canadian Idol,* which had declining audiences. Other popular programs such as *Survivor* and *The Apprentice* manage to inject elements of newness into each season, thereby keeping the shows popular with viewers.

A company follows one of three strategies to deal with a declining product. It will either delete the product, as seen in the television entertainment industry; reinvent the product, as seen in the technology industry; or harvest the product, as sometimes seen in the food industry. Deletion is when a product is discontinued, while **harvesting** is when a company keeps the product but reduces marketing support in an attempt to reap some minor profits at this stage in the life cycle.

Shape of the Product Life Cycle

The length of a product life cycle varies according to the industry, the competition, technological innovation, and approaches to marketing the product. Television shows such as *The Apprentice* and products such as the Kindle may follow a consistent product life cycle curve as illustrated by the *generalized life cycle* shown in Figure 8–1. This consistent curve, however, does not always apply to all products. Products such as smartphones have very short product life cycles, moving from introduction to decline in only about 18 months. Other products, such as Heinz Ketchup, have extended product life cycles that have continued for years, driven by marketing approaches that keep the product relevant. Figure 8–4 shows four product life cycle curves that apply to different types of products. These products and

New sports' programming is added by TSN to refresh its product life cycle.

Figure 8–4
Alternate product life cycles

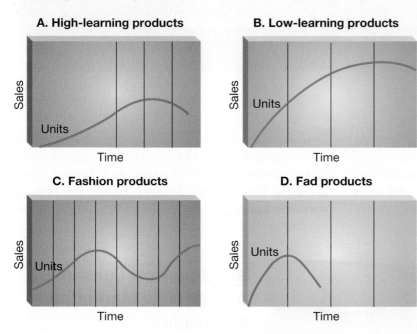

their life cycles can be categorized into four main areas: (1) high-learning products, (2) low-learning products, (3) fashion products, and (4) fad products.

A **high-learning product** is one where there is an extended introductory period due to the significant efforts required to educate customers on the usage and benefits of the product. DVDs are examples of such a product. The DVD technology required consumers to understand the advantages of the new technology, how to use it, and what to do with their old VHS players and cassettes. It also required the entertainment industry to adopt this new technology for its movie releases instead of the traditional VHS format. It took considerable time for consumers and the industry to fully adopt this technology, resulting in an extended introductory period for DVDs.

In contrast, a **low-learning product** has a short introductory stage in the product life cycle. In these instances, the benefits of purchasing these products are self-evident and very little learning is required. An example of a successful low-learning product is the Apple iPad, which required little education on behalf of consumers. Consumers trusted the Apple brand, were often familiar with its touch technology from use of the Apple iPhone, and found the interface intuitive and easy to use. Within 28 days, the iPad had sold more than a million units.[7]

The product life cycle for a **fashion product** is cyclical. The length of the cycle will vary, but it is relatively short, going from introduction to decline, generally within a two- to three-year period, only to resurface again a few years later. Life cycles for fashion products most often appear in men's and women's footware and apparel. UGG Australia boots is an interesting example of a fashion product that managed to extend its product life cycle well beyond the typical few years for a fashion product.

UGG boots, originally from rural Australia, were virtually unknown in North America until UGG Australia was purchased by Deckers Outdoor Corporation in 1995. The company repositioned the brand and started to market it in the early 2000s as a high-end, premium boot. In its introductory phase, the product was high-priced, not advertised, and available only at a few premium stores. The boots came in only a few colours and in very limited quantities. In its early stages, the company gave the boots to a few select celebrities who boosted demand; Pamela Anderson, Kate Hudson, and Jessica Simpson all wore the boots at highly publicized events. Oprah featured the boots on her show in 2000, 2003, and 2005, which immediately catapulted the boots into a rapid growth phase. By 2008, UGGs could commonly be found at regular shoe stores in a wide assortment of styles and colours. Now in its maturity stage, UGGs compete with similar sheepskin-type boots that can be found across the country.[8]

---

ask yourself

1. *What are the four stages in the product life cycle? How do they differ in terms of sales and profits?*

2. *How do high-learning and low-learning products differ?*

3. *What is the shape of the product life cycle for a smartphone in today's marketplace?*

---

high-learning product
Significant consumer education is required for these products, which have an extended introductory period

low-learning product
Little consumer education is required, resulting in a short introductory stage for the product

fashion product
The life cycle for fashion is relatively short and cyclical, going from introduction to decline within two to three years, only to resurface again a few years later

A **fad** refers to a product with a very short product life cycle. It typically experiences immediate rapid growth, followed by an equally rapid decline, with no real maturity stage at all. These products tend to be novelties. Children's toys often fall into this category.

as a soup but also to use it as an ingredient in main dish recipes. Another example is Rice Krispies, which often promotes its cereal usage as a baking ingredient for Rice Krispie Squares. Follow the links at **www.kelloggs.ca** to see the extended usage recipes used to market Rice Krispies.

Product Life Cycle Strategies

LO² It is important for a firm to manage its products through their life cycles, profitably extending and prolonging their relevance in the market. Product life cycles can be extended in a number of ways, namely by (1) targeting current users with extended usage strategies, (2) targeting new consumers through new marketing approaches, (3) revitalizing a product with product improvements and line extensions, (4) repositioning a product, (5) introducing a new product, and (6) finding new uses for a product. It is important to realize that a combination of these approaches is most often used to keep products fresh and relevant.

Kraft keeps its product lines fresh with new items and marketing campaigns.

Targeting New Consumers through New Marketing Approaches

Companies may decide that their current product is underrepresented with certain consumer groups and may see an opportunity to target these consumers. Marketers are often cautious and somewhat reluctant to follow this approach as it can be an expensive proposition that yields few results. This approach is currently followed by Kraft with its gourmet salad dressing line, Pure Kraft Refrigerated Dressings. This line is targeting a new user group—the premium-priced, high-quality gourmet salad dressing market—with top-quality, premium ingredients such as asiago cheese, extra virgin olive oil, and aged balsamic vinegar, as well as no artificial flavours, colours, or preservatives.

Targeting Current Users with Extended Usage Strategies

This approach is typically used by marketers for products with strong brand equity and a loyal consumer base. Current consumers are encouraged to consume more of the product in a variety of new ways. In the food industry, Knorr soup follows this approach by encouraging its users not only to consume the product

Revitalizing a Product with Product Improvements and Line Extensions

Product improvements and line extensions are often used by marketers to ensure that products remain competitive and address new trends in the market. Examples can be seen in the food industry, where marketers are addressing consumers' demand for smaller portion sizes, healthier foods, and greener products. PC Blue Menu, for example, introduced

fad
Novelty products with very short product life cycles that experience immediate rapid growth, followed by an equally rapid decline

marketing NewsFlash

New Products Bolster Coffee Wars

The Canadian coffee market continues to morph, boosted by a highly competitive market where consumers love their coffee. The Coffee Association of Canada tells us that 65 percent of Canadians drink coffee every day and about 37 percent of them do so outside the home. This leaves coffee as one of the most highly requested products in food establishments, and with its high margins, competitors work hard to hang on to market share.

Tim Hortons is the coffee shop of choice. It enjoys a hefty 77 percent share of the out-of-home coffee business, followed by McDonald's at 11 percent, leaving the remaining 12 percent to independent coffee shops and smaller coffee chains (in Canada) such as Starbucks and Second Cup. However, being number one in the business is no easy task, and between 2009 and 2013, Tim Hortons' market share slipped 3 share points from 80 percent to 77 percent, feeling the direct hit from McDonald's premium McCafé beverage brand, which was launched in 2009 with an annual free coffee giveaway. Since 2009, McDonald's share of the out-of-home coffee market has increased 5 share points, from 6 percent to 11 percent.

McDonald's restaurants now sell a line of McCafé beverages that includes made-to-order premium hot coffees such as Premium Roast brewed coffee, as well as upscale varieties including mocha, latte, cappuccino, Americano, espresso, and iced coffees from freshly ground beans. McDonald's also sells 350-gram packages of McCafé

Tim Hortons introduced single-serve capsules for home brewing in Tassimo machines.

Premium Roast ground coffee for home brewing.

In 2012, not to be outdone, and needing to shore up its own coffee business that consisted of original and decaf premium blends and flavoured cappuccinos, Tim Hortons added a new line of coffees made with premium espresso beans, lattes, mocha lattes, and cappuccinos. In addition, in 2012, Tim Hortons introduced Tassimo single-serve coffee T DISCs for coffee lovers who use the Tassimo single-serve brewing machines at home, followed by the launch of Tim Hortons Single Serve Coffee Cups compatible for use in Keurig single-serve brewers in 2013. In 2013, it also test-marketed a dark roast coffee blend in London, Ontario, and Columbus, Ohio, to see how it fared in the market. In 2014, Tim Hortons launched this product in Canada and the U.S.

So where is Starbucks in this equation? Starbucks is holding its own and also attempting to take business away from Tim Hortons. In 2012, it introduced a Blonde roast to target Canadians that prefer the milder coffees they can buy at Tim Hortons, and in 2013, it announced the opening of Starbucks coffee shops within Target stores in Canada.[9] ●

Questions

1. Why do you think Tim Hortons is so successful in the coffee business?

2. In what stage of the product life cycle are single-serve coffee capsules?

---

products infused with omega-3s, and Knorr reformulated many of its Sidekick side dishes with 25 percent less sodium. A **line extension** is the term used when a new item is added to an already existing product line, such as Cheerios adding its Banana Nut Cheerios to the already well-established Cheerios product line or Tim Hortons adding premium espresso lattes, mocha lattes, and cappuccinos to its original brewed coffee products (see the Marketing NewsFlash, "New Products Bolster Coffee Wars").

Some of the most successful and long-lasting Canadian brands use product improvements and line extensions to extend their product

> **line extension**
> The addition of a new item to an already existing product line

Infographic

The Coffee Business

CANADIANS LOVE THEIR COFFEE

Tim Hortons leads the pack in out-of-home coffee consumption

11% McDonalds

12% other

77% Tim Hortons

Market Share
Tim Hortons is #1 in the out-of-home coffee business with a 77% market share

Coffee drinking

65% of Canadians drink coffee daily

37% drink coffee out-of-home

Average cups per day

3.2 cups of coffee are consumed daily by coffee drinkers in Canada

20% single portion in-home brewing has reached 20%

Preferred Types of Coffee

Traditional coffees are still preferred by most, accounting for over half of coffee consumption in Canada

- Traditional brew — 55%
- Expresso — 12%
- Instant — 9%
- Iced/frozen — 6%
- Decaf — 5%

(Percentage vs Types of Coffee)

Source: Hollie Shaw, "Tim Hortons to offer new dark roast coffee blend in two test markets," *Financial Post*, October 28, 2013, accessed at http://business.financialpost.com/2013/10/28/tim-hortons-dark-roast-coffee; "Coffee remains dominant," *Canadian Vending and Office Coffee Service* magazine, October 28, 2013, accessed at www.canadianvending.com/content/view/3423/57.

brands based on reputation, products, innovation, workplace, citizenship, leadership, and performance. The top three Canadian brands were identified as (1) Tim Hortons, (2) WestJet, and (3) McCain Foods. Tim Hortons' strength lies in its reputation, innovation, and citizenship as seen through its community sports involvement and its children's camp programs.[10]

Repositioning a Product

Once a product has reached its maturity stage, it often needs an injection of newness to focus the market on the product and to provide it with a renewed competitive advantage. Many products appear tired at this stage and require a renewed focus. This can be achieved through new product development initiatives and/or repositioning the product to meet changing consumer needs more readily.

We look to the Knorr brand as an example of a brand that over the years has repositioned itself to remain relevant to consumers. Knorr is a well-known food brand that grew its business on the back of powdered soup mixes and stock cubes. Over the years, it

Knorr continues to revitalize its product mix with new products, line extensions, and marketing approaches.

life cycles. They also include innovative marketing approaches to stay relevant to consumers. A *Canadian Business* special report, *Canada's Top Brands 2013*, highlighted the results of the Reputation Institute's annual survey of Canadians and how they rate their brands. A survey of over 5,000 Canadians ranks has been refreshed and revitalized numerous times, with new products and new packaging to reflect the times. Today, the brand that was once known for salty dried seasonings, dried soups, and stock cubes, has 286 chefs and teams of product innovators that work to bring international flavours and high-quality recipes and products to its consumers.

Knorr continues to evolve with a renewed focus on healthier eating. This is communicated through many of its low-salt products as well as its marketing communication tools that provide consumers with meal plans, recipes, and cooking tips. Knorr products now include bouillons, soups, stocks, seasonings, sauces, side dishes, dressings, and gravies, many of them formulated to be low in salt for healthier eating. Check out the Knorr website at **www.knorr.ca** to see its latest products and marketing approaches.

Introducing a New Product

Refreshing a new product or adding a new one to the line can provide the focus that a mature product needs, bringing it back in the product life cycle to either the growth or early maturity stage. Apple has done this successfully by regularly introducing new versions of its iPhones, iPads, iPods, and computers with updates to its technology and design. Regardless of the type of product, new products have a greater chance of success if they provide meaningful benefits to its target market.

Drivers of Product Success When it comes to new products, the 2013 *BrandSpark Canadian Shopper Study: Critical Insights for Engaging Shoppers* reviewed the opinions and attitudes of over 100,000 respondents in Canada. The study tells us that there are four critical drivers for product success: (1) value, (2) convenience,

(3) health, and (4) innovation. Shoppers explain that they derive satisfaction when products save them money; that they want products that are easy to use and save time; that they are concerned about family health; and that they enjoy trying new products and want to know which ones best suit their needs. Specifically, 62 percent of respondents look for products that are innovative, and 76 percent like trying new products.[11]

The BrandSpark Best New Products Awards of 2013 echo the drivers for product success. These annual awards include the opinions of over 93,000 consumers on new products in the consumer packaged goods industry (everyday food, beverage, health, beauty, and household products). The winning products all provided good value and convenience, were innovative, and in some instances, provided health benefits. In the health and beauty category, Colgate My First Toothpaste was a winner with its innovative infant and toddler low-foaming mild toothpaste that encourages young ones to brush their teeth. Nestle Mini Drumsticks won in the food and beverage category for its mini cones of only 110 calories each. Mr. Clean Magic Eraser Bath Scrubber was awarded first place in household products, for its product that was 30 percent larger, more durable, and infused with a soap scum cleanser to make bathroom cleaning easier.[12]

Finding New Uses for a Product

Finding new uses for an existing product is not a simple task because many products do not lend themselves to this approach. A few exceptions exist such as Aspirin and Arm & Hammer baking soda. Aspirin is sold

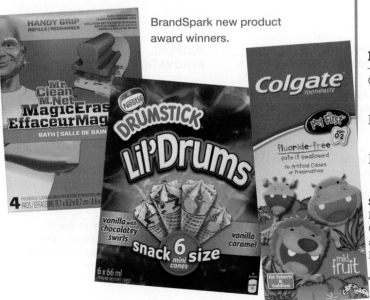

BrandSpark new product award winners.

Best New Product Award Winners

Product	Category
Colgate My First Toothpaste	Health and beauty products
Nestle Mini Drumsticks Dessert	Food and beverage products
Mr. Clean Magic Eraser Bath Scrubber	Household products

Source: "The 2013 Best New Product Award Winners announced: More than 93,000 Canadians choose the best new products in Canada's largest consumer study," press release, January 7, 2013, accessed at www.bestnewproductawards.biz/canada/pdf/2013_BNPA_Winners_Jan07_2013.pdf.

> *New products are the lifeblood of a company, helping to make products relevant and to bring future revenues into the company.*

mainly as a pain medication but it is also marketed as a heart and stroke preventative. Arm & Hammer baking soda is sold as a baking ingredient but it is also marketed as a product that eliminates odours, unblocks sinks, and cleans various household items.

New Products

Types of New Products

LO3 New products are the lifeblood of a company, helping to make products relevant and to bring future revenues into the company. There are many types of new products, ranging from a slight product modification to a more radical innovation. How new products are categorized depends on the degree of newness involved, and how much time a consumer needs to learn to use the product. Based on these factors, we classify innovations as (1) minor innovations, (2) continuous innovations, and (3) radical innovations (see Figure 8–5).

Minor innovations refer to minor product modifications that require no adjustments on behalf of the consumer. Marketing a minor modification requires marketers to generate awareness for the

innovation and to continue to market along current lines. Consumers do not need to be educated on how to use the product.

These types of innovations are relatively common and can be seen with new and improved products such as detergents and diapers, or updates to software and apps that are frequently provided to users.

ask yourself

1. *What approaches can be used to extend a product's life cycle?*

2. *If you were the marketer of a large sport-utility vehicle, what approach would you use today to extend its product life cycle?*

3. *Tim Hortons introduced single-serve Tassimo products for home brewing. What approach is Tim Hortons using to extend the product life cycle of its coffee products?*

Figure 8–5
Degree of product innovation

	MINOR INNOVATION	CONTINUOUS INNOVATION	RADICAL INNOVATION
Definition	Requires no new learning by consumers	Changes consumer's normal routine but does not require totally new learning	Requires new learning and consumption patterns by consumers
Examples	New and improved detergents or diapers	Electric toothbrushes or digital cameras	E-readers, GPS devices, smart watches, and other wearables such as Google Glass
Marketing emphasis	Gain consumer awareness and wide distribution	Advertise points of difference and benefits to consumers	Educate consumers through advertising, product trial, and personal selling; public relations can play a major role

Continuous innovations refer to new products that include more than just a minor product improvement but do not require radical changes in consumer behaviour. Continuous innovations are not common and require extensive product development by a company. Marketers must invest in marketing communication programs to launch these innovative products and to communicate their benefits to consumers. An example of a continuous innovation is Instagram. Instagram was introduced as a mobile app where users can quickly snap a photo on a mobile device and, in an instant, add filters and captions to share it with others in their social networks. The simplicity of this app and its immediate popularity with iPhone users boosted its success to the point where approximately 18 months after launch, Facebook announced the purchase of the app for $1 billion in cash and equity. Today, Instagram is the world's largest photo-sharing site and has over 150 million active users (see the Marketing NewsFlash, "Instagram—New Product Success").

Radical innovations are the least common form of innovation. They involve the introduction of a product that is entirely new to the market. The success of these products is often dependent on the education of the consumer, usually through advertising and/or public relations efforts. Public relations can add credibility to a radical innovation with the media encouraged through launch events, press kits, and press releases to discuss the product in its broadcasts or publications. This can result in considerable media coverage, which can boost sales by giving the public an objective and credible point of view.

Google Glass, as a voice-activated wearable mobile device, is a radical innovation.

Google Glass is an example of a radical innovation. It is a wearable mobile computer device that is designed into a pair of glasses. It accesses the Internet through voice commands and presents the information in a screen that is mounted on the glasses. It can also take pictures, record video, share images and multimedia, get directions, and send messages. This product is currently in limited supply in the U.S., but Google is working with sunglass manufacturers Ray-Ban and Oakley to make it more fashionable so that it appeals to a wider base of consumers.

The Adoption Curve

LO 4 The success of a new product and how quickly it is adopted by consumers is demonstrated in Figure 8-6, which shows the **adoption curve**. The adoption curve takes the point of view that some consumers are more ready than others to buy a product innovation. North American research (statistics vary across the world) shows that 2.5 percent of the population are innovators, risk takers who

Figure 8–6
The adoption curve

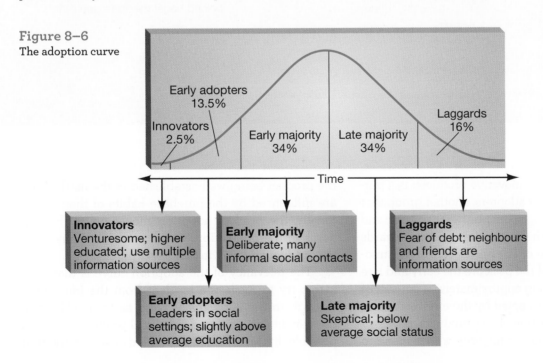

continuous innovations
New products with more than just a minor product improvement, but that do not require radical changes by the consumer

radical innovations
New products that involve the introduction of a product that is entirely new and innovative to the market

adoption curve
The sequential diffusion and acceptance of an innovation into the market by consumers

Instagram—New Product Success

In October 2010, the new free iPhone app Instagram was launched in the Apple app store, the brainchild of Kevin Systrom, a Stanford University graduate with an entrepreneurial spirit and a passion for photography. Influenced by a university study-abroad photography course in Italy, inspired by a trip to Mexico where he created an app to make mobile photography easier, and with an entrepreneurial spirit coaxed by an internship at start-up Odeo (which morphed into Twitter) and two years working at Google, Systrom knew he had an idea with legs, and the passion to make it happen.

The idea was to create an open mobile platform for visual media that could be accessed anywhere in the world, whether this be a sporting event, a protest, a natural disaster, or just a personal experience. What started off as an idea for a mobile check-in app where photos could be added, turned into a photo app with optional location check-in; Systrom realized that Foursquare had cornered the market on check-in apps and changed his approach.

As with most starts-ups, Systrom needed funds to help get his idea off the ground. He secured $500,000 in start-up seed money but it was dependent on Systrom taking a partner. Enter Mike Krieger, also a Stanford grad, and together they launched Instagram as an iPhone camera app with social and commenting options.

The new product was an instant success, boosted in its early days by tweets from Jack Dorsey, owner of Twitter, and articles in the *TechCrunch* and *Bits* blogs. In 24 hours, the app was downloaded 25,000 times, and the entrepreneurs were challenged to prevent its servers from crashing. Reaching out to their contacts, the hosting was transferred to Amazon's servers, and after a month, the app had 1 million users. In December 2011, Apple selected Instagram as its app of the year, boosting it into further success. Four months later, in April 2012, an Android version was launched, and Facebook announced its intention to purchase the start-up for a deal worth $1 billion in cash and equity, although Instagram had yet to make any money.

Instagram has over 150 million active users.

Today, Instagram is the world's largest photo-sharing site, has over 150 million active users, and runs ads to help monetize the platform. The app allows users to instantly and easily create square photos with borders and filters that give them a hip, retro feel. Images can be tagged and immediately shared with a user's Instagram network for comments and likes, and also shared on Twitter, Facebook, Flickr, or through e-mail. Images can be "hashtagged" for search functionality, and short video clips (up to 15 seconds) can also be shared with the network.

Passion, hard work, creativity, and an entrepreneurial spirit helped make this happen. But let's not forget the role of funding, word-of mouth marketing, and the impact of subtle recommendations from tech gurus such as Jack Dorsey and tech blogs that helped boost the app's popularity.[13] ●

Questions

1. Which drivers of new product success are included in the Instagram product?

2. Do you think Instagram will lose its lustre once ads become a regular feature of the app?

---

are the first to purchase innovative products; 13.5 percent are considered early adopters, another group that will accept a new offering sooner rather than later; and another 16 percent of the population are the laggards who are either reluctant or late purchasers of the innovation. In the middle of the pack are the early and late majority, each comprising approximately 34 percent of the population. Once accepted by the innovators and early adopters, the adoption of new products moves on to the early majority and late majority, who respond to

the product being well-established in the market and are influenced by the purchase habits of their peers. Finally, the product adoption moves on to the laggards of the population, who are reluctant buyers of the product and may in fact never purchase it.

The relevancy of the adoption curve is that marketers try to move the product from the innovators through to the early majority so as to quickly reap the benefits of increased sales and profits as soon as possible. In this manner, marketers design marketing programs to target these specific groups in different ways and separately focus their marketing programs on the demographic and psychographic needs, interests, and drivers of these target groups.

An example of how the adoption curve applies to new product diffusion can be seen with Twitter and, separately, with 3-D TVs. In the social media market, Twitter followed an interesting approach when introducing its updated interface in 2010, treading carefully so as to not alienate its then-current users—innovators and early adopters. Instead of migrating users immediately over to the new interface and its improved functionality, which may have resulted in a backlash, Twitter embedded a button on its homepage so that users could choose when to move over to the new interface. This button also allowed users to switch back to the old version if they wished. This flexible approach existed for many months, until the new Twitter interface became a permanent fixture and its users were familiar with its new design.

A new product currently struggling to move along the adoption curve is 3-D TV. Introduced in 2010 after its successful adoption in movie theatres, 3-D TVs have gained little traction among the TV-buying public. Not innovative enough to attract the attention of innovators and early adopters, and lacking the substantial easy-to-recognize benefits that appeal to the early and late majority, the long-term viability of this product is questionable.

Why New Products Succeed or Fail

LO5 We are familiar with successful new products and brands such as Google, Xbox, Twitter, and iPad, yet only one in ten new products are successful over time.[14] It is important at this point to remember that new products become successful over time and that marketers work to finesse these new products with upgrades and improvements that better meet consumer needs and expectations. Marketers are tasked to implement meaningful changes to the marketing mix by listening and reacting to consumer needs, and not to be focused only on the innovation itself.

Reasons for New-Product Failures Research from several studies on new product successes and failures identify critical marketing factors that often spell failure for new product launches:[15]

1. **Insignificant point of difference:** Shown as one of the most important factors, a distinctive and meaningful point of difference is essential for a new product to compete in the market. In 2010, TV manufacturers introduced 3-D TVs to the market, expecting consumers to readily buy these units. Disappointing sales have pundits questioning the benefit of this technology, particularly when very little programming is available in 3-D. In an attempt to boost sales, manufacturers are joining forces with TV networks to provide 3-D programming. Sony has worked with a TV network in Japan to create a 3D drama series, while Panasonic has created a 3-D music program for satellite TV.[16]

2. **Incomplete new-concept definition:** Ideally, before a new product is developed, it needs a well-defined, consumer-based reason for being. Its consumer insights must be clearly identified. If these areas are not clarified, the new products will have no meaningful positioning in the market. Coca-Cola Blak, a coffee-flavoured cola, is such an example. Introduced in Canada in August 2006, this new product took on both coffee shops and energy drinks with a beverage that had less caffeine than coffee and Red Bull and more caffeine than Coca-Cola—clearly a confusing proposition. Its target market, according to Coca-Cola, was the "adult that appreciates a good cup of coffee who is looking for something a little different, a little more premium."[17] However, the product missed its mark and was discontinued in Canada and the U.S. in 2007.

An unsuccessful new product from Coca-Cola.

3. **Insufficient market attractiveness:** Market attractiveness refers to a product having strong consumer appeal in a category with both growth and profit potential. Often, a target market can be too small or too competitive to result in a profitable entry. The Canadian theatre production *Lord of the Rings: The Musical* was a $27 million flop with poor sales that forced the production to be pulled after only five months. The three-and-a-half-hour production was deemed too lengthy for the traditional theatre-going audience and criticized for being neither a play nor a musical, which limited its appeal.[18]

4. **Inadequate marketing support:** Companies often launch products with little marketing support or a marketing mix that does not adequately support the innovation. Although Coca-Cola Blak was a poorly defined concept, it also lacked marketing support that could have better positioned the product with consumers.

5. **Insensitivity to critical customer needs:** Ignoring a critical consumer insight can kill a product, even though the general concept may be well-accepted. For example, the Japanese, like the British, drive on the left side of the road, resulting in right-hand-drive vehicles on their roads. Until 1996, North American car makers continued to sell left-hand-drive options to Japan with little success. Contrast this with the German car manufacturers that successfully exported right-hand-drive models for a number of their brands to this market.[19]

6. **Bad timing:** A product can suffer negative consequences if it is introduced too soon, too late, or at a time when consumer tastes are shifting. An example exists in the aircraft industry. In March 2001, Boeing announced it would start the multi-billion dollar development of its Sonic Cruiser, designed to cross oceans with over 400 passengers at almost the speed of sound. However, the tragic attacks of September 11, 2001, caused such a decline in air travel that the project was postponed.[20]

7. **Limited access to buyers:** It is often difficult to obtain the necessary distribution to reach a target market. Consumer products typically need a retailer to list and display their products in-store, but this distribution network is not always readily available. A new product may have tested well with consumers, but if a retailer does not carry the product, its distribution will be limited.

   Cottonelle Fresh Rollwipes from Kimberly-Clark is an example of a product that suffered from poor distribution. This moist toilet-tissue on a roll was launched in the U.S. in 2001 in a plastic dispenser that clipped on to the side of a regular toilet-paper dispenser. Kimberly-Clark spent $100 million on research and development and protected the product with 30 patents. Within 10 months, sales had reached only a third of forecasts, and distribution was so sporadic that 18 months after launch, the product was available only in specific southern markets. Despite a national advertising campaign, the product could not be found at most retailers across the U.S.[21] Perhaps the journey of product development required more time and marketing adjustments to be successful.

ask yourself

1. Describe the three types of product innovation and explain which ones are most common.

2. How does the adoption curve apply to the diffusion of new products in the marketplace?

3. What are the main reasons that new products fail?

New Product Development

Developing and launching new products is an expensive undertaking with a high risk of failure. Research costs are high, as is the time and effort spent on developing prototypes and marketing materials. Product launches may also include expensive listing fees required to secure retail distribution. Product failure can result in expensive product write-offs and a lack of future credibility in the market. Hundreds of thousands of dollars are often at stake. In order to avoid expensive product failures, companies can use a number of different approaches to develop these new products. These range from providing clear strategic direction, to creating particular company structures, to instituting rigorous product development processes. We look at these areas in more detail in the sections that follow.

Approaches to New Product Development

Strategic Direction From a strategic point of view, companies can follow different approaches to innovation (see Figure 8–7). It is somewhat dependent on the degree of risk and investment that companies are willing to take. The most common forms of innovation take either a market penetration or product development slant, focusing on current consumers with promotional tactics (market penetration), or looking to develop a new product for these current consumers (product development). Higher-risk considerations include either a market development or diversification strategy, taking the more expensive approach of either targeting new markets with current products (market development), or moving out into new arenas with totally new products (diversification).

Company Structure Companies use different structures to encourage innovation. Some companies, such as Loblaw Companies, use teams to help marshal successful new products to Canadian consumers. They use a *team-based approach* that includes chefs, nutrition researchers, registered dieticians, nutritionists, product developers, quality assurance specialists, regulatory affairs experts, and marketers.

Cross-functional teams reduce new product development time.

> *New product development success ultimately requires the expertise of people with different specializations.*

Other companies may follow a more individualized approach, appointing a new product development manager to concentrate entirely in this area. In other instances, full departments are tasked with this responsibility, or new product development is included in the role of the general marketer. In some instances, new venture teams are used to concentrate on all innovation projects for the company, which could include new products, new processes, or new business ventures.

Regardless of the formal structure, new product development success ultimately requires the expertise of people with different specializations and from varied backgrounds to ensure that the best product ideas are developed. These experts are either fully involved in the process from the start, or brought in along the way to contribute to the journey.

Figure 8–7
Strategic approaches to innovation

	PRODUCTS	
Markets	**Current**	**New**
Current	**Market Penetration** Finding ways to make current products appeal to current customers	**Product Development** Reaching current customers with a new product
New	**Market Development** Reaching new customers with a current product	**Diversification** Reaching new customers with a new product

The New Product Development Process

LO 6 In order to avoid expensive product failures, companies use rigorous product development processes to minimize the risk. Each step in the process requires an individual or team to assess whether the project is still viable and should continue down the road to innovation. The **new product development process** includes the seven steps shown in Figure 8-8 and summarized in Figure 8-9, and starts with a clearly defined strategy. This is followed by a number of brainstorming, research, product development, and business analysis steps. A successful trip down this road faces many twists and turns, and any new product development team needs to be flexible, creative, and responsive to the insights learned at each step.

Step 1: New Product Development Strategy

New product development success relies on many factors. Having a clear definition and understanding of what you are trying to achieve with the innovation is one of the most important building blocks in this process. A **new product development strategy** involves setting the new product strategic direction for the company as a whole, as well as the precise objectives for the project at hand. There must be consistency between the two.

An example can be seen with Procter & Gamble, which refocused its new product development strategy from "new-to-the-world" products and brands to evolving current brands such as Crest, Tide, and Pampers with new initiatives. The result was products such as Crest Whitestrips for teeth whitening and Crest SpinBrush for better dental care. These innovations helped boost global sales for the Crest brand by 50 percent within two years.[22]

Step 2: Idea Generation

Once the purpose and direction for the product development project is clarified, the second step of **idea generation** comes into play. This includes brainstorming sessions focused on participants coming up with new ideas for the project at hand. Ideas can come from inside or outside the company, depending on the organization's approach to new product development. It is important for these brainstorming sessions to include individuals who are creative, have varied experiences, and have differing areas of expertise. This should stimulate a more varied and interesting pool of ideas.

Brainstorming sessions can result in a host of interesting ideas, but for this approach to work, participants must be willing to share their most ludicrous or boring ideas with the group. Participants need to be open-minded, energetic, flexible, and willing to build on each other's ideas. Often, companies hire an outside moderator, skilled in these types of sessions, to promote creativity sessions that render results. As a rule of thumb, it takes at least 60 ideas to generate an inspired idea with some potential.

Step 3: Screening and Evaluation

The third stage of the new product development process, **screening and evaluation**, attempts to reduce the array of brainstorming ideas down to a manageable list of promising concepts. Ideas are initially screened internally by the new product development team, which eliminates ideas that do not meet the objectives, as well as those that are clearly not feasible. The short list of ideas is then developed by the team into concepts. A concept is a more detailed idea, couched in consumer terms, with added particulars for clarification. A concept is then presented to consumers for initial feedback in the form of a concept test. This presents consumers with a short descriptive paragraph and an accompanying visual.

Concept tests are external evaluations of the new product idea, rather than the actual product itself. Several key issues are addressed during concept testing, such as

Figure 8–8
Steps in the new product development process

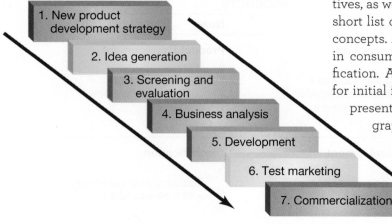

1. New product development strategy
2. Idea generation
3. Screening and evaluation
4. Business analysis
5. Development
6. Test marketing
7. Commercialization

Figure 8–9
Elements in each stage of the new product development process

STAGE OF PROCESS	PURPOSE OF STAGE	MARKETING INFORMATION AND METHODS USED
New product development strategy	Identify new-product development focus that meets company objectives	Company objectives; SWOT analysis of company/product/brand
Idea generation	Brainstorm new ideas	Ideas from employees, co-workers, and consumers
Screening and evaluation	Evaluate product ideas and develop concepts	Internal evaluation of technical requirements, external concept tests
Business analysis	Identify the product's features and its marketing strategy, and make financial projections	Product's key features and anticipated marketing mix; assessment of production, legal, and profitability issues
Development	Create the prototype, and test it internally at the company and externally with consumers	Internal company assessments and external tests on product prototypes
Test marketing	Test the product and marketing strategy in the marketplace on a limited scale (if necessary)	Test marketing in defined areas
Commercialization	Launch and fully market the product in the marketplace	Implement all areas of the marketing mix; possible regional rollout

how the customer perceives the product, who would use it, and how it would be used. The purpose of these evaluations is to get feedback on the strengths and weaknesses of the concepts and to understand what further modifications are required. Concept tests will result in some concepts being eliminated and others surfacing as more-promising opportunities that require further investigation. One may ask why product prototypes are not presented to consumers at this point. Product prototypes are typically expensive to develop, and a basic concept test avoids this unnecessary expense until a final concept is determined.

Once a clear concept has surfaced during this stage, further research is required to determine the specific elements of the marketing mix that will help the product succeed in the marketplace. Consumers need to be probed on elements such as pricing, brand names, and advertising ideas.

Step 4: Business Analysis After the concept tests have determined which product, or line of products, are strong new product candidates, the **business analysis** step is necessary. This involves determining financial projections on bringing the new product to market and selling it in the future. Typical financial projections for a new product cover a three-year period and often look five years into the future. Financial projections involve sales and revenue forecasts, cost projections, and budget requirements for marketing support. Marketers need to initially establish the positioning of the product in the market and what marketing elements are needed for a successful launch. The new product is also studied to determine whether it can, and should, be protected with a patent, trademark, or copyright.

The business analysis step requires marketers to determine market share projections, price points, cost parameters, special discounts, distribution requirements, research needs, and all the marketing communication programs needed to ensure product

business analysis
Financial projections on the impact of bringing the new product to market and selling it in the future

success. Marketers also need to understand whether a product will require an investment in infrastructure, software, machinery, people, or training programs, and whether it will cannibalize the sales of existing products. At this point in the new product development process, marketers are checking the commercial viability of the new product. This requires strong analytical skills and the ability to understand the dynamics of the market. A marketer must also be able to anticipate competitive reactions and foresee target market needs.

The business analysis stage results in profit projections. Marketers review these projections, taking a realistic view of the product and the market to decide whether the concept has real financial merit. Often at this stage, one can easily take an optimistic view, but it is important for marketers to be as realistic as possible and to consider severe competitive reactions to their launch. If the product can meet sales, profit, and market share targets, then the new product development process will continue to the next step. If not, marketers may reassess the concept, going back to consumers to conduct further research. It is important for marketers at this point to stop the process if the concept has little merit and weak profit forecasts. This is usually the last checkpoint before significant resources are invested in creating a *prototype,* a full-scale operating model of the product.

Step 5: Development
New product ideas that survive the business analysis step proceed to actual **development**, turning the idea into a prototype for further consumer research and manufacturing tests. This step is considerably complex, involving laboratory and consumer tests to ensure that the product consistently meets legal and quality control requirements. Manufacturing trials are also conducted to eliminate manufacturing problems and to reduce costs.

This step can be time-consuming, with some products requiring extensive testing before they can be safely brought to market.

> *The business analysis stage results in profit projections.*

Pharmaceutical products, children's toys, cars, and food products that require shelf-life tests are examples that fall into this category. The TACKLA QuikBlade Shift251 hockey skate, discussed in this chapter's opening vignette, explained the three months of product safety testing the product had to undergo before securing the required certification for Canadian Tire and the additional testing implemented by Multimatic.

The advantage of the development step is that it allows marketers to take actual product prototypes into consumer research or show them to potential buyers. This provides a platform to probe preliminary sales strategies with key accounts or marketing ideas with consumers. In some instances, ambivalence may still exist on the subtleties of brand names, packaging, and pricing. Advertising campaigns may also require feedback on the clarity of the communication.

Step 6: Test Marketing
Test marketing involves offering a product for sale on a limited basis in a defined geographic area. This test is done to determine whether consumers will actually buy the product, and to what extent. Marketers may use this opportunity to test different marketing approaches to support the product.

Tim Hortons test-marketed its new dark roast coffee product in London, Ontario, and Columbus, Ohio, subsequently launching it in Canada and the U.S.

In Canada, test markets are conducted in cities such as London, Edmonton, and Moncton. These cities are good candidates as their populations are representative of Canada in general. The media in these cities is also isolated, meaning that a company can advertise and test special promotions and be able to measure their success. Using tracking systems by firms such as Nielsen, marketers can try to correlate local advertising campaigns to in-store purchases by using data from store scanners. In 2014, Tim Hortons introduced its new dark roast coffee product in Canada and the U.S. after having conducted successful test markets in London, Ontario, and Columbus, Ohio.

The main drawbacks of test markets are that they are expensive to conduct and they immediately alert the competition. Competitors can easily sabotage test markets by altering their own pricing and marketing support to render the test market unsuccessful. These issues are so real that many marketers do not embark on test markets, relying instead on research to provide good direction for a full product launch.

Technology is assisting marketers by creating simulated test markets through a number of software programs. An emerging trend uses virtual reality testing to allow marketers to present consumers with a range of experiences such as simulated store environments. Ipsos is an example of a reputable market research firm that conducts simulated test marketing services for its clients.

Step 7: Commercialization **Commercialization** is the step when the new product is brought to market with full-scale production, sales, and marketing support. Companies proceed very carefully at the commercialization stage because this is the most expensive stage for most new products. To minimize the risk of financial failure, many companies use regional rollouts, introducing the product sequentially into geographic areas of the country to allow production levels and marketing activities to build gradually. Grocery product manufacturers and some telecommunication service providers are examples of firms that use this strategy.

Marketing plays a crucial role in the success of a new product, and marketers need to intimately understand their consumers and what is important to their purchase decisions. Each element of the marketing mix needs to be carefully crafted to help make a new product successful.

ask yourself

1. *What occurs in the screening and evaluation step of the new product development process?*

2. *What is the purpose of the business analysis step in the new product development process?*

3. *What are the advantages and disadvantages of a test market?*

Summary...*just the facts*

LO 1 • Product life cycles are the stages that a new product goes through from its initial introduction through to growth, maturity, and decline.

• The shape of a product life cycle varies depending on the industry, the competition, technological innovation, and the marketing of the product.

LO 2 • Product life cycles can be extended through various marketing techniques that encourage new and current users to keep purchasing the product and to use it in new ways.

• Extending a product life cycle can be done by following one or a combination of these approaches: 1) targeting current users with extended usage strategies, (2) targeting new consumers through new marketing approaches, (3) revitalizing a product with product improvements and line extensions, (4) repositioning a product, (5) introducing a new product, and (6) finding new uses for a product.

LO 3 • There are many types of new products, ranging from slight product modifications, to more innovative changes, to the more radical innovations that we see in the market. We term these minor innovations, continuous innovations, and radical innovations.

LO 4 • The adoption curve shows the sequential diffusion and acceptance of an innovation into the market by consumers. It categorizes people into five groupings: innovators, early adopters, early majority, late majority, and laggards.

LO 5 • A new product must have a distinct point of difference to enjoy long-term success in the market.

• Reasons for new product failures are (1) insignificant point of difference, (2) incomplete new-concept definition, (3) insufficient market attractiveness, (4) inadequate marketing support, (5) insensitivity to critical customer needs, (6) bad timing, and (7) limited access to buyers.

• From a strategic point of view, companies can follow a combination of approaches to innovation, including market penetration, product development, market development, and diversification.

LO 6 • The new product development process follows seven steps: (1) new product development strategy, (2) idea generation, (3) screening and evaluation, (4) business analysis, (5) development, (6) test marketing, and (7) commercialization.

Key Terms and Concepts...*a refresher*

adoption curve
business analysis
commercialization
concept tests
continuous innovations
development
fad

fashion product
harvesting
high-learning product
idea generation
line extension
low-learning product
minor innovations

new product development process
new product development strategy
product life cycle
radical innovations
screening and evaluation
test marketing

Hands-on...*apply your knowledge*

New Product Development Assignment Impact Machine's TACKLA QuikBlade Shift251 hockey skate was created as an innovative hockey skate in the competitive sports market. Review this chapter's opening vignette on this skate and gather additional information about this and other products in this category by going online to visit brand websites and social media sites. Also review the latest news in this category, and if appropriate, visit sporting goods stores to review the products in a retail environment. Brainstorm on how the online environment can be used to market the TACKLA QuikBlade Shift251 hockey skate to consumers, and present your ideas to the class.

Chapter Vignette...reminder

This chapter's opening vignette explains the development and launch of the TACKLA QuikBlade Shift251 hockey skate. Answer the Reality Check questions at the end of the vignette by carefully reading the chapter sections on the product life cycle and new products.

Video Clip...questions

Review the *TACKLA Shift251 Skate* video from the CONNECT website to hear Morgan Matthews talk about this new product. Answer the following questions:

▶ Video
TACKLA

- Which drivers of new product success are incorporated into the TACKLA QuikBlade Shift251 hockey skate?
- Considering the adoption curve (Figure 8–6), which group of consumers do you think is most likely to purchase the TACKLA QuikBlade Shift251 hockey skate?

Infographic...data analysis

Review the Infographic on the coffee business that details consumer preferences and the dynamics of the coffee market. Research the latest changes in the Canadian retail coffee business by reviewing news articles on this topic and navigating to the Coffee Association of Canada website at **www.coffeeassoc.com** and the *Canadian Vending and Coffee Service* magazine website at **www.canadianvending.com**.

Create a new infographic with the latest data gleaned from these sites and write a short analysis that highlights the trends and changes that are occurring in this industry. (*Infographic tip:* Use Microsoft Excel and Word to create charts and place them in a single PowerPoint slide to combine the visuals.)

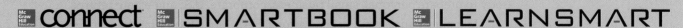

For more information on the resources available from McGraw-Hill Ryerson, go to **www.mheducation.ca/he/solutions**.

pricing

Creativity is definitely a talent associated with marketing; however, successful marketing campaigns and strategies benefit from another important skill. In order to generate an appropriate return on investment, organizations need to implement effective pricing strategies for their goods and services. In this chapter, we discuss different pricing strategies and constraints that companies consider when determining final prices for their products and services.

Pore over historical quotes and you will find many that discuss the certainty, dread, or complexity of taxation. By April of every year, Canadians search for options and evaluate alternatives for filing their personal and business taxes. Whether they are students, professors, or business professionals, Canadians who seek help for tax preparation services have a number of different options. After careful evaluation of their alternatives, Canadians remain loyal to only a few of them. Tax preparers who have discovered the correct strategy for effective pricing have realized the lifetime value of their clients.

Not only does H&R Block have an effective pricing strategy, it effectively trains the future tax preparers of Canada. Each year, more than 10,000 students enroll in H&R Block's Income Tax School. Graduates of the school may become H&R Block employees, but they also may work for major banks, mutual fund companies, and brokerage firms in Canada. The training offered includes a written guarantee that the training is the strongest in the industry. H&R Block's guarantee to its clients is just one element of its customer relationship management strategy and its success. Furthermore, H&R Block values students as future clients. Its tax preparation services in Canada offer student pricing offers. For example, from August 2013 through July 2014, H&R Block offered a promotion giving students Student Price Cards (SPC) valid for savings at over 100 retailers.

The organization aspires to be the preferred tax and financial partner of its clients in every market it serves. This vision is led by Rick Brown, president of H&R Block Canada, and communicated by the company's director of marketing, Hilary Zaharko. From its headquarters in Calgary, H&R Block manages the preparation of tax returns from more than 1,200 offices across Canada. Not only do H&R Block's tax professionals have the best training in the industry, they also use the latest technology to prepare personal, small business, corporate, U.S., and estate returns.

Like many successful organizations, H&R Block took time to develop its effective strategy, but had excellent values to draw from. In the 1940s, Henry and Richard

H&R BLOCK

Chapter Features

Priced Right
H&R Block uses customer feedback to drive pricing strategies.

Perfect Promotion
Accenture, the management consulting firm, considers various factors when recommending trade promotions for businesses.

High Credit Card Fees Still an Issue
Consider the continuing challenges of fees associated with the services offered by VISA and MasterCard and their impact on pricing.

Zipping Our Wallets through Car Sharing
Explore the car-sharing trend as consumers try to keep more disposable income for their purchases.

Death by Chocolate
Hershey's Canada pleads guilty to price-fixing.

Chapter Outline:

- Priced right
- Nature and importance of price
- General pricing approaches
- Estimating demand and revenue
- Determining cost, volume, and profit relationships
- Pricing objectives and constraints
- Setting a final price

Bloch started a company called United Business Company that provided bookkeeping services to small businesses. To add value to the offering, the brothers prepared individual income tax returns of the executives of the client companies. Through word-of-mouth advertising, the organization's reputation grew, and H&R Block Inc. was formed.

H&R Block opened its first franchised operation in Canada in 1964 and opened its first company-owned operation in Canada the following year. This was its first venture into multichannel offerings for its clients, but definitely not its last. As the organization grew in U.S. and Canada, it also expanded into 13 foreign companies and it services Canadians home and abroad.

It may seem difficult for such a large organization to keep its service offering consistent among so many locations, but H&R Block finds a way to do it. Hilary explains, "H&R Block spends a great deal of time educating its employees on the value they offer clients. Through effective training on position pricing, H&R Block employees explain the value their services offer in the context of perceived benefits in relation to price." The value of the organization's services increase as the benefits clients receive increase.

Pricing strategy is an important element of H&R Block's business. When determining if the prices for the services the organization offers are appropriate, H&R Block researches its competitors. This allows the company to decide if it should be offering prices at, above, or below market pricing. More importantly, H&R Block conducts research on its clients. As director of marketing, Hilary leads the market research efforts. She explains the rationale behind the key questions clients are asked. "We first want to understand if our clients know what price they are paying for the service. From there, we determine the price they are willing to pay for the service." What Hilary has noticed is that clients are actually willing to pay more if they receive a level of service that exceeds their expectations. "We also ask if clients are willing to pay a certain price for a service to see if it is appropriately positioned for the market."

In addition to its at- and below-market pricing strategies, H&R Block also uses odd-even pricing strategies. "You will notice that some of our prices are shown below the whole dollar amount. That is just the beginning of the conversation. As I mentioned before, clients are willing to pay more for our services when they see the value-added service we offer."[1]

To get a sense of H&R Block's customer experience from a customer's perspective, consider Tony, an H&R Block client. When Tony moved into his new home, he also made a decision to change accountants. "There were a lot of individuals at work that were speaking highly of H&R Block," shares Tony. "It made sense to try them out." Going through his consumer purchase decision, Tony identified that "I did not want the hassle of doing taxes on my own." Encouraged by work colleagues, Tony decided to investigate H&R Block as an option. His decision to go with the company over private accounting firms was finalized when he walked into the company's convenient neighbourhood office location. "There was a sandwich board in the H&R Block office," recounts Tony. "I knew right there what I was going to pay and I had the assurance that my taxes would be done accurately. I also received my money right there."

▶ Video
H&R Block
Canada

reality CHECK ✓

As you read Chapter 9, refer back to this opening vignette to answer the following questions:

- As a professional service provider, what approaches to pricing should H&R Block consider when determining the prices for the services it offers?
- What are some of the major constraints H&R Block should consider when setting prices?

Price has many implications for marketing. Beyond it being a key element of the 4Ps of the marketing mix, marketers need to know how pricing impacts their target markets and competitors. The infographic from Accenture illustrates the number of different factors being considered in pricing and promotion.

Nature and Importance of Price

LO 1 The price paid for goods and services goes by many names. You pay *tuition* for your education, *rent* for an apartment, *interest* on a bank credit card, and a *premium* for car insurance. Your dentist or physician charges you a *fee*, a professional or social organization charges *dues*, and airlines charge a *fare*. And what you pay for clothes or a haircut is termed a *price*.

What Is a Price?

From a marketing viewpoint, **price** is the money or other considerations, including other goods and services, exchanged for the ownership or use of a product. An example of other considerations includes Wilkinson Sword exchanging some of its knives for advertising that promotes its razor blades. This practice of exchanging goods and services for other goods and services rather than for money is called barter. Barter transactions account for billions of dollars annually in domestic and international trade.

For most products, money is exchanged. How much money is paid is not always consistent with the list, or quoted, price because of discounts, allowances, and extra fees. While discounts, allowances, and rebates make the effective price lower, other marketing tactics raise the real price. One new pricing tactic is to use "special fees" and "surcharges." This practice is driven by consumers' zeal for low prices combined with the ease of making price comparisons on the Internet. Buyers are more willing to pay extra fees than a higher list price, so sellers use add-on charges as a way of having the consumer pay more without raising the list price. Consider this when you purchase a cellphone. Examples of such special fees include the Telus Mobility "system licensing charge" and "911 emergency service access charge" that increase the monthly cellphone bill. You may also encounter an environmental surcharge on new tires and batteries for cars in some provinces.

Infographic

Accenture Perfect Promotion

The Win/Win/Win/Win Machine: Accenture's business services model allows CPG manufacturers to add advanced TPM/TPO capabilities faster and at a lower cost

Source: www.accenture.com/SiteCollectionDocuments/PDF/Accenture-Perfect-Promotion-Graphic.pdf.

The different factors that increase or decrease the price are put together in a "price equation," which is shown for several different products in Figure 9–1.

Suppose that you decide you want to buy a Bugatti Veyron, the world's fastest production car, which can move you from 0 to 100 km/h in 2.5 seconds, with a top speed of 422 km/h. The Veyron has a list price of $2.5 million, but you want the clear coat paint option, so it will cost an extra $430,000. An extended warranty will add an additional $70,000 to the cost. However, if you put $500,000 down now and finance the balance over the next year, you will receive a rebate of

price
Money or other considerations exchanged for the ownership or use of a good or service

value
The ratio of perceived benefits to price

Figure 9–1

The price of three different purchases

ITEM PURCHASED	PRICE EQUATION			
	PRICE	= LIST PRICE	− INCENTIVES AND ALLOWANCES	+ EXTRA FEES
New car bought by an individual	Final price	= List price	− Rebate Cash discount Old car trade-in	+ Financing charges Special accessories Destination charges
Term in university bought by a student	Tuition	= Published tuition	− Scholarship Other financial aid	+ Special activity fees
Merchandise bought from a wholesaler by a retailer	Invoice price	= List price	− Quantity discount Cash discount Seasonal discount Functional or trade discount	+ Penalty for late payment

$50,000 off the list price. For your 2005 Honda Civic DX 4-door sedan that has 100,000 kilometres and is in fair condition, you are given a trade-in allowance of $5,000. Assume another $300,000 for additional taxes and charges. Finally, your total finance charge at an annual interest rate of five percent over a five-year period is $378,640.[2]

Applying the price equation (as shown in Figure 9–1) to your purchase, your final price is:

Final price = List price − (Incentives + Allowances) + Extra fees

= $2,500,000 − ($500,000 + $50,000 + $5,000) + ($430,000 + $70,000 + $300,000 + $378,640)

= $3,173,640

Are you still interested in buying this car? If so, put yourself on the waiting list.

Price as an Indicator of Value

From a consumer's standpoint, price is often used to indicate value when it is compared with the perceived benefits such as quality, durability, and so on of a product or service. Specifically, **value** is the ratio of perceived benefits to price,[3] or

$$\text{Value} = \frac{\text{Perceived benefits}}{\text{Price}}$$

This relationship shows that for a given price, as perceived benefits increase, value increases. If you can purchase a medium or a large pizza for $13.99, which pizza would you choose? Would having more pizza to eat be more valuable? Many marketers often engage in the practice of *value pricing*—increasing product or service benefits while maintaining or decreasing price. McDonald's understands the importance of price to consumers and launched its McValue® Menu.

Consider all the costs when purchasing items like the Bugatti Veyron.

This menu offered special pricing on select menu items and everyday low prices on some Extra Value Meal combinations in 2000.

Marketers must be careful when using price as an indicator of value. For example, for many consumers, a low price would imply poor quality, and ultimately, poor perceived value. This is particularly true for services. For example, what would be your perception of a dentist who charges only $25 for a checkup and cleaning, when the average dentist charges between $150 and $200? Consumers make comparative value assessments, so it is important for marketers to know what their competitors are charging.

In a survey of home-furnishing buyers, 84 percent agreed with the statement, "The higher the price, the higher the quality." In turn, firms may use high prices to signify high quality.[4] For example, Kohler introduced a walk-in bathtub that is safer for children and the elderly. Although priced higher than conventional step-in bathtubs, it has proven very successful because buyers are willing to pay more for what they perceive as the benefit of extra safety.

Price in the Marketing Mix

Pricing is a critical decision made by a marketing executive because price has a direct effect on a firm's profits. This is apparent from a firm's **profit equation**:

$$\text{Profit} = \text{Total revenue} - \text{Total cost}$$
$$= (\text{Unit price} \times \text{Quantity sold}) - \text{Total cost}$$

McDonald's increases value to consumers by reducing the overall price of food items purchased in a combo.

What makes this relationship even more complicated is that price affects the quantity sold, as illustrated with demand curves later in this chapter, because the quantity sold sometimes affects a firm's costs because of efficiency of production, price also indirectly affects costs. Thus, pricing decisions influence both total revenue (sales) and total cost, which makes pricing one of the most important decisions marketing executives face.

General Pricing Approaches

LO² A key to a marketing manager's setting a final price for a product is to find an "approximate price level" to use as a reasonable starting point. Four common approaches to helping find this approximate price level are demand-oriented, cost-oriented, profit-oriented, and competition-oriented approaches (see Figure 9–2). Although these approaches are discussed separately below, some of them overlap, and an effective marketing manager will consider several in searching for an approximate price level.

Demand-Oriented Approaches

Demand-oriented approaches emphasize factors underlying expected customer tastes and preferences more than such factors as cost, profit, and competition when selecting a price level.

Pricing decisions influence both total revenue (sales) and total cost, which makes pricing one of the most important decisions marketing executives face.

Figure 9–2
Four approaches for selecting an approximate price level

Demand-oriented approaches	Cost-oriented approaches	Profit-oriented approaches	Competition-oriented approaches
• Skimming • Penetration • Prestige • Odd-even • Target • Bundle • Yield management	• Standard markup • Cost-plus	• Target profit • Target return on sales • Target return on investment	• Customary • Above, at, or below market • Loss leader

profit equation
Profit =
Total revenue −
Total cost

Skimming Pricing   A firm introducing a new product can use *skimming pricing,* setting the highest initial price that those customers really desiring the product are willing to pay. These customers are not very price-sensitive because they weigh the new product's price, quality, and ability to satisfy their needs against the same characteristics of substitutes. As the demand of these customers is satisfied, the firm lowers the price to attract a more price-sensitive segment. Thus, skimming pricing gets its name from skimming successive layers of "cream," or customer segments, as prices are lowered in a series of steps.

In early 2003, many manufacturers of flat-screen TVs were pricing them at about $5,000 and using skimming pricing because many prospective customers were willing to buy the product immediately at the high price. Over time, prices of flat-screen TVs have dropped considerably.

Penetration Pricing   Setting a low initial price on a new product to appeal immediately to the mass market is *penetration pricing,* the exact opposite of skimming pricing. This strategy makes sense when consumers are price-sensitive; Nintendo consciously chose a penetration strategy when it introduced the Nintendo Wii, its popular video game console.

In addition to offering the potential to build sales, market share, and profits, penetration pricing discourages competitors from entering the market because the profit margin is relatively low. Furthermore, if the costs to produce drop because of the accumulated volume, competitors that enter the market will face

> *Creative marketers, aware that consumers often compare value between competing products, engage in value pricing.*

higher unit costs, at least until their volume catches up with the early entrant. Walmart comes to mind when one thinks about penetration pricing. The same holds true for the very successful chain Dollarama, which is constantly increasing its number of stores in Canada.

In some situations, penetration pricing may follow skimming pricing. A company might price a product high in the early stages of the product life cycle to attract price-insensitive consumers. After the company has earned back the money spent on research and development and introductory promotions, it uses penetration pricing in the later stages of the product life cycle to appeal to a broader segment of the population and increase market share.[5]

Prestige Pricing   Although consumers tend to buy more of a product when the price is lower, sometimes the reverse is true. If consumers are using price as a measure of the quality of an item, a company runs the risk of appearing to offer a low-quality product if it sets the price below a certain point. *Prestige pricing* involves setting a high price so that quality- or status-conscious consumers are attracted to the product and buy it. Rolls-Royce cars, Chanel perfume, and Cartier jewellery have an element of prestige pricing in them and may not sell as well at lower prices than at higher ones.[6]

The higher the price of a prestige product, the greater the status associated with it and the greater its exclusivity, because fewer people can afford to buy it. Unlike products such as flat-panel TVs, which have decreased in price over the product life cycle, prices of prestige products remain high throughout the product life cycle.

An example of prestige pricing is the All Day Heels® collection of women's high-heeled shoes developed by Canadian retailer Ron White. This fashionable line of women's shoes combines elegance as well as comfort. The All Day Heels collection is set at a high price that matches its superior quality. The shoes provide arch support, built-in cushioning materials, and thin lightweight insoles made of Poron, a flexible high-tech elastic polymer developed by NASA.

Price Lining   Often, a firm that is selling not just a single product but a line of products may price them at a number of different specific pricing points, which is called *price lining.* For example, a discount department store manager may price a line of women's dresses at

Nintendo used a penetration pricing strategy to introduce its Wii video game console.

$59, $79, and $99. In some instances, all the items may be purchased at the same cost and then marked up to different percentages to achieve these price points, based on colour, style, and expected demand. In other instances, manufacturers design products for different price points, and retailers apply approximately the same markup percentages to achieve the three price points offered to consumers.

Odd-Even Pricing

If you are in Canadian Tire, you may see a Mastercraft mitre saw for $399.99. In Walmart, you may find Windex glass cleaner on sale for 97 cents. These firms are using *odd-even pricing*, which involves setting prices a few dollars or cents under an even number. The presumption is that consumers see the mitre saw as priced at "something over $300" rather than "about $400." The effect this strategy has is psychological: $399.99 *feels* significantly lower than $400—even though there is only one cent difference. There is some evidence to suggest this does work. However, research suggests that overuse of odd-ending prices tends to mute its effect on demand.[7]

Target Pricing

Manufacturers will sometimes estimate the price that the ultimate consumer would be willing to pay for a product. They then work backward through markups taken by retailers and wholesalers to determine what price they can charge for the product. This practice, called *target pricing*, results in the manufacturer deliberately adjusting the composition and features of a product to achieve the target price to consumers.

Airlines use yield management pricing to help fill empty seats.

> ## ask yourself
>
> 1. What is the profit equation?
> 2. What is the difference between skimming and penetration pricing?
> 3. What is odd-even pricing?

Companies may use odd-even pricing to make products like power tools seem less expensive.

Bundle Pricing

A frequently used demand-oriented pricing practice is *bundle pricing*, which is the marketing of two or more products in a single "package" price. For example, Air Canada offers vacation packages that include airfare, car rental, and hotel. Bundle pricing is based on the idea that consumers value the package more than the individual items. This is due to benefits received from not having to make separate purchases as well as increased satisfaction from one item in the presence of another. Bundle pricing often provides a lower total cost to buyers and lower marketing costs to sellers.[8]

Yield Management Pricing

Have you ever been on an airplane and discovered the person next to you paid a lower price for her ticket than you paid? Annoying, isn't it? But what you observed is *yield management pricing*, the charging of different prices to maximize revenue for a set amount of capacity at any given time.[9] Airlines, hotels, and car rental firms engage in capacity management by varying prices based on time, day, week, or season to match demand and supply.

High Credit Card Fees Still an Issue

The fees charged to merchants for processing credit card purchases may affect store prices.

Every time a merchant swipes a customer's credit card, it costs the retailer about 2 percent of the value of the purchase. That's $2 on every $100 worth of goods or services. To the customer, this little expense is invisible. It isn't added at the cash register. Instead, like heat and hydro and other costs of doing business, it's buried in the overall price of the merchandise, whether the consumer buys with a card or cash. It might not sound like a very high price to pay for all the convenience, rewards, and financial flexibility that credit cards offer both consumers and merchants, but some Canadian retailers say credit card fees now take $5 billion a year out of their pockets, and they're spiralling out of control. Consumers argue it is they who are paying the $5 billion in hidden credit card fees because the retailers are passing on these hidden costs to the consumer in the price.

With two very large multinational companies, Visa and MasterCard, dominating the card market, retailers say it can only get worse unless government intervenes. Peter Woolford, vice-president of policy development and research at the Retail Council of Canada, says, "We don't disagree that credit cards are useful means of payment. Customers love them. They are a reasonably effective and efficient way of paying for goods. Our main concern is that they're exorbitantly expensive." In 2013, in an attempt to gain more negotiating power over the fees being charged, merchants argued that Visa and MasterCard were engaging in anti-competitive behaviour. A federal Competition Tribunal dismissed the case.

The fee that retailers pay is called *interchange,* the percentage of each transaction that Visa and MasterCard banks collect from merchants every time a credit card is used to pay for a purchase. The fee varies with type of card, size of merchant, and other factors, but as much as $2 of every $100 a consumer spends goes to card issuers. Interchange fees are higher in Canada, an average of 2 percent, compared with less than 1 percent in most other industrialized countries.[10]

Questions

1. What is your preferred method of payment when shopping?

2. Do you believe that the fees merchants pay in order to accept Visa and MasterCard should be factored into the prices they charge for their products?

Cost-Oriented Approaches

With cost-oriented approaches, a price is more affected by the cost side of the pricing problem than the demand side. (See, for example, the Marketing NewsFlash, "High Credit Card Fees Still an Issue.") Price is set by looking at the production and marketing costs and then adding enough to cover direct expenses, overhead, and profit.

Standard Markup Pricing In order to make a profit, firms sell their products at a price that exceeds their costs of producing or sourcing the items and the costs of marketing them. Conventionally, the difference between the selling price of an item and its cost is referred to as the **markup** and this is normally expressed as a percentage. Markup is also often referred to as gross margin.

Manufacturers commonly express markup as a percentage of cost, which is the difference between selling price and cost, divided by cost. This is also referred to as *standard markup.* Manufacturers use this approach because they are concerned most of the time with costs.

Parties who buy and resell products—for example, wholesalers and retailers—are nearly always dealing with selling prices. They often express markup as a percentage of price, which is the difference between selling price and cost, divided by the selling price.

markup
The difference between selling price and cost, usually expressed as a percentage of cost

Using the same markup percentage for both of the above approaches will result in a different selling price (see the example in Figure 9–3).

Consider the example of a product that is produced by a manufacturer and sold to a wholesaler, who in turn sells it to a retailer, who then sells it to a consumer. The product will be subjected to a series of markups as shown below.

Manufacturer's cost:	**$50.00**
Markup % (based on manufacturer's cost):	40%
Markup $:	$20.00
Selling price to wholesaler:	**$70.00**
Wholesaler cost:	**$70.00**
Markup % (based on selling price to retailer):	15%
Markup $:	$12.35
Selling price to retailer:	**$82.35**
Retailer cost:	**$82.35**
Markup % (based on retailer selling price):	35%
Markup $:	$44.34
Retailer selling price:	**$126.69**

This may surprise you to find out that a product costing $50 to produce can end up costing a consumer more than twice that much when bought at a retailer, but this is not unusual. It is important to remember that markup is necessary at each stage so that companies involved can cover their costs of purchasing the item, can pay to market it to the next stage in the distribution channel, and can generate some profit. The markups shown would be representative of some items such as designer furniture.

Figure 9–3
Markup examples

MARKUP TABLE BASED ON SELLING PRICE		
	$	**%**
Selling price	$75.00	100%*
– (minus) Cost	$60.00	80%
= (equals) Markup	$15.00	20%

* Price is always 100% when markup is relative to price.

MARKUP TABLE BASED ON COST		
	$	**%**
Selling price	$72.00	120%
– (minus) Cost	$60.00	100%**
= (equals) Markup	$12.00	20%

** Cost is always 100% when markup is relative to cost.

This percentage markup varies depending on the type of retail store (such as furniture, clothing, or grocery) and on the product involved. High-volume products usually have smaller markups than do low-volume products. Supermarkets such as Loblaws and Sobeys mark up staple items such as sugar, flour, and dairy products 10 to 25 percent, whereas they mark up discretionary items such as snack foods and candy 25 to 47 percent. These markups must cover all expenses of the store, pay for overhead costs, and contribute something to profits. For supermarkets, these markups, which may appear very large, can result in only a 1 percent profit on sales revenue.

Cost-Plus Pricing Many manufacturers, professional services, and construction firms use a variation of standard markup pricing. *Cost-plus pricing* involves summing the total unit cost of providing a product or service and adding a specific amount to the cost to arrive at a price. Cost-plus pricing is the most commonly used method to set prices for business products.[11] Increasingly, however, this method is finding favour among business-to-business marketers in the service sector. For example, the rising cost of legal fees has prompted some law firms to adopt a cost-plus pricing approach. Rather than billing business clients on an hourly basis, lawyers and their clients agree on a fixed fee based on expected costs plus a profit for the law firm. Many advertising agencies now use this approach. Here, the client agrees to pay the agency a fee based on the cost of its work plus some agreed-on profit.[12]

Profit-Oriented Approaches

A company may choose to balance both revenues and costs to set price using profit-oriented approaches. These might involve either setting a target of a specific dollar volume of profit or expressing this target profit as a percentage of sales or investment.

Target Profit Pricing When a firm sets an annual target of a specific dollar amount of profit, this is called *target profit pricing*. For example, if you owned a picture frame store and wanted to achieve a target profit of $7,000 in the coming year, how much would you need to charge for each frame? Because profit depends on revenues and costs, you would have to know your costs and then estimate how many frames you would sell. Let's assume, based on sales in previous years, you expect to frame 1,000 pictures next year. The cost of your time and materials to frame an average picture is $22, while your overhead expenses (rent, manager salaries, and so on) are $26,000. Finally, your goal is to achieve a profit of $7,000. How do you calculate your price per picture?

Profit = Total revenue − Total costs

$$= \text{(Pictures sold} \times \text{Price/picture)} \\ - [\text{(Cost/picture} \times \text{Pictures sold)} \\ + \text{overhead cost]}$$

Solving for price per picture, the equation becomes:

$$\text{Price/picture} = \frac{\text{Profit} + [\text{(Cost/picture} \times \text{Pictures sold)} + \text{overhead costs}]}{\text{Pictures sold}}$$

$$= \frac{\$7,000 + [(\$22 \times 1,000) + \$26,000]}{1,000}$$

$$= \frac{\$7,000 + \$48,000]}{1,000}$$

$$= \$55 \text{ per picture}$$

Clearly, this pricing method depends on an accurate estimate of demand. Because demand is often difficult to predict, this method has the potential for disaster if the estimate is too high. Generally, a target profit pricing strategy is best for firms offering new or unique products, without a lot of competition. What if other frame stores in your area were charging $40 per framed picture? As a marketing manager, you'd have to offer increased customer value with your more expensive frames, lower your costs, or settle for less profit.

Target Return-on-Sales Pricing Firms such as supermarkets often use *target return-on-sales pricing* to set prices that will give them a profit that is a specified percentage—say, 1 percent—of the sales volume. This pricing method is often used because of the difficulty in establishing a benchmark of sales or investment to show how much of a firm's effort is needed to achieve the target.

Target Return-on-Investment Pricing Firms such as General Motors and many public utilities use *target return-on-investment pricing* to set prices to achieve a return-on-investment (ROI) target, such as a percentage that is mandated by its board of directors or regulators. For example, a hydro utility may decide to seek 10 percent ROI. If its investment in plant and equipment is $50 million, it would need to set the price of hydro to its customers at a level that results in $5 million a year in profits. The importance of achieving ROI estimates will be explored later in this chapter.

Competition-Oriented Approaches

Rather than emphasize demand, cost, or profit factors, a company's approach may be based on an analysis of what competitors are doing.

Customary Pricing For some products where tradition, a standardized channel of distribution, or other competitive factors dictate the price, *customary pricing* is used. Candy bars offered through standard vending machines have a customary price of a dollar, and a significant departure from this price may result in a loss of sales for the manufacturer. Hershey typically has changed the amount of chocolate in its candy bars depending on the price of raw chocolate, rather than vary its customary retail price so that it can continue selling through vending machines.

Above-, at-, or below-Market Pricing The "market price" of a product is what customers are generally willing to pay, not necessarily the price that the firm sets. For most products, it is difficult to identify a specific market price for a product or product class. Still, marketing managers often have a subjective feel for the competitors' price or the market price. Using this benchmark, they then may deliberately choose a strategy of *above-, at-,* or *below-market pricing.*

Items on a supermarket shelf may be priced using target return-on-sales pricing.

Zipping Our Wallets through Car Sharing

As gasoline prices and traffic volumes continue to rise, roughly 20,000 Toronto residents have become members of AutoShare and Zipcar. These are two car-sharing services in the city that have enjoyed rapid growth in recent years. In North America, membership in car-share services is expected to balloon more than eight-fold between now and 2016, a trend that could trim the market for new auto sales by up to one million vehicles.

David Zhao, an automotive research analyst with Frost & Sullivan, says it's a wake-up call for the automakers. "Once that population of shared vehicles gets bigger, the impact on the car market will become more serious," says Zhao, who published a report on car sharing. He predicts car-share membership in North America will reach 4.4 million by 2016, translating into a car-share fleet of more than 70,000 vehicles. There will be a million fewer cars on North American streets by 2016. "It's a trend that will happen and vehicle manufacturers need to carefully gauge the potential impact on their total sales," Zhao concludes.

Such predictions are no surprise for Kevin McLaughlin, founder and president of 12-year-old AutoShare. As big cities improve public transit, as the cost of car ownership rises, and as young people rely more on their iPhones and other technologies to connect and socialize, buying a car is becoming less of a priority, said McLaughlin.

McLaughlin says that in just four years, the number of Torontonians using car-sharing services such as AutoShare has gone from 2,000 to over 20,000. AutoShare, which operates only in Toronto, has roughly 10,000 members. The company has a fleet of about 210 cars representing 13 different models, from minivans to Mini Coopers to hybrids.

Cambridge, Massachusetts–based Zipcar has 350,000 members and a fleet of 6,500 vehicles operating in dozens of North American cities. Its Toronto fleet has grown to about 260 cars since 2006.

Promoting car sharing also reduces air pollution and greenhouse-gas emissions. It is estimated that car-share members drive 31 percent less than they would if they owned their own vehicle. A consumer who owns a car wants to get as much use out of it as possible. Faced with the option of driving a few blocks, walking, or taking transit, most people hop in the car. Paying by the hour from a car-sharing company means that a consumer makes every trip a financial calculation and forces consideration of other options. The pay-as-you-go model encourages conservation every time, whether it's applied to mobile phone minutes, hydro use, or water consumption.

A third player in the car-sharing market is Shelby Clark, a former Zipcar member. The 27-year-old Harvard MBA grad recently launched his own company called RelayRides, which is attempting to pioneer "peer-to-peer" car sharing. Here's how it works: A person who owns a car but doesn't use it very often signs up to RelayRides and offers to let other members drive his or her car for an hourly fee. The Boston-based RelayRides maintains an online reservation system, provides the insurance, does the background checks, confirms that a safety inspection has been done, and acts as a payment clearinghouse. In return, it takes a 15 percent cut of the action.[13]

Zipcar memberships help price-conscious consumers save money.

Questions

1. What do you see as the main benefits in a car-sharing service?

2. Do you feel car-sharing popularity will increase or decrease in the next few years? Give reasons.

"Among watch manufacturers, Rolex takes pride in emphasizing that it makes one of the most expensive watches you can buy—a clear example of above-market pricing."

Rolex watches
are priced above market.

Among watch manufacturers, Rolex takes pride in emphasizing that it makes one of the most expensive watches you can buy—a clear example of above-market pricing. Manufacturers of national brands of clothing such as Christian Dior and retailers such as Holt Renfrew deliberately set higher prices for their products than those seen at Sears.

Large mass-merchandise chains such as Hudson's Bay generally use at-market pricing. These chains often are seen as establishing the going market price in the minds of their competitors. They also provide a reference price for competitors that use above- and below-market pricing.

In contrast, a number of firms use below-market pricing. Walmart positions itself this way. Manufacturers of generic products and retailers that offer their own private brands of products ranging from peanut butter to shampoo deliberately set prices for these products about 8 percent to 10 percent below the prices of nationally branded competitive products such as Skippy peanut butter or Pantene Pro-V shampoo.

Loss-Leader Pricing   Retailers sometimes deliberately sell commonly used products, such as paper towels, soft drinks, and facial tissues, at very low prices to attract consumers who, the retailer hopes, will also buy other, regularly priced merchandise. The downside to loss-leader pricing is that some consumers move from store to store, making purchases only on those products that are loss leaders. This purchasing pattern, called cherry-picking, effectively foils the strategy underlying loss-leader pricing—to attract customers who will also buy products with healthier profit margins. For example, video game consoles may be sold at a loss to create the opportunity to profit from high-margin video games.

Estimating Demand and Revenue

LO 3   Creating the correct price for a product begins the process of forecasting. With the product's price known, marketers try to determine the extent of customer demand for it given their marketing efforts and the efforts of their competitors. Once an estimate for demand is known, marketing executives must translate this information to an estimate of revenues the firm expects to receive.

The Importance of Accurate Forecasting

The forecasts created by the marketing department impact decisions made in other areas of an organization, including production and finance. Inaccurate information and poor estimates can be detrimental to the profitability of a marketing campaign. Similar to market research, both quantitative and qualitative analysis are used to make projections for an organization. Still, a forecast is still an estimate, so given the importance of the estimate, research continues to identify methodologies that can help marketers forecast more accurately.[14]

Forecasting Methods   There are various methods that can be used to forecast. For our introductory purposes, consider the four broad categories of qualitative methods, regression methods, multiple equation methods, and time-series methods. Qualitative methods involve market experts coming to consensus using non-quantitative means to achieve projections. Regression methods link the forecast to a number of other variables through an equation. Multiple equations related to one another can also be used to forecast. Finally, time-series methods assume that the variable being forecast is affected by time.[15]

Profit and Loss   Accurate profit and loss statements help organizations measure financial performance. The statement summarizes the revenues, costs, and expenditures outlined in a particular time frame and helps organizations project their ability for achieving future cash flow. For marketers, it is one of the best tools to gauge the success of a given marketing campaign or initiative.[16]

Return on Investment (ROI)

With profit and loss capturing the performance of a given campaign, return on investment (ROI), or return on marketing investment (ROMI), evaluates the dollars invested in the initiative. When investing in a marketing campaign, marketers are essentially "risking" capital to achieve a desired result. The profit achieved from their initiatives in comparison to what was invested results in the return on marketing investment. Since this model assumes that an infinite number of customers are available to the firm, additional measures such as return on customer (ROC) are being explored to help marketing departments measure campaigns more accurately.[17]

$$\text{return on investment (\%)} = \frac{\begin{pmatrix} \text{gain attributable to investment} \\ - \text{ cost of investment} \end{pmatrix}}{\text{cost of investment}}$$

If a marketing investment of $10,000 in additional advertising and promotion was directly related to an increase in profits of $20,000, then the return on investment would be 100%.

$$\text{return on investment} = \frac{(\$20,000 - \$10,000)}{(\$10,000)} = 100\%$$

Fundamentals of Estimating Demand

Demand for a product or service can be estimated in different ways. An organization can study the marketplace by reviewing historical results from its sales and its competitors' sales. An organization can also conduct tests to gauge the demand of its product. In 1986, *Newsweek* decided to conduct a pricing experiment at newsstands in 11 cities. In one city, newsstand buyers paid $2.25. In five other cities, newsstand buyers paid the regular $2.00 price. In another city, the price was $1.50, and in the remaining four cities it was only $1.00. By comparison, the regular newsstand price for a competing magazine, *Time,* was $1.95. Why did

Newsweek conduct the experiment? According to a *Newsweek* executive, "We wanted to figure out what the demand curve for our magazine at the newsstand is."[18]

As discussed earlier, forecasting is challenging as the marketplace for different products and services continues to change. In December 2012, *Newsweek* published its last print edition and is now under new management with goals to grow the brand in the digital age.[19]

The Demand Curve

A **demand curve** shows the number of products that will be sold at a given price. Demand curve D1 in Figure 9–4A shows the newsstand demand for *Newsweek* under the pricing conditions when it still offered a print version. Note that as price falls, more people decide to buy and unit sales increase. But price is not the complete story in estimating demand. Economists emphasize three other key factors:

1. **Consumer tastes:** These depend on many factors such as demographics, culture, and technology. Because consumer tastes can change quickly, up-to-date marketing research is essential. For example, although older readers prefer paper books, research finds it is easier for them to read from electronic tablets.[20]

2. **Price and availability of similar products:** The laws of demand work for one's competitors, too. Consider *Newsweek* in its print format again. If the

demand curve
Graph relating quantity sold and price, which shows how many units will be sold at a given price

The last print issue of *Newsweek* was due to laws of demand.

> **"We first want to understand if our clients know what price they are paying for the service. From there, we determine the price they are willing to pay for the service."**
>
> –Hilary Zaharko, director of marketing, H&R Block Canada

price of *Time* magazine falls, more people will buy it. Fewer people will buy *Newsweek* since *Time* is considered by economists to be a substitute for *Newsweek*. In 2012, other online magazines were considered substitutes, so if their prices fell or their availability increased, the demand for a product (*Newsweek* magazine, in this case) would fall. The result was *Newsweek* magazine moving online.

3. **Consumer income:** In general, as real consumer income (allowing for inflation) increases, demand for a product also increases. More disposable income allows for additional purchases that are not necessarily necessities. In 2014, Canada's inflation rate rose 1.5 percent.

The first of these two factors influences what consumers *want* to buy, and the third affects what they can buy. Along with price, these are often called *demand factors,* or factors that determine consumers' willingness and ability to pay for goods and services. It is often very difficult to estimate demand for new products, especially because consumer likes and dislikes are often so difficult to read clearly. (See the Marketing NewsFlash, "Zipping Our Wallets through Car Sharing," to find out how these factors are impacting demand for owning a car.)

Movement along versus Shift of a Demand Curve

Demand curve *D*1 in Figure 9–4A shows that as the price is lowered from $2.00 to $1.50, the quantity demanded increases from 3 million (*Q*1) to 4.5 million (*Q*2) units per year. This is an example of a *movement along a demand curve* and assumes that other factors (consumer tastes, price and availability of substitutes, and consumer income) remain unchanged.

What if some of these factors change? For example, if advertising causes more people to want *Newsweek*, newsstand distribution is increased, or if consumer incomes rise, then the demand increases. Now the original curve, *D*1 (the blue line in Figure 9–4B), no longer represents the demand; a new curve must be drawn (*D*2). Economists call this a *shift in the demand*

curve—in this case, a shift to the right, from *D*1 to *D*2. This increased demand means that more *Newsweek* magazines are wanted for a given price: At a price of $2, the demand is 6 million units per year (*Q*3) on *D*2 rather than 3 million units per year (*Q*1) on *D*1.

While print magazine were still in demand, what price did *Newsweek* select after conducting its experiment? It kept the price at $2.00. However, through expanded newsstand distribution and more aggressive advertising, *Newsweek* was later able to shift its demand curve to the right and charge a price of $2.50 without affecting its newsstand volume.

Price Elasticity of Demand

Marketing managers must also pay attention to *price elasticity,* a key consideration related to the product's demand curve. Price elasticity refers to how sensitive consumer demand and the firm's revenues are to changes in the product's price.

A product with *elastic demand* is one in which a slight decrease in price results in a relatively large increase in demand, or units sold. The reverse is also true: With elastic demand, a slight increase in price results in a relatively large decrease in demand. Marketing experiments on products that are price-sensitive, such as cola, coffee, and snack foods, show them often to have elastic demand. So marketing managers may cut prices to increase the demand, the units sold, and total revenue for one of these products, depending

Figure 9–4
Illustrative demand curves for *Newsweek*

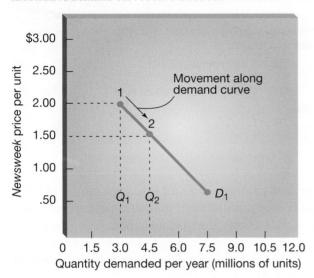

A Demand curve under initial conditions

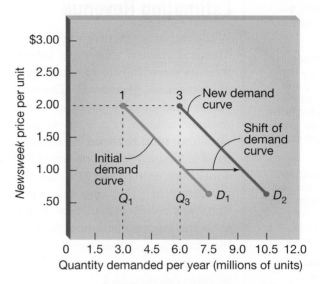

B Shift in the demand curve with different conditions

on what competitors' prices are. The demand for many consumer products is elastic—think jeans, DVDs, and car stereos.

One major factor influencing the elasticity of demand is the availability of substitute products. If consumers can easily find close substitutes for a good or service, the product's demand tends to be elastic.

In contrast, a product with *inelastic demand* means that slight increases or decreases in price will not significantly affect the demand, or units sold, for the product. Products and services considered as necessities, such as hydro or going to the dentist, usually have inelastic demand. What about gasoline for your car? Will an increase of a few cents per litre cause you to drive fewer kilometres and buy less gasoline? No? Then you're like millions of other consumers, which is why gasoline has inelastic demand. This means that an increase of a few cents per litre may have a relatively minor impact on the number of litres sold, and may actually increase the total revenue of the gasoline producer. Inelastic demand is usually a relatively short-term phenomenon. Consumers, when they are faced with high prices for something they have to have, will seek out an alternative, and/or producers will see an opportunity to develop a new product. A hybrid car is, in some ways, a producer's response to high gas prices. Or maybe you could learn to love the bus!

Another example of inelastic demand is when buyers are less price-sensitive when the product they are buying is unique or is high in quality and prestige. In this case, consumers perceive that the high price means more quality and the demand for that product

will not suffer very much. In some cases, a higher price may result in higher sales, which results in the demand curve actually sloping upwards.

The Internet has changed the elasticity of demand for some products. In the past, a consumer's choice when considering buying a product was limited to the number of bricks-and-mortar stores available. Now, with the Internet, there are many more choices of suppliers to choose from. The large number of suppliers competing with each other has led to lower prices on products that were once available only in stores. The availability of different suppliers on the Internet combines to create more products with elastic demand.

ask yourself

1. *What is loss-leader pricing?*

2. *What are three demand factors other than price that are used in estimating demand?*

3. *What is the difference between movement along a demand curve and a shift in a demand curve?*

total revenue

Total money received from the sale of a product

total cost

Total expenses incurred by a firm in producing and marketing a product; total cost is the sum of fixed cost and variable costs

fixed cost

A firm's expenses that are stable and do not change with the quantity of product that is produced and sold

variable cost

Sum of the expenses of a firm that vary directly with the quantity of products that is produced and sold

break-even analysis

Examines the relationship between total revenue and total cost to determine profitability at different levels of output

Fundamentals of Estimating Revenue

While economists may talk about "demand curves," marketing executives are more likely to speak in terms of "revenues generated." Demand curves lead directly to an essential revenue concept critical to pricing decisions: **total revenue**. As summarized in Figure 9–5, total revenue (TR) equals the unit price (P) times the quantity sold (Q). Using this equation, let's recall our picture frame shop and assume our annual demand has improved so that we can set a price of $100 per picture and sell 400 pictures per year. So,

$$TR = P \times Q$$
$$= \$100 \times 400$$
$$= \$40,000$$

This combination of price and quantity sold annually will give us a total revenue of $40,000 per year. Is that good? Are you making money, making a profit? Total revenue is only part of the profit equation that we saw earlier:

$$\text{Total profit} = \text{Total revenue} - \text{Total cost}$$

The next section covers the other part of the profit equation: cost.

Determining Cost, Volume, and Profit Relationships

LO 4 While revenues are the monies received by the firm from selling its products or services to customers, costs or expenses are the monies the firm pays out to its employees and suppliers. Marketing managers often use break-even analysis to relate revenues and costs, topics covered in this section.

The Importance of Controlling Costs

Understanding the role and behaviour of costs is critical for all marketing decisions, particularly pricing decisions. Many firms go bankrupt because their costs get out of control, causing their total costs to exceed

Figure 9–5
Total revenue concept

Total revenue (TR) is the total money received from the sale of a product. If

    TR = Total revenue
    P = Unit price of the product
    Q = Quantity of the product sold

Then

    TR = P × Q

their total revenues over an extended period of time. This is why sophisticated marketing managers make pricing decisions that balance both their revenues and costs. Three cost concepts are important in pricing decisions: **total cost**, **fixed cost**, and **variable cost** (Figure 9–6).

Break-Even Analysis

LO 5 Marketing managers often employ an approach that considers cost, volume, and profit relationships, based on the profit equation. **Break-even analysis** is a technique that analyzes the relationship between total revenue and total cost to determine profitability at various levels of output. The *break-even point (BEP)* is the quantity at which total revenue and total cost are equal. Profit comes from any units sold after the BEP has been reached. In terms of the definitions in Figure 9–6,

$$\text{BEP}_{\text{Quantity}} = \frac{\text{Fixed cost}}{\text{Unit price} - \text{Unit variable cost}}$$

Figure 9–6
Total cost concept

Fixed cost (FC) is the sum of the expenses of the firm that are stable and do not change with the quantity of product that is produced and sold. Examples of fixed costs are rent on the building, executive salaries, and insurance.

Variable cost (VC) is the sum of the expenses of the firm that vary directly with the quantity of product that is produced and sold. Examples are the direct labour and direct materials used in producing the product. Variable cost expressed on a per unit basis is called *unit variable cost (UVC)*.

TC = FC + VC

Total cost (TC) is the total expense incurred by a firm in producing and marketing the product. Total cost is the sum of fixed cost and variable cost.

Calculating a Break-Even Point Consider again your picture frame store. Suppose that you wish to identify how many pictures you must sell to cover your fixed cost at a given price. Let's assume demand for your framed pictures has increased, so the average price customers are willing to pay for each picture is $100. Also, suppose your fixed cost (FC) has grown to $28,000 (for real estate taxes, interest on a bank loan, and other fixed expenses) and unit variable cost (UVC) for a picture is now $30 (for labour, glass, frame, and matting). Your break-even quantity ($BEP_{Quantity}$) is 400 pictures, as follows:

$$BEP_{Quantity} = \frac{\text{Fixed cost}}{\text{Unit price} - \text{Unit variable cost}}$$

$$= \frac{\$28,000}{\$100 - \$30}$$

$$= 400 \text{ pictures}$$

The row shaded in blue in Figure 9–7 shows that your break-even quantity at a price of $100 per picture is 400 pictures. At less than 400 pictures, your picture frame store incurs a loss, and at more than 400 pictures it makes a profit. Figure 9–7 also shows that if you could double your annual picture sales to 800, your store would make a profit of $28,000—the row shaded in brown in the figure.

Figure 9–8 shows a graphic presentation of the break-even analysis, called a *break-even chart*. It shows that total revenue and total cost intersect and are equal at a quantity of 400 pictures sold, which is the break-even point at which profit is exactly $0. You want to do better? If your frame store could double the quantity sold annually to 800 pictures, the graph in Figure 9–8 shows that you can earn an annual profit of $28,000, as shown by the row shaded in brown in Figure 9–7.

ask yourself

1. **What is the difference between fixed costs and variable costs?**

2. **What is a break-even point?**

Applications of Break-Even Analysis Because of its simplicity, break-even analysis is used extensively in marketing, most frequently to study the impact on profit of changes in price, fixed cost, and variable cost. The mechanics of break-even analysis are the basis of the widely used electronic spreadsheets such as Microsoft Excel that permit managers to answer hypothetical "what if" questions about the effect of changes in price and cost on their profit.

Pricing Objectives and Constraints

LO 6 With such a variety of alternative pricing strategies available, marketing managers must consider the pricing objectives and constraints that will impact their decisions. While pricing objectives frequently reflect corporate goals, pricing constraints often relate to conditions existing in the marketplace.

Figure 9–7
Calculating a break-even point for a picture frame store

Quantity of pictures sold (Q)	Price per picture (P)	Total revenue (TR) = (P × Q)	Unit variable cost (UVC)	Total variable cost (TVC) = (UVC × Q)	Fixed cost (FC)	Total cost (TC) = (FC + TVC)	Profit = (TR − TC)
0	$100	$0	$30	$0	$28,000	$28,000	−$28,000
200	100	20,000	30	6,000	28,000	34,000	−14,000
400	100	40,000	30	12,000	28,000	40,000	0
600	100	60,000	30	18,000	28,000	46,000	14,000
800	100	80,000	30	24,000	28,000	52,000	28,000
1,000	100	100,000	30	30,000	28,000	58,000	42,000
1,200	100	120,000	30	36,000	28,000	64,000	56,000

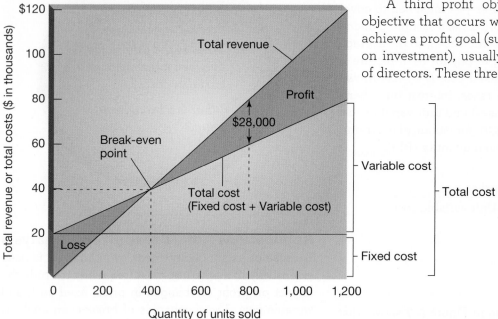

Figure 9–8
Break-even analysis for a picture frame store

Identifying Pricing Objectives

Pricing objectives specify the role of price in an organization's marketing and strategic plans. To the extent possible, these pricing objectives are carried to lower levels in the organization, such as in setting objectives for marketing managers responsible for an individual brand. These objectives may change, depending on the financial position of the company as a whole, the success of its products, or the segments in which it is doing business. H. J. Heinz, for example, has specific pricing objectives for its Heinz ketchup brand that vary by country.

Profit Three different objectives relate to a firm's profit, which is often measured in terms of return on investment (ROI). These objectives have different implications for pricing strategy. One objective is *managing for long-run profits,* in which a company—such as many Japanese car or TV set manufacturers—gives up immediate profit in exchange for achieving a higher market share. Products are priced relatively low compared to their cost to develop, but the firm expects to make greater profits later because of its high market share.

A *maximizing current profit* objective, such as for a quarter or year, is common in many firms because the targets can be set and performance measured quickly. North

American firms are sometimes criticized for this short-run orientation.

A third profit objective is a *target return* objective that occurs when a firm sets its price to achieve a profit goal (such as 20 percent for return on investment), usually determined by its board of directors. These three profit objectives have different implications for a firm's pricing objectives.

Another profit consideration for firms such as movie studios and manufacturers is to ensure that those firms in their channels of distribution make adequate profits. For example, Figure 9–9 shows where each dollar of your movie ticket goes. The 51 cents the movie studio gets must cover its profit plus the cost of making and marketing the movie. Although the studio would like more than 51 cents of your dollar, it settles for this amount to make sure theatres and distributors are satisfied and willing to handle its movies.

Sales As long as a firm's profit is high enough for it to remain in business, an objective may be to increase sales revenue, which will in turn lead to increases in market share and profit. Cutting the price on one product in a firm's line may increase its sales revenue but reduce those of related products. Objectives related to sales revenue or unit sales have the advantage of being translated easily into meaningful targets for marketing managers responsible for a product line or brand.

Market Share Market share is the ratio of the firm's sales to those of the industry (competitors plus the firm itself). Companies often pursue a market share objective when industry sales are relatively flat or declining. For example, the cola market is declining, but Coke wants to keep its market share by retaining its piece of a dwindling pie. Although increased market share is a primary goal of some firms, others see it as a means to increasing sales and profits.

Adopting a market share objective does not always imply low price. The lowest-priced brand rarely has the highest market share. Tropicana orange juice, French's mustard, and Heinz ketchup are market share leaders and are all premium-priced. Brands such as these retain their market share positions because they offer value to consumers.

Figure 9–9
Where each dollar of your movie ticket goes

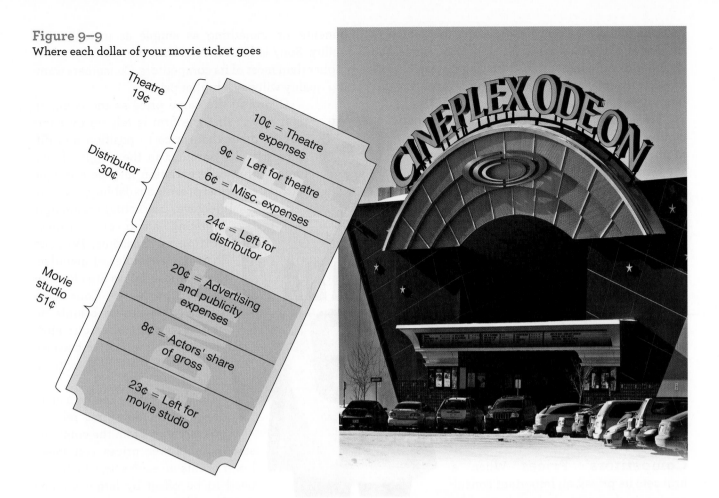

Theatre 19¢
Distributor 30¢
Movie studio 51¢

10¢ = Theatre expenses
9¢ = Left for theatre
6¢ = Misc. expenses
24¢ = Left for distributor
20¢ = Advertising and publicity expenses
8¢ = Actors' share of gross
23¢ = Left for movie studio

Volume Many firms use volume, the quantity produced or sold, as a pricing objective. These firms often sell the same product at several different prices, at different times, or in different places in an attempt to match customer demand with the company's production capacity. Using volume as an objective can sometimes be misleading from a profit standpoint. Volume can be increased by using sales incentives (lowering prices, giving rebates, or offering lower interest rates). By doing this, the company chooses to lower profits in the short run to sell its product quickly. For example, a new health club might focus on getting a certain number of people to join by lowering its membership prices and accepting less profit, at first.

Survival In some instances, profits, sales, and market share are less important objectives of the firm than mere survival. Air Canada has struggled to attract passengers with low fares and aggressive promotions to improve the firm's cash flow. This pricing objective has helped Air Canada to stay alive in the competitive airline industry.

Social Responsibility A firm may forgo higher profit on sales and follow a pricing objective that recognizes its obligations to customers and society in general. Gerber supplies a specially formulated product free of charge to children who cannot tolerate foods based on cow's milk.

Identifying Pricing Constraints

Factors that limit the range of price a firm may set are **pricing constraints**. Consumer demand for the product clearly affects the price that can be charged. Other constraints on price vary from factors within the organization to competitive factors outside it.

Demand for the Product Class, Product, and Brand The number of potential buyers for a product class (cars), product (sports cars), and brand (Bugatti Veyron) clearly affects the price a seller can charge. So does whether the item is a luxury, like a Bugatti Veyron, or a necessity, like bread and a roof over your head.

Newness of the Product: Stage in the Product Life Cycle The newer the product and the earlier it is in its life cycle, the higher the price

pricing constraints
Factors that limit the range of price a firm may set

that can usually be charged. Consider the launch of the Apple iPad. With its new technology, Apple had no other direct competition at first, so it was possible to ask consumers to pay a high initial price for this innovative product.

Sometimes, such as when nostalgia or fad factors are present, prices may rise later in the product's life cycle. The legendary hockey jersey worn by Paul Henderson in the 1972 Summit Series was sold for over $1 million at an auction. Henderson was wearing the jersey when he scored the winning goal in Team Canada's emotional win over the Soviets.[21]

Cost of Producing and Marketing the Product
In the long run, a firm's price must cover all the costs of producing and marketing a product. If the price doesn't cover these costs, the firm will fail; so in the long run, a firm's costs set a floor under its price.

Competitors' Prices
When a firm sets its prices, an important consideration is the prices being charged by the competition. As we talked about previously, a firm has three choices: It can charge a higher price, the same price, or a lower price than its competitors. Each choice conveys a message to customers. For example, e-readers such as Amazon's Kindle and the Sony Reader were developed as single-function devices, meant solely for use as a reader. The iPad, on the other hand, is a multi-function appliance that allows the user to surf the Internet as well as use it as a reader. Because the e-readers made by Sony and Amazon have a limited use, they were forced to drop their prices dramatically when the iPad came on the scene.[22] Amazon has gone on to develop its own multi-function device, introducing the Kindle Fire in November 2011, which includes Internet, video, app, and gaming functionality to go along with its reader. Amazon's price for its Kindle Fire is significantly lower than the iPad, a strategy to reach consumers who are price-sensitive.

A high price signifies that the firm believes its offering represents a higher value in comparison to competing products—value being quality, brand image, benefits and unique features offering extra

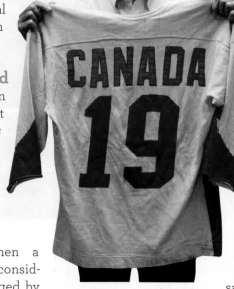

Canadian hockey legend Paul Henderson, who scored the game-winning goal during the 1972 Summit Series against the Soviet Union, holds his original 1972 Team Canada sweater.

benefits, or something as simple as instant availability. Sony is known as a firm that typically prices higher than most of its competitors. Consumers wanting quality will pay a higher price.

Charging the same price as the competition means that the firm is relying on some aspect other than price to position and differentiate its products in the minds of customers—that differentiation may be a unique attribute, widespread availability, or an intensive marketing campaign. Thinking again of consumer electronics, Panasonic, JVC, and Sharp are examples of manufacturers whose prices are close for similar products. Consumers typically buy these brands on the basis of some unique attribute of the product, or because they prefer to deal with a specific retailer.

Lower prices can be a challenge, but many firms rely on this strategy. From the company standpoint, lower prices can mean lower profits on each sale, which may need to be offset by larger volume sales. In addition, larger volumes can result in production efficiencies and lower costs. Less well-known brands and some of the larger manufacturers such as RCA use this strategy. For consumers, the lower prices often mean forgoing some aspect such as quality or brand image.

The decision to charge a certain price is impacted by marketing and pricing objectives. If winning market share is an objective, lower prices may be the solution. If being perceived as the "best brand" is an objective, higher prices may be part of the answer. Being known as a *market leader* based on pricing is a title that could be ascribed to firms using either strategy.

Charging prices in line with the competition earns firms the title of *market follower*. This is a conscious choice of many smaller firms manufacturing and selling similar or often the same products. Emphasis is shifted away from price to some other aspect of the marketing mix.

There are occasions where other objectives override any consideration of competitor pricing, such as selling off discontinued models or time-sensitive items (summer-vacation packages, for example).

Legal and Ethical Considerations

Deciding on a final price is a complex process. In addition to the considerations we have just presented, there are laws and regulations that also play a role in the price decision. We will look at four of the most prominent considerations.

Price Fixing When competitors collaborate and conspire to set prices, they agree to increase, decrease, or stabilize a price for their benefit. This is called *price fixing,* and it is illegal—the *Competition Act* prohibits this practice. The *Competition Act* consists of federal regulations governing most business conduct in Canada. Price fixing usually occurs where price is the most important factor in the marketing mix. Twelve global airlines that ran a cargo price-fixing cartel for years were hit with fines totalling $1.1 billion by European Union regulators. The European Commission slapped Air Canada with the third-smallest fine at $29.2 million.[23] Read the Focus on Ethics, "Death by Chocolate," below for another story on price fixing.

Price Discrimination If different prices are charged to different customers for the same or very similar goods and the same terms, *price discrimination* has occurred. The *Competition Act* prohibits this, but in order for a firm to be charged with the offence, there has to be evidence of a "practice" of price discrimination—that is, that it is not just a one-time or occasional event.

Deceptive Pricing Price offers that mislead the consumer are considered *deceptive pricing,* and this is prohibited under the *Competition Act.* Figure 9–10 shows the most common deceptive pricing practices. Many companies across the country have been accused of deceptive pricing, but it can be difficult to police and the laws are hard to enforce. Often, regulators rely on the ethical standards of those making and publicizing pricing decisions. The Canadian Code of Advertising Standards provides guidelines for various aspects of promotion, and pricing is one of these; advertising industry members are expected to follow this Code and to self-regulate (ensure that they and their colleagues adhere to the Code).

An example of deceptive pricing is menswear retailer Grafton-Fraser Inc. The retailer agreed to pay a $1.2 million penalty to settle an advertising case regarding misleading sale prices. The Competition Bureau found that Grafton-Fraser had significantly inflated the regular price of certain garments sold in its stores, resulting in an overstatement of the savings to consumers when these garments were on sale. The retailer joins other merchants, including Suzy Shier, Sears Canada Ltd., and Forzani Group Ltd., that the Competition Bureau found were inflating an item's regular price and thereby overstating the savings of the sale price. Grafton-Fraser, the bureau found, was tagging garments with both a regular and a sale price; however, the items did not sell "in any significant quantity or for any reasonable period of time at the regular price," the Bureau said. Grafton-Fraser runs stores across the country that operate under several names, among them Tip Top Tailors, George Richards Big & Tall, and Grafton & Co.[24]

Predatory Pricing Charging a very low price for a product with the intent of undercutting competitors and possibly driving them out of the market is called *predatory pricing.* After the competitors have been driven out, the offending firm raises its prices. If a company can genuinely operate more efficiently than others, and this lets them offer its products at a lower

Figure 9–10
Most common deceptive pricing practices

Deceptive Practice	Description
Bait and switch	A firm offers a very low price for a product (the bait), and when consumers come to purchase it, they are persuaded to buy a more expensive product (the switch). Uses techniques such as downgrading the advertised item or not having it in stock.
Bargains conditional on other purchases	A firm advertises "buy one, get one free" or "get two for the price of one." If the first items are sold at the regular price, this is legal. If the price for the first items is inflated for the offer, it is not.
Price comparisons	Advertising "retail value $100—our price $85" is deceptive if a substantial number of stores in the area are not using the $100 price—in other words, if it is not the "going price." Advertising "below manufacturer's suggested list price" is deceptive if no sales occur at the manufacturer's list price. Advertising that the price is reduced 50% is deceptive if the item was not offered for sale at the higher price for a substantial previous period of time.
Double ticketing	When more than one price tag is placed on an item, it must be sold at the lower price; this practice is not illegal, but the law requires that the lower price be charged.

Death by Chocolate

Lovers of chocolate have jokingly associated it with sin. Ironically, one of the largest confectionery and snack companies around the world was accused of deceptive pricing practices. In 2013, Hershey Canada was fined $4 million for its role in a price-fixing chocolate cartel. The six-year investigation found that Hershey was guilty of conspiring, agreeing, or arranging to fix prices in the Canadian chocolate industry in 2007. Hershey Canada cooperated with the Competition Bureau's investigation and plans to continue to cooperate on any further issues. The class action lawsuit resulted in Cadbury Adams Canada Inc., Nestlé Canada Inc., Mars Canada Inc., and Hershey Canada Inc. agreeing to pay more than $23 million to settle.

In a statement, John Pecman, commissioner of competition, said, "Price-fixing is a serious criminal offence, regardless of whether it is in the chocolate confectionary market or any other industry."

Hershey stated that its senior employees spoke with members of the cartel in 2007. Hershey also stated that its current Canadian management and the rest of Hershey Company had no involvement in the cartel. Nonetheless, this news may leave a bad taste in the mouth for some.[25]

Hershey Canada and other Canadian chocolate companies were accused of price fixing.

Questions

1. If a company such as Hershey's can be accused of deceptive pricing practices, what other companies could as well? Give an example from your own experience where you encountered deceptive pricing practices.

2. Price fixing is a key concern for the Competition Bureau. Figure 9–10 highlights four deceptive pricing practices. Which of the four do with you feel is the most unethical and unlawful? Give reasons.

price, should this be classified as predatory pricing? No! It's not easy to prove that the intent of the lower price is to eliminate a competitor, and that the prices set are unreasonably and artificially low, so there are many more charges of predatory pricing than there are convictions.

Global Pricing Strategy

Global companies face many challenges in determining a pricing strategy as part of their worldwide marketing effort. Individual countries, even those with free trade agreements, may place considerable competitive, political, and legal constraints on the pricing

ask yourself

1. *What is the difference between pricing objectives and pricing constraints?*

2. *Explain what bait and switch is and why it is an example of deceptive pricing.*

flexibility of global companies. For example, Walmart was told by German antitrust authorities that the prices in its stores were too low, relative to competitors, and faced a fine for violating the country's trade if the prices weren't raised![26]

Pricing too low or too high can have dire consequences. When prices appear too low in one country, companies can be charged with dumping, a practice subject to severe penalties and fines. **Dumping** occurs when a firm sells a product in a foreign country below its domestic price or below its actual cost. A recent trade dispute involving U.S. apple growers and Mexico is a case in point. Mexican trade officials claimed that U.S. growers were selling their red and golden delicious apples in Mexico below the actual cost of production. They imposed a 101 percent tariff on U.S. apples, and a severe drop in U.S. apple exports to Mexico resulted. Later negotiations set a price floor on the price of U.S. apples sold to Mexico.[27]

When companies price their products very high in some countries but competitively in others, they face a grey market problem. A **grey market**, also called *parallel importing,* is a situation where products are sold through unauthorized channels of distribution. A grey market comes about when individuals buy products in a lower-priced country from a manufacturer's authorized retailer, ship them to higher-priced countries, and then sell them below the manufacturer's suggested retail price through unauthorized retailers. Many well-known products have been sold through grey markets, including Olympus cameras, Seiko watches, and Mercedes-Benz cars. Parallel channels are not strictly illegal in Canada, but there are mounting legal challenges to them. Parallel importing is legal in the United States. It is illegal in the European Union.[28]

Setting a Final Price

LO 7 The final price set by the marketing manager serves many functions. It must be high enough to cover the cost of providing the product *and* meet the objectives of the company. Yet it must be low enough that customers are willing to pay it. But not too low, or customers may think they're purchasing an inferior product. Confused? Setting price is one of the most difficult tasks the marketing manager faces, but four generalized steps are useful to follow.

Step 1: Select an Approximate Price Level

Before setting a final price, the marketing manager must understand the market environment, the features and customer benefits of the particular product, and the goals of the firm. A balance must be struck between factors that might drive a price higher (such as a profit-oriented approach) and other forces (such as increased competition from substitutes) that may drive a price down.

Marketing managers consider pricing objectives and constraints first, and then choose among the general pricing approaches—demand-, cost-, profit-, or competition-oriented—to arrive at an approximate price level. This price is then analyzed in terms of cost, volume, and profit relationships. Break-even analyses may be run at this point, and finally, if this approximate price level "works," it is time to take the next step: setting a specific list or quoted price.

Step 2: Set the List or Quoted Price

A seller must decide whether to follow a one-price or flexible-price policy.

One-Price Policy A *one-price policy* involves setting one price for all buyers of a product or service. For example, when you buy a product at Walmart, you are offered the product at a single price. You can decide to buy it or not, but there is no variation of the price under the seller's one-price policy. Some retailers such as Dollarama married this policy with a below-market approach and used to sell mostly everything in their stores for $1! Recently, Dollarama has added more products at prices ranging from $1.25 to $3.

dumping
Occurs when a firm sells a product in a foreign country below its domestic prices or below its actual cost

grey market
Situations where products are sold through unauthorized channels of distribution

Dollarama previously used a one-price policy.

3920 BROCK ST. N.
DOLLARAMA

Flexible-Price Policy In contrast, a *flexible-price policy* involves setting different prices for products and services depending on individual buyers and purchase situations in light of demand, cost, and competitive factors. Dell Computer adopted flexible pricing as it continually adjusts prices in response to changes in its own costs, competitive pressures, and demand from its various personal computer segments (home, small business, corporate, and so on). "Our flexibility allows us to be [priced] different even within a day," says a Dell spokesperson.[29]

Flexible pricing is not without its critics because of its discriminatory potential. For example, car dealers have traditionally used flexible pricing on the basis of buyer-seller negotiations to agree on a final price. Is it any wonder that 60 percent of prospective car buyers dread negotiating the price?

> *Is it any wonder that 60 percent of prospective car buyers dread negotiating the price?*

Step 3: Make Special Adjustments to the List or Quoted Price

LO 8 When you pay $2 for a bag of M&Ms in a vending machine or receive a quoted price of $10,000 from a contractor to renovate a kitchen, the pricing sequence ends with the last step just described: setting the list or quoted price. But when you are a manufacturer of M&M candies and sell your product to dozens or hundreds of wholesalers and retailers in your channel of distribution, you may need to make a variety of special adjustments to the list or quoted price. Wholesalers also must adjust list or quoted prices they set for retailers. Three special adjustments to the list or quoted price are discounts, allowances, and geographical adjustments.

Discounts *Discounts* are reductions from list price that a seller gives a buyer as a reward for some activity of the buyer that is favourable to the seller. Four kinds of discounts are especially important in marketing strategy: quantity, seasonal, trade (functional), and cash.[30]

- **Quantity discounts:** To encourage customers to buy larger quantities of a product, firms at all levels in the channel of distribution offer quantity discounts, which are reductions in unit costs for a larger order. For example, an instant photocopying service might set a price of 10 cents a copy for 1 to 24 copies, 9 cents a copy for 25 to 99, and 8 cents a copy for 100 or more.

Because the photocopying service gets more of the buyer's business and has longer production runs that reduce its order-handling costs, it is willing to pass on some of the cost savings in the form of quantity discounts to the buyer.

- **Seasonal discounts:** To encourage buyers to stock inventory earlier than their normal demand would require, manufacturers often use seasonal discounts. A firm such as Toro that manufactures lawn mowers and snow blowers offers seasonal discounts to encourage wholesalers and retailers to stock up on lawn mowers in January and February and on snow blowers in July and August—months before the seasonal demand by ultimate consumers. This enables Toro to smooth out seasonal manufacturing peaks and troughs, thereby contributing to more-efficient production. It also rewards wholesalers and retailers for the risk they accept in assuming increased inventory carrying costs and gives them the benefit of having supplies in stock at the time they are wanted by customers.

Toro uses seasonal discounts to stimulate consumer demand and smooth out seasonal manufacturing peaks and troughs.

- **Trade (functional) discounts:** To reward wholesalers and retailers for marketing functions they will perform in the future, a manufacturer often gives trade, or functional, discounts. These reductions off the list or base price are offered to resellers in the channel of distribution on the basis of where they are in the channel and the marketing activities they are expected to perform in the future.

  Traditional trade discounts have been established in various product lines such as hardware, food, and pharmaceutical items. Although the manufacturer may suggest trade discounts, the sellers are free to alter the discount schedule depending on their competitive situation. Suppose that a manufacturer quotes prices in the following form:

  List price — $100, less 30/10/5

  The first number in the percentage sequence (in this example, 30/10/5) always refers to the retail end of the channel, and the last number always refers to the wholesaler or jobber closest to the manufacturer in the channel. The trade discounts are simply subtracted one at a time. This price quote shows that $100 is the manufacturer's suggested retail price:

  - For the retailer, 30 percent of the suggested retail price ($100 × 0.3 = $30) is available to cover costs and provide a profit;

  - Wholesalers closest to the retailer in the channel get 10 percent of their selling price ($70 × 0.1 = $7); and

  - The final group of wholesalers in the channel (probably jobbers) that are closest to the manufacturer get 5 percent of their selling price ($63 × 0.05 = $3.15).

  Thus, starting with the manufacturer's retail price and subtracting the three trade discounts shows that the manufacturer's selling price to the wholesaler or jobber closest to the manufacturer is $59.85 (see Figure 9–11).

- **Cash discounts:** To encourage retailers to pay their bills quickly, manufacturers offer them cash discounts. Suppose that a retailer receives a bill quoted at $1,000, 2/10 net 30. This means that the bill for the product is $1,000, but the retailer can take a two percent discount ($1,000 × 0.02 = $20) if payment is made within 10 days and send a cheque for $980. If the payment cannot be made within 10 days, the total amount of $1,000 is due within 30 days. It is usually understood by the buyer that an interest charge will be added after the first 30 days of free credit.

  Retailers provide cash discounts to consumers as well, to eliminate the cost of credit granted to consumers. These discounts take the form of discount-for-cash policies.

Figure 9–11
How trade discounts work

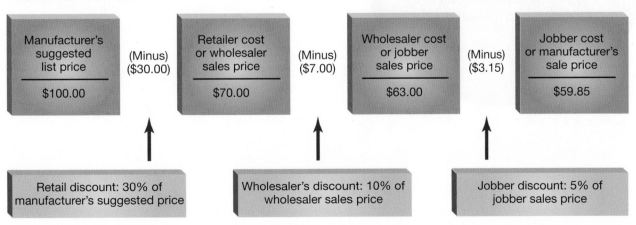

Allowances Allowances—like discounts—are reductions from list or quoted prices to buyers for performing some activity.

- **Trade-in allowances:** A new car dealer can offset the list price of that new Toyota Camry by offering you a trade-in allowance of $500 for your old Honda. A trade-in allowance is a price reduction given when a used product is part of the payment on a new product. Trade-ins are an effective way to lower the price a buyer has to pay without formally reducing the list price.

- **Promotional allowances:** Sellers in the channel of distribution can qualify for promotional allowances for undertaking certain advertising or selling activities to promote a product. Various types of allowances include an actual cash payment or an extra amount of "free goods" (as with a free case of pizzas to a retailer for every dozen cases purchased). Frequently, a portion of these savings is passed on to the consumer by retailers.

Geographical Adjustments Geographical adjustments are made by manufacturers or even wholesalers to list or quoted prices to reflect the cost of transportation of the products from seller to buyer. The two general methods for quoting prices related to transportation costs are FOB origin pricing and uniform delivered pricing.

- **FOB origin pricing:** FOB means "free on board" some vehicle at some location, which means the seller pays the cost of loading the product onto the vehicle that is used (such as a barge, railroad car, or truck). FOB origin pricing usually involves the seller's naming the location of this loading as the seller's factory or warehouse (such as "FOB Montreal" or "FOB factory"). The title and ownership to the goods passes to the buyer at the point of loading, so the buyer becomes responsible for picking the specific mode of transportation, for all the transportation costs, and for subsequent handling of the product. Buyers furthest from the seller face the big disadvantage of paying the higher transportation costs.

- **Uniform delivered pricing:** When a uniform delivered pricing method is used, the price the seller quotes includes all transportation costs. It is quoted in a contract as "FOB buyer's location," and the seller selects the mode of transportation, pays the freight charges, and is responsible for any damage that may occur because the seller retains title to the goods until delivered to the buyer.

Step 4: Monitor and Adjust Prices

Rarely can a firm set a price and leave it at that. As you have learned, there are many constraints that affect setting prices, and the firm has objectives that it also takes into account. Things change both in the external business environment and within the firm itself; as a result, prices need to be reviewed and revised if necessary. A key activity is the monitoring of competitor activity, legislative changes, economic conditions, and—the ultimate measure—consumer demand! These factors, and their potential impact on the firm's ability to achieve its marketing goals, have to be examined and action taken when necessary.

ask yourself

1. *Why would a seller choose a flexible-price policy over a one-price policy?*

2. *What is the purpose of (a) quantity discounts and (b) promotional allowances?*

ad Alyze

Keep more money in your pocket.

When you file with your taxes with H&R Block, you keep more money in your pocket. You'll also get great pricing, the best refund possible and a free SPC† card.

For more information, speak to an H&R Block Tax Professional today.

Province
) 456-7890
45@hrblock.ca

H&R BLOCK®

hrblock.ca | 800-HRBLOCK (472-5625)

What pricing strategies has H&R Block used in this advertisement?

How does the ad make you feel about working for or with this company?

Summary...*just the facts*

LO¹ • Price is the money or other considerations exchanged for the ownership or use of a product or service.

• Price typically involves money and the amount exchanged can be different from the list or quoted price because of allowances and extra fees.

• When reviewing the perceived benefits of a good or service, price is used as an indicator of value by consumers.

LO² • Four general approaches for finding an approximate price level for a product or service:

- Demand-oriented pricing approaches stress consumer demand and revenue implications of pricing and include eight types: skimming, penetration, prestige, price lining, odd-even, target, bundle, and yield management.
- Cost-oriented pricing approaches emphasize the cost aspects of pricing and include two types: standard and cost-plus pricing.
- Profit-oriented pricing approaches focus on a balance between revenues and costs to set a price and include three types: target profit, target return-on-sales, and target return-on-investment pricing.
- Competition-oriented pricing approaches emphasize what competitors or the marketplace are doing and include three types: customary; above-, at-, or below-market; and loss-leader pricing.

LO³ • A demand curve shows the maximum number of products consumers will buy at a given price and for a given set of (a) consumer tastes, (b) price and availability of other products, and (c) consumer income.

• The price elasticity of demand relates to the reaction of consumer demand and a firm's revenue when a price changes.

LO⁴ • Marketers need to understand the total revenue and total costs when considering pricing decisions as they will determine their ability to generate an appropriate profit.

LO⁵ • Break-even analysis shows the relationship between total revenue and total cost at various quantities of output for given conditions of price, fixed cost, and variable cost.

• The break-even point is where total revenue and total cost are equal.

LO⁶ • Pricing objectives, which specify the role of price in a firm's marketing strategy, may include pricing for profit, sales revenue, market share, unit sales, survival, or some socially responsible price level.

• Pricing constraints such as demand, product newness, costs, competitors, other products sold by the firm, and the type of competitive market restrict a firm's pricing range.

LO⁷ • In setting a final price, Step 1 is to set an approximate price level.

• Setting the list or quoted price is Step 2.

• Step 3 involves making special adjustments to prices through discounts and allowances.

• Finally, Step 4 requires marketers to monitor and adjust prices.

LO⁸ • Geographical adjustments to price reflect the cost of transportation.

• Organizations can reward buyers by offering discounts such as quantity discounts or seasonal discounts that also work in favour of the seller.

• When buyers perform an activity, they can sometimes receive allowances or reductions to listed or quoted prices.

Key Terms and Concepts...*a refresher*

break-even analysis	markup	total cost
demand curve	price	total revenue
dumping	pricing constraints	value
fixed cost	pricing objectives	variable cost
grey market	profit equation	

Hands-on *...apply your knowledge*

Pricing Your Services Review the opening vignette about H&R Block. Consider that you are the individual offering similar professional services and review the textbook section on break-even analysis. Determine how many hours you would have to work in order to break even if your annual fixed costs for your professional practice were $12,000 annually and variable costs for an hour of work were $25 dollars on average.

Chapter Vignette *...reminder*

Effective marketing requires individuals with a variety of skill sets. Although creativity is an important skill in this discipline, the ability to analyze figures and data is critical in developing marketing strategy. Review this chapter's vignette about H&R Block and the importance of key marketing calculations for developing an appropriate pricing strategy. Ensure that you are comfortable completing break-even analysis and return-on-investment calculations.

Video Clip *...questions*

Although the CONNECT video on H&R Block Canada does not explicitly discuss pricing, there is a pricing strategy at play. Watch the video and answer the following questions:

▶ Video
H&R Block
Canada

- What customer-oriented pricing approach do you think H&R Block Canada is taking with its Second Look strategy?
- Have you ever felt that you were not receiving value from a product or service? If so, how do you think the video appeals to Canadians feeling that way about the preparation of their tax returns?
- Once a Canadian feels they deserve a Second Look from H&R Block Canada, what price do you believe he or she would pay to re-file their taxes?

Infographic *...data analysis*

The Accenture Perfect Promotion infographic illustrates the number of factors being considered when developing promotions and prices for companies. Consider an item you recently purchased and use the infographic to help you determine how the final price of the product was determined.

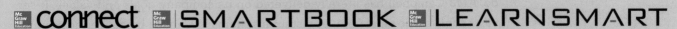

marketing channels and supply chain

Before the sun comes up and your local mall opens, people may have already visited your favourite store. To prevent congestion during peak times and ensure your products are available when you want them, key partners in marketing channels visit your local retailers and provide them with their required inventory. These partners are key in delivering goods to your doorstep as the "last mile" of many supply chains.

Businesses that are part of the marketing channel are crucial components to the client experience. They are trusted partners that ensure that manufacturers deliver their products to consumers in a timely manner. AMJ Campbell has become Canada's largest moving company. Lenny Malley is one of the partners of his AMJ Campbell franchise. He is responsible for the overall operations of his transportation company and has over 20 years of experience in logistics and supply chain management. "A critical skill marketers need is an appreciation of logistics," Lenny says with a grin. "Individuals with that appreciation help us reasonably negotiate deadlines and delivery dates. They help foresee obstacles to getting products from point A to point B and work with us to find solutions that meet the needs of all parties."

When planning his delivery schedules, Lenny considers the many challenges of geography and terrain. "We have had situations where the target date of delivery is not realistic due to our knowledge and experience of logistics. In those situations, creative thinking and managing expectations with clients is critical to our success."

Aside from moving, AMJ Campbell has a specialized products division where it diversifies its service offering. The goal of the division is to ensure on-time delivery of goods to their destination. Many times, the company's expertise in logistics and special care of the merchandise delivered leads to exceptional client experiences from manufacturers, retailers, and the end customer. "There is a cost to keeping things safe," describes Lenny. "We believe we are better at it than a general carrier." AMJ Campbell uses blanket wrap services to ensure the safety of the products being delivered. Potential clients may choose another provider, but they run the risk of products being damaged during the process.

The unsung heroes of marketing channels are extremely talented in what they do. AMJ Campbell has literally delivered on its company goals and values. It services some of the most popular restaurant chains in Canada by delivering required equipment to create a consistent retail environment. When a new franchise in the

AMJ CAMPBELL™
MAKE YOUR BEST MOVE

Chapter Outline:

The last mile → Nature and importance of marketing channels → Channel structure and organization → Vertical marketing systems → Channel choice and management → Logistics and supply chain management

chain opens, it may require AMJ Campbell to visit 13 locations across multiple provinces before delivering all retailing fixtures to the final destination.

"The time and organization required to coordinate multiple suppliers is sometimes taken for granted by marketers," explains Lenny. "Our clients want us to figure things out for them, and we do that. But we understand that there are some parts of the process out of our control that we have to be prepared to address." Lenny is referring to experiences where their truck may be 90 percent full and ready to leave, but requiring an item from another supplier that is arriving late to their warehouse. Fortunately, Lenny's experience and ingenuity allows AMJ Campbell to address many of these challenges. "We plan our trips starting with target delivery dates, but then use a logistical setup that is cost-effective and timely." Other challenges include parts of the supply chain being too efficient. "Manufacturers may not receive their purchase order until the delivery van has been waiting there for 15 minutes!"

As Lenny leads a tour of his warehouse, he identifies another key need his company fulfills. One of their customers is a major appliance retailer that relies on their services to complete the client experience. "We want to ensure that every client receives their purchase on time and in good working order," shares Lenny. "Our experience allows us to pack our trucks efficiently, ensuring the safest delivery process for what we are carrying." Clients browsing, evaluating, and purchasing products in store may complete the sale from the retailer's perspective, but the delivery of the purchase is just as important as the consumer purchase decision itself. "A reliable supply chain is a safety net for the manufacturers to ensure satisfied customers."

Lenny describes the role of AMJ Campbell as the "last mile" of the marketing channel. It uses a form of cross-docking that allows trucks from manufacturers to unload at their warehouse, allowing them to determine the best setup and delivery system to get the final product out on time. "There are many ways to organize trips," suggests Lenny. "It all depends on how much we have to deliver and how many stops there will be along the way." Throughout the tour, Lenny shows that most deliveries are organized by destination; however, when a 53-foot truck is not conducive to a certain destination, AMJ Campbell uses smaller vehicles to complete the more local "last mile" for their customers.

Not only does it service marketing systems, AMJ Campbell is part of a vertical marketing system. In particular, it is a franchise system. "This is an excellent business model," explains Paul Paquette. Paul is Lenny's partner responsible for the company's sales efforts. "We can leverage our corporate brand, but also have the ability to make decisions for our particular franchise. It is a great balance for individuals with an entrepreneurial spirit, creativity, and good business sense."

A great example of ingenuity is how AMJ Campbell utilizes its warehouse space. The company has partnered with a popular energy drink to store products and keep them fresh for delivery. Although the energy drink company handles the delivery of its drinks to its retailer customers, AMJ Campbell is still an important part of the supply chain, acting as the hub of distribution. Paul comments that the flexibility he has as a franchisee allows him and his partners to think outside the box. "We know what our potential business opportunities are, and we have the flexibility and support to secure it." From being the "last mile" in various marketing channels, an integral part of many supply chains, and running a successful franchise, the business leaders at AMJ Campbell appreciate the importance of logistics in marketing.[1]

---

reality CHECK ✓

As you read Chapter 10, refer back to the AMJ Campbell vignette to answer the following questions:

- Why do you believe that the logistics of marketing channels are challenging and sometimes taken for granted?
- What skills are required for the individuals that plan the logistics of a supply chain?

Getting the product to the consumer is another key component of the marketing mix. In order to ensure an established place for consumers to acquire the product or service, marketers need to understand the distribution and supply chain aspects of bringing a product to market. Good marketers understand the value of the supply chain to perform the activities required to deliver a good or service to customers.

Nature and Importance of Marketing Channels

LO¹ Reaching potential buyers is obviously a critical part of successful marketing. Buyers benefit from well-structured and efficient distribution systems. The route to do this is direct in some cases and indirect in others.

What Is a Marketing Channel?

You see the results of distribution every day. You may have purchased Lay's potato chips at Mac's convenience store, a book through chapters.indigo.ca, or Levi's jeans at Hudson's Bay. Each of these items was brought to you by a marketing channel of distribution, or simply a marketing channel. A **marketing channel** consists of individuals and firms involved in the process of making a product or service available.

Marketing channels can be compared with a pipeline through which water flows from a source to an endpoint. Marketing channels make possible the flow of goods from a producer, through **intermediaries**, to a buyer. There are several types of intermediaries, as shown in Figure 10–1. Intermediaries go by various names and perform various functions. Some intermediaries actually purchase items from the producer, store them, and resell them to buyers. For example, Nestlé Canada produces Aero chocolate bars and sells them to wholesalers. The wholesalers then sell the bars to independent convenience and grocery stores, which in turn sell them to consumers. Other intermediaries, such as brokers and agents, represent sellers but do not actually ever own the products; their role is to bring a seller and buyer together. Real estate agents are examples of this type of intermediary.

Value Is Created by Intermediaries

Few consumers appreciate the value created by intermediaries; however, producers recognize that intermediaries make selling goods and services more efficient because the intermediaries minimize the number of sales contacts necessary to reach a target market. Figure 10–2 shows a simple example of how this

> **marketing channel**
> The set of individuals or firms involved in the process of making a product available
>
> **intermediaries**
> Individuals or firms performing a role in the marketing channel, involved in making a product available

Figure 10–1
Terms used for marketing intermediaries

TERM	DESCRIPTION
Middleman	Another name for intermediary
Agent or broker	Any intermediary with legal authority to act on behalf of another channel member (for example, a manufacturer)
Wholesaler	Any intermediary who sells to other intermediaries, usually to retailers—this term usually applies to intermediaries who deal in consumer goods
Retailer	An intermediary who sells to consumers
Distributor	A general term used to describe intermediaries who perform a variety of functions, including selling, maintaining inventories, extending credit, and others—usually used for those in business markets
Dealer	A general term that can mean the same as a distributor, a retailer, or a wholesaler

Figure 10–2
How intermediaries minimize transactions

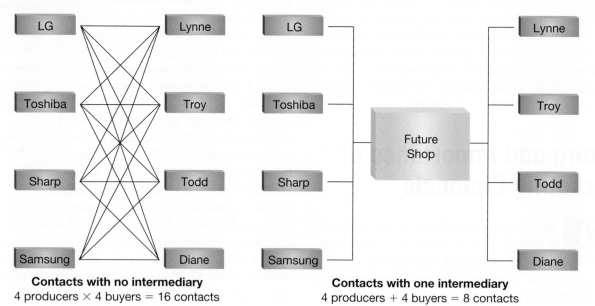

Contacts with no intermediary
4 producers × 4 buyers = 16 contacts

Contacts with one intermediary
4 producers + 4 buyers = 8 contacts

comes about in the flat-panel TV market. Without a retail intermediary (such as Future Shop), LG, Toshiba, Sharp, and Samsung would each have to make four contacts to reach the four consumers shown, who are in the target market. When Future Shop acts as an intermediary, each producer has to make only one contact, reducing the number of industry transactions from 16 to 8, which reduces producer costs.

Functions Performed by Intermediaries

Intermediaries make possible the flow of products from producers to ultimate consumers by performing three basic functions (see Figure 10–3).

- **Transactional function:** Intermediaries perform a transactional function when they buy and sell goods or services. But an intermediary such as a wholesaler also performs the function of sharing risk with the producer when it stocks merchandise in anticipation of sales. If the stock is unsold for any reason, the intermediary—not the producer—suffers the loss.

- **Logistical function:** The logistics of a transaction involve the details of preparing and getting a product to buyers. Gathering, sorting, and dispersing products are some of the logistical functions of the intermediary. Consider the critical role played by AMJ Campbell for its clients in the opening vignette.

- **Facilitating function:** Finally, intermediaries perform facilitating functions that, by definition, make a transaction *easier* for buyers. For example, Hudson's Bay issues credit cards to consumers so that they can buy now and pay later.

All three groups of functions must be performed in a marketing channel, even though each channel member may not participate in all three. Channel members often negotiate which specific functions they will perform. Sometimes, disagreements result, and a breakdown in relationships among channel members occurs. This happened when Pepsi-Cola's bottler in Venezuela switched to Coca-Cola. Given the intermediary's logistical role—storing and transporting Pepsi to Venezuelan customers, in this case—Pepsi-Cola either had to set up its own bottling operation to perform these marketing channel functions, or find another bottler, which it did. Since then, Pepsi has continued to improve its bottling procedures to control costs in difficult years.[2]

Consumer Benefits from Intermediaries

Consumers also benefit from the actions of intermediaries. Having the goods and services you want, when you want them, where you want them, and in the form you want them is the ideal result of marketing channels. In more specific terms, marketing channels help create value for consumers through these five utilities: time, place, form, information, and possession.

- *Time utility* refers to having a product or service when you want it. For example, Purolator provides next-morning delivery.

- *Place utility* means having a product or service available where consumers want it, such as having a Petro-Canada gas station located on a long stretch of a provincial highway.

Figure 10–3
Marketing channel functions performed by intermediaries

TYPE OF FUNCTION   **ACTIVITIES RELATED TO FUNCTION**

Transactional function
- *Buying*: Purchasing products for resale
- *Selling*: Contacting potential customers, promoting products, and seeking orders
- *Risk taking*: Assuming business risks in the ownership of inventory

Logistical function
- *Selection*: Putting together a selection of products from several different sources
- *Storing*: Assembling and protecting products at a convenient location
- *Sorting*: Purchasing in large quantities and dividing into smaller amounts
- *Transporting*: Physically moving a product to customers

Facilitating function
- *Financing*: Extending credit to customers
- *Marketing information and research*: Providing information to customers and suppliers, including competitive conditions and trends

- *Form utility* involves enhancing a product or service to make it more appealing to buyers. For example, retail stores such as Harry Rosen and Roots provide appealing displays of their products and an environment that caters to their customers.

- *Information utility* means providing consumers with the information they need to make an informed choice; information-packed websites and user manuals provide this type of utility.

- *Possession utility involves* efforts by intermediaries to help buyers take possession of a product or service, such as providing various ways for payment to be made for a product—by credit card, debit card, cash, or cheque.

Purolator adds value by offering time utility to customers.

Channel Structure and Organization

LO² A product can take many routes on its journey from producer to buyer, and marketers search for the most efficient route from the many alternatives available. As you'll see, there are some important differences between the marketing channels for consumer goods and those for business goods.

Marketing Channels for Consumer Goods and Services

Figure 10-4 shows the four most common marketing channel configurations for consumer goods and services. It also shows the number of levels in each marketing channel—that is, the number of intermediaries between a producer and ultimate buyers. As the number of intermediaries between a producer and

ask yourself

1. *What is meant by a marketing channel?*

2. *What are the three basic functions performed by intermediaries?*

Figure 10–4
Common marketing channels for consumer goods and services

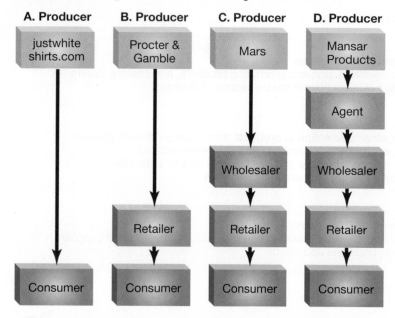

buyer increases, the channel is viewed as increasing in length. The producer → wholesaler → retailer → consumer channel is longer than the producer → consumer channel.

Channel A in Figure 10-4 represents a *direct channel* because a producer and ultimate consumers deal directly with each other. Many products and services are distributed this way. A number of insurance companies sell their financial services using a direct channel and branch sales offices. The online store **justwhiteshirts.com** designs and produces high-quality men's shirts that are sold online and by catalogue to consumers around the world. Because there are no intermediaries with a direct channel, the producer must perform all channel functions.

The remaining three channel forms are *indirect channels* because intermediaries are inserted between the producer and consumers and perform numerous channel functions. Channel B, with a retailer added, is most common when the retailer is large and can buy in large quantities from a producer. Packaged goods companies such as Procter & Gamble use this channel with large retailers such as Loblaws and Sobeys. These retailers buy in sufficient quantities to make it cost-effective for a producer to deal with only a retail intermediary. Adding a wholesaler in channel C is most common when the wholesaler sells to small retailers, such as independent convenience stores and small grocery stores that do not buy enough to warrant a producer selling to these

retailers directly. Channel C is most common for low-cost, low-unit value items that are frequently purchased by consumers, such as candy, confectionary items, and magazines. For example, Mars sells its line of candies to wholesalers in case quantities; wholesalers can then break down (sort) the cases so that individual small retailers can order in boxes of much smaller quantities.

Channel D, the most indirect channel, is employed when there are many small manufacturers and many small retailers and an agent is used to help coordinate a large supply of the product. Mansar Products, Ltd., is a Belgian producer of specialty jewellery that uses agents to sell to wholesalers, which then sell to many small retailers.

Marketing Channels for Business Goods and Services

The four most common channels for business goods and services are shown in Figure 10-5. In contrast with channels for consumer products, business channels typically are shorter and rely on one intermediary or none at all because business users are fewer in number, tend to be more concentrated geographically, and buy in larger quantities. For these reasons, business channels can be served directly or by a limited number of intermediaries.

Channel A, represented by IBM's large, mainframe computer business, is a direct channel. Firms using this kind of channel maintain their own sales force and perform all channel functions. This channel

Figure 10–5
Common marketing channels for business goods and service

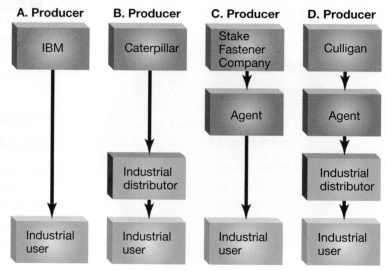

is employed when buyers are large and well-defined, the sales effort requires extensive negotiations, and the products are of high unit value and require hands-on expertise in terms of installation or use. Bombardier and Airbus Industries would be other examples.

Channels B, C, and D are indirect channels with one or more intermediaries to reach industrial users. In channel B, an *industrial distributor* performs a variety of marketing channel functions, including selling, stocking, and delivering a full product assortment and financing. In many ways, industrial distributors are like wholesalers in consumer channels. Caterpillar relies on industrial distributors to sell and service its construction and mining equipment in almost 200 countries.

Channel C introduces another intermediary, an agent, who serves primarily as the independent selling arm of producers and represents a producer to industrial users. For example, Stake Fastener Company, a producer of industrial fasteners, has an agent call on industrial users rather than employing its own sales force.

Channel D is the longest channel and includes both agents and distributors. For instance, Culligan, a producer of water treatment equipment, uses agents to call on distributors who sell to industrial users.

Electronic Marketing Channels

The marketing channels that we have just discussed for consumer and business goods and services are not the only routes to the marketplace. Advances in electronic commerce have opened new avenues for reaching buyers and creating customer value.

Interactive electronic technology has made possible **electronic marketing channels**, which employ the Internet to make goods and services available to consumers or business buyers. A unique feature of these channels is that they can combine electronic and traditional intermediaries to create time, place, form, information, and possession utility for buyers.[3]

Figure 10–6 shows the electronic marketing channels for books (**Amazon.ca**), travel reservation services (**Travelocity.ca**), and personal computers (**Dell.ca**). Are you surprised that they look a lot like common marketing channels? An important reason for the similarity resides in the channel functions detailed in Figure 10–3. Electronic intermediaries can and do perform transactional and facilitating functions effectively and at a relatively lower cost than traditional intermediaries because of efficiencies made possible by information technology. However, electronic intermediaries are incapable of performing elements of the logistical function, particularly for products such as books and automobiles. This function remains

Figure 10-6

Examples of electronic marketing channels

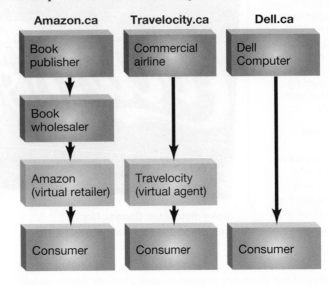

with traditional intermediaries or with the producer, as seen with Dell and its direct channel.

Many services are distributed through electronic marketing channels, such as travel services marketed by **Travelocity.ca**, financial securities by Royal Bank, and insurance by Metropolitan Life. Software, too, can be marketed this way. However, many other services, such as health care and auto repair, still involve traditional intermediaries.

Multiple Channels and Strategic Alliances

In some situations, producers use **dual distribution**, an arrangement whereby a firm reaches different buyers by employing two or more different types of channels for the same basic product. For instance, GE sells its large appliances directly to home and apartment builders but uses retail stores, including Walmart, to sell to consumers. In some instances, firms pair multiple channels with a multibrand strategy. This is done to minimize cannibalization of the firm's family brand and to differentiate the channels. For example, Hallmark sells its Hallmark greeting cards through Hallmark stores and select department stores, and its Ambassador brand of cards through discount and drugstore chains.

A recent development in marketing channels is the use of *strategic channel alliances*, whereby one firm's

electronic marketing channels
Channels that use the Internet to make goods and services available to consumers or business buyers

dual distribution
Arrangement whereby a firm reaches buyers by using two or more different types of channels for the same basic product

Coke distributes Canada Dry soft drinks to stores in Canada.

Integrating Multiple Channels with Multichannel Marketing

Companies often employ multiple marketing channels for their products and services. Multichannel marketing bears some resemblance to dual distribution. For example, different communication and delivery channels are used, such as catalogues, kiosks, retail stores, and websites. However, the resemblance ends at this point. **Multichannel marketing** is the *blending* of different communication and delivery channels that are *mutually reinforcing* in attracting, retaining, and building relationships with consumers who shop and buy in the traditional marketplace and in the online marketspace. Multichannel marketing seeks to integrate a firm's communication and delivery channels, not differentiate them. In doing so, consumers can browse and buy anytime, anywhere, any way, expecting that the experience will be similar regardless of channel.

Multichannel marketing is essential to success. Allowing business to measure results and make changes rapidly is one benefit, while ensuring a seamless customer experience is another benefit. At Eddie Bauer, for example, every effort is made to make the apparel shopping and purchase process for its customers the same in its retail stores, through its catalogues, and at its website. According to an Eddie Bauer marketing manager, "We don't distinguish between channels because it's all Eddie Bauer to our customers."[5]

Multichannel marketing can also leverage the value-adding capabilities of different channels. For example, retail stores leverage their physical presence by allowing customers to pick up their online orders at a nearby store, or return or exchange non-store purchases at the store if they wish. For instance, a consumer can purchase a laptop computer on the Staples website and pick up the computer at any Staples store.

Another example of multichannel marketing is the **cross-channel shopper**, who researches products online and then purchases them at a retail store. These shoppers represent both genders equally. Cross-channel shoppers want the right product at the best price, and they don't want to wait several days for delivery. The top reasons these shoppers look online before buying in stores include (1) the desire to compare products among different retailers, (2) the need for more information than is available in stores, and (3) the ease of comparing options without having to trek to multiple retail locations.

marketing channel is used to sell another firm's products.[4] An alliance between Canada Dry and Coke is a case in point. Coke distributes Canada Dry soft drinks to stores in Canada. Strategic alliances are popular in global marketing, where the creation of marketing channel relationships is expensive and time-consuming. For example, General Mills and Nestlé have an extensive alliance that spans 70 international markets from Brazil to Poland to Thailand.

Multichannel Marketing to the Online Consumer

Consumers and companies populate two market environments today. One is the traditional marketplace, where buyers and sellers engage in face-to-face exchange relationships in an environment characterized by physical facilities (stores and offices) and mostly tangible objects. The other is the *marketspace,* an Internet/web-enabled digital environment characterized by "face-to-screen" exchange relationships and electronic images and offerings.

The existence of multiple market environments has benefited consumers tremendously. Today, consumers can shop for and purchase a wide variety of products and services in either market environment. Many consumers now browse and buy in multiple environments, and more are expected to do so in the future. With so many consumers browsing and buying in different environments, few companies limit their marketing programs exclusively to the traditional marketplace or to the online marketspace. Today, it is commonplace for companies to maintain a presence in both market environments. This dual presence is called *multichannel marketing.*

Omni-Channel Marketing at Best Buy Canada

Just as Walmart has been a technology leader in logistics, Best Buy is at the front of the line with its omni-channel strategy. As Canada's fastest-growing specialty retailer and e-tailer of consumer electronics, Best Buy offers a unique shopping experience for its customers. Although many smaller businesses may be concerned about how to execute an omni-channel marketing strategy for themselves, Best Buy's size and resources allows it to take bold steps in this frontier.

Omni-channel retailing evolved from the concept of multichannel retailing. Technology has given consumers the choice to acquire objects in store, over the phone, via mail, and online. Omni-channel retailing creates a seamless process and consistent experiences to the consumer across all these channels. By allowing information found online to match the offering in store, retailers avoid the concerns of *showrooming* (the practice of using mobile devices in

Shopping using QR codes is becoming more commonplace.

store to check competitive online product reviews and prices and to then purchase the cheaper product online) and facilitate the completion of more sales. Although omni-channel retailing is a technology-enabled evolution, it is not limited to technology

companies. For example, Canadian Tire is working toward improving its connections among its mobile, in-store, and online technologies to provide consistency. The move toward omni-channel marketing seems inevitable for most retailers, given the competitive landscape.

In Canada, Best Buy is preparing for the competitive landscape with a price beat guarantee. It has extended its lowest price guarantee to match any Canadian online retailer's price and address potential showrooming. Best Buy's chief operating officer, Mike Pratt, believes that this strategy changes the showrooms from the Best Buy or Future Shop stores to the websites of its competitors. With price eliminated from its competitive advantage, Best Buy believes it will stay number one. Furthermore, with increased sales on the horizon and multiple marketing channels being managed, Best Buy needs to ensure that it has a good understanding of the value of its supply chain.[6] ●

Questions

1. How will the success of omni-channel retailing affect Best Buy's supply chain?

2. What other companies could implement omni-channel retailing to help address showrooming?

The evolution of how individuals make purchases leads us to the trend of omni-channel retailing. Omni-channel retailing creates a seamless experience among all available shopping channels. Since technology has made it difficult to distinguish between online and physical retail opportunities, the next step for retailers is to make the process seamless; see, for example, the Marketing NewsFlash, "Omni-Channel Marketing at Best Buy Canada." Both online and offline retailers need to be ready for the changes in the competitive landscape. It will become an expectation for them to invest resources toward omni-channel retailing to meet the demand of consumers.[7]

Implementing Multichannel Marketing It should not be surprising to you that not all companies use websites for multichannel marketing the same way. Different companies apply the value-creation capabilities of Internet/web technology differently depending on their overall marketing program. Websites can play multiple roles in multichannel marketing because they can serve as either a communication or delivery channel, or as both. There are two general types of websites, classified based on their intended purpose: transactional websites and promotional websites.

Transactional websites are essentially electronic storefronts. They focus mainly on converting an online

The Gap generates more sales volume from its website than any one of its stores, except for one.

Global Channel Strategy

Distribution is of critical importance in global marketing. The availability and quality of retailers and wholesalers as well as transportation, communication, and warehousing facilities are often determined by a country's economic infrastructure. Figure 10–7 outlines the channel through which a product manufactured in one country must travel to reach its destination in another country. The first step involves the seller; its headquarters is responsible for the successful distribution to the ultimate consumer.

The next step is the channel between two nations, moving the product from one country to another. Intermediaries that can handle this responsibility include resident buyers in a foreign country, independent merchant wholesalers who buy and sell the product, and agents who bring buyers and sellers together.

Once the product is in the foreign nation, that country's distribution channels take over. These channels can be very long or surprisingly short, depending on the product line. In Japan, fresh fish go through three intermediaries before getting to a retail outlet. Conversely, shoes go through only one intermediary. The sophistication of a country's distribution channels increases as its economic infrastructure develops. Supermarkets are helpful in selling products in many nations, but they are not popular or available in many others where culture and a lack of refrigeration dictate shopping on a daily rather than a weekly basis. For example, when Coke and Pepsi entered China, both had to create direct distribution channels, investing in refrigerator units for small retailers.

browser into an online, catalogue, or in-store buyer using website design elements. Transactional websites are most common among store and catalogue retailers such as Lee Valley. The Gap, for instance, generates more sales volume from its website than from any one of its stores, except for one. The company has built on its online success and prepared for the future by forming an innovation and digital strategy group in 2013.[8]

Transactional websites are used less frequently by manufacturers of consumer products, but a recurring issue for manufacturers is the threat of channel conflict by harming their relationships with their retailing intermediaries. Hudson's Bay, for instance, would not be very happy if a brand of jeans it carries is being sold online directly from the manufacturer to the consumer; however, Ethan Allen, the furniture manufacturer, markets its product line at **www.ethanallen.com** whenever feasible. Ethan Allen has attempted to address channel conflict by having retailers fill online orders and receive 25 percent of the sales price. For items shipped directly from the Ethan Allen factory, the store nearest the customer receives 10 percent of the sales price.[9]

Promotional websites have a different purpose than transactional sites: No actual selling takes place on them, but they showcase products and services and provide information.

Vertical Marketing Systems

LO³ The traditional marketing channels described so far represent a network of independent producers and intermediaries brought together to distribute goods and services. However, channel arrangements have emerged for the purpose of improving efficiency in performing channel functions and achieving greater marketing effectiveness.

Figure 10–7
Channels of distribution in global marketing

| Seller | Seller's international marketing headquarters | Channels between nations | Channels within foreign nations | Final consumer |

Tiffany & Co. and H&R Block represent two different types of vertical marketing systems.

These arrangements are called vertical marketing systems. **Vertical marketing systems** are professionally managed and centrally coordinated marketing channels designed to achieve channel economies and maximum marketing impact. They encourage collaboration, shared responsibility, and partnership between the manufacturers and retailers in a system.[10] Figure 10–8 depicts the major types of vertical marketing systems: corporate, contractual, and administered.

Corporate Systems

Under a *corporate vertical marketing system,* a firm at one level of a channel owns the firm at the next level or owns the entire channel.

For example, a producer might own the intermediary at the next level down in the channel. This practice, called *forward integration,* is exemplified by Polo/Ralph Lauren, which manufactures clothing and also owns apparel shops. Another example of forward integration is Goodyear, which distributes its tires not only through preferred stores but also through its own retail stores. Alternatively, a retailer might own a manufacturing operation, a practice called *backward integration.* For example, Tiffany & Co., the exclusive jewellery retailer, manufactures about half of the fine jewellery items for sale through its 150 stores and boutiques worldwide.

Figure 10–8
Types of vertical marketing systems

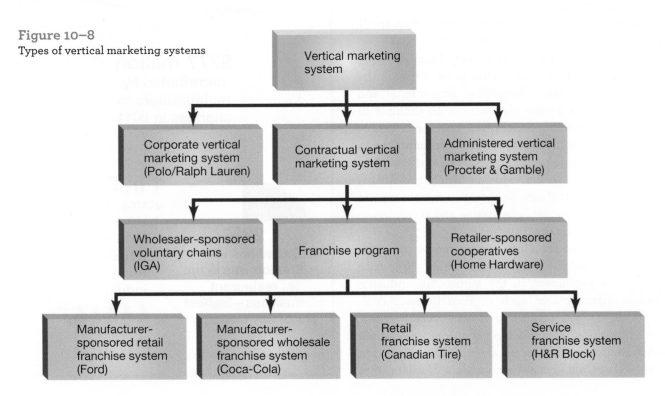

franchising
Contractual arrangement in which a parent company (the franchiser) allows an individual or firm (the franchisee) to operate a certain type of business under an established name and according to specific rules set by the franchiser

Companies seeking to reduce distribution costs and gain greater control over supply sources or resale of their products pursue forward and backward integration. Many companies favour contractual vertical marketing systems to achieve channel efficiencies and marketing effectiveness.

Contractual Systems Under a *contractual vertical marketing system,* independent production and distribution firms combine their efforts on a contractual basis to obtain greater functional economies and marketing impact than they could achieve alone. Contractual systems are the most popular among the three types of vertical marketing systems. They account for about 40 percent of all retail sales.

Three variations of contractual systems exist. The first contractual system, *wholesaler-sponsored voluntary chains,* involve a wholesaler that develops a contractual relationship with small, independent retailers to standardize and coordinate buying practices, merchandising programs, and inventory management efforts. With the organization of a large number of independent retailers, economies of scale and volume discounts can be achieved to compete with chain stores. Independent Grocers Alliance (IGA) was the largest group of independent grocers in Canada and pursued this strategy. The group garnered the interest of Sobeys, which purchased the stores and incorporated a different business model.

Retailer-sponsored cooperatives exist when small, independent retailers form an organization that operates a wholesale facility cooperatively. Member retailers then concentrate their buying power through the wholesaler and plan collaborative promotional and pricing activities. Home Hardware is an example of a retailer-sponsored cooperative. The most visible variation of contractual systems is **franchising**, a contractual arrangement between a parent company (a franchiser) and an individual or firm (a franchisee) that allows the franchisee to operate a certain type of business under an established name and according to specific rules set by the franchiser.

Four types of franchise arrangements are most popular. *Manufacturer-sponsored retail franchise systems* are prominent in the automobile industry, where a manufacturer such as Ford licenses dealers to sell its cars subject to various sales and service conditions. *Manufacturer-sponsored wholesale franchise systems* appear in the soft-drink industry, where Pepsi-Cola licenses wholesalers (bottlers) that

Infographic

Canada's Restaurant Industry

We are part of every community: There are more than 81,000 restaurants, bars, and caterers across the country.

68 billion
in annual sales generated by the restaurant industry

6.6% of the country's workforce

4% of the country's GDP

1.1 million people directly employed in the restaurant industry

250,000 indirect jobs in related industries

$24 billion in food and beverage products purchased every year

18 million visits to restaurants every day by Canadians

$277 million contributed by restaurateurs to charities in 2011

22% Canadians whose first job was in the restaurant business—highest of any industry

1 in 5 young people between the ages of 15 and 24 are employed in the restaurant industry

Source: Restaurants Canada.

Maxed Out on McDonald's

McDonald's has more than 1,400 restaurants with over 80,000 employees in Canada—a fraction of its 33,000 restaurants and 1.7 million employees worldwide. With franchising being a key to its success, McDonald's has expanded over six continents into almost 120 countries.

Franchising is a popular method for businesses to expand internationally, and Canada has historically been the most popular country for U.S. companies to expand into. More recently, with changing markets and ever-evolving opportunities, franchise growth has expanded to South America, Asia, and Mexico.

Franchising has many benefits to a business as it facilitates the entry into consumer segments where there is demand. As a franchisee, the key to success is to follow direction from the corporate offices and leverage support of their resources and the company brand. For Canadian McDonald's franchises, a great

> Innovative menu items help franchisees attract and retain consumers.

example of leveraging resources was the national launch of the Signature McWrap in 2013. This new menu item was specifically designed for Canadian tastes, but modified the recipe of a similar, successful global menu item in McDonald's Europe.

Keeping in mind that business-model benefits are usually balanced with challenges, McDonald's U.S. franchisees faced increased store fees and raised concerns with their corporate parent. Franchisees were impacted by rent, training fees, and software. The concern among franchisees is that the business model is no longer as profitable as it has been in the past. To help

address this rising channel conflict, McDonald's spokespeople have commented that "We are continuing to work together with McDonald's owner/operators and our supplier partners to ensure that our restaurants are providing a great experience to our customers, which involves investments in training and technology."

Being part of the marketing channels and supply chains, a number of Canadian companies have a vested interest in the success of McDonald's in Canada. McDonald's is considered a channel captain in Canada with the ability to influence the behaviour of its partners and support success for all parties concerned.[11]

Questions

1. What are some of the challenges McDonald's franchisees face in their contractual vertical marketing system?

2. What are some of the key benefits of being part of a franchising arrangement?

---

purchase concentrate from Pepsi-Cola and then carbonate, bottle, promote, and distribute its products to supermarkets and restaurants. *Retail franchise systems* are provided by firms that have designed a unique approach for selling merchandise to consumers. Canadian Tire and McDonald's represent this franchising approach (see the Marketing NewsFlash, "Maxed Out on McDonald's").

Service franchise systems exist when franchisers license individuals or firms to dispense a service under a trade name and specific guidelines. An example is H&R Block tax services. Service franchise arrangements are the fastest-growing type of franchise.

Administered Systems Ownership of a marketing system is not always necessary to achieve desired results. *Administered vertical marketing systems* achieve coordination at successive stages of production and distribution by the size and influence of one channel member. Procter & Gamble, given its broad product assortment ranging from disposable diapers to detergents, is able to obtain cooperation from supermarkets in displaying, promoting, and pricing its products. Given its position as the world's largest retailer, Walmart can obtain cooperation from manufacturers in terms of product specifications, price levels, and promotional support.

Where Do You Go for Coffee?

Canadians have plenty of options when choosing their morning brew.

McDonald's	Over 1,400 locations
Second Cup	Over 350 locations
Starbucks	Over 600 locations
Tim Hortons	Over 3,450 locations

Source: Tim Hortons corporate website, "The History of Tim Hortons," accessed August 20, 2013, at www.timhortons. com/ca/en/about/media-history.html; Second Cup corporate website, "Investors Relations," accessed August 20, 2013 at www.secondcup.com/investors-relations/investor-relations; Starbucks website "The Story of Starbucks Coffee Canada," accessed August 20, 2013 at www.starbucks.ca/about-us/ company-information; McDonald's Canada corporate website, "FAQs," accessed August 20, 2013, at www.mcdonalds.ca/ca/en/ contact_us/faq.html.

Channel Choice and Management

LO 4 Marketing channels not only link a producer to its buyers but also provide the means through which a firm executes various elements of its marketing strategy. Therefore, choosing a marketing channel is a critical decision.

Factors Affecting Channel Choice

The final choice of a marketing channel by a producer depends on a number of market, product, and company factors.

Market Factors

- **Geographic concentration of the market:** When most of a firm's customers are concentrated in a few geographic areas, a direct sale to customers is practical. When customers are geographically dispersed, a direct sale is likely to be impractical due to high travel costs. Sellers may establish sales branches in densely populated markets and use intermediaries in less-concentrated markets.

- **Number of potential customers:** A manufacturer with few potential customers may use its own sales force to sell directly to ultimate consumers or business users. Bombardier uses this approach in selling its jet aircrafts and subway cars. For a large number of customers, the manufacturer would probably use intermediaries. For example, Tim Hortons relies on numerous franchisee outlets to reach the large number of consumers buying coffee.

- **Type of market:** Consumer products are made available through retailers, while business products are sold either direct to customers or through intermediaries.

- **Order size:** Direct distribution makes sense when an order size is large. For example, Campbell's delivers its soups directly to large

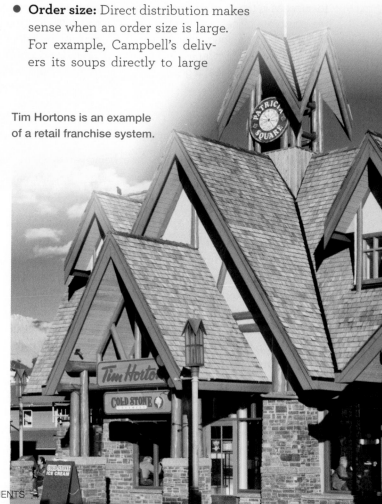

Tim Hortons is an example of a retail franchise system.

grocery chains. On the other hand, Campbell's uses wholesalers to reach small independent grocery and convenience stores, whose orders are usually too small to justify a direct sale.

Product Factors

- **Technical factors:** In general, highly sophisticated products, such as custom-built machinery and scientific computers, are distributed direct to buyers. The producer's sales force must provide considerable pre-purchase and post-purchase service for these types of products, and typically, wholesalers do not do these tasks.

- **Perishability:** Some goods, such as milk and bread, deteriorate fairly quickly. As a result, these types of products go directly from the producer to the retailer, no matter the size of the order.

- **Unit value:** The price attached to each unit of a product affects the amount of funds available for distribution. For example, a company like Bombardier can afford to use its own employees to sell aircrafts costing millions of dollars. But it would not make sense for Hershey Canada to call on households to sell an Oh Henry! chocolate bar. That's why intermediaries such as convenience stores, vending machines, and gasoline service stations carry low unit-value products.

- **Product life cycle:** Over time, some products, such as the Apple iPad, become very popular, easy to operate, and available in more mainstream channels such as Walmart and Best Buy.

Company Factors

- **Financial resources and ability of management:** A business with limited financial resources may be unable to employ its own salespeople, and thus resorts to using intermediaries such as selling agents or manufacturer's agents to reach customers. Also, businesses that have limited or no marketing know-how may elect to use intermediaries.

    A manufacturer of jams and marmalades may face limited markets for its products because it cannot afford the listing fees that supermarkets demand for the privilege of carrying the product. The manufacturer chooses instead to sell to small fruit and vegetable–type stores, who do not demand a listing fee and whose clientele enjoys buying products that are not available everywhere. The retailer may command a premium price for the jam because of its perceived quality and limited distribution.

- **Desire for channel control:** Some producers establish direct channels because they want to control their product's distribution, even though a direct channel may be more costly than an indirect channel. For example, Gap Inc. employs designers to come up with the styles that consumers want. Instead of selling Gap products to independent retailers, Gap Inc. assures distribution with its more than 3,000 Gap stores. Having its own stores assures Gap that its products are marketed properly and merchandised prominently.

Channel Design Considerations

Marketing executives consider three questions when choosing a marketing channel and intermediaries:

1. Which channel and intermediaries will best reach the target market?

2. Which channel and intermediaries will best serve the needs of the target market?

3. Which channel and intermediaries will lead to the most cost-efficient and profitable results?

Target Market Coverage Achieving the best coverage of the target market requires attention to the density—that is, the number of stores in a given geographical area—and type of intermediaries to be used at the retail level of distribution. Three degrees of distribution intensity exist: intensive, exclusive, and selective.

Intensive distribution means that a firm tries to place its products and services in as many outlets as possible. Intensive distribution is usually chosen for convenience products or services, such as candy, newspapers, and soft drinks. For example, Coca-Cola's retail distribution objective is to place its products "within an arm's reach of desire."

Exclusive distribution is the extreme opposite of intensive distribution because only one retail outlet in a specified geographical area carries the firm's products. Exclusive distribution is typically chosen for specialty products or services such as specialty automobiles, some women's fragrances, men's and women's apparel and accessories, and yachts. Sometimes, retailers sign exclusive distribution agreements with manufacturers and suppliers.

Selective distribution lies between these two extremes and means that a firm selects a few retail outlets in a specific geographical area to carry its products. Selective distribution combines some of the market coverage benefits of intensive distribution with the control measures possible with exclusive distribution. For this reason, selective distribution is the most common form of distribution intensity. It is usually associated with products such as Rolex watches, Levi's jeans, and Samsung flat-panel TVs.

Satisfying Buyer Requirements

A second objective in channel design is gaining access to channels and intermediaries that satisfy at least some of the interests buyers might have when they purchase a firm's products or services. These requirements fall into four categories: information, convenience, variety, and pre- or post-sale services.

Information is an important requirement when buyers have limited knowledge or desire specific data about a product or service. Properly chosen intermediaries communicate with buyers through in-store displays, demonstrations, and personal selling. Electronics manufacturers such as Apple and Sony have opened their own retail outlets, with highly trained personnel to inform buyers about their products and how they can meet the buyers' needs.

Convenience has multiple meanings for buyers, such as proximity or driving time to a retail outlet or hours of operation. For example, Mac's convenience stores, with outlets nationwide, many of which are open 24 hours a day, satisfy this interest for buyers. Candy and snack food firms benefit by gaining display space in these stores.

For other consumers, convenience means a minimum of time and hassle. Jiffy Lube and Mr. Lube, which promise to change engine oil and filters quickly, appeal to this aspect of convenience. Another example of convenience is Tim Hortons, which has locations in Esso service stations across Canada.

Variety reflects buyers' interest in having numerous competing and complementary items from which to choose. Variety is seen in both the breadth and depth of products carried by intermediaries, which enhances their attractiveness to buyers. Thus, manufacturers of pet food and supplies seek distribution through pet stores such as PetSmart and PJ's Pets.

Services provided by intermediaries are an important buying requirement for products such as large household appliances that require delivery, installation, and credit. Therefore, Whirlpool seeks dealers that provide such services.

The late Steve Jobs, formerly Apple's CEO, was one person who believed that computer retailers have failed to satisfy the buying requirements of today's consumer. Believing that "buying a car is no longer the worst purchasing experience; buying a computer is number one," he launched Apple Stores.[12]

Profitability

The third consideration in designing a channel is profitability, which is determined by the revenues earned minus cost for each channel member and for the channel as a whole. Cost is the critical factor of channel profitability. These costs include distribution, advertising, and selling expenses. The extent to which channel members share these costs determines the profitability of each member and of the channel as a whole.

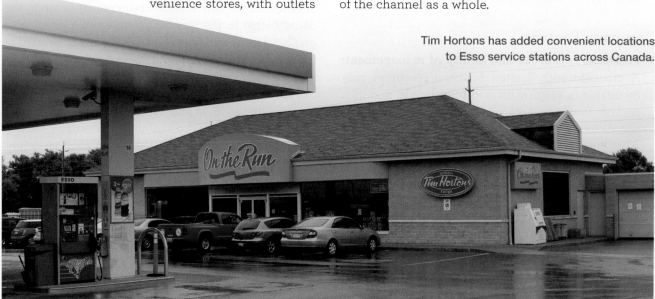

Tim Hortons has added convenient locations to Esso service stations across Canada.

Channel Relationships: Conflict and Cooperation

Unfortunately, because channels consist of independent individuals and firms, there is always potential for disagreements concerning who performs which channel functions, how profits are distributed, which products and services will be provided by whom, and who makes critical channel-related decisions. These channel conflicts necessitate measures for dealing with them.

Conflict in Marketing Channels
Channel conflict arises when one channel member believes another channel member is engaged in behaviour that prevents it from achieving its goals. Two types of conflict occur in marketing channels: vertical conflict and horizontal conflict. Although channel conflict may have a negative effect on channel performance, it can also encourage channels to find better efficiencies to deliver results.[13]

Vertical conflict occurs between different levels in a marketing channel—for example, between a manufacturer and a wholesaler or between a manufacturer and a retailer. An example of vertical conflict was when Coke and Costco had a disagreement on price. Costco claimed that Coke's selling price to Costco was too high. As a result, Costco stopped carrying Coke products. It took a month for the two channel members to resolve their differences before Coke once again was made available at Costco.[14]

Another type of vertical conflict arises when a channel member bypasses another member and sells directly to consumers, a practice called **disintermediation**. Apple is an excellent example of how disintermediation works. Before Apple Stores existed, Apple products were sold through independent retailers. When Apple started opening its own stores, its retailers began to complain. In 2005, independent Apple retailers filed a lawsuit against Apple, accusing the company of giving preferential treatment to its own stores and harming their sales. The lawsuit claimed that Apple had favoured Apple Stores by providing significant discounts that were unavailable to independent retailers. It also claimed that Apple was holding back product from the independent retailers.

> *"Conflict can have disruptive effects on the workings of a marketing channel."*

Horizontal conflict occurs between intermediaries at the same level in a marketing channel, such as between two or more retailers or two or more wholesalers that handle the same manufacturer's brands. For instance, one Toyota dealer might complain to Toyota that another Toyota dealer has located too close to its dealership and is affecting its business.

Cooperation in Marketing Channels
Conflict can have disruptive effects on the workings of a marketing channel, so it is necessary to secure cooperation among channel members. One means is through a *channel captain,* a dominant channel member that coordinates, directs, and supports other channel members. Channel captains can be producers, wholesalers, or retailers. Procter & Gamble assumes this role because it has a strong consumer following in brands such as Crest, Tide, and Pampers. Therefore, it can set policies or terms that supermarkets will follow. Walmart and Home Depot are retail channel captains because of their strong consumer image, number of outlets, and purchasing volume.

A firm becomes a channel captain because it is the channel member with the ability to influence the behaviour of other members.[15] Influence can take four forms. First, economic influence arises from the ability of a firm to reward other members because of its strong financial position. Microsoft Corporation and Toys "R" Us have such influence. Expertise is a second source of influence. Third, identification with a particular channel member creates influence for that channel member. For example, retailers may compete to carry the Ralph Lauren line, or clothing manufacturers may compete to be carried by Hudson's Bay or Holt

Vertical conflict occurred between Coke and Costco.

channel conflict
Arises when one channel member believes another channel member is engaged in behaviour that prevents it from achieving its goals

disintermediation
Vertical channel conflict that arises when a channel member bypasses another member and sells directly to consumers

Renfrew. In both instances, the desire to be associated with a channel member gives that firm influence over others. Finally, influence can arise from the legitimate right of one channel member to direct the behaviour of other members. This situation occurs under contractual vertical marketing systems where a franchiser can legitimately direct how a franchisee behaves.

Logistics and Supply Chain Management

LO 5 A marketing channel relies on logistics to make products available to consumers and industrial users. **Logistics** involves those activities that focus on getting the right amount of the right products to the right place at the right time at the lowest possible cost. The performance of these activities is *logistics management,* the practice of organizing the cost-effective flow of raw materials, in-process inventory, finished goods, and related information from point of origin to point of consumption to satisfy *customer requirements*. Although logistics primarily provide distribution services, there is underlying value to the supply chain.[16]

Three elements of this definition deserve emphasis. First, logistics deals with decisions from the source of raw materials to consumption of the final product—that is, the *flow* of the product. Second, those decisions have to be *cost-effective*. Third, while it is important to drive down logistics costs, there is a limit: A firm needs to drive down logistics costs as long as it can deliver expected *customer service,* while satisfying customer requirements. The role of management is to see that customer needs are satisfied in the most cost-effective manner. When properly done, the results can be spectacular. Procter & Gamble is a case in point. Beginning

logistics
Activities that focus on getting the right amount of the right products to the right place at the right time at the lowest possible cost

supply chain
Sequence of firms that perform activities required to create and deliver a product to consumers or industrial users

ask yourself

1. *What are the three degrees of distribution intensity?*

2. *What are the three questions marketing executives consider when choosing a marketing channel and intermediaries?*

in the 1990s, the company set out to meet the needs of consumers more effectively by collaborating and partnering with its suppliers and retailers to ensure that the right products reached store shelves at the right time and at a lower cost. The effort was judged a success when, during an 18-month period, Procter & Gamble's retailers recorded a US$65 million savings in logistics costs while customer service increased.[17]

The Procter & Gamble experience is not an isolated incident. Companies now recognize that getting the right items needed for consumption or production to the right place at the right time in the right condition at the right cost is often beyond their individual capabilities and control. Instead, collaboration, coordination, and information sharing among manufacturers, suppliers, and distributors are necessary to create a seamless flow of goods and services to customers. This perspective is represented in the concept of a supply chain and the practice of supply chain management.

Supply Chains versus Marketing Channels

A **supply chain** is a series of firms that perform activities required to create and deliver a good or service to consumers or industrial users. It differs from a marketing channel in terms of the firms involved. A supply chain is longer and includes suppliers that provide raw material inputs to a manufacturer as well as the wholesalers and retailers that deliver finished goods to you. The management process is also different. **Supply chain management** is the integration and organization of information and logistics activities across firms in a supply chain for the purpose of creating and delivering goods and services that provide value to consumers. The relation among marketing channels, logistics management, and supply chain management is shown in Figure 10–9. An important feature of supply chain management is its use of sophisticated information technology that allows companies to share and operate systems for order processing, transportation scheduling, and inventory and facility management.

supply chain management
Integration and organization of information and logistics activities across firms in a supply chain for the purpose of creating and delivering goods and services that provide value to consumers

Figure 10–9
How distribution channels work: the relationships between supplier networks, marketing channels, logistics management, and supply chain management

Sourcing, Assembling, and Delivering a New Car: The Automotive Supply Chain

All companies are members of one or more supply chains. A supply chain is essentially a series of linked suppliers and customers in which every customer is, in turn, a supplier to another customer until a finished product reaches the ultimate consumer. Even a simplified supply chain diagram for carmakers shown in Figure 10–10 illustrates how complex a supply chain can be.[18] A carmaker's supplier network includes thousands of firms that provide the 5,000 or so parts in a typical automobile. They provide items ranging from raw materials such as steel and rubber to components, including transmissions, tires, brakes, and seats, to complex subassemblies and assemblies such as in chassis and suspension systems that make for a smooth, stable ride. Coordinating and scheduling material and component flows for their assembly into actual automobiles by carmakers is heavily dependent on logistical activities, including transportation, order processing, inventory control, materials handling, and information technology. A central link is the carmaker supply chain manager, who is responsible for translating customer requirements into actual orders and arranging for delivery dates and financial arrangements for automobile dealers.

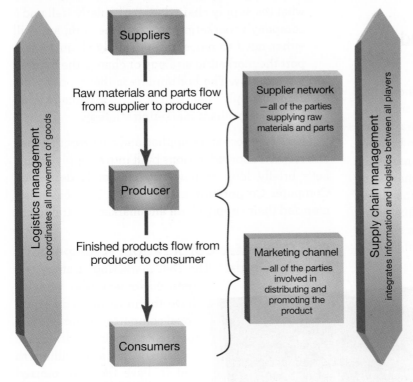

Figure 10–10
The automotive supply chain

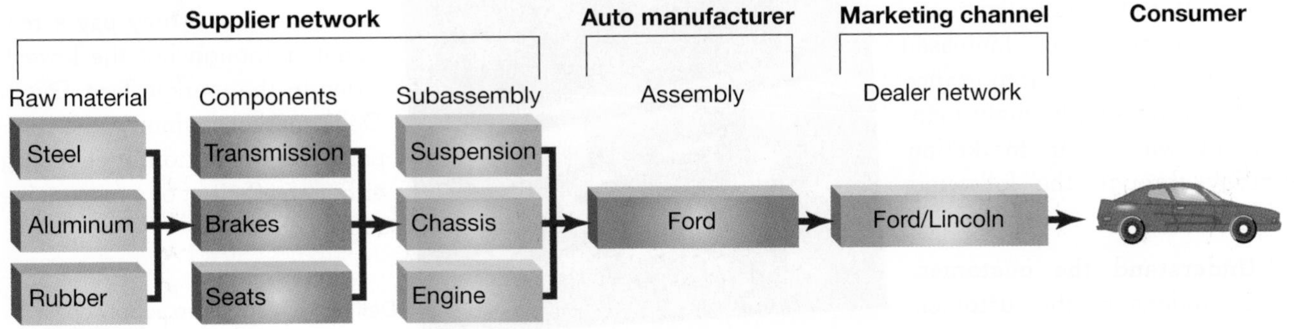

Logistical aspects of the automobile marketing channel are also an important part of the supply chain. Major responsibilities include transportation (which involves the selection and management of external carriers—trucking, airline, railroad, and shipping companies—for cars and parts to dealers), the operation of distribution centres, the management of finished goods inventories, and order processing for sales. Supply chain managers also play an important role in the marketing channel. They work with extensive car dealer networks to ensure that the right mix of automobiles is delivered to each location. In addition, they make sure that spare and service parts are available so that dealers can meet the car maintenance and repair needs of consumers. All of this is done with the help of information technology that links the entire automotive supply chain. What does all of this cost? It is estimated that logistics costs represent 25 percent to 30 percent of the retail price of a typical new car.

Supply Chain Management and Marketing Strategy

The automotive supply chain illustration shows how logistics activities are interrelated and organized across firms to create and deliver a car for you. What's missing from this illustration is the linkage between a specific company's supply chain and its marketing strategy. Just as companies have different marketing strategies, they also manage supply chains differently. The goals to be achieved by a firm's marketing strategy determine whether its supply chain needs to focus on being more responsive or more efficient in meeting customer requirements.

Aligning a Supply Chain with Marketing Strategy There are a variety of supply chain configurations, each of which is designed to perform different tasks well. Marketers today recognize that the choice of a supply chain follows from a clearly defined marketing strategy. With the globalization of the world economy and increased competition, see the importance of integrating supply chain management with their marketing strategy through the following three steps:[19]

1. **Understand the customer.** To understand the customer, a company must identify the needs of the customer segment being served. These needs, such as a desire for a low price or convenience of purchase, help a company define the relative importance of efficiency and responsiveness in meeting customer requirements.

2. **Understand the supply chain.** A company must understand what a supply chain is designed to do well. Supply chains range from those that emphasize being responsive to customer requirements and demand to those that emphasize efficiency with a goal of supplying products at the lowest possible delivered cost.

3. **Harmonize the supply chain with the marketing strategy.** A company needs to ensure that what the supply chain is capable of doing well is consistent with the targeted customer's needs and its marketing strategy. If a mismatch exists between what the supply chain does particularly well and a company's marketing strategy, the company will either need to redesign the supply chain to support the marketing strategy or change the marketing strategy. The bottom line is that a poorly designed supply chain can do serious damage to an otherwise brilliant marketing strategy.

How are these steps applied and how are efficiency and response considerations built into a supply chain? Let's briefly look at how two market leaders—Dell Computer Corporation and Walmart, Inc.—have harmonized their supply chain and marketing strategy.

Dell Computer Corporation: A Responsive Supply Chain The Dell marketing strategy targets customers who want to have the most up-to-date personal computer equipment customized to their needs. These customers are also willing to wait to have their customized personal computer delivered in a few days, rather than picking out a pre-packaged model at a retail store, and they pay a reasonable, though not the lowest, price in the marketplace. Given Dell's market segments, the company has the option of choosing either an efficient or a responsive supply chain.

Dell has a responsive supply chain.

Walmart operates with an efficient supply chain.

An efficient supply chain may use inexpensive but slower modes of transportation, emphasize economies of scale in its production process by reducing the variety of PC configurations offered, and limit its assembly and inventory storage facilities to a single location, say Austin, Texas, where the company is headquartered. If Dell opted only for efficiency in its supply chain, it would be difficult if not impossible to satisfy its target customer's desire for rapid delivery and a wide variety of customizable products. Dell instead has opted for a responsive supply chain. It relies on more expensive express transportation for receipt of components from suppliers and delivery of finished products to customers. The company achieves product variety and manufacturing efficiency by designing common platforms across several products and using common components. Dell also has invested heavily in information technology to link itself with suppliers and customers.

Walmart, Inc.: An Efficient Supply Chain

Walmart's marketing strategy is to be a reliable, lower-price retailer for a wide variety of mass-consumption consumer goods. This strategy favours an efficient supply chain designed to deliver products to consumers at the lowest possible cost. Efficiency is achieved in a variety of ways. For instance, Walmart keeps relatively low inventory levels, and most inventory is stocked in stores available for sale, not in warehouses gathering dust. The low inventory arises from Walmart's use of *cross-docking*—a practice that involves unloading products from suppliers, sorting products for individual stores, and quickly reloading products onto its trucks for a particular store. No warehousing or storing of products occurs, except

> *Walmart keeps relatively low inventory levels, and most inventory is stocked in stores available for sale, not in warehouses gathering dust.*

for a few hours or, at most, a day. Cross-docking allows Walmart to operate only a small number of distribution centres to service its vast network of Walmart Stores and Supercentres, which contributes to efficiency. On the other hand, the company runs its own fleet of trucks to service its stores.

This does increase cost and investment, but the benefits in terms of responsiveness justify the cost in Walmart's case. Walmart has invested significantly more than its competitors in information technology to operate its supply chain. The company feeds information about customer requirements and demand from its stores back to its suppliers, which manufacture only what is being demanded. This large investment has improved the efficiency of Walmart's supply chain and made it responsive to customer needs.

RFID, which stands for *radio frequency identification,* is a tag that is incorporated in a product for tracking purposes. RFID improves the efficiency of inventory tracking and management. Walmart has already asked its suppliers to use RFID. Walmart says that RFID will result in a 30 percent reduction of out-of-stock items and less excess inventory in the supply chain.[20] Some suppliers have complied but many to date have not. The cost of using this new technology is the reason for them not going ahead.

Three lessons can be learned from these two examples. First, there is no one best supply chain for every company. Second, the best supply chain is the one that is consistent with the needs of the customer segment being served and complements a company's marketing strategy. And finally, supply chain managers are often called upon to make trade-offs between efficiency and responsiveness on various elements of a company's supply chain.

The SmartWay

For decades, the impact of vehicle emissions on our environment has been a concern. Many business have used the reduction of greenhouse emissions in their business as a key focus of their corporate social responsibility. In 2013, the SmartWay program was introduced in Canada. Natural Resources Canada and Supply Chain & Logistics Association Canada partnered to bring this program across the border from the U.S. The U.S. Environmental Protection Agency originally launched the program, which shares industry best practices on supply chain transportation with its members.

The SmartWay program boasts a tool that allows its members to benchmark supply chain fleets. It then measures its progress with respect to various emissions categories. This year-over-year analysis provides feedback to transportation companies and elicits accountability of each company's carbon footprint. Now, program members that can potentially have a negative impact on our environment can work together to create greener process within the supply chain.[21]

Questions

1. What are the main benefits that organizations receive from being members of SmartWay?

2. What Canadian companies do you believe need to join SmartWay if they have not already?

Key Logistics Functions in a Supply Chain

The four key logistics functions in a supply chain are transportation, order processing, inventory management, and warehousing. These functions have become so complex that many companies are outsourcing them to third-party logistics providers. Ultimately, successful logistics management minimize the total costs to logistics while delivering the appropriate level of customer service factors of time, dependability, communication, and convenience.

Transportation

There are five basic modes of transportation—railroads, motor carriers, air carriers, water carriers, and pipelines—as combinations involving two or more modes, such as highway trailers on a rail flatcar. Although many manufacturers pay transportation expenses, some retailers negotiate with their vendors to absorb this expense. The transportation modes can be evaluated on six basic service criteria:

- **Cost:** Charges for transportation
- **Time:** Speed of transit
- **Capability:** What can be realistically carried with this mode, such as controlled temperatures and humidity levels
- **Dependability:** Reliability of service regarding time, loss, and damage
- **Accessibility:** Ability to move products over a specific route or network; for example, some destinations, such as remote areas in northern parts of Canada, may be unavailable by truck or water
- **Frequency:** Refers to how often a marketer can ship products by a specific transportation mode. Pipelines provide continuous shipments whereas railways and water carriers follow specific schedules for moving products from one location to another.

Order Processing

Order processing is much more sophisticated these days with the use of **electronic data interchange (EDI)**. EDI is the computer-to-computer exchange of business documents from a retailer to a supplier and back. Purchase orders and invoices can be transmitted back and forth electronically, replacing manual processing. Walmart is a pioneer in using EDI. Now, many other retailers also use this system. The use of EDI increases the speed, accuracy, and streamlining of operations between retailer and supplier.

electronic data interchange (EDI)
A computer-to-computer exchange of business documents from a retailer to a supplier and back

Inventory Management

Inventory management entails maintaining the delicate balance between keeping too little and too much inventory. For example, a retailer that carries too much inventory ends up with a lot of capital tied up in storing products in a warehouse. Too little inventory means that there is an increased risk for being out of stock and having unhappy customers.

A solution to this problem is the **just-in-time (JIT) inventory system**, which is designed to deliver less merchandise on a more frequent basis than traditional inventory systems. This system requires fast on-time delivery. The firm gets the merchandise "just-in-time" for it to be used in production of another product, or for sale when the customer wants it, in the case of consumer products.

Although firms achieve great benefits from a just-in-time system, it is not without its costs. The logistics function becomes more complicated with more frequent deliveries. Greater order frequencies result in smaller orders, which are more expensive to transport and more difficult to coordinate.

Inventory management helps companies maintain optimal levels of inventory.

Warehousing

There are two types of warehouses: a public warehouse offering storage for small companies or individuals and a private warehouse is used usually by large firms. Most storage warehouses are located in the outskirts of the city where rail and truck transportation are easily available. Warehouses are places to store products whereas distribution centres described below receive, store, and redistribute goods to customers.

Distribution centres can be divided into three types: traditional, cross-docking, and combination. In a traditional distribution centre, merchandise is unloaded from trucks and placed on shelves for storage. When the merchandise is required in stores, a worker goes to the shelf, picks up the item, and places it in a bin. A conveyer transports the merchandise to a staging area, where it is consolidated and made ready for shipment to stores.

The second type of distribution centre is called cross-docking. For example, Heinz ships ketchup prepackaged in the quantity required for each Walmart store. It is then sent to a staging area rather than into storage. When all the merchandise going to a particular Walmart store has arrived in the staging area, it is loaded onto a Walmart truck that goes directly to the store.

The third type of distribution centre consists of a combination of the two types explained above. Most modern distribution centres are comprised of the third type. It is difficult for a company to operate without some storage facilities, even if merchandise is stored for only a few days.

ask yourself

1. *Explain the concept of cross-docking.*

2. *Describe a just-in-time inventory system.*

LO 1
- A marketing channel consists of individuals and firms involved in the process of making a product or service available for use by consumers or business users.
- Intermediaries make possible the flow of products and services from producers to buyers by performing transactional, logistical, and facilitating functions thereby creating time, place, form, information, and possession utility.

LO 2
- Multichannel marketing is the blending of different communication and delivery channels that are mutually reinforcing in attracting, retaining, and building relationships with consumers.
- When consumers shop and buy in the traditional marketplace as well as in the online marketspace, marketers reinforce the consumer benefits of time, place, form, information, and possession utility.

LO 3
- Vertical marketing systems are channels designed to achieve channel function economies and marketing impact. A vertical marketing system may be one of three types: corporate, contractual, or administered.
  - Corporate systems display ownership of the next level or the entire channel.
  - Contractual systems benefit from functional economies and marketing impact by combining efforts on a contractual basis.
  - Administered systems achieve coordination through size and influence rather than ownership.

LO 4
- The final choice of a marketing channel by a producer depends on a number of factors. They are market factors, product factors, and company factors.
- Channel design considerations are based on the target market coverage sought by producers, the buyer requirements to be satisfied, and the profitability of the channel.
- Target market coverage comes about through one of three levels of distribution density: intensive, exclusive, or selective distribution.
- Buyer requirements are evident in the amount of information, convenience, variety, and service sought by consumers.
- Profitability—of each channel member and the channel as a whole—is largely affected by costs and whether or not costs can be shared by members.

LO 5
- A supply chain is a sequence of firms that perform activities required to create and deliver a good or service to consumers or industrial users.
- Supply chain management is the integration and organization of information and logistics across firms for the purpose of creating value for consumers.
- The goals to be achieved by a firm's marketing strategy determine whether its supply chain needs to be more responsive or efficient in meeting customer requirements. Marketers today recognize that the choice of a supply chain involves three steps: (1) understand the customer, (2) understand the supply chain, and (3) harmonize the supply chain with the marketing strategy.

Key Terms and Concepts...*a refresher*

channel conflict
cross-channel shopper
disintermediation
dual distribution
electronic data interchange (EDI)
electronic marketing channels

exclusive distribution
franchising
intensive distribution
intermediaries
just-in-time (JIT) inventory system
logistics

marketing channel
multichannel marketing
selective distribution
supply chain
supply chain management
vertical marketing systems

Hands-on...*apply your knowledge*

The Importance of Supply Chain in Marketing The opening vignette describes an intermediary performing a logistical function for a major Canadian franchisee in setting up new store locations. Review Figures 10-1 and 10-3 and create a list of companies that could potentially work with Canadian restaurants to perform the transactional and facilitating function of the marketing channel. Keep in mind that AMJ Campbell transports all of the "finished product" to locations, so consider the components of a "finished product" and how the supply chain is integral to allowing a new store location to open on time.

Chapter Vignette...*reminder*

In the opening vignette, AMJ Campbell executives describe their role in the supply chain as they warehouse a popular energy drink. Considering their comments in the vignette as well as the figures describing intermediaries and the marketing function channels they perform, answer the Reality Check questions at the end of the vignette.

Video Clip...*questions*

The idea behind **Amazon.com** was to use the Internet to transform book buying into the fastest, easiest, and most enjoyable shopping experience possible. What consumers take for granted is the amount of work and planning needed for Amazon to execute its logistics and supply chain management strategies. Review the CONNECT video and answer the following questions:

▶ Video Amazon

- How do **Amazon.com**'s logistics and supply chain management activities help the company create value for its customers?
- What systems did Amazon develop to improve the flow of products from suppliers to Amazon distribution centres? What systems improved the flow of orders from the distribution centres to customers?
- How will the Internet play an important role in the future success of **Amazon.com**?

Infographic...*data analysis*

Review the Infographic providing a snapshot of the Canadian restaurant industry provided by Restaurants Canada (previously known as the Canadian Restaurant and Foodservices Association). Consider the number of individuals directly employed by the industry. Now consider the different components of the restaurant supply chain. How many other jobs do you think are reliant on the success of the Canadian restaurant industry?

retailing and wholesaling

The physical or online space that consumers frequent to acquire products and services is a key element of the marketing mix. Thanks to technology, the concept of creating a place or distribution strategy has evolved. Even though stores no longer require a physical storefront to get goods in the hands of their customers, the need for viewing items in a tangible fashion is still alive in retailing. By partnering with organizations in their supply chain, businesses benefit from a multichannel approach to appeal to the varied purchasing practices of their customers.

TELUS has delivered innovative telecommunications solutions to Canadians for over 100 years. Starting in British Columbia and Alberta, the company has spanned across Canada to become the country's second-largest telecommunications company. Leveraging the Internet, TELUS offers communications products and services solutions to over 13 million Canadians at home, at work, and on the move. These products and services include voice, data, wireless, entertainment, and video. Using forward integration, TELUS launched its first retail stores, and with its passion for growth, TELUS provides coverage that is available to 97 percent of the Canadian population.

These days, Canadians play many roles, including employees, business owners, spouses, parents, and community leaders. In their hurried lives, it is challenging to keep up with the various bits of information sent to them each day. Knowing that Canadians have limited time and seemingly endless information to consume, Aaron Surkis has a challenging role. As manager of in-store communications for TELUS, Aaron leads a team of business professionals to communicate consistent messages to consumers through its corporate and franchise stores. The corporate stores allow for centralized decision-making on marketing initiatives, and the franchises leverage the corporate marketing investment.

"At TELUS, we believe that the strength of our team is linked to our overall success. As a team, our goal is to inspire consumers to buy," shares Aaron. "Even if they have already decided to purchase a particular product, we ensure that we guide them through the consumer purchase decision process by providing them with important information about products to allow them to evaluate their alternatives."

Aaron is amazed at how many consumers walk into their stores with a set solution in mind. Although that could be a quick sale at the retail level, the TELUS representatives ensure that they ask, "What do you plan to do with your device?" After

the future is friendly

Chapter Features

Simplicity Is Key
TELUS sends a consistent message to customers through almost 3,000 points of distribution.

Turning Loonies into Billions
Dollarama's continued success keeps the loonies (and toonies) rolling in.

It's Not Easy Going Green
Greentailing in Canada is led by Roots.

The Cashless Future
Smartphones are taking over Canadian wallets.

Online Presents
Discover the Top Ten Sites Where Canadians Shop.

Likes or Buys
Do the Top Five Canadian Brands, According to Facebook Fans, Make Sense?

The Best Buy on the Fly
Best Buy uses non-traditional retailing to bring customers what they need.

courage

Chapter Outline:

Simplicity is key

The value of retailing

Classifying retail outlets

Target market selection and positioning

Retailing mix

Non-store retailing

Online retailing

Retailer's usage of the mobile channel

Wholesaling

determining how much they plan to use their smartphone, for example, on the Internet or for pictures, TELUS representatives can provide the appropriate advice to consumers during various levels of the conversations. The retail store setup is evolving, and new technology launches will continue to require change at the retail store level. That is why the overarching philosophy for Aaron's team is to keep communications to consumers clear and simple while highlighting a consumer benefit. "It's all about consistent storytelling," affirms Aaron. "Our goals in-store around the spring, back-to-school, or holiday marketing campaigns are to create a message that resonates with consumers and ties back to our paid advertising campaigns."

Now that individuals are in the store, Aaron considers the strategy TELUS uses to provide the depth and breadth of products to its clients. Aaron suggests that the correct mix of inventory is a challenge for any retailer. Reflecting on his experience as a wholesale representative in the sporting goods industry, Aaron shares that retailers are normally risk averse. "You want to carry what is very likely to sell," explains Aaron. "TELUS works with amazing partners that allow us to hold the more popular inventory. We know the latest and greatest devices are not for everyone, but they help draw attention to the store." The bottom line, according to Aaron, is that TELUS representatives ensure that the device fits the consumers' needs. With aggressive competition and the challenges of inventory management, putting the customer first will help TELUS succeed.

Coordination is a key for Aaron's team to achieve its goals. There are 900 TELUS branches plus 2,000 other points of distribution through which the in-store communications team delivers the corporate message. Many points of contact can yield differing opinions, all driven by an entrepreneurial spirit. The chief responsibility of Aaron's team is to be the collaborative voice of dealers and negotiate a corporate message and strategy that all parties will agree to. Aaron shares that "the key to successful in-store

communications is to keep the message clear and simple." With the development of more digitized and interactive stores, there are multiple points of communication to reinforce the message TELUS wants consumers to hear. With retail stores and an online presence, TELUS uses innovative multichannel strategies to attract and retain customers. The evolution of the in-store experience is just the beginning. As a member of a forward-thinking company, Aaron sees the future of retailing to be in omni-channel retailing. As the next step in the evolution of multichannel marketing, omni-channel retailing creates a seamless and consistent experience for consumers across the different marketing channels available.

Creating a seamless and consistent experience is easy to describe, but it can be challenging for smaller companies to execute. "Consider business persons who want to purchase a phone accessory," explains Aaron. "They visit the store, do their research on their mobile device, and begin to make their purchase. After filling out their contact information on their mobile device, they pause and realize that they would prefer to provide their payment information through the security of their work computer. When they re-engage in the purchase process on their work computer, they are able to continue from where they left off." Such an experience is delightful for consumers, but it requires an investment of time and resources by the retailer. Nonetheless, TELUS plans to be a leader in this strategy, keeping with the innovative solutions that have made it so successful over the last 100 years.[1]

reality CHECK ✓

As you read Chapter 11, refer back to the TELUS vignette to answer the following questions:

- What types of form of ownership are the TELUS distribution outlets?
- How does Aaron's team help ensure a consistent message among the different consumer touch points?

Distribution involves creating a place where the customer can access a product. It is a key and evolving component of the marketing mix. As technology enables customers to access multiple channels of distribution, the challenge of retailers becomes to anticipate customer needs and provide them with favourable purchasing options.

The Value of Retailing

LO 1 **Retailing** includes all activities involved in selling, renting, and providing goods and services to ultimate customers for personal, family, or household use.

It is an important marketing activity that engages the consumers by offering a place for showcasing products and creates interest and excitement. Shopping is not only a way to acquire necessities but also a social activity and often an adventure—retailing makes this possible. Producers and consumers are brought together through retailing actions, and retailing also creates customer value and has a significant impact on the economy. Retailing's economic value is represented by the number of people employed in retailing as well as by the total amount of money exchanged in retail sales.

Consumer Utilities Offered by Retailing

The utilities provided by retailers create value for consumers. Time, place, form, information, and possession utilities are offered by most retailers in varying degrees, but one utility is often emphasized more than others. Look at Figure 11–1 to find out how well you can match the retailer with the utility being emphasized in the description.

Placing minibanks in supermarkets puts the bank's products and services close to the consumer, providing place utility. Retail kiosks continue to grow in supermarkets and drugstores as this self-source technology is meant to improve service.[2] Hudson's Bay makes the purchase easier by offering different ways to pay for the purchase, providing possession utility.

> **retailing**
> All activities involved in selling, renting, and providing goods and services to ultimate consumers for personal, family, or household use

Figure 11-1
Which company best represents which utilities?

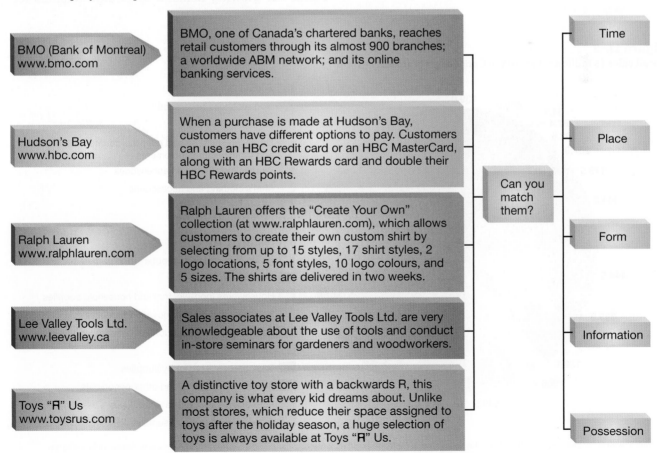

BMO (Bank of Montreal) www.bmo.com — BMO, one of Canada's chartered banks, reaches retail customers through its almost 900 branches; a worldwide ABM network; and its online banking services.

Hudson's Bay www.hbc.com — When a purchase is made at Hudson's Bay, customers have different options to pay. Customers can use an HBC credit card or an HBC MasterCard, along with an HBC Rewards card and double their HBC Rewards points.

Ralph Lauren www.ralphlauren.com — Ralph Lauren offers the "Create Your Own" collection (at www.ralphlauren.com), which allows customers to create their own custom shirt by selecting from up to 15 styles, 17 shirt styles, 2 logo locations, 5 font styles, 10 logo colours, and 5 sizes. The shirts are delivered in two weeks.

Lee Valley Tools Ltd. www.leevalley.ca — Sales associates at Lee Valley Tools Ltd. are very knowledgeable about the use of tools and conduct in-store seminars for gardeners and woodworkers.

Toys "R" Us www.toysrus.com — A distinctive toy store with a backwards R, this company is what every kid dreams about. Unlike most stores, which reduce their space assigned to toys after the holiday season, a huge selection of toys is always available at Toys "R" Us.

Can you match them?

Time
Place
Form
Information
Possession

Form utility—production or alteration of a product—is offered by Ralph Lauren through its online "Create Your Own" program, which offers shirts that meet each customer's specifications. Finding toy shelves well-stocked year-round is the time utility dreamed about by every child (and many parents) who enters Toys "R" Us. Many retailers offer a combination of the four basic utilities. Some supermarkets, for example, offer convenient locations (place utility) and are open 24 hours (time utility). In addition, consumers may seek additional utilities such as entertainment, recreation, or information.

The Canadian Retail Scene

Retail is a vibrant and important part of the Canadian economy as retailers develop strong ties with Canadians throughout their everyday lives.

In 2012, Canadian retailers had revenues of over $485 billion.[3] In Canada, Alimentation Couche-Tard, Loblaw, and Empire Company Limited (Sobeys) are the top three in terms of sales, while Walmart, Tesco, and Costco Wholesale Corporation are the top three globally.[4]

Figure 11–2 tells us that $103.4 billion is spent on food per year. It follows logically that the three largest retailers in the country are predominantly in the food business.

ask yourself

1. When Ralph Lauren makes shirts to a customer's exact preferences, what utility is provided?

2. The customer has different ways to pay for a purchase at Hudson's Bay. What utility is provided?

There is a growing trend for American retailers to open locations in Canada. For example, HBC sold the bulk of its weakest chain Zellers Inc. to the U.S. retail giant Target. The chain assumed control of up to 220 Zellers stores. The move, which came after years of rumours and discussion about Target's desire to acquire space in Canada, has dramatically reshaped the domestic retail landscape. It underscores the growing demand by foreign retailers for

Figure 11–2
Retail sales ($ millions) for 2013 in Canada by commodity group

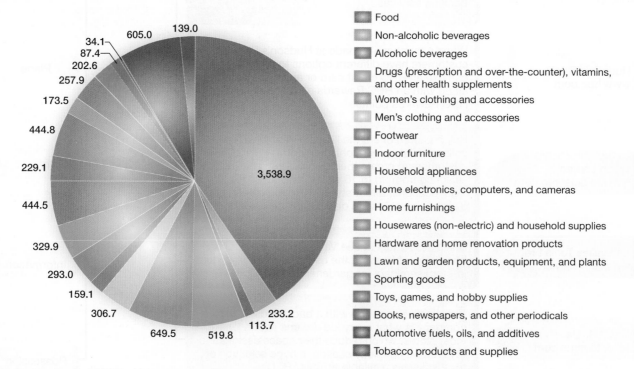

Legend:
- Food
- Non-alcoholic beverages
- Alcoholic beverages
- Drugs (prescription and over-the-counter), vitamins, and other health supplements
- Women's clothing and accessories
- Men's clothing and accessories
- Footwear
- Indoor furniture
- Household appliances
- Home electronics, computers, and cameras
- Home furnishings
- Housewares (non-electric) and household supplies
- Hardware and home renovation products
- Lawn and garden products, equipment, and plants
- Sporting goods
- Toys, games, and hobby supplies
- Books, newspapers, and other periodicals
- Automotive fuels, oils, and additives
- Tobacco products and supplies

Source: Statistics Canada, CANSIM, table 080-0009, September 19, 2013; retrieved from www.statcan.gc.ca/tables-tableaux/sum-som/l01/cst01/trad44a-eng.htm.

Canadian locations to take advantage of the country's relatively healthy economy as well as the importance of Canadian retailers to be competitive to keep Canadians shopping at home.[5]

The Global Retail Picture

Retailing is also a very important factor in the global economy, and it is a difficult retail climate for store owners. In the past few years, the worldwide economy has been challenged by issues such as terrorism, economic downturn, reduced tourism, political crises, and low consumer confidence. All of these issues translate into lower sales for retail. At the same time, consumers are empowered, and it is more difficult to gain and maintain their loyalty. Profits have to be worked at very diligently. Technology is making the industry more sophisticated and streamlined, and consolidation makes some competitors large and very powerful. It is a demanding and thorny business.

Not all countries have experienced the soft demand and market challenges that have characterized the major industrialized nations. Some of the developing countries or emerging markets in Asia and Eastern Europe are experiencing solid growth and are developing modern types of retailing. China, India, and Russia are seen as some of the biggest growth opportunities for retail in the next few years.

On a global scale, Walmart is number one, followed by Carrefour and Tesco. A study of the top 250 global retailers by Deloitte ranks the world's biggest retailers. The chart accompanying Figure 11–3 shows that most of the top 10 global retailers have sought opportunities to serve consumers outside their country of origin.

Classifying Retail Outlets

LO² For manufacturers, consumers, and the economy, retailing is an important component of marketing that has several variations. Because of the large number of alternative forms of retailing, it is easier to understand the differences among retail institutions by recognizing that outlets can be classified by ownership. **Form of ownership** distinguishes retail outlets on the basis of whether individuals, corporate chains, or contractual systems own or control the outlet. Each form has its own benefits and challenges.

Form of Ownership

INDEPENDENT RETAILER One of the most common forms of retail ownership is the independent business, owned by an individual. Small independent retailers

account for more than 60 percent of the total retail trade in Canada. They tend to be retailers such as bakeries, sporting goods stores, jewellery stores, or gift stores. Other types of small independent retailers include restaurants, automotive supply stores, bookstores, paint stores, flower shops, and women's accessories outlets. The advantage of this form of ownership for the owner is that he or she can be his or her own boss. For customers, the independent store can offer convenience, quality personal service, and lifestyle compatibility. This is mainly due to the smaller organization being able to adapt and to be more efficient than its larger competitors.[6]

CORPORATE CHAIN A second form of ownership, the corporate chain, involves multiple outlets under common ownership. If you've ever shopped at Hudson's Bay, Sears, or Real Canadian Superstore, you've shopped at a chain outlet. Read the Marketing NewsFlash, "Turning Loonies into Billions," to find out about one of Canada's fastest-growing corporate chains.

In a chain operation, centralization of decision-making and purchasing is common. Chain stores have advantages in dealing with manufacturers, particularly as the size of the chain grows. A large chain can bargain with a manufacturer to obtain good service or volume discounts on orders. Loblaw's large volume makes it a strong negotiator with manufacturers of most products. The buying power of chains is obvious to consumers who compare prices at chain stores with other types of stores. Consumers also benefit in dealing with chains because there are multiple outlets with similar merchandise and consistent management policies.

Retailing has become a high-tech business for many large chains. Walmart, for example, has developed a sophisticated inventory-management and cost-control system that allows rapid price changes for each product in every store. In addition, stores such as Walmart are implementing pioneering new technologies such as radio frequency identification (RFID) tags to improve the quality of information available about products. RFID is a tag that is incorporated in a product for tracking purposes, which improves the efficiency of inventory tracking and management.

CONTRACTUAL SYSTEM Contractual systems involve independently owned stores that use leverage to act like a chain. Contractual systems include retailer-sponsored cooperatives, wholesaler-sponsored voluntary chains, and franchises. One retailer-sponsored cooperative is

Figure 11–3
Where do we find the top retailers in the world? Who are they?

Rank	Country of Origin	Name of Company	2012 Retail Revenue (US$ Millions)	Countries of Operation
1	U.S.	Wal-Mart Stores, Inc.	$469,162	Argentina, Brazil, Canada, China, Costa Rica, El Salvador, Guatemala, Honduras, Japan, Mexico, Nicaragua, Puerto Rico, U.K., U.S.
2	U.K.	Tesco PLC	$101,269	China, Czech Republic, Hungary, Japan, Malaysia, Poland, Republic of Ireland, Slovakia, South Korea, Taiwan, Thailand, Turkey, U.K., U.S.
3	U.S.	Costco Wholesale Corporation	$99,137	Canada, Japan, Mexico, Puerto Rico, South Korea, Taiwan, U.K., U.S.
4	France	Carrefour S.A.	$98,757	Algeria, Argentina, Belgium, Brazil, Chile, China, Colombia, Dominican Republic, Egypt, France, Greece, Guadeloupe, Indonesia, Italy, Japan, Malaysia, Martinique, Oman, Poland, Portugal, Qatar, Romania, Saudi Arabia, Singapore, Spain, Switzerland, Taiwan, Thailand, Tunisia, Turkey, UAE
5	U.S.	The Kroger Co.	$96,751	U.S.
6	Germany	Schwarz Unternehmens Treuhand KG	$87,236	Austria, Belgium, Bulgaria, Croatia, Cyprus, Czech Republic, Denmark, Finland, France, Germany, Greece, Hungary, Italy, Luxembourg, Netherlands, Norway, Poland, Portugal, Republic of Ireland, Romania, Slovakia, Spain, Sweden, U.K..
7	Germany	Metro AG	$85,832	Austria, Belgium, Bulgaria, China, Croatia, Czech Republic, Denmark, France, Germany, Greece, Hungary, India, Italy, Japan, Luxembourg, Moldova, Morocco, Netherlands, Pakistan, Poland, Portugal, Romania, Russia, Serbia, Slovakia, Spain, Sweden, Switzerland, Turkey, U.K., Ukraine, Vietnam
8	U.S.	The Home Depot	$70,395	Canada, China, Guam, Mexico, Puerto Rico, U.S., Virgin Islands
9	Germany	Aldi Einkauf GmbH & Co. oHG	$73,035	Australia, Austria, Belgium, Denmark, France, Germany, Luxembourg, Netherlands, Portugal, Republic of Ireland, Slovenia, Spain, Switzerland
10	U.S.	Target Corporation	$71,960	Canada, U.S.

Source: Deloitte, *Global Powers of Retailing 2014: Beyond Retailing*. Retrieved from www.deloitte.com/assets/Dcom-Kenya/Local%20Assets/Documents/CB_Global-Powers-of-Retailing-2014.pdf.

Home Hardware, which is a collection of independent hardware and home-renovation stores across Canada. Home Hardware actually created its own wholesale operation to take full advantage of dealings with manufacturers and suppliers. As a cooperative, members can take advantage of volume discounts commonly available to chains and also give the impression of being a large chain, which may be viewed more favourably by some consumers. Wholesaler-sponsored voluntary chains such as Independent Grocers' Association (IGA) try to achieve similar benefits.

In a franchise system, an individual or firm (the franchisee) contracts with a parent company (the franchiser) to set up a business or retail outlet. McDonald's, Holiday Inn, and Subway all offer franchising opportunities. The franchiser usually assists in selecting the store location, setting up the store, advertising, and training personnel. In addition,

Turning Loonies into Billions

Dollarama is the largest dollar-store chain in Canada, with well over 800 stores across the country with the potential to grow further. Founded in 1992 by third-generation retailer Larry Rossy, this publicly traded company is focused on providing customers with compelling value in convenient locations, and offering a broad assortment of everyday consumer products, general merchandise, and seasonal items.

All stores are corporate-owned and provide customers with a consistent shopping experience. Dollarama's uncomplicated approach to its business involves operating clean stores, maintaining a consistent inventory of name brands and house brands, and dealing directly with suppliers. Under this no-frills strategy, the company has seen growth every year since it opened in 1992. The stores have accepted debit cards since 2008. Dollarama introduced new price points in 2009 and again in 2012 and now sells $1.25, $1.50, $2.00, $2.50, and $3.00 items alongside its traditional $1.00 items, as well as select items at $0.69. A leader in the industry, Dollarama knows the importance of investing in technology as it invested heavily in this area to increase efficiency during its growth.

An estimated 4,000 items line Dollarama's shelves year-round, and an additional 700 or so are seasonal products. This ability to capitalize on seasonal demand is widely admired.

"They run it like the U.S. Marines," says John Williams, a retail consultant. "When Christmas is out, they go into Valentine's Day, and when that's out, they go into Easter."

Food, drinks, and other so-called consumables, currently represent 37 percent of a Dollarama's store stock. These items are not obscure, low-quality brands being sold cheaply, but a mix of Dollarama house brands and name brands. Popular brand names such as Pepsi and Lay's chips are prominently displayed.

Sometimes, rather than seeking out brand-name merchandise, Dollarama creates its own. Kids now seek out Studio notebooks, made for Dollarama, the same way they once sought out Hilroy for back-to-school. Dollarama sources many of its suppliers directly and gets involved with the product design, packaging, and labelling. Dollarama has 70 house brands, still a novel concept in the dollar-store world.

There is no denying that Dollarama dominates the Canadian dollar-store sector. There are thousands of "mom and pop" dollar stores, but only one other national dollar-store chain, Dollar Tree Canada. It has just 160 stores. There are also three large franchise operations—Dollar Store with More, Great Canadian, and Buck or Two— but combined they operate less than 300 stores.

What percentage of Dollarama's customers fall into each of those two camps—rich and poor—is not entirely clear? In the United States, dollar stores undeniably rely on the lower class for business. But Canadian dollar stores seem to draw from a wider demographic. "There's a type of consumer who may drive a Mercedes but get their stationery from a dollar store," says retail consultant Wendy Evans. "You'll see them buying a no-name brand and driving luxury cars and wearing designer clothing. They care about brands for some things and not others."

Retail analyst John Williams argues that the dollar-store industry is now in a "mature phase." Others contend there is still plenty of room for growth. In Canada, there is a dollar store for every 32,000 people, far less than the one per 15,500 people in the United States. Dollarama's current plans call for opening an additional 70 to 80 stores per year across the country.[7] ●

Questions

1. What benefits does a corporate chain business model offer Dollarama?

2. Given the price of its typical product, how do you explain the success of Dollarama?

McDonald's offers franchising opportunities.

McDonald's and Subway look at demographics— population, family, and age characteristics—to determine where new restaurants should be located and what formats to offer.

the franchiser provides step-by-step procedures for major aspects of the business and guidelines for the most likely decisions a franchisee will confront. The franchisee pays a one-time franchise fee and an annual royalty, usually tied to the store's sales. By selling franchises, an organization reduces the cost of expansion, although they lose some control. To ensure mutual benefits to all parties involved, a good franchiser concentrates on enhancing the image and reputation of the franchise name.[8]

Target Market Selection and Positioning

LO 3 Retailing involves many decisions and considerations. In this section, we look at the issues in selecting a target market and the concept of retail positioning.

Selecting a Target Market

The first task in developing a retail strategy is to define a target market, describing it in detail. Without customers, even the best-conceived retail concept is nothing, so focusing on customers is the guiding principle of successful retail businesses. This focus involves understanding wants and needs, knowing customer preferences, analyzing behaviour, and deciding how to craft all of the dimensions of the retail concept to appeal to the targeted customer.

Look at any mall or shopping district, and you will see the varied selection of retail offerings the customer has to choose from. This provides a challenge to retailers. It is no longer enough to appeal to customers; now the retailer has to interest, engage, and delight customers in order to foster loyalty.

How do we define target markets? The most common descriptors are geographics, demographics, psychographics, and behaviouristics. Retailers study these factors and adjust their retail mix accordingly. McDonald's and Subway look at demographics—population, family, and age characteristics—to determine where new restaurants should be located and what formats to offer. Retailers such as Target and Canadian Tire look at consumers' trends and tastes and adjust their product offerings and store composition to match customer preferences. Staples and Shoppers Drug Mart have adjusted their store hours to respond to the behaviour of consumers; many now prefer to shop and do errands in the evening after working during the day.

Retail Positioning

Just as marketers of packaged goods position their products to differentiate themselves from competitors, so do retailers. For example, Harry Rosen is a high-end men's clothing retailer. It would be a mistake in times of recession for Harry Rosen to start carrying lower-quality, low-priced suits. Larry Rosen, CEO and chairman of Harry Rosen Inc., and son of founder Harry Rosen, says, "The customer who is used to the quality and calibre of our product is not looking for a cheaper product. Maybe he'll buy slightly less this year but it's not about reducing quality. It's about sticking to your guns, to who you are." The confidence to be able to do so comes from a deep understanding of your customers and their buying habits.[9]

retailing mix
The goods and services, pricing, physical distribution, and communications tactics chosen by a store

Harry Rosen, a high-end men's clothing retailer, provides a good example of retail positioning.

Shopper Marketing

Shopper marketing is a hot trend in marketing today. It is a discipline designed to understand how consumers behave as shoppers in different channels and formats. Consequently, shopper marketing practices extend well outside of the store, to the place and time when a consumer first thinks about purchasing a product. That might be on a treadmill at the gym, at home reading a magazine, or in the car while driving to work. That means that shopper marketing is by necessity a multichannel practice that makes use of traditional media, new media, direct marketing, loyalty, trade promotion, and innumerable other marketing techniques.

Underneath it all is one area that is largely alien to traditional marketers, whose focus has been almost exclusively on understanding *consumers*—that is, the consumption of goods and services. What's been ignored is understanding *shoppers*—that is, consumers when they are in the shopping mode. Shopper marketing is new to Canada, but the distinction in understanding shoppers is important.[10]

Retailing Mix

LO 4 The marketing mix, or the 4 Ps (product, price, place, and promotion), are used in retail just as they are in other businesses, but with some unique considerations. In this section, we look at the retailing mix, which includes product and service considerations, retail pricing, physical location factors, and communications, as shown in Figure 11–4. All of these components of the mix focus on the consumer. In retail, it is often said that the consumer is king, and treating them that way is a winning idea for successful retailing.

The positioning of a retail store must be consistent with the store's **retailing mix**. The four elements must be coordinated so that they portray a clear position to consumers. For example, Winners is positioned as a store providing upscale designer clothing at a discount price. If prices suddenly rose and consumers came to the conclusion that they were not getting a bargain, Winners' positioning would not be effective.

Figure 11—4
The retailing mix

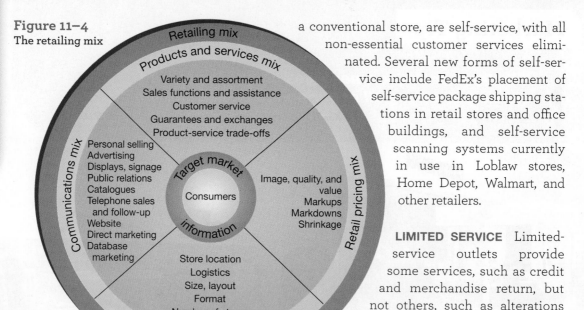

Products and Services

One of the first decisions that retailers make is what they are going to sell. Usually, both services and products are offered. McDonald's offers a hamburger, which is the tangible product, but the smiles, thank yous, and clean washrooms make up some of the service components. A department store such as Hudson's Bay sells many products—from clothing to housewares—and also provides services such as bridal registries. First Choice Hair Cutters provides services such as haircuts, colouring, and styling, but also sells hair care products. The balance between products and services involves a trade-off between costs and customer satisfaction.

Level of Service Most customers perceive little variation in retail outlets by form of ownership. Rather, differences among retailers are more obvious in terms of level of service. **Level of service** is used to describe the degree of service provided to the customer. Three levels of service include self-, limited-, and full-service retailers. Stores such as Costco do not offer bags, while outlets such as Holt Renfrew provide a wide range of customer services from gift wrapping to wardrobe consultation.

SELF-SERVICE Self-service is at the extreme end of the level-of-service continuum because the customer performs many functions and little is provided by the outlet. Home building-supply outlets and gas stations are often self-service. Warehouse stores such as Costco, usually in buildings several times larger than

a conventional store, are self-service, with all non-essential customer services eliminated. Several new forms of self-service include FedEx's placement of self-service package shipping stations in retail stores and office buildings, and self-service scanning systems currently in use in Loblaw stores, Home Depot, Walmart, and other retailers.

LIMITED SERVICE Limited-service outlets provide some services, such as credit and merchandise return, but not others, such as alterations to clothes. General merchandise stores such as Shoppers Drug Mart and Ikea are usually considered limited-service outlets. Customers are responsible for most shopping activities, although salespeople are available in departments such as cosmetics at Shoppers Drug Mart.

FULL SERVICE Full-service retailers, which include most specialty stores and department stores, provide many services to their customers. Holt Renfrew, a Canadian specialty fashion retailer with nine stores across the country, is very committed to exemplary customer service. Its stores feature more salespeople on the floor than other similarly sized stores, and Holt Renfrew offers a national concierge service, as well as personal shopping in each store. Employees are trained in customer follow-up, and many call their clients to advise them of new merchandise and send thank-you notes after purchase. With an eye kept fixed on customers and their evolving needs, Holt Renfrew is a leader in merchandise assortments and in innovations in customer services demonstrated by its previous successes and future expansion plans.[11]

Merchandise Mix Merchandise selection is one of the major attracting factors for customers, so choices and combinations must be made carefully and continually updated to reflect current trends and tastes. This involves finding sources of supply of the products, or having them manufactured, as well as managing inventory and warehousing. The **merchandise mix** describes how many different types of products a store carries and in what assortment.

Retail outlets vary by their merchandise mix, the key distinction being the breadth and depth of the

It's Not Easy Going Green

According to the Environmental Careers Organization (ECO) Canada, the green economy includes "inputs, activities, outputs, and outcomes as they relate to the production of green products and services." In essence, by "reducing resource consumption, harmful emissions, and minimizing all forms of environment impact," a new economy is created that can not only save money and our world, but also create career opportunities. ECO Canada is a non-profit organization whose vision is to build the world's leading environmental workforce. It does this by creating online resources for careers and training.

Since consumers are becoming more and more aware of the impact of their purchases on the environment, green products become increasingly available and more emphasis is being placed on marketing these strategies. For example, apparel companies have begun to produce environmentally friendly clothing. For example, Roots employs sustainable practices through using eco-friendly materials and manufacturing clothes out of organic or recycled cottons. The company continues to develop more eco-friendly products each year.

Roots has made protecting the environment a core value. It believes the environment is one of the most critical issues of our time. Along with some of the world's leading environmentalists, Roots demonstrates its commitment through its actions and financial support of environmental organizations. A partial list of environmental organizations that Roots works with includes the David Suzuki Foundation, the Canadian Wildlife Federation, and the Jane Goodall Institute of Canada.

The larger strategy being considered in Canadian retailing and business is corporate social responsibility (CSR), where companies voluntarily conduct business in a manner that is sustainable from an economic, social, and environmental standpoint. Not only is CSR important locally, but Canadian companies see the value of incorporating their practices on an international scale. Considering what Roots is doing with its stores and apparel, it is surprising not to see them in *Maclean's* list of the "Top 50 Socially Responsible Companies 2013." Seeing Roots' competitors, such as Adidas, Nike, and Gap, get recognized helps confirm the importance of CSR in Canadian retailing.[12]

▶ Video
Roots

Questions

1. Describe the target market that retailers such as Roots are trying to reach by adopting green practices.

2. Considering a retailer you have made a purchase from, identify three changes it can make to its practices that would support a green economy.

---

items offered to customers (see Figure 11–5). **Depth of product line** means the assortment of products within each product line, such as a shoe store that offers running shoes, dress shoes, and children's shoes. **Breadth of product line** refers to the variety of different lines a store carries, such as women's clothing, men's clothing, children's clothing, cosmetics, and housewares.

DEPTH OF LINE Stores that carry a large assortment (depth) of a related line of items are limited-line stores. Sport Chek sporting goods stores carry considerable depth in sports equipment, ranging from golf accessories to running shoes. Stores that carry tremendous depth in one primary line of merchandise are single-line stores. Victoria's Secret, a nationwide chain, carries great depth in women's lingerie. Both limited- and single-line stores are often referred to as *specialty outlets*.

Specialty outlets focus on one type of product, such as electronics (Future Shop), office supplies (Staples), or books (Indigo Books &

depth of product line
Assortment of products within each product line that a store carries

breadth of product line
The variety of different lines a store carries

Figure 11–5
Breadth versus depth of merchandise lines

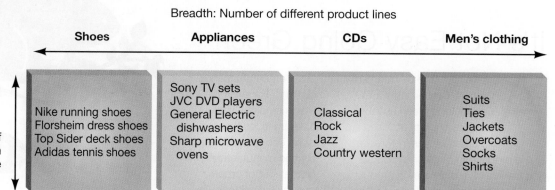

Breadth: Number of different product lines

Shoes	Appliances	CDs	Men's clothing

Depth: Number of items within each product line

Nike running shoes
Florsheim dress shoes
Top Sider deck shoes
Adidas tennis shoes

Sony TV sets
JVC DVD players
General Electric dishwashers
Sharp microwave ovens

Classical
Rock
Jazz
Country western

Suits
Ties
Jackets
Overcoats
Socks
Shirts

Likes or Buys?

Brands That Have the Most Canadian Fans on Facebook

Rank	Brand
1	Tim Hortons
2	Subway Canada
3	Skittles
4	Target Canada
5	iTunes

Source: Social Bakers, "Canada Facebook Statistics (2013)." Retrieved from www.socialbakers.com/facebook-pages/brands/canada.

Music) at very competitive prices. These outlets are referred to in the trade as category killers because they often dominate the market. Indigo Books & Music, for example, controls a large percentage of the retail book market in Canada.

BREADTH OF LINE Stores that carry a variety of product lines, with limited depth, are referred to as *general merchandise stores*. For example, large department stores such as Hudson's Bay, Sears, and Target carry a wide range of different lines of products but not unusual sizes. The breadth and depth of merchandise lines are important decisions for a retailer. Traditionally, outlets carried related lines of goods. Today, however, **scrambled merchandising**, offering several unrelated

Indigo
Enrich your life

Indigo Books & Music is the largest book retailer in Canada and is a category killer.

product lines in a single store, is common. The modern drugstore carries food, cosmetics, camera equipment, magazines, paper products, toys, small hardware items, and pharmaceuticals. Supermarkets rent carpet-cleaning equipment, operate pharmacy departments, and sell flowers.

Scrambled merchandising makes it convenient for consumers because it eliminates the number of stops required in a shopping trip. However, for the retailer, this merchandising policy means that there is competition between very dissimilar types of retail outlets, or **intertype competition**. A local bakery may compete with a department store, discount outlet, or even a local gas station. Scrambled merchandising and intertype competition make retailing more challenging.

PLANOGRAMS A planogram is a visual diagram or drawing of fixtures and products that illustrates how and where retail products should be placed on a store shelf. It also illustrates how many facings should be allocated for each stock-keeping unit (SKU). The planogram is arranged so that the fastest-moving high-margin products get the most space on the shelf. For example, Procter & Gamble works closely with Walmart by providing the retailer with planograms, which lead to higher profits than if products were placed indiscriminately on the shelf.

As competition increases, we're seeing suppliers and retailers becoming more aware of the importance of correctly merchandising their products. Some retailers produce their own planograms while others, such as Walmart, receive planograms from suppliers such as Procter & Gamble.

Apple offers a store atmosphere allowing consumers to engage with Apple products.

Discounting a product, or taking a *markdown*, occurs when the product does not sell at the original price and an adjustment is necessary. Often, new models or styles force the price of existing models to be marked down. Discounts may also be used to increase demand for related products.[14] For example, retailers might take a markdown on DVD players to increase sales of DVDs or reduce the price of cake mix to generate frosting purchases. The *timing* of a markdown can be important. Many retailers take a markdown as soon as sales fall off, to free up valuable selling space and obtain cash. However, other stores delay markdowns to discourage bargain hunters and maintain an image of quality. There is no clear answer, but retailers must consider how the timing might affect future sales.

Although most retailers plan markdowns, many retailers use price discounts as a part of their regular merchandising policy. In Canada, retailers such as Walmart and Bed, Bath & Beyond emphasize consistently low prices and eliminate most markdowns with a strategy often called *everyday low pricing*.[15] Consumers often use price as an indicator of product quality; however, the brand name of the product and the image of the store become important decision factors in these situations.[16]

A special issue for retailers trying to keep prices low is **shrinkage**, or breakage and theft of merchandise by customers and employees. What is surprising is that more than 50 percent of thefts are made not by consumers but by employees.

> *What is surprising is that more than 50 percent of thefts are made not by consumers but by employees.*

Store Atmosphere

Store atmosphere is related to the positioning of a store. For example, Costco has a warehouse appearance that is consistent with the low prices that it offers. Store atmosphere refers to the physical characteristics of a store that provide an overall impression to the consumer. These characteristics consist of the exterior and interior appearance and physical layout of the store. The Apple Store's customer-friendly layout encourages consumers to mingle and sample the products. Apple successfully trademarked its store design in 2013, and continues to trademark the distinctive design and layout of its retail store in Canada. It filed an application with the Canadian Intellectual Property Office in 2010.[13] If approved, Canadian competitors will not be able to copy the Apple layout for their retail stores.

The Apple Store is usually quite crowded. This frenetic atmosphere draws in even more people who want to be part of the "event." Every Apple Store offers a range of services designed to help customers get the most out of their Apple products, including face-to-face support and advice at the Genius Bar, hands-on workshops, and special programs for kids.

Retail Pricing

In setting prices for merchandise, retailers must decide on the markup. The markup refers to how much should be added to the cost the retailer paid for a product to reach the final selling price. We discussed the calculation of markup in Chapter 9. The difference between the final selling price and retailer cost is called the gross margin.

ask yourself

1. *What are the four components of the retailing mix?*

2. *What are some examples of stores with scrambled merchandising?*

3. *Would a shop for big men's clothes carrying pants in sizes 40 to 60 have a broad or deep product line?*

shrinkage
Breakage and theft of merchandise by customers and employees

Off-price retailing is a retail pricing practice that is used by retailers such as Winners. **Off-price retailing** involves selling brand-name merchandise at lower than regular prices. The difference between the off-price retailer and a discount store is that off-price merchandise is bought by the retailer from manufacturers with excess inventory at prices below wholesale prices, whereas the discounter buys at full wholesale price but takes less of a markup than do traditional department stores. Because of this difference in the way merchandise is purchased by the retailer, selection at an off-price retailer is unpredictable, and searching for bargains has become a popular activity for many consumers. Savings to the consumer at off-price retailers are reported as high as 70 percent off the prices of a traditional department store.

Physical Location

Another aspect of the retailing mix involves deciding where to locate the store and how many stores to have. Department stores, which started downtown in most cities, have followed customers to the suburbs, and in recent years, more stores have been opened in large regional malls. Most stores today are near several others in one of five settings: the central business district, the regional centre, the community shopping centre, the strip, or the power centre.

The **central business district** is the oldest retail setting, the community's downtown area. Until the regional outflow to suburbs, it was the major shopping area, but the suburban population has grown at the expense of the downtown shopping area.

Regional shopping centres consist of 50 to 150 stores that typically attract customers who live or work within a 5- to 15-km range. These large shopping areas often contain two or three anchor stores, which are well-known national or regional stores such as Sears and Hudson's Bay. One of the largest variations of a regional centre is the West Edmonton Mall in Alberta. The shopping centre is a conglomerate of over 800 stores, 7 amusement centres, 110 restaurants, and a 355-room Fantasyland hotel.[17]

A more limited approach to retail location is the **community shopping centre**, which typically has one primary store (usually a department store branch) and often about 20 to 40 smaller outlets. Generally, these centres serve a population of consumers who are within a 2- to 5-km drive.

Not every suburban store is located in a shopping mall. Many neighbourhoods have clusters of stores, referred to as a **strip location**, to serve people who are within a 5- to 10-minute drive. Gas station, hardware, laundry, grocery, and pharmacy outlets are commonly found in a strip location. Unlike the larger shopping centres, the composition of these stores is usually unplanned. A variation of the strip shopping location is called the **power centre**, which is a large shopping strip with many national stores. Power centres are seen as having the convenient location found in many strip centres and the added power of national stores. These large strips often have two to five anchor stores plus a supermarket, which brings the shopper to the power centre on a weekly basis.[18]

Communications

The elements of the retailing communication mix described in Figure 11–4 represent an exciting menu of choices for creating customer value in the marketplace. Each format allows retailers to offer unique benefits

Power centres are unenclosed shopping centres.

and meet particular needs of various customer groups. Today, retailers combine many of the formats to offer a broader spectrum of benefits and experiences. These **multichannel retailers** utilize and integrate a combination of traditional store and non-store formats such as catalogues and online retailing. Indigo Books & Music, for example, created **chapters.indigo.ca** to compete with Amazon. As discussed in the opening vignette, TELUS has integrated a number of its communications options.

Integrated channels can make shopping simpler and more convenient. A consumer can research choices online or in a catalogue and then make a purchase online, over the telephone, or at the closest store. In addition, the use of multiple channels allows retailers to reach a broader profile of customers. While online retailing may cannibalize catalogue business to some degree, a web transaction costs about half as much to process as a catalogue order. Multichannel retailers also benefit from the synergy of sharing information among the different channel operations.

ask yourself

1. *Explain how shrinkage impacts retailers.*

2. *A large shopping strip with multiple anchor stores is a _____ centre.*

3. *How do multichannel retailers make shopping simpler and more convenient?*

Non-Store Retailing

LO5 Most of the retailing examples discussed earlier in the chapter, such as corporate chains, department stores, and limited- and single-line specialty stores, involve the consumer physically being in the store. Many retailing activities today, however, are not limited to sales in a store. Non-store retailing occurs outside a retail outlet through activities that involve varying levels of customer and retailer involvement. Forms of non-store retailing include automatic vending, television home shopping, and direct marketing (direct mail and catalogue retailing, telemarketing, direct selling, and online buying). Many traditional "bricks and mortar" stores are involved in non-store retailing, making them "click and mortar" concepts; for example, Indigo Books & Music has developed **chapters.indigo.ca**, its online store. Dell Computers, in contrast, relies mainly on non-store retailing for its consumer sales.

Automatic Vending

Non-store retailing includes vending machines, which make it possible to serve customers when and where stores cannot. Maintaining and operating vending machines is expensive, so product prices in vending machines tend to be higher than those in stores. Typically, small convenience products are available in vending machines. In Japan, products available in vending machines include dried squid, hair tonic, boxers, green tea, beer, CDs, books, clothing, and even music downloaded from a satellite transmission system. The Marketing NewsFlash, "The Best Buy on the Fly," discusses the Best Buy Express automatic vending kiosks.

Improved technology will soon make vending machines easier to use by reducing the need for cash. In Europe, for example, Marconi Online Systems has installed 6,000 vending machines that allow consumers to pay for products using a cellphone. Similarly, the world's largest vending machine company, Canteen Services Inc., is testing a cashless system called FreedomPay, which allows consumers to wave a small wand in front of a sensor to make a purchase.

Another improvement in vending machines—the use of wireless technology to notify retailers when their machines are empty—is one reason automatic merchandising sales are expected to increase in the future.[19]

Television Home Shopping

Television home shopping is possible when consumers watch a shopping channel on which products are displayed; orders are then placed over the telephone or the Internet. One popular network is The Shopping Channel, which has 24-hour programming and calls itself a broadcast retailer. A limitation of TV shopping

The Best Buy on the Fly

Great companies not only seize opportunities but also adapt to their changing environment. As the consumer landscape changed, Best Buy began expanding its web presence and its Best Buy Express kiosks. With these non-traditional retailing options in place, Best Buy considered subleasing some of its space. For example, it created a store-within-a-store kiosk for Samsung products.

In early 2013, Best Buy Canada launched its Best Buy Express kiosk in the Halifax Stanfield International Airport. At that time, there were 14 Best Buy Express vending machines across Canada, with plans to continue growing.

Although the product offerings are not as robust as a traditional retail store, Best Buy Express uses target marketing to offer 60 different products, including headphones, digital cameras, and tablets. Forgetting your important technology accessories can

reduce the pleasantries of travel. According to Peter Spurwa, VP of concession and development at the Halifax International Airport Authority, "It's been a pleasure working with Best Buy to bring this innovation to our airport—another example of our commitment to providing our passengers with new and creative retail options."

Looking west, Best Buy Express automated kiosks are also available in Toronto Pearson International Airport as well as on BC Ferries. Further expansions of this option are coming.

Back in 2008, the concept of Best Buy Express began with Chris Stidman, VP of strategic planning at Best Buy. The vision was to create a solution to help the customer who shows up for a flight without his

BlackBerry. Prices at kiosks match the Best Buy stores, except for any clearance promotions. Similar to purchasing a can of soda or bottle of water from a vending machine, Best Buy Express kiosks allow you to browse the selection, choose your item, and then pay by debit card or credit card.[20]

Questions

1. What does the introduction of Best Buy Express kiosks mean for its retail stores?

2. What other products would you feel comfortable purchasing through this non-traditional retailing method?

---

has been the lack of buyer-seller interaction. New Internet technologies, however, now allow consumers to explore different possibilities.

Direct Marketing from a Retailing Perspective

We talk in detail about direct marketing in Chapter 12; here we introduce the idea, as it is an important form of retailing. In its simplest terms, direct marketing is an interactive process of marketing that uses advertising media or direct consumer contact to offer products or services. When a direct communication to a

consumer or a business market is intended to generate a response from the recipient, direct marketing is the tactic being used.

Direct Mail and Catalogues   Direct mail and catalogue retailing is attractive because it eliminates the cost of a store and clerks. It costs a traditional retail store more than twice the amount to acquire a new customer than it costs a catalogue retailer. Why? Because catalogues improve marketing efficiency through segmentation and targeting. In addition, they create customer value by providing a fast and convenient means of making a purchase. In Canada, the amount spent on direct mail catalogue merchandise

IKEA delivers over 210 million copies of its catalogue.

IKEA delivers 210 million copies of its catalogue to 36 countries in 28 languages, including 5 million in Canada.

continues to increase; internationally, spending is also increasing. IKEA delivers over 210 million copies of its catalogue to 36 countries in 28 languages, including over 5 million in Canada.[21]

One reason for the growth in catalogue sales is that traditional retailers are adding catalogue operations. Another reason is that many Internet retailers, such as Amazon, have also added catalogues. As consumers' direct mail purchases have increased, the number of catalogues and the number of products sold through catalogues have increased. A typical Canadian household now receives dozens of catalogues every year, and there are billions circulated around the world. The competition, combined with recent increases in postal rates, however, have caused catalogue retailers to focus on proven customers rather than "prospects." Another successful new approach used by many catalogue retailers is to send specialty catalogues to market niches identified in their databases. L.L. Bean, a longstanding catalogue retailer, has developed an individual catalogue for fly-fishing enthusiasts. Lee Valley Tools Ltd. sends out specialized catalogues for hardware, woodworking, gardening, and Christmas.

Telemarketing Another form of non-store retailing, called **telemarketing**, involves using the telephone to interact with and sell directly to consumers. Compared with direct mail, telemarketing is often viewed as a more efficient means of targeting consumers, although the two techniques are often used together. Sears Canada utilizes telemarketing to increase sales of extended warranty programs and other services. Communications companies such as Bell Mobility telemarket new potential customers, and financial institutions such as HSBC and MBNA use telemarketing for customer follow-up and cross-selling. Telemarketing has grown in popularity as companies search for ways to cut costs but still provide convenient access to their customers. In 1991, the telemarketing industry generated $3.1 billion in sales and planned to employ one million Canadians by the year 2000. By 2007, there were approximately 250,000 Canadians employed by the industry, and it generated $17 billion in sales annually.[22]

As the use of telemarketing grows, consumer privacy has become a topic of discussion among consumers, governments, and businesses. Issues such as industry standards, ethical guidelines, and new privacy laws are evolving to provide a balance between the varying perspectives. In September 2008, the Canadian Radio-television and Telecommunications Commission (CRTC) instituted a national Do Not Call List (DNCL), which was created to enable Canadian consumers to reduce the number of unsolicited telemarketing calls they receive. Every year, thousands of Canadians raise concerns about receiving unwanted telemarketing calls, despite being on the DNCL list.

Direct Selling Direct selling, sometimes called door-to-door retailing, involves direct sales of goods and services to consumers through personal interactions and demonstrations in their home or office. A variety of companies, including familiar names such as Avon, Tupperware, and Mary Kay Cosmetics, have created an industry with billions in sales by providing consumers with personalized service and convenience. However, sales have been declining as retail chains begin to carry similar products at discount prices and as the increasing number of dual-career households reduces the number of potential buyers who can be found at home.

In response to change, many direct-selling retailers are expanding online and into other markets. Avon, for example, already has over

telemarketing
Using the telephone to interact with and sell directly to consumers

Walmart.ca and **ebay.ca** are two examples of online retailing.

six million sales representatives in over 100 countries with over 10,000 reps trained to sell online. In Canada, the Avon sales force is 65,000 strong.[23] Direct selling is likely to continue to grow in markets where the lack of effective distribution channels increases the importance of door-to-door convenience and where the lack of consumer knowledge about products and brands will increase the need for a person-to-person approach. Furthermore, it will help maximize growth and customer loyalty.[24]

Online Retailing

LO 6 Online retailing allows customers to search for, evaluate, and order products through the Internet. For many consumers, the advantages of this form of retailing are the 24-hour access, the ability to comparison shop, and the in-home privacy. Four in ten Canadians aged 16 and over use the Internet to purchase products and services. This is a space that can no longer be ignored by Canadian retailers, as reported by a Forrester Research study. Canadians may begin foregoing their loyalty to Canadian retailers if prices are cheaper online from non-Canadian retailers. Furthermore, Forrester Research believes that the online retail sales market will increase from $20 billion to $34 billion by 2018, creating a huge opportunity cost for Canadian retailers who have not ventured into an online retailing strategy.[25]

Studies of online shoppers indicated that men were initially more likely than women to buy something online. As the number of online households increased to more than 50 percent, however, the profile of online shoppers changed to include all shoppers. In addition, the number of online retailers grew rapidly for several years but then declined as many stand-alone, Internet-only businesses failed or consolidated. Today, there has been a melding of traditional and online retailers—"bricks and clicks"—that are using experiences from both approaches to create better value and experiences for customers.

Online buying is getting a boost from the comments that consumers are leaving on social media sites such as Facebook and Twitter. These sites are having an influence on what consumers are buying online. Research shows that Facebook and Twitter influences online buying decisions.[26]

Mobile Banking and Cashless Future

One of the biggest problems that online retailers face is that nearly two-thirds of online shoppers make it to "checkout" and then leave the website to compare shipping costs and prices on other sites. Of the shoppers who leave, 70 percent do not return. One way online retailers are addressing this issue is to offer consumers a comparison of competitors' offerings. Online retailers are also trying to improve the online retailing experience by adding experiential, or interactive, activities to their websites. Montreal-based My Virtual Model Inc. develops software for apparel stores so that consumers can create models of themselves online to assist with the purchase process and help with product selection.[27] Car manufacturers such as BMW and Toyota encourage website visitors to build a vehicle by selecting interior and exterior colours, packages, and options and then view the customized virtual car.

Why Consumers Shop and Buy Online

Consumers typically offer six reasons why they shop and buy online: convenience, choice, communication, customization, cost, and control (see Figure 11-6).

- **Convenience:** Online shopping and buying is *convenient,* so websites must be easy to locate and navigate, and image downloads must be fast.

- **Choice:** There are two dimensions to choice: *selection*—numerous websites for almost anything consumers want—and *assistance*—interactive capabilities of Internet/web-enabled technologies assist customers to make informed choices.

Infographic

Mobile Banking in Canada and the Cashless Future

Categories more popular than banking: **games, weather, messaging, navigation, social networking**

Categories banking apps have eclipsed: **music, news, video, entertainment**

2.5 million the amount of Canadians who have downloaded a mobile banking app

1 in 3 Canadians with a smartphone and data plan bank on the go

43% already don't carry cash.

36% would buy a latte—or an iPad—with their device.

security is the #1 cause of concern.

56% percent of Canadians who would be comfortable never handling cash again.

online banking | mobile banking
In 14 months, mobile banking has reached the same level of penetration in Canada as online banking did after four years.

4 years

14 months

The dollar value of global payments via mobile devices will triple over the four years from 2011 to 2015

240 billion 2011

670 billion 2015

Source: Techvibes, created from data from Solutions Research Group, Leger Marketing, and Juniper Research.

Online Presents
The Top 10 Online Shopping Sites in Canada

Rank	Retailer
1	Old Navy Canada
2	chapters.indigo.ca
3	Groupon
4	FragranceX
5	Gap Canada
6	Dell Canada
7	Sephora
8	Expedia.ca
9	Banana Republic Canada
10	The Source Canada

Source: Sarah Kelsey, "Online Shopping Canada: Top Ten Sites Canadians Shop At," *The Huffington Post,* September 26, 2012. Retrieved from www.huffingtonpost.ca/2012/09/26/online-shopping-canada-to_n_1916479.html.

Figure 11–6
Why do consumers shop and buy online?

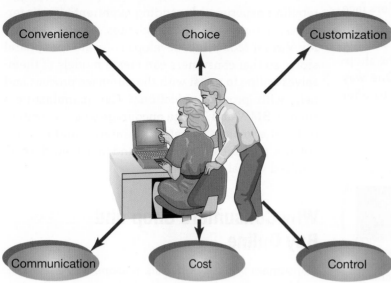

Convenience, choice, communication, customization, cost, and control result in a favourable customer experience.

- **Communication:** Communication can take three forms: marketer-to-consumer e-mail notification, consumer-to-marketer buying and service requests, and consumer-to-consumer chat rooms and instant messaging.[28]

- **Customization:** Internet/web-enabled capabilities make possible a highly interactive and individualized information and exchange environment for shoppers and buyers. Consumers get what they want and feel good about the experience. An example is Dell, which allows consumers to choose the components of their computer rather than purchase a computer off the shelf at a bricks-and-mortar retailer.

- **Cost:** Many popular items bought online can be purchased at the same price or cheaper than in retail stores. Lower prices also result from Internet/web-enabled software that permits *dynamic pricing,* the practice of changing prices for products and services in real time in response to supply and demand conditions.

- **Control:** Online shoppers and buyers are empowered consumers. They readily use Internet/web-enabled technology to seek information, evaluate alternatives, and make purchase decisions on their own time, terms, and conditions.

When and Where Online Consumers Shop and Buy

Shopping and buying also happen at different times in the online marketspace than in the traditional marketplace. Though most online retail sales occur Monday through Friday, the busiest shopping day is Monday. Canadians are the world's heaviest Internet users, spending on average 34 hours online monthly. However, Canadians are not the heaviest online consumers, with one in five stating they have never purchased anything online.[29]

Describing the Online Consumer

Research indicates that more than 80 percent of Canadians over the age of 16 are now connected to the Internet. Ninety-four percent of Canadians say they use the Internet to compare prices, and 60 percent go online to read or write reviews. As a result, consumers are becoming smarter, increasingly informed, and more demanding. This trend will continue as more and more Canadians are now embracing mobile technologies from smartphones to iPads.[30]

Many consumers are spending online time at social media sites such as Facebook and Twitter as well as purchasing products and services on company websites. The following points describe the effects of social media on the online consumer:

- Research suggests that social media recommendations tend to increase the chances of people buying products or services. For instance, a study

Social media can impact consumer purchases.

found that 50 percent of people under 35 followed the recommendations of their social media friends, compared to only 17 percent who bought because of celebrity endorsements.

● Another study reveals that while, on average, 7 percent of visitors to an online store make a purchase, if directed to the retailer via a social media site, the percentage of visitors who will make a purchase goes up to 71 percent. This means that people accessing an online retailer via social media are 10 times more likely to buy something than other users.[31]

● Research has also shown that becoming a follower of a brand on Twitter or a fan on Facebook has a positive impact on the possibility of buying and recommending a product or service.

Recommendations from personal acquaintances or opinions posted by consumers online are the most trusted forms of advertising, according to a Nielsen *Global Online Consumer Survey* of over 25,000 Internet consumers from 50 countries. Ninety percent of consumers surveyed noted that they trust recommendations from people they know, while 70 percent trusted consumer opinions posted online. The influence of word of mouth on consumer purchases is still strong, be it face to face or on social media sites.[32]

What Online Consumers Buy

There is a lot marketers have to learn about online consumer purchase behaviour. Although research has documented the most frequently purchased products and services bought online, marketers also need to know why these items are popular in the digital marketplace.

Retailer Usage of the Mobile Channel

LO 7 Retailers are becoming increasingly aware of the value of smartphone-equipped customers. Like they did with the emergence of the Internet, many retailers initially approached the mobile channel with a bit of trepidation. Today, retailers are looking at mobile as another important customer touch point. Cellphones, smartphones, and other handheld devices are a convenient way for customers to gather more information about a retailer's products or even conduct transactions on a mobile basis. In-store shoppers can research products and prices on their handsets using cameras, barcode scanners, QR codes, and other mobile applications. QR (quick response) codes are two-dimensional images that look like blobs of black on a white background. They are similar to standard barcodes but have much more functionality. QR codes are encoded with information ranging from text to photos to website addresses and are scanned by smartphones. They can be used to send consumers who scan the codes to places online and are very effective marketing tools.[33]

Retailers can provide immediate incentives by knowing the specific in-store location of the shopper via GPS technology. The customer can make the purchase in-store or over a mobile cellphone or smartphone. The key is to provide methods to retain customer interest and loyalty via a consistent shopping and branding experience across channels. Smartphones are being used to engage consumers and help them make better shopping choices.

The following scenarios demonstrate how mobile can be used:[34]

● Riding the chairlift of a major western ski resort, a customer of a ski apparel retailer pulls out a smartphone and clicks on the retailer's specialty application. The mobile software uses GPS technology to determine the skier's location, and the customer sees feedback on this specific mountain's terrain and recommendations on how to approach its trails.

● Walking through the pet food section of a major discount chain, a customer receives a text message with a digital coupon good for 20 percent off Iams dog food. The store has detected the shopper's presence in the pet food aisle, and knows that this particular shopper generally purchases the competitor's product, Purina. For the retailer's suppliers, this provides a chance to encourage a brand switch. For the retailer, it enhances loyalty from a customer who has opted in to participate in the mobile program.

Smartphones are being integrated into the shopping experience.

- Two teenage girls rifle through the racks of tops in a major department store chain's juniors section. Stopping on one she likes, one girl takes out her phone and scans a QR code on the shelf next to the shirt. On the screen of her phone, she sees product reviews from other shoppers, and also gets a special offer on a pair of shoes to complete the outfit.

- As he jockeys to make his flight at Toronto's Pearson Airport, a Montreal-bound traveller realizes he's forgotten to pack his laptop's power cord. He turns to his cellphone and brings up Best Buy's wireless website. He orders a replacement cord, finds the store location closest to his hotel, and picks it up on his way to check in.

The above are examples of just a handful of customer interactions taking place today in the mobile commerce (*m-commerce*) channel. In each instance, a retailer uses mobile as a way to enhance customer engagement and loyalty. And it is the pervasiveness of cellphones, smartphones, and other mobile devices that is leading a growing number of retailers to explore what additional opportunities await in the mobile space.

> *Sephora, the beauty products retailer, uses mobile strategy.*

Here's an example of how Sephora, the beauty products retailer, uses mobile strategy. It created a specific mobile website with thousands of product reviews intended to help shoppers evaluate and compare items on their smartphones when they are in the stores. All the shopper has to do to retrieve the reviews is type in the SKU number or the name of the product in their smartphone.

The increasing number of shoppers arriving at stores with smartphones can also pose a threat for retailers. The threat comes from in-store shoppers using their phones to check prices at other retailers. Retailers that ignore the growing number of mobile Internet users will see their customers defect to competitors. A retailer's best defence for maintaining customer loyalty is to develop a mobile website, with information on the site that differentiates itself from competitors. This can take the form of such intangibles as product reviews, warranty information, customer service, product knowledge, and return policy.

Retailers should take note that their websites might have to be adapted for smartphones. Regular websites are not configured for mobile, which may lead to frustration as a shopper, for example, tries to read words that are too tiny to read on a phone. By providing mobile access to their extensive online product information, retailers can help customers feel more comfortable about making a purchase at that store as opposed to fleeing to another store solely for the low price.[35]

Wholesaling

LO 8 Many retailers rely on intermediaries to provide them with selection and availability of the products sold in their retail operations. Many other businesses also use intermediaries to provide them with selection and availability plus value-added services for products that they need to operate their businesses. Those intermediaries are commonly called wholesalers and agents (described briefly in Chapter 10), according to the functions that they fulfill in the distribution process. In addition, there are manufacturers' sales offices operated by the original manufacturers of the products. All of these wholesaling

Truck jobbers are small wholesalers that have a small warehouse from which they stock their trucks for distribution to retailers.

intermediaries play an important role in the retailing process and in helping other businesses get the products they need.

Merchant Wholesalers

Merchant wholesalers are independently owned firms that take title to—that is, they buy—the merchandise they handle. They go by various names, described in detail below. About 83 percent of the firms engaged in wholesaling activities are merchant wholesalers.

Merchant wholesalers are classified as either full-service or limited-service wholesalers, depending on the number of functions performed. Two major types of full-service wholesalers exist. General merchandise (or full-line) wholesalers carry a broad assortment of merchandise and perform all channel functions. This type of wholesaler is most prevalent in the hardware, drug, and clothing industries. However, these wholesalers do not maintain much depth of assortment within specific product lines. Specialty merchandise (or limited-line) wholesalers offer a relatively narrow range of products but have an extensive assortment within the product lines carried. They perform all channel functions and are found in the health foods, automotive parts, and seafood industries.

Four major types of limited-service wholesalers exist. Rack jobbers furnish the racks or shelves that display merchandise in retail stores and perform all channel functions. They sell on consignment to retailers, which means they retain the title to the products

displayed and bill retailers only for the merchandise sold. Familiar products such as hosiery, toys, housewares, and health and beauty aids are sold by rack jobbers. Cash and carry wholesalers take title to merchandise but sell only to buyers who call on them, pay cash for merchandise, and furnish their own transportation for merchandise. They carry a limited product assortment and do not make deliveries, extend credit, or supply market information. This wholesaler commonly deals in electric supplies, office supplies, hardware products, and groceries. Drop shippers, or desk jobbers, are wholesalers that own the merchandise they sell but do not physically handle, stock, or deliver it. They simply solicit orders from retailers and other wholesalers and have the merchandise shipped directly from a producer to a buyer. Drop shippers are used for bulky products such as coal, lumber, and chemicals, which are sold in large quantities. Truck jobbers are small wholesalers that have a small warehouse from which they stock their trucks for distribution to retailers. They usually handle limited assortments of fast-moving or perishable items that are sold for cash directly from trucks in their original packages. Truck jobbers handle products such as bakery items, dairy products, and meat.

Agents and Brokers

Unlike merchant wholesalers, agents and brokers do not take title to merchandise and typically provide fewer channel functions. They make their profit from

manufacturers' agents
Work for several producers and carry non-competitive, complementary merchandise in an exclusive territory

selling agents
Represent a single producer and are responsible for the entire marketing function of that producer

brokers
Independent firms or individuals whose main function is to bring buyers and sellers together to make sales

commissions or fees paid for their services, whereas merchant wholesalers make their profit from the sale of the merchandise they have bought and resold.

Manufacturers' agents and selling agents are the two major types of agents used by producers. **Manufacturers' agents**, or manufacturers' representatives, work for several producers and carry non-competitive, complementary merchandise in an exclusive territory. Manufacturers' agents act as a producer's sales arm in a territory and are principally responsible for the transactional channel functions, primarily selling. They are used extensively in the automotive supply, footwear, and fabricated steel industries. By comparison, **selling agents** represent a single producer and are responsible for the entire marketing function of that producer. They design promotional plans, set prices, determine distribution policies, and make recommendations on product strategy. Selling agents are used by small producers in the textile, apparel, food, and home furnishing industries.

Brokers are independent firms or individuals whose main function is to bring buyers and sellers together to make sales. Brokers, unlike agents, usually have no continuous relationship with the buyer or seller but negotiate a contract between two parties and then move on to another task. Brokers are used extensively in the real estate industry.

A unique broker that acts in many ways like a manufacturer's agent is a food broker, representing buyers and sellers in the grocery industry. Food brokers differ from conventional brokers because they act on behalf of producers on a permanent basis and receive a commission for their services. For example,

food giant Nabisco uses food brokers to sell its candies, margarine, and Planters peanuts, but it sells its line of cookies and crackers directly to retail stores.

Manufacturer's Branches and Offices

Unlike merchant wholesalers, agents, and brokers, manufacturer's branches and sales offices are wholly owned extensions of the producer that perform wholesaling activities. Producers assume wholesaling functions when there are no intermediaries to perform these activities, customers are few in number and geographically concentrated, orders are large or require significant attention, or they want to control the distribution of their products. A *manufacturer's branch office* carries a producer's inventory and performs the functions of a full-service wholesaler. A *manufacturer's sales office* does not carry inventory, typically performs only a sales function, and serves as an alternative to agents and brokers.

ask yourself

1. Describe how smartphones are being used by retailers to engage consumers and help them make better shopping choices.

2. What is the difference between merchant wholesalers and agents?

adAlyze

Summary...just the facts

LO 1 ● Retailing provides customer value in the form of various utilities: time, place, form, information, and possession.

● Economically, retailing is important in terms of the people employed and money exchanged in retail sales.

LO 2 ● Retailing outlets can be classified by forms of ownership, such as independent retailer, corporate chain, and contractual system.

LO 3 ● The first task in developing a retail strategy is to define the target market and positioning of the retail store.

LO 4 ● The retailing mix consists of goods and services, retail pricing, physical location, and communications.

● In retailing, the product P (of the 4 Ps of the marketing mix) includes level of service, merchandise mix, and store atmosphere.

● Stores vary in the level of service they provide. Three levels are self-service, limited service, or full service.

● Retail outlets vary in terms of the breadth and depth of their merchandise lines. Breadth refers to the number of different items carried, and depth refers to the assortment of each item offered.

● In retail pricing, retailers must decide on the markup. Off-price retailers offer brand-name merchandise at lower than regular prices.

● Retail store location is an important retail mix decision. The common alternatives are the central business district, regional shopping centre, community shopping centre, or strip location. A variation of the strip location is the power centre, which is a strip location with multiple national anchor stores.

LO 5 ● Non-store retailing includes automatic vending, television home shopping, online retailing, and direct marketing (direct mail and catalogue retailing, telemarketing, and direct selling).

LO 6 ● Online retailing allows consumers to search for, evaluate, and purchase products and services online. The increasing sales and number of people purchasing online suggest that the profile of the online consumer is becoming more and more like the profile of the consumer of the traditional marketplace.

● Consumers refer to six reasons they shop and buy online: convenience, choice, communication, customization, cost, and control.

LO 7 ● Retailers are becoming increasingly aware of the value of smartphone-equipped customers:
  - Retailers are looking at mobile as another important customer touch point.
  - Cellphones, smartphones, and other handheld devices are a convenient way for customers to gather more information about a retailer's products or even conduct transactions on a mobile basis.
  - Many retailers depend on the numerous types of intermediaries that engage in wholesaling activities.

LO 8 ● The main difference between the various types of wholesalers lies in whether they take title to the items they sell.

Key Terms and Concepts...a refresher

breadth of product line
brokers
central business district
community shopping centre
depth of product line
form of ownership
intertype competition
level of service

manufacturers' agents
merchandise mix
merchant wholesalers
multichannel retailers
off-price retailing
power centre
regional shopping centres

retailing
retailing mix
scrambled merchandising
selling agents
shrinkage
strip location
telemarketing

Hands-on...*apply your knowledge*

Online Retailing Assignment TELUS has a number of strategies to distribute its products. Online retailing is a key component to the TELUS strategy. It is able to do so because of its size and resources. Interview an independent retailer in your local community to determine the benefits and challenges of providing an online retailing offering to the organization's clientele.

Chapter Vignette...*reminder*

In the opening vignette of this chapter, TELUS's manager of in-store communications discusses how simplicity is the key to sending a consistent message through 3,000 distribution outlets. Review the Marketing NewsFlash, "Turning Loonies into Billions," to help answer the Reality Check questions at the end of the vignette.

Video Clip...*questions*

While watching the CONNECT video about Roots, pay particular attention to the store location and layout and answer the following questions:

▶ Video Roots

- How would you describe the store's merchandise mix?
- What is the store atmosphere?
- Why do you believe Roots chose that location?
- What retail positioning strategy has Roots taken?
- How does an online retailing strategy complement this store?

Infographic...*data analysis*

"Share of wallet" refers to the percentage of a customer's purchases that a company has in a specific product category. The irony of the term is that as technology evolves, more Canadians are discarding their wallets for more mobile alternatives. The Infographic shows that more than half of Canadians would be comfortable never having to use cash again. Furthermore, the dollar value of global payments using mobile devices could almost triple from its 2011 numbers. Review the different alternatives to cash, including Visa, MasterCard, PayPal, and Interac, and try to determine the "share of wallet" these different services have on the mobile banking dollars of Canadians. Use this information to create your own infographic.

connect | **SMARTBOOK** | **LEARNSMART**

For more information on the resources available from McGraw-Hill Ryerson, go to **www.mheducation.ca/he/solutions**.

marketing communications

The digital world brings a wealth of new tools and opportunities to marketing communications. This chapter looks at these digital approaches as well as traditional offline marketing communications tools that are used to communicate with target audiences.

We begin by speaking with Rosanne Caron, president of the Out-of-Home Marketing Association of Canada (OMAC), who tells us that while consumers increasingly tune out media messages, attention to out-of-home advertising is high, making it an effective tool for integrated campaigns and stand-alone platforms. Out-of-home advertising refers to billboards, transit shelters, posters, washroom ads, floor decals, installations, wall murals, and ads that appear in subway stations and on or in buses and subways, just to name a few. Many of these forms of advertising now take advantage of digital technology to interact with consumers in new and creative ways. We see digital transit shelters turned into interactive games, billboards that invite consumers to text to receive offers, QR codes that can be scanned for further information, or near field communication (NFC) tags (NFC uses high-frequency wireless technology) that can be tapped by a smartphone for more details—creativity and relevancy that can get results.

"Out-of-home advertising cannot be turned off, and marketers use it to raise awareness with creative approaches that get results," states Caron, who explains that often out-of-home components are built into integrated campaigns that also use other forms of media such as print, broadcast media, and online platforms. There are numerous award-winning campaigns that stand out due to their creativity and ability to increase campaign awareness: the non-profit Raising the Roof organization built a cardboard house and placed it in an alleyway to draw attention to the homeless; a three-dimensional poster by Allegra allergy medication portrayed a man blowing his nose on the poster paper; and a McDonald's coffee promotion filled bus shelter ads with coffee beans and added small holes to the ad casing so that people could smell the coffee.

"Creativity that yields results is the intention," explains Caron. She points to a creative seasonal gift campaign, "Spread the Cheer," that had exceptional results for money transfer company Western Union. The holiday season is the busiest and most competitive time of year for money transfer companies, and Western Union, with service to over 200 countries, is the dominant player in Canada, but not the cheapest. Western Union's objective was to boost business by rising above the advertising clutter of the holiday season. It wanted to give globally connected Canadians a memorable reason to send money-gifts to loved ones overseas with Western Union, rather than with other less expensive options.

LONG
GIFT LIST

SEND $50
FOR $5
TRANSFER FEE*
ACROSS CANADA.
WORLDWIDE.
Valid December 1-31, 2011

MORE TIME
TO BE MERRY

SPREAD THE CHEER... SCAN HERE

Chapter Outline:

Spread the Cheer campaign → Recent developments in marketing communications → Online and offline approaches → Advertising → Public relations → Sales promotion

Event marketing and sponsorship → Personal selling → Alternative approaches → Unique online tools → Planning and evaluation

spreadthecheer.ca

WESTERN UNION
moving money for better

The "Spread the Cheer" campaign focused on multicultural communities in Vancouver, Saskatoon, Halifax, Toronto, and Montreal, and consisted of local mall posters, event marketing, ethnic print ads, transit ads, social media ads, and in-store signage that used QR codes to drive people to a microsite. Local TV and radio ads also built on this familiar gift-giving approach and sent people to the same site to send e-cards and, for a $5 fee, send $50 to loved ones (total price, $55). Let's look at this integrated campaign in more detail:

Shopping Centre Elements   Western Union worked with its advertising agency AV Communications to create virtual holiday-card stores that appeared as oversized posters in shopping centres. There, these eye-catching posters could not be missed due to their location as well as their colourful selection of carefully designed holiday e-cards, created with multicultural preferences in mind.

QR codes were placed beneath each e-card to allow for easy scanning. The QR codes took users to a microsite, www.spreadthecheer.ca, to personalize and send free e-cards. Once an e-card was sent, users were asked if they wanted to send a gift of $50 for a $5 fee (total cost, $55), a $3 discount off Western Union's regular rates. The money-gift could be purchased immediately online using Visa or MasterCard, or through mobile wallet applications such as Zoompass for an additional fee.

If you happened to be in a shopping centre and missed the holiday-card posters, Western Union used event marketing and organized groups of carolers, complete with "Spread the Cheer" buttons and song books, to periodically sing holiday songs in close proximity to the promotional posters, thus adding to the cheerful ambience and drawing attention to the promotion.

Transit Components   In addition to the mall posters and events, interior transit ads were placed inside buses and streetcars where a smaller selection of e-cards, again complete with QR codes, drew attention to the promotion and invited people to send free e-cards. Similar ads also appeared as posters in transit stations in highly trafficked areas. Specific stations and transit routes were selected to reach multicultural target groups.

Online Features   Online elements included the microsite at www.spreadthecheer.ca as well as online ads that appeared in online ethnic community newspapers such as *Diaryo Filipino*, where Western Union ads, translated into Tagalog, targeted people from the Philippines.

Understanding the popularity of social media with this target group, ads were also placed on Facebook to appear around local multicultural pages.

Multicultural Community Outreach   An outreach to multicultural community centres was layered over the advertising elements. Seasonal community events, complete with Western Union signage, were sponsored and spread the message through prizes and giveaways at local festivities.

Independent food stores in multicultural communities were also involved in the promotion and given window signs, posters, and shelf danglers to further raise campaign awareness. Local ethnic community newspapers also featured Western Union "Spread the Cheer" ads, while TV and radio ads were broadcast on local ethnic stations to send listeners and viewers to the campaign's microsite.

"This program was a resounding success for Western Union," states Caron, "It creatively used out-of-home media with other marketing communications tools to get results. It turned a price discount into a memorable campaign that overshot its business goals." Caron explains that the "Spread the Cheer" campaign resulted in over 130,000 page visits to its microsite (versus a 50,000 objective), a sales increase of 30 percent (versus an expected 10 percent), and QR code interactions of over 4,400 scans. "This is creativity that works," emphasizes Caron, who advises students to take note of changing mobile technologies that, coupled with other marketing communication tools, get excellent results. Western Union's "Spread the Cheer" campaign won a 2013 Cassie Award for campaigns that build seasonal business.

For further information on the Out-of-Home Marketing Association of Canada and to read about the latest data, campaigns, cases, and webinars, visit **www.omaccanada.ca**. There you will find detailed information on the out-of-home industry, research updates, cases, and a gallery of recent campaigns.[1]

reality CHECK ✓

As you read Chapter 12, refer back to this Western Union vignette to answer the following questions:

- Why was out-of-home media a good choice for this campaign?
- What forms of media were not used by Western Union in this campaign? Suggest the reasons why they were not considered appropriate.

Developments in Marketing Communications

LO 1 This chapter provides readers with a realistic view of marketing communications, bringing to the forefront the online and offline approaches that are used by marketers to reach consumers. We examine how the online digital world continues to change and explain how traditional offline approaches are used to reach ever-elusive consumers. Frequently, online and offline marketing communications work together, hand-in-hand, to reach consumers in their worlds, relying on metrics and analytics to measure and evaluate success and to make improvements.

Self-expression has become the new form of entertainment.

Today, marketing communications is in an *age of selective reception*, where social media keeps marketers and advertisers honest in 140-character bursts and where marketers increasingly interact in two-way conversations with consumers through digital formats such as social networks, mobile messaging, and blogs, just to mention a few. Whereas once marketers wholly controlled the messaging, today consumers are largely in control of whether they receive marketing communication messages, and if so, when, where, and on what device.

In this age of selective reception, consumers choose how, if, and when to listen to advertising messages and whether they want to engage in the conversations. Arianna Huffington, co-founder of the *Huffington Post*, succinctly summarizes that self-expression has become the new form of entertainment, with people posting comments, writing blogs, and creating videos as forms of self-expression.[2] Initial concerns around baby boomers zapping TV ads and generation Xers changing channels during commercial breaks pale in comparison to the new reality: where young adults often catch the news online rather than in newspapers; where TV programs can be watched on laptops, tablets, and smartphones rather than on TVs; where music is streamed from apps or downloaded rather than listened to on the radio; where magazines can be read on laptops or accessed through apps on mobile devices; and where smartphones interact with marketing messages through text messages, barcodes, and apps.

We start by looking at facts about how consumers, marketers, and the media are adapting to the digital world, and then review some of the new and evolving marketing communications approaches that are being used.

A Changing Landscape

Let's look at the facts in terms of the media and consumers in Canada.

Connected Consumers Affordable Internet technology provides consumers in Canada with easy-to-use services and devices that facilitate marketing communications. Free online services such as e-mail, search engines, and social media have democratized the media so that two-way communication now exists between marketers and consumers, and between consumers and their friends. Many individuals multitask with the media, spending time on the Internet while watching TV, and using tablets and smartphones interchangeably, depending on the circumstance.[3] Consumers in Canada are connected throughout the day on mobile devices.

The use of mobile devices in Canada (cellphones, tablets, e-readers, handheld gaming devices, and portable MP3 players) continues to grow. In 2013, there were over 28 million mobile subscribers in Canada,[4] with usage expected to climb over the next few years. Data plans are used by over 47 percent of subscribers, and tablets are owned by 20 percent of cellphone users.[5] Smartphone penetration in Canada has reached 62 percent and continues to increase.[6] Chapter 13 reviews mobile marketing in detail.

Research studies tell us that consumers in Canada are among the most connected in the world. Data from comScore highlights that, on average, individuals in Canada spend over 34 hours per month online. Online video viewing is particularly high, with 74 percent watching video on the Internet. Social networking is a popular online activity, with people in Canada increasingly accessing social networks on their mobile devices.[7] **Social networks** are online websites that allow members to create a network of friends and contacts to share messages, comments, videos, and images as a form of self-expression.

The most popular social networking sites in Canada are Facebook, YouTube, Google+, Twitter, LinkedIn, Instagram, Tumblr, and Pinterest.[8] Chapter 13 provides an in-depth look at social media in Canada.

Media Usage

The amount of time consumers spend with the media has changed significantly over the last few years, prompting marketers to take note and adapt marketing communications approaches. Younger consumers spend more time on the Internet than with other forms of media, while older consumers gravitate toward TV viewing. Specifically, 18- to 34-year-olds clock an average of 30 hours per week on the Internet and 16.6 hours on TV, while Internet time

Time Spent with Canadian Media Varies by Age				
Average Weekly Hours per Capita				
Age	**Adults 18+**	**18–34**	**35–49**	**50+**
Internet	19.7	30.0	20.1	12.7
TV	24.2	16.6	21.4	31.0
Radio	17.5	13.5	17.5	20.0
Daily newspaper	1.9	0.6	0.9	3.3
Magazine	0.6	0.2	0.4	0.9

Source: "Cross-Media Reach and Time Spent 2013," RTS data. TVB Canada, November 2013, accessed at www.tvb.ca/pages/RTS.

for 35- to 49-year-olds drops to 20.1 hours per week, with TV coming in first at 21.4 hours per week.[9]

Marketers tailor messages accordingly and are shifting advertising dollars online to respond to changing media habits. The Internet is now the largest recipient of advertising dollars in Canada, ahead of TV and newspaper (see Figures 12–1 and 12–2).

Evolving Media

The digital reality that sees consumers aggregate online is impacting the revenues of media companies that see advertising budgets move to online destinations, and consumers gravitate to digital online services such as Netflix to consume content. This is encouraging magazines, newspapers, radio, and TV stations to create their own online assets to remain competitive and relevant. Major news organizations, such as the CBC, for example, use YouTube

> *The most popular social networking sites in Canada are Facebook, YouTube, Google+, Twitter, LinkedIn, Instagram, Tumblr, and Pinterest.*

Popular social networking sites in Canada.

social networks
Online websites that allow members to create a network of friends and contacts to share messages, comments, videos, and images as a form of self-expression

Figure 12–1
Advertising expenditures in Canada, 2015 forecasts ($ millions)

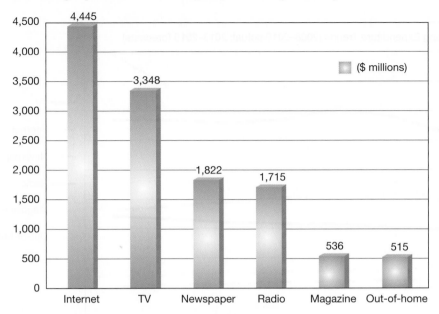

Internet reaches top spot in advertising expenditures.

Source: Anne Austin, Jonathan Barnard, and Nicola Hutcheon, "Advertising Expenditure Forecasts—September 2013," ZenithOptimedia.

channels and apps to deliver content, despite having websites and TV channels of their own. Radio stations stream content online and write articles for their websites. Magazines create content specifically for online reading, and in this new media universe, we see newspapers such as the *Globe and Mail* undergo redesigns to compete with online news and the 24/7 news cycle. News blogs such as the *Huffington Post* (launched as recently as 2005) became so reputable that six years

Online and offline approaches are used by the *Globe and Mail*.

after launch it was purchased by AOL for $315 million.[10] The media most severely impacted by this digital disruption is the newspaper industry. In 2008, annual newspaper advertising revenues in Canada stood at $2,489 million but 2015 forecasts stand at only $1,882 million.

We look to the *Globe and Mail* for a more detailed view of how the newspaper industry is adjusting to the new media reality. Online tools are constantly tweaked at the *Globe and Mail* so that content is accessible on computers, e-readers, mobile devices, and hard copy. Readers can receive e-newsletters and e-mail alerts, and follow the *Globe and Mail* on Facebook and Twitter. In 2010, the *Globe and Mail* resized its hard-copy format to be slightly smaller and to include sections with glossy, colourful, smudge-proof pages. The front page was totally overhauled and reformatted as a type of "home page" that pointed to interesting content within the publication. In October 2012, the *Globe and Mail* addressed its decline in advertising revenues by introducing a metered paywall for digital access. Plans started at 10 free digital articles per month and reached as high as $19.99 for an unlimited monthly subscription. This resulted in the *Globe and Mail* increasing its digital subscribers and shifting its focus to profitable loyal readers.[11]

In 2013, the *Globe and Mail* continued its focus on profitability and stopped physical distribution to Newfoundland and Labrador, as well as to remote areas of British Columbia, which saved the newspaper over $1 million per year. The newspaper also improved its use of analytics to determine what content drives subscriptions and tasked a core team to create content to improve results.[12]

Advertising Expenditures
Marketers are adjusting marketing communications approaches to increasingly communicate with consumers online by shifting advertising expenditures to the Internet. The latest data on advertising expenditures shows that the Internet is the largest form of media in Canada, with 2015 forecasts coming in at $4,445 million in annual expenditures,

real-time marketing
A planned tactical approach where brands make themselves relevant online during events or newsworthy occurrences by diving into conversations as they occur with aligned short-term messaging that takes advantage of the current buzz

content marketing
Creating and sharing information and expertise that is designed to inform and engage with tools such as research papers, e-books, infographics, how-to videos, blogs, webinars, e-newsletters, case studies, and events that can readily be found by search engines

Figure 12–2

Trends—advertising expenditures ($ millions)

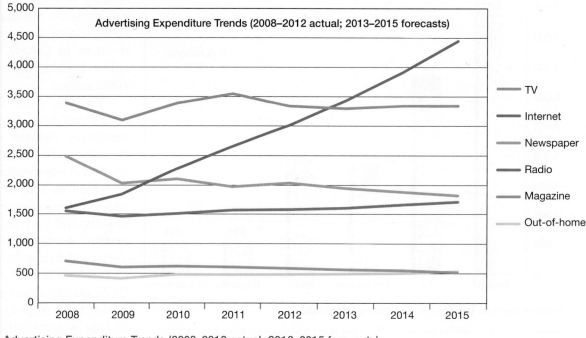

Advertising Expenditure Trends (2008–2012 actual; 2013–2015 forecasts)

Source: Anne Austin, Jonathan Barnard, and Nicola Hutcheon, "Advertising Expenditure Forecasts - September 2013," ZenithOptimedia.

followed by TV at $3,348 million. Looking at other forms of media, newspaper and magazine advertising revenues continue a slow decline, while radio and out-of-home show slight increases.[13]

New and Evolving Marketing Communications Approaches

Marketing communications approaches are constantly evolving to meet changing media habits and to take advantage of new technologies. Four new marketing communication approaches are evolving: (1) real-time marketing, (2) content marketing, (3) social media marketing, and (4) mobile marketing. We examine these approaches in more detail here.

Real-time marketing is a planned tactical approach where brands make themselves relevant online during events or newsworthy occurrences by diving into conversations as they occur with aligned short-term messaging that takes advantage of the current buzz. Simple approaches empower front-line social media managers on a continuous basis to monitor social media conversations and to respond to issues, questions, and conversations as they occur.[14] Sophisticated approaches use large-scale media events such as the Super Bowl, the Olympic Games, or the Academy

Awards as pivotal points, and organize a team of real-time marketing experts to creatively engage in online conversations. The intent is to take advantage of the buzz and reach a wide audience. Teams of real-time marketing experts may include marketers, ad agency writers and art directors, and the company's legal marketing experts so that messaging can be immediately approved and deployed in real time.

A well-known example of real-time marketing surfaced during the 2013 Super Bowl, when, during a lengthy power outage, Oreo cookies posted a tweet, "Power out? No problem," with a link to a visual showing an Oreo cookie with the caption, "You can still dunk in the dark." This real-time marketing tweet was retweeted almost 15,000 times, increased Oreo's Twitter followers by 8,000, received 20,000 likes on Facebook, and increased its Instagram following by 34,000. It is important to note that this real-time marketing effort was no fluke. Oreo had identified the Super Bowl as a focus for its real-time marketing efforts and had a real-time marketing command centre set up, complete with marketers and advertising experts—with senior managers on call for approvals. In this manner, Oreo was ready and poised to respond to whatever situation presented itself at the game.[15]

Content marketing is when brands or companies reach out by creating and sharing expertise and brand

310 | **PART 3** DESIGNING MARKETING STRATEGIES AND MARKETING MIX ELEMENTS

social media marketing
Reaching out to consumers online through social networks where people connect with friends and contacts to share comments, articles, opinions, videos, and images as a form of self-expression

Oreo cookies' real-time marketing efforts used Twitter during the 2013 Super Bowl to get results.

information that is designed to inform and engage with tools such as research papers, e-books, infographics, how-to videos, blogs, webinars, e-newsletters, case studies, and events. This information can be readily found by search engines.[16] In the business-to-business market, the e-mail service provider Constant Contact uses this approach with how-to videos and in-person seminars to help businesses use its services. In the consumer market, the children's toy company

LEGO uses content marketing to spark the imagination of children who play with LEGO. It has microsites that narrate stories containing LEGO characters, online LEGO cartoons that help children imagine the world of their creations, videos that contain LEGO characters, LEGO wallpapers for downloading, and *LEGO Club* magazines for reading. In February 2014, Warner Brothers released *The LEGO Movie*, which continues LEGO's efforts to reach out to children with content that makes playing with LEGO richer and more enjoyable.[17]

Social media marketing is when brands reach out to consumers online through social networks where people connect with friends and contacts to share comments, articles, opinions, videos, and images as a form of self-expression. Brands engage on these platforms by creating their own social media accounts to join in conversations and to send out offers or updates. Brands may also place ads on social networks that accept advertising to increase awareness. The most popular social networks in Canada are Facebook, YouTube, Twitter, Google+, LinkedIn, Instagram, Tumblr, and Pinterest, although numerous other niche social networks exist around particular topics of interest. Social media marketing is discussed in detail in Chapter 13.[18] When Oreo uses Twitter to engage with its followers in real time, it is also using social media marketing approaches.

Content marketing approaches by LEGO provide imaginative ideas on playing with LEGO.

Mobile marketing includes a set of practices that enables organizations to communicate and engage with target audiences in an interactive and relevant manner through any mobile device or network. It typically uses cellphones, tablets, e-readers, handheld gaming devices, or portable MP3 players to communicate with consumers. It mainly refers to the use of cellphones and tablets. Elements in the mobile marketer's toolkit range from the mobile web, mobile apps, and mobile advertising, and include various mobile sales promotional and proximity marketing tools that are discussed in Chapter 13.[19] Simple examples include using text messaging to vote for winners of TV reality shows, creating mobile apps to facilitate interactions, or using mobile games to encourage brand loyalty. In 2013, Murphy's Irish Stout created an app, When It Rains It Pours, to reward its loyal consumers in Cork, Ireland, with free beer during the wettest summer in 50 years. The brand created an app for the months of August and September, and whenever it rained more than two millimetres in Cork, the people in Cork could claim one of 1,000 free pints of Murphy's brew at their local pub by using the app. Almost 30,000 free pints were claimed during the two months, and the app won a Gold Cannes Lion award for mobile marketing at the Cannes International Festival of Creativity.[20]

Numerous examples of mobile marketing exist in Canada, with the Hospital for Sick Children's Pain Squad app worth noting. The hospital designed this app specifically for its young patients to help doctors monitor and research their pain and to then tweak treatments. Realizing it was difficult for children to keep pain journals, advertising agency Cundari created the Pain Squad app so that children could more easily record their pain levels. The app was created in the form of a police game where patients were recruited to the Pain Squad Special Police Unit and given an iPhone with the app. Twice a day, push notifications reminded patients to update their information by tapping on the app. The app contained specially designed video clips where actors from well-known police shows such as *Flashpoint* and *Rookie Blue* spoke directly to patients, inspiring them to continue the mission. By updating information, recruits could earn badges and be promoted through the ranks from rookies to junior detectives, detectives, sergeants, lieutenants, and chiefs. The results were very positive with patient compliance rates averaging 90 percent (much higher than the typical 80 percent for paper-based approaches). The app is now available for other children's hospitals in Canada.[21]

The Marketing Communications Industry

LO² The marketing communications industry consists of five main areas that work together to form an industry that is ethical, trustworthy, cohesive, and measurable. These areas include the following: (1) the media, (2) marketing communication agencies, (3) research companies, (4) associations, and (5) regulatory bodies. Let's look at these areas in more detail.

The Media

The main forms of media are Internet, TV, newspaper, magazine, radio, out-of-home, and mobile. **Out-of-home advertising**, casually referred to as *outdoor*, reaches consumers outside the home in outdoor locations, in transit, or in commercial or business locations. It can take many forms such as billboards, posters, transit, electronic signage, closed-circuit TV, or street furniture.

New media terms have surfaced in the Internet era: *paid media, owned media*, and *earned media*. **Paid media** is the media time that is purchased so that messages can be disseminated through channels that are controlled by others—TV advertising is an example. **Owned media** refers to the media channels that a company controls, either fully or partially, such as a website, microsite, or social media page that is used to directly communicate with consumers. **Earned media**, a term with origins in the public relations industry, refers to the free publicity secured through unpaid media mentions and consumers who spread the word through word of mouth or the Internet.

Successful campaigns use integrated approaches that creatively use paid media and owned media as springboards to secure earned media. The 2013 Campaign for Real Beauty from Dove is a notable

---

mobile marketing
A set of practices that enables organizations to communicate and engage with their audiences in an interactive and relevant manner through any mobile device or network

out-of-home advertising
Casually referred to as *outdoor;* reaches consumers outside the home in outdoor locations, in transit, or in commercial or business locations

paid media
The media time purchased so that messages can be disseminated through channels that are controlled by others

owned media
The media channels that a company controls, either fully or partially, such as a website, microsite, or social media page that is used to directly communicate with consumers

earned media
The free publicity secured through unpaid media mentions and consumers who spread the word through word of mouth or the Internet

example that drew attention to women's negative perceptions of their own beauty and to the struggle that young girls have with body image. Globally, the 2013 campaign's focal point was owned media with six short films, *Dove Real Beauty Sketches,* that showed how adult women negatively view their appearance. These videos were shared by Dove on the campaign's branded website, as well as its YouTube channels, Google+ accounts, and Facebook pages, and they were sent out through Twitter. Paid media was used to boost campaign awareness by pointing viewers to the short films through ads placed online on sites such as YouTube, using pre-roll video ads, home-page masthead banner ads, and pay-per-click search ads to draw attention to the short films. These paid- and owned-media elements worked together with public relations overlays that used press releases and a media, blogger, and social media outreach to help spread the word through earned media. Campaign results were exceptionally strong, with YouTube views of the six short films reaching over 66 million views in nine months. Total video views from its combined channels, including its branded website, reached over 163 million views, with public relations activities securing 4.6 billion media impressions. The *Dove Real Beauty Sketches* campaign won the 2013 Titanium Grand Prix at the Cannes Lions International Festival of Creativity.

In addition to the *Dove Real Beauty Sketches* short films, in 2013, the Campaign for Real Beauty had a secondary focus: to draw attention to young girls' negative body image. Two short films with the theme "Girls Unstoppable" were uploaded to YouTube, and in Canada, two billboards on the same topic drew attention to why young girls stop playing soccer and quit swimming activities. These billboards were covered with actual bathing suits and soccer shoes (not photos) to emphasize the magnitude of the issue, and included the alarming statistics that 50,405 Canadian girls quit swimming and 112,670 girls stop playing soccer because they are unhappy with their bodies. A Mother's Day short film was also created for the Canadian market to demonstrate the inner beauty of mothers and their daughters.[22]

Dove Canada uses paid and owned media to secure earned media.

Dove Real Beauty Sketches Ignites Debate

The skincare brand Dove uses its Campaign for Real Beauty to prompt public debate about the media's portrayal of women's beauty and to nurture an emotional bond with women who relate to its cause. After 10 years in the spotlight, the campaign is still going strong with periodic peaks from new campaigns that reignite the debate. The campaign uses actual women (not models) to show that real beauty does not come in the form of skinny, tall supermodels and celebrities. It uses thought-provoking online short films, TV spots, and billboards, as well as websites and workshops, to show that inner and outer beauty come in all forms, colours, shapes, and sizes. Communication elements are designed to improve women's self-esteem and to create a lasting emotional bond between Dove and the women who relate to its message.

In 2013, Dove used short films and billboards to draw attention to the issue. The short films, *Dove Real Beauty Sketches*, were the focal point and

prompted considerable media attention and discussion by individuals, the press, women's advocates, and media critics. These powerful clips focused on the tagline "You Are More Beautiful Than You Think," and portrayed a forensic composite artist sketching women based on how they describe themselves and then based on a stranger's description. The final portraits highlighted that the women were overly critical of their appearance and missed how their inner beauty and personalities were also etched in their features.

The campaign was designed to go viral on the Internet with online ads and public relations activities directing people to watch the short films on the brand's website or on its social media assets. In a few short weeks, the films had secured 163 million views and 4.6 billion media impressions.

The campaign, however, was not without controversy. Its detractors vocally criticized Dove and its parent company Unilever for hypocrisy, given that Axe deodorant, marketed with sexy young girls, is also a Unilever brand. The campaign was also negatively viewed by people who saw it as patronizing, perpetuating beauty as an aspirational value for women, and using women's insecurities to sell more beauty products.

Ultimately, on the positive side, the campaign was praised for attempting to boost women's self-confidence and prompting a provocative and open dialogue about society's unrealistic standards of beauty and the resultant self-esteem issues.[23]

Dove Real Beauty Sketches prompted debate.

Questions

1. Navigate to the YouTube channel at **www.youtube.com/user/DoveCanada** to view *Dove Real Beauty Sketches* and point out why you think these short films resonate highly with women.

2. Navigate to the AXE YouTube website at **www.youtube.com/user/AXE** to view its approaches to marketing AXE products and comment on whether you think it is hypocritical for Unilever to be using these two diverse approaches to market its products.

Marketing Communication Agencies

Marketing communication agencies provide marketers with expertise on how best to communicate messages to their audiences. Agencies can be broad-spectrum and offer a variety of services to their clients, or they can be specialty agencies providing expertise in media, creative, public relations, event marketing, product placement and branded integration, direct marketing, or sales promotion. These terms are discussed in more detail later in this chapter.

Research Companies

Metrics are central to the smooth functioning of the marketing communications industry. Data on audience measurement, readership, consumer trends, and the quality of communication messages is needed to provide transparent and reliable information to the media, agencies, and clients. Most major media sectors publish third-party data for the industry, which is used to determine advertising rates and trends. In addition, other research companies, such as Forrester Research, comScore, and the Nielsen Company, provide data to keep the industry apprised on the latest developments.

Associations

The marketing communications industry has a number of active associations that provide research data and host informative events and educational workshops for the industry. Three top events are worth noting: Digital Day, hosted by the Canadian Marketing Association (CMA) and *Marketing* magazine, is an annual event focused on digital innovation; the MIXX Canada Conference Series, put on by the Interactive Advertising Bureau of Canada (IAB), presents full-day conferences on the digital and interactive industry, highlighting what is new and evolving; and FFWD Advertising and Marketing Week, created by the Institute of Communication Agencies (ICA), is a week-long series of presentations and events focused on the latest developments in the industry with a number of well-priced events available for students. Its Next Generation Day is a full-day event designed specifically for students that are interested in advertising—see the Marketing NewsFlash, "Inspiring—Next Generation Day," for more about this event. The Out-of-Home Marketing Association is also worth noting for its informative website and top-quality online webinars.

Regulatory Bodies

Prior to embarking on a marketing communications program, marketers need to be well-versed on the limitations and restrictions placed on them by regulatory bodies. Marketers are well-advised to become familiar with their specific industry associations and to stay up-to-date on marketing regulations, business restrictions, and best practices. Chapter 2 provides details on these regulatory bodies and the regulations that guide marketing communications in Canada. It is advisable

marketing communication agencies
Broad-spectrum integrated agencies or specialist agencies that provide marketers with expertise on how best to communicate messages to their audiences

Looking for Media Data?

Alliance for Audited Media (AAM)	www.auditedmedia.com
Numeris (formerly BBM Canada)	www.numeris.ca
Canadian Out-of-Home Measurement Bureau (COMB)	www.comb.org
comScore	www.comscore.com
Forrester Research	www.forrester.com
Interactive Advertising Bureau of Canada (IAB)	www.iabcanada.com
Media Digest	www.cmdc.ca
Newspaper Audience Databank (NADBank)	www.nadbank.com
Nielsen Company	http://ca.nielsen.com
Print Measurement Bureau (PMB)	www.pmb.ca
Television Bureau of Canada (TVB)	www.tvb.ca

Inspiring—Next Generation Day

The theatre at the Bell Lightbox buzzed with anticipation as 260 college and university students waited for the Institute of Communication Agencies (ICA) to kick off 2014 Next Generation Day, a day-long event that annually inspires and motivates dozens of young people interested in the advertising industry. Students from various programs, such as marketing, advertising, media, and copywriting, spend the morning listening to seasoned experts who share their perceptions of the industry and to fresh-faced professionals who more recently entered the field. The afternoon hosts the anticipated agency-immersion sessions, where 26 advertising agencies welcome the students (now divided into small groups), conduct agency tours, and involve them in brainstorming and strategy sessions on a live project.

"Don't be shy," advises Gillian Graham, president and CEO of the ICA. "This is your opportunity to shine and get involved in an innovative industry that touches and influences popular culture. For some, this event is a game-changer, a catalyst that attracts many of the best and the brightest marketing minds to the industry." The day ends with a casual networking event where students and agency folk mingle to socialize and exchange information.

So how does a student get into the advertising industry? Seasoned experts at Next Generation Day explain that the task is not linear and the answers are many—knock on doors, check online job boards, intern,

Next Generation Day provides a glimpse into the advertising industry.

network, start in a related field. Often, it is being at the right place at the right time, standing out, and proving yourself. The industry looks for smart, inventive, curious, and energetic people who can think on their feet and have a passion for the industry. They need to be genuine, authentic team players, and be able to build lasting relationships. They must also be hard-working, self-motivated, resilient, and adept at selling themselves and their ideas. However, this business is not for everyone. The challenges lie in unpredictable days, long hours, a frenetic pace, and frustration when ideas are rejected. Nevertheless, for those who are resilient, thrive on change, have a passion for the industry, and possess the skills and personality that fit, this business provides an adrenaline rush that works. Next Generation Day gives students a taste of what it is like to work in this business.

Next Generation Day runs during FFWD Marketing and Advertising Week, an annual week-long event hosted by the ICA in Canada. FFWD Marketing and Advertising Week runs during the last week of January to shine a spotlight on the marketing and advertising industry, and celebrates its achievements and creativity through high-profile speaking events, workshops, marketing awards, boot camps, student outreach, and social hubs. You can see more details on its website at **www.advertisingweek.ca** and catch updates on its Twitter and Facebook streams at @adweekcdn and **www.facebook. com/advertisingweekcdn**. FFWD Marketing and Advertising Week is highly recommended for marketing and advertising professionals, and Next Generation Day is tops for students interested in the advertising business.[24]

▶ Video
Next
Generation
Day

Questions

1. What is the purpose of FFWD Advertising and Marketing Week?

2. What are the characteristics of people who flourish in the advertising industry?

ASC helps protect Canadians from false messaging in advertising. Because among all the pretty words and pictures – truth matters.

ASC Advertising Standards Canada
adstandards.ca

This ASC ad encourages honest communications.

at this point for you to re-visit these pages to obtain details. The following is only a brief reminder.

In Canada, there are five main regulatory groups that work toward limiting intentional and unintentional deceptive marketing practices: (1) Advertising Standards Canada (ASC), (2) the Competition Bureau, (3) the Canadian Radio-television and Telecommunications Commission (CRTC), (4) the Canadian Marketing Association (CMA), and (5) the Canadian Wireless Telecommunications Association (CWTA). Specialist areas and industry groups such as the public relations and the mobile marketing

Deceptive price claims are illegal.

industries also have associations that provide codes of ethics and guidelines on best practices to assist members.

1. **Advertising Standards Canada (ASC)** is a self-regulatory, non-government association that sets and regulates advertising standards. It uses a consumer-complaint process to review questionable ads that are withdrawn from the media if they contravene its guidelines and are not fixed. The ASC also provides advice and pre-clearance services for advertisers but has no legal jurisdiction and does not levy fines. Its guidelines discourage advertisers from misleading consumers with messages that are untrue, vague, fraudulent, or against the standards of public decency. Special care is taken to protect impressionable members of society from testimonials, claims, and images that misrepresent products. Detailed guidelines can be found at **www.adstandards.com**.

2. **The Competition Bureau** is an independent law-enforcement agency with jurisdiction in many areas. In the marketing communications area, it looks at fraudulent advertising and misleading representation to sell products, including price and warranty claims. Deceptive price claims and contests that do not publish the required terms and conditions are illegal and heavily scrutinized. Failure to comply with regulations can result in fines and jail time. To see more about the Competition Bureau, visit its website at **http://competitionbureau.gc.ca**.

3. **The Canadian Radio-television and Telecommunications Commission (CRTC)** is another government agency. It regulates the broadcast and telecommunications industry in Canada, including the licensing of stations. It also provides guidelines on Canadian content and sets limitations on the amount of advertising permitted during broadcasts. It oversees the advertising of alcoholic beverages and works with the ASC on advertising to children. It also oversees the CRTC Wireless Code, which sets industry standards related to wireless contracts, cancellation fees, the unlocking of mobile devices, the notification of roaming charges, and ceilings for overages in data plans and roaming fees. Find more about the CRTC at **www.crtc.gc.ca**.

> *Deceptive price claims and contests that do not publish the required terms and conditions are illegal and heavily scrutinized.*

4. **The Canadian Marketing Association (CMA)** uses a *Code of Ethics and Standards of Practice* to guide the marketing industry in Canada on telemarketing, e-mail marketing, mobile marketing, Internet marketing, promotional contests, fundraising, database marketing, and marketing to children and teenagers. It also provides guidelines on privacy issues and anti-spam practices. It liaises with the Mobile Marketing Association (MMA) to bring the best practices and ethical approaches in mobile marketing to marketers in Canada. Visit **www.the-cma.org** for more information.

5. **The Canadian Wireless Telecommunications Association (CWTA)** administers the CWTA Short Code Guidelines, a strict set of guidelines on pricing and practices for mobile text messaging. This includes pricing guidelines, the use of keyword protocols, opt-in rules, privacy requirements, and terms and conditions. To find out more about the CWTA, go to **www.cwta.ca**.

Failure to abide by marketing communication regulations can have dire consequences for marketers—campaigns may be forced off air, companies and individuals may be fined, and legal action can result in jail time. In 2012, the Competition Bureau ruled against specific companies that intentionally scammed businesses and organizations by misrepresenting themselves as marketers of Yellow Pages directories; the companies were fined $8 million and its two principles slapped with a $500,000 penalty. In addition, the companies had to publish corrective notices on their websites, send letters to their victims, and pay full restitution.[25]

Approaches to Marketing Communications

Outbound and Inbound Marketing Communications

LO3 There are two terms that we need to understand in marketing communications: outbound marketing and inbound marketing. **Outbound marketing** refers to the traditional marketing approach where marketers seek out consumers by widely broadcasting messages using advertising, direct mail, e-mail marketing, telemarketing, and personal-selling approaches. It includes advertising methods that consumers increasingly avoid, such as ads on TV and radio, ads in newspapers and magazines, as well as Internet display ads. **Inbound marketing** is when interested consumers find the product and its messaging by using online techniques that marketers facilitate. It involves search engine optimization, pay-per-click ads, and the use of social media to connect with consumers through social networks, blogs, social bookmarks, social media releases, and microsites. It is the result of paid, earned, and owned media.

These two approaches often work together to communicate with consumers in ways they prefer. Smaller businesses may rely more on inbound marketing, which is cheaper, while larger businesses, depending on the target market, may use a combination of both techniques.

Integrated Marketing Communications

The concept of designing a marketing communications program that coordinates all promotional activities to provide a consistent message to a target audience is referred to as **integrated marketing communications (IMC)**.

The key to developing successful IMC programs is to use a process that makes it easy to design and evaluate. In an IMC program, each element has a distinct role as well as a purpose in the overall campaign. For example, TV ads and Internet display advertising might be used to build awareness and to drive consumers to a website; print advertising may be used to provide details on technical specs; social media interactions may be used to encourage engagement; sales promotional offers may be needed to encourage product trial; direct marketing programs through e-mail marketing approaches may be required to create a database of the target market; and personal selling might be needed to complete a transaction. Each tool is used for a different reason and needs to be evaluated against that purpose and its contribution to the overall success of the marketing communications program.

Baskin-Robbins Canada's "Indulgence That Fits" campaign presents an example of an IMC program that garnered positive results. This campaign promoted its new line of flavours, BRight Choices, that

outbound marketing
Marketers seek out consumers by widely broadcasting messages using advertising, direct mail, e-mail marketing, telemarketing, and personal-selling approaches

inbound marketing
When consumers find a product and its messaging by using online techniques that marketers facilitate, including search engine optimization, pay-per-click ads, and the use of social media to connect with consumers

integrated marketing communications (IMC)
A communications approach that coordinates all promotional activities to provide a consistent message to a target audience

consisted of light ice cream, real fruit sorbets, low-fat frozen yogourts, and mini-ice cream cakes. It used event marketing, public relations, in-store sampling, consumer promotions, and social media to build product awareness and trial as follows:

- **Event marketing:** Baskin-Robbins made Toronto Fashion Week central to its product launch and partnered fashion with ice cream by becoming the inspiration for top fashion designer Pat McDonagh, who designed clothes for the Beatles, Princess Diana, Veronica Tennant, and Grace Jones. Her designs flaunted ice cream cake–type hats and dresses reflecting the new ice cream flavours.

- **Public relations:** Press releases alerted the media and fashion bloggers to the Baskin-Robbins fashion-inspired collection.

- **In-store sampling:** In-store merchandising and sampling directed people to the Baskin-Robbins website and Facebook page to enter a contest to win front-row tickets to McDonagh's Fashion Week show.

- **Consumer promotions:** An online contest ran for six weeks, leading up to Fashion Week, and asked participants to name two of the collection's dresses. The winning names, Cherry Poppins and Decadent Diva, secured VIP tickets for its creators to see the Pat McDonagh fashion show.

- **Social media:** Facebook, Twitter, and YouTube were used to reach consumers. Facebook announced the new products and publicized the Fashion Week contest, while online videos were posted to all Baskin-Robbins social media accounts with behind-the-scenes interviews and footage.

The IMC campaign for Baskin-Robbins was carefully monitored in real time to determine its success. The public relations aspect was particularly strong, with over 50 million impressions acquired through free coverage in newspapers, magazines, and blogs, as well as on radio and TV stations. Media highlights included articles in the *National Post,* the *Toronto Sun,* and *Flare,* with online articles appearing in **thestar.com, eyeweekly. com, metronews.ca,** blogTO, and **CTV.ca.** On-air mentions were noted on the MIX and CHFI radio stations. Sales results for Baskin-Robbins increased 15 percent for this two-month launch compared to the previous year.[26]

An IMC campaign by Baskin-Robbins successfully launched its new product line.

marketing communication tools
Advertising, public relations, sales promotion, direct response, event marketing and sponsorship, and personal selling

ask yourself

1. *How is marketing communications regulated in Canada?*
2. *What is the role of the ASC?*
3. *What is IMC?*

Marketing Communication Tools

In this diverse media environment, a wide range of marketing communication tools is available to reach consumers in the best possible way. **Marketing communication tools** consist of advertising, public relations, sales promotion, direct response, event marketing and sponsorship, and personal selling. Figure 12–3 summarizes the relative strengths and weaknesses of these six elements.

this definition is important because advertising space is normally purchased, with the exception of some public service announcements, which may use donated media.

Advertising can exist in many forms in Canada. In the broadcast media, there are TV and radio. In the print media, there are newspapers and magazines. In the out-of-home media, there are billboards, posters, bus shelter ads, transit ads, washroom ads, and a variety of non-conventional methods such as aerial advertising. In the digital media space, ads can be placed on websites, blogs, social networks, search engines, and apps as well as on e-newsletters, permission-based e-mails, and mobile messaging platforms.

Advertising

LO 4 **Advertising** is a paid form of media used to communicate to consumers about an organization, good, service, or idea. The *paid* aspect of

Figure 12–3
Strengths and weaknesses of communication tools

Promotional Tool	Strengths	Weaknesses
Advertising	• An efficient means of reaching large numbers of people both online and offline • Many affordable online options exist for marketers with small budgets • Online and offline options can work together to enhance messaging • Advertisers control messaging	• High cost of offline approaches • Difficult to evaluate offline approaches • High clutter both online and offline • Low credibility of messaging • Viewers avoid both online and offline messaging
Public relations	• Highly credible messages when spread by the media • Inexpensive, particularly when using social media • New measurable tools available due to social media • Can be well-integrated into IMC programs	• Unable to control media messaging • Difficult to influence the number of messages spread through the media • Results can be difficult to evaluate
Sales promotion	• Effective at increasing short-term sales • Many options are available both online and offline • Social media provides an affordable way to disseminate offers • Results are measurable • Can be well-integrated into IMC programs	• Fraudulent involvement can occur • Can lead to promotional wars • Promotions can be easily duplicated by competitors • Consumers may wait for a sales promotion before purchasing • Legal regulations are complex
Direct response	• Messages can be targeted through online and offline approaches • Facilitates customer relationships • Results are measurable	• High cost of offline and online approaches • Negative customer reactions • Clutter • Requires a database to be done properly
Event marketing and sponsorship	• Small branded events can be used to create a buzz and spread viral messages • Major event sponsorships can reach large audiences and create positive associations • Can be integrated into IMC programs • Sponsorships can be carried into the online environment • Buzz can be affordably created through micro-sites and social media	• Large event-sponsorships can be limited to awareness-building messages • Sponsorships can be costly and difficult to evaluate • Results are difficult to measure
Personal selling	• Personal interactions can build lasting relationships with consumers • Online approaches can be used to enhance relationships • An important approach for expensive products • Can be used in large and small businesses • Can be a strong form of product differentiation	• Can become expensive when large salesforces are involved • Consistency in approach and messaging is difficult to achieve • People may not want to engage

> *Marketers have a number of media options from which to choose. Selection is based on campaign objectives as well as the product, the target market, and budget constraints.*

Advertising can be very expensive. A one-time, national rate for a full-page, four-colour ad in the hard copy of *Maclean's* magazine, for example, costs $39,330, with digital tablet ads running at $4,965 per page.[27] Television ads are even more expensive, with average production costs running at approximately $200,000 and media prices running over $150,000 to run a 30-second spot during a top, prime-time, highly viewed TV broadcast. Media prices will vary, depending on when and where an advertiser wishes to run the spot.

A more recent form of advertising is the *webisode* with companies such as Ikea, Sara Lee, and Maybelline creating short online episodes with storylines that entertain and subtly weave in the product. In 2013, RBC launched a three-episode YouTube reality series in Canada featuring one of its top executives returning to university and trying to survive on a student budget.[28]

Advertising Media Choices   Marketers have a number of media options from which to choose. Selection is based on campaign objectives as well as the product, the target market, and budget constraints. Figure 12–4 summarizes the advantages and disadvantages of the major forms of advertising: Internet, TV, newspaper, magazine, radio, and out-of-home. These media choices are described in more detail in the following pages.

INTERNET   Advertising on the Internet provides marketers with numerous tools to reach online audiences.

Many options exist, such as online display ads, pay-per-click ads, search engine optimization, social networking, e-mail marketing, affiliate marketing, mobile marketing, and the use of promotional microsites and corporate websites.

When it comes to online advertising, companies can create display ads that can be placed on various online destinations, such as media websites, web portals, blogs, social networks, e-mail platforms, and online gaming sites. Pay-per-click ads can also be placed on search engines, content networks, and social networks such as Facebook, LinkedIn, or YouTube, while online classified ads can be placed on websites such as Craigslist or Kijiji.

Display advertising refers to the use of online ads with graphics, video, or animation. Display ads can be static or dynamic, sometimes with video or animation playing within the ad, and can be expandable, float on to a page, or be transitional by appearing between the loading of two content pages. Display ads can also be formatted as *home page takeovers* where an entire ad obscures a website home page. Display ads are commonly called **banner ads**, and come in a variety of shapes and sizes—leaderboards, rectangles, big boxes, or skyscrapers. **Leaderboards** stretch across the top of a web page, while rectangles and big boxes typically appear lower down, on the right-hand side of a webpage. **Skyscrapers** are tall, slim, vertical ads placed along the side of a web page.

Figure 12–4
Advertising options—advantages and disadvantages

MEDIUM	ADVANTAGES	DISADVANTAGES
Internet	• Video and audio capabilities • Animation and sound can get attention • Ads can be interactive • Ad can be placed on websites, web portals, search engines, or social networks • Detailed information can be conveyed • Many creative options • Easy to measure • Can be low cost	• Animation and interactivity require large files that can have long load-times • High avoidance • Short attention spans on the Internet
Television	• Reaches a wide audience • Uses sight, sound, and motion • Can target specific audiences • Excellent for products requiring demonstration • Highly visible	• High cost to create ads • High cost to purchase media • Short exposure time • Perishable message • Difficult to convey complex information • High avoidance • Difficult to measure
Newspapers	• Strong in local markets • Short lead-times for ad placement • Flexible ad sizes • Ads can be clipped and saved • Detailed information can be conveyed • Can be low cost for local placements	• Ads compete for attention with other newspaper features • Advertising clutter • Short lifespan • Poor colour reproduction • Relatively high cost for national ads
Magazines	• Can target specific audiences • High-quality colour • Pass-along readership • Ads can be clipped and saved • Complex information can be conveyed	• Long lead-times • Relatively high cost • Advertising clutter • Ads compete for attention with other magazine features
Radio	• Low cost of media and production • Good for local businesses • Short lead-times • Theatre of the mind gets attention	• No visual elements • Perishable message • Background media • Difficult to convey complex information • Difficult for national campaigns
Outdoor/Transit	• Relatively low cost • Local market focus • High visibility • Strong opportunity for repeat exposures • Good for building awareness in short time • Cannot be turned off	• Message must be short and simple • Low selectivity of audience • Visual pollution

advergaming
Placing ads in online or offline video games

pre-roll video advertising
The use of TV-type ads that play before video segments are watched online

The most successful banner ads are interactive in nature and commonly link to an advertiser's promotional website. Gaming websites embed banner ads within their online games so that ads appear as billboards or posters within the games. This is called **advergaming**, an opportunity that allows marketers to dynamically rotate display ads as appropriate by time of day or day of the week. Ads can also be placed within offline games.

Pre-roll video advertising refers to the use of TV-type ads that play before video segments are watched online, for example, on social media sites such as YouTube. These types of ads are increasingly popular with marketers but have the disadvantage of being more expensive to produce than static or display ads.

An Internet marketing approach pioneered by search engines and now also used by a few websites, blogs, and social media sites is called **pay-per-click advertising (PPC)**. It is often referred to as *search advertising* because it primarily appears on search engines in the form of mini-text ads that are served during keyword searches on either the top or right-hand side of the search page. The search engine is paid by the PPC advertiser only when the ads are clicked. Pay-per-click image ads also exist on some blogs and social media sites.

TELEVISION   Television is a valuable medium because it communicates with sight, sound, and motion and gets attention from large target audiences. Digital technology now allows TV viewing to be flexible, whether this means watching it on the go on a smartphone or tablet, time-shifting to watch it in a different time zone, or using a digital recording device to watch a program at a more convenient time. The rapid adoption of Internet-based services such as Netflix offers consumers more choices. It now exists in over 25 percent of anglophone homes in Canada and is changing how consumers view TV-type programming and how marketers view TV as an advertising platform.[29]

When TV ads are well-designed and appropriately placed in the media, this tool can deliver very impactful and effective messages. Many TV advertisers complement their ads with other advertising options that meet target audiences online through online display ads or with pre-roll video ads that play before an online broadcast of a TV program. Marketers are aware that consumer behaviour is placing the effectiveness of stand-alone TV advertising into question. TV viewers frequently change channels when ads appear during commercial breaks, and many use digital recording devices to watch programs at a later date. Sometimes, people prefer to watch TV programs online where fewer ads exist, or catch a show at another time through on-demand digital programming. Concern exists that a portion of younger viewers may cut the TV cord altogether, preferring to hop online and use Internet-based services such as Netflix and iTunes, or TV network apps to watch their favourite programs.

NEWSPAPERS Newspapers are an important advertising medium that are highly trusted by consumers and well-recognized in the market for providing

The Print Measurement Bureau provides readership and circulation data on print publications.

reliable information. They have excellent reach, particularly for local retailers. There are three types of newspapers: daily paid circulation newspapers, free daily newspapers, and free community newspapers. The highest circulation of a paid daily newspaper in Canada is the *Toronto Star* followed in order by the *Globe and Mail,* the *National Post,* and *Le Journal de Montreal.* The two free daily newspapers, *Metro* and *24 Hours,* are enjoying high circulation numbers that rival the traditional paid circulation newspapers.[30] Community newspapers are published either weekly or monthly and are an excellent media choice for local retailers and for community events. As noted earlier, newspapers are challenged with lower advertising revenues in this digital age where the news is accessible through multiple avenues.

MAGAZINES   Magazines provide advertisers with a high-quality media environment and present data to marketers on the profile of their readers, so advertisers can match magazines to their target market profile. *Ski Canada* magazine, for example, provides data (see the related Infographic on the next page) on the skiing expertise of its readers as well as the types of ski vacations they take, the ski equipment they purchase, and their shopping habits for ski gear. This is all relevant data for sporting goods manufacturers, sporting goods stores, travel companies, and holiday destinations that may wish to place ads in the publication.

Infographic

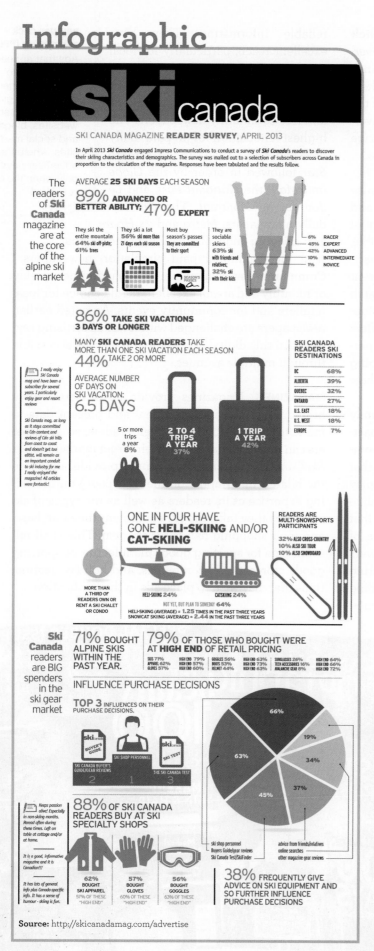

ski canada

SKI CANADA MAGAZINE READER SURVEY, APRIL 2013

In April 2013 *Ski Canada* engaged Impresa Communications to conduct a survey of *Ski Canada*'s readers to discover their skiing characteristics and demographics. The survey was mailed out to a selection of subscribers across Canada in proportion to the circulation of the magazine. Responses have been tabulated and the results follow.

The readers of **Ski Canada** magazine are at the core of the alpine ski market

AVERAGE 25 SKI DAYS EACH SEASON

89% ADVANCED OR BETTER ABILITY; 47% EXPERT

They ski the entire mountain 64% ski off-piste; 61% trees

They ski a lot 56% ski more than 21 days each ski season

Most buy season's passes They are committed to their sport

They are sociable skiers 63% ski with friends and relatives; 32% ski with their kids

6%	RACER
45%	EXPERT
42%	ADVANCED
10%	INTERMEDIATE
1%	NOVICE

86% TAKE SKI VACATIONS 3 DAYS OR LONGER

MANY **SKI CANADA READERS** TAKE MORE THAN ONE SKI VACATION EACH SEASON **44% TAKE 2 OR MORE**

AVERAGE NUMBER OF DAYS ON SKI VACATION: **6.5 DAYS**

5 or more trips a year 8%

2 TO 4 TRIPS A YEAR 37%

1 TRIP A YEAR 42%

SKI CANADA READERS SKI DESTINATIONS

BC	68%
ALBERTA	39%
QUEBEC	32%
ONTARIO	27%
U.S. EAST	18%
U.S. WEST	18%
EUROPE	7%

I really enjoy Ski Canada mag and have been a subscriber for several years. I particularly enjoy gear and resort reviews

Ski Canada mag, as long as it stays committed to Cdn content and reviews of Cdn ski hills from coast to coast and doesn't get too elitist, will remain as an important conduit to ski industry for me I really enjoyed the magazine! All articles were fantastic!

ONE IN FOUR HAVE GONE **HELI-SKIING** AND/OR **CAT-SKIING**

MORE THAN A THIRD OF READERS OWN OR RENT A SKI CHALET OR CONDO

HELI-SKIING 24%

CATSKIING 24%

NOT YET, BUT PLAN TO SOMEDAY 64%
HELI-SKIING (AVERAGE) = 1.25 TIMES IN THE PAST THREE YEARS
SNOWCAT SKIING (AVERAGE) = 2.44 IN THE PAST THREE YEARS

READERS ARE MULTI-SNOWSPORTS PARTICIPANTS

32% ALSO CROSS-COUNTRY
10% ALSO SKI TOUR
10% ALSO SNOWBOARD

Ski Canada readers are BIG spenders in the ski gear market

71% BOUGHT ALPINE SKIS WITHIN THE PAST YEAR.

79% OF THOSE WHO BOUGHT WERE AT HIGH END OF RETAIL PRICING

SKIS 71%	HIGH END 79%	GOGGLES 56%	HIGH END 63%	SUNGLASSES 26%	HIGH END 64%
APPAREL 62%	HIGH END 57%	BOOTS 53%	HIGH END 73%	TECH ACCESSORIES 16%	HIGH END 66%
GLOVES 57%	HIGH END 60%	HELMET 44%	HIGH END 63%	AVALANCHE GEAR 8%	HIGH END 72%

INFLUENCE PURCHASE DECISIONS

TOP 3 INFLUENCES ON THEIR PURCHASE DECISIONS.

SKI CANADA BUYER'S GUIDE/GEAR REVIEWS — 2

SKI SHOP PERSONNEL — 1

THE SKI CANADA TEST — 3

Keeps passion alive! Especially in non-skiing months. Reread often during these times. Left on table at cottage and/or at home.

It is a good, informative magazine and it is Canadian!!!

It has lots of general info plus Canada-specific info. It has a sense of humour - skiing is fun.

88% OF SKI CANADA READERS BUY AT SKI SPECIALTY SHOPS

62% BOUGHT SKI APPAREL 57% OF THESE "HIGH END"

57% BOUGHT GLOVES 60% OF THESE "HIGH END"

56% BOUGHT GOGGLES 63% OF THESE "HIGH END"

38% FREQUENTLY GIVE ADVICE ON SKI EQUIPMENT AND SO FURTHER INFLUENCE PURCHASE DECISIONS

66%
19%
34%
37%
45%
63%

ski shop personnel
Buyers Guide/gear reviews
Ski Canada Test/SkiFinder

advice from friends/relatives
online searches
other magazine gear reviews

Magazines have adapted well to the online environment by providing added online content such as searchable databases, blogs, contests, and polls, as well as mobile versions that can be accessed on tablets and other mobile devices. Magazines such as *Canadian Living* and *Chatelaine* offer expansive recipe databases and in-depth coverage. News magazines such as *Maclean's* include added features such as blogs, polls, quizzes, and videos, and *Canadian Business* follows a similar approach.

The Canadian Print Measurement Bureau (PMB) issues topline reports detailing two-year data for circulation, readership, and target market information on many Canadian newspapers and magazines. The spring 2014 report shows that Canadian magazines with the highest readership are *Reader's Digest* and *Canadian Living;* the top 10 magazines are noted in Figure 12–5.[31] Navigate to the PMB website at **www.pmb.ca** to review its latest data.

RADIO Radio reaches 91 percent of Canadians over the age of 12, but listening continues to decline among teens who prefer to access music on a variety of devices.[32] The main characteristics of radio are that it is local and has a relatively low production cost. This makes it affordable for both small and large advertisers. There are 699 private commercial radio stations in Canada, many of which focus on specific listener interests, including news and talk, or music genres such as adult contemporary, country, contemporary hits, rock, classical, and the oldies. Stations also exist for specific ethnic groups that broadcast content in foreign languages. Radio stations

Figure 12–5

Top magazines (readership in Canada)

Ranking	Magazine
1	*Reader's Digest*
2	*Canadian Living*
3	*What's Cooking*
4	*Canadian Geographic*
5	*Chatelaine*
6	*Cineplex Magazine*
7	*People*
8	*CAA magazine*
9	*Maclean's*
10	*Food and Drink*

Source: *PMB 2014 Spring Topline Report,* Canadian Print Measurement Bureau, accessed at www.pmb.ca/public/e/pmb2014_spring/release/pmb2014spring_topline.pdf (rolling two-year data).

have responded to the Internet with online broadcasts, downloadable podcasts, apps, and blogs. Satellite radio, with its commercial-free programming, is available through SiriusXM Radio in Canada for $21.99 per month, which limits its appeal.

OUT-OF-HOME Out-of-home advertising is an effective medium for quickly building awareness and interest in a product. It is also an excellent reminder for current products. Over the last few years, this media has experienced slight increases due to its participation in IMC programs and the realization by marketers that this media cannot be turned off. Out-of-home advertising can reach people where they live, work, and socialize with traditional and digital formats that include outdoor digital video billboards. Examples can be seen at Yonge-Dundas Square in Toronto where Canada's first media tower dominates with 20,000 square feet of advertising in the form of digital billboards, full-motion video, and customized displays.

Out-of-home advertising includes outdoor and transit advertising. Outdoor includes billboards, back-lit posters, superboards (large billboards), mall posters, digital signs, video signage/displays, wall banners, murals, and street-level columns. It also includes *place-based media* where messages are placed in out-of-home destinations such as shopping malls, airports, parking lots, doctors' offices, health clubs, gas stations, elevators, and washrooms in restaurants, bars, and post-secondary schools. Transit advertising refers to ads placed on the interior and exterior of buses, subway cars, and taxis as well as in subway stations and on transit shelters. An example of how out-of-home campaigns can be used to increase awareness is discussed in the Marketing NewsFlash "Repackaging Help Raises Funds for Non-Profit," which describes how the creativity of the advertising agency Leo Burnett helped raise funds for the non-profit organization Raising the Roof by putting a spotlight on homelessness in Canada.

Public Relations

LO⁵ Public relations is an area that is increasingly used by marketers to deliver messages to consumers. While advertising may be viewed with suspicion, messages that come through a third party, such as the media, are often seen as more reliable and credible. In addition, for marketers with small budgets, public relations efforts can be a more affordable way to communicate with a wide audience. The Childhood Cancer Foundation in Canada, for example, is a non-profit organization with very small budgets, and it turns to public relations to help spread messages using direct contacts with the media, event-marketing programs, social media, and community relations to encourage donations.

Public relations is a communications tool that seeks to influence the opinions and attitudes of target groups through the use of unpaid media exposure. Public relations professionals build relationships with the media and stakeholders and use tools such as press releases, social media releases, press kits, news

public relations
A communications tool that seeks to influence the opinions and attitudes of target groups through the use of unpaid media exposure; targets the media in an attempt to generate positive publicity for a company, product, or individual

Digital media tower at Yonge-Dundas Square in Toronto.

Repackaging Help Raises Funds for Non-Profit

Raising the Roof is a small non-profit organization that works with partners across Canada at the grassroots community level to reduce homelessness. Its purpose is to provide long-term solutions to homelessness so that individuals have access to safe and stable homes, as well as the support needed to thrive. It embraces diversity and believes that everyone should be met with compassion, respect, and without discrimination. It encourages businesses, community groups, schools, and individuals to get involved to help reduce homelessness.

Since its inception in 1996, Raising the Roof has provided over $3.5 million to agencies across Canada that work to reduce homelessness at the community level. Since 2010, it has worked with advertising agency Leo Burnett to raise awareness on homelessness. Leo Burnett provides its services pro-bono (free) for this charitable organization and works with media organizations and other marketing companies and organizations so that media time, media

space, and marketing services and support are also provided at no cost. Its "Repackaging Help" campaign focused on the charity's annual fund-raiser that sells winter hats to raise donations for homelessness.

Annually, and for over 17 years in the middle of winter, Raising the Roof runs its Toque Tuesday to raise funds to combat homelessness in Canada. It sells toques (winter hats) for $10 each, now allowing people to also buy them online. However, recognizing that the charity suffers from low awareness and that people are hesitant to purchase toques from an organization with low recognition, Raising the Roof and Leo Burnett created a campaign, "Repackaging Help," that pointed out how funds are used and why people should donate to this cause.

The campaign created special packaging for the toques to explain the fund-raiser and used a mobile street-level billboard as a pop-up type store to communicate and sell the toques that were displayed on the billboard. Each hat was packaged in transparent

cellophane with large letters sprawled across the front with messages such as "This hat will help a homeless woman find a job," or "This hat will help a homeless man eat tonight," or "This hat will help a homeless teen connect with a mentor." Many other messages were created that focused on different homeless situations, whether for an adult, a child, or a family trying to get back on its feet.

The hats were mounted on the mobile street-level billboard with a bold headline that stated, "Every hat sold helps the homeless. Find the toque that connects with you." Rows of hats with individual messages supported this headline and encouraged people to purchase a toque. The messages explained that funds would help provide basic necessities for homeless people such as medication for a child, a warm shower, or a safe place to sleep.

In three months, Raising the Roof reached its annual sales goal of 40,000 hats by demonstrating that every hat makes a difference.[33]

▶ Video
Raising
the Roof

Street-level out-of-home installations helped raise funds for the homeless.

Questions

1. What forms of marketing communication were integrated into this campaign?

2. How could social media be used to further spread awareness?

conferences, and events to spread the word. Public relations specialists target the media in an attempt to generate positive publicity for a company, product, or individual. While public relations specialists are paid to create public relations campaigns, the intent is to generate positive publicity that by far outweighs its cost. Public relations can also take the form of crisis management and image management.[34]

Crisis management can be an important aspect of public relations, as seen with various incidences over the last few years that have severely impacted people's lives and forced companies to answer to the public outcry. Public relations professionals, well-versed in crisis management, help companies navigate these difficult circumstances by advising on what strategies should be followed to rectify situations and salvage a company's image. Three examples are worth noting. The first example refers to the 2008 Maple Leaf Foods *listeria* food contamination issue that was linked to 20 deaths in Canada and prompted Maple Leaf Foods to voluntarily provide honest, daily media updates on the issue and tighten its food-safety practices.[35] The second example lies with the 2010 BP Deepwater Horizon oil spill that killed 11 people and leaked 4.9 million barrels of oil into the Gulf of Mexico with dire repercussions on local wildlife, natural habitat, and local businesses. BP was not as transparent, honest, and forthcoming as Maple Leaf Foods and was negatively portrayed in the media, which severely impacted its company image. BP was fined billions of dollars by the U.S. government for the damage it caused.[36] The third example is rooted in the 2013 Bangladesh garment factory collapse that killed over 1,100 people. The public outcry over poor working conditions demanded an explanation, and companies were compelled to explain their involvement and moral compass in purchasing products from poor countries with substandard wages, building codes, and working conditions. Unlike many other manufacturers, Loblaw was transparent and immediately forthright in noting that its Joe Fresh products were manufactured in one of the collapsed buildings and immediately set out to try to improve building standards for workers in Bangladesh. In a few short months, it signed the Bangladesh Accord on Fire and Building Safety, implemented a policy that required all off-shore manufacturing abide by local building codes, audited all its vendors in Bangladesh, removed manufacturing from seven facilities that

were not compliant, and established a team of experts in Bangladesh to ensure supplier compliance. In addition, Loblaw voluntarily compensated the survivors and the families of the victims that lost their lives in the tragedy.[37] This transparent and open approach to crisis management is widely respected in Canada.

It is important to understand that while public relations efforts can yield positive results, ultimately the media decides if, what, and when it may spread a message about a company, brand, or individual. The publicity is not controlled by the company itself, and the company has no control over what is discussed. **Publicity** is a non-personal form of communication that appears in the media and is not paid for directly by the organization.

The Dove Campaign for Real Beauty's short films, *Dove Real Beauty Sketches,* discussed earlier in this chapter, are examples of how public relations can be used to drum up positive publicity for a campaign. Online ads and an outreach to the media and bloggers resulted in 163 million views of the short films, and 4.6 billion media impressions were also prompted by the public relations program.[38]

Public Relations Tools Public relations activities need to be ethical and integrated into marketing communications efforts. Several tools and tactics are available for marketers, including press

> *Crisis management can be an important aspect of public relations.*

publicity
A non-personal form of communication that appears in the media and is and not paid for directly by the organization

ask yourself

1. *What types of advertising opportunities are available on the Internet?*

2. *How are newspapers in Canada dealing with the decline in advertising revenues?*

3. *What are the reasons online advertising is the largest forms of media in Canada?*

releases, press conferences, special events, and company reports. Social media releases and social media initiatives are relatively new tools that can come under the guise of public relations. Let's look at the tools:

PRESS RELEASES One of the most frequently used public relations tools is the **press release**, an announcement written by the organization and sent to the media.

PRESS CONFERENCES Another commonly used publicity tool is the **press conference**, when representatives of the media are invited to an informational meeting with the company. Advanced materials and press releases are often distributed ahead of time. This tool is often used during crisis management situations.

SPECIAL EVENTS This growing area of public relations involves the creation, support, or sponsorship of special events such as company-sponsored seminars, conferences, and sporting or entertainment events. The goal of these events is to create a forum to disseminate company information and to create positive brand associations for participants or viewers.

COMPANY REPORTS Formal company information that is published in annual reports, brochures, newsletters, or videos and sent out to the company's publics are also public relations tools that help spread positive messages.

SOCIAL MEDIA This tool is seen as a hybrid of advertising and public relations and is often managed by public relations professionals to seed messages and spread the word. Public relations companies and advertising agencies often use social media specialists to manage these efforts.

A **social media release** is a tool available for marketers to efficiently and effectively communicate information to the media and the public. Unlike press releases, which exist online and offline with mainly text-based information, social media releases use online multimedia to communicate with recipients. Video,

ask yourself

1. *What are the advantages and disadvantages of using public relations?*

2. *What is a social media release?*

3. *What role do company reports play in public relations?*

images, and text are included in online releases, with comment areas and share buttons so that readers can easily share the release on blogs or social networks such as Twitter and Facebook.

Sales Promotion

LO 6 **Sales promotion** is a communications tool that provides short-term incentives to generate interest in a product or cause and encourages purchase or support. Social media sites such as Facebook and Twitter are often used to deliver promotional offers to fans and followers, while microsites provide online destinations where contests can be communicated and people can interact. While coupons, rebates, samples, and sweepstakes are some of the traditional sales promotion tools, the digital age has spawned new creative forms. We see agencies developing online promotions where consumers can create and share their own user-generated content. **User-generated content (UGC)** is consumer content that is created by participants. We define it as original online content that has been created by users in the form of blogs, posts, images, audio, or video. We see sales promotions directed through mobile devices with specific smartphone apps and text-message contests allowing for interaction. We see augmented reality options embedded into magazines, postcards, and product labels so that when viewers hold the images up to a live webcam or interact with a GPS signal, it overlays additional information over the image. Such was the case with Coke Zero during the launch of the movie *Avatar* in the U.S., where augmented reality allowed people to interact with the movie's microsite.

press release
An announcement written by an organization and sent to the media

press conference
A planned event where representatives of the media are invited to an informational meeting with the company

social media release
A multimedia online press release platform that includes video, text, and images, as well as social media buttons for sharing on social networks and comment areas where viewers can leave comments

sales promotion
A communications tool that provides short-term incentives to generate interest in a product or cause and encourages purchase or support

user-generated content (UGC)
Original online content that has been created by users in the form of blogs, posts, images, audio, or video

> ❝ *Facebook and Twitter are often used to deliver promotional offers.* ❞

Augmented reality (AR) uses a webcam or mobile device to capture an image that is then supplemented with graphics, audio, video, or GPS data to provide additional information or an enhanced experience. Another digital sales promotion tool is the **matrix 2D barcode**, a two-dimensional square or rectangular response code that, when scanned by a mobile barcode reader or app, provides additional information. It can launch a website, prompt a download, send a text message, or deploy an e-mail. A popular brand of matrix 2D barcode is the QR code.

There are two basic types of sales promotion: (1) consumer promotions and (2) trade promotions. **Consumer promotions** are short-term marketing

Tim Hortons' "Roll Up The Rim To Win" is one of Canada's most-successful consumer promotions.

tools used to encourage immediate consumer purchase. They include incentives such as coupons, premiums, contests, sweepstakes, samples, continuity programs, point-of-purchase materials, and rebates, which are outlined in Figure 12–6.

Tim Hortons' "Roll Up The Rim To Win" promotion is one of Canada's most-successful consumer promotions; in 2016, it is celebrating its 30th anniversary. The promotion's simplicity plays a major role in its success. Consumers just have to roll up the rim of their paper Tim Hortons coffee cup to reveal whether they have won a prize, which could be an item such as a free cup of coffee or perhaps a car. The complexity of creating the program for Tim Hortons is another matter, with the program requiring detailed negotiations with program partners and complex dealings with promotional agencies and legal experts to pull together the online and in-store communication components and legal requirements. Contest regulations include over 3,500 words of contest rules and regulations that are posted online and in restaurants.[39]

Figure 12–6
Consumer promotions

Consumer Promotions	Promotional Tools	Explanation
Short-term marketing tools used to encourage immediate consumer purchase	Coupons	Price reductions offered in exchange for tickets/documents. Can be distributed online, on-pack, through flyers, or on shelf.
	Premiums	Offers that provide merchandise in exchange for proof-of-purchase. Extra funds may also be required.
	Contests	Offers where participants require a skill to win a prize such as creative submissions.
	Sweepstakes	Offers which are pure games-of-chance and where consumers often participate by completing an entry form and, if selected as a winner, answering a skill-testing question.
	Samples and free trials	The provision of free products or free trials to encourage consumers to try and purchase a product.
	Loyalty programs	Continuity programs that reward customers for ongoing purchases with points that can be redeemed for rewards.
	Rebates	A price reduction supplied via mail in exchange for proof-of-purchase.
	Bonus packs/ special packs	The provision of oversized packs or bonus items attached to the original product. Special packs can also be created.
	Point-of sale materials	The use of in-store merchandising such as display materials, banners, floor decals, and posters to draw attention.

Consumer promotions are an effective way to increase short-term sales.

augmented reality (AR)
The use of webcams or mobile devices to capture an image that is then supplemented with graphics, audio, video, or GPS data to provide additional information or an enhanced experience

matrix 2D barcode
A two-dimensional response code that, when scanned by a mobile barcode reader or app, provides additional information, launches websites, prompts downloads, sends text messages, or deploys messages

consumer promotions
Short-term marketing tools used to encourage immediate consumer purchase

Consumer promotions must adhere to legal marketing practices and regulations.

Trade promotions are short-term promotional tools used to generate support with wholesalers, distributors, or retailers. Common approaches include trade shows, trade allowances and discounts, and cooperative advertising (see Figure 12–7).

Direct Response

LO 7 **Direct response** is a marketing communications tool designed to communicate with consumers one-on-one and to elicit a direct action either online or offline. This action can be in the form of an order, a supportive gesture, a request for further information, or a visit to a retail outlet or website. In many instances, a direct marketing program is multifaceted and designed with short-term communication blasts to build long-term relationships with the company and brand loyalty. In this manner, e-mail newsletters, updates on points' programs, pre-recorded telephone messages, or letters received in the mail are designed

as reminders that build relationships, increase product awareness, and build business in the long run.

Offline approaches include face-to-face selling, direct mail pieces, catalogues, telemarketing, and direct-response advertising on TV, radio, or print where telephone numbers or web addresses drive an immediate call to action. Online approaches look to the Internet to facilitate one-on-one interactions and use tools such as e-mail campaigns, online display ads, pay-per-click ads, and social media interactions to drive consumers to landing pages, websites, or microsites. In many instances, offline and online direct-response approaches work together to encourage consumers to go to a store or an e-commerce site to complete a transaction.

Direct response programs use metrics to evaluate success, such as business leads, traffic generation, and direct orders. **Lead generation** is the resultant request for additional information. **Traffic generation** is the resultant visit to a location or website.

A successful direct-marketing approach that uses a loyalty CRM (customer relationship marketing) database is the Shoppers Drug Mart Optimum program. The program collects purchase data from its

ask yourself

1. *What types of consumer promotions are available to marketers?*

2. *How do trade promotions differ from consumer promotions?*

3. *What trade promotional tools are available to marketers?*

---

trade promotions
Short-term promotional tools used to generate support with wholesalers, distributors, or retailers

direct response
A marketing communications tool designed to communicate with consumers one-on-one and elicit a direct action either online or offline

lead generation
The requests for additional information that result from direct-response marketing

traffic generation
The visits to a location or website that result from direct-response marketing

---

Figure 12–7
Trade promotions

Trade Promotions	Promotional Tools	Explanation
Short-term promotional tools given to wholesalers, distributors, or retailers	Trade shows	Participation in industry events that showcase new products and initiatives.
	Off-invoice allowances	A price reduction taken off the invoice of a purchase that is made within a specific time frame.
	Merchandising allowances	A price reduction taken off a purchase in return for displaying the product.
	Co-op advertising	The contribution of funds for inclusion in a wholesaler, distributor, or retailer advertising program such as a flyer.

Trade promotions are often required to encourage retail support.

Optimum card members and then tailors messages using print ads, flyers, direct mail, e-mail messages, and in-store signage to encourage retail purchases. The intent is to obtain a greater share of wallet from its customers

While CRM direct-response approaches are one of the fastest-growing forms of promotion, it poses several challenges. First, it requires a comprehensive and up-to-date database of respondent information, including demographics, purchase habits, and offer responses. Second, developing and maintaining this database is expensive. And third, some consumers avoid participation in these programs due to concerns over privacy issues.

A successful CRM program by Shoppers Drug Mart uses the Optimum card.

Event Marketing and Sponsorship

Event marketing refers to the creation or involvement of a brand in an experience or occasion that heightens its awareness, creates positive associations, and generates a desired response. Event marketing and sponsorship often go hand-in-hand with brands lending their names to established events. Companies often weave event marketing into integrated campaigns that use public relations, social media, and consumer promotions to make connections with consumers and create a buzz. The Baskin-Robbins Canada example noted earlier is such as example. It used all these elements to launch a new line of ice cream, BRight Choices, weaving it into a Toronto Fashion Week event.

Sponsorship involves a company paying a fee in exchange for inclusion in an event, involvement in its advertising opportunities, or exposure within the event itself. Sponsorship programs can encompass a multitude of approaches that range from placing ads or logos in brochures, to setting up banners at events, to the naming of the event itself. An example of event marketing and sponsorship can be seen with the annual international tennis tournament hosted by Tennis Canada—the Rogers Cup that occurs in Toronto and Montreal. This event provides wide media coverage as well as significant brand exposure at the events. The events are viewed by more than 6 million viewers in Canada and 150 million worldwide through seven consecutive days of coverage that results in more than 8,000 national print/online news clippings, over 14 million website impressions, and broadcasts to over 165 countries. In 2014, the title sponsor was Rogers, the presenting sponsor was the National Bank, and platinum sponsors included Buick, Casino Montreal, Emirates airlines, Corona beer, and Iris eye care. Sponsorship opportunities depended on the

"Companies often weave event marketing into integrated campaigns."

negotiated package and ranged from print ads within the event brochure, to on-site giveaways and ads, as well as on-air mentions and promotional TV spots that run during broadcasts.[40]

Personal Selling

LO 8   **Personal selling** involves the two-way flow of communication between a buyer and seller, often face-to-face or facilitated through communication devices, to influence an individual or group purchase-decision. Unlike advertising, personal selling is usually face-to-face communication, although telephone and electronic communication is also used.

Sales positions include account management positions, manufacturing sales personnel, real estate brokers, stockbrokers, and salesclerks who work in retail stores. In reality, virtually every occupation that involves customer contact has an element of personal selling with the salespeople representing the company. **Relationship selling** is the practice of building long-term loyalty from customers based on a salesperson's attention and commitment to customer needs over time.

The personal selling process consists of six stages: prospecting, pre-approach, approach, presentation, close, and follow-up as detailed in Figure 12–8.

event marketing
The creation or involvement of a brand in an experience or occasion that will heighten its awareness, create positive associations, and generate a desired response

sponsorship
When an advertiser pays a fee in exchange for inclusion in an event, involvement in its advertising opportunities, or exposure within the event itself

personal selling
The two-way flow of communication between a buyer and seller, often face-to-face or facilitated through communication devices, to influence an individual or group purchase decision

relationship selling
The practice of building long-term loyalty from customers based on a salesperson's attention and commitment to customer needs over time

Figure 12–8
Stages and objectives in the personal selling process

Stage	Objective	Comments
1. Prospecting	Search for and qualify prospects	Start of the selling process; prospects generated through advertising, referrals, and cold canvassing
2. Pre-approach	Gather information and decide how to approach the prospect	Information sources include personal observation, other customers, and company salespeople
3. Approach	Gain prospect's attention, stimulate interest, and make transition to the presentation	First impression is critical; gain attention and interest through references to common acquaintances, a referral, or product demonstration
4. Presentation	Begin converting a prospect into a customer by creating a desire for the product or service	Different presentation formats are possible; involving the customer is critical; responding to objections is key; a professional ethical approach is needed
5. Close	Obtain a purchase commitment from the prospect and secure a customer	Salesperson asks for the order; different approaches include the trial close and assumptive close; trial close can be used at any stage
6. Follow-up	Ensure that the customer is satisfied with the product or service	Resolve any problems faced by the customer to ensure customer satisfaction and future sales possibilities

ask yourself

1. **What are the differences between advertising and public relations?**

2. **Which promotional tools can generate immediate, short-term responses?**

3. **What are the stages in the personal selling process?**

Personal selling plays a central role in many industries.

word-of-mouth marketing
The spread of positive messages about a product by listening to consumers, identifying influential individuals that can spread the word, and making it easier for them to do so

Alternative Marketing Communication Approaches

Marketing communication is often avoided by consumers who view it suspiciously and as a general annoyance. Marketers turn to alternative approaches to help deal with this avoidance, using word-of-mouth marketing techniques and product placement or branded entertainment initiatives to strengthen communications.

Word-of-Mouth Marketing Word-of-mouth communication is based on transparent and honest communication. It starts with organizations understanding where, when, and how opinions are being shared by listening and responding to supporters, detractors, and neutrals. **Word-of-mouth marketing** works by listening to consumers, identifying influential individuals, providing important information, and making it easier for them to spread the word.

Word-of-mouth communications typically works on three levels. On a *viral level*, it tries to create buzz through public relations events and social media that seed fun and interesting messages with influential people that spread the word. On a *grassroots level*, it identifies key communities, opinion leaders, and product advocates who get personally involved with the brand and have the ability to influence others. On a *professional level*, official referral programs may be put in place to reward satisfied customers who refer the brand to friends and contacts.[41]

One of the best examples of successful word-of-mouth marketing is the group-buying phenomenon pioneered by Groupon. Groupon, whose memorable name is a hybrid of the words *group* and *coupon,* started in 2008 in the U.S. Within a year, it had an e-mail database of over 1.5 million people. Today it exists in 48 countries.

This is how it works. Instead of clipping coupons, subscribers receive daily local deep-discounted deals from Groupon via e-mail or through their Twitter and Facebook feeds or mobile app. Subscribers designate their location and the deals start rolling in. Deals go live only when enough people have purchased the offer. Customers are encouraged to pass the deal on to others. For small businesses, Groupon helps reach local customers who may not be aware of their products. Deals are time-sensitive, come in limited quantities, and need to be redeemed within a few months.[42]

Product Placement and Branded Entertainment

The fact that consumers avoid TV ads by muting the sound, changing the channel, or leaving the room is encouraging marketers to include products in TV shows and movies. This can be done through **product placement**, the inclusion of a product such as a soft drink in a movie or TV program, or the creation of an entire TV episode around a brand, which is referred to as **branded entertainment**. When Coca-Cola pays *American Idol* to display its product on set in front of the judges, this is an example of product placement. When Embassy Suites hotels pays the reality series *The Apprentice* to create an episode focused on its hotels, this is branded entertainment.

Unique Online Tools

LO 9 While online advertising approaches were discussed earlier in this chapter, the Internet has a number of unique online tools that marketers use to engage individuals. These are namely search engine marketing, social network marketing, affiliate marketing, e-mail marketing, and mobile marketing.

Search engine marketing (SEM) is an Internet marketing approach that includes two areas: (1) search engine optimization and (2) pay-per-click advertising. **Search engine optimization (SEO)** looks at website design, technical coding, written content, incoming links, and website updates to ensure that websites are highly rated and properly indexed by search engines such as Google and Bing. Marketers

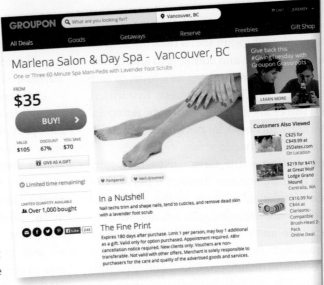

Groupon appeals as a marketing tool for online and offline retailers.

often work with specialists to maximize search engine optimization.

When it comes to websites, their design and content is central to successful ranking on search engines, which facilitates discovery by consumers. Content needs to be fresh and frequently updated, thus the inclusion of blogs on many websites as a means of routinely adding fresh new content. Visual website appeal is also important. Consumers decide to click on a web page within seconds; therefore, content and visual appeal need to work together to present an appealing proposition.

Microsites are promotional websites created for short-term promotional purposes, often providing consumers with the ability to enter contests and access promotional offers. **Corporate websites** are important destination sites for consumers and the media that want to quickly access company and product information.

Social media marketing, discussed earlier in this chapter and in more detail in Chapter 13, refers to the use of online communities or social networks to openly interact within the communities by sharing ideas, activities, events, and offers. Social media marketing reaches

product placement
The inclusion of a product in a movie or TV program in return for payment

branded entertainment
The creation of an entertainment program, such as a TV episode, that is highly focused on a brand in exchange for payment

search engine marketing (SEM)
Includes the use of search engine optimization and pay-per-click advertising to market on search engines

search engine optimization (SEO)
Ensuring that websites are written, indexed, and coded so that they are highly rated and ranked by the search engines

microsites
Promotional websites created for short-term promotional purposes, often allowing consumers to enter contests and access promotional information

corporate websites
Websites that provide corporate and brand information to consumers and the media

> *Microsites are promotional websites created for short-term promotional purposes.*

out to consumers online through social networks where people connect with friends and contacts to share messages, comments, videos, and images as a form of self-expression. Facebook, YouTube, Pinterest, Instagram, LinkedIn, and Twitter are examples of popular social networks, with many niche social networks also existing, such as Last.fm for music lovers.

Affiliate marketing is the term used when companies promote their businesses through a network of online associates (affiliates) to drive traffic, leads, and purchases. Affiliates are provided with ads and links to the business website and rewarded with commissions for resultant business. Amazon and Indigo Books & Music use this business model, providing affiliates with online ads and links to display on their own websites or blogs.

Mobile marketing, also discussed earlier in this chapter and in more detail in Chapter 13, includes a set of practices that enables organizations to communicate and engage with target audiences in an interactive and relevant manner through any mobile device or network.

E-mail marketing includes the use of opt-in e-mail lists where consumers register and give permission to receive online communications. The Groupon phenomenon, mentioned earlier in this chapter, is such an example. The Canadian Marketing Association (CMA) strictly advises members not to use spam. **Permission-based e-mail** is when a recipient chooses to receive e-mail from a marketer, while **spam** is unsolicited e-mail that clutters the Internet.

Planning and Evaluation

Designing Marketing Communication Programs

LO 10 Marketing communications can be a fun yet daunting task for marketers. Its subjective nature and the ability of social media to make or break a campaign can make it unnerving. However, the creativity required to pull it together, and the ability of metrics to measure success, can make it rewarding.

Marketers turn to marketing communication experts to navigate this terrain. Communication agencies provide expertise on communication approaches with access to insights on new opportunities, consumer trends, and media research. They help guide strategy development, creative development, and media planning and buying, as well as program evaluation. Marketers shape the backdrop by providing company, product, and target market information, as well as insights into product positioning, previous campaigns, the competition, and budgetary constraints. They explain the balance between consumer and trade promotion, as well as how push and pull strategies are used. They are also involved in program creation and evaluation.

A **push strategy** is when marketers focus communication efforts on the distribution channel to gain support from retailers, distributors, and wholesalers through listings, sales, merchandising, featured pricing, and the inclusion in flyers. A **pull strategy** is when marketers focus communication efforts on ultimate consumers to build awareness, trial, and demand for a product. These approaches should work together (see Figure 12–9).

The Customer Advocacy Funnel

Marketers use integrated marketing communications approaches to ensure that all communication elements speak with the same messaging and use a shared visual platform. This approach involves developing, executing, and evaluating each element of a promotional program so that it encourages customers to become loyal supporters that spread positive messages. We call this *advocacy*.

The **Customer Advocacy Funnel** (Figure 12–10) encompasses the latest in marketing approaches where, over time, the positive connections that customers make with brands encourage them to become brand advocates who recommend the brand to others. This funnel has consumers moving from an initial awareness stage through to interest, engagement, trial, purchase, loyalty, and advocacy.

Let's look at the online environment to understand how marketers can use specific tools to drive customers through the funnel:

- **Awareness:** A company trying to raise online product awareness may use a website, search engine, and online display ads to drive consumers to a website for more information.

---

affiliate marketing
When companies promote their businesses through a network of online associates (affiliates) to drive traffic, leads, and purchases

e-mail marketing
The use of e-mail to market products

permission-based e-mail
When a recipient chooses to receive e-mail from a marketer

spam
Unsolicited e-mail

push strategy
When marketers focus communication on the distribution channel to gain support from retailers, distributors, and wholesalers

pull strategy
When marketers focus communication efforts on ultimate consumers to build awareness, trial, and demand for a product

Customer Advocacy Funnel
A communications approach that takes consumers down a path of initial product awareness through to brand advocacy

retargeted ads
Display ads that
ad networks redirect
to a computer's
IP address when
a consumer
previously clicked
on an ad but did
not respond to
its contents

Figure 12–9
Push and pull communication
strategies

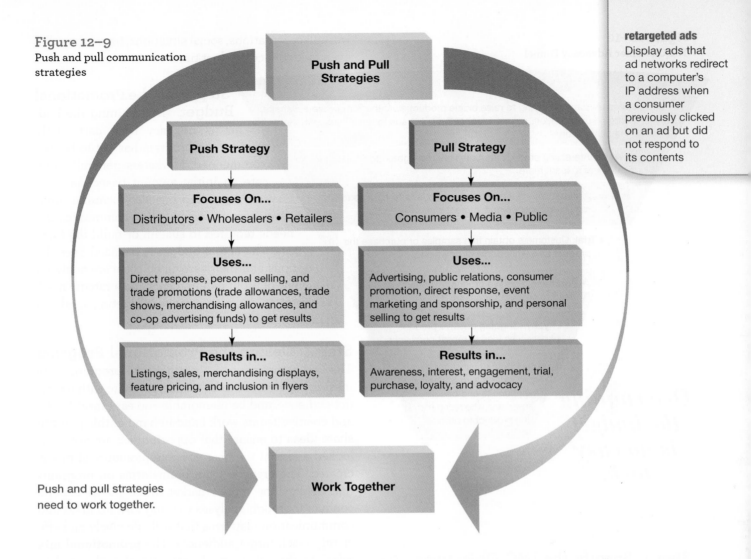

Push and Pull Strategies

Push Strategy

Focuses On...
Distributors • Wholesalers • Retailers

Uses...
Direct response, personal selling, and
trade promotions (trade allowances, trade
shows, merchandising allowances, and
co-op advertising funds) to get results

Results in...
Listings, sales, merchandising displays,
feature pricing, and inclusion in flyers

Pull Strategy

Focuses On...
Consumers • Media • Public

Uses...
Advertising, public relations, consumer
promotion, direct response, event
marketing and sponsorship, and personal
selling to get results

Results in...
Awareness, interest, engagement, trial,
purchase, loyalty, and advocacy

Work Together

Push and pull strategies
need to work together.

- **Interest:** A company may use online video to increase interest in the product, this time using experts to demo the product and add credibility.

- **Engagement:** Social media can be added to the mix to encourage engagement by using networks such as Facebook, YouTube, Pinterest, Instagram, and Twitter to deliver promotional messages.

- **Trial:** Contests, samples, free downloads, and limited trials can be communicated through microsites, social media networks, and display ads.

- **Purchase:** Search engine optimization, display ads, pay-per-click ads, e-mail campaigns, and retargeted display ads and apps can be used to prompt viewers to purchase products. **Retargeted ads** are display ads that are redirected to a computer's IP address when a consumer previously clicked on an ad but did not respond to its contents.

- **Loyalty:** Customer loyalty can be encouraged through CRM programs that reward continued purchases through loyalty programs. Social media can help encourage interaction with the brand.

- **Advocacy:** Ongoing communications, often one-to-one, through e-mail newsletters, social networks, branded communities, and blogs can solidify connections with loyal customers, providing them with information and experiences to share with others.

Steps in the Marketing Communications Process

Today, with the multitude of communication tools available, and consumers fragmented over a wide array of touch points, marketers follow an integrated approach to marketing communications, making sure all elements work together to reach specific target audiences. The steps in this process, outlined in Figure 12–11, require a marketer to (1) specify the IMC objectives, (2) identify the target audience, (3) set the promotional budget, (4) design the promotional program, (5) schedule and run the IMC elements, and (6) evaluate the program and recommend changes. These steps are explained below.

Figure 12–10
The Customer Advocacy Funnel

Figure 12–10
The Customer Advocacy Funnel

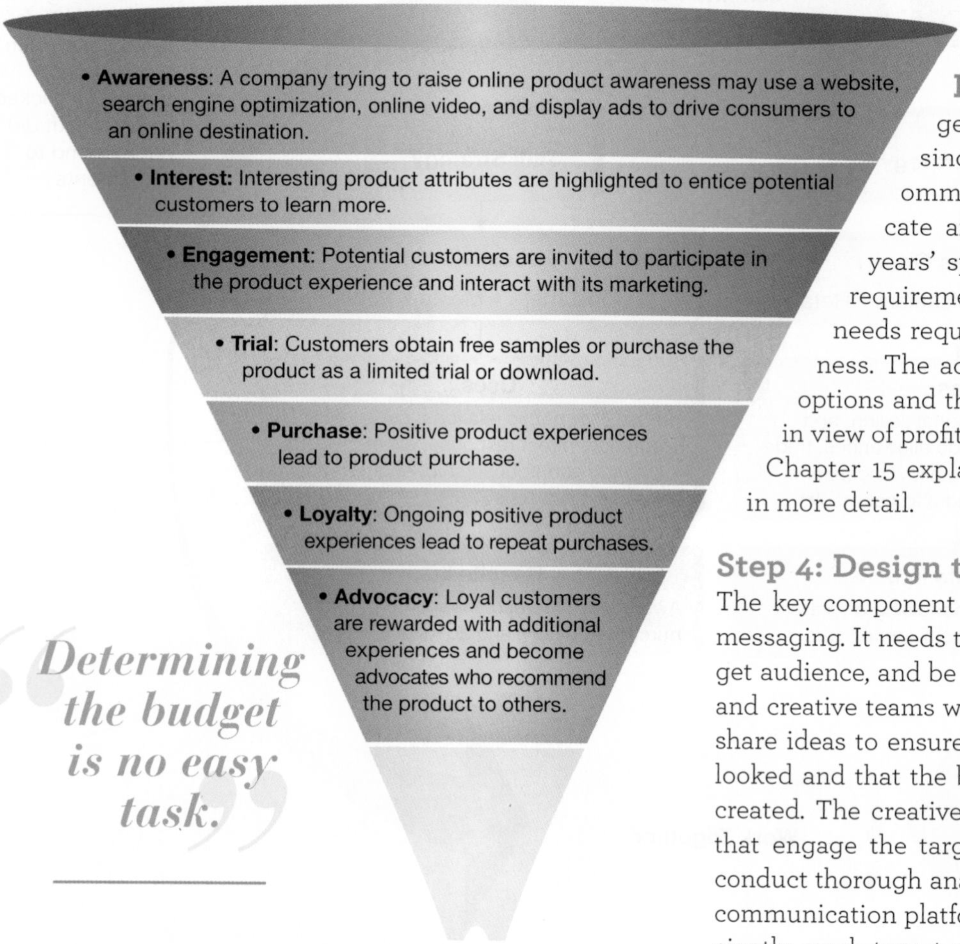

- **Awareness:** A company trying to raise online product awareness may use a website, search engine optimization, online video, and display ads to drive consumers to an online destination.

- **Interest:** Interesting product attributes are highlighted to entice potential customers to learn more.

- **Engagement:** Potential customers are invited to participate in the product experience and interact with its marketing.

- **Trial:** Customers obtain free samples or purchase the product as a limited trial or download.

- **Purchase:** Positive product experiences lead to product purchase.

- **Loyalty:** Ongoing positive product experiences lead to repeat purchases.

- **Advocacy:** Loyal customers are rewarded with additional experiences and become advocates who recommend the product to others.

> *Determining the budget is no easy task.*

workplace situations, social situations, travel time, and even face-to-face product time.

Step 3: Set the Promotional Budget

Determining the budget is no easy task, particularly since the program has yet to be recommended. Marketers generally allocate an initial amount based on prior years' spending but also examine profit requirements and the communication needs required to sustain or build the business. The actual budget is finalized once the options and their associated costs are analyzed in view of profit requirements and strategic need. Chapter 15 explains various budgeting methods in more detail.

Step 4: Design the Promotional Program

The key component of a promotional program is its messaging. It needs to be visible, resonate with its target audience, and be memorable—no easy task! Media and creative teams work hand-in-hand at this point to share ideas to ensure that opportunities are not overlooked and that the best possible promotional mix is created. The creative team brainstorms on programs that engage the target market, while media experts conduct thorough analyses to bring forward ideas and communication platforms that will effectively and efficiently reach target audiences. The **promotional mix** refers to the selection of promotional tools used to communicate with a target market. It can encompass online and offline approaches and include advertising, public relations, sales promotion, direct response, event marketing and sponsorship, and personal selling.

When determining the promotional program, marketers carefully consider their product's life cycle and the competitive nature of the market so that their programs are engaging, and meaningful to target markets (see Figure 12–12). Product life cycle considerations include the knowledge that during introductory stages, marketing communication builds awareness, provides information, and encourages trial. In the growth stage, promotional focus changes and starts to persuade and differentiate the brand from the competition. In the maturity stage, promotional efforts are designed as a reminder of the brand and to encourage repeat purchases through special offers. The decline stage often has little to no promotion at all.

Step 5: Schedule and Run the IMC Elements

The sequencing of promotional elements is carefully planned so that individual aspects seamlessly

Step 1: Specify the IMC Objectives

The first step formalizes the purpose of the promotional program, such as building brand awareness, creating customer engagement, or increasing brand loyalty. Specific numerical targets are often included at this point and used later to evaluate the program. The Customer Advocacy Funnel noted earlier may help determine these objectives.

Step 2: Identify the Target Audience

The second step pinpoints the audience that is to be targeted by the promotional program, identifying geographic, demographic, psychographic, and behavioural data. Media information is also provided, as well as insights on consumer touch points. **Consumer touch points** are the points of interaction that can be used to connect with consumers, including personal time in the home, shopping time,

consumer touch points
The points of interaction that can be used to connect with consumers, including personal time in the home, shopping time, workplace situations, social situations, travel time, and even face-to-face product time

promotional mix
The selection of promotional tools used to communicate with a target market

Figure 12–11
Steps in the marketing communications process

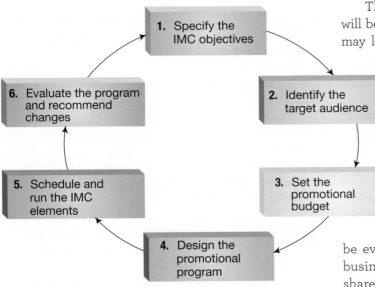

1. Specify the IMC objectives
2. Identify the target audience
3. Set the promotional budget
4. Design the promotional program
5. Schedule and run the IMC elements
6. Evaluate the program and recommend changes

work together to communicate with target audiences. Awareness is the prime concern of any program, built during its early stages with the subsequent rollout of different elements to support and develop the program. Throughout the campaign, marketers carefully monitor developments, particularly in social media, to immediately answer questions, respond to comments, and carefully deal with negative feedback.

Step 6: Evaluate the Program and Recommend Changes Promotional programs are evaluated on four levels. First, messaging is often evaluated before a program is fully developed to gauge responses so that adjustments can be made before launch.

Second, once the program is live, research may be fielded to measure campaign awareness and messaging elements such as *likeability, message comprehension,* and *attitude changes* toward the brand.

Third, upon completion, each individual element will be evaluated against expectations. Online aspects may look at impressions, click-throughs, unique visitors, page views, time on site, and return on investment (ROI). Social media campaigns may be evaluated on the basis of social mentions, buzz, shares, fans, and ROI. Public relations efforts may be measured on publicity mentions, media equivalency values, and ROI. Offline approaches may refer back to the *awareness, likeability, message comprehension,* and *attitude changes* mentioned earlier.

Fourth, the promotional program will be evaluated against its objectives. This will look at business results such as sales, profitability, market share, and return on investment (ROI).

All of these metrics will be used to determine campaign success and what elements can be strengthened in the future.

ask yourself

1. *What are the stages in the Customer Advocacy Funnel?*
2. *What approaches are used to set the promotional budget?*
3. *How are marketing communications programs evaluated?*

Figure 12–12
Product life cycle considerations for promotional programs

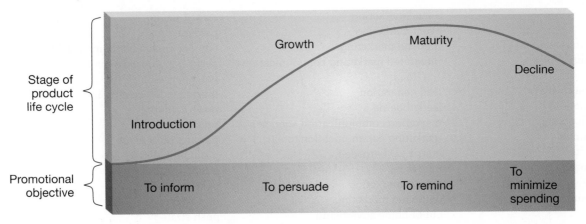

Stage of product life cycle

Introduction — Growth — Maturity — Decline

Promotional objective

To inform — To persuade — To remind — To minimize spending

Summary...just the facts

LO¹ ● New and evolving marketing communications approaches include (1) real-time marketing, (2) content marketing, (3) social media marketing, and (4) mobile marketing.

LO² ● The marketing communications industry consists of the media, marketing communications agencies, research companies, associations, and regulatory bodies.

● The marketing communications industry is regulated by Advertising Standards Canada (ASC), the Competition Bureau, the Canadian Radio-television and Telecommunications Commission (CRTC), the Canadian Marketing Association (CMA), and the Canadian Wireless Telecommunications Association (CWTA).

LO³ ● Marketing communications approaches can include inbound and outbound approaches with marketers commonly using an integrated marketing communications (IMC) approach.

● Marketing communication tools include advertising, public relations, sales promotion, direct response, event marketing and sponsorship, and personal selling.

LO⁴ ● Advertising media choices include Internet, TV, newspaper, magazine, radio, out-of-home, and mobile marketing.

LO⁵ ● Public relations initiatives include press releases, press conferences, special events, company reports, and the use of social media.

● Consumer promotional tools include contests, sweepstakes, samples, free trials, loyalty programs, rebates, bonus packs, and point-of-sale materials.

LO⁶ ● Trade promotions include trade shows, trade allowances, merchandising allowances, and co-op advertising.

LO⁷ ● Direct-response marketing tools include face-to-face selling, direct mail, catalogues, telemarketing, and direct-response advertising on TV, radio, and print, as well as e-mail marketing, online ads, and social media interactions.

● Event marketing and sponsorship refers to the involvement of a brand in an event through either an advertising package or on-site involvement.

LO⁸ ● The personal selling process consists of six stages: prospecting, pre-approach, approach, presentation, close, and follow-up.

● Alternative marketing communication approaches include word-of-mouth marketing, product placement, and branded entertainment.

LO⁹ ● Unique online approaches include the use of corporate websites, microsites, social networks, affiliate marketing, mobile marketing, and e-mail marketing, as well as search engine marketing (SEM) and search engine optimization (SEO).

LO¹⁰ ● The promotional planning process requires marketers to (1) specify the IMC objectives, (2) identify the target audience, (3) set the promotional budget, (4) design the promotional program, (5) schedule and run the IMC elements, and (6) evaluate the program and recommend changes.

● Evaluation approaches look at the program in general as well as each individual element.

Key Terms and Concepts...a refresher

advergaming
advertising
affiliate marketing
augmented reality (AR)
banner ads
branded entertainment
consumer promotions
consumer touch points
content marketing
corporate websites
Customer Advocacy Funnel
direct response
display advertising
earned media

e-mail marketing
event marketing
inbound marketing
integrated marketing communications (IMC)
lead generation
leaderboards
marketing communication agencies
marketing communication tools
matrix 2D barcode
microsites
mobile marketing
outbound marketing
out-of-home advertising

owned media
paid media
pay-per-click advertising (PPC)
permission-based e-mail
personal selling
pre-roll video advertising
press conference
press release
product placement
promotional mix
public relations
publicity
pull strategy
push strategy

real-time marketing
relationship selling
retargeted ads
sales promotion
search engine marketing (SEM)
search engine optimization (SEO)

skyscrapers
social media marketing
social media release
social networks
spam
sponsorship

trade promotions
traffic generation
user-generated content (UGC)
word-of-mouth marketing

Hands-on...*apply your knowledge*

Promotion Assignment Assume that Western Union wishes to create a new IMC campaign that focuses on the same target audience but wants to increase participation by testing a promotion during the summer months. Review the opening vignette on Western Union and the varied marketing communications approaches discussed in this chapter.

Brainstorm on an IMC campaign for the summer months and outline the following factors: (1) IMC objectives, (2) target market profile, (3) central promotional idea, (4) recommended promotional mix, and (5) how the promotion will be evaluated. Assume that your promotional budget is similar to that from the previous campaign.

Chapter Vignette...*reminder*

This chapter's opening vignette examines Western Union's "Spread the Cheer" campaign. Answer the Reality Check questions at the end of the vignette by carefully reading this chapter's section on marketing communications tools.

Video Clip...*questions*

Review the video *Next Generation Day* from the CONNECT website to get a glimpse inside this event. Answer the following questions:

▶ Video
Next
Generation
Day

- What is the benefit of attending this event?
- What element of this event do you think will provide the most insights to students?

Infographic...*data analysis*

Review the Infographic that details information on the *Ski Canada* magazine and navigate to its website at **http://skicanadamag.com** to see issues of its magazines and

updated infographics. Based on the data you retrieve, determine a list of potential advertisers that may be appropriate for this publication.

Chapter 13

mobile marketing and social media marketing

LEARNING OBJECTIVES

LO¹ Explain mobile marketing and its approaches

LO² Describe the tools involved in mobile marketing

LO³ Outline the best practices and regulations that guide mobile marketing

LO⁴ Explain social media marketing and its tools

LO⁵ Outline the main social networks used in social media marketing

LO⁶ List the best practices in social media marketing

Have you ever wondered who came up with the app you just downloaded—how and why they came up with the idea? The answers are many, but for mobile marketing tools, we need look no further than Toronto digital agency Rich Media, which creates easy-to-use mobile marketing tools and websites that make consumers' lives a little easier. Whether this is with a TV selector tool, a home-buying app, or a mortgage calculator, Rich Media knows how to make the complicated simple. This is why Rich Media is one of the go-to digital marketers for companies like Scotiabank and Samsung in Canada.

Rich Media sets itself apart in the mobile marketing space through a solid foundation of 20 years' experience in new media and the fact that it creates innovative projects with an in-house approach to building clients' business. Its expertise lies in designing interactive website discovery tools, apps, mobile web, and video animation that go beyond client expectations to tell stories that engage.

Clients turn to Rich Media for its ability to quickly take projects from start to finish, including strategy development, creative design, technology adaptation, and in-house testing—all with high levels of customer service that they call the *Rich Experience*. The Rich Experience involves the agency going above and beyond with all its interactions, whether this be with couriers, video extras, its staff, or its clients. The Rich Experience is memorable, positive, fun, playful, personal, and professional.

Rich Media's approach ensures that projects are not farmed out to specialists, but instead created by its own lean team of carefully selected designers, coders, writers, videographers, and client services experts who share the same space to collaborate on projects. This ensures that the best work is created and exceeds client expectations. If a technical problem surfaces, or a client suggests an opportunity, no one needs to track down an expert in another organization. Instead, a walk across the hallway lands you with the in-house experts who can quickly resolve problems and discuss opportunities.

richmedia
www.richmedia.com

Chapter Outline:

Jake Rich, president and founder of Rich Media, explains that every project at Rich Media must adhere to its three-pillar approach of strategy, creativity, and technology. First, projects must meet the objectives and strategies set out at the start in the creative brief. Second, they must uniquely engage users and tell a client's story. Third, they must use technology to make the customer journey easier and more memorable through intuitive, interactive, and informative tools. Its agile approach includes strategy, creativity, and technology all wrapped up in one to achieve excellent results. Rich Media's clients include, among others, Scotiabank, Samsung, and Sun Life Financial, as well as ING Direct, TD Insurance, Great West Life, and RBC Financial Group.

"Mobile has disrupted marketing as a new and interactive communication channel. It connects, it informs, and it communicates, all in one," explains Rich. "Often, people are hung up on technology and miss the opportunity it presents—the opportunity to engage, to experience, and to communicate to individuals on their personal devices." He explains that intrusion is not welcome on mobile devices, and so marketers must learn to engage customers to be invited into their coveted mobile space. Rich does not see technology as mobile's biggest challenge, but instead points to understanding how consumers use the technology and how it is changing cultural norms. Mobile devices are always on, consumers are always connected, and marketers must learn how to communicate across these new and exciting channels.

We look to Scotiabank and Samsung, two of Rich Media's clients, to gain an understanding into the mobile space and how Rich Media has created mobile experiences that help build business. The Scotiabank Dream Home Finder is a mobile application for prospective home buyers that makes house hunting easier and more enjoyable. Instead of home buyers muddling through stacks of feature sheets and trying to recall the homes they have visited, the Scotiabank Dream Home Finder cleverly organizes all elements on a computer or mobile device. On a mobile device, people merely download the free app and, in a few short minutes, register to set up a profile that includes required home features (number of bedrooms and bathrooms, price ranges, etc.) as well as important locations such as work, schools, gyms, and babysitters. Then, as prospective homes are visited, the user uploads photos of the homes and adds information on addresses, price points, features, and personal notes for future reference. The app automatically plots the properties on Google Maps in relation to important locations and then rates the prospective homes based on the originally selected features. A report can then be printed or viewed on the mobile device. The app also includes a simple mortgage calculator and a list of Scotiabank specialists who can be contacted for mortgage advice.

"The beauty of this tool is its simplicity," states Rich. "We wanted to ensure that users were not weighed down by complicated registrations or confusing interfaces. It's all very intuitive and helps any house hunter—whether they are Scotiabank clients or just casual browsers—more easily find a home. Its integration with Google Maps and mobile images makes it very useful, and having a comparison tool to assess different properties is highly rated." The Scotiabank Dream Home Finder fits into Rich Media's three business pillars—strategy, creativity, and technology. It creatively uses new technology to help clients more enjoyably go through the daunting house-hunting process and to easily envision their lives in a new location.

The Scotiabank Dream Home Finder took Rich Media a number of months to design to its high standards and since then it has been enhanced and periodically updated to keep pace with operating systems, the real estate industry, as well as new mobile devices for iOS, Android, and BlackBerry. The mobile space requires constant attention to ensure that applications remain compatible with updated software and hardware. The Scotiabank Dream Home Finder is a free application and desktop destination that comes in English and French.

The Samsung TV selector tool is another Rich Media project that helps make consumer decision-making easier and more enjoyable. It was born out of a need to make TV purchasing easier for consumers who are confused about LED and plasma options. Rich Media turned to its three pillars and created a tool that takes the pain out of the purchase with the Samsung HDTV and Sound Solution Selector, which is strategic and creative, and uses technology to tell a story. Consumers simply answer a few questions on a computer or mobile device about TV location, room dimensions, lighting, TV usage, pricing, and Internet applications. This results in a TV recommendation from Samsung that includes TV features, pricing, and size. These suggestions can then be shared with friends via e-mail, Twitter, or Facebook to solicit advice. This tool has been very successful for Samsung, helping it stay top-of-mind with consumers on their path-to-purchase.

Rich leaves us with a few final thoughts to consider on our journey to learn about mobile marketing. He wants students to understand that mobile is merely a step in the development of the digitally connected world; it allows consumers to more richly explore and connect with marketers and brands. Separately, he advises students to follow their passions, to work hard, to use their creativity to engage with others, and to follow their dreams. Rich Media was born out

of his desire to run his own business, as well as his passion for design, creativity, and technology. Now, a motivated team of digital experts create the Rich Experience at Rich Media with annual growth rates of over 20 percent. Thank you, Jake Rich![1]

► Video
Rich Media

reality CHECK ✓

As you read Chapter 13, refer back to the Rich Media opening vignette on mobile marketing to answer the following questions:

- Why is it important that the Samsung TV selector tool be mobile-friendly?
- Download the Scotiabank Dream Home Finder app and identify what mobile marketing tools and social media marketing tools are used to engage users.

Mobile Marketing and Social Media Marketing

Mobile marketing and social media marketing are two rapidly evolving areas in marketing, and a marketer needs to understand how consumers and marketers use them to stay connected and engaged. Today, consumers connect with each other and to brands using social media, whether this is with Facebook to locate an offer, Twitter to lodge a complaint, or various other social networks to stay connected with friends. Mobile marketing is often the platform consumers use to reach out on social networks, checking statuses and posting updates to share with friends throughout the day and on the go. Marketers in turn connect brands with consumers on these networks and use mobile marketing approaches to reach consumers on mobile devices, whether this be on a smartphone, tablet, e-reader, or other handheld mobile device. The penetration of mobile devices is rapidly increasing in Canada, and so marketers are engaging consumers on this platform in multiple ways that engage and inform.

This chapter is designed to provide students with an understanding of how mobile marketing and social media are used for marketing purposes. We start with

mobile marketing, explaining the approaches used, and move into social media, again touching on the ways it is used by marketers so that brands make connections with consumers.

The Mobile Marketing Landscape

The Mobile Market

LO 1 Mobile has become a driving force in marketing, a central connector to other forms of media. It is used by consumers to communicate, to gather information, and to be entertained. It is a pillar in a multi-screen era where consumers connect in and out of home using portable devices such as tablets and cellphones, and use them to complement desktop/laptop usage and TV viewing. Mobile devices are no longer accessories, but tools that help manage the daily bustle.

Global data tells us that in 2013, smartphones and tablets reached over 1.5 billion devices worldwide to surpass laptops and desktop computers.[2] Unlike other platforms, mobile devices are personal, portable, and usually on. They accompany us in the home, at work, and into our social spaces. They help manage our lives in real time, letting us access messages, set reminders, e-mail, text, and update calendars. They entertain us with photo apps, video viewing, and social networking. They help us find local restaurants, read product reviews, and shop for products.

Importantly, people use mobile devices to help in the path-to-purchase. People check mobile devices multiple times a day, providing numerous touch points for marketers to engage on this journey. Whether gathering information, evaluating alternatives, interacting with a brand, checking recommendations, or making a purchase, mobile devices are used to help in the path-to-purchase, even if this is just to create a final shopping list. People may start by researching a product on a smartphone on the go, then gravitate to a tablet for better viewing at home, and eventually purchase the product online from a laptop or add it to a shopping list to purchase from a bricks-and-mortar store. Unlike other marketing tools, mobile marketing allows marketers to communicate directly with consumers at the point-of-purchase, which can be persuasive and compelling.

Smartphones and tablets reached over 1.5 billion devices worldwide to surpass laptops and desktop computers.

We find that mobile marketing budgets currently lag behind the opportunities that exist in this area, partly due to its newness and to a lack of understanding of the tools and standard practices. Over time, mobile marketing spending is expected to increase substantially to meet consumers in this space, as it did with Internet marketing.[3]

Mobile marketing is defined by the Mobile Marketing Association (MMA) as a set of practices that enables organizations to communicate and engage with their audiences in an interactive and relevant manner through any mobile device or network.[4] Mobile marketing refers to the use of mobile devices that can connect to the Internet, such as cellphones, tablets, e-readers, handheld gaming devices, or portable MP3 players, to communicate with consumers.

Elements in the mobile marketer's toolkit are the mobile web, mobile apps, mobile advertising, mobile sales promotional tools, and proximity marketing practices, which are discussed later in the chapter.

Mobile Devices

The mobile industry is complex due to the wide range of handsets, screen sizes, operating systems, browsers, and products that exist in this space. Devices include feature phones, smartphones, tablets, Internet-enabled handheld gaming devices, Internet-enabled MP3 players, and e-readers, not to mention wearable devices such as Google Glass, the Apple Watch, and the Pebble Smartwatch. Growth is currently driven by smartphones and tablets, but wearable devices are expected to increase in popularity once privacy issues are overcome.

A **feature phone** is a cellphone that is Internet-enabled and that allows for e-mailing, texting, and browsing, but unlike smartphones, it cannot download or use apps.[5] Feature phones tend to be cheaper and make the mobile landscape more complex as they are often built with their own unique technology, which makes consistent viewing across all devices difficult.

A **smartphone** is a more advanced cellphone that uses cutting-edge applications and sophisticated operating systems to function like a mobile personal computer. It has the capability to call, text, e-mail, browse the Internet, listen to music, take photos and video, watch videos, and use apps to enhance its features and capabilities. Smartphones tend to have larger screens.

A wide range of mobile devices complicates mobile marketing.

mobile marketing

A set of practices that enables organizations to communicate and engage with their audiences in an interactive and relevant manner through any mobile device or network

feature phones

Cellphones that are Internet-enabled and that allow for e-mailing, texting, and browsing but cannot download or use apps

smartphones

Advanced cellphones that use cutting-edge applications and sophisticated operating systems to function like a mobile personal computer

Figure 13–1
Smartphone platform market share in Canada

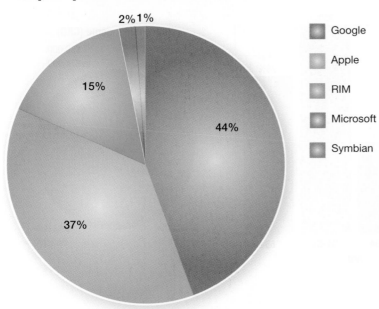

Legend:
- Google
- Apple
- RIM
- Microsoft
- Symbian

Pie chart values: 44%, 37%, 15%, 2%, 1%

Google with its Android platform leads the market in smartphones.

Source: "Canada Digital Future in Focus 2014," comScore, April 2014. Accessed at www.comscore.com/Insights/Presentations-and-Whitepapers/2014/2014-Canada-Digital-Future-in-Focus. Used with permission.

Top 10 Activities on a Smartphone

Activity	Percent
Took a photo or video	86%
Used e-mail or messaging	85%
Browsed the Internet	81%
Used a search engine	78%
Used an app	76%
Accessed directions/maps	76%
Connected to a social network	72%
Played a game	71%
Conducted a product search	68%
Listened to music	66%

Source: "Our Mobile Planet: Canada Understanding the Mobile Consumer," Ipsos MediaCT, May 2013, accessed at www.thinkwithgoogle.com/mobileplanet/en.

From a platform perspective, there are three main mobile device platforms in Canada (Figure 13–1): Android (Google), iOS (Apple), and BlackBerry. In the smartphone market in Canada, Android is the market leader with a 44 percent market share, followed by Apple at 37 percent, and BlackBerry at 15 percent.[6]

In 2013, there were almost 28 million mobile subscribers in Canada, with numbers expected to climb over the next few years (Figure 13–2). Data plans are used by over 47 percent of subscribers, and tablets are owned by 20 percent of cellphone users. Smartphone penetration in Canada has reached over 75 percent and continues to climb.[7]

Consumers and Mobile Devices

Canadian demographic data (Figure 13–3) tells us that consumers who use mobile devices are almost equally male and female (49 and 51 percent, respectively), with two-thirds between the ages of 18 and 55 years and an annual household income over $50 thousand.[8]

Research from Internet analytics company comScore reveals that electronic devices play different roles throughout the day. A typical consumer starts the day at home checking e-mails on a smartphone, uses a desktop or laptop computer at work for business purposes, and returns home in the evening where relaxation often occurs in front of a TV, with a tablet and smartphone close at hand to respond to text messages, connect on social media, surf the Internet, and check apps. At all times during the day, a smartphone is close at hand for personal communication and is on.[9] People have become device agnostic, switching seamlessly between

Figure 13–2
Mobile subscribers—Canada (millions)

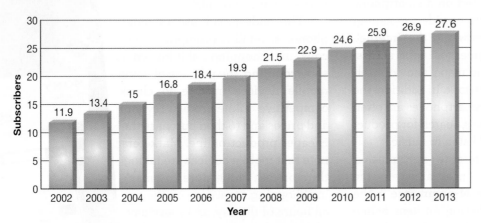

Bar chart data (Subscribers vs. Year):
- 2002: 11.9
- 2003: 13.4
- 2004: 15
- 2005: 16.8
- 2006: 18.4
- 2007: 19.9
- 2008: 21.5
- 2009: 22.9
- 2010: 24.6
- 2011: 25.9
- 2012: 26.9
- 2013: 27.6

The number of mobile subscribers is growing rapidly in Canada.

Source: Canadian Wireless Telecommunications Association, "Facts & Figures: Wireless phone subscribers in Canada," accessed from http://cwta.ca/facts-figures.

Figure 13–3
Canadian mobile demographic breakdown

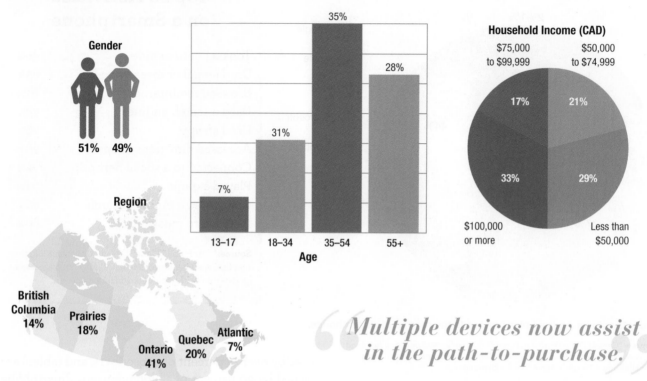

Gender
51%   49%

Age
13–17: 7%
18–34: 31%
35–54: 35%
55+: 28%

Household Income (CAD)
$75,000 to $99,999: 17%
$50,000 to $74,999: 21%
$100,000 or more: 33%
Less than $50,000: 29%

Region
British Columbia 14%
Prairies 18%
Ontario 41%
Quebec 20%
Atlantic 7%

> *Multiple devices now assist in the path-to-purchase.*

Source: "2013 Canada Digital Future in Focus," comScore, March 2013, accessed at www.comscore.com/Insights/Presentations_and_Whitepapers/2013/2013_Canada_Digital_Future_in_Focus. Used with permission.

devices depending on location, circumstance, and device availability.

Looking at smartphone usage, the 2013 Canadian study by Ipsos MediaCT for Google Canada, "Our Mobile Planet: Canada," notes that the top activities conducted on a smartphone are taking a photo or video, e-mailing or messaging, browsing the Internet, using search engines and apps, accessing directions and maps, and connecting to a social network. In addition, the study notes that smartphones are often used to play games, search for product information, and listen to music.[10]

When it comes to m-commerce, multiple devices now assist in the path-to-purchase. **M-commerce** is the process of purchasing an item online through a mobile device. Smartphones may initially help consumers research products and gather information, while final transactions are finally completed in-store, or online on a tablet or personal computer. While consumer attitudes are expected to change, current research from Quorus Consulting Group on consumer attitudes to cellphone usage notes that only 32 percent of respondents would use a mobile device for banking, 28 percent for m-commerce, with only 24 percent positively viewing mobile wallets. **Mobile wallets** are apps that allow users to store payment and loyalty information on mobile devices to then swipe at retail.[11]

The widespread use of smartphones at retail is prompting a new consumer shopping habit known as **showrooming**, the practice of using mobile devices in-store to check competitive online product reviews and prices and to then purchase the cheaper product online. Marketers note that mobile devices are taking the store out of the store and making shopping accessible on the go, all hours of the day, and every day of the week.

What is "showrooming"?

m-commerce
The process of purchasing an item online through a mobile device

mobile wallets
Apps that store payment and loyalty information on a mobile device that can be then be swiped or tapped at retail

showrooming
The practice of using mobile devices in-store to check competitive online product reviews and prices and to then purchase the cheaper product online.

Infographic

Smartphone Usage Canada

Our Mobile Planet Research

OurMobilePlanet.com is an annual global study on smartphone usage and attitudes that started in 2011.

OurMobilePlanet.com

Commissioned by Google and conducted by Ipsos *MediaCT* and TNS *Intratest* in conjunction with the Mobile Marketing Association and the Interactive Advertising Bureau.

Number of Apps on Smartphone

Over **40** countries surveyed

1,000 Canadians polled annually

Bar chart — Number of Apps on Smartphone (y-axis 0 to 40), x-axis Canada Country:
- 30
- 12
- 8

Canada – Top Activities Conducted on a Smartphone

- E-mailed/messaged **85%**
- Took photo/video **86%**
- Browsed the Internet **81%**
- Connected to a social network **72%**
- Accessed directions/maps **76%**
- Used a search engine **78%**
- Used an app **76%**

Activities on Smartphone – Canada 2013

Bar chart (% on y-axis, 0 to 100):

Activity	%
Used an app	76
Browsed the Internet	81
Purchased a product or service	39
Accessed a social network	72
E-mailed/messaged	85
Watched videos on a video-sharing website	65
Read news on newspaper or magazine portals	51
Looked up directions or used a map	76
Took a photo or video	86
Listened to music	66
Played games	71
Online-banking or other finance-related activities	57

Source: "Our Mobile Planet: Canada Understanding the Mobile Consumer," Ipsos MediaCT, May 2013; data charts accessed at www.thinkwithgoogle.com/mobileplanet/en.

---

ask yourself

1. *What is mobile marketing?*

2. *How does consumer behaviour differ on mobile devices throughout the day?*

3. *What is showrooming?*

Mobile Marketing Tools

LO² Mobile marketing provides marketers with a platform for one-to-one personalized communications where targeting can be more precise, not only demographically but also by device, by interest, and in real time by exact location. Marketers note that consumers carefully guard their mobile devices and are reticent to invite marketers in. However, market research also points out that consumer brand attitudes improve when mobile marketing is used to send reminders, deliver offers, or provide free useful tools such as apps, organizers, shopping lists, or calendars.[12] Marketers are therefore advised to follow best practices, provide added value through non-disruptive mobile marketing approaches, show respect for the privacy of the mobile user, and in all instances, follow regulatory guidelines and ethical approaches. Remember that in most instances, consumers need to opt-in to receive mobile messaging, so unless a mobile marketer can provide exceptional value and interest, a marketer will not be invited in.

Here we examine the mobile marketing tools that are used to engage consumers: mobile web, mobile applications, mobile advertising, mobile sales promotional tools, and proximity marketing.

> *Consumers carefully guard their mobile devices and are reticent to invite marketers in.*

Mobile Web

Websites that render on mobile devices need to be fast and functional and easier to use than a brand's desktop website. People do not want to scroll across screens on small mobile devices or pinch and zoom to read content. Mobile websites are created and designed for the smaller mobile screen with screens that load quickly, display clearly, and offer unique mobile features that satisfy the goal-oriented mobile user. **Mobile web** is when a website is designed for the smaller screens of mobile devices.

Companies use one of three approaches with mobile web. They either optimize a desktop website for the mobile web by using responsive design platforms that use flexible layouts, flexible images, and flexible file options so that websites automatically adjust and resize to render on mobile devices. Alternatively, they can design separate mobile websites with streamlined content and finger- and thumb-friendly navigation. The third option uses a combination of these approaches. Some companies will create three different interfaces: one for a desktop site, which is information rich; one for tablets, which has heavy image-based content; and one for cellphones, which has less content and fewer images.

Mobile Applications (Apps)

Mobile applications (apps) are software programs designed for mobile devices so that with a quick tap or click, they engage with information, entertainment, or other forms of interactivity. The Canadian Marketing Association's mobile marketing task force flags the importance of apps, quoting data that indicates app stores have over 22 billion downloads, 90 percent of them free. Apple's App Store and Google's Play store each boast over 1 million apps, a huge leap from July 2008 when Apple launched the first app store.[13] The Gartner Institute predicts that by 2016, brand apps will be used more often than brand websites.[14]

Research reveals that 70 percent of smartphone users in Canada download apps, resulting in 30 apps per device. Only 12 apps are used regularly.[15] The

Popularity of Apps in Canada

Type of App	Used by Percent of Smartphone Users
Weather	84%
Social networking/instant messaging/blogs	79%
Travel/transit/navigation/mapping	73%
YouTube	64%
Gaming	61%
News	53%

Source: "2012 Cell Phone Consumer Attitudes Study," Le groupe Conseil Quorus Consulting group, April 23, 2012, accessed at http://cwta.ca/facts-figures.

most popular apps are for weather, social networking/messaging/blogs, travel/transit/navigation/maps, YouTube, gaming, and news.[16]

Apps are highly rated when they are free, are quick to download, are simple to use, do not crash, clearly explain updates, and are available across platforms.[17] Apps need to have added functionality over a website, and the Scotiabank Dream Home Finder, discussed in this chapter's opening vignette, is an example of such an app, with exceptional functionality over its website.

Apps can be free or paid, and can also host ads, sell products, or just provide content. They are downloaded from online device-specific app stores. App developers pay small annual fees to these app stores, and typically pay 30 percent commission to the app stores from the revenues generated from the app (downloads, product sales, or ad revenues).

Technically, three types of apps can be created for marketing programs: (1) native apps, (2) web apps, or (3) hybrid apps. Depending on the choice, the app creation can become more or less expensive for marketers. For the end user, it is the app functionality that is important, and most users will not understand the nuances between these types of apps. Marketers, however, need to understand the differences.

- **Native apps** are created specifically to be hosted and run on a mobile device. They are downloaded from app stores and reside on mobile devices. They can provide a rich experience by interacting with mobile features such as the device's GPS, camera,

> *The most popular apps are for weather.*

▶ *"Follow your passions, work hard, and be creative."*

—Jake Rich, president and founder, Rich Media

web apps
Websites designed to simulate an app experience by placing a shortcut that runs off a browser on a mobile device

hybrid apps
Apps that combine the functionality of native apps with the flexibility of web apps

or notification system. They can also work offline. Technology differences dictate that separate native apps need to be designed for iOS, Android, Windows, and BlackBerry devices. This can be an expensive undertaking.

- **Web apps** are websites designed to simulate a native app experience. They run off browsers rather than the actual mobile device, and ask users to add a shortcut to the home screen. These apps are not hosted on the mobile device, or accessed through an app store as they run off a browser. They can therefore run on any platform, making them cheaper to develop. The user experience is not as rich as on a native app, as these apps do not interact with the mobile device features, such as its GPS or image files. These apps do not pay app store developer fees or require app store approval. They do not share revenue with the app stores.

- **Hybrid apps** combine the superior functionality of a native app with the flexibility of a web app. They can interact with mobile features, but render in a browser and so can be used across mobile platforms with minimal changes and therefore lower costs. Hybrid apps are generally cheaper to develop than native apps as they require minimal development changes for cross-platform use. Typically, hybrid apps do not provide the same rich experience as native apps, but they are becoming increasingly popular.[18]

Marketers use apps in various ways to engage with users. For example, Chipotle Mexican Grill created a fun Chipotle Scarecrow game app, Virgin Mobile created a Selfserve app to view phone usage and pay phone bills, Twitter created an app to conveniently provide its service on the go, and Starbucks has an app for its payment card and loyalty card. Other marketers use apps to provide functionality and to also generate

revenue. For example, the Weather Network and the 680News apps both sell advertising space on their apps to marketers, while Groupon sells discounted offers directly from its app that have been negotiated with local small businesses.

The Marketing NewsFlash, "Apps Are Not Just for Consumers," describes how apps can be used in the B2B market. Figure 13–4 offers a checklist that marketers should consider when working with mobile application developers to create apps.

Mobile Advertising

Advertising that renders on mobile devices is a small but rapidly growing area of mobile marketing. It can help build brand awareness and positive interactions with brands. In 2013, mobile advertising in Canada almost tripled from the previous year to reach $443 million, an increase of 177 percent versus the previous year. These revenue leaps are expected to grow exponentially over the next decade due to the rapid adoption of smartphones and tablets, the standardization of mobile ad sizes, the use of mobile ad networks, the growth in mobile analytics platforms, and the implementation of best practices.[19]

Research tells us that mobile ads are viewed positively when they are timely, relevant, and engaging, and provide information that answers questions, solves problems, or facilitates decision-making. They are negatively received when they take up too much screen space, interfere with the user's online activity, appear harmful to the device, or are unclear.[20] Marketers should therefore tread cautiously in this area to ensure that messaging is not disruptive and intrusive, but instead is useful and viewed positively.

Advertising options on mobile devices include placing displays ads on highly trafficked mobile-optimized websites, or placing ads within third

Figure 13–4
App developer's checklist

- ☑ Determine the purpose of the app.
- ☑ Outline the functionality of the app.
- ☑ Identify how consumers will use the app.
- ☑ Estimate the frequency of app updates.
- ☑ Decide what mobile platforms will be used.
- ☑ Establish what app analytics will be used to measure success.
- ☑ Finalize how the app will be marketed.

Apps Are Not Just for Consumers

Business apps can boost productivity in the B2B market.

I f you thought apps were just for consumers, think again. In November 2013, Salesforce, the world's leader in customer relationship management tools (over 620,000 clients in over 125 countries), launched its Salesforce1 Customer Platform so that business customers can access updates and data, and communicate on the go to better connect with clients. The Salesforce1 Customer Platform also allows developers to create their own business-facing apps that target businesses that are built on the Salesforce1 platform, and to integrate them into company programs, connecting apps, devices, and data together in one place.

Compatible across Android and iOS platforms, Salesforce1 provides real-time access to critical business information at all times using the cloud to offer downloadable business apps through its Salesforce AppExchange platform. Agents can collaborate,

communities can help each other, and users can search a knowledge bank to help troubleshoot problems to deliver outstanding customer service. Salesforce1 is generally included with user licences of Salesforce CRM and the Salesforce Platform.

This approach is no surprise, considering Salesforce's forward-thinking approach to helping

Salesforce provides marketers with many data management and data analytics tools.

businesses put their customers first by becoming more mobile and social. Salesforce calls this revolution the Internet of Customers, whereby companies can be more productive by connecting employees, partners, and products, as needed, from anywhere, at any time, and on any device. Salesforce believes that the Internet of Customers is the future and that the brands that get there first will win the hearts and minds of consumers everywhere.[21]

▶ Video
Salesforce

Questions

1. What business practices and consumer expectations do you think prompted Salesforce to create a business app for its customers?

2. What general benefits can apps bring to business users?

> *Marketers should ensure that mobile ad messaging is not disruptive and intrusive, but instead is useful and viewed positively.*

party apps such as the Weather Network app, which delivers ads for many companies such as Tim Hortons with its Find a Tims location finder or Starbucks with

its Discover Your Favourite Flavour tool. Pay-per-click mobile ads can also be placed around mobile search results, and mobile video ads can be created to appear as pre-roll video ads that are seen before watching a video on a mobile device.

An example of how marketers meticulously design ads for mobile devices and carefully select the appropriate devices to deliver their advertising message can be seen with the *Toronto Star* website properties:

- The *Toronto Star* desktop site at **www.thestar.com** hosts display ads for Porter Airlines with discounted airfares appearing in leaderboards across the top as well as in big box ads on the right that lead to the Porter Airlines website.

mobile messaging
Comes in the form of common short codes (CSC), short messaging services (SMS), multimedia messaging services (MMS), e-mail messaging, in-person voice phone calls, and voice messaging

common short codes (CSC)
Dedicated short messaging codes of typically five to six digits that are used to trigger subscriptions, donations, alerts, or downloads, or to access promotional content

- The *Toronto Star* mobile site for cellphones at **http://m.thestar.com** has no ads on its home page. Instead, small leaderboard banner ads appear at the top of the screen when articles are selected for reading. Bell Canada and local car dealerships are placing ads on these web pages.

- The *Toronto Star* tablet site at **http://read.thestar.com** has no visible advertising within the site except for a sponsorship reference to the **HelloBC.com** website on the landing page, where readers are invited to go to the tablet or desktop version of the site. Periodically, after reading articles on a tablet, a full-screen transitional ad appears for **HelloBC.com**. The ad shows snow-covered mountains with an interactive skier that readers can drag down the mountain by using their fingers on a touch screen. This results in an invitation to go to **www.SkiItToBelieveIt.com** for further information.

The Weather Network app is very popular in Canada.

This experience could not have been duplicated on the desktop *Toronto Star* website or on its cellphone interface.

Mobile Sales Promotional Tools

Sales promotions provide short-term incentives for people to interact with brands whether through a discount, an offer, or another form of engagement. These elements can be communicated through the advertising approaches mentioned above, but in the mobile space, other more-direct tools can encourage engagement and interaction. In the sales promotion space, mobile marketers can use mobile messaging, matrix 2D barcodes, and proximity marketing approaches. Common examples include text message alerts, app notifications, mobile loyalty card storage, and various mobile downloads (mobile coupons, wallpapers, ringtones, and games).

Mobile Messaging **Mobile messaging** comes in five forms. There are (1) common short codes (CSC), (2) short messaging services (SMS), (3) multimedia messaging services (MMS), (4) e-mail messaging, and (5) in-person voice phone calls and voice messaging. SMS is experiencing rapid growth in Canada with 96.5 billion SMS person-to-person text messages sent in 2012, a 24 percent increase over 2011 levels. MMS messaging is also booming, with 636 million MMS sent in 2012, a 95 percent increase over 2011 levels, with 2013 data showing an average 3.5 million MMS messages sent in Canada per day.[22]

Common short codes (CSC) are dedicated short messaging codes of typically five to six digits that trigger subscriptions, donations, alerts, or downloads, or the ability to access promotional content. Mobile

Canadian Wireless
Telecommunications Association

Checkout the Canadian Wireless Telecommunications Association at **http://cwta.ca/**.

ask yourself

1. *What types of apps exist and how do they differ?*

2. *What are common short codes (CSC) and how are they used in mobile marketing?*

3. *What forms of advertising are used on mobile devices?*

marketers often use these codes in conjunction with keywords to involve consumers in a program. CSC numbers are provided by the Canadian Wireless Telecommunications Association (CWTA). There are numerous examples of CSC programs in Canada, such as the Weather Network that for $3 per month allows people to subscribe to text message weather alerts. Charitable foundations also use CSC programs in Canada to fund-raise for disaster relief. In 2013, the Canadian Red Cross raised disaster relief funds for the Philippines with this approach; mobile subscribers texted REDCROSS to 30333 to automatically donate $5, which was added to their cellphone bills.

CSC programs are administered by the Canadian Wireless Telecommunications Association, which charges for its services and provides strict guidelines that must be followed. Failure to abide by these regulations can result in substantial penalties. For example, in 2012, the Competition Bureau started legal proceedings against Bell Canada, Rogers Communications Inc., TELUS Corporation, and the CWTA for misleading consumers with premium texting services that did not adequately disclose the associated fees to consumers. The Competition Bureau is requesting full customer refunds in the misleading situations, administrative penalties of $10 million against each of the named carriers, and a $1 million fine against the CWTA.[23]

In terms of guidelines, all CSC programs in Canada must abide by the Canadian Wireless Telecommunications Association guidelines, which are discussed later in this chapter and can be found in more detail at **www.txt.ca**. The standard marketing regulations that guide marketing practices in Canada also apply; these are outlined in Chapter 2.

Short messaging services (SMS) and **multimedia messaging services (MMS)** are mobile communication approaches that allow marketers to send text messages or multimedia messages that contain graphics, video, or audio to an opted-in customer's mobile device. Customers must opt-in to SMS/MMS programs to receive ongoing communication that might include, among other things, text message alerts, offers, discounts, or coupons. Virgin Mobile routinely uses this approach to provide subscribers with SMS bill-notification reminders and discounts on clothing or entertainment.

Mobile e-mail is an important tool in a mobile marketer's arsenal. Mobile devices are personal communication gadgets, and retrieving and sending e-mails is widely used on these devices. Research from 2013 indicates that 49 percent of sent e-mails were opened on mobile devices, so when designing e-mails, marketers must consider that an e-mail may be viewed on a desktop, a laptop, a tablet, or a cellphone, which may render e-mails differently.[24] E-mail marketing communications can be deployed by using e-mail service providers that provide analytics on open rates, forward rates, bounce rates, and clicks. These metrics allow marketers to test different subject lines, headlines, and content so that, over time, the most effective

short messaging services (SMS)
Standard text messaging that uses protocols of 160 characters per message

multimedia messaging services (MMS)
Standard text messaging services that include audio, video, or images

mobile e-mail
E-mail sent and/or received using a mobile device

e-mail campaigns are deployed. When using e-mail campaigns, marketers must adhere to Canada's anti-spam legislation and other marketing regulations as outlined in Chapter 2.

Mobile voice can be a useful marketing tool; however, marketers acknowledge that consumers do not want to be interrupted by marketing phone calls or voice messages on their personal mobile devices. Marketers therefore steer away from using this approach.

Matrix 2D Barcodes
A **matrix 2D barcode** is a two-dimensional square or rectangular response code that, when scanned by a mobile barcode reader or app, provides additional information, launches websites, prompts downloads, or sends SMS or e-mail messages. A popular brand of matrix 2D barcode is the QR code.

Matrix 2D barcodes can be placed on flat surfaces such as print ads, posters, business cards, or even at the bottom of TV screens so that they can be scanned by mobile devices. During the 2013 holiday season, Walmart Canada teamed up with Mattel toys and used QR codes to make holiday shopping easier for commuters. Colourful oversized posters were placed in subway stations and on GO Trains, complete with images of toys that had their own scannable QR codes. Commuters were invited to scan the codes to purchase toys that would be delivered to their homes. Posters appeared at Toronto's Union Station, Montreal's McGill Station, and Vancouver's Waterfront Station.[25]

Proximity Marketing
Proximity marketing is the local distribution of marketing content to

> *" A popular brand of matrix 2D barcode is the QR code. "*

mobile devices that have opted-in at a specific geo-location. A shopping mall may use proximity marketing to provide mobile coupons to shoppers who are using its free Wi-Fi network. A local coffee shop may use Bluetooth technology to invite people in the immediate vicinity to come in and try a new coffee. **Bluetooth** technology refers to the use of low-power radio waves that wirelessly transfer text, images, and audio or video data through a local hotspot to Bluetooth-enabled and -activated devices. Early Bluetooth items were baby monitors, garage door openers, and cordless phones. Today many smartphones come with Bluetooth technology that is easily activated to receive local messages.

Proximity marketing can also use other technologies such as near field communications (NFC), radio frequency identification (RFID) tags, and augmented reality (AR) approaches to provide consumers with information.

- **Near field communications (NFC)** is the two-way radio communication between smartphones and smartphone-type devices that can transfer images, documents, or monetary transactions when the two devices touch or are within a few inches of each other. The mobile wallet app Google Wallet is an example of NFC. NFC approaches

Walmart and Mattel used QR codes to make holiday shopping easier for commuters.

mobile voice
Voice messaging left or received using mobile devices

matrix 2D barcode
Two-dimensional response code that, when scanned by a mobile barcode reader or app, provides additional information, launches websites, prompts downloads, or sends SMS or e-mail messages

proximity marketing
The local distribution of marketing content to mobile devices that have opted-in at a specific geo-location

Bluetooth
The use of low-power radio waves to wirelessly transfer text, images, audio, or video data through a local hotspot to a Bluetooth-enabled and -activated device

near field communications (NFC)
The two-way radio communication between smartphones and smartphone-type devices to transfer images, documents, or monetary transactions when the two devices touch or are within a few inches of each other

Near field communications.

are used at industry events and conferences where NFC-enabled mobile devices can tap a centrally located hotspot to download complementary white papers, research studies, or speaker information.

- **Radio frequency identification (RFID) tags** are physical tags that use radio signals to provide information in the form of text, images, or video. These tags are commonly embedded in pets, in case they go missing, and have been used for years to track and identify farm animals and items for production processes. More recently, these tags are being used by mobile marketers to provide consumers with information. The luxury clothing brand Burberry, for instance, uses RFID technology within its flagship London store so that when RFID-tagged items come in close proximity to mirrors within the store, the mirrors become digital screens that play videos on how the product was made or snippets from a related fashion show.

- **Augmented reality (AR)** uses a webcam or mobile device to capture an image or GPS signal that is then supplemented with graphics, audio, video, or location data to provide additional information or an enhanced experience. The Wikitude app is such an app, which is used by international travelers; the app uses AR and GPS data to superimpose local attraction information over a current location.

Proximity marketing also includes mobile check-in services and mobile discovery apps that provide consumers with offers from local merchants. **Mobile**

check-in services are when consumers check into locations using apps such as Foursquare or Yelp to post their whereabouts and then receive offers from local merchants on their mobile devices. **Mobile discovery** refers to the use of mobile apps such as Google Maps, Yelp, or Urbanspoon to find local services that are rated in the area.

Mobile Marketing Regulations and Best Practices

Mobile Marketing Regulations

LO 3 The mobile marketing industry is regulated by the same guidelines that apply to the marketing industry in general, but with the addition of further regulations for mobile marketing practices. In this manner, the regulations, guidelines, and policies discussed in Chapter 2 all need to be followed. Mobile marketers need to be keenly aware of Canada's privacy legislation as well as Canada's anti-spam legislation (CASL), which was revised and is being implemented in stages over the 2014–2017 period.

In the mobile space, the Canadian Radio-television and Telecommunications Commission (CRTC), the Canadian Wireless Telecommunications Association (CWTA), and the Mobile Marketing Association (MMA) have additional regulations and codes of conduct to protect consumers and to help standardize the industry. The mobile marketing industry is rapidly changing, and so, in all instances, marketers are strongly advised to obtain regulatory updates and to consult with marketing lawyers and mobile marketing experts to ensure approaches adhere to regulatory and legislative updates.

The Wireless Code In mobile marketing, the CRTC regulates the Wireless Code. This was introduced in 2013 as a mandatory code of conduct for all wireless service providers. It ensures that wireless contracts are easy to understand and that contracts can be cancelled after two years. In addition, data overages are capped for notification at $50 per month, roaming fees are capped at $100 per month, and data plan providers need to notify users when these limits are reached.[26] For more details on the CRTC Wireless Code, navigate to **http://crtc.gc.ca**.

Complaints against wireless service providers can be lodged at the website for the Commissioner for Complaints for Telecommunications Services at **www.ccts-cprst.ca**.

Common Short Code (CSC) Guidelines These guidelines are administered by the CWTA to provide direction on CSC pricing and marketing practices. Mobile marketers must provide participants with mandatory keyword protocols (stop/arret to stop participation, help/aide to access information on terms of use and privacy policies, and info to retrieve company and customer service information). In addition, consumers must double opt-in to CSC programs and be aware of its terms, conditions, and pricing.[27] Updates on CSC regulations can be found at **www.cwta.ca** and **www.txt.ca**.

The CRTC Wireless Code helps protect consumers.

The MMA Global Code of Conduct The MMA Global Code of Conduct is administered by the Mobile Marketing Association, which guides the industry with standards, guidelines, and best practices. The MMA has over 700 members and is represented in over 20 countries. The MMA Global Code of Conduct specifically notes that privacy policies and terms and conditions must be clear, and opt-in and opt-out protocols must be used. Messaging should be limited to its initial purpose, personal data must be protected, and all MMA members must demonstrate compliance with the code.[28] You can see more about the MMA and its code of conduct at **www.mmaglobal.com**.

The website **txt.ca** provides data on text messaging in Canada.

Mobile Marketing Best Practices

The mobile marketing industry is rapidly changing, with new technologies, devices, and regulations keeping marketers on their toes and associations busy sharing knowledge on how best to approach mobile consumers. Best practices see marketers abiding by marketing regulations and using a *mobile first* approach to make connections. A mobile first approach means that mobile becomes a central element in a marketing program and is integrated throughout the consumer path-to-purchase. Mobile is not added as an after-thought, but instead it is integrated into marketing programs from the start.

Best practices also use market research to stay abreast of how technology impacts consumer behaviour and to learn how mobile devices are integrated into daily lives. Changes in shopping habits are noted and mobile analytics programs are used to glean insights on how best to approach, engage, and connect with consumers.

The Mobile Marketing Association (MMA) advises mobile marketers to keep the following best practices in mind:[29]

● Think *mobile first* and start with a mobile perspective.

Best practices use a mobile first approach, which places mobile as a pivotal element in marketing programs.

- Leverage concurrent multi-screen usage so that consumers can simultaneous connect using smartphones and tablets.

- Utilize a full spectrum of mobile tools to interact with consumers.

- Integrate mobile marketing programs into traditional marketing campaigns.

- Create campaigns that work across multiple screens and devices.

- Leverage every phase of the sales funnel, understanding that mobile is used for search and discovery as well as connecting and purchasing.

- Test your way to success by tracking, measuring, and making adjustments to improve results and ROI.

ask yourself

1. What is proximity marketing?

2. Which associations and commissions regulate mobile marketing in Canada?

3. What best practices have surfaced in mobile marketing?

The Social Media Landscape

LO 4 Mobile marketing is often intertwined with social media marketing, with marketers understanding that most consumers access social media on mobile devices. These two areas are rapidly evolving, and we often find them working together to help brands make connections with consumers. We start by looking at the characteristics of social media and move into a discussion on social media marketing practices and tools. We continue by examining the top social media sites in Canada and end this chapter noting the best social media marketing practices.

social media
A form of online media that allows members to create their own network of friends and contacts to share comments, articles, opinions, videos, and images

Characteristics of Social Media

Social media is a form of online media that allows members to create their own network of friends and contacts to share comments, articles, opinions, videos, and images. It is helpful for marketers to understand that social media broadly falls into five areas, as shown in Figure 13–5. There are *social communities* such as Facebook, Twitter, Google+, and LinkedIn for sharing opinions, articles, images, and videos with friends, contacts, and associates; there are *social bookmarking sites* such as Pinterest for primarily sharing images; there are *social review sites* such as Urbanspoon and Yelp for posting reviews on local restaurants and services; there are *social gaming sites* such as Xbox Live for video games and Zynga for social games (Draw Something); and there are *social creation and discovery sites* such as YouTube, Tumblr, and Instagram for sharing video or image-based content. In all instances, members of these social media sites can share content and post comments to express their thoughts and opinions.

The various forms of social media share common characteristics. They run off cloud-based software that does not have to be downloaded on a computer; they can be accessed from mobile or desktop devices; they often use apps for easy mobile access; they are generally free to join; they allow members to interact with content providers by sharing content, participating in conversations, and posting comments and opinions; they categorize content so it can be searched and accessed by others; and they continuously evolve with new elements for users. Many social networks allow marketers to place ads on the social network to help build their social presence and to increase awareness; however, not all social networks have this opportunity.

A single social media site, such as Facebook or YouTube, is called a *social network*. The most popular social networks in Canada are Facebook, YouTube, Twitter, Google+, LinkedIn, Instagram, Tumblr, and Pinterest, although numerous other niche social networks exist, built around particular topics of interest. Social networks rely on users to share content that has been created by others, upload their own original content if they wish, and comment on content that has already been shared. Original

What are the characteristics of social media networks?

Figure 13–5
Social media categories and examples

Social bookmarks
Delicious
Digg
Pinterest
Reddit
StumbleUpon

Social communities
Facebook
Google+
LinkedIn
Path
Twitter

Social reviews
Foursquare
Goodreads
TripAdvisor
Urbanspoon
Yelp

Social creation and discovery
Blogger
Etsy
Flickr
Instagram
Last.fm
SlideShare
Tumblr
YouTube
Vine
Wikipedia

Social gaming
Kongregate
QuizUp
Xbox Live
Zynga

an application with which multiple users can create, add, edit, or delete content.

The Conversation Prism is a useful tool for marketers as it may point to social networks that may be useful for their brands. You can see more about this tool at **https://conversationprism.com/**.

Social Media Marketing

Social media marketing is when brands reach out to consumers online through social networks where people connect with friends and contacts to share comments, articles, opinions, videos, and images as a form of self-expression. Brands engage on these platforms by hiring experts and social media community managers to create brand pages on social media platforms, to join online conversations, to monitor and respond to questions and comments, to use metrics to measure performance and engagement, and to send out updates and offers. Brands may also place ads on the social networks that accept advertising.

Consumers in Canada live in a wired world and are exposed to marketing messages in a variety of formats, whether this be online or offline. Social media marketing is similar to

online content that has been created by users is called **user-generated content (UGC)**. It can be in the form of blogs, posts, images, audio, or video.

Brian Solis developed the Conversation Prism to visually demonstrate the vastness of the social media landscape and all that it has to offer. It tracks dominant, niche, and promising new social networks. It shows that social media is much larger than the popular sites that we hear about every day—Facebook, Twitter, LinkedIn, YouTube, Pinterest, Tumblr, Instagram, and Google+. It shows that social media includes blogs and wikis as well as countless other social networks, such as Quora for asking questions, last.fm for listening to music, SlideShare for sharing presentations, Goodreads for book lovers, Foodspotting for food enthusiasts, tvtag for TV buffs, and so many more. A **blog** is a website in the form of an online diary that is used by organizations and individuals to post updates that include personal opinions, activities, and experiences. Readers can subscribe to blogs, post comments, and share content. A **wiki** is a collaborative website (such as Wikipedia) that uses

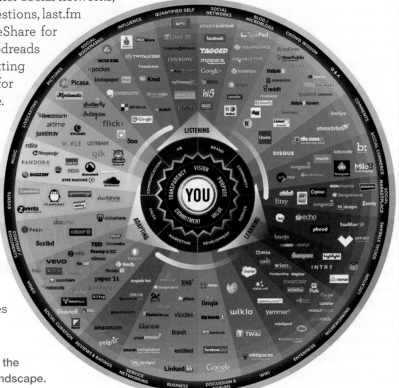

The Conversation Prism shows the vastness of the social media landscape.

user-generated content (UGC)
Original online content that has been created by users in the form of blogs, posts, images, audio, or video

blog
A website in the form of an online diary that is used by organizations and individuals to post updates that include personal opinions, activities, and experiences with readers able to subscribe and post comments

wiki
A collaborative website that uses an application with which multiple users can create, add, edit, or delete content

social media marketing
Reaching out to consumers online through social networks where people connect with friends and contacts to share comments, articles, opinions, videos, and images as a form of self-expression

Sharpie engages
teens on social networks.

other forms of marketing communications in that it can reach mass audiences or niche markets, but it is different in that consumers participate in this platform, and therefore marketers do not have full control over the messaging that appears for their brands.

Social media differs from conventional forms of marketing communications in important ways that marketers need to consider. It is inexpensive and easy to use, and advertising on these platforms is relatively cheap. It does, however, need dedicated attention and is labour-intensive in that it requires real-time monitoring and nurturing to ensure messaging stays current and responsive. Questions and comments should not go unanswered; advertisements should be monitored and adjusted for engagement; advocates should be noted; and newsworthy items should be posted for fans and followers to keep the content fresh and engaging.

Social media is a public venue, and marketers need to delicately deal with detractors and negative interactions, understanding that vehemently defending a brand in the court of public opinion can rapidly escalate on social media with negative repercussions. In order to avoid negative situations on social media, companies create social media policies and guidelines to help guide social media programs and interactions.

An example of how negative situations can play out in social media can be seen with the environmental group Greenpeace. Greenpeace chose to protest publicly outside Nestlé's offices and to use social media to chastise Nestlé for using palm oils in its products, a practice that was adding to the deforestation of rainforests and the elimination of habitat for orangutans. Nestlé's heavy-handed responses on social media caused an uproar, which put further pressure on the company to change its procurement practices. The Marketing NewsFlash, "Greenpeace and Nestlé's Kit Kat Social Media Showdown," discusses this in more detail.

The writing tool Sharpie provides a good example of a company that effectively uses social media marketing to engage its teenage target audience. This brand is very visual and uses this to its advantage.

Sharpie noted that teens like to create images with Sharpies but are easily bored. It therefore followed a strategy of frequently updating its images and sharing those created by its fans. Social media community managers at Sharpie work to showcase the passion people have for its product by commenting, sharing, and engaging with Sharpie enthusiasts. Sharpie frequently changes its Facebook cover photos with hand-drawn Sharpie images submitted by its fans. It uses Instagram to showcase its own Sharpie images. It frequently changes its Twitter backgrounds with fun and vibrant hand-drawn images and focuses numerous tweets on the Sharpie creations it finds on social networks. Its blog at **http://blog.sharpie.com/** encourages people to upload their Sharpie creations, while its Tumblr account tags Sharpie doodles and musings for others to find. Sharpie's Pinterest account pins everything from Sharpie designs etched on backpacks and running shoes, to fun creations for Halloween. Sharpie has over 4 million fans on Facebook, more than 200,000 followers on Twitter, over 111,000 followers on Instagram, and over 9,000 followers on Pinterest.[30]

Social Media Marketing Tools

LO 5 Social media marketing requires knowledge of the social networks that can be used to drive engagement as well as an understanding of the tools that exist to help manage and measure these programs.

Greenpeace and Nestlé's Kit Kat Social Media Showdown

In March 2010, in London, England, Greenpeace demonstrated outside Nestlé's offices protesting the company's use of palm oil, which contributes to deforestation and threatens the environment and the lives of orangutans. Protestors dressed as orangutans screeched animal sounds outside Nestlé's offices and held placards that used the Kit Kat colours, slogan, and graphic elements to turn the brand name into the word "Killer." The protest invited people to go to Greenpeace.org to read more and to be directed to a YouTube ad that spoofed the Kit Kat brand to draw attention to the issue. The Greenpeace message was simple: "We're asking Nestlé to give rainforests and orangutans a break and stop buying palm oil from destroyed forests."[31]

In April 2010, a similar protest surfaced at Nestlé's annual general shareholders' meeting with the addition of activists dropping down over shareholders just as the meeting began. The Wi-Fi connection at the meeting was also hijacked so that when people logged on, they were directed to the Greenpeace website.

The YouTube video spoof was central to the campaign's success.

It used the Kit Kat slogan *Have a Break* and showed a man snacking on a Kit Kat bar that turned out to be dried fingers of an orangutan. When he bit into the Kit Kat bar, orangutan blood gushed onto his keyboard. With less than 1,000 views on YouTube, Nestlé demanded that YouTube remove the video due to copyright infringement. It was replaced with the words, "This video is no longer available due to a copyright claim by Société des Produits Nestlé S.A."

Nestlé's heavy-handed approach provoked a major social media backlash. Greenpeace quickly posted the video on Vimeo, another video-sharing site, and used social media to drum up support and chastise the company for its censorship and environmental practices. Video spin-offs of the ad also appeared on YouTube, and total video views from all sites rapidly reached 1.5 million. The confrontation quickly escalated and became very public on Facebook and Twitter. Kit Kat's Facebook page was bombarded with fan complaints, online protesters changed their profile pics to Greenpeace's Kit Kat "Killer" logo, and Nestlé's Twitter feed was flooded with negative comments. Nestlé also received over 200,000 e-mail complaints.

Social media gives companies less control over their brand assets.

Nestlé responded aggressively on social media to this backlash, threatening to remove negative Facebook comments from its Kit Kat page and to sue those who used the modified Kit Kat "Killer" logo. It also posted sarcastic responses such as, "Oh please," which further portrayed the company in a negative light.

The result was that two months after the protests began, Nestlé's announced it would no longer work with the palm oil producers that were linked to deforestation and it affirmed its commitment to the environment and ending deforestation.[32]

Questions

1. How do you think Nestlé should have responded to the social media attacks?

2. What can companies do to avoid these types of social media confrontations?

Social Media Networks in Canada

Social media is used by marketers in many ways to help connect consumers with a brand. For example, Facebook can send out offers, updates, and contests; Twitter can post newsy updates and answer customer service questions; Pinterest and Instagram can post inspiring images and contests; Google+ can be used to interview experts; YouTube can be used for storytelling, how-to content, and engaging videos; and LinkedIn can profile a company's expertise. The most developed social media programs use multiple social media sites to profile a brand in creative, engaging, and imaginative ways. Before creating social media marketing programs, marketers need to check any restrictions that these social media sites may have for running elements such as contests, which should also always adhere to the marketing regulations in Canada that were outlined in Chapter 2.

In 2014, the most popular social networks in Canada were Facebook, YouTube, LinkedIn, Google+, Twitter, Pinterest, Tumblr, and Instagram. While the life cycle of social media sites can be rather fickle since these sites grow and die based on public perceptions, current comScore data shows that Facebook and YouTube dominate the social media space in Canada with Facebook at approximately 18.9 million unique visitors per month and YouTube at 17.7 million. Other popular social media sites follow, with LinkedIn and Google+ at 6.1 million unique visitors each, Twitter at 5.6 million, Pinterest at 3.7 million, Tumblr at 3.2 million, and Instagram at 3.1 million.[33] The databox below, "Comparing Social Media Networks," shows how these accounts fare globally.

These social media sites are carefully managed to maintain their popularity since the demise of a social media site can happen rather quickly, as seen with the once-popular MySpace.

Launched in 2004, MySpace quickly became a popular social network for young people. It defined youth culture with its funky pages and was seen as a place where young people could discover friends and music, and find out about hip movies and pop culture. In less than a year, the social media site had over 5 million global users, and in 18 months, it was purchased by newspaper giant News Corp for $580 million. At its peak, it had approximately 75 million global users. Its demise, however, came quickly after this buyout, as the entrepreneurial spirit was replaced by a focus on revenues and monetization. Advertising started to clutter the site, and new features were not always well-executed or required. The technology became dated, and it lacked the flexibility, security, and privacy options needed to curb spam. In 2011, after years of attrition, News Corp sold MySpace for $35 million, only 6 percent of its 2005 purchase price. It was purchased by Specific Media Group and Justin Timberlake and has been re-launched as a destination for music enthusiasts and musicians. It now has 36 million global users, but its long-term viability is still in question as it competes with other social media sites such as Facebook and YouTube, which have quicker and easier ways to connect people with music.[34] The MySpace journey has put other social media sites on alert, reminding them to step cautiously into monetization and to always put the user experience first.

Here we look at eight mainstream social media networks to understand how they are used for marketing purposes. Specifically, we look at Facebook, YouTube, Google+, Twitter, LinkedIn, Instagram, Tumblr, and Pinterest.

Comparing Social Media Networks—Global Users

facebook	Facebook	1.23 billion
You Tube	YouTube	1 billion
Google+	Google+	300 million
twitter	Twitter	243 million
LinkedIn	LinkedIn	227 million
Instagram	Instagram	150 million
tumblr.	Tumblr	108 million
Pinterest	Pinterest	70 million

Source: Statistics accessed March 2014 from individual social media networks and Simply Measured and Digital Marketing Ramblings.

Facebook Founded in 2004, Facebook sees its mission as "giving people the power to share and make the world more open and connected." It is a free social network where people connect with friends and family, share what matters to them, and "discover what's going on in the world."[35] Social media analytics company Simply Measured tells us that Facebook is used for marketing purposes by 98 percent of Interbrand's top 100 brands, with 60 percent of brands posting at least once a day. Facebook dominates social media with 1.23 billion global monthly active users.[36] Due to its dominance and well-developed platform, Facebook is usually the centre of a brand's social media program, and it accounts for most of its social media audience.

Facebook is a social network with three tracks. First, there is the *personal track*, which is how Facebook started, where users create a personal profile; add other users as friends; exchange comments, photos, videos, and "likes"; and receive updates through notifications in the News Feed feature. Private messages can also be sent, a popular feature that is used to quickly message people without using e-mail. Second, there is the *group track*, which uses Facebook Groups to allow Facebook

Social Media Marketing Example: Netflix's *House Of Cards**

facebook { "Like" if you're addicted to *House of Cards*.

twitter { Netflix releases season 3 #HouseofCards #FrancisUnderwood.

You Tube { See Netflix trailer for *House of Cards*, season 3.

Linked in { Spruce up your networking skills with *House of Cards*, season 3.

{ Post a selfie watching #HouseofCards3 with #mydog.

Pinterest { BBQ rib recipe from Frank's on *House of Cards* #BBQ #ribs #HouseofCards.

Google+ { Countdown to Google+ Hangout On Air with Kevin Spacey #HouseofCards.

tumblr. { Quotes from *House of Cards* #HouseofCards #quotes.

*This is a hypothetical example.

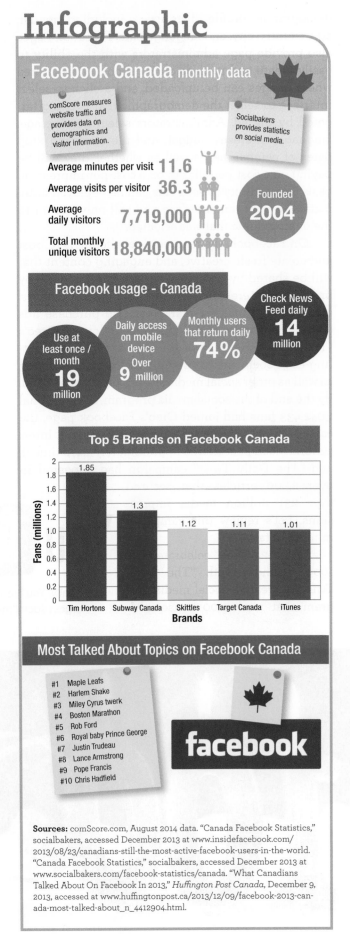

Infographic

Facebook Canada monthly data

comScore measures website traffic and provides data on demographics and visitor information.

Socialbakers provides statistics on social media.

Average minutes per visit **11.6**

Average visits per visitor **36.3**

Average daily visitors **7,719,000**

Total monthly unique visitors **18,840,000**

Founded **2004**

Facebook usage - Canada

Use at least once / month **19 million**

Daily access on mobile device Over **9 million**

Monthly users that return daily **74%**

Check News Feed daily **14 million**

Top 5 Brands on Facebook Canada

Fans (millions)

- Tim Hortons 1.85
- Subway Canada 1.3
- Skittles 1.12
- Target Canada 1.11
- iTunes 1.01

Brands

Most Talked About Topics on Facebook Canada

#1 Maple Leafs
#2 Harlem Shake
#3 Miley Cyrus twerk
#4 Boston Marathon
#5 Rob Ford
#6 Royal baby Prince George
#7 Justin Trudeau
#8 Lance Armstrong
#9 Pope Francis
#10 Chris Hadfield

facebook

Sources: comScore.com, August 2014 data. "Canada Facebook Statistics," socialbakers, accessed December 2013 at www.insidefacebook.com/2013/08/23/canadians-still-the-most-active-facebook-users-in-the-world. "Canada Facebook Statistics," socialbakers, accessed December 2013 at www.socialbakers.com/facebook-statistics/canada. "What Canadians Talked About On Facebook In 2013," *Huffington Post Canada*, December 9, 2013, accessed at www.huffingtonpost.ca/2013/12/09/facebook-2013-canada-most-talked-about_n_4412904.html.

members to create public or private groups where members are focused on a particular interest, such as a high school reunion group or a group on pets, fitness, marketing, or an educational course. Facebook Groups allow members to post comments to everyone in the group at once. Facebook Groups provide members with notifications and have the added benefit of allowing people to upload documents. Third, there is the commercial *page track* that allows artists, public figures, businesses, brands, and non-profits to create pages that people can like and follow to receive notifications and updates in their News Feed.

Facebook Pages are used by organizations and brands to engage consumers with relevant updates, news, and offers that may be of interest to its followers. This feature provides marketers with *insights*, a term Facebook uses to describe the metrics it provides for Facebook Pages on likes, reach, engagement, and visits. These insights also show which posts have the most traction, and the aggregated demographic profile of its users, including gender, age, country, city, and language data. Facebook Pages also provide page administrators with the ability to easily create and run ads on Facebook, with an area where images can be uploaded, and a click-to-select interface to select the demographic that is being targeted by the ad. Administrators select gender, age, language, interests, budget, and the start and stop dates of campaigns, as well as whether they will be paying on a cost-per-click or on a cost-per-impression basis (opportunity to see). Ads can be deployed automatically from this interface and will only appear to the demographic that was selected.

On Facebook, the marketer's challenge is to post and create fresh, creative, and engaging content that will be shared by its followers. This is often done by providing interesting updates and posting offers, contests, and images. Marketers also purchase ads on this network to rapidly increase followers. Oreo's "The Daily Twist" campaign is an example of a cutting-edge social media program that ran on Facebook as well as other social media sites to profile the brand. By the end of the social media program, an additional 1,042,433 fans had joined Oreo's Facebook page, the campaign had prompted 1.3 million Facebook interactions (each post shared approximately 1,472 times), and "The Daily Twist" campaign had appeared in over 2,600 articles that secured over 231 million media impressions. Let's review this campaign in more detail.

In 2012, Oreo celebrated its 100th birthday with "The Daily Twist," a creative social media program that made 100 consecutive days an Oreo day. Every morning, Oreo's social media team scoured the Internet for trending topics, iconic birthdays, headlines, and pop-culture happenings. It then selected one of these occurrences and set to work to portray it with a unique Oreo twist. By 6 p.m. each evening, a poster-like image with Oreo as the focus had been created, approved, and posted on social media sites for others to share. Facebook, Twitter, and Pinterest were the main social sites used for this program, and fun images were posted that celebrated daily landmarks such as Twitter's birthday, the birth of a giant panda, the Mars Rover launch, and Gay Pride Day, just to name a few. The gay pride image is an example of what can happen on social media. The rainbow image was very popular for its support of the LGBT community and made the rounds of the late-night talk shows, such as *Jimmy Kimmel Live* and *The Colbert Report,* as well as numerous articles written in the mainstream media, such as the *Huffington Post,* the *New York Times,* and CNN. Nonetheless, a few Facebook fans were not pleased and unliked the page and posted negative comments. However, the net result was that within a few hours, the image was positively shared 14,800 times and had 87,000 likes.[37]

YouTube   In 2005, YouTube was launched as a free video-sharing social network for people to discover and be inspired by interesting, entertaining, and informative videos. In 2006, it was purchased by Google and today it has more than 1 billion global users who collectively watch over 6 billion hours of video per month. More than 100 hours of video are uploaded every minute. YouTube

Globally, YouTube is the second-largest social media network.

"The Daily Twist" social media campaign posted a unique newsworthy image of an Oreo cookie every day for 100 consecutive days.

is localized across 61 countries and allows individuals to create their own YouTube channels, subscribe to other channels, and to upload, watch, and share videos. The platform also allows users to post comments and share videos across other social media sites, such as Facebook, Twitter, Google+, Tumblr, and Pinterest. YouTube is widely used by marketers who upload short films, how-to videos, and video ads on their products, relying on the platform to engage with storytelling. Marketers can also purchase advertising on this site.[38]

Marketers understand that YouTube provides a robust marketing tool: Brands can create YouTube channels, upload videos, access YouTube analytics, and purchase advertising. Marketers target ads on YouTube in the form of banner ads, sponsored/featured videos, or in-stream video ads. They can also optimize their YouTube channels and videos for the search engines through the use of keywords.

In a few instances, marketers use YouTube to upload videos that are designed to go *viral*. This is generally a carefully orchestrated approach that involves creating catchy content that is often humorous or very creative to appeal to a wide audience that will quickly view, share, and rate the video, sending it to the top of YouTube's recommended videos, which will immediately boost its popularity. These videos are generally *seeded* with influential journalists and celebrities and sometimes through already well-established YouTube channels so that people will hear about the video in live broadcasts or tweets and share it. The *Gangnam Style* video from the popular South Korean pop star Psy was created by his record label with this in mind. The music video included popular South Korean celebrities as well as catchy universal lyrics and medleys, and was launched through a well-established YouTube channel. In 24 hours, the video had gone viral in South Korea with 500,000 views in the first day. Over the next few months, as its popularity spread to North America and Europe, the video continued to go viral, with 1.9 million views, 5.1 million comments, 2.3 million shares, and an increase in channel subscriptions by 1.1 million users.[39]

Google+

Google+ is a free social networking site that was launched in 2011 and is becoming more widely used. It currently has over 300 million global users, although the number of engaged actual users is judged to be substantially lower. Google automatically creates Google+ accounts for people with Google or YouTube

> *Marketers understand that YouTube provides a robust marketing tool.*

accounts (difficult to delete), and these users do not necessarily use the social network regularly. Google+ allows users to post and share images, articles, and videos to their networks as well as to the site in general. It allows users to follow others in the Google+ network, like their posts, and add comments. It is unique in that it also has Google+ Communities for users to share related content, and Google+ Hangouts where groups can chat through a video interface. It also has Google+ Hangouts On Air for live broadcasts to an unlimited number of people on Google+ and YouTube. Google+ members can also create their own communities, hangouts, and private circles that group like-minded individuals together for easy sharing.[40]

Google+ provides marketers with business pages to share content and engage others. It is experimenting with advertising opportunities for brands. Posting content on the site may help optimize brand posts for the search engines. Many brands start engaging on Google+ but do not do so consistently, finding it difficult to determine what it offers over other existing social networks. It is the Hangouts On Air that will make the difference for brands, with their ability to cheaply host live events and post them online to reach a wide audience. Print publications such as *National Geographic* host Hangouts On Air to interview experts from around the world. These Hangouts On Air automatically save the event on video. This video can then be edited and uploaded to YouTube to share with others.

Twitter

Twitter was launched in 2006 as a free social media site for individuals and organizations to post and receive short newsworthy text updates and links in 140 characters from accounts of interest, whether this be from friends, journalists, media outlets, or experts that are followed. Its advantage is the speed with which people can scan updates and decide whether they warrant additional reading. In this way, people are updated on developments in areas of interest, whether this be for business purposes or related to a passion or hobby. Twitter users can create lists, *favourite* tweets, send out other people's tweets through a *retweet*, and receive notifications recommending whom to follow. The platform encourages users to use hashtags (#) so that topics and conversations are searchable in the Twitter database. Twitter is home to 243 million global users, with a combined volume of 500 million tweets per day. It is supported in 35 languages.[41]

Organizations use Twitter for customer service and marketing purposes. Companies can use analytics platforms to monitor the Twitter landscape for brand and company mentions, to answer questions, and to respond to comments and suggestions in real time. On Twitter, brands post newsworthy content related to areas of expertise and engage brand advocates that have influential social networks. Simply Measured notes that 98 percent of Interbrand's top 100 brands are active on Twitter, with 58 percent of these brands having over 100,000 followers, and most accounts tweeting more than once a day.[42] Brand tweets may be pre-planned and pre-approved to coincide with marketing events and integrated into marketing communication programs, while others may task social community managers with the responsibility to deploy real-time tweets that respond to opportunities and buzz. Some marketers also use Twitter chats to profile their expertise and to build their following on social media platforms. These pre-scheduled chats revolve around a certain topic and occur on Twitter by using a predetermined hashtag to monitor the conversations. These chats typically run for about an hour and are hosted by a brand that will ask five to ten questions during the session and sometimes allocate prizes for the best responses.

Twitter offers marketers advertising opportunities through Twitter ads that take the form of *promoted accounts* or *promoted tweets*. A promoted account will appear in the *Who to follow* section of a Twitter account, while a promoted tweet will appear in an individual's timeline. The advertiser only pays when followers are added or tweets are clicked, retweeted, or favourited, or when they result in a reply. Ads can be targeted by interest.

Oreo's "The Daily Twist" campaign mentioned earlier in this chapter is an example of how a carefully planned social media program can use Twitter in conjunction with Facebook and Pinterest to drive engagement. An example of how Twitter can take advantage of real-time marketing and create buzz can be seen with the fast-food chain Arby's. During the TV broadcast of the 2014 Grammy Awards, the Arby's Twitter account noted that music artist Pharrell Williams was wearing a hat that was getting humorous comments; to Arby's, this hat resembled the Arby's logo, which triggered the tweet, "Hey @Pharrell, can we have our hat back? #GRAMMYs."

Arby's real-time tweet during the Grammy Awards boosted awareness for Arby's and its social media following.

The tweet resulted in over 83,000 retweets, almost 49,000 favourites, and 6,000 new followers, with coverage surfacing in the subsequent days in the mainstream entertainment and business press. This was all very positive for Arby's awareness, particularly when Pharrell responded the following day with, "Y'all tryna start a roast beef?" which was then retweeted by over 17,000 people with over 14,000 favourites.[43]

LinkedIn LinkedIn is a freemium (some services are free, and others require payment) business networking social media site for professionals that was launched in 2003. It has over 277 million global members and is used in over 200 countries. Students and post-secondary graduates are its fastest-growing demographic and account for over 30 million members. LinkedIn is free for its basic usage, which allows members to create professional profiles, connect to their network of business people, join business-oriented groups on particular interests, and use its job-search function to see recent job postings and company profiles. A free membership also allows members to post and share updates, endorse individuals, write recommendations, add comments, like articles, answer questions, contribute to discussions, follow companies, view profiles of individuals in their network, and see basic information on other LinkedIn members. LinkedIn members identify areas of interest and can receive notifications on job postings, network updates, and relevant news stories and articles.

Premium LinkedIn services are not free, but for a monthly or annual fee, LinkedIn provides upgraded services that range in price for recruiters, job seekers, and business professionals. These services include, among others, advanced search, increased e-mail capacity, and extended profile access. A premium service for job seekers moves a person to the top of a recruiter's list, provides comparisons with other applicants, and gives advice through its job seekers' group where webinars can be accessed. For a fee, companies on LinkedIn can post job openings and receive real-time analytics on who has viewed the posting as well as profiles on the applicants.

In the business-to-business market, LinkedIn can be used as a successful marketing tool. It is used by organizations to profile their expertise and to target individuals, companies, and sectors who may be interested in their services. On the marketing front, LinkedIn allows companies to create company pages, access visitor analytics, and create groups that profile expertise. Companies can also run ads on LinkedIn with razor-sharp targeting, whether this be a job posting, a branded display ad, or a sponsored story. LinkedIn has the advantage of having fewer distractions than the other social networks as it is focused on business and work-related topics. Display ads and sponsored stories that relate to business expertise are therefore placed in the appropriate environment and tend to perform well. LinkedIn display ads and sponsored stories are on a cost-per-click or a cost-per-impression basis. These ads can target by location, keyword, and interest. They stand out for B2B marketers in that they also target by company, job title, job function, and group, which can result in very high-quality responses and business leads.

Social media analytics company Simply Measured tells us that 88 percent of Interbrand's top 100 brands have LinkedIn company accounts and that 55 percent use LinkedIn to drive engagement on company pages. These organizations recognize the opportunity to use LinkedIn to share company values, expertise, and updates with current and potential customers. Simply Measured points to Microsoft as an example of a company that uses LinkedIn to promote its services and

expertise. It averages 2.7 updates per day, has about 127 people commenting on these updates, and is followed by 1,082,305 people on LinkedIn.[44]

Instagram Instagram is a free social network that was launched in 2010 as a mobile app and purchased by Facebook in 2012. It is the world's largest photo-sharing site with over 150 million active users who quickly and easily share their lives through photos and short videos that are taken with a mobile device, instantly adding filters and captions to customize the image before it is shared. Instagram's interface is very simple and allows users to add comments and likes, as well as use hashtags for easy search. Users can connect accounts to other social media sites so that images seamlessly appear on Facebook, Twitter, and Tumblr—an element that makes Instagram very popular.

Instagram is a relatively new platform but is quickly being recognized by marketers as an essential tool to share visual content. Simply Measured tells us that 71 percent

LinkedIn is widely used by businesses to establish credibility.

> *LinkedIn provides upgraded services that range in price for recruiters, job seekers, and business professionals.*

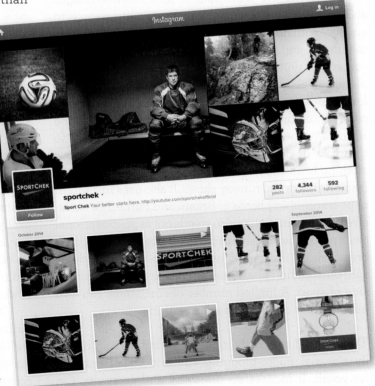

Interesting images work for Sport Chek on Instagram.

Quirky images, creative photos, and interesting quotes engage youth on Tumblr.

of Interbrand's top 100 companies use Instagram, with the highest engagement going to luxury brands, automotive brands, and media publications. Instagram can be used by marketers to post interesting behind-the-scenes footage from events as well as stunning product shots and contests.[45]

Marketers use Instagram to post creative images and add hashtags and captions that invite people to engage with the brand by adding comments, liking the image, and posting their own images of the brand, sometimes tying into a contest. A coffee shop, for example, asked people to dress up their branded coffee cups for Halloween and post and hashtag photos to win a gift card. Visual brands do well on Instagram, such as the British fashion house Burberry that uses Instagram to showcase its new collections. It posts images of its new clothing lines and shows behind-the-scene photos from fashion shoots and runway shows. It also uses Instagram to post stunning photos of Britain and Burberry's exclusive music events. Nike also stands out as an exceptional example of how to use Instagram. It posts inspiring and breathtaking images of people, places, and products with outstanding photography that captures the human side of sport. A limited number of companies can also purchase ads on the Instagram platform.

Tumblr Launched in 2007, Tumblr is primarily a visual micro-blogging site and social network for youth. It focuses on discovery and creativity. On Tumblr, people creatively share the things they love

with short posts that often reblog content from other sites on the network. Users can design creative-looking blogs and add posts that contain text, images, audio, and video. Tumblr users can add comments, like a post, reblog content, search for topics, and follow interesting blogs. Tumblr blog posts are generally short, are very visual, and contain little text. They use hashtags so that content is searchable and can be easily discovered and reblogged by others. Users are encouraged to share blogs and to add photos, quotes, links, text, and audio and video. Tumblr is home to 176 million blogs and has 108 million active accounts. It was purchased by Yahoo! in 2013.

While Tumblr is a top social networking destination for people under 35 years of age, it is not as widely used by brand marketers as the other social networks as it does not lend itself to quickly sharing content that was posted on other social media sites. On Tumblr, content needs to be more creative to fit in with the Tumblr platform. Brands also shy away from Tumblr as its users are often criticized for illegally lifting copyrighted content from the Internet and sharing it without attribution, links, or permission. Tumblr is used by 31 percent of Interbrand's top 100 companies, far below the 98 percent enjoyed by Facebook and Twitter, or 71 percent enjoyed by Instagram.

Marketers that understand Tumblr realize that creative images continue to be shared over a number of weeks on Tumblr, a practice that is not evident on the other social media networks. While Facebook and Twitter drive immediate real-time engagement, 29 percent of content on Tumblr is shared after 30 days, which results in content living longer on this site than on other social networks. Marketers therefore work to create original visual content that is creative and lasts on Tumblr, realizing that if it resonates, it will be curated and reblogged numerous times, often getting the most traction by being shared and amplified in other blogs in subsequent weeks. When creating content for Tumblr, marketers must consider why and how its content will appear and be shared on other blogs.

Many youthful brands use Tumblr as they understand that it is a popular place to engage fans. Sprite and MTV, for example, use Tumblr to share content that is reblogged countless times. The Sprite Tumblr includes short films, cool images of celebrity basketball athletes, and GIFs and sounds related to basketball—all presented in a mosaic of its recognizable green colour. Marketers can also advertise on the Tumblr website.[46]

Pinterest Pinterest is a free virtual bookmarking and content-sharing social network that was launched in 2010 and has over 70 million global users. Pinterest allows people to visually bookmark (or pin) and share images or videos of their favourite things, hobbies, and interests to a digital scrapbook. It visually places images, videos, and articles (and their links) in a bulletin board–type space, with users naming their boards to organize content under categories such as "quotes," "breakfast ideas," "DIY projects," "fall fashion," "vintage cars," or "bucket list." Pinterest members can pin content that they find on the Internet to their boards, follow other members or individual boards, and repin content that they find on Pinterest. Pinned images can also be shared on Facebook and Twitter. Simply Measured notes that 76 percent of the Interbrand's top 100 companies use Pinterest to drive business. Pinterest stands out versus Instagram in its

attractive multi-board interface and the fact that content links back to its original source—a feature not currently available on Instagram.

Marketers can create business accounts on Pinterest to pin interesting product-related images that drive traffic to a website for further information on usage, tips, ideas, promotions, or purchase. Marketers can also create group boards where others can pin content, an interesting way to build community around a brand. Contests also run on Pinterest, such as travel companies that ask people to create vacation boards and pin images from the brand's websites to win a free holiday. Marketers can purchase Promoted Pins and Rich Pins on Pinterest to increase awareness, and they can access its analytics to measure success. Fashion, food, and lifestyle brands do well on Pinterest as they have ample visual content and appeal to the Pinterest demographic.

Pinterest has spiked a growth in infographics as an interesting way to present facts about a product, its heritage, or how it is used. It has also sparked the growth in the visual web trend where brands have redesigned their websites to include visual board–type interfaces to access further content.[47]

Pinterest's strong visual platform is popular with female audiences.

cost-per-thousand (CPM)
The cost of reaching one thousand people

cost-per-acquisition (CPA)
The cost of acquiring a new follower or sale

cost-per-click (CPC)
The cost of getting someone to click on a link or ad

Creating and Measuring Social Media Marketing Programs

Marketers need to carefully plan their social media marketing efforts to ensure that they are supportable and measurable, and can help drive brand engagement and a positive return on investment.

Creating Social Media Marketing Programs Marketers can start the process of building social media programs into their marketing initiatives by answering the questions outlined in Figure 13–6, which will help steer content and the tools of engagement. Questions refer to a range of elements such as understanding a company's social media policies, selecting which social networks are appropriate for a brand, and determining an analytics platform to monitor, measure, and deploy social media programs, as well as many other important elements that you can see in Figure 13–6.

Figure 13–6
Planning social media marketing

Answer these questions to help steer your social media marketing programs:

SOCIAL MEDIA MARKETING QUESTIONS

1. What are your company's social media policies and guidelines?

2. What voice and tone do you want to use for your brand?

3. How does your target market use social media and what drives engagement?

4. What social media networks are appropriate for your brand and target group?

5. What type of content is suitable for your brand on your selected social media sites?

6. Who will be creating social media content for your brand and what is the budget?

7. What are your daily/weekly targets for social media posts and interactions?

8. Who will be running the social media programs?

9. What analytics platforms will be used to deploy, monitor, measure, engage, and evaluate social media programs?

10. How will social media be integrated into other brand marketing programs?

Measuring Social Media Marketing Programs Social media analytics platforms have surfaced to help marketers measure success in this environment. Social networks, such as Facebook and, to a lesser degree, YouTube and Pinterest, will often provide marketers with analytics on their accounts, but these metrics are not always in real time, do not provide the required depth, and cannot be aggregated across platforms. Third-party social media analytics and monitoring tools have surfaced to help marketers measure and manage multiple social media platforms, an important consideration since many brands engage across multiple platforms.

Social media analytics platforms vary by provider, but generally identify online brand mentions and monitor consumer sentiment, buzz, engagement, and amplification. These platforms often allow marketers to respond in real time to customer questions and complaints, to pre-schedule posts, and to identify brand advocates with strong influence scores that can amplify and spread positive brand messages. Hootsuite, Salesforce Marketing Cloud Radian6, and Simply Measured are examples of social media analytics platforms that can help marketers manage social media programs.

Many performance metrics can be used to measure social media marketing programs, but marketers are advised to use no more than 10 to make this process manageable and actionable. Generally, marketers will look at **cost-per-thousand (CPM)**, the cost of reaching 1,000 people; **cost-per-acquisition (CPA)**, the cost of acquiring a new follower or sale; and **cost-per-click (CPC)**, the cost of getting someone to click on a link, image, or ad. Other important metrics include measuring followers, views, comments, likes, shares, sentiment, engagement, and return on investment (ROI), with additional website metrics accessed if the intent is to drive people to a website.

Best Practices in Social Media Marketing

LO 6 The Canadian Marketing Association cautions marketers that in this fast-moving and intricate world of social media, marketers need to be aware of the trends and changes that are occurring and to be prepared for the unexpected. Marketers need to understand that a new generation of consumers exists—one that is less guarded on public platforms, one that is constantly connected on mobile devices, and one that uses social networks to gather information and connect.[48] Brands need to be seen as a trusted source of information on all platforms and they need to use social media to connect.

Brands initially approached social media with caution, seeing it as a youthful fad, but as its popularity expanded, and research revealed its role in the path-to-purchase, companies started to use social media to interact with consumers. Data tells us that 45 percent of people regularly look up brands on social networks, whether this is to access an offer, voice an opinion, access information, or read an update. For people under 35 years of age, this percentage jumps to 54 percent; it falls to 31 percent for people over 50.[49]

Organizations and brands are advised to use the following best practices when starting to use social media:

- Obtain senior management commitment.
- Set company-wide governance for social media.
- Create detailed social media policies, guidelines, and rules of engagement.
- Set clearly defined and measurable social media marketing objectives.
- Select a scalable platform that will be used to deploy, monitor, and measure social media activity.
- Identify the social networks that will be used.
- Establish metrics that will be used to evaluate approaches.
- Dedicate, train, and hire social media marketing experts.
- Understand that negative comments will surface on social networks.
- Realize that mistakes will be made.
- Integrate social media programs into marketing practices.

> *Brands need to be seen as a trusted source of information on all platforms and they need to use social media to connect.*

These best practices will help organizations and brands set the voice and tone for their social media marketing programs so that they genuinely reflect brand images and authentically communicate through multiple social networks. These best practices will also help organizations plan for negative situations that may surface and flag when scenarios should be escalated to a senior level. Social media marketing should be integrated into paid, owned, and earned media programs so that it positively impacts on the consumers' path-to-purchase.

ask yourself

1. *What two approaches are used to measure social media marketing programs?*

2. *What cost metrics are used to measure social media marketing programs?*

Summary...*just the facts*

LO¹ ● Mobile marketing is a set of practices that enables organizations to communicate and engage with audiences in an interactive and relevant manner through any mobile device or network.

● Mobile marketing provides marketers with an additional platform to communicate with consumers one-to-one. It can target by location, by device, by interest, and by demographic.

● Consumers use a wide array of mobile devices to stay in touch, to explore, and to stay informed. They are tech-savvy and platform agnostic, switching seamlessly between devices based on need and occasion.

● Mobile platforms are changing consumers' path-to-purchase with mobile devices used to gather information, to engage with brands, to make decisions, and to purchase products.

LO² ● Mobile marketing uses a variety of tools: the mobile web, mobile apps, mobile advertising, and mobile sales promotional tools. Mobile sales promotional tools include mobile messaging, matrix 2D barcodes, and proximity marketing approaches.

LO³ ● Best practices for mobile marketing advise marketers to think mobile first, and to plan programs across devices and screens by using multiple mobile tools that can integrate offline and online approaches.

● Standard marketing regulations in Canada also apply to mobile marketing.

● Specific mobile marketing regulations are administered by the Canadian Radio-television and Telecommunications Commission (CRTC), the Canadian Wireless Telecommunications Association (CWTA), and the Mobile Marketing Association (MMA).

LO⁴ ● Social media marketing is when brands reach out to consumers online through social networks where people connect with friends and contacts to share comments, articles, opinions, videos, and images as a form of self-expression.

● Companies hire experts and social media community managers to create brand pages on social media platforms.

● On social media networks, brands post updates and offers, join online conversations, respond to questions and comments, and use metrics to measure performance and engagement.

● Brands can place ads on social networks that accept advertising.

LO⁵ ● The main social networks used in Canada for marketing purposes are Facebook, YouTube, Twitter, Google+, LinkedIn, Instagram, Tumblr, and Pinterest.

LO⁶ ● The best social media marketing practices include obtaining senior management commitment, setting company-wide governance, creating social media policies, setting clear and measurable objectives, and selecting a scalable platform to use to deploy, monitor, and measure social media activity. It also involves identifying the social networks that will be used, establishing metrics, training and hiring experts, understanding that negative circumstances will occur, realizing that mistakes will be made, and integrating social media programs into marketing practices.

Key Terms and Concepts...*a refresher*

augmented reality (AR)
blog
Bluetooth
common short codes (CSC)
cost-per-acquisition (CPA)
cost-per-click (CPC)
cost-per-thousand (CPM)
feature phones
hybrid apps
matrix 2D barcode
m-commerce
mobile applications (apps)

mobile check-in services
mobile discovery
mobile e-mail
mobile marketing
mobile messaging
mobile voice
mobile wallet
mobile web
multimedia messaging services (MMS)
native apps
near field communications (NFC)

proximity marketing
radio frequency identification (RFID) tags
short messaging services (SMS)
showrooming
smartphones
social media
social media marketing
user-generated content (UGC)
web apps
wiki

Hands-on...*apply your knowledge*

Mobile Marketing and Social Media Marketing Assignment Rich Media creates mobile marketing tools and designs websites that make consumers' decisions easier. Navigate to its website at **www.richmedia.com** to review its latest portfolios. Identify a mobile marketing program that has assisted in consumer decision-making and analyze it in detail to see what specific decisions it is making easier for consumers. Brainstorm and recommend other elements that could be incorporated into the mobile marketing tool, including social media elements that could enhance the program for consumers.

Chapter Vignette...*reminder*

This chapter's opening vignette explains Rich Media's three-pillar approach to mobile marketing. Answer the Reality Check questions at the end of the vignette by carefully reading this chapter's sections on mobile marketing tools and social media marketing tools.

Video Clip...*questions*

Review the *Salesforce—Become a Customer Company* video from the CONNECT website to see how Salesforce views consumers in the age of mobile marketing, and then answer the following questions:

▶ Video
Salesforce

- Salesforce notes that technology has changed consumer expectations and is pushing organizations to become *customer companies*. What are the characteristics of a customer company and how does mobile fit into this?
- What customer elements does Salesforce respect and protect in the mobile environment?

Infographic...*data analysis*

Review the Infographic on smartphone activities in Canada and navigate to the source of the research at **www.thinkwithgoogle.com/mobileplanet/en**. Review the latest information on smartphone usage in Canada and create a new infographic with the latest data and write a short analysis of industry changes that have occurred over the last year. (*Infographic tip:* Use Microsoft Excel and Word to create charts and place them in a single PowerPoint slide to combine the visuals.)

connect **SMARTBOOK** **LEARNSMART**

For more information on the resources available from McGraw-Hill Ryerson, go to **www.mheducation.ca/he/solutions**.

customer relationship management

Whether an organization develops video games or curates digital artwork, building trusted relationships among customers and supporters is essential to the organization's success. Loyalty leads to deep relationships that yield multiple benefits for customers and companies. As an industry's landscape becomes more competitive, maintaining strong, long-term relationships becomes more challenging. In order to enhance customer relationships, organizations turn to two key strategies: customer relationship management (CRM) and customer experience management (CEM).

Although a customer relationship management (CRM) strategy may begin with a software solution, to maximize the benefits of this solution, the company's top management creates a culture incentivizing employees to buy in to the overall strategy. Effective execution of a CRM strategy offers faster and better results in sales and marketing. By leveraging CRM data, organizations place their customers in the centre of all business decisions. Furthermore, organizations need to ensure that they have an effective customer experience management (CEM) strategy in place. By creating positive experiences at all customer touch points, CEM facilitates a personalized experience for consumers. In essence, the two strategies work together to help organizations deepen relationships and retain customers.

Since CRM and CEM programs can be difficult to develop from scratch, organizations seek trusted partners such as OpenText to assist in their customer engagement strategies. In 1991, OpenText incorporated its enterprise information management business. From its global headquarters in Waterloo, Ontario, it began developing five key pillars of business, including one of its main areas of focus: customer experience management (CEM).

As the senior director of customer experience management at OpenText, Marci Maddox has the opportunity to see first-hand the CRM and CEM strategies her company develops. Realizing the implementation of such strategies requires integration with a company's culture, Marci believes, "There should be a shared emphasis between investing in the right technology and ensuring your workforce uses it to enhance the customer experience effectively." With so many touch points for customers to engage with, companies need "to evolve the one-to-one message into a multi-dimensional relationship driven by the customer." By placing the customer in the centre and allowing the customer to customize the information experience, organizations will create deeper relationships and better experiences.

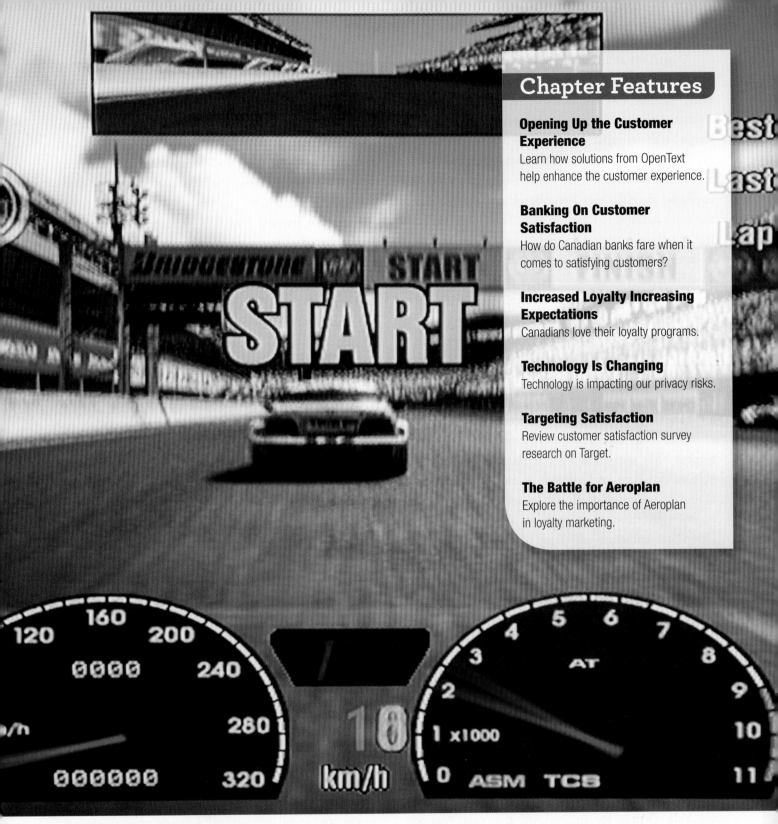

Chapter Features

Opening Up the Customer Experience
Learn how solutions from OpenText help enhance the customer experience.

Banking On Customer Satisfaction
How do Canadian banks fare when it comes to satisfying customers?

Increased Loyalty Increasing Expectations
Canadians love their loyalty programs.

Technology Is Changing
Technology is impacting our privacy risks.

Targeting Satisfaction
Review customer satisfaction survey research on Target.

The Battle for Aeroplan
Explore the importance of Aeroplan in loyalty marketing.

Chapter Outline:

Opening up the customer experience

Customer relationship management (CRM)

Social media and CRM

Customer acquisition and retention

Database marketing

CRM and customer reacquisition

OpenText solutions have helped a leading global interactive entertainment software company. By delivering games and content online, the reach of this company and its client base seemed endless. The challenge for the company was to establish control over its global brand by offering a consistent look-and-feel for local markets. Since there was so much content that could be shared, OpenText offered a strategy to send the right content to the right user. The OpenText solution involved creating a warehouse of digital content, allowing its global users to access the content for their specific needs. Now, marketers of games from all over the world can customize their solutions specifically to the needs of their local markets.

The benefits of the OpenText solution is explained best by Marci: "From a marketing perspective, organizations are looking at ways to elevate their brand and increase the loyalty and advocacy they have with their customers." The end goal for companies is to create brand advocates who cannot stop talking about experiences that exceeded their expectations. So being able to measure and manage customer information is just one component of customer experience management. Additional components are offered through OpenText solutions allowing businesses to control and customize the information being sent to customers with the goal of enhancing the customer experience. "We are seeing customers, employees, and even suppliers and distributors demanding better online self-service from companies."

OpenText solutions can positively impact non-profit organizations as well. The Yale Digital Collections Center (YDC2) is an initiative to create and establish a digital preservation method and best practices to manage and share Yale University collections, research, and projects. The content represents the valuable holdings from Yale's museums and libraries—the Beinecke Rare Book and Manuscript Library, the Yale Center for British Art, the Yale Peabody Museum of Natural History, and the Yale University Art Gallery. Yale's academic and research institutions, libraries, and museums generate and consume enormous quantities of content that must now be managed in the context of the global digital environment. Yale strives to remain competitive in an era when knowledge creation, dissemination, and preservation are increasingly dependent on digital content infrastructure. Yale has set a goal to develop an infrastructure that represents an intersection of content, technology, policy, shared practice, and community with the aim to better steward Yale's intellectual output in the digital age. "Making sure you understand how your rich media gets created, how it is being used, and where it has already been sent is critical to creating a successful and exciting customer experience," explains Marci. The Yale Digital Collections Center (or YDC2) is a website that offers research support, an imaging lab, and an area to develop digital content. The power of centralizing Yale University's cultural heritage and natural history collections offers consistency, accuracy, and accessibility to researchers globally.

Customizing the customer experience relies heavily on how much a consumer wants to share. As Marci reflects on permission marketing, she says, "Millennials are not shy about sharing personally identifiable information. Organizations will leverage the information you share about yourself to deliver a more targeted and relevant experience." Marci explains that companies still need to maintain corporate and regulatory governance when doing this, especially since not all countries allow personal data to be used by companies without explicit permission approval. The users of OpenText solutions can rest assured that the company's heritage is built on ensuring governance is adhered to, as it is a legal risk for the organizations involved otherwise.

When consumers make a purchase from a company, they are essentially aligning their personal brand and reputation with that company. "Consumers do not want to feel abandoned by the organization they trusted with their business," shares Marci. "That is why the customer relationship has to offer ongoing support and evolve into trusted social interaction." As companies think and act globally, the opportunities for employment grow globally. OpenText plans to double its workforce across the globe over the next few years. This growth will allow OpenText to continue to grow its enterprise information management strategy and leadership.[1]

reality CHECK ✓

As you read Chapter 14, refer back to the OpenText vignette to answer the following questions:

- What exactly do you think is meant by companies needing to take a joint approach when considering a CRM or CEM solution?
- How much personal data would you share to have a better customer experience?
- How should organizations use data in the public domain, such as tweets or uploaded videos, to enhance the customer experience?

After consumers have initiated and completed their purchase decision, they become customers. Customer relationship management (CRM) considers the purchase decision from the point of view of the business. It engages three interactions with customers, including customer acquisition, customer retention, and customer reacquisition. To be executed effectively, CRM requires support from the company's top management.

Customer Relationship Management (CRM)

LO 1 **Customer relationship management (CRM)** is the overall process of building and maintaining profitable customer relationships by delivering superior customer value and satisfaction. Executing CRM may involve technology, business rules, and operational processes, as well as the cooperation of key stakeholders within the organization.[2]

Customer relationship management (CRM) strives to build and maintain profitable customer relationships.

This involves many aspects within an organization, including how consumers become customers, how they are retained as customers, and how well a company manages information on customers. The strategies that companies put into place around how they manage data will help them be successful in the customer relationship management discipline.[3]

Customer Satisfaction

Information about customers can be used to create marketing programs that result in customer satisfaction. Information technology and database systems are a great starting point for CRM; however, for CRM to be successful, there must be attitude changes in the organization. CRM started out as a tool to help the sales force keep track of customers and prospects, but it has evolved into so much more. A large corporation may spend tens of millions of dollars on a CRM system. Among the big suppliers are Oracle, SAP, and IBM; dozens of other companies specialize in components such as telephone call centre technology, database software, and Internet systems. The whole idea is to customize each system to a specific company's needs. Funnelling information to one place that otherwise would be dispersed in a big company allows all employees to access one customer profile instead of bits and pieces of information about the customer scattered throughout the company.

Call your local bank about your chequing account and you may discover that the person on the phone is looking at a screen that summarizes your previous calls and displays information about your mortgage and credit card as well. Visit your local bank and you may be surveyed about your experiences and your likelihood to recommend the branch.

customer relationship management (CRM)
The overall process of building and maintaining profitable customer relationships by delivering superior customer value and satisfaction

customer experience management (CEM)
Managing customer interactions with the goal of increasing satisfaction and loyalty

touch point
Any situation in which a customer comes into contact with a brand or company

Customer Experience Management

A concept similar to CRM is a process called **customer experience management (CEM)**. CEM involves managing customer interactions to build brand equity and improve long-term profitability. It requires strategy to manage all points of the customer experience, as keeping customers satisfied will be more important than simply making a sale.[4] CEM focuses on customer interactions, or touch points. A **touch point** describes any customer interaction with the brand or company.

Customer interactions include every point in which the customer interacts with a business, product, or service. For the Starbucks customer, this may include the anticipation of going to Starbucks, walking up to a shop, opening the door, ordering and paying for the coffee, talking to the server, getting the coffee, and sitting down in the relaxed atmosphere of the shop to enjoy the coffee. In the case of MacBooks, Apple ascertained that its customers disliked the touch point of impersonal technical support calls.

Instead, Apple resolves this issue by creating Genius Bar touch points that offer face-to-face help at the Apple Store. Furthermore, your banking touch points include experiences with automatic bank machines (ABMs), online banking, and customer service representatives. Alternatively, read about how Target may have misread its consumers' touch points when it expanded into Canada in the Marketing NewsFlash, "Targeting Satisfaction."

Companies should measure and improve customer interactions on an ongoing basis. Levels of customer satisfaction at each touch point can be a better measure of customer loyalty than just measuring overall customer satisfaction. It starts by understanding and listing each individual interaction or touch point that influences customer satisfaction. Whether human (such as sales staff or a call centre), interactive (such as websites, e-mail, or Twitter), or static (such as radio or newspaper ads), each touch point is an opportunity to improve customer experience.[5]

CEM and touch points are used to maintain profitable relationships with customers and are used in various industries to enhance customer satisfaction. Canadian Pacific Hotels (CP Hotels) was not well-regarded by business travellers, a notoriously demanding and diverse group to serve, but also very lucrative and much coveted by other hotel chains. By investing time and money in learning what would most satisfy this segment, the company discovered that customers wanted recognition of their individual preferences and lots of flexibility with check-ins and check-outs. CP Hotels mapped each step of customer interactions from check-in to check-out, and set a standard of performance for each activity. Along the way, the management structure was revamped so that each hotel had a champion with broad cross-functional ability to ensure that the hotel lived up to its ambitious goals.[6]

Ideally, CEM information is analyzed to gain insight into each customer's needs and behaviour, and then it is used to improve the customer's dealings with the company. This can be as simple as freeing the customer from having to repeat his mailing address every time he places an order, to something like being able to instantly tell the customer the status of a shipment. The analysis might guide promotion efforts so that the customer receives mailings, calls, e-mails, or website advertising tailored to his or her likes.

> *Listening to customers is as important as—if not more important than— talking to them.*

Banking On Customer Satisfaction

J.D. Power creates a customer satisfaction index ranking based on a 1,000-point scale. The big 5 banks are ranked as follows:

TD Canada Trust	781
Big 5 Average	765
BMO Bank of Montreal	764
RBC Royal Bank	763
Scotiabank	759
CIBC	750

Source: J.D. Power, "Canadian Retail Banking Customer Satisfaction Improves as Customers Increasingly Understand Fees and Services; However, Customers Still Perceive Banks as Profit Driven, Lagging in Innovation and Not Customer Focused," press release, July 18, 2013. Retrieved from www.jdpower.com/content/press-release/MnoDBJD/2013-canadian-retail-banking-customer-satisfaction-study.htm.

Apple knows that customers dislike the touch point that consists of impersonal technical support calls, so it has created the Genius Bar in its retail stores.

Cultural Changes

CRM databases allow companies to get closer to their customers to establish a mutually beneficial relationship. A company's failure with CRM is often the result of approaching CRM as a software project rather than an overall company strategy. A company may spend millions of dollars on software, but doesn't bother changing the cultural attitudes of the organization. A company may be looking for a quick fix for its problems. Companies feel that if they purchase CRM software, their problems will disappear. Collecting and managing data is just one component of CRM. A more important component is the organizational culture and support from top management.

A hotel that is suffering from poor employee customer-service skills cannot use software alone to solve the issue. CRM requires a top-down long-run commitment and attitude change by management. If the hotel employees see that management treats them with respect and rewards customer satisfaction, there is a larger incentive for employees to treat customers with respect.

▶ Video
Xerox

In 1997, Xerox Canada refocused a 5,100-person organization with annual revenues over $1.1 billion and underwent a change in structure and compensation incentives to

> *A company's failure with CRM is often the result of approaching CRM as a software project rather than an overall company strategy.*

ensure that its employees focused on customer satisfaction. Although the change was not an easy one, it was necessary to achieve the result of customers being more satisfied with the company's service offerings.[7]

Although not always noticed by customers, the cultural change that organizations undergo requires an investment of time and resources. In the same year that Xerox Canada underwent its cultural change, the 407 ETR opened in the Greater Toronto Area, allowing an all-electronic tolling feature for drivers on this highway. Customer loyalty is increasing for this service due to a lack of competition and the additional convenience offered by the highway. Unfortunately, more resources should be allocated to understanding customer complaints from this organization.[8]

CRM at Four Seasons Hotels and Resorts

Four Seasons Hotels and Resorts grew from a modest hotel in downtown Toronto to a luxury hotel chain consisting of 91 hotels in 38 countries around the world. Founder Isadore Sharp has spent decades developing a culture in which all employees are empowered to take responsibility and make decisions, rather than exclusively relying on orders from management. Mr. Sharp says that culture has to start from the top, the person who really is able to control and make the decisions to reinforce the culture in a meaningful way. "The Golden Rule guides our interactions with our guests, our business partners and investors, but most importantly, with each other," says Sharp. "We also believe in investing in our employees and promoting from within. Many of our senior managers began their careers with Four Seasons and continue to be culture ambassadors." CRM involves tracking guest information and preferences, such as extra pillows, into a database. This information should be used by employees the next time the guest returns to the hotel. Satisfied employees will take this extra step to make guests feel important and recognized. However, if hotel employees are not feeling engaged or appreciated themselves, they may not take that extra step and may fail to enhance the guest experience. It has been estimated that in a 200- to 300-room luxury hotel, there are as many as 5,000 interactions between guests and staff per day; in other words, thousands of opportunities for high performance or for mishaps. Four Seasons Hotels and Resorts excels in making its interactions with guests very positive.[9]

The cultural attitudes of the organization must change internally to what is called a CRM culture if the company is really interested in instituting positive customer service. Management must understand the customer and drive its company to developing the best experience. Top-management support to align internal processes toward a company's CRM strategy is critical to a CRM program's success.[10]

CRM at WestJet

WestJet is an excellent example of a company that has embraced CRM from the top management down. Every employee literally takes ownership in what they do. As shareholders of the company, WestJet employees have a heightened sense of customer service responsibility uncharacteristic of many employees. Seeing this as a differentiator, WestJet launched a series of ads that focused on WestJet's theme of ownership.

Employees who take ownership in what they do have a heightened sense of customer service responsibility.

The average business executive goes into CRM thinking it's only about technology, but if cultural attitudes don't change, employees won't benefit from the information collected and analyzed. Without employees using the system, the software becomes useless. The most senior levels of management need to embrace the business strategy of CRM and move the message and tactics of CRM throughout the organization. CEOs need to get the message out to their VPs and have them get it out to their managers, down to supervisors, and down to the front line.

Gaining loyal customers is critical to a successful CRM strategy. In that strategy, you can ask questions similar to these below:

- Who are your most profitable customers?
- Why do your customers buy from you and not the competition?
- What percentage of your customers are profitable?
- How can you make profitable customers do more business with you?
- How do you plan on managing less profitable customers?

Ulitimately, a company should consider the answers to these questions to evaluate the state of the firm's CRM strategy and what culture changes need to be made in order to effectively execute the strategy. In the end, technology is an enabler of CRM, but a successful CRM strategy is executed by high-performing employees.[11]

CRM at TD Canada Trust

Customer relationship management involves building and maintaining profitable customer relationships. After the merger of TD and Canada Trust banks, the newly formed organization invested $15 million in informing its clients of what to expect of the new company. The investment was part of its strategy of client retention and profitability. In recent TD Canada Trust customer loyalty polls, customers are expecting a higher level of customer service and are receiving it.[12]

But if they don't receive positive customer service, they may not be coming back. Businesses are constantly looking for ways to show customers that they care, such as through reward programs. Many customers appreciate the perks, but according to the findings of the TD Canada Trust loyalty poll, customers want to be treated well. When asked which form of appreciation they are most interested in, 49 percent ranked "just good customer service" as number one. This was followed by just 18 percent who cited reward programs. According to the results, respondents' definition of good service was friendly staff followed by quick and helpful service.

Social Media and CRM

LO² A growing number of companies are keeping track of what's said about their brands on social media platforms such as Facebook and Twitter. This activity falls in line with the process of CRM because it's an excellent way to build and maintain a relationship with customers. Dell, General Motors, H&R Block, Kodak, and Whole Foods Market are among a growing number of companies monitoring Twitter to see what people are saying about their brands as well as to provide solutions to customers' concerns. With the ability to create a conversation between companies and customers, social media provides an excellent platform for the consumer voice and a great resource for marketers. The attention to Twitter reflects the power of new social media tools in letting consumers shape public discussion over brands.[13] A single Twitter message—known informally as a tweet—sent in frustration over a product or a service's performance, can be read by hundreds or thousands of people. Similarly, positive interaction with a representative of the company can help turn an unhappy customer into a more loyal one.

Some companies are hiring social media analytics consultants to monitor social media sites such as Facebook and Twitter in order to digest and understand what consumers are saying about their brands. These consultants have developed specialized software for their clients to scour these sites in real time and to provide actionable insights for smarter business decisions.

Tourism and Social Media

Hotels and airlines were among the first industries to recognize the value of social media platforms such as Twitter and Facebook, and to monitor them to respond to angry customers. Increasingly, companies are taking the tactic to a new level, trying to listen in on every mention of their brands for a real-time gauge of what people think of their offerings, competitors, and industry trends.[14]

Consumers are increasingly using tools such as Twitter to contact an airline as opposed to the old way of phoning the company. For flyers who have lost luggage or missed a flight, the immediacy of social media–based feedback could render toll-free numbers and website feedback forms obsolete in the near future. In an industry where every airline essentially

Porter Airlines employees scanned social media sites to help identify and resolve a customer complaint.

Dave Carroll got his revenge when United Airlines broke his guitar.

sells the same commoditized service, airlines that use social media to turn disappointed customers into happy ones, or to simply enhance the travel experience, are already setting themselves apart and building loyalty.

Consider this scenario, which actually took place at Porter Airlines. When an unhappy passenger found herself waiting in a check-in line that wasn't moving quickly enough, she tweeted her dissatisfaction from her smartphone. At the same time that this was occurring, Porter Airlines employees were scanning Twitter traffic and came across the woman's complaint. By the time that passenger got to the front of the line, Porter staff were on hand to directly deal with her complaint.[15]

The engagement created by social media cannot be ignored as it may have consequences. United Airlines baggage handlers damaged Halifax songwriter David Carroll's $3,500 custom-made bass guitar on a flight from Halifax to Chicago. Carroll spent nine months seeking compensation by sending e-mails, writing letters, and calling airline representatives, all to no avail. Carroll, deeply frustrated and out of options, wrote a song entitled "United Breaks Guitars" and uploaded it to YouTube. The catchy song went viral, with 150,000 views the day it went live and nearly 10 million since then. United Airlines finally relented and, at Carroll's request, donated the $1,200 he paid for repairs to charity. It's interesting to note that within four days of the song going online, the bad PR caused United Airlines' stock price to suffer a plunge of 10 percent, costing shareholders $180 million. After the incident, United Airlines created a Twitter presence, but approaches social media with a more controlled strategy.[16]

Credibility Issues of Social Media

One of the temptations for a company is to encourage consumers to say positive things about its brand on a social media platform. In 2009, Ford promoted its new Fiesta subcompact by letting 100 consumers drive the car for free for six months, gas included. All they had to do was blog, tweet, and post about the car. There exists the possibility that they were more likely to say good things about the car as a result of the freebie, instead of truly giving their unbiased opinions. Although credibility may have suffered as a result of this campaign, the underlying strategy for Ford was engagement. Even though there are not a lot of Fiestas on the road, Ford believes in social media as a means to attract the tech-savvy consumer, and it relaunched a similar social media campaign in 2014.[17]

Customer Acquisition and Retention

LO3 CRM starts by building customer relationships. Data-driven programs can examine the profiles of a company's most-popular customers and use these characteristics to find prospective customers. After a company has found commonalities among profitable customers, it can use this information to accurately target potential customers with the same profile.

Once customer relationships are established, CRM shifts to maintaining profitable customer relationships. A company that builds strong relationships with customers will retain these customers, resulting in more sales and profits than the company would have if it focused only on getting new customers. It's important to note that making a sale to a current

Ford used social media to promote its Fiesta subcompact car.

▶ *"Making sure you understand how your rich media gets created, how it's being used, and where it has already been sent is critical to creating a successful and exciting customer experience."*

—*Marci Maddox, senior director, customer experience management, OpenText*

ask yourself

1. *What is customer relationship management all about?*

2. *Describe how companies are using social media in their relationships with customers.*

customer is way less expensive than making a sale to a new customer.

Listening to customers is as important as—if not more important than—talking to them. Some business-to-business (B2B) companies are now making a special effort to ask customers when and how they would like to be contacted by the company. This information is placed in a database so that it is readily available. This practice shows respect for loyal customers' time and allows companies to direct the brand communication in a way that is appropriate.

The increased profitability that is associated with customer retention is due to several factors that occur after a relationship has been established with a customer. Furthermore, by choosing the right customer, nurturing the right customer, and allocating resources to the right customer, profitability can be further enhanced. Among Canadian respondents in the financial services industry, more than three out of five say that the greatest benefit of CRM is in understanding, acquiring, and retaining customers. Why CRM can help increase profitability through customer retention is explained by the following factors:[18]

- The cost of acquiring a customer occurs only at the beginning of a relationship, so the longer the relationship, the lower the amortized cost.

- Long-term customers tend to be less inclined to switch, and also tend to be less price-sensitive.

- Long-term customers may initiate word-of-mouth activity and referrals.

Loyalty Programs

One way to retain customers is through **loyalty programs**. In Canada, customers have created emotional connections to loyalty programs such as the Air Miles Reward Program.[19] Air Miles is Canada's largest loyalty program; Air Miles can be earned through more than 100 different sponsors, and there are almost 1,000 different rewards that can be redeemed. BMO Bank of Montreal offers an Air Miles–sponsored program, and CIBC offers an Aeroplan program (see the Marketing NewsFlash, "The Battle for Aeroplan," for more detail). Loyalty programs were not always as advanced as Air Miles. In fact, the oldest and best-known loyalty program in Canada is Canadian Tire money.

Loblaw offers the President's Choice Financial MasterCard, with which consumers can get PC points that can be redeemed for groceries. And the Shoppers Drug Mart Optimum card is a very successful loyalty program. Loyalty programs have become a way for one company to differentiate itself from another, but these differentiations have high expectations from Canadians.[20]

Although businesses appreciate all their customers, CRM practices allow them to distinguish between the loyalty habits of their customers. In most product categories, a small number of heavy users accounts for a large percentage of a brand's sales and profits. Heavy users are customers who buy an above-average amount of a given brand. According to **Pareto's Rule**, a marketing rule of thumb named after Italian economist Vilfredo Pareto, 80 percent of a brand's sales come from 20 percent of its customers. Heavy users should be rewarded differently than light users.

loyalty programs
Programs specifically designed for customer retention

Pareto's Rule
The concept that 80 percent of a brand's sales come from 20 percent of its customers

Increased Loyalty, Increasing Expectations

Loyalty programs participation
    per Canadian (2012)   6.4
Loyalty programs participation
    per Canadian (2013)   7.3
Number of members wanting to
    receive relevant communications   9 out of 10

Source: S. Robinson and K. Davies, *The 2013 Maritz Loyalty Report, Canadian Edition*. Maritz Canada.

The implication here is to take special care of the 20 percent by offering them better rewards than the remaining 80 percent. Databases allow companies to do more than merely recognize their customers. Companies that surprise and delight their high-profit customers with reward programs are more likely to keep these customers in the long run.

Consider the loyalty program at Starwood Hotels & Resorts, which has such brands as Sheraton and Westin. The chain offers a different twist on personalizing a loyalty program. As well as the usual system of accumulating points that can be redeemed for free rooms, Starwood Preferred Guest program members can use their points to bid for special experiences. The Moments program allows members to take part in online auctions to bid for "insider access" to red-carpet premieres, closed rehearsals with top musicians, private dinners with celebrity chefs, or rounds of golf with PGA Tour pros.

Members of the Moments program can hone their golf skills with a hands-on clinic led by PGA TOUR Professional Jason Gore. Members learn golfing techniques from Gore and then test out their new skills with 18 holes of challenging play, where Jason

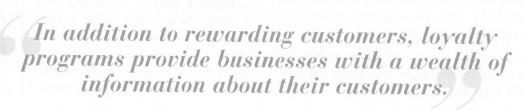

HMV's purehmv program recently had a Disturbed-Autographed Schecter Diamond Series Guitar as a reward.

joins the member for several holes and offers tips along the way.[21]

HMV also has a unique loyalty offering through its purehmv program. Over and above giving points to customers to redeem for merchandise, the HMV program offers rewards such as autographed memorabilia, limited-edition products, and celebrity meet-and-greets. One expensive reward recently on offer was a Disturbed-Autographed Schecter Diamond Series Guitar.[22]

In addition to rewarding customers, loyalty programs provide businesses with a wealth of information about their customers. This information is the raw material for data mining, which is discussed in the next section.

Privacy

With technology becoming more pervasive in our culture and companies having access to more and more consumer information, the Canadian government has extended the responsibilities of the Office of the Privacy Commission of Canada to the private sector. This office acts as an advocate for Canadians on their rights to privacy. The *Personal Information Protection and Electronic Documents Act (PIPEDA)* established rules for how personal information is handled during the course of business. Personal information can be collected only through lawful means. Consumers need to consent to the information being collected, while companies need to protect the information and cannot use it for purposes other than what was originally intended. Furthermore, in 2014, the Canadian government introduced anti-spam legislation. Given the ease of accessibility to consumer information, this legislation is intended to protect Canadians from unwanted communications and threats.[23] The "Technology Is Changing" Infographic demonstrates how one Australian jurisdiction is dealing with privacy issues.

> *In addition to rewarding customers, loyalty programs provide businesses with a wealth of information about their customers.*

Infographic

TECHNOLOGY IS *changing...*

THEN | **NOW**

We wrote letters | We send messages via **social media**

BUSINESS WAS DONE IN PERSON AND IN PRINT | Business is done **online** using our personal information

We stored information on a bookshelf | We store information **in the cloud**

...*so are* THE PRIVACY RISKS

166,801 Privacy complaints in Korea in 2011-12

68% of 2012 internet privacy complaints were about social media and smartphone applications **in Hong Kong**

30% increase in privacy investigations each year from 2007-12 in Macau

78% of Australians have refused to provide personal information online

NT 100% **increase** in time spent providing privacy advice from 2007-12

QLD 86% of people think privacy is important when using or installing mobile apps

NSW 300% increase in privacy enquiries from 2007-12

VIC 33% of complaints in 2011-12 were about data security

92% of Canadians say companies should ask permission to track them online

88% increase in public education and outreach in **British Columbia** in 2011-12

$33.85M assessed in US for privacy violations in 2011-12

65% of school children **in Mexico** learn about online privacy at school

88% of New Zealanders say to punish businesses that misuse personal information

What are you doing TO PROTECT YOUR PRIVACY?

APPA

WWW.PRIVACYAWARENESSWEEK.ORG

Source: "Technology is changing," accessed at www.privacy.vic.gov.au/privacy/web2.nsf/files/privacy-awareness-week-2013-appa-poster/$file/paw_2013_appa_poster.pdf. Used by permission of the Office of the Victorian Privacy Commissioner (Privacy Victoria).

Targeting Satisfaction

Target focuses on customer satisfaction, summarized well by its tagline: "Our promise is simple: Expect More. Pay Less.®" It aims to create an environment in which team members and guests have an experience that exceeds their expectations. Part of the appeal of Target is that it partners with chic designer fashions and promotes their fashions at a reasonable price. This strategy led to a relatively high customer satisfaction index among its American customers and opportunities for further expansion into Canada.

When Target opened its first stores in Canada in 2013, it got off to a slow start with respect to customer satisfaction. By starting with 17 stores and with plans to expand to 124 stores, Target planned to bring the same customer experience it had in the United States to Canada. Shortly after its expansion, however, a Forum Research survey found that less than three out of ten consumers said they were "very satisfied" with Target. The main concerns of Canadian consumers included low inventory and high prices. Unfortunately, the touch points in the United States that attracted Canadians to the brand were not identical in the Canadian stores. The media companies that reported the findings also received feedback from their readers through social media. These comments offered a balanced view, yet commenters were split on their perspectives of Target.

The concerns from shoppers drove Target to the bottom of the Forum Research survey list among major retailers in Canada. With Costco Canada leading the pack and Target's main competitor Walmart Canada clearly improving, Target has a lot of opportunity for growth and is confident that its core customers will continue showing their loyalty.[24]

Questions

1. Describe the attributes of a Canadian retailer that provides excellent customer service?

2. How do customer expectations affect customer relationship management?

database marketing
The use of databases to customize communications to customers and potential customers for the purpose of promoting a product or service

data mining
The processing of large amounts of data using sophisticated software and algorithms to find insightful correlations and patterns that lead to better business decisions

Database Marketing

LO 4 **Database marketing** is an essential practice for enhancing the customer experience. It is significant to a company's success in identifying its customers and customizing its service offerings. Over time, company's collect, process, and analyze information on their customers, potential customers, and competitors. Through careful analysis, companies can better recognize customer needs and adjust accordingly to meet and exceed expectations. Whether through traditional means or social networks, database marketing can help companies improve customer loyalty.[25]

Data Mining

How does a company use the reams of information in its databases? One answer is data mining. **Data mining** is an efficient way to sort through large amounts of data to find relationships between variables. It is a process of analyzing customer patterns and insights to make better marketing decisions. By spotting trends and relationships among the reams of information, data mining can help specifically target customer segments to meet their needs. Since data mining is

ask yourself

1. *What is Pareto's Rule?*
2. *Give some examples of loyalty programs.*
3. *What is data mining?*

bar called "Sharx" were a higher risk. "If you show us what you buy, we can tell you who you are, maybe even better than you know yourself," a former Canadian Tire exec said.[28]

A third example of data mining involves Metro, a chain of supermarkets in Ontario and Quebec. Its bottled juices traditionally were placed on the shelves by brand. But data mining information showed that consumers preferred the juices to be shelved by flavour. Metro made the change and sales of juices increased.[29]

data warehouse
A central repository of an organization's electronically stored data

customer lifetime value
The potential sales that will be generated by a customer if the customer remains loyal to that company for a lifetime

growing in its impact to customer satisfaction and developing business opportunities, companies need to place more emphasis in getting customer information in the hands of sales and support staff to make a difference. Effective integration of data mining in a company's CRM strategy will allow for improved customer service and sales performance.[26]

Loyalty programs supply a lot of information that can be used for data mining purposes. Information that customers supply when they apply for a loyalty program can be tied to their purchase behaviour. Data mining can then be used to find patterns in consumer behaviour and also help marketers with customer segmentation.

All the data about customers is stored in a central place, called the **data warehouse**. A data warehouse can be thought of as an electronics library where all the information is indexed. Once the data warehouse brings the data together, the company uses data mining techniques to find insights about customers.

There are multiple examples of how CRM and data mining techniques positively impact retail organizations in Canada. For example, since 1995, Royal Bank of Canada has invested over $100 million in its CRM strategy and has considered it a core strategy. It attributes CRM as having a positive impact to its revenue growth and profitability, while still allowing the organization to reduce costs. The deeper the data can be analyzed, the better insights that can be made.[27]

A second example is Canadian Tire. Data mining enabled the retailer's credit card division to create psychological profiles of its cardholders that were built upon alarmingly precise correlations. Data mining revealed that cardholders who purchased carbon-monoxide detectors, premium birdseed, and felt pads for the bottoms of their chair legs rarely missed a payment. On the other hand, those who bought cheap motor oil and visited a Montreal pool

Customer Lifetime Value

In customer relationship management, a company focuses on its relationship with customers with the ultimate goal of creating an unbreakable bond with its customers. Companies are starting to focus on the value of a customer if that customer remains loyal to the firm over the customer's lifetime. This is referred to as **customer lifetime value**.

Carl Sewell, a successful car dealer-owner and author of a book called *Customers for Life,* looks at each customer as an investment. If he can provide each customer with excellent customer service, that customer will likely remain loyal to Carl's dealership in the future. In a sense, that customer may have a lifetime value to Carl of hundreds of thousands of dollars. Knowing this, Carl keeps an insightful perspective in dealing with customers.[30]

An example of Carl's insight involved a customer who came to pick up his car after servicing and noticed that his tennis racquet, which he had left in the car, was gone. Under normal circumstances, a dealer would say that it is not responsible for items left in a car. Carl

ask yourself

1. *Why is customer lifetime value important for companies to calculate?*
2. *What does share of wallet mean?*

The Battle for Aeroplan

Loyalty cards are normally associated with rewards. In the fall of 2011, Groupe Aeroplan underwent a change. It began conducting business under a new brand name, Aimia. Aeroplan is the consumer-facing brand in Canada that allows travellers to collect points for travel rewards with Air Canada and its strategic alliances. Owned by Aimia, Aeroplan is considered Canada's premier coalition loyalty program since it has over 75 world-class partners and represents over 150 brands in the retail, travel, and financial industries.

Having celebrated its 30th anniversary in July 2014, Aeroplan has more than 4.6 million active members, making it a sought-after partner in a variety of industries. Well-known Canadian companies such as Esso, Home Hardware, and Sobeys were added as partners in 2005. In the financial services industry, Aeroplan partnered with American Express® and CIBC to offer rewards credit cards. Aeroplan's relationship with CIBC began in 1991 when Aeroplan and CIBC partnered to launch the CIBC Aerogold® VISA Card, considered one of the most popular credit cards in Canada.

Although the 20-year-plus partnership has been a successful one, Aeroplan recently had another suitor. In 2013, TD Bank entered into the Aeroplan loyalty business by becoming the primary credit card issuer for the Aeroplan loyalty rewards program. For a few months, this caused friction between all parties involved. Fortunately, a few months later, TD Bank Group and Canadian Imperial Bank of Commerce were able to reach an agreement. With half of the Aeroplan card portfolio shifting from CIBC to TD, it seemed like a negative situation for CIBC. Over 550,000 cardholder accounts were changing banks. As compensation for this change, CIBC received over $312.5 million from TD and Aimia, with Aimia paying $150 million of that figure. For CIBC, transferring loyalty cards had its rewards.[31]

Questions

1. In terms of customer loyalty, why do you believe TD was so interested in becoming an Aeroplan partner?

2. What benefits does Aeroplan gain by expanding its partners in the financial services sector?

Sewell, on the other hand, went over to the customer and apologized for the mishap. He then proceeded to write a cheque for replacement of the racquet. Carl surmised that it was not worth jeopardizing an investment of hundreds of thousands of dollars over the price of a tennis racquet.

A concept very close to customer lifetime value is **share of wallet**. CRM techniques can help marketers get a larger share of a customer's purchases from that company. Here's an example of how a bank can increase its share of wallet. The bank that holds a customer's mortgage and chequing account may learn at some point that the customer has children and may then try to sell the customer a registered education savings plan. Another example of a company increasing share of wallet is Shoppers Drug Mart. A customer with an Optimum card who

share of wallet
The percentage of a customer's purchases that a company has in a specific product category

purchases cosmetics may receive subsequent communications from Shoppers that offer coupons for related cosmetic products.

CRM and Customer Reacquisition

LO⁵ Companies are realizing that losing a customer means more than losing a sale. It means losing the entire future stream of purchases that the customer would make over a lifetime of patronage. Customers stop buying from a company for a variety of reasons. Very often, the reason can be poor customer service as opposed to something inherently wrong with the brand. The first step in customer recovery is to find the customer who is in jeopardy of being lost to the company. The longer customers stay away from a business, the less likely they are to return. Because customer databases capture purchases, computers can be programmed to periodically examine transaction frequencies and create a list of all customers who have not made a purchase within a set period of time. Because each customer generally has a certain purchase frequency, software can determine when each customer's purchase frequency has been broken. After lapsed customers are identified, the next step is to contact them to determine why they have stopped buying.[32] If the problem is resolved, the lapsed customer may become a very loyal customer because the firm has shown interest in the customer.

Retaining Marginal Customers

CRM allows firms to use information technology to quantify the value of individual customers in terms of sales and profits. High-value customers are provided with better privileges, discounts, or other inducements. CRM analysis shows that a small proportion of customers contribute to a large percentage of profits, and that many customers are unprofitable. Many firms are beginning to jettison or fire their low-value customers and are focusing their time on their high-valued customers. In 2007, CNN reported that Sprint had dropped about 1,000 customers who were calling the customer-care centre too frequently—40 to 50 times more than the average customer every month over an extended period.[33]

Firing low-value customers seems to be a common-sense approach, but in some cases there is a danger. If a company is left with only high-value customers, this leaves the company open to poaching by competitors if they are aware of its customer base.

ask yourself

1. *What does firing a customer mean?*

2. *Describe the two steps in customer recovery.*

Summary...*just the facts*

LO¹ • Customer relationship management (CRM) focuses on using information about customers to build and maintain profitable customer relationships.

• Customer experience management (CEM) involves managing customer interactions to build brand equity and improve long-term profitability.

LO² • A growing number of companies are keeping track of what's said about their brands on social media platforms such as Facebook and Twitter. This activity falls in line with the process of CRM, because it's an excellent way to build a relationship with customers.

LO³ • One way to retain customers is through loyalty programs. It should be noted that all customers should be rewarded, but not all customers are the same. In most product categories, a small number of heavy users account for a large percentage of a brand's sales and profits.

LO⁴ • Companies use database marketing to collect, process, and analyze information on their customers, potential customers, and competitors with a goal to improve customer loyalty.

• Data mining is an efficient way to sort through large amounts of data to find relationships between variables.

• Companies are starting to focus on the value of a customer if that customer remains loyal to the firm over the customer's lifetime.

LO⁵ • Many firms are beginning to jettison or fire their low-value customers and are focusing their time on their high-value customers.

• Companies are instituting customer reacquisition programs to prevent losing customers.

Key Terms and Concepts...*a refresher*

customer experience management (CEM)
customer lifetime value

customer relationship management (CRM)
database marketing

data mining
data warehouse
loyalty programs

Pareto's Rule
share of wallet
touch point

Hands-on...*apply your knowledge*

Online CEM Assignment Visit the OpenText website at **www.opentext.com/customer-stories**. Review another customer success story and put into your own words how an OpenText customer experience management solution helped the company.

Chapter Vignette...*reminder*

In the opening vignette, customer relationship management and customer experience management are discussed. Answer the questions at the end of the vignette by reviewing the vignette as well as the Marketing NewsFlash boxes, "Targeting Satisfaction" and "The Battle for Aeroplan."

Video Clip...*questions*

Anne Mulcahy, former chairman and CEO of Xerox Corporation, helped Xerox shift to a consultative selling model when she became CEO in 2001. While watching the CONNECT video, consider these questions that concern customer relationships:

▶ Video
Xerox

- What are the six stages of building customer relationships at Xerox? How do they align with the strategies outlined in this chapter?
- Why was Anne Mulcahy's experience as a sales representative an important part of Xerox's growth?
- Why is the Xerox training program so important to the company's success?

Infographic...*data analysis*

According to a 2013 whitepaper by Maritz Canada, almost one in four Canadians avoid loyalty programs because of privacy issues. The irony is that more Canadians are expecting personalized communications, and collecting personal information is necessary for marketers to customize their messages. What is interesting is that the majority of Canadians are not letting privacy concerns act as barriers to their loyalty programs. Review the Infographic in this chapter on privacy risks and offer your thoughts about what loyalty marketers can do to address these issues.

For more information on the resources available from McGraw-Hill Ryerson, go to **www.mheducation.ca/he/solutions**.

Chapter 15

strategic marketing planning

LEARNING OBJECTIVES

LO¹ Describe how strategy is developed at the corporate, business unit, and functional levels in an organization

LO² Define the concepts of business, mission, and goals, and explain why they are important in organizations

LO³ Explain why managers use marketing dashboards and marketing metrics

LO⁴ Discuss how organizations formulate strategies

LO⁵ Outline the strategic marketing process

Strategic planning is a continuous process used by large and small companies to set direction and organizational objectives. Businesses and not-for-profit organizations use this approach to help set, and then work toward, achieving a long-term vision for an organization and to satisfy stakeholders' expectations. With limited resources and increasing competition from local, national, and global competitors, Canadian businesses face many challenges each day. Strategic planning and the development of marketing plans help keep these businesses competitive.

Whether it is a non-profit organization seeking donors or a business firm creating new customers, the right decisions and effective use of resources contribute to an organization's success. Always making the right decisions is challenging, so business leaders need guidelines and feedback mechanisms to support their direction. The strategy a business chooses helps define this framework. If developing and setting strategy seems like a daunting task, a good reference point is to start with the organization's mission statement.[1]

For example, ESPN's mission is "to serve sports fans wherever sports are watched, listened to, discussed, debated, read about, or played." In order to be pervasive among sports fans, ESPN needs to attract and retain good people to execute its mission. In fact, the organization sees people as its most valuable resource, making effective talent acquisition a key component of its strategy.[2]

More and more companies see talent as a important component to executing strategy. Finding the right people to execute business strategy well is a challenging and rewarding task, as the effective utilization of people, processes, and capital helps organizations achieve their long-term vision.[3]

As vice president of strategy with webTactics, Mike Jackson reviews the strategic planning process with business leaders and helps them develop marketing plans specific to talent acquisition. Located in Toronto, webTactics' business focuses on management consulting, digital strategy development, and data analysis related to all aspects of talent acquisition. It is led by three individuals bringing together more than 20 years of digital industry experience.

webTactics' focus is on problem resolution. Mike shares that "since one of the most important commitments of time and resources is a company's hiring and development of employees, an organization has to determine how much of an investment it wants to make toward its recruitment marketing strategy." Creating a strategic marketing plan for talent acquisition has many steps. The first step begins with understanding the target audience. This is complemented by an analysis of the organization's culture. Mike believes that determining how well candidates will fit in a culture is an important part of the hiring process.

One of the key questions Mike asks is, "What is your employee value proposition?" If the client can articulate this well, Mike's team determines how the value proposition was derived. He believes it is important to evaluate and validate a client's answer, and that process involves examining past successes and failures in hiring. This can involve external surveys asking job seekers how the company is perceived in the marketplace. If resources cannot be allocated toward gathering external research, Mike looks deeper within the company.

Similar to how products and services marketers receive feedback from customers, Mike will evaluate an organization by the people that already work for it. Satisfied and successful employees are confidentially interviewed to get a sense of how they consume information. By understanding what the current employees feel are the competitive strengths and weaknesses of the organization, by specifically targeting the employees the organization wants to hire more of, Mike gains a better understanding of the personality of the candidate that would match the personality of the company helping the client organization excel. Finding this fit helps candidates reach professional and personal fulfillment, allowing the company to reduce turnover. Mike's team can develop a strategy to find individuals with similar media habits and, ideally, similar fits for the organization.

Mike invests a lot of time helping clients understand the importance of the four key elements in the discovery phase of a marketing plan. It begins with an understanding of the existing recruitment brand to determine the company's strengths, weaknesses, opportunities, and threats against the talent pool. Once that is complete, the organization reviews its existing recruitment process and the corresponding candidate experience. The next element reviews the tools and technologies in place, which are designed to support the overall talent acquisition goal, and tie them into the last element, which is the tracking and analysis of key metrics against the recruitment process and brand. Based on these four elements, the marketing program is then put together based on a budget and the media habits of the target job seeker.

Once the recruitment marketing plan is put into practice, it is immediately (and continually) evaluated. Measuring the results of a recruitment marketing plan is a key step in achieving client satisfaction. Reviewing website traffic and keeping in contact with prospective candidates are additional steps in the implementation and evaluation phases. As we discuss marketing metrics and dashboards, Mike laments that "the tools and technology we are discussing today may be either obsolete or irrelevant in a few years." Notwithstanding, he definitely sees the value that technology has added to measuring the results from the investments made in marketing research and creative. When describing the importance of metrics to his clients, Mike illustrates the value using Angry Birds, the video game by Rovio. "Before metrics and dashboards, our recruitment marketing plans would be executed with a ready-aim-fire approach whereby guesstimates and research were the key." That is, his marketers would not receive feedback until the campaign was complete. "The digital age we are in right now allows us to execute recruitment marketing plans with an aim-fire-adjust approach." To illustrate this further, Mike clarifies, "After we execute a part of the recruitment marketing plan, we use the metrics to quickly adjust our plan and get closer to our desired result. This will lead to adjustments to and revised investments in the campaigns."

Although some organizations can develop and execute their own strategic recruitment marketing plans, many look for help from agencies. Knowing when to develop strategy using internal resources or an external agency depends on an organization's commitment to mobilizing resources to avoid the risks of insularity. Mike finds that developing strategy works best when he works with management, requiring external perspective, a reality check, and/or insight into the best practices of an industry. He has implemented marketing plans for various organizations, appealing to graduating students or requiring specific needs for targeted talent. Mike ends the interview with a final piece of advice for developing recruitment marketing plans and strategies. As business continues to evolve, and technology continues to enable, Mike suggests that marketers "focus some energy on what's next, rather than all energy on what's now."[4]

reality CHECK ✓

As you read Chapter 15, refer back to the webTactics vignette to answer the following questions:

• How is the strategic marketing process described by Mike Jackson aligned with the process described in the chapter?

• If Mike Jackson was helping organizations create more loyal customers, what modifications (if any) would you make to its strategic marketing process?

Organizational Structure and Strategy

LO¹ Chapter 15 describes how organizations set their mission and overall direction and link these activities to marketing strategies. As consumers become more concerned about a company's impact on society, marketing strategy may need to be linked to the social goals of the company's mission statement. Chapter 15 focuses on strategic planning and the role it plays in the marketing process.

Kinds of Organizations

Today's organizations can be divided into business firms and not-for-profit organizations. A *business firm* is an organization that serves its customers in order to earn a profit. **Profit** is the excess of revenues over costs, the reward to a business for the risk it undertakes in offering a product for sale. In contrast to business firms, a *not-for-profit organization* is an organization that serves its customers but does not have profit as an organizational goal. For simplicity, however, we use the terms *firm, company, corporation,* and *organization* to cover both business and not-for-profit operations.

Marketing and the Three Organizational Levels

All organizations should have a strategic direction—that is, they should have an idea of what they hope to achieve and how they plan to achieve it. Marketing not only helps set the direction but also helps the organization get there. Large organizations are complex and may consist of three organizational levels whose strategies are linked to marketing. Figure 15–1 illustrates the three levels of strategy in an optimal organization.

At the *corporate level,* top management directs overall strategy for the entire organization. Multimarket, multiproduct firms such as General Electric or Unilever really manage a group of different businesses, variously termed strategic business units (SBUs), strategic business segments, or product-market units (PMUs).[5] Each of these units markets a set of related products to a clearly defined group of customers. Management at the corporate level focuses on the interests of the shareholders of the firm, as measured by stock performance and profitability.

Similar to adjusting trajectory in the game Angry Birds, marketers make slight adjustments after executing their strategy.

profit
The excess of revenues over costs, the reward to a business for the risk it undertakes in offering a product for sale

The *business unit level* has business unit managers set the direction for individual products and markets. Strategic direction is more specific at the business unit level of an organization. For less complex firms with a single business focus, the corporate and business unit strategies may merge. Unilever has provided products such as Sunlight and Vaseline to Canadians for over 100 years. Another example of one of their strategic business units is Ben & Jerry's, a premium ice cream company with fun flavour names.[6]

At the *functional level,* each business unit has marketing and other specialized activities such as finance, manufacturing, or human resources. The name of a *department* generally refers to its specialized function, such as the marketing department or information systems department. At the functional level, the strategic direction becomes very specific and focused.

In a large corporation with multiple business units, marketing may be called on to assess consumer trends as an aid to corporate planning. At the business unit level, marketing may be asked to provide leadership in developing a new, integrated customer service program across all business units. At the functional level, marketing may implement an advertising campaign.

Strategy Issues in Organizations

LO² Organizations need a reason for their existence—and a direction. This is where their business, mission, and goals converge. We'll discuss each below. Figure 15–1 illustrates the different organizational levels in a business. Business and mission apply to the corporate and business unit levels, while goals relate to all levels.

Strategy Defined for Business Plans and Marketing Plans
As discussed earlier, an organization has limited resources available to produce and market its offerings. Since it cannot possibly do everything, it must develop strategies to focus and direct the resources it has to achieve its goals. Unfortunately, the definition of strategy is debated among management and marketing theorists, so for our purposes, we will define **strategy** as an organization's long-term course of action designed to deliver a unique customer experience while achieving its goals.[7] Once the strategy of an organization or an organizational initiative is defined, business leaders collaborate to develop a marketing plan.

Getting ideas and goals down on paper is the first step to making them into reality. The business plan becomes a valuable tool for organizations to do this. It is a document that can help convey the value of your company to investors, employees, and future partners. Business plans help identify the strengths, weaknesses, opportunities, and threats of a business, as well as help develop accurate financial forecasts. Essential to the overall business plan, a marketing plan helps a business develop the right products to address customer needs, establish the best way to promote the business, and determine where the product will be distributed. Advertising and communications are also important components of the marketing plan.[8]

The Business Organizations such as Canadian Blood Services and your college or university exist for a purpose—to accomplish something for someone. At the beginning, most organizations have clear ideas about what "something" and "someone" mean. But as the organization grows over time, often its purpose becomes fuzzy and continually unclear.

Figure 15–1
The three levels of strategy in organizations: corporate, business unit, and functional

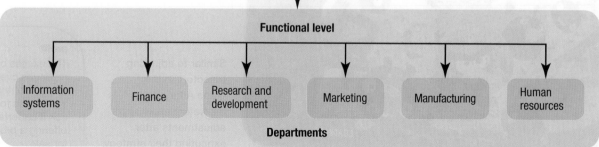

Board of directors → Corporate level → Strategic business unit level → Functional level → Departments: Information systems, Finance, Research and development, Marketing, Manufacturing, Human resources

This is where the organization repeatedly asks some of the most difficult questions it ever faces: What business are we in? Who are our customers? What offerings should we provide to give these customers value? One guideline in defining the company's business is to try to understand the people served by the organization and the value they receive, which emphasizes the critical customer-driven focus that successful organizations have.

In a now-famous article entitled "Marketing Myopia," Harvard professor Theodore Levitt cited railroads as organizations that had a narrow, production-oriented statement of their business: "We are in the railroad business!" This narrow definition of their business lost sight of who their customers were and what their needs were. Railroads saw only other railroads as competitors and failed to design strategies to compete with airlines, barges, pipelines, trucks, bus lines, and cars. Railroads would probably have fared better over the past century by recognizing they are in "the transportation business."[9] Examining business from a broader perspective allows you apply this concept to companies such as Disney. Disney is *not* in the movie and theme park business, but rather it *is* in the business of entertainment, creating fun and fantasy for customers.

The Mission By understanding its business, an organization can take steps to define its **mission**, a statement of the organization's scope, often identifying its customers, markets, products, technology, and values. Today, often used interchangeably with *vision,* the *mission statement* frequently has an inspirational theme—something that can ignite the loyalty of customers, employees, and others with whom the organization comes in contact.

Inspiration and focus appear in the mission statements of business and non-profit organizations. Even if the businesses are different, their mission statements can exhibit similar qualities:

- **Ben & Jerry's (Product Mission):** "To make, distribute and sell the finest quality all natural ice cream and euphoric concoctions with a continued commitment to incorporating wholesome, natural ingredients and promoting business practices that respect the Earth and the Environment."

- **Canadian Blood Services:** "... operates Canada's blood supply in a manner that gains the trust, commitment and confidence of all Canadians by providing a safe, secure, cost-effective, affordable and accessible supply of quality blood, blood products and their alternatives."

- **Mountain Equipment Co-op:** "... to support our members to lead active outdoor lifestyles."

Ben & Jerry's, the maker of premium ice cream, has a mission statement consisting of three parts: social, product, and economic.

Each mission statement illustrates clear direction and challenging and compelling pictures for their futures. Ben & Jerry's goes so far as to add a mission focused on social responsibility as well as a mission for its product. IBM has put strategy in place to create a "smarter planet." It is driven by three core values that help it create its mission statement.

▶ Video IBM

ask yourself

1. *What are the three levels of organization in today's large corporations?*

2. *What is the purpose of an organization's mission?*

3. *What are stakeholders?*

mission
Statement of the organization's purpose and direction

Organizations must connect not just with their customers but with all their *stakeholders*. Stakeholders are the people who are affected by what the company does and how well it performs. This group includes employees, owners, and board members, as well as suppliers, distributors, unions, local communities, governments, society in general, and, of course, customers. Communicating the mission statement is an important corporate-level marketing function. Some companies publish their mission statement on their website or in their annual reports. One British Columbia company has its mission statement on a huge wall poster in its manufacturing facility, and every employee reads and signs it!

Goals Goals or **objectives** take an organization's mission and translate it into targeted levels of performance to be achieved within a specific time frame. These goals measure how well the mission is being accomplished. Goals exist at the corporate, business unit, and functional levels, which were shown in Figure 15–1. All lower-level goals must contribute to achieving goals at the next highest level.

Business firms can pursue several different types of goals:

- **Profit:** Most firms seek to maximize profits—to get as high a financial return on investment (ROI) as possible.

- **Sales:** A firm may elect to maintain or increase its sales level even though profitability may not be maximized.

- **Market share:** A firm may choose to maintain or increase its market share, sometimes at the expense of greater profits if industry status or prestige is a desired goal. **Market share** is the ratio of sales revenue of the firm to the total sales revenue of all firms in the industry, including the firm itself.

- **Quality:** A firm may target the highest quality, as Rolex does with its luxury wristwatches.

- **Customer satisfaction:** Customers are the key to an organization's success, so their perceptions and actions are of vital importance. Their satisfaction can be measured directly with surveys.

- **Employee welfare:** A firm may recognize the critical importance of its employees by having an explicit goal stating its commitment to good employment opportunities and working conditions.

Canada's Most Profitable Companies in 2013

1. Royal Bank of Canada
2. Bank of Nova Scotia
3. Toronto-Dominion Bank
4. Bank of Montreal
5. Imperial Oil
6. Canadian Imperial Bank of Commerce
7. Suncor Energy
8. BCE Inc.
9. Canadian National Railway Co.
10. Potash Corporation of Saskatchewan

Source: Based on "Canada's top performing companies: by the data," *Canadian Business*, May 10, 2013, accessed at www.canadianbusiness.com/lists-and-rankings/canadas-top-performing-companies/; and Jamie Henry, "Insurers among Canada's most profitable companies," *Insurance Business*, July 2, 2014, accessed at www.insurancebusiness.ca/news/insurers-among-canadas-most-profitable-companies-178673.aspx.

- **Social responsibility:** A firm may seek to balance conflicting goals of stakeholders to promote overall welfare, even at the expense of profits. (See, for example, the discussion of the emphasis on corporate social responsibility at Mountain Equipment Co-op in the Focus on Ethics box, "MEC Believes Accountability Is Key to Corporate Social Responsibility.")

Many organizations (for example, museums, symphony orchestras, and private schools) do not seek profits as a primary goal. These organizations strive to serve consumers as efficiently as possible. Government agencies also perform marketing activities in trying to achieve their goal of serving the public good.

Marketing Budgets and Financials Clearly stating goals in a marketing plan is important. Aligning marketing objectives and financial objectives of a company is also important since discrepancies between chief marketing officer (CMO) and chief financial officer (CFO) activities can have a negative impact on financial results.[10]

The break-even analysis and profit equation, discussed in Chapter 9, help develop a pricing strategy for products and services. With key assumptions, marketing plans need to generate sales forecasts to determine the amount of money or sales that will be generated. These sales help the business's finance team forecast a company's cash flow and profit and loss for its overall

MEC Believes Accountability Is Key to Corporate Social Responsibility

Mountain Equipment Co-op (MEC) set challenging goals for itself in 2013. When sourcing its apparel materials, it focused on using facilities with environmental management systems and products with environmentally preferred materials. The additional steps MEC made for the benefit of the environment were not in vain. It surpassed its targets with respect to how it designs its products, how it operates as an organization, and how it supports the community.

MEC did not stop at achieving some of its goals. It held itself accountable through an accountability report shared with the public. This report highlighted where it succeeded and where it needed to improve. Furthermore, to ensure that results were conveyed in an unbiased yet fair manner, MEC looked to its stakeholders to form an accountability review panel to help compile and submit the findings.[11] Mountain Equipment Co-op is not the only company focused on corporate social responsibility. According a recent article in *Maclean's,* applying socially responsible practices makes good business sense and adds to the bottom line of many Canadian companies.[12]

Questions

1. Give some examples of other companies practising corporate social responsibility.

2. Would you pay more for more environmentally friendly apparel? Discuss.

business plan. Marketers rely on historical information, emerging trends, and assumptions to look forward, and then suggest the potential impact that marketing will have on the company's success.[13]

Determining how marketing spending impacts company profitability is an ongoing challenge for CMOs.[14] With this challenge looming, marketers need to be able to prepare accurate budgets for their marketing plans. Since forecasts in marketing plans may be relied upon for other decisions, it is important for marketers to ensure that more than one forecast is created. Considering realistic, optimistic, and pessimistic forecasts helps decision makers see expected, best-case, and worst-case scenarios. Preparing forecasts and budgets provides an opportunity for companies to predict future revenues and expenses while looking for ways to cut costs. To help improve accuracy in budgeting and forecasting for marketing, marketers may review past sales, consider upcoming contracts, and propose predictions to potential changes in the market.[15]

Tracking Strategic Performance

LO³ Although marketing managers can set strategic directions for their organizations, how do they know if they are making progress in getting there? One answer is to measure performance by using marketing dashboards.

Marketing Dashboards A **marketing dashboard** is the visual display of the essential information related to achieving a marketing objective. Often, it is a computer-based display with real-time information and active hyperlinks to provide further detail. For example, a CMO may want to see daily what the effect of a new TV advertising campaign is on a product's sales in order to allocate future marketing resources effectively. Dashboards can track other parts of an organization's business, including the impact of its corporate social responsibility endeavours. Similar to a dashboard in a car, marketing dashboards can give feedback at a quick glance.

> **marketing dashboard**
> A visual computer display of essential marketing information

> "We use the metrics to quickly adjust our plan and get closer to our desired result."
>
> —Mike Jackson, vice president, strategy, webTactics

"What the marketing dashboard shows are the key marketing metrics that the organization believes will drive it to success."

Figure 15–2
Example of a marketing dashboard

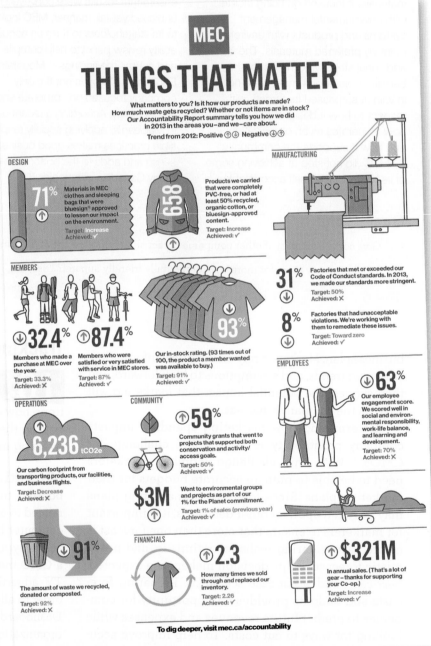

Marketing Metrics Most companies keep their marketing dashboards and metrics proprietary, as the information in the dashboard gives an indication as to the organization's strategy. Marketing dashboards are similar to the accountability report dashboard shown in Figure 15–2. The graphic displays of marketing dashboards are key performance measures of a product category, such as sales versus cost of sales. Each variable in a marketing dashboard is a **marketing metric**, which is a measure of the quantitative value or trend of a marketing activity or result. The choice of which marketing metrics to display is critical for a busy marketing manager, who can be overwhelmed with too much or inappropriate information.

Dashboard designers take great care to show graphs and tables in easy-to-understand formats to enable clear interpretation at a glance. What the marketing dashboard shows are the key marketing metrics that the organization believes will drive it to success.

marketing metric
A measure of the value or trend of a marketing activity or result

An effective dashboard, like this one from Mountain Equipment Co-op, helps managers assess their corporate social responsibility impact at a glance.

Setting Strategic Directions

LO⁴ The webTactics vignette at the beginning of this chapter described key questions that clients are asked when developing a talent acquisition strategy. Setting strategic direction for drawing employees or consumers closer to an organization involves answering challenging questions: Where are we now? Where do we want to go? How will we get there?

A Look Around: Where Are We Now?

Asking an organization where it is at the present time involves identifying its customers, competencies, and competitors. More-detailed approaches of assessing "where are we now?" include SWOT analysis, discussed later in this chapter, and environmental scanning (Chapter 2). It is important for an organization to look internally and externally to assess its starting point. These approaches may be carried out at each of the three levels in the organization.

Customers Tilley Endurables is a Canadian retailer that knows that its customers appreciate the fine hats and travel clothing that Tilley makes. Tilley provides an example of a clear focus on customers. Its stores and website give a remarkable statement about its commitments to customer relationships and the quality of its products. The Tilley guarantee for its legendary hats has always been an unconditional one: "Tilley Hats will be replaced free if they ever wear out, mildew, or shrink." The same guarantee applies to some of their shorts, vests, jackets, pants, and skirts. They are replaced free if they ever wear out.[16]

The crucial point: Strategic directions must be customer-focused and provide genuine value and benefits to existing and prospective customers.

Competencies "What do we do best?" asks about an organization's competencies—an organization's special capabilities, including skills, technologies,

Mountain Equipment Co-op distributes Garmin products, another company committed to being a good corporate citizen.

Each year, *Maclean's* recognizes companies and their socially responsible practices. Companies recognized in 2013 include Loblaw and Canadian Tire.

and resources that distinguish it from other organizations. Exploiting these competencies can lead to success.[17] In Tilley's case, its competencies include an obsession with quality. To quote the founder Alex Tilley, "I'll make travel clothing! I'll make it the best in the world! And then I'll make it even better!" Tilley Endurables is one of the last remaining companies to manufacture all its products in Canada.[18]

Competitors After understanding your business internally, it is important to set your analysis externally. In today's global competition, the lines among competitive sectors are increasingly blurred. This may not be as evident in the apparel industry, but consider Loblaws. Loblaws competes directly with other supermarkets such as Sobeys. At the same time, it also competes against mass merchandisers such as Walmart Supercentres, which also carry groceries, and it competes with warehouse clubs such as Costco. Loblaws also carries many pharmacy items, which puts it into direct competition with pharmacies such as Shoppers Drug Mart and Pharma Plus. Shoppers Drug Mart carries many lines of cosmetics, which puts it in direct competition with department stores such as Hudson's Bay, which traditionally carries cosmetics.

Growth Strategies: Where Do We Want to Go?

Knowing where the organization is at the present time enables managers to set a direction for the firm and commit resources to move in that direction. Two techniques to aid in these decisions are the business portfolio analysis and the market-product analysis.

Business Portfolio Analysis Developed by the Boston Consulting Group (BCG), *business portfolio analysis* uses quantified performance measures and market growth rates to analyze a firm's strategic business units as though they were a collection of separate investments.[19] While used at the business unit level here, the BCG analysis has also been applied at the product line or individual product or brand level. This kind of portfolio analysis is very popular; most large firms have used it in some form.

BCG, a leading management consulting firm, advises its clients to locate the position of each of its SBUs on a growth-share matrix (Figure 15–3). The vertical axis is the *market growth rate,* which is the annual rate of growth of the specific market or industry in which a given SBU is competing. The horizontal axis is the *relative market share,* defined as the sales of the SBU divided by the sales of the largest firm in the industry.

BCG has given specific names and descriptions to the four resulting quadrants in its growth-share matrix based on the amount of cash they generate for or require from the firm:

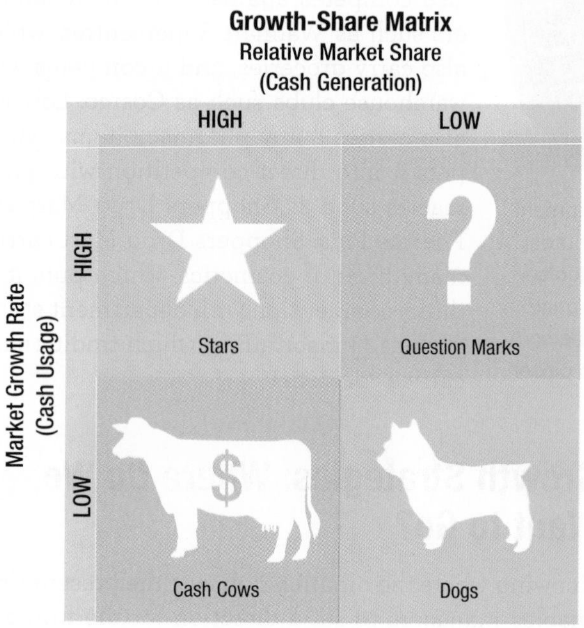

- *Cash cows* are SBUs that typically generate large amounts of cash, far more than they can invest profitably in their own product line. They have a dominant share of a slow-growth market and provide cash to pay large amounts of company overhead and to invest in other SBUs.

- *Stars* are SBUs with a high share of high-growth markets that may need extra cash to finance their own rapid future growth. When their growth slows, they are likely to become cash cows.

- *Question marks* or *problem children* are SBUs with a low share of high-growth markets. They require large injections of cash just to maintain their market share, and even more to increase it. Their name implies management's dilemma for these SBUs: choosing the right ones to invest in and phasing out the rest.

- *Dogs* are SBUs with a low share of low-growth markets. Although they may generate enough cash to sustain themselves, they do not hold the promise of ever becoming real winners for the firm. Dropping SBUs that are dogs may be required, except when relationships with other SBUs, competitive considerations, or potential strategic alliances exist.[20]

Market-Product Analysis Firms can also view growth opportunities in terms of markets and products. Think of it this way: For any product, there is both a current market (consisting of existing customers) and a new market (consisting of potential customers). And for any market, there is a current product (what they're now using) and a new product (something they might use if it were developed). Four possible market-product strategies are shown in Figure 15–4.

As Unilever attempts to increase sales revenues of its Ben & Jerry's business, it must consider all four of the alternative market-product strategies shown in

Figure 15–3
Boston Consulting Group's growth-share matrix for a strong, diversified firm showing some strategic plans

Growth-Share Matrix
Relative Market Share
(Cash Generation)

Figure 15–4
Four market-product strategies: Alternative ways to expand sales revenues for Ben & Jerry's

Markets	PRODUCTS	
	Current	New
Current	**Market penetration** Selling more Ben & Jerry's super premium ice cream in North America	**Product development** Selling a new product such as frozen yogourt under the Ben & Jerry's brand in North America
New	**Market development** Selling Ben & Jerry's super premium ice cream in Brazil for the first time	**Diversification** Selling a new product such as breakfast cereal in China for the first time

Figure 15-4. For example, it can try to use a strategy of *market penetration*—increasing sales of present products in its existing markets, in this case by increasing sales of Ben & Jerry's present ice cream products to consumers. There is no change in either the basic product line or the market served, but increased sales are possible—either by selling more ice cream (through better promotion or distribution) or by selling the same amount of ice cream at a higher price to its existing customers.

Market development is a marketing strategy to sell current products to new markets. For Ben & Jerry's, Brazil is an attractive new market. There is good news and bad news for this strategy: As household incomes of Brazilians increase, consumers can buy more ice cream; however, the Ben & Jerry's brand may be unknown to Brazilian consumers.

An expansion strategy using *product development* involves selling a new product to existing markets. When Ben and Jerry's launched sorbet and frozen yogourt products, the firm was following a product development strategy. Figure 15-4 shows that the firm could try leveraging the Ben & Jerry's brand by selling its own frozen yogourt in North America.

Diversification involves developing new products and selling them in new markets. This is a potentially high-risk strategy for Ben & Jerry's—and for most firms—because the company has neither previous production experience nor marketing experience on which to draw. For example, in trying to sell a Ben & Jerry's brand of breakfast cereal in China, the company has expertise neither in producing cereals nor in marketing to consumers in China. Fast-food giant McDonald's has implemented diversification strategies to gauge success prior to introducing new product development in an established market. An example of this is its McCafé launch in Australia in 1993, many years before it came to North America.

Diversification can take different forms to open a company to new opportunities and threats. When Rogers purchased the Toronto Blue Jays, it got into a completely new area of business. Diversification can also consist of a company introducing a variation of a product to a new market. For example, McDonald's introduced product variations in India including the Veg McMuffin™ and the McVeggie™ to appeal to the high population of vegetarians.

McDonald's introduced McCafé in Australia, as well as the Veg McMuffin and the McVeggie in India, all examples of its diversification strategy.

ask yourself

1. **Why is it important to know what your competencies are?**

2. **How can you use business portfolio analysis to help improve your business?**

3. **What are the four market-product strategies?**

The Strategic Marketing Process

LO5 The Marketing NewsFlash, "The Netflix Launch and Its Continually Changing Business Model," describes how Netflix changed its business model to benefit from the digital age. It is a great example of the strategic marketing process in action. In general, after an organization assesses where it's at and where it wants to go, it must work out how it will get there. Specifically, it must decide the following:

● How to allocate resources

● How to convert plans into actions

● How results compare with plans, and whether deviations (results that differ from expectations) require new plans and actions

This approach is used in the **strategic marketing process**, whereby an organization allocates its marketing mix resources to reach its target markets and achieve its goals. The strategic marketing process is so central to the activities of most organizations that they formalize

strategic marketing process
Approach whereby an organization allocates its marketing mix

The Netflix Launch and Its Continually Changing Business Model

If in 1997 a customer had been charged a late fee of $40 for a VHS tape of *Apollo 13,* what might she or he have done? Maybe just grumble and pay it?

In the case of Reed Hastings, he was embarrassed, apparently paid the $40 late fee, and—this is where he's different—got to thinking that there's a big market out there. "So I started to investigate the idea of how to create a movie-rental business by mail," he told a *Fortune* magazine reviewer.

The Original Business Model

"Early on, the first concept we launched was rental by mail, but it wasn't subscription-based so it worked more like Blockbuster," says Hastings, the founder and chief executive officer of Netflix. It wasn't very popular. So in 1999, he relaunched his idea with a new business model—as a subscription service, pretty much the mail business you see today. "We named the company Netflix, not DVDs by Mail, because we knew that eventually we would deliver movies directly over the Internet," Hastings says.

Netflix's Changing Business Model

The Netflix DVDs-by-mail model delivered movies on DVD to customers for a fixed monthly fee—and drove Blockbuster to seek bankruptcy protection. But the Netflix business model changed over eight months in 2008: from "Watch Now," enabling subscribers to watch any of 1,000 streaming movies on a PC, to partnering with TiVo, Xbox, and others to enable their systems to let you see

one of about 12,000 movies on your television.

The movie distribution channel has also expanded with web-ready TVs such as Sony's Bravia, game consoles such as Xbox 360, and tablets such as Apple's iPad.

With Netflix breaking a series of technology barriers, its "any movie, any time" business is just around the corner. In mid-2011, Netflix introduced controversial new pricing options: DVD only, streaming only, or both. Then in late-2011, when customer reaction exploded, Reed Hastings cancelled the plan to separate Netflix's DVD-by-mail business from its movie streaming service. Change is a constant in the Netflix business model.

Netflix alters its "business model" to respond to changing consumer demand and technologies. Many organizations need to continually improve their businesses in order to stay ahead of the changes that are evident now and predicted for the future.

Questions

1. Netflix's leadership was able to foresee the change from watching movies on DVD to watching movies over the Internet. How does this success validate the final words from Mike Jackson in this chapter's opening vignette?

2. What media do you access to get your news and entertainment? How can Netflix reach consumers like you?

it as a **marketing plan**, which is a road map for the marketing activities of an organization for a specified future period of time, such as one year or five years. The marketing plan is divided into three phases: planning, implementation, and evaluation (Figure 15–5). See the Appendix, available in CONNECT, for an example of a marketing plan, which also includes an executive summary.

This chapter's opening vignette focuses on the strategic marketing process for a talent acquisition marketing plan. Both profit and not-for-profit industries use this approach to help achieve their long-term visions and to satisfy stakeholders' requirements. The following sections give an overview of the marketing plan that puts Chapters 1 through 15 of this book in perspective.

The Planning Phase of the Marketing Plan

As shown in Figure 15–5, the planning phase of the marketing plan consists of the three steps shown at the top of the figure: situation analysis, market-product focus and goal setting, and the marketing program. Let's use the recent marketing planning experiences of several companies to look at each of these steps.

Step 1: Situation Analysis

The essence of a **situation analysis** is taking stock of the firm's or product's past performance, where it is now, and where it is headed in light of the organization's plans and the external factors and trends affecting it. The situation analysis box in Figure 15–5 is the first of the three steps in the planning phase.

Step 1 starts with a **SWOT analysis**, which describes an organization's appraisal of its internal **S**trengths and **W**eaknesses and its external **O**pportunities and **T**hreats. Both the situation and SWOT analyses can be done at the level of the entire

marketing plan
Road map for the marketing activities of an organization for a specified future period of time

situation analysis
Taking stock of a firm's or product's past performance, where it is now, and where it is headed

SWOT analysis
Organization's appraisal of its internal strengths and weaknesses and its external opportunities and threats

Figure 15–5
Outline of a marketing plan

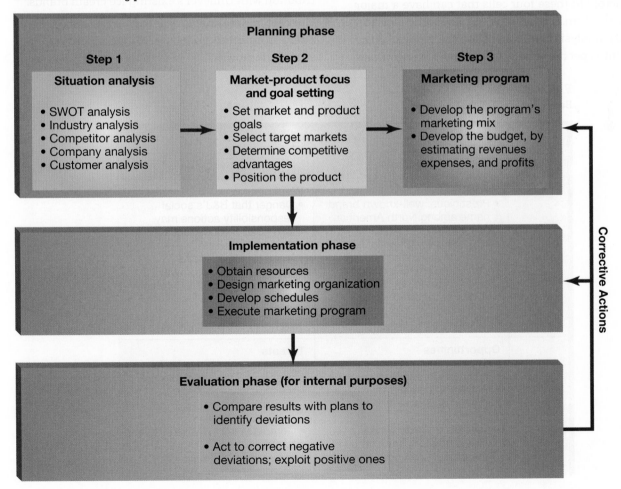

One of Ben & Jerry's 75 flavours of ice cream.

organization, the business unit, the product line, or the specific product. As an analysis moves from the level of the entire organization to the specific product, it, of course, gets far more detailed. For small firms or those with basically a single product line, an analysis at the firm or product level is really the same thing.

Let's assume you are the Unilever vice president responsible for integrating Ben & Jerry's into Unilever's business. You might do the SWOT analysis shown in Figure 15–6. Note that your SWOT table has four cells formed by the combination of internal versus external factors (the rows) and favourable versus unfavourable factors (the columns) that summarize Ben & Jerry's strengths, weaknesses, opportunities, and threats.

A SWOT analysis helps a firm identify the strategy-related factors in these four cells that can have a major effect on the firm. The goal is not simply to develop the SWOT analysis but to translate the results of the analysis into specific actions to help the firm grow and

succeed. The ultimate goal is to identify the critical factors affecting the firm and then build on vital strengths, correct glaring weaknesses, exploit significant opportunities, and avoid or prepare for disaster-laden threats. That is a big order.

The Ben and Jerry's SWOT analysis in Figure 15–6 can be the basis for these kinds of specific actions. An action in each of the four cells might be as follows:

- **Build on a strength.** Find specific efficiencies in distribution with Unilever's existing ice cream brands.

- **Correct a weakness.** Recruit experienced managers from other consumer product firms to help stimulate growth.

> "A SWOT analysis helps a firm identify the strategy-related factors that can have a major effect on the firm."

Figure 15–6
Ben & Jerry's: A SWOT analysis

Location of Factor	TYPE OF FACTOR	
	Favourable	**Unfavourable**
Internal	**Strengths** • Prestigious, well-known brand name among North American consumers • Major share of the super premium ice cream market • Can complement Unilever's existing ice cream brands • Widely recognized for its social responsibility actions	**Weaknesses** • Danger that B&J's social responsibility actions may add costs, reduce focus on core business • Need for experienced managers to help growth • Flat sales and profits in recent years
External	**Opportunities** • Growing demand for quality ice cream in overseas markets • Increasing demand for frozen yogourt and other low-fat desserts • Success of many firms in extending successful brand in one product category to others	**Threats** • Consumer concern with fatty desserts; B&J customers are the type who read new government-ordered nutritional labels • Competes with Haagen-Dazs brand • Increased competition in international markets

- **Exploit an opportunity.** Develop a new line of low-fat yogourts to respond to consumer health concerns.
- **Avoid or prepare for a disaster-laden threat.** Focus on less risky international markets, such as Mexico.

The next areas to consider in step 1 are as follows:

- The *industry analysis* section focuses on the industry and trends.
- The *competitor analysis* section looks at the firm's competitors.
- The *company analysis* section provides details of the company itself.
- The *customer analysis* section addresses the question: Who are the customers of the firm's products?

Step 2: Market-Product Focus and Goal Setting

Determining which products will be directed toward which customers (step 2 of the planning phase in Figure 15–5) is essential for developing an effective marketing program (step 3). This decision is often based on **market segmentation**, which involves considering prospective buyers in terms of groups, or segments. These groups have common needs and will respond similarly to a marketing program. Ideally, a firm can use market segmentation to identify the segments on which it will focus its efforts—its target market segments—and develop one or more marketing programs to reach them.

Goal setting involves setting measurable marketing objectives to be achieved. For organizations launching recruitment marketing campaign, the objective is applications and hires. Entertainment companies such as Netflix measure the number of members as well as the number of hours of television shows and movies that are downloaded. An organization selling apparel, such as Tilley Endurables, sets objectives for its product categories and offerings. When viewing the entire marketing program, objectives are often a series of actions to be implemented over several years.

Using the marketing plan outline shown in Figure 15–5, step 2 can be illustrated using Sleep Country Canada as an example:

- **Set market and product goals.** Based on listening to what is important to customers, Sleep Country Canada offers lots of choice in mattresses. It also makes each experience before, during, and after the sale an enjoyable one for the customer. One of its market goals may be to increase its market share by a certain percentage in the retailing mattress business in Canada. It's important to quantify the percentage so that the company can measure whether it successfully meets its goals.

- **Select target markets.** Sleep Country Canada targets consumers who want a quality mattress as well as a positive customer service experience.
- **Determine competitive advantages. Competitive advantages** are those characteristics of a product that make it superior to competing substitutes. Sleep Country Canada offers the mattress purchaser an enjoyable customer service experience unparalleled in this market. It offers clean, bright stores; sleep experts who put the customer's comfort and budget needs first; and courteous delivery people.
- **Position the product.** Sleep Country Canada is positioned as a mattress specialist that offers quality products with the added benefit of courteous and knowledgeable staff, an attractive in-store setting, and a convenient delivery service.

Details in these four elements of step 2 provide a solid foundation to use in developing the marketing program—the next step in the planning phase of the marketing plan.

market segmentation
Sorting potential buyers into groups that have common needs and will respond similarly to a marketing program

competitive advantages
Those characteristics of a product or service that make it superior to competing substitutes

---

Ben & Jerry's Contest for Canadian Ice Cream Flavour

Ben & Jerry's had a contest to give a Canadian name to its newest creation, a combination of vanilla ice cream, fudge-covered waffle cone pieces, and a fudge swirl. Some contest submissions:

1. Le Leonard Cone
2. Laid Back and Lovin' It
3. It's Good, Eh!
4. Oh, Cone-ada!
5. Canucks Deluxe
6. Canadian Rocky Road

Winner: Oh, Cone-ada!

Source: Judy Creighton, "Burlington woman scoops ice cream naming contest," *Toronto Star*, July 26, 2010, accessed at www.thestar.com/news/gta/article/840310--gta-woman-wins-ben-jerry-s-contest-with-flavour-name-oh-cone-ada.

Step 3: Marketing Program Activities in step 2 tell the marketing manager which customers to target and which customer needs the firm's product offerings can satisfy—the *who* and *what* aspects of the marketing plan. The *how* aspect—step 3 in the marketing plan—involves developing the program's marketing mix and its budget.

Figure 15–7 shows components of each marketing mix element that are combined to provide a cohesive marketing program. For Sleep Country Canada, the marketing mix activities can include the following:

- **Product strategy:** Offer consumers one of the largest selections of top, name-brand mattresses.
- **Price strategy:** Offer consumers a low-price guarantee. If consumers find a comparable product at a competitor that is equal to or lower than Sleep Country Canada's price, the company will beat that figure by 5 percent.
- **Promotion strategy:** Sleep Country Canada uses mass media advertising to communicate its unique retail experience to prospective and current customers.
- **Place (distribution) strategy:** Sleep Country Canada is conveniently located in six Canadian provinces with 240 stores in total.

Putting a marketing program into effect requires that the firm commit time and money to it, prepare a sales forecast, and establish a budget that must be approved by top management. In some organizations, this is referred to as financial data and projections.

The Implementation Phase of the Marketing Plan

A firm's marketing plan is the result of the many hours spent in the planning phase of the strategic marketing process. Implementation, the second phase of the marketing plan, involves implementing the marketing

Figure 15–7
Elements of the marketing mix that comprise a cohesive marketing program

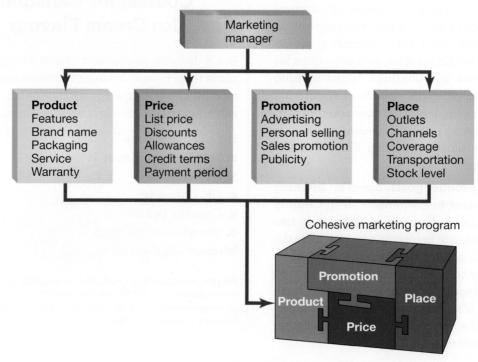

program that emerges from the planning phase. An organization needs to invest time and resources into the planning phase of the marketing plan, but just as is important is the implementation phase. The implementation phase is the part of the process that executes the individual tactics that support the marketing strategy. Figure 15–5 shows the four components of the implementation phase: obtaining resources, designing the marketing organization, developing schedules, and actually executing the marketing program designed in the planning phase.

Obtaining Resources

Most companies have numerous options for growth. But such growth requires an investment. Corporate leadership within an organization determines the best options for growth and how they should be funded. Tying back to the three levels within an organization, it can sometimes be challenging to get support from all stakeholders. Ideally, this part of the process is already introduced during the planning phase and is more of a formality at this point.

Designing the Marketing Organization

A marketing program needs marketing staff to implement it. Figure 15–8 shows the organization chart of a typical manufacturing firm, giving some details of the marketing department's structure. Four managers of marketing activities are shown to report to the vice president of marketing. Several regional sales managers and an international sales manager may report to the manager of sales. This marketing organization is responsible for converting marketing plans to reality.

Developing Schedules

Effective implementation requires developing appropriate schedules and determining specific deadlines for the creation and execution of marketing activities. For example, if a company wants to place an ad in the *Globe and Mail's Report on Business* magazine, it must reserve space a month prior to the date that the ad appears in the magazine. Also, the company must allow time for creating and producing the ad. Digital advertising allows for shorter advanced notice and tweaks to the creative process.

Executing the Marketing Program

Marketing plans are meaningless unless they are put into action. This requires attention to detail to both marketing strategies and marketing tactics. A **marketing strategy** is the means by which a marketing goal is to be achieved, usually characterized by a specified target market and a marketing program to reach it. Although the term strategy is often used loosely, it implies both the end sought (target market) and the means to achieve it (marketing program).

> **marketing strategy**
> Means by which a marketing goal is to be achieved

Figure 15–8

Organization of a typical manufacturing firm, showing a breakdown of the marketing department

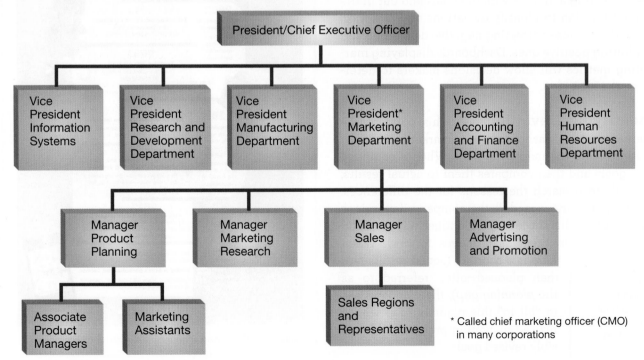

To implement a marketing program successfully, hundreds of detailed decisions are often required, such as writing ads or setting prices. These decisions, called **marketing tactics**, are detailed day-to-day operational decisions essential to the overall success of marketing strategies.

The Evaluation Phase of the Marketing Plan

The evaluation phase of the marketing plan is used to determine if the plan is moving in the right direction. The marketing manager compares the results of the marketing activities with the goals laid out in the marketing plan to identify deviations and to act on these deviations—correcting negative deviations and exploiting positive ones. Dashboards displaying marketing metrics will allow decisions makers to determine the next step.

Identifying Deviations At this point of the marketing plan, dashboards and marketing metrics help evaluate the marketing plan. When a company sets goals and then compares them to actual results, it needs to research the reasons for the differences. Where plans are exceeded, the company determines the drivers of this success and identifies ways to build on them as it moves forward. When there is a shortfall (actual results less than planned—often referred to as the *planning gap*), the company has to "fill in" this planning gap with a revised marketing program and possibly revised goals.

marketing tactics
Detailed day-to-day operational decisions essential to the overall success of marketing strategies

Infographic

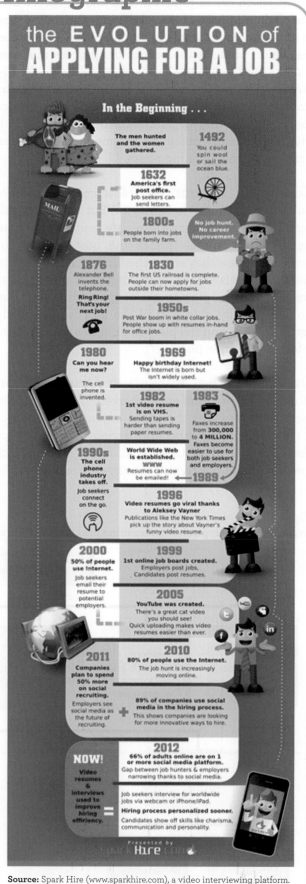

the EVOLUTION of APPLYING FOR A JOB

In the Beginning . . .

The men hunted and the women gathered.

1492 You could spin wool or sail the ocean blue.

1632 America's first post office. Job seekers can send letters.

1800s People born into jobs on the family farm.

No job hunt. No career improvement.

1876 Alexander Bell invents the telephone. Ring Ring! That's your next job!

1830 The first US railroad is complete. People can now apply for jobs outside their hometowns.

1950s Post War boom in white collar jobs. People show up with resumes in-hand for office jobs.

1980 Can you hear me now? The cell phone is invented.

1969 Happy birthday Internet! The Internet is born but isn't widely used.

1982 1st video resume is on VHS. Sending tapes is harder than sending paper resumes.

1983 Faxes increase from 300,000 to 4 MILLION. Faxes become easier to use for both job seekers and employers.

1990s The cell phone industry takes off. Job seekers connect on the go.

World Wide Web is established. www Resumes can now be emailed! **1989**

1996 Video resumes go viral thanks to Aleksey Vayner. Publications like the New York Times pick up the story about Vayner's funny video resume.

2000 50% of people use Internet. Job seekers email their resume to potential employers.

1999 1st online job boards created. Employers post jobs, Candidates post resumes.

2005 YouTube was created. There's a great cat video you should see! Quick uploading makes video resumes easier than ever.

2011 Companies plan to spend 50% more on social recruiting. Employers see social media as the future of recruiting.

2010 80% of people use the Internet. The job hunt is increasingly moving online.

89% of companies use social media in the hiring process. This shows companies are looking for more innovative ways to hire.

NOW! Video resumes & interviews used to improve hiring efficiency.

2012 66% of adults online are on 1 or more social media platform. Gap between job hunters & employers narrowing thanks to social media.

Job seekers interview for worldwide jobs via webcam or iPhone/iPad. Hiring process personalized sooner. Candidates show off skills like charisma, communication and personality.

Presented by Spark Hire.com

Source: Spark Hire (www.sparkhire.com), a video interviewing platform.

Acting on Deviations Generally speaking, results of a marketing plan will not be exactly as anticipated. Sometimes, the marketing program falls short of its goals. When this occurs, managers need to take corrective action. This is called *correcting a negative deviation*. For example, if Sleep Country Canada is experiencing less-than-desired sales from an Internet campaign, it may re-evaluate where they are advertising. Alternatively, when actual results are far better than the plan called for, creative managers find ways to exploit the situation. This is called *exploiting a positive deviation*. Continuing with the example, if Sleep Country Canada's sales are more than expected from certain digital media ads, it may consider investing more money into that part of the marketing program.

Whether an organization is selling ice cream, box-spring mattresses, or the opportunity to work at the company, technology impacts its strategic marketing process. The Infographic entitled "The Evolution of Applying for a Job" shares how job seekers changed the way they look for. Companies use this insight to review their recruitment marketing strategies. Furthermore, organizations focused on the strategic marketing process know that the business world is changing. Not only can we review results through dashboards quicker, but our world is changing so that strategy and marketing plans need to change with it.

webTactics

Summary...*just the facts*

LO 1 ● Large corporations can be complex. This complexity among business firms and not-for-profit organizations requires the division into three functional levels: the corporate, business unit, and functional levels.

● At the *corporate level,* top management directs overall strategy for the entire organization.

● The *business unit level* has business unit managers set the direction for individual products and markets.

● At the *functional level,* each business unit has marketing and other specialized activities such as finance, manufacturing, or human resources.

LO 2 ● Businesses exist for various purposes and establish missions and goals. A business's mission is the statement of its direction. Goals are the targets the organization has set to be achieved within a specific time frame.

● Missions and goals are important to businesses as they help them establish direction and maintain their course.

LO 3 ● In order to gauge the success of a marketing program, managers use marketing dashboards and marketing metrics to determine the performance of various elements of the marketing plan.

LO 4 ● An organization develops its strategy and direction by first understanding its current status. This involves asking "Where are we now?" to assess the organization's customers, competencies, and competitors. Asking "Where do we want to go" with techniques such as portfolio analysis and market-product analysis also help develop strategy. Furthermore, questions like "How will we get there?" helps create the marketing plan.

LO 5 ● The strategic marketing process involves an organization allocating its marketing mix resources to reach its target markets using three phases: planning, implementation, and evaluation.

● The planning phase of the marketing plan has three steps, each with more specific elements: situation (SWOT) analysis, market-product focus and goal setting, and marketing program.

● The implementation phase of the marketing plan has four key elements: obtaining resources, designing the marketing organization, developing schedules, and executing the marketing program.

● The evaluation phase of the marketing plan is used for internal purposes and involves comparing results with the planned targets to identify deviations and take actions to correct negative deviations and exploit positive ones.

Key Terms and Concepts...*a refresher*

competitive advantages
goals (objectives)
marketing dashboard
marketing metric
marketing plan

marketing strategy
marketing tactics
market segmentation
market share
mission

profit
situation analysis
strategic marketing process
strategy
SWOT analysis

Hands-on...*apply your knowledge*

Strategic Marketing Planning Assignment webTactics uses strategic planning and marketing to develop recruitment programs for a number of different organizations. This chapter's opening vignette outlines steps in the strategic planning process. Assume you have been approached by a major sports entertainment network to help recruit from colleges and universities across Canada. Using the ideas from the vignette and Figure 15–5 as a guide, outline a strategic marketing plan to recruit students for this organization.

Chapter Vignette...*reminder*

In this chapter's opening vignette, we gain a better understanding of how strategic marketing plans are developed in recruitment advertising agencies. Although the audience and desired result would be different, the strategic marketing process used in the vignette can also be used to develop loyal customers. Answer the Reality Check questions at the end of the vignette by reviewing the strategic marketing process in detail throughout the chapter.

Video Clip...*questions*

IBM recently celebrated its 100th anniversary! Its record of success is testimony to the resilience of a business model that encourages long-term strategies that can say "Welcome to a Smarter Planet." Review the IBM video on creating a smarter planet. Reflecting on this perspective, answer the following questions:

▶ Video
IBM

- What is IBM's "Smarter Planet" business strategy? How does this strategy relate to IBM's mission and values?
- Conduct a SWOT analysis for IBM's Smarter Planet initiative. What are the relevant trends to consider for the next three to five years?
- How can IBM communicate its strategy to companies, cities, and governments?
- What are the benefits of the Smarter Planet initiative to (a) society and (b) IBM?
- How should IBM measure the results of the Smarter Planet strategy?

Infographic...*data analysis*

The Infographic explaining how the candidate job search has changed over the years illustrates the importance of being able to execute and adjust a marketing strategy well. Using more recent insights about job-seeking tactics, add them as extensions to the Infographic and suggest what might be the next change that recruitment advertisers may need to be ready for.

Glossary

Numbers in parentheses following the definitions indicate chapters where the terms are identified. Consult the index for page references.

adoption curve The sequential diffusion and acceptance of an innovation into the market by consumers (8)

advergaming Placing ads in online or offline video games (12)

advertising A paid form of media used to communicate to consumers; includes broadcast, print, out-of home, and digital media (12)

affiliate marketing When companies promote their businesses through a network of online associates (affiliates) to drive traffic, leads, and purchases (12)

analytics The process of taking metrics data and applying smart thinking and technology to gain actionable insights that can help make better business decisions (1, 4)

attitude Tendency to respond to something in a consistently favourable or unfavourable way (3)

augmented reality (AR) The use of webcams or mobile devices to capture an image that is then supplemented with graphics, audio, video, or GPS data to provide additional information or an enhanced experience (12, 13)

baby boomers Generation of people born between 1946 and 1965 (2)

back translation Retranslating a word or phrase back into the original language by a different interpreter to catch errors (3)

banner ads Online ads that can stretch across the top of a web page or be formatted in various sizes, such as leaderboards, rectangles, big boxes, and skyscrapers (12)

behaviouristics How and why consumers buy and use a product, including the desired product benefits, how often it is purchased, how frequently it is used, and whether consumers are brand loyal in their purchase behaviour (6)

beliefs Consumer's perceptions of how a product or brand performs (3)

big data Massive amounts of data characterized as high-volume, high-velocity, and high-variety information (4)

binge viewing Watching complete or partial seasons of TV shows over a few days (2)

blog A website in the form of an online diary that is used by organizations and individuals to post updates that include personal opinions, activities, and experiences with readers able to subscribe and post comments (13)

Bluetooth The use of low-power radio waves to wirelessly transfer text, images, audio, or video data through a local hotspot to a Bluetooth-enabled and -activated device (13)

brand A name or phrase uniquely given by a company to a product to distinguish it from the competition (7)

brand development index (BDI) An index that shows how well a brand's sales are developed in a region relative to the region's population size (4)

branded entertainment The creation of an entertainment program, such as a TV episode, that is highly focused on a brand in exchange for payment (12)

brand equity The value of a brand that results from the favourable exposure, interactions, associations, and experiences that consumers have with a brand over time (7)

brand extension When new goods or services are introduced under an existing flagship brand name (7)

brand loyalty Favourable attitude toward and consistent purchase of a single brand over time; the degree of target market commitment toward a brand over time that results in varying levels of purchase insistence (3, 6, 7)

brand personality A set of human characteristics associated with a brand (7)

breadth of product line The variety of different items a store carries (11)

break-even analysis Examines the relationship between total revenue and total cost to determine profitability at different levels of output (9)

brokers Independent firms or individuals whose main function is to bring buyers and sellers together to make sales (11)

business analysis Financial projections on the impact of bringing the new product to market and selling it in the future (8)

business market Products that are purchased either to run a business or to be used as a component in another product or service (6)

business marketing Marketing to firms, governments, or non-profit organizations (5)

business products Products that are purchased either to run a business or to be used as a component in another product or service (7)

business sustainability The long-term viability of a business related to its financial results, social performance, and environmental impact (1)

buy classes Three types of organizational buying situations: straight rebuy, modified rebuy, or new buy (5)

buying centre Group of people in an organization who participate in the buying process (5)

causal research Research designed to identify cause-and-effect relationships among variables (4)

central business district The oldest retail setting, the community's downtown area (11)

channel conflict Arises when one channel member believes another channel member is engaged in behaviour that prevents it from achieving its goals (10)

commercialization When the new product is brought to market with full-scale production, sales, and marketing support (8)

common short codes (CSC) Dedicated short messaging codes of typically five to six digits that are used to trigger subscriptions, donations, alerts, or downloads, or to access promotional content (13)

community shopping centre Retail location that typically has one primary store and 20 to 40 smaller outlets, serving a population of consumers within a 2- to 5-km drive (11)

competitive advantages Those characteristics of a product or service that make it superior to competing substitutes (15)

competitive forces Alternative products that can satisfy a specific market's needs (2)

concept tests External evaluations of a new product idea, rather than the actual product itself (8)

consumer behaviour Actions a person takes when purchasing and using products and services (3)

consumer market Products, ideas, and services that a person can purchase, use, or support for personal use (6)

consumer products Products purchased for their personal use by the ultimate consumer (7)

consumer promotions Short-term marketing tools used to encourage immediate consumer purchase (12)

consumer touch points The points of interaction that can be used to connect with consumers, including personal time in the home, shopping time, workplace situations, social situations, travel time, and even face-to-face product time (12)

content marketing Creating and sharing expertise, information, or branded content that is designed to inform and engage with tools such as research papers, e-books, infographics, how-to videos, blogs, webinars, e-newsletters, case studies, and events that can readily be found with search engines (1, 12)

continuous innovations New products with more than just a minor product improvement, but that do not require radical changes by the consumer (8)

convenience products Items purchased frequently that are inexpensive and require minimum risk and shopping effort (7)

copyrights Used to legally protect the written word, a sound-recording, or a form of communication from being copied by others (7)

corporate social responsibility (CSR) When organizations voluntarily consider the well-being of society by taking responsibility for how their businesses impact consumers, customers, suppliers, employees, shareholders, communities, the environment, and society in general (1)

corporate websites Websites that provide corporate and brand information to consumers and the media (12)

cost-per-acquisition (CPA) The cost of acquiring a new follower or sale (13)

cost-per-click (CPC) The cost of getting someone to click on a link or ad (13)

cost-per-thousand (CPM) The cost of reaching one thousand people (13)

cross-channel shopper An online consumer who researches products online and then purchases them at a retail store (10)

cross-cultural analysis Study of similarities and differences among consumers in two or more societies (3)

cultural symbols Objects, ideas, or processes that represent a particular group of people or society (3)

culture A set of values, ideas, and attitudes that are learned and shared among the members of a group (3)

Customer Advocacy Funnel A communications approach that takes consumers down a path of initial product awareness through to brand advocacy (12)

customer experience management (CEM) Managing customer interactions with the goal of increasing satisfaction and loyalty (14)

customer lifetime value The potential sales that will be generated by a customer if that customer remains loyal to that company for a lifetime (14)

customer relationship management (CRM) The overall process of building and maintaining profitable customer relationships by delivering superior customer value and satisfaction (1, 14)

customer value The unique combination of benefits received by targeted buyers that includes quality, price, convenience, delivery, and both before-sale and after-sale service (1)

customs Norms and expectations about the way people do things in a specific country or culture (3)

dashboards The visualization of data and key performance indicators using graphs, charts, and numbers so that numerical information tells a story that is insightful and easy to use and understand (1,4)

data mining The processing of large amounts of data using sophisticated software to find insightful correlations and patterns that lead to better business decisions (4, 14)

data warehouse A central repository of an organization's electronically stored data (14)

demand curve Graph relating quantity sold and price, which shows how many units will be sold at a given price (9)

demographics The statistical data on a population according to characteristics such as gender, age, ethnicity, income, education, and occupation (2, 6)

depth of product line   Assortment of products within each product line that a store carries (11)

derived demand   Demand for industrial products and services driven by demand for consumer products and services (5)

descriptive research   Research designed to describe basic characteristics of a given population or to clarify its usage and attitudes (4)

development   The new product idea is turned into a prototype for further consumer research and manufacturing tests (8)

digital marketing   Using digital technology to reach consumers through computers, gaming devices, out-of-home electronic screens, or mobile devices such as smartphones, tablets, MP3 players, and e-readers (1)

direct competitors   Similar products sold in the same category (2)

direct response   A marketing communications tool designed to communicate with consumers one-on-one and elicit a direct action either online or offline (12)

discretionary income   Money that consumers have left after paying taxes and buying necessities (2)

disintermediation   Vertical channel conflict that arises when a channel member bypasses another member and sells directly to consumers (10)

display advertising   The use of online ads with graphics or animation that are placed on websites (12)

disposable income   Balance of income left after paying taxes; income that is used for spending and savings (2)

Do Not Call List (DNCL)   Gives customers the ability to elect to not receive telemarketing calls on cellphones, landline phones, and fax machines by registering the numbers of their communication devices (2)

dual distribution   Arrangement whereby a firm reaches buyers by using two or more different types of channels for the same basic product (10)

dumping   Occurs when a firm sells a product in a foreign country below its domestic prices or below its actual cost (9)

durable good   An item that lasts over an extended number of uses (7)

earned media   The free publicity secured through unpaid media mentions and consumers who spread the word through word of mouth or the Internet (12)

economy   The collective income, expenditures, and resources that affect the cost of running a business or a household (2)

electronic data interchange (EDI)   A computer-to-computer exchange of business documents from a retailer to a supplier and back (10)

electronic marketing channels   Channels that use the Internet to make goods and services available to consumers or business buyers (10)

e-mail marketing   The use of e-mail to market products (12)

e-marketplaces   Online trading communities that bring together buyers and supplier organizations (5)

event marketing   The creation or involvement of a brand in an experience or occasion that will heighten its awareness, create positive associations, and generate a desired response (12)

exchange   The trade of things of value between buyers and sellers so that each benefits (1)

exclusive distribution   Only one retail outlet in a specific geographical area carries the firm's products (10)

experiential marketing   Creating opportunities for consumers to directly interact with brands (1)

experiment   In marketing, changing a variable involved in a customer purchase to find out what happens (4)

exploratory research   Preliminary research conducted to clarify the scope and nature of the marketing problem or opportunity (4)

fad   Novelty products with very short product life cycles that experience immediate rapid growth, followed by an equally rapid decline (8)

family brand   When a company uses a brand name to cover a number of different product categories (7)

family life cycle   A family's progression from formation to retirement, with each phase bringing distinct needs and purchasing behaviours (3)

fashion product   The life cycle for fashion is relatively short and cyclical, going from introduction to decline within two to three years, only to resurface again a few years later (8)

feature phones   Cellphones that are Internet-enabled and that allow for e-mailing, texting, and browsing but cannot download or use apps (13)

fixed cost   Firm's expenses that are stable and do not change with the quantity of product that is produced and sold (9)

fluctuating demand   Demand for business products and services fluctuates more than demand for consumer products and services (5)

focus group   A research technique where a small group of people (usually six to ten) meet for a few hours with a trained moderator to discuss predetermined areas (4)

form of ownership   Distinguishes retail outlets on the basis of whether individuals, corporate chains, or contractual systems own the outlet (11)

franchising   Contractual arrangement in which a parent company (the franchiser) allows an individual or firm (the franchisee) to operate a certain type of business under an established name and according to specific rules set by the franchiser (10)

Generation X   People born between 1966 and 1971 (2)

Generation Y   People born between 1972 and 1992 (2)

Generation Z   People born in 1993 and beyond (2)

generic brand   A product that has no branding and is produced as a cheap alternative to a manufacturer's brand and to branded private label products (7)

geographics   Where a target market lives, using variables such as country, region, province, city size, and type of location, such as urban, suburban, or rural (6)

global brands Brands that are sold in a variety of international markets and that enjoy wide recognition in these markets (7)

goals (objectives) Targets of performance to be achieved within a specific time frame (15)

good A product you can touch and own (1)

greenwashing The deceptive use of marketing practices to give the impression that a good, service, or organization is environmentally friendly (1)

grey market Situations where products are sold through unauthorized channels of distribution (9)

gross income Total amount of money made in one year by a person, household, or family unit, including taxes (2)

harvesting When a company keeps a product but reduces marketing support in an attempt to reap some minor profits (8)

high-learning product Significant consumer education is required for these products, which have an extended introductory period (8)

hybrid apps Apps that combine the functionality of native apps with the flexibility of web apps (13)

idea A concept that typically looks for support (1)

idea generation Focuses on brainstorming sessions to prompt new ideas (8)

idle production capacity When the supply of a service exceeds its demand (7)

inbound marketing When consumers find a product and its messaging by using online techniques that marketers facilitate, including search engine optimization, pay-per-click ads, and the use of social media to connect with consumers (12)

in-depth interviews Detailed interviews where a researcher questions an individual at length in a free-flowing conversational style in order to discover information that may help solve a marketing problem (4)

indirect competitors Products competing for the same buying dollar in a slightly different, but related category (2)

individual brand When a company uses a brand name solely for a specific product category (7)

individualized marketing One-to-one marketing that involves customizing offers and, in some cases, products to fit individual needs (6)

inelastic demand Demand for products does not change because of increases or decreases in price (5)

inflation A period when the cost to produce and buy products and services gets higher as prices rise (2)

integrated marketing communications (IMC) A communications approach that coordinates all promotional activities to provide a consistent message to a target audience (12)

intensive distribution A firm tries to place its products or services in as many outlets as possible (10)

intermediaries Individuals or firms performing a role in the marketing channel, involved in making a product available (10)

intertype competition Competition between very dissimilar types of retail outlets (11)

involvement Personal, social, and economic significance of a purchase to the consumer (3)

just-in-time (JIT) inventory system A system designed to deliver less merchandise on a more frequent basis than traditional inventory systems (10)

leaderboards Banner ads that stretch across the top of a web page (12)

lead generation The requests for additional information that result from direct-response marketing (12)

learning Behaviours that result from repeated experience or reasoning (3)

legacy data Data that is difficult to use as it has been collected and stored in an obsolete format or system that is no longer compatible with current computer systems and databases (4)

level of service The degree of service provided to the customer by self-, limited-, and full-service retailers (11)

line extension The addition of a new item to an already existing product line (8)

logistics Activities that focus on getting the right amount of the right products to the right place at the right time at the lowest possible cost (10)

low-learning product Little consumer education is required, resulting in a short introductory stage for the product (8)

loyalty programs Programs specifically designed for customer retention (14)

macroeconomic forces The state of a country's economy as a whole as indicated by its growth rates, inflation rates, unemployment rates, and consumer confidence indexes (2)

manufacturers' agents Work for several producers and carry non-competitive, complementary merchandise in an exclusive territory (11)

manufacturer's brand A brand owned and produced by the manufacturer (7)

market Potential consumers with both the willingness and ability to buy (1)

marketing The process of planning and managing goods, services, or ideas to meet consumer needs and organizational objectives. It includes the conception of these products and the pricing, promotion, and distribution programs designed to make a profit and generate revenue or support for an organization. (1)

marketing channel The set of individuals or firms involved in the process of making a product available (10)

marketing communication agencies Broad-spectrum integrated agencies or specialist agencies that provide marketers with expertise on how best to communicate messages to their audiences (12)

marketing communication tools Advertising, public relations, sales promotion, direct response, event marketing and sponsorship, and personal selling (12)

marketing concept The idea that an organization should strive to satisfy the needs of consumers while also trying to achieve organizational goals (1)

marketing dashboard A visual computer display of essential marketing information (15)

marketing environmental scan The process of continually acquiring information on events occurring outside an organization to identify trends, opportunities, and threats to a business (2)

marketing information system (MIS) A set of procedures and processes for collecting, sorting, analyzing, and summarizing information on an ongoing basis (4)

marketing metric A measure of the value or trend of a marketing activity or result (15)

marketing mix The 4 Ps—product, price, place, and promotion (1)

marketing orientation Focusing organizational efforts to collect and use information about customers' needs to create customer value (1)

marketing plan Road map for the marketing activities of an organization for a specified future period of time (15)

marketing process The process of (1) identifying consumer needs, (2) managing the marketing mix to meet these needs, and (3) realizing profits (1)

marketing strategy Means by which a marketing goal is to be achieved (15)

marketing tactics Detailed day-to-day operational decisions essential to the overall success of marketing strategies (15)

market research The process of planning, collecting, and analyzing information in order to recommend actions to improve marketing activities (4)

market segmentation The aggregation of prospective buyers into groups that have common needs and respond similarly to marketing programs (6, 15)

market share The percentage of sales volume for a product, relative to the entire sales volume of the category in which it competes; ratio of a firm's sales to the total sales of all firms in the industry (4, 15)

markup The difference between selling price and cost, usually expressed as a percentage of cost (9)

mass marketing Marketing a product with broad appeal to the entire market without any product or marketing differentiation (6)

matrix 2D barcode A two-dimensional response code that, when scanned by a mobile barcode reader or app, provides additional information, launches websites, prompts downloads, sends text messages, or deploys messages (12, 13)

m-commerce The process of purchasing an item online through a mobile device (13)

merchandise mix How many different types of products a store carries and in what assortment (11)

merchant wholesalers Independently owned firms that take title to the merchandise they handle (11)

metrics Numeric data that is collected and grouped to track performance, often presented in spreadsheets and dashboards (1, 4)

microeconomic forces The supply and demand of goods and services and how this is impacted by individual, household, and company decisions to purchase (2)

microsites Promotional websites created for short-term promotional purposes, often allowing consumers to enter contests and access promotional information (12)

millennials People born between 1980 and 2000, a subset of generation Y and generation Z (2)

minor innovations Minor product modifications that require no adjustments on behalf of the consumer (8)

mission Statement of the organization's purpose and direction (15)

mobile applications (apps) Software programs that can be down-loaded on a smartphone or tablet to engage consumers with information, entertainment, or interactivity (13)

mobile check-in services When consumers check into locations using apps to post their whereabouts and to receive offers from local merchants on their mobile device (13)

mobile discovery The use of mobile apps to help find local businesses, services, and attractions (13)

mobile e-mail E-mail sent and/or received using a mobile device (13)

mobile marketing A set of practices that enables organizations to communicate and engage with their audiences in an interactive and relevant manner through any mobile device or network (1, 12, 13)

mobile messaging Comes in the form of common short codes (CSC), short messaging services (SMS), multimedia messaging services (MMS), e-mail messaging, in-person voice phone calls, and voice messaging (13)

mobile voice Voice messaging left or received using mobile devices (13)

mobile wallets Apps that store payment and loyalty information on a mobile device that can then be swiped or tapped at retail (13)

mobile web A website designed for the smaller screens of mobile devices (13)

monopolistic competition Type of competition where a large number of sellers compete with each other, offering customers similar or substitute products (2)

monopoly When only one company sells in a particular market (2)

motivation Energizing force that stimulates behaviour to satisfy a need (3)

multichannel marketing Blending of different communication and delivery channels that are mutually reinforcing in attracting, retaining, and building relationships with customers (10)

multichannel retailers Use a combination of traditional store formats and non-store formats such as catalogues and online retailing (11)

multimedia messaging services (MMS)   Standard text messaging services that include audio, video, or images (13)

native apps   Apps downloaded from app stores that are specifically created to be hosted and run on a mobile device (13)

near field communications (NFC)   The two-way radio communication between smartphones and smartphone-type devices to transfer images, documents, or monetary transactions when the two devices touch or are within a few inches of each other (13)

new product development process   Sequence of steps that a firm takes to develop a new product idea and take it to market (8)

new product development strategy   Setting the new product strategic direction for the company as a whole, and the precise objectives for the project at hand (8)

niche marketing   Marketing a limited product line to a narrow but profitable segment of the market that is of marginal interest to major competitors (6)

non-durable good   An item that does not last and is consumed only once, or for a limited number of times (7)

non-probability sampling   Selecting a sample so that the chance of selecting a particular element of a population is either unknown or zero (4)

North American Industry Classification System (NAICS)   Provides common industry definitions for Canada, Mexico, and the United States (5)

objectives   Specific, measurable goals (4, 15)

observational research   Obtained by watching how people behave, in person or by using a machine to record the event (4)

off-price retailing   Selling brand-name merchandise at lower than regular prices (11)

oligopoly   Type of competition that occurs when a few companies control a market (2)

omnibus survey   The voluntary participation of respondents in routine research surveys that allow marketers to add a small number of questions to an existing survey to receive cost-effective data (4)

online behavioural advertising (OBA)   The use of web-based programs to track consumers' online activity so as to serve ads that correspond to browsing interests (2)

online research bulletin boards   Private online static forums, without real-time dialogue, where respondents can post their responses to questions posed by researchers (4)

online research communities   The use of consumer groups, brought together privately in an online environment, to answer questions, respond to ideas, and collaborate with researchers in real time (4)

opinion leaders   Individuals who have social influence over others (3)

organizational buyers   Manufacturers, wholesalers, retailers, and government agencies that buy goods and services for their own use or for resale (5)

organizational buying behaviour   Process by which organizations determine the need for goods and then choose among alternative suppliers (5)

outbound marketing   Marketers seek out consumers by widely broadcasting messages using advertising, direct mail, e-mail marketing, telemarketing, and personal-selling approaches (12)

out-of-home advertising   Casually referred to as *outdoor*; reaches consumers outside the home in outdoor locations, in transit, or in commercial or business locations (12)

owned media   The media channels that a company controls, either fully or partially, such as a website, microsite, or social media page that is used to directly communicate with consumers (12)

paid media   The media time purchased so that messages can be disseminated through channels that are controlled by others (12)

panel   A large sample of respondents that voluntarily complete questionnaires on a regular basis so that researchers can assess changes in behaviour and attitudes (4)

Pareto's Rule   The concept that 80 percent of a brand's sales come from 20 percent of its customers (14)

partnership marketing   The creation of formal associations between brands that will result in incremental business for both brands that could not have been achieved separately (1)

patents   Used to legally protect new technologies, unique processes, or formulations from usage by other companies (7)

pay-per-click advertising (PPC)   Ads that appear in response to keyword triggers on search engines, as well as on some websites, blogs, and social media sites, where the advertiser pays only when the ad is clicked (12)

perceived risk   Anxiety felt when a consumer cannot anticipate possible negative outcomes of a purchase (3)

perception   Process by which someone selects, organizes, and interprets information to create a meaningful picture of the world (3)

perfect competition   Type of competition where there are many sellers with nearly identical products and little differentiation (2)

perishability   When products cannot be stored for long periods of time to use at a later date (7)

permission-based e-mail   When a recipient chooses to receive e-mail from a marketer (12)

personality   A person's character traits that influence behavioural responses (3)

personal selling   The two-way flow of communication between a buyer and seller, often face-to-face or facilitated through communication devices, to influence an individual and group purchase decision (12)

personas   Character descriptions of a typical customer in the form of fictional character narratives, complete with images that capture the personalities, values, attitudes, beliefs, demographics, and expected interactions with a brand (6)

place   Distribution channels, retail formats, and merchandising used to sell a product (1)

positioning maps   Visual representations of how products are positioned in a category to consumers (6)

positioning statement   A formalized statement that identifies the image a branded product represents in the market and what sets it apart from the competition (6)

power centre   Large shopping strip with multiple anchor stores, a convenient location, and a supermarket (11)

predictive analytics   The combination of data from varied sources to reveal consumer behaviour patterns that are modelled to customize offers and predict business outcomes (4)

pre-roll video advertising   The use of TV-type ads that play before video segments are watched online (12)

press conference   A planned event where representatives of the media are invited to an informational meeting with the company (12)

press release   An announcement written by an organization and sent to the media (12)

price   Expected retail or sale price of a product; money or other considerations exchanged for the ownership or use of a good or service (1, 9)

pricing constraints   Factors that limit the range of price a firm may set (9)

pricing objectives   Expectations that specify the role of price in an organization's marketing and strategic plans (9)

primary data   Data that is original and specifically collected for a project (4)

private label brand   Otherwise known as a store brand, a brand owned by a retailer that contracts its manufacturing to major suppliers, and then sells the product at its own retail stores, under its own store-brand name (7)

probability sampling   Selecting a sample so that each element of a population has a specific known chance of being selected (4)

product   Attributes that make up a good, a service, or an idea, including product design, features, colour, packaging, warranty, and service levels (1, 7)

product depth   The variety of product lines and products sold within a company's product categories, groups, or lines (7)

product differentiation   Positioning a product to a target group so that it appears distinct from competitive offerings (6)

production orientation   Focusing organizational efforts on the manufacture of goods (1)

product life cycle   The stages that a new product goes through, starting with introduction and evolving into growth, maturity, and decline (8)

product line   A group of similar products with the same product and brand name that is directed at the same general target market and is marketed together (7)

product mix   The combination of product lines offered by a company (7)

product placement   The inclusion of a product in a movie or TV program in return for payment (12)

product positioning   The impression of the product you want to establish in consumers' minds relative to their needs and the competition (6)

product width   The number of different categories offered by a company (7)

profit   The excess of revenues over costs, the reward to a business for the risk it undertakes in offering a product for sale (15)

profit equation   Profit = Total revenue – Total cost (9)

promotion   Communication tools needed to inform consumers about a product, including advertising, public relations, sales promotion, direct response, event marketing and sponsorship, and personal selling (1)

promotional mix   The selection of promotional tools used to communicate with a target market (12)

promotional partnerships   Simple short-term promotional offers between brands (1)

proximity marketing   The distribution of marketing content to mobile devices that have opted in at a particular local geo-location to receive information (1, 13)

psychographics   Understanding consumers' attitudes to life, values, personalities, general interests, opinions, and activities (6)

publicity   A non-personal form of communication that appears in the media and is and not paid for directly by the organization (12)

public relations   A communications tool that seeks to influence the opinions and attitudes of target groups through the use of unpaid media exposure; targets the media in an attempt to generate positive publicity for a company, product, or individual (12)

pull strategy   When marketers focus communication efforts on ultimate consumers to build awareness, trial, and demand for a product (12)

purchase decision process   Stages that a buyer passes through when making choices about which products or services to buy (3)

push strategy   When marketers focus communication on the distribution channel to gain support from retailers, distributors, and wholesalers (12)

qualitative research   A form of research that uses approaches such as focus groups, in-depth interviews, online communities, online bulletin boards, and social listening to provide insightful and directional information (4)

quantitative research   Statistically reliable information that uses observational and/or questioning techniques such as observations, surveys, and experiments (4)

questionnaire   Obtaining information by posing standardized questions through surveys that can be conducted in person, through the mail, on the telephone, or through the Internet (4)

radical innovations   New products that involve the introduction of a product that is entirely new and innovative to the market (8)

radio frequency identification (RFID) tags   The use of physical tags on products so that its radio signals can interact with an electronic device to provide information in the form of text, images, or video (13)

real-time marketing A planned tactical approach where brands make themselves relevant online during events or newsworthy occurrences by diving into conversations as they occur with aligned short-term messaging that takes advantage of the current buzz (1, 12)

recession A time of slow economic activity with two consecutive periods of negative growth (2)

reference group A group of people who influence a person's attitudes, values, and behaviour (3)

regional shopping centres Consist of 50 to 150 stores that typically attract customers who live within a 5- to 15-km range; often containing two or three anchor stores (11)

regulations Restrictions placed on marketing practices by government and industry associations (2)

relationship marketing When organizations create long-term links with customers, employees, suppliers, and other partners to increase loyalty and customer retention (1)

relationship selling The practice of building long-term loyalty from customers based on a salesperson's attention and commitment to customer needs over time (12)

repositioning A revamping of a product and its marketing mix to more accurately meet consumer needs (6)

retailing All activities involved in selling, renting, and providing goods and services to ultimate consumers for personal, family, or household use (11)

retailing mix The goods and services, pricing, physical distribution, and communications tactics chosen by a store (11)

retargeted ads Display ads that ad networks redirect to a computer's IP address when a consumer previously clicked on an ad but did not respond to its contents (12)

reverse auction Occurs when a buyer communicates a need for something and would-be suppliers bid in competition with each other (5)

RFM analysis The rating of customers on the basis of how recently products were purchased (recency), how often products were purchased (frequency), and the dollar value of the transactions (monetary value) (4, 6)

sales orientation Focusing organizational efforts on selling as many products as possible (1)

sales promotion A communications tool that provides short-term incentives to generate interest in a product or cause and encourages purchase or support (12)

sampling The process of gathering data from a subset of the total population rather than from all members of that particular group (4)

scrambled merchandising Offering several unrelated product lines in a single retail store (11)

screening and evaluation Reduces the list of brainstorming ideas down to a list of promising concepts (8)

search engine marketing (SEM) Includes the use of search engine optimization and pay-per-click advertising to market on search engines (12)

search engine optimization (SEO) Ensuring that websites are written, indexed, and coded so that they are highly rated and ranked by the search engines (12)

secondary data Facts and figures that have already been recorded by a third party (4)

segment marketing Marketing a range of different products and brands to specifically meet the needs of an organization's varied target markets (6)

selective distribution A firm selects a few retail outlets in a specific geographical area to carry its products (10)

selling agents Represent a single producer and are responsible for the entire marketing function of that producer (11)

semi-structured data A hybrid data format that consists of structured and unstructured data (4)

service A product that is intangible; an activity, benefit, or satisfaction that you cannot touch (1, 7)

service continuum A range from tangible goods to intangible services (7)

share of wallet The percentage of a customer's purchases that a company has in a specific product category (14)

shopping products Items that require comparison-shopping between different brands and an investment of shopping time (7)

short messaging services (SMS) Standard text messaging that uses protocols of 160 characters per message (13)

showrooming Using mobile devices in-store to check online competitive product reviews and prices, which results in the online purchase of a cheaper product (2, 3, 13)

shrinkage Breakage and theft of merchandise by customers and employees (11)

situation analysis Taking stock of a firm's or product's past performance, where it is now, and where it is headed (15)

skyscrapers Banner ads that are tall, slim, and vertical and appear along the side of a web page (12)

smartphones Advanced cellphones that use cutting-edge applications and sophisticated operating systems to function like a mobile personal computer (13)

social listening Research that monitors public online consumer conversations on social media sites such as social networks, blogs, and forums (4)

social media A form of online media that allows members to create their own network of friends and contacts to share comments, articles, opinions, videos, and images as a form of self-expression (1, 13)

social media analytics The real-time measurement, interaction, and analysis of social media to assess social media campaign performance, message resonation and amplification, consumer sentiment, and common themes (4)

social media marketing Reaching out to consumers online through social networks where people connect with friends and contacts to share comments, articles, opinions, videos, and images as a form of self-expression (1, 12, 13)

social media monitoring The monitoring of brand mentions, as well as consumer sentiment, buzz, and engagement, on the Internet (2)

social media release A multimedia online press release platform that includes video, text, and images, as well as social media buttons for sharing on social networks and comment areas where viewers can leave comments (12)

social networks Online websites that allow members to create a network of friends and contacts to share messages, comments, videos, and images as a form of self-expression (12)

social TV Watching TV programming while adding comments on social networks (2)

societal marketing concept Marketing programs that focus on the consumer *and* the well-being of society (1)

socio-cultural forces Cultural values, ideas, and attitudes, as well as society's morals and beliefs (2)

spam The dissemination of unsolicited electronic messages to recipients (2, 12)

specialty products Items for special occasions that require a specific product or brand and require considerable time and effort to purchase (7)

sponsorship When an advertiser pays a fee in exchange for inclusion in an event, involvement in its advertising opportunities, or exposure within the event itself (12)

strategic alliance Long-term arrangement between companies with similar values and marketing objectives that extend beyond short-term promotional offers into long-term formal business agreements (1)

strategic marketing process Approach whereby an organization allocates its marketing mix (15)

strategy An organization's long-term course of action that delivers a unique customer experience while achieving its goals (15)

strip location A cluster of stores serving people who live within a 5- to 10-minute drive (11)

structured data Data that can be easily tagged, stored, and searched in a database using consistently identifiable terms that are systematically organized into columns, rows, and tables (4)

sub-brand A brand that uses the family brand name as well as its own brand name and identity so that it can take on the strengths of the parent brand but also differentiate itself (7)

subcultures Subgroups within a larger culture that have unique values, ideas, and attitudes (3)

supply chain Sequence of firms that perform activities required to create and deliver a product to consumers or industrial users (10)

supply chain management Integration and organization of information and logistics activities across firms in a supply chain for the purpose of creating and delivering goods and services that provide value to consumers (10)

supply partnership Relationship between a buyer and supplier that adopt mutually beneficial objectives, policies, and procedures (5)

SWOT analysis The assessment of how well an organization or brand is servicing its businesses and target markets by evaluating its internal strengths and weaknesses, and its external opportunities and threats (2, 15)

syndicated studies A hybrid of primary and secondary research whereby the cost of a research study is shared among clients and made available at a price to interested parties (4)

target market The specific group of existing and potential consumers to which marketers direct their marketing efforts (1,6)

target market profile A description of the target market that contains specific information about the target group in four areas: geographics, demographics, psychographics, and behaviouristics (6)

technological forces Inventions from science or engineering research (2)

telemarketing Using the telephone to interact with and sell directly to consumers (11)

test market An in-market localized regional approach, or short-term online destination, used to test the success of promotional offers, new services, or new-product launches (4)

test marketing Offering a new product for sale on a limited basis in a defined geographic area to assess its success (8)

total cost Total expenses incurred by a firm in producing and marketing a product; total cost is the sum of fixed cost and variable costs (9)

total revenue Total money received from the sale of a product (9)

touch point Any situation in which a customer comes into contact with a brand or company (14)

trademarks Used to legally protect brand images, names, and designs from usage by others (7)

trade promotions Short-term promotional tools used to generate support with wholesalers, distributors, or retailers (12)

traditional auction Occurs when a seller puts an item up for sale and would-be buyers bid in competition with each other (5)

traffic generation The visits to a location or website that result from direct-response marketing (12)

unsought products Unknown items or those of no interest to the purchaser (7)

unstructured data Data that comes from word-processed documents, presentations, audio files, images, video, and e-mail or social media messages that cannot be easily categorized and tagged in a database using fixed terms and definitions (4)

user-generated content (UGC) Original online content that has been created by users in the form of blogs, posts, images, audio, or video (12, 13)

value The ratio of perceived benefits to price (9)

values Socially preferable modes of conduct or states of existence that tend to persist over time (3)

variable cost Sum of the expenses of the firm that vary directly with the quantity of products that is produced and sold (9)

vertical marketing systems Professionally managed and centrally coordinated marketing channels designed to achieve channel economies and maximum marketing impact (10)

virtual services Services that exist only online and have no person-to-person interaction (7)

web analytics The measurement and analysis of website data, looking at elements such as page views, time on site, bounce rate, new visitors, returning visitors, and referral traffic (4)

web apps Websites designed to simulate an app experience by placing a shortcut that runs off a browser on a mobile device (13)

wiki A collaborative website that uses an application with which multiple users can create, add, edit, or delete content (13)

word of mouth People influencing each other in personal conversations (3)

word-of-mouth marketing The spread of positive messages about a product by listening to consumers, identifying influential individuals that can spread the word, and making it easier for them to do so (12)

Chapter Notes

Chapter 1

1. Interview with Mike Welling, president and brand strategist doug and serge agency, June 2013; interview with Norm Pickering, director of marketing, North America, Mucho Burrito, June 2012; Mucho Burrito Fresh Mexican Grill 2011 franchise brochure, accessed at www.muchoburrito.com/documents/Franchise_Brochure.pdf and www.muchoburrito.com/wp-content/uploads/MB_FranchiseBrochure_2011_WEB.pdf; Brianne Binelli, "In the News," *Foodservice World,* February 1, 2009, accessed at www.muchoburrito.com/media-center/news/02012009.php; Kelly Olive, "Much Burrito Goes Urban," Maverick PR, press release, January 18, 2012, accessed at www.maverickpr.com/blogs/latestnews/mucho-burrito-goes-urban; Jeff Beer, "Fast food: Invasion of the burger joints," *Canadian Business,* November 9, 2012, accessed at www.canadianbusiness.com/lifestyle/fast-food-invasion-of-the-burger-joints/; "Mucho Burrito launches epicurean tacos: la Taqueria Trio," Maverick Public Relations, press release, accessed at Reuters at www.reuters.com/article/2013/03/18/idUSnCCNrwbDMa+1c6+MKW20130318; Amritraj Gupta, "Mucho Burrito—Ghost Pepper Burrito Poster," About.me, accessed at www.artraj.com/folio/?projects=mucho-burrito; "Mucho Burrito Introduces the Ghost Pepper to Canadian Heat-Seekers," Maverick Public Relations, press release, September 24, 2012, accessed at Market Wired at www.marketwire.com/press-release/mucho-burrito-introduces-the-ghost-pepper-to-canadian-heat-seekers-1704620.htm; Jordan Twiss, "Mucho Burrito does a taco tango," *Strategy Online,* May 26, 2013, accessed at http://strategyonline.ca/2013/03/26/mucho-burrito-does-a-taco-tango/; Jonathon Paul, "Mucho Burrito launches first ad effort," *Strategy Online,* August 3, 2011, accessed at http://strategyonline.ca/2011/08/03/mucho-burrito-launches-first-ad-effort/; Jonathon Paul, "Mucho Burrito bows spicy ad effort," *Strategy Online,* August 31, 2011, accessed at http://strategyonline.ca/2011/08/31/mucho-burrito-bows-spicy-ad/; "Mucho Burrito Selects the 'SAMY' Mobile Marketing and Engagement Solution in Celebration of Cinco de Mayo," Yahoo Finance, press release, May 6, 2013, accessed at "http://finance.yahoo.com/news/mucho-burrito-selects-samy-mobile-153356234.html; Wendy Leung, "How fancy can fast food get?" *Globe and Mail,* August 23, 2012, accessed at http://m.theglobeandmail.com/life/food-and-wine/food-trends/how-fancy-can-fast-food-get/article567669/?service=mobile.

2. StatsCounter Global Stats for Jan 2013–Jan 2014, accessed at http://gs.statcounter.com/#search_engine-CA-monthly-201301-201401-bar.

3. Stan Schroeder, "Google Sets Up Person Finder and Relief Map for Typhoon Haiyan," *Mashable,* November 11, 2013, accessed at http://mashable.com/2013/11/11/google-tools-typhoon-yolanda/; Affan Chowdhry, "How typhoon survivors and Filipino expats are trying to connect," *Globe and Mail,* November 12, 2013, accessed at www.theglobeandmail.com/news/world/how-typhoon-survivors-and-filipino-expats-are-trying-to-connect/article15387907/; Google, Typhoon Yolanda, Philippines, November 2013, accessed at www.google.org/crisisresponse/2013-yolanda/index.html.

4. NRF Stores, "2013 Top 100 Retailers," accessed at www.stores.org/2013/Top-100-Retailers; AmazonPrime Canada, accessed at www.amazon.ca/gp/prime and AmazonPrime in the US accessed at www.amazon.com/Amazon-Services-LLC-Prime/dp/B00DBYBNEE.

5. Adapted from "Marketing," Business Dictionary website, 2010, accessed at www.businessdictionary.com/definition/marketing.html.

6. Steve Ladurantaye and Susan Krashinsky, "'Let's Talk' campaign a boost for mental health and Bell," *Globe and Mail,* February 14, 2013, accessed at www.theglobeandmail.com/report-on-business/industry-news/marketing/lets-talk-campaign-a-boost-for-mental-health-and-bell/article8644553/; Niamh Scallan, "Clara Hughes: 'I want to erase the stigma' of mental health issues," *Toronto Star,* February 12, 2013, accessed at www.thestar.com/news/gta/2013/02/12/clara_hughes_i_want_to_erase_the_stigma_of_mental_health_issues.html; "'Let's Talk' day puts mental health in the spotlight," *Globe and Mail,* January 28, 2014 accessed at www.theglobeandmail.com/life/health-and-fitness/health/20-million-tweets-and-counting-bells-lets-talk-day-puts-mental-health-in-the-spotlight/article16542407/; Bell Let's Talk, accessed at http://letstalk.bell.ca/en/; "109,451,718 tweets, texts, calls and shares: Thank you Canada for another record setting Bell Let's Talk Day!" CNW, news release, January 29, 2014, accessed at www.newswire.ca/en/story/1296879/109-451-718-tweets-texts-calls-and-shares-thank-you-canada-for-another-record-setting-bell-let-s-talk-day; Sasha Nagy, "It's Wrong to Hate the "Bell" in Bell Let's Talk Day," *Huffington Post Living Canada,* January 29, 2014, accessed at www.huffingtonpost.ca/sasha-nagy/bell-lets-talk-day_b_4689983.html.

7. "Scene adds Milestones Grill + Bar to its Points Program Menu," Marketwire, news release, March 30, 2010, accessed at www.marketwire.com/press-release/SCENE-Adds-Milestones-Grill-Bar-to-its-Points-Program-Menu-1139906.htm.

8. American Marketing Association, Marketing Power Resource Library, Dictionary, June 2010, accessed at www.marketingpower.com/_layouts/dictionary.aspx?dLetter=M.

9. Philip Kotler, Gary Armstrong, and Peggy H. Cunningham, *Principles of Marketing,* Seventh Canadian Edition (Toronto: Pearson, 2008).

10. "Good For Business: Corporate Social Responsibility Report 2010," *Maclean's,* June 4, 2010, accessed at www2.macleans.ca/2010/06/14/jantzi-macleans-csr-report-2010; BMO Financial Group, "2013 Corporate Responsibility Report," accessed at www.bmo.com/home/about/banking/corporate-responsibility/our-approach/reporting#cr.

11. "Top 50 Socially Responsible Companies 2013," *Maclean's* and Sustainalytics, accessed at www2.macleans.ca/canada-top-50-socially-responsible-corporations-2013/; "Tim Hortons Sustainability and Responsibility 2012 Performance Report," accessed at http://sustainabilityreport.timhortons.com/pdf/performance_summary_2012.pdf.

12. "Top 50 Socially Responsible Companies 2013," *Maclean's* and Sustainalytics, accessed at www2.macleans.ca/canada-top-50-socially-responsible-corporations-2013/.

13. Adapted from "Definition of Business Sustainability," *Financial Times Lexicon,* accessed at http://lexicon.ft.com/term?term=business-sustainability.

14. "Simon Creet on social marketing," *Globe and Mail Report on Business,* June 4, 2009, accessed at www.theglobeandmail.com/

report-on-business/article1133378.ece; "Cadbury Inspires Canadians to Make the World a Better Place, One Bicycle at a Time," Marketwire, news release, April 16, 2009, accessed at www.marketwire.com/press-release/Cadbury-Inspires-Canadians-to-Make-the-World-a-Better-Place-One-Bicycle-at-a-Time-975667.htm; The Bicycle Factory website, June 2010, April 2011, February 2014, accessed at www.thebicyclefactory.ca/Landing.aspx; Katherine Dorell, "Hope, Survival, Freedom," *Canadian Living*, May 2010, pp. 93–96; The Bicycle Factory Facebook page, February 2014, accessed at www.facebook.com/BicycleFactory.

15. "The Mobile Marketing Roadmap: How Mobile is Transforming Marketing for Targeting Next Generation Consumers," Mobile Marketing Association, accessed December 2013, at http://www.mmaglobal.com/.

16. "Mobile Future in Focus 2013," comScore, February 2013, accessed at www.comscore.com/.

17. "2013 Canada Digital Future in Focus," comScore, March 2013, accessed at www.comscore.com/Insights/Presentations_and_Whitepapers/2013/2013_Canada_Digital_Future_in_Focus; "2014 Canada Digital Future in Focus," comScore, April 2014, accessed at www.comscore.com/Insights/Presentations_and_Whitepapers/2014/2014_Canada_Digital_Future_in_Focus.

18. Cross Media Reach and Time Spent 2013, RTS data, TVB Canada, November 2013, accessed at www.tvb.ca/pages/RTS.

19. "Real-time Marketing is Madison Avenues's Next Big Challenge," *The Economist Group*, March 21, 2013, accessed at www.economistgroup.com/leanback/social-media/real-time-marketing-is-madison-avenues-next-big-challenge/; Steve Hall, "7 Steps to Becoming a World-Class Real-Time Marketer," *HubSpot* blog, March 26, 2013, accessed at http://blog.hubspot.com/how-to-be-a-world-class-real-time-marketer; Rebecca Lieb, "7 Inspiring Examples of Real-Time Marketing in Action," *HubSpot* blog, October 12, 2012, accessed at http://blog.hubspot.com/blog/tabid/6307/bid/33696/7-Inspiring-Examples-of-Real-Time-Marketing-in-Action.aspx.

20. Jennifer Rooney, "Behind the Scenes of Oreo's Real-Time Super Bowl Slam Dunk," *Forbes*, February 4, 2013, accessed at www.forbes.com/sites/jenniferrooney/2013/02/04/behind-the-scenes-of-oreos-real-time-super-bowl-slam-dunk/; Ryan Caligiuri, "Four ways to build on Oreo's winning Super Bowl marketing play," *Globe and Mail*, February 15, 2013, accessed at www.theglobeandmail.com/report-on-business/small-business/sb-marketing/advertising/four-ways-to-build-on-oreos-winning-super-bowl-marketing-play/article8616201/; Gian LaVecchia, "Oreo's 'Dunk in the Dark' Strategy and the Future of Real-Time Marketing," *Fast Company*, April 18, 2013, accessed at www.fastcompany.com/3008486/oreos-dunk-dark-strategy-and-future-real-time-marketing; Brian Morrissey, "The 5 Best Real-Time Marketing Moments of the Super Bowl," *Digiday*, February 2, 2014, accessed at http://digiday.com/brands/best-real-time-marketing-super-bowl/; Megan Buerger, "Who Won (and Lost) the Social Media Ad Super Bowl?" *Wall Street Journal*, February 3, 2014, accessed at http://blogs.wsj.com/speakeasy/2014/02/03/who-won-and-lost-the-social-media-ad-super-bowl/.

21. "What is Content Marketing?" Content Marketing Institute, accessed at http://contentmarketinginstitute.com/what-is-content-marketing/; "Content Marketing: Harnessing the Power of Content to Fuel Your Brand," American Marketing Association, events, April 2013, brochure accessed at www.marketingpower.com/Calendar/Documents/FY13%20Training%20Series/Q4/ContentMarketing_Apr_Brochure.pdf.

22. "MMA Updates Definition of Mobile Marketing," accessed December 2013 at www.mmaglobal.com/node/11102.

23. David Moth, "How Red Bull uses Facebook, Twitter, Pinterest and Google+," *Econsultancy* blog, February 21, 2013, accessed at http://econsultancy.com/blog/62178-how-red-bull-uses-facebook-twitter-pinterest-and-google; Nate Smitha, "Brand Profile: Red Bull's Cross-Channel Success," *Simply Measured* blog, April 1, 2013 accessed at http://simplymeasured.com/blog/2013/04/11/brand-profile-red-bulls-cross-channel-success.

24. "2000 visitors tour Street House," Raising the Roof, news update, summer 2012, accessed at www.raisingtheroof.org/RaisingTheRoof/media/RaisingTheRoofMedia/Documents/RTR_News_Summer2012_Web.pdf; "Leo Burnett and Raising the Roof see great potential in homeless youth," Leo Burnett, press release, February 24, 2011, accessed at www.raisingtheroof.org/RaisingTheRoof/media/RaisingTheRoofMedia/Documents/Releases/Ad-Campaign-Media-Release.pdf; Raising the Roof website, accessed at www.raisingtheroof.org/; "Cardboard house on King Street promises tour of a different kind," Raising the Roof, media release, May 24, 2012, accessed at, www.raisingtheroof.org/RaisingTheRoof/media/RaisingTheRoofMedia/MediaRelease-StreetHouse-May2011.pdf; Leo Burnett Worldwide, "Raising the Roof—The Street House," YouTube video, September 12, 2012, accessed at www.youtube.com/watch?v=WRLqs8dokHc&list=PL3IbgymsTKo68VHl1NR-eJeaw-fOrXiEd; "A Cardboard Installation to Raise Awareness of Homelessness: The Street House," CBC, *George Stroumbouloupolos Tonight*, May 25, 2012, accessed at www.cbc.ca/strombo/news/seeing-how-the-homeless-live-the-street-house.html; "The Street House – a tour of a different kind," Raising the Roof, news release, May 25, 2012, accessed at www.raisingtheroof.org/News-and-Events/News/The-Street-House-%E2%80%93-a-tour-of-a-different-kind.aspx.

25. "Top 10 Ways to Use Chatter," Salesforce.com, accessed at www.salesforce.com/chatter/overview/top10ways/; "Burberry builds deeper customer connections, from the runway to the retail store," Salesforce.com, accessed at www.salesforce.com/customers/stories/burberry.jsp; "Duha Group Innovates by Inviting Their Customers into Their Manufacturing Process Using Salesforce," Salesforce.com, accessed at www.salesforce.com/ca/customers/stories/duha.jsp; "G Adventures Explores New Customer Experiences with Salesforce," Salesforce.com, accessed at www.salesforce.com/ca/customers/stories/gadventures.jsp.

26. "Partnership Marketing Seminar—Part 1," CMA website, June 2010, accessed at www.the-cma.org/?WCE=C=47|K=229840; Rod Kurtz, "Effective Affinity Marketing Programs," *Bloomberg BusinessWeek*, October 8, 2007, accessed at www.businessweek.com/smallbiz/tips/archives/2007/10/effective_affinity_marketing_programs.html.

27. Sean B. Pasternak, "Scotiabank Adds 100,000 New Accounts in SCENE Loyalty Program," *Bloomberg*, July 24, 2008, accessed at www.bloomberg.com/apps/news?pid=newsarchive&sid=az7BZ9e5b5CE.

28. "Telus Case Study," Ontario Science Centre website, June 2010, accessed at www.ontariosciencecentre.ca/sponsor/partners/telus.asp.

29. "Tougher consumer protection bill lauded," CBC News, June 10, 2010, accessed at www.cbc.ca/consumer/story/2010/06/10/con-consumer-bill-reax.html; "Federal consumer protection bill unveiled," CBC News, June 9, 2010, accessed at www.cbc.ca/consumer/story/2010/06/09/con-consumer-legislation.html; Tony Van Alphern and Dana Flavelle, "Toyota's troubles an example of consumer safety power," *Toronto Star*, February 20, 2010, accessed at www.thestar.com/news/insight/article/767771-toyota-s-troubles-an-example-of-consumer-safety-power.

Chapter 2

1. Personal interview with Mohammed Asaduallah, founder and CEO GrapeTrail Inc., February 2014; "Per capita Canadian wine consumption now 15 litres a year," Canadian Press and CBC News, January 22, 2013, accessed at www.cbc.ca/news/business/story/2013/01/22/business-wine-canada.html; "Canada's Wine Consumption us Growing," CNW Canada Newswire, press release, February 17, 2011, accessed at www.newswire.ca/en/story/749099/canada-s-wine-consumption-is-growing; Benjamin Travis, "Android vs. iOS: User Differences Every Developer Should Know," comScore, March 6, 2013, accessed at www.comscore.com/esl/Insights/Blog/Android_vs_iOS_User_Differences_Every_Developer_Should_Know; Neil Hughes, "New study shows

iPhone users to be in a class by themselves," *AppleInsider*, June 12, 2009, accessed at http://appleinsider.com/articles/09/06/12/new_study_shows_iphone_users_to_be_in_a_class_by_themselves.

2. "The Canadian Population in 2011: Population Counts and Growth," Statistics Canada, accessed at www12.statcan.gc.ca/census-recensement/2011/as-sa/98-310-x/98-310-x2011001-eng.cfm#a2.

3. "The Canadian Population in 2011: Age and Sex," Statistics Canada, accessed at www12.statcan.gc.ca/census-recensement/2011/as-sa/98-311-x/98-311-x2011001-eng.cfm.

4. "Centenarians in Canada," Statistics Canada, accessed at www12.statcan.gc.ca/census-recensement/2011/as-sa/98-311-x/98-311-x2011003_1-eng.cfm.

5. *Marketing Facts: Statistics and Trends for Marketing in Canada*, Canadian Marketing Association, 2012, p. 4.

6. "Fifty Years of Families in Canada: 1961 – 2011," Statistics Canada, accessed at www12.statcan.gc.ca/census-recensement/2011/as-sa/98-312-x/98-312-x2011003_1-eng.cfm.

7. Michael Callahan, "Retirement Planning," Advocis Forum, September 2012, accessed at www.advocis.ca/forum/FMarchives12/FM-sep/caseStudy.html.

8. "Census in Brief: Generations in Canada, Age and Sex, 2011 Census," Statistics Canada, accessed at www12.statcan.gc.ca/census-recensement/2011/as-sa/98-311-x/98-311-x2011003_2-eng.pdf; "Generations in Canada," Statistics Canada, accessed at www12.statcan.gc.ca/census-recensement/2011/as-sa/98-311-x/98-311-x2011003_2-eng.cfm.

9. "Canadian Baby Boomers Testing the Waters of New Technology," Ipsos, November 20, 2012, accessed at www.ipsos-na.com/news-polls/pressrelease.aspx?id=5903.

10. "Census in Brief: Generations in Canada, Age and Sex, 2011 Census," Statistics Canada, accessed at www12.statcan.gc.ca/census-recensement/2011/as-sa/98-311-x/98-311-x2011003_2-eng.pdf; "Generations in Canada," Statistics in Canada, accessed at www12.statcan.gc.ca/census-recensement/2011/as-sa/98-311-x/98-311-x2011003_2-eng.cfm.

11. "Getting Inside Gen Y," *American Demographics*, September 2001, p. 44.

12. "Census in Brief: Generations in Canada, Age and Sex, 2011 Census," Statistics Canada, accessed at www12.statcan.gc.ca/census-recensement/2011/as-sa/98-311-x/98-311-x2011003_2-eng.pdf; "Generations in Canada," Statistics in Canada, accessed at www12.statcan.gc.ca/census-recensement/2011/as-sa/98-311-x/98-311-x2011003_2-eng.cfm.

13. David Coletto and Jaime Morrison, "R U Ready 4 Us? An Introduction to Canadian Millennials," Abacus Data Inc., January 22, 2012, accessed at http://canadianmillennials.ca/wp-content/uploads/2012/01/R-U-Ready-for-Us-An-Introduction-to-Canadian-Millennials.pdf.

14. "Census in Brief: Generations in Canada, Age and Sex, 2011 Census," Statistics Canada, accessed at www12.statcan.gc.ca/census-recensement/2011/as-sa/98-311-x/98-311-x2011003_2-eng.pdf; "Generations in Canada," Statistics in Canada, accessed at www12.statcan.gc.ca/census-recensement/2011/as-sa/98-311-x/98-311-x2011003_2-eng.cfm.

15. "What's The Big Deal with Facebook," Abacus Data, Millennial Research Practice, January 13, 2011 accessed at http://abacusdata.ca/wp-content/uploads/2011/01/Facebook-report-final.pdf; Rick Fergerson, "Born This Way The Canadian Millennial Loyalty Survey How Generation Y Will Shape Customer Loyalty," Aimia, 2012, accessed at www.aimia.com/files/doc_downloads/Aimia_GenY_WhitepaperCanada_Final.pdf; Jonathan Becher, "A Multitude of Myths about Millennials," *Forbes*, October 15, 2012, accessed at www.forbes.com/sites/sap/2012/10/15/a-multitude-of-myths-about-millennials/; "Generation Y In Canada: Highlights of National Poll of Millennials," *Huffington Post*, November 20, 2012, accessed at www.huffingtonpost.ca/2012/11/20/generation-y-in-canada-survey-2012_n_2151488.html.

16. "The Canadian Population in 2011: Population Counts and Growth Population and Dwelling Counts, 2011 Census," Statistics Canada, accessed at www12.statcan.gc.ca/census-recensement/2011/as-sa/98-310-x/98-310-x2011001-eng.pdf and www12.statcan.gc.ca/census-recensement/2011/as-sa/98-310-x/98-310-x2011001-eng.cfm#a1.

17. Tobi Cohen, "Canada Census 2011: Immigrants and newcomers drive population growth," *National Post*, Feb 8, 2012, accessed at http://news.nationalpost.com/2012/02/08/canada-census-2011-immigrants-and-newcomers-drive-population-growth/.

18. "Canada Facts and Figures, Immigration Overview, Permanent and Temporary Residents, 2011" Citizen and Immigration Canada, accessed at www.cic.gc.ca/english/pdf/research-stats/facts2011.pdf.

19. "Figure 1: Number of Canadians whose mother tongue is one of the 22 immigrant languages reported by more than 100,000 persons, Canada, 2011," Statistics Canada, accessed at www12.statcan.gc.ca/census-recensement/2011/as-sa/98-314-x/2011003/fig/fig3_2-1-eng.cfm; "Census in Brief, Immigrant Languages in Canada, Language, 2011 Census of Population," Statistics Canada, accessed at www12.statcan.gc.ca/census-recensement/2011/as-sa/98-314-x/98-314-x2011003_2-eng.pdf; "Linguistic Characteristics of Canadians," Statistics Canada, accessed at www12.statcan.gc.ca/census-recensement/2011/as-sa/98-314-x/98-314-x2011001-eng.cfm; "An overview of language data, 2011 Census," Statistics Canada, October 24, 2012, accessed at http://youtu.be/BFpS6h3t2yA.

20. "European population compared with world population," European Commission, November 2012 data, accessed at http://epp.eurostat.ec.europa.eu/statistics_explained/index.php/European_population_compared_with_world_population.

21. "Portrait of Families and Living Arrangements in Canada," Statistics Canada, accessed at www12.statcan.gc.ca/census-recensement/2011/as-sa/98-312-x/98-312-x2011001-eng.cfm.

22. Gregor Smith, "The Impact of Connected Devices on Consumer Behaviour," comScore, Mobile World Congress presentation, February 2013, accessed at www.comscore.com/Insights/Presentations_and_Whitepapers/2013/The_Impact_of_Connected_Devices_on_Consumer_Behavior; Brent Bernie, "Brave New Digital World—What media measurement business must address," comScore, IAB Canada Mixx presentation, March 21, 2013.

23. James Russo and Carman Allison, "What's in Store 2013 Think Small for Big Results," Nielsen, accessed April 2013 at www.nielsen.com/ca/en/news-insights/reports-downloads/2013/webinar--what-s-in-store--think-small-for-big-results.html.

24. "2013 Canada Digital Future in Focus," comScore, March 2013, accessed at www.comscore.com/Insights/Presentations_and_Whitepapers/2013/2013_Canada_Digital_Future_in_Focus.

25. "To Binge or Not to Binge, That is the Question," SRG, March 7, 2013, accessed at www.srgnet.com/index.php/2013/03/07/to-binge-or-not-that-is-the-question/; "New Stars, Channels Increase YouTube's Popularity," SRG, March 29, 2013, accessed at www.srgnet.com/2013/03/29/new-stars-channels-increase-youtubes-popularity/; "More than a Quarter of Online Canadians are 'Social TV' Viewers," SRG, November 11, 2012, accessed at www.srgnet.com/index.php/2012/11/11/more-than-a-quarter-of-online-canadians-are-social-tv-viewers/.

26. "Canadian Food Trends to 2020," *Agriculture and Agri-Food Canada*, February 24, 2009, accessed at www4.agr.gc.ca/AAFC-AAC/display-afficher.do?id=1170944121865&lang=eng.

27. Beth Hoffman, "How 'Millennials' Are Changing Food as We Know It," *Forbes*, September 4, 2012, accessed at www.forbes.com/sites/bethhoffman/2012/09/04/how-millenials-are-changing-food-as-we-know-it/.

28. mySupermarket website, April 2013, accessed at http://mysupermarket.co.uk/; Kristopher Kubicki, "For Grocers, After Years of Shunning Internet, Digital Starts to Click," *AdAge* dataworks, March 18, 2013, accessed at http://adage.com/article/

data-at-work/u-s-grocers-stop-shunning-internet-finally-embrace-digital/240371/; "Food trends to watch in 2013," *Canadian Grocer*, October 24, 2012, accessed at www.canadiangrocer.com/top-stories/food-trends-to-watch-in-2013-17136.

29. SupperWorks website, April 2013, accessed at www.supperworks.com.

30. Pamela L. Ramage-Morin and Didier Garriguet, "Nutritional risk among older Canadians," Statistics Canada, March 2013, accessed at www.statcan.gc.ca/pub/82-003-x/2013003/article/11773-eng.pdf; Karen C. Roberts, Margot Shields, Margaret de Groh, Alfred Aziz, Joanne Gilbert, "Overweight and obesity in children and adolescents: Results from the 2009–2011 Canadian Health Measures Survey," Statistics Canada, August 2012, accessed at www.statcan.gc.ca/pub/82-003-x/2012003/article/11706-eng.pdf.

31. "An Analysis of Consumer Health Apps for Apple's iPhone 2012," *MobiHealthNews*, accessed April, 2013 at http://mobihealthnews.com/research/an-analysis-of-consumer-health-apps-for-apples-iphone-2012/; Jonathon Kantor, "Happtique Launches mRx; Pilot Program," *Happtique* blog, August 19, 2012, accessed at http://blog.happtique.com/blog/bid/214860/; Dave Chase, "Prescribable Mobile Apps Huge Threat for Pharma," *Forbes*, April 14, 2012, accessed at www.forbes.com/sites/davechase/2012/05/14/prescribable-mobile-apps-huge-threat-for-pharma/; "10 Trends for 2013," trendwatching.com, accessed at www.trendwatching.com/trends/10trends2013/.

32. "Standards Matter 2011 – 2012 Annual Report," Advertising Standards Canada, accessed April 2013 at www.adstandards.com/en/AboutASC/2012AnnualReport.pdf; "Canadian Children's Food and Beverage Advertising Initiative," Advertising Standards Canada, accessed April 2013 at www.adstandards.com/en/childrensinitiative/default.htm; "Canadian Children's Food and Beverage Advertising Initiative Year One Compliance Report," Advertising Standards Canada, accessed April 2013 at www.adstandards.com/en/childrensinitiative/yearOneComplianceReport.pdf; "Canadian Children's Food and Beverage Advertising Initiative 2009 Compliance Report," Advertising Standards Canada, accessed April 2013 at www.adstandards.com/en/childrensinitiative/2009ComplianceReport.pdf; "Canadian Children's Food and Beverage Advertising Initiative 2010 Compliance Report," Advertising Standards Canada, accessed April 2013 at www.adstandards.com/en/childrensinitiative/2010ComplianceReport.pdf; "Canadian Children's Food and Beverage Advertising Initiative 2011 Compliance Report," Advertising Standards Canada, accessed April 2013 at www.adstandards.com/en/childrensinitiative/2011ComplianceReport.pdf.

33. "Kruger report looks at green consumers, and how to help them," *Canadian Grocer*, September 26, 2012, accessed at www.canadiangrocer.com/top-stories/kruger-report-looks-at-green-consumers-and-how-to-help-them-16077; Paulette S. Padanyi, "Helping Canadian Households Achieve Their Sustainability Goals," Kruger Products White Paper, accessed at http://bppgcreative.ca/pdfs/g/SustainabilityGoals.pdf.

34. "A Greener Tomorrow Starts Today," Canadian Tire, accessed April 2013 at www.canadiantire.ca/AST/browse/Green.jsp?locale=en&bmLocale=en; ECOLOGO website, accessed April 2013 at www.ecologo.org/en/.

35. Carly Weeks, "The drive to go green—saving the environment or money?" *Globe and Mail*, March 14, 2011, accessed at www.theglobeandmail.com/life/health-and-fitness/the-drive-to-go-green---saving-the-environment-or-money/article572773/; "Households and the Environment Survey, 2011," Statistics Canada, March 18, 2013, accessed at www.statcan.gc.ca/daily-quotidien/130318/dq130318b-eng.pdf; "Synovate Survey Reveals Latest Green Habits and Consumption Across the World," Ipsos, April 7, 2011, accessed at www.ipsos-na.com/news-polls/pressrelease.aspx?id=5480.

36. "Does Gender Matter?" Newswire Nielsen Global, March 8, 2013, accessed at www.nielsen.com/us/en/newswire/2013/does-gender-matter-.html; Andrea Gordon, "Grocery stores targeting male shoppers," *Toronto Star*, November 30, 2011, accessed at www.thestar.com/life/2011/11/30/grocery_stores_targeting_male_shoppers.html.

37. Nielsen, "Consumer Confidence: A Canadian Perspective, Q4 2012," accessed April 2013 at www.nielsen.com/content/dam/nielsen/en_ca/documents/pdf/reports/Consumer-Confidence%20-%20A-Canadian-Perspective-Q4-2012.pdf.

38. Scott Deveau, "'Year of the truck' pushes Canadian auto sales to record in 2013," *National Post*, January 4, 2014, accessed at http://business.financialpost.com/2014/01/03/chrysler-december-auto-sales/; Dana Flavelle, "Auto sales hit new high in Canada," *Toronto Star*, January 3, 2014, accessed at www.thestar.com/business/2014/01/03/auto_industry_headed_for_yearend_high.html; Associated Press, "2013 auto sales up 4% in Canada, 8% in U.S.," CBC, January 3, 2014, accessed at www.cbc.ca/news/business/2013-auto-sales-up-4-in-canada-8-in-u-s-1.2483065; Alastair Sharp, "Canada auto sales best ever in 2013, Ford still tops," Reuters, January 4, 2014, accessed at http://ca.reuters.com/article/businessNews/idCABREA020OS20140104.

39. "OECD says Canada to lead G7 in growth for next 50 years," CBC News, November 9, 2012, accessed at www.cbc.ca/news/business/story/2012/11/09/oecd-canada-growth.html; "Canada to face period of weak economic growth: OECD," Canadian Press, March 11, 2013, accessed at www.ctvnews.ca/business/canada-to-face-period-of-weak-economic-growth-oecd-1.1191243.

40. The Bensimon Byrne Consumerology Report: Technology and Canadian Consumers, January 2010, accessed at www.consumerology.ca.

41. Gregor Smith, "The Impact of Connected Devices on Consumer Behaviour," comScore, February 2013, accessed at www.comscore.com/Insights/Presentations_and_Whitepapers/2013/The_Impact_of_Connected_Devices_on_Consumer_Behavior; "2013 Canada Digital Future in Focus," comScore, March 2013, accessed at www.comscore.com/Insights/Presentations_and_Whitepapers/2013/2013_Canada_Digital_Future_in_Focus.

42. Aidan Foster, "Responsive Web Design: What is it and why should I care?" *Responsive Web Design* blog, February 12, 2012, accessed at http://responsivedesign.ca/blog/responsive-web-design-what-is-it-and-why-should-i-care; Pete Cashmore, "Why 2013 is the year of Responsive Web Design," *Mashable*, December 11, 2012, accessed at http://mashable.com/2012/12/11/responsive-web-design/.

43. "The Ipsos Canadian inter@ctive Reid Report 2012 Fact Guide," Ipsos, accessed April, 2012 at www.ipsos.ca/common/dl/pdf/Ipsos_InteractiveReidReport_FactGuide_2012.pdf.

44. "Retailers in Canada Make Strides in the Ecommerce Channel," *eMarketer*, October 19, 2012, accessed at www.emarketer.com/Article/Retailers-Canada-Make-Strides-Ecommerce-Channel/1009427; "Canada Grabs Greater Share of Ecommerce sales in North America," *eMarketer*, September 7, 2012, accessed at www.emarketer.com/Article/Canada-Grabs-Greater-Share-of-Ecommerce-Sales-North-America/1009328.

45. "The Ipsos Canadian inter@ctive Reid Report 2012 Fact Guide," Ipsos, accessed April, 2012 at www.ipsos.ca/common/dl/pdf/Ipsos_InteractiveReidReport_FactGuide_2012.pdf.

46. "Canadian Teens Increasingly Paying for Music Downloads," Ipsos, March 2012, accessed at www.ipsos-na.com/news-polls/pressrelease.aspx?id=5537.

47. Michael Oliveira, "Report looks at 'tuned out' Canadians who don't pay for TV, mostly stream video," *Canadian Business*, April 3, 2013, accessed at www.canadianbusiness.com/business-news/report-looks-at-tuned-out-canadians-who-dont-pay-for-tv-mostly-stream-video/.

48. "More Canadians "tuning out" conventional TV: report," *Marketing*, April 3, 2013, accessed at www.marketingmag.ca/news/media-news/more-canadians-tuning-out-conventional-tv-report-75618?P=75618?Utm; "Take two tablets and watch last

night's TV show in the morning," Deloitte, January 17, 2012, accessed at www.deloitte.com/view/en_CA/ca/pressroom/ca-pressreleases-en/cd1c728f536e4310VgnVCM3000001c-56f00aRCRD.htm .

49. "New Stars, Channels Increase YouTube's Popularity," SRG, March 29, 2013, accessed at www.srgnet.com/index.php/2013/03/29/new-stars-channels-increase-youtubes-popularity.

50. "TMT Predictions 2013," Deloitte Canada, January 15, 2013, accessed at www.deloitte.com/view/en_CA/ca/industries/tmt/tmt-predictions-2013/index.htm; "TMT Predictions 2013 Insights. In advance," Deloitte, accessed April 2013 at www.deloitte.com/assets/Dcom-Canada/Local%20Assets/Documents/TMT/ca_en_tmt_canadian_predictions_2013_011513.pdf.

51. "Close to Half of Canadians Now Own a Smartphone," Ipsos, February 21, 2013, accessed at www.ipsos-na.com/news-polls/pressrelease.aspx?id=6005; "The Mobile Marketing Roadmap: How Mobile is Transforming Marketing for Targeting Next Generation Consumers," Mobile Marketing Association, accessed December 2013, at www.mmaglobal.com; "Mobile Future in Focus 2013," comScore, February 2013, accessed at www.comscore.com; "2012 Cell Phone Consumer Attitudes Study," Canadian Wireless Telecommunications Association and Quorus Consulting Group, April 23, 2012, accessed at http://cwta.ca/wordpress/wp-content/uploads/2011/08/CWTA-2012ConsumerAttitudes1.pdf.

52. Betsy Frank, "Consumer and context with smartphones versus tablets," *Mobile Commerce Daily*, April 2, 2013, accessed at www.mobilecommercedaily.com/consumer-and-context-with-smartphones-versus-tablets; "Connected device usage diverges," WARC, April 3, 2012, accessed at www.warc.com/LatestNews/News/Connected_device_usage_diverges.news?ID=31219.

53. Ibid.

54. "Canada's Anti-Spam Law Casts a Wide Net – Requires all Organizations to take Action," Osler, Hoskin & Harcourt LLP, January 2014, accessed at www.osler.com/uploadedFiles/Expertise/Areas_of_Expertise/Areas_Of_Practice/Privacy_Law/CASL-Canada%E2%80%99s-Anti-Spam-Law-Casts-a-Wide-Net.pdf.

55. "Competition Bureau Secures Over $9 Million and Money Back to Victims for Business Scam," Competition Bureau, March 2, 2012, accessed at www.competitionbureau.gc.ca/eic/site/cb-bc.nsf/eng/03439.html; Ashley Weber, "Canadian court comes down hard on misleading business directory scam," Stikeman Elliott, March 15, 2012, accessed at www.thecompetitor.ca/2012/03/articles/competition/competition-bureau/canadian-court-comes-down-hard-on-misleading-business-directory-scam/#more; "Competition Bureau Sues to Shut Down Business Directory Scam," Competition Bureau, July 28, 2011, accessed at www.competitionbureau.gc.ca/eic/site/cb-bc.nsf/eng/03394.html.

56. Tamara Baluja, "OMG: They referenced the F-word on a billboard," *Globe and Mail*, March 22, 2011, updated August 23, 2012, accessed at www.theglobeandmail.com/news/toronto/omg-they-referenced-the-f-word-on-a-billboard/article1951865/; "Canadian Marketing, Advertising & Regulatory Law Update," *Heenan Blaikie*, September 2011, Issue 10, page 6, accessed at www.heenanblaikie.com/en/Publications/2011/Canadian-Marketing,-Advertising-Regulatory-Law-Update.pdf; "Ad Complaints Reports - Q2 2011," Advertising Standards Canada, accessed April 2012 at http://adstandards.com/en/Standards/adComplaintsReports.aspx?periodquarter=2&periodyear=2011.

57. "Broadcast Advertising Basics: Revenue, Limits and Content," Consumers-Radio and Television—Advertising, Canadian Radio-television and Telecommunications Commission, February 18, 2010, accessed at www.crtc.gc.ca/eng/info_sht/b300.htm.

58. "CRTC announces that Bell Canada has paid a $1.3 million penalty for violating the National Do Not Call List Rules," Canadian Radio-television and Telecommunications Commission, news release, December 20, 2010, accessed at www.crtc.gc.ca/eng/com100/2010/r101220.htm; "In settlement with the CRTC, Comwave Telenetworks Inc. agrees to stop violating the do not call rules

and pays $100,000," Canadian Radio-television and Telecommunications Commission, news release, April 3, 2012, accessed at www.crtc.gc.ca/eng/com100/2013/r130403.htm.

59. "The CRTC Wireless Code," The Canadian Radio-television and Telecommunications Association, accessed December 2013 at www.crtc.gc.ca/eng/info_sht/t13.htm; "CRTC wireless code comes into force: Canadians can cancel their contracts without penalty after two years," Canadian Radio-television and Tele-communications Association, news release, December 2, 2013, accessed at http://crtc.gc.ca/eng/com100/2013/r131202.htm#.UqMX0MRDuSo.

60. CCTS accessed at www.ccts-cprst.ca.

61. CWTA accessed at http://cwta.ca.

62. Jason Kerr, "Text Messaging in Canada," Canadian Wireless Telecommunications Association; "Canadian Common Short Code Application Guidelines Version 2.2," Canadian Wireless Telecommunications Association, August 9, 2012, accessed at www.txt.ca/english/business/doc/Canadian%20Common%20Short%20Code%20Application%20Guidelines.pdf; "Canada standard rate short code pricing," Clickatell, November 18, 2010, accessed at www.clickatell.com/downloads/Clickatell_Canadian_Shortcode_pricing_revenue_share.pdf.

63. MMA accessed at www.mmaglobal.com.

64. "Global Code of Conduct," Mobile Marketing Association, July 15, 2008, accessed at www.mmaglobal.com/bestpractice.

65. "Payment processor for scareware cyber crime ring sentenced to 48 months in prison," FBI, Seattle division, December 4, 2012, accessed at www.fbi.gov/seattle/press-releases/2012/payment-processor-for-scareware-cyber-crime-ring-sentenced-to-48-months-in-prison; Leon Erlanger, "Happy Halloween! Defence against scareware and randsomeware," McAfee blog, October 30, 2012, accessed at http://blogs.mcafee.com/security-connected/happy-halloween-defense-against-scareware-and-ransomware; "Scareware" scam warning," Canadian Anti-Fraud Centre, accessed June 2013 at www.antifraudcentre-centreantifraude.ca/english/Scareware.html; Jody Porter, "Scam locks up computers, accuses users of downloading porn," CBC News, February 21, 2013, accessed at www.cbc.ca/news/technology/story/2013/02/20/hamilton-scareware-child-porn-scam.html?cmp=rss; "Computer porn 'scareware' seen in Canada," UPI, April 20, 2012, accessed at www.upi.com/Top_News/World-News/2012/04/20/Computer-porn-scareware-seen-in-Canada/UPI-96431334934804/.

66. Fact Sheets, "Privacy Legislation in Canada," Office of the Privacy Commissioner of Canada, March 2009, accessed at www.priv.gc.ca/resource/fs-fi/02_05_d_15_e.asp; Privacy Act, amended February 28, 2013, Minister of Justice, accessed at http://laws-lois.justice.gc.ca/PDF/P-21.pdf and http://laws-lois.justice.gc.ca/eng/acts/P-21/index.html.

67. Personal Information Protection and Electronic Documents Act, amended April1, 2011, Minister of Justice, accessed at http://laws-lois.justice.gc.ca/PDF/P-8.6.pdf; "PIPEDA Guide for Businesses and Organizations Your Privacy Responsibilities," Office of the Privacy Commissioner of Canada, February 2010, accessed at www.priv.gc.ca/information/guide_e.pdf; "CMA Privacy Compliance Guide," Canadian Marketing Association, May 2010, accessed at www.the-cma.org/regulatory/code-and-guidelines/privacy.

68. "Canada's Anti-Spam Legislation, Fast Facts," accessed February 2014 at http://fightspam.gc.ca/eic/site/030.nsf/eng/h_00039.html; "Canada's Anti-Spam Law Casts a Wide Net – Requires All Organizations to Take Action," Osler, Hoskin & Harcourt LLP, January 2014, accessed at www.osler.com/uploadedFiles/Expertise/Areas_of_Expertise/Areas_Of_Practice/Privacy_Law/CASL-Canada%E2%80%99s-Anti-Spam-Law-Casts-a-Wide-Net.pdf; Canada's Anti-Spam Legislation website, accessed February 2014 at http://fightspam.gc.ca/eic/site/030.nsf/eng/home; "Canada's anti-spam legislation," Canadian Radio-television and Telecommunication Commission, accessed February 2014 at www.crtc.gc.ca/eng/casl-lcap.htm; Bernice Karn, Christopher

Hersh, Imran Ahmad and Chad Matheson, "Canada: Canada's Anti-Spam Legislation Coming Into Force In 2014: Are You Ready?," Mondaq, December 6, 2013, accessed at www.mondaq.com/canada/x/279700/advertising+marketing+branding/Canadas+AntiSpam+Legislation+Coming+Into+Force+In+2014+Are+You+Ready; "CMA Guide to Canada's Anti-Spam Law (CASL)," Canadian Marketing Association, April2, 2014, accessed at http://www.the-cma.org/regulatory/code-and-guidelines/cma-guide-to-canada-anti-spam-law.

69. Adapted from Brenda Pritchard and Mathew Marinett, "Canada: Are you compliant? Online behavioural advertising in Canada, the US, and Europe," Gowlings blog, December 2012, accessed at http://m.gowlings.com/knowledgecentre/article.asp?pubID=2718

70. "New program gives consumers more online choice," Canadian Marketing Association, press release, September 2013, accessed at www.the-cma.org/newsroom/2013/new-program-gives-consumers-more-online-choice; Digital Advertising Alliance of Canada website, accessed February 2014 at http://youradchoices.ca/; "New Online Behavioural Advertising Guidelines Issued by the Federal Privacy Commissioner," Gowlings blog, December 2011, accessed at www.gowlings.com/KnowledgeCentre/article.asp?pubID=2599.

71. "Canadian Marketing Association Guide to Promotional Contests," Canadian Marketing Association, May 2010, accessed from www.the-cma.org/?WCE=C=47|K=225856.

72. Mohammed Asaduallah, founder and CEO GrapeTrail Inc., February 2014.

Chapter 3

1. Personal Interview with Nick Gaudreau – Chief Marketing Officer, Yellow Pages Group, October 2013.

2. Chris Sorensen, "Living beyond our means," Maclean's, March 22, 2014; Bryan Borzykowski, "Managing your debt-to-income ratio," Maclean's, November 19, 2012; Canada Country Profile, 2013, 1-82.

3. Gordon C. Bruner II and Richard J. Pomazal, "Problem Recognition: The Crucial First Stage of the Consumer Decision Process", Journal of Consumer Marketing 5, 1988, pp. 53–63; James F. Engel, Roger D. Blackwell, and Paul Miniard, Consumer Behavior, 9th ed. (Fort Worth, TX: Dryden Press, 1998).

4. For thorough descriptions of consumer expertise, see Joseph W. Alba and J. Wesley Hutchinson, "Knowledge Calibration: What Consumers Know and What They Think They Know," Journal of Consumer Research, September 2000, pp. 123–56.

5. For in-depth studies on external information search patterns, see Sridhar Moorthy, Brian T. Ratchford, and Debabrata Tulukdar, "Consumer Information Search Revisited: Theory and Empirical Analysis," Journal of Consumer Research, March 1997, pp. 263–277; and Joel E. Urbany, Peter R. Dickson, and William L. Wilkie, "Buyer Uncertainty and Information Search," Journal of Consumer Research, March 1992, pp. 452–463.

6. Personal interview with Aby Alameddine, Co-Founder of Core Online Marketing, June 2013; C. Loudon and P. Ferriss, "100 thought leaders look to the future," Marketing, November 10, 2008; Ben Carter, "Fulfilling potential," Marketing, July 5, 2006.

7. For an extended discussion on evaluative criteria, see Del J. Hawkins, Roger J. Best, and Kenneth A. Coney, Consumer Behavior, 8th ed. (New York: Irwin/McGraw-Hill, 2001), pp. 566–83.

8. Jochen Wirtz and Anna S. Mattila, "The effects of consumer expertise on evoked set size and service loyalty," Journal of Services Marketing 17, 2003, pp. 649–665; John A. Howard, Buyer Behavior in Marketing Strategy, 2nd ed. (Englewood Cliffs, NJ: Prentice Hall, 1994), pp. 101, 128–89.

9. Peter Weill and Stephanie L. Woerner, "Optimizing your digital business model," MIT Sloan Management Review, March 19, 2013, pp. 71–78; Joerg Koenigstorfer and Andrea Groeppel-Klein, "Consumer acceptance of the mobile Internet," Marketing Letters, August 31, 2012, pp. 917–928; Sheena Leek and George Christodoulides, "Next-Generation Mobile Marketing: How Young Consumers React to Bluetooth-Enabled Advertising," Journal of Advertising Research, March 2009, pp. 44–53.

10. Ann Zimmerman, "Showdown over showrooming," Wall Street Journal, January 23, 2012, accessed at http://online.wsj.com/article/SB10001424052970204624204577177242516227440.html; "Target Battles 'Showrooming,'" Music Trades, March 2012, p. 34; "Target fights showrooming with price-match policy," SCTWeek, January 11, 2013.

11. Jagdish N. Sheth, Banwari Mitral, and Bruce Newman, Consumer Behavior (Fort Worth, TX: Dryden Press, 1999), p. 22.

12. Monika Koller and Thomas Salzberger, "Heterogeneous development of cognitive dissonance over time and its effect on satisfaction and loyalty," Journal of Customer Behaviour, Autumn 2012, pp. 261–280; Thomas Salzberger and Monika Koller, "Investigating the impact of cognitive dissonance and customer satisfaction on loyalty and complaint behaviour," REMark, Jan/Apr 2010, pp. 5–16.

13. For an overview of research on involvement, see John C. Mowen and Michael Minor, Consumer Behavior, 6th ed. (Upper Saddle River, NJ: Prentice Hall, 2001), pp. 64–68; and Frank R. Kardes, Consumer Behavior (Reading, MA: Addison-Wesley, 1999), pp. 256–58.

14. For an overview on the three problem-solving variations, see Hawkins, Best, and Coney, Consumer Behavior, pp. 506–7; and Howard, Buyer Behavior, pp. 69–162.

15. Hollie Shaw, "Fast Food Makes You Think Fast," National Post, April 23, 2010, page FP10; "Importance of Brand Recognition," accessed June 2010 at www.syncrat.com/articles/importance-of-brand-recognition; and "Logo Can Make You Think Different," Duke University, March 18, 2008, accessed at today.duke.edu/2008/03/apple_ibm.html.

16. Kenneth C. Gehrt and Ruoh-Nan Yan, "Situational, consumer, and retailer factors affecting internet, catalog, and store shopping," International Journal of Retail & Distribution Management, January 2004, pp. 5–18; Sydney Roslow, Tiger Li, and J.A.F. Nicholls, "Impact of situational variables and demographic attributes in two seasons on purchase behaviour," European Journal of Marketing, October 2000, pp. 1167–1180; Russell Belk, "Situational Variables and Consumer Behavior," Journal of Consumer Research, December 1975, pp. 157–163.

17. "Shopping As Therapy: Good Health Comes in Small Packages," Discover Fit & Health, accessed June 2011 at http://health.howstuffworks.com/wellness/women/general/shopping-as-therapy.htm.

18. A. H. Maslow, Motivation and Personality (New York: Harper & Row, 1970).

19. "Brand Papers: Challenging Maslow," Brand Strategy, 2003; Francis Buttle, "The social construction of needs," Psychology & Marketing, September 15, 2006, p. 197.

20. Arthur Koponen, "The Personality Characteristics of Purchasers," Journal of Advertising Research, September 1960, pp. 89–92; Joel B. Cohen, "An Interpersonal Orientation to the Study of Consumer Behavior," Journal of Marketing Research, August 1967, pp. 270–78; and Rena Bartos, Marketing to Women Around the World (Cambridge, MA: Harvard Business School, 1989).

21. Michael R. Solomon, Consumer Behavior, 5th ed. (Upper Saddle River, NJ: Prentice Hall, 2002), p. 61.

22. "BMW Service and Warranties," BMW Canada website, accessed at www.bmw.ca/ca/en/owners/service/warranty/warranty_1.html.

23. Martin Fishbein and I. Aizen, Belief, Attitude, Intention and Behavior: An Introduction to Theory and Research (Reading, MA: Addison-Wesley, 1975), p. 6.

24. Richard J. Lutz, "Changing Brand Attitudes through Modification of Cognitive Structure," Journal of Consumer Research, March 1975, pp. 49–59; "Pepsi's Gamble Hits Freshness Dating Jackpot," Advertising Age, September 19, 1994, p. 50; and "Every Which Way to Color, Whiten, Brighten," Brandweek, June 17, 2002, p. 558.

25. "How many hours of sleep are enough?" Mayo Clinic website, accessed September 2014 at www.mayoclinic.com/health/how-many-hours-of-sleep-are-enough/AN01487.

26. "The VALS™ Types," www.strategicbusinessinsight.com, downloaded July 1, 2013.

27. Personal interview with Michael Weiss, chief marketing officer, Environics Analytics, July 2013.

28. "Maximizing the Market with Influentials," *American Demographics*, July 1995, p. 42; also see, "I'll Have What He's Having," *American Demographics*, July 2000, p. 22.

29. Representative recent work on positive and negative word of mouth can be found in Geok Theng Lau and Sophia Ng, "Individual and situational factors influencing negative word-of-mouth behaviour," *Canadian Journal of Administrative Sciences*, April 8, 2009, pp. 163–178; Robert E. Smith and Christine A. Vogt, "The Effects of Integrating Advertising and Negative Word-of-Mouth Communications on Message Processing and Response," *Journal of Consumer Psychology* 4 (1995), pp. 133–151; Paula Bone, "Word-of-Mouth Effects on Short-Term and Long-Term Product Judgments," *Journal of Business Research* 32 (1995), pp. 213–23; Chip Walker, "Word of Mouth," *American Demographics*, July 1995, pp. 38–45; and Dale F. Duhan, Scott D. Johnson, James B. Wilcox, and Gilbert D. Harrell, "Influences on Consumer Use of Word-of-Mouth Recommendation Sources," *Journal of the Academy of Marketing Science*, Fall 1997, pp. 283–295.

30. For an extended discussion on reference groups, see Wayne D. Hoyer and Deborah J. MacInnis, *Consumer Behavior*, 2nd ed. (Boston: Houghton Miffin, 2001), chap. 15.

31. For an extensive review on consumer socialization of children, see Deborah Roedder John, "Consumer Socialization of Children: A Retrospective Look at Twenty-Five Years of Research," *Journal of Consumer Research*, December 1999, pp. 183-213.

32. This discussion is based on "The American Family in the 21st Century," *American Demographics*, August 2001, p. 20; and J. Paul Peter and Jerry C. Olson, *Consumer Behavior and Marketing Strategy*, 5th ed. (New York: Irwin/McGraw-Hill, 1999), pp. 341–43.

33. "Canadian households in 2011: Type and growth," Statistics Canada, September 2012, accessed at www12.statcan.gc.ca/census-recensement/2011/as-sa/98-312-x/98-312-x2011003_2-eng.cfm.

34. Diane Crispell, "Dual-Earner Diversity," *American Demographics*, July 1995, pp. 32–37.

35. "There She Is . . . ." *American Demographics*, August 2001, p. 6; "Wearing the Pants," *Brandweek*, October 20, 1997, pp. 20, 22; "Look Who's Shopping," *Progressive Grocer*, January 1998, p. 18.

36. "Call It 'Kid-fluence,'" *U.S. News & World Report*, July 30, 2001, pp. 32–33; "Special Report: Superstars of Spending," *Advertising Age*, February 20, 2001, pp. S1, S10; Teen Research Unlimited, www.teenresearch.com, downloaded September 4, 2001.

37. "I.AM.Canadian by Molson," CBC Digital Archives, accessed at www.cbc.ca/archives/categories/economy-business/business/selling-suds-the-beer-industry-in-canada/i-am-canadian.html; and Susan Krashinsky, "I am Canadian, and so are they: Molson's new nationalist pitch," *Globe and Mail*, February 6, 2013, accessed at www.theglobeandmail.com/report-on-business/industry-news/marketing/i-am-canadian-and-so-are-they-molsons-new-nationalist-pitch/article8280376/.

38. Word of Mouth Marketing Association (WoMMA),

39. "French and the francophonie in Canada," Statistics Canada, October 2012, accessed at www12.statcan.gc.ca/census-recensement/2011/as-sa/98-314-x/98-314-x2011003_1-eng.cfm.

40. Danny Kucharsky, "French Lessons," *Marketing* magazine, March 27, 2006, p. 8.

41. Ed Crain, "Say 'Oui' to the Quebec Market," *Electronic Retailer*, August 2010, accessed at www.electronicretailermag.com/er0810_quebec.

42. Rebecca Harris, "Embrace and Prosper," *Marketing* magazine, January 23, 2006.

43. For comprehensive references on cross-cultural aspects of marketing, see Paul A. Herbig, *Handbook of Cross-Cultural Marketing* (New York: Halworth Press, 1998); and Jean-Claude Usunier, *Marketing across Cultures*, 2nd ed. (London: Prentice Hall Europe, 1996). Unless otherwise indicated, examples found in this section appear in these excellent sources.

44. "Pepsi's second global campaign 'embrace your past, but live for now' featuring Beyonce," *Economic Times*, April 11, 2013, accessed at http://articles.economictimes.indiatimes.com/2013-04-10/news/38434267_1_pepsi-international-brad-jakeman-global-brand-ambassador; Kia Makarechi, "Beyoncé on Pepsi Criticism: 'It's All About Choices,'" *Huffington Post*, July 10, 2013, accessed at www.huffingtonpost.com/2013/07/10/beyonce-pepsi-criticism-choices_n_3572582.html.

45. "McDonald's Adapts Mac Attack to Foreign Tastes with Expansion," *Dallas Morning News*, December 7, 1997, p. 3H; and "Taking Credit," *The Economist*, November 2, 1996, p. 75.

46. Patricia Adams, "Foreign aid corruption case puts Canada on trial," *National Post*, August 20, 1999.

47. These examples appear in Del I. Hawkins, Roger J. Best, and Kenneth A. Coney, *Consumer Behavior*, 8th ed. (Burr Ridge, IL: McGraw-Hill/Irwin, 2001), chap. 2.

48. "Greeks Protest Coke's Use of Parthenon," *Dallas Morning News*, August 17, 1992, p. D4.

49. Valentina Vescovi and Aixa Rocca, "In Argentina, Pepsi Becomes 'Pecsi,'" *Advertising Age*, July 15, 2009, accessed at http://adage.com/globalnews/article?article_id=137946.

50. "Global Thinking Paces Computer Biz," *Advertising Age*, March 6, 1995, p. 10.

51. "If only Krispy Kreme makes you smarter," *Business 2.0*, August 2005, p. 108.

Chapter 4

1. Svetlana Sicular, "Gartner's Big Data Definition Consists of Three Parts, Not to Be Confused with Three "V"s," Gartner, Inc, featured in *Forbes*, March 27, 2013, accessed at www.forbes.com/sites/gartnergroup/2013/03/27/gartners-big-data-definition-consists-of-three-parts-not-to-be-confused-with-three-vs/.

2. Susan Krashinsky, "I am Canadian, and so are they: Molson's new nationalist pitch," *Globe and Mail*, February 6, 2013, accessed at www.theglobeandmail.com/report-on-business/industry-news/marketing/i-am-canadian-and-so-are-they-molsons-new-nationalist-pitch/article8280376/; "Molson's Canadians: Are beer and patriotism a potent brew?" CBC News Community, February 6, 2013, accessed at www.cbc.ca/news/yourcommunity/2013/02/are-beer-and-patriotism-a-potent-brew.html; Curtis Rush, "New Molson Canadian ad shows wild, crazy side of this nation's beer drinkers," *Toronto Star*, February 6, 2013, accessed at www.thestar.com/news/canada/2013/02/06/new_molson_canadian_ad_shows_wild_crazy_side_of_this_nations_beer_drinkers.html; "Molson Canadian Ad Goes Viral: Proud Patriotism Or Cynical Exploitation?" *Huffington Post Canada*, February 6, 2013, accessed at www.huffingtonpost.ca/2013/02/06/molson-canadian-ad-viral_n_2631017.html.

3. Interview with Luke Sklar, partner and founder of Sklar Wilton and Associates, May 2013; discussion with Jennifer Roberts, director at Sklar Wilton and Associates, June 2013.

4. For an expanded definition, consult the American Marketing Association's website at www.marketingpower.com; for a researcher's comments on this and other definitions of marketing research, see Lawrence D. Gibson, "Quo Vadis, Marketing rch?" *Marketing Research*, Spring 2000, pp. 36–41.

5. Michael Grant and Catharine Johnston, "1 + 1 = 3: CMO & CIO Collaboration Best Practices That Drive Growth," CMA and The Conference Board of Canada's Organizational Effectiveness and Learning Division, June 2013; "Big Data 101: Unstructured Data Analytics," Intel Corporation, June 2012, accessed at www.intel.com/content/www/us/en/big-data/unstructured-data-analytics-paper.html www.intel.com/content/dam/www/public/us/en/documents/solution-briefs/big-data-101-brief.pdf (June 2012); Sicular, "Gartner's Big Data Definition Consists of Three Parts, Not to Be Confused with Three "V"s."

6. Grant and Johnston, "1 + 1 = 3: CMO & CIO Collaboration Best Practices That Drive Growth."

7. "Increase Marketing ROI with New Analytics Techniques," IBM Business Analytics Summit 2013, "Gain insights. Drive performance," Toronto, April 2013; "Connect to Your Customers in a Whole New Way," Salesforce Company Tour, Toronto, June 19, 2013.

8. Tim Peterson, "Salesforce takes marketing into the cloud," *Adweek*, September 19, 2012, accessed at www.adweek.com/news/technology/salesforce-takes-social-marketing-cloud-143807; "Salesforce.com Delivers Next Generation Social Analytics for the Marketing Cloud," Salesforce.com, press release, October 19, 2012, accessed at www.salesforce.com/company/news-press/press-releases/2012/10/121019.jsp; Mike Rosenbaum, "Become a Customer Company—connect with your customer in a whole new way," Salesforce Company Tour, keynote presentation, Toronto, June 19, 2013; "Case Study: Air Canada. How Air Canada Uses Social Media to Help Customers when Snowstorms Strike," Salesforce Marketing Cloud, accessed September 2014 at www.salesforcemarketingcloud.com/resources/case-studies/social-media-and-snow-storms-how-air-canada-used-the-social-web-to-help-customers/; "Case Study: Brock University. The higher education industry has long been receptive to social media, valuing its ability to create connections between institutions, organizations and their various supporters," Salesforce Marketing Cloud, accessed September 2014 at www.salesforcemarketingcloud.com/resources/case-studies/brock-uses-social-media-to-build-a-connected-campus/; Trish Forant, "5 Ways to Connect Social media to Your Business Goals," Salesforce Marketing Cloud Blog, May 22, 2013, accessed at www.salesforcemarketingcloud.com/blog/2013/05/social-media-business-goals/.

9. Interview with Lucy Brun, partner Agnew Peckham and Associatates, June 2013.

10. Kathy Sheenan, "The Consumer Journey to 2020. Five Trends Driving the Future of Brands," GFK Roper webinar for CMA, July 30, 2013.

11. Jessica Hogue, "Building a Better Burger? Try Listening for Product Development," *Nielsenwire* blog, April 2010, accessed at http://blog.nielsen.com/nielsenwire/online_mobile/building-a-better-burger-try-social-listening-for-product-development; Paul M. Banas, "Social Listening: Focusing on Insights," *Insight Buzz* blog, January 2010, accessed at www.insightbuzz.com/2010/01/18/social-listening-focusing-on-insights; Suresh Vittal, "Listening Metrics that Matter. Avoid Data Overload by Targeting Metrics that Support Specific Listening Goals," Forrester Research, May 29, 2009, accessed at www.forrester.com/rb/Research/listening_metrics_that_matter/q/id/54700/t/2.

12. BBM Canada, "The Portable People Meter (PPM)," accessed July 2013 at www.bbm.ca/en/products-services/the-portable-people-meter.

13. Conversation with John Vavrik, director of the B.C. Centre for Strategic Management of Risk in Transportation, n.d.

14. Leger Marketing, "Online Surveys," accessed August 2010 at www.legermarketing.com/eng/webstudies.asp.

Chapter 5

1. Personal interview with Sharon Metz, vice president, vertical marketing, at Rovi Corporation , September 2013.

2. Peter LaPlaca, "From the Editor," *Journal of Business and Industrial Marketing* 3 (1992); D. Lawin, "Business-to-business marketing: A defined strategy," *Franchising World* 36 (2004), pp. 24–25; Nicole E. Coviello and Roderick J. Brodie, "Contemporary marketing practices of consumer and business-to-business firms: How different are they?" *Journal of Business & Industrial Marketing* 16 (2001), pp. 382–400.

3. This figure is based on *Statistical Abstract of the United States: 2002*, 122nd ed. (Washington, DC: U.S. Census Bureau, 2002).

4. "Key Small Business Statistics (2013)," Industry Canada, September 2013, accessed at www.ic.gc.ca/eic/site/061.nsf/eng/02804.html.

5. Canadian Press, "Federal Budget 2013: Government stays the course on cuts, 2015 balanced budget," *Huffington Post*, March 21, 2013, accessed at www.huffingtonpost.ca/2013/03/21/federal-budget-2013_n_2883904.html; Joel Eastwood, "New database will allow Canadians to track government spending data," Canadian Press, April 22, 2013, accessed at http://globalnews.ca/news/502224/new-database-will-allow-canadians-to-track-government-spending-data/; "Expenditure database," Treasury Board of Canada Secretariat, April 12, 2013, accessed at www.tbs-sct.gc.ca/ems-sgd/edb-bdd/edb-bdd-eng.asp.

6. "Charities Listings," Canada Revenue Agency, April 4, 2013, accessed at www.cra-arc.gc.ca/tax/charities/online_listings/canreg_interim-e.html; "Charities Program Update," Canada Revenue Agency, April 18, 2013, accessed at www.cra-arc.gc.ca/chrts-gvng/chrts/bt/chrtsprgrm_pdt-eng.html.

7. North American Industry Classification System (NAICS) Canada 2012, Statistics Canada, October 24, 2013, accessed at www23.statcan.gc.ca/imdb/p3VD.pl?Function=getVDPage1&TVD=118464.

8. Joe Pulizzi, "The transformation of content marketing," *EContent*, December 2012, pp. 20–21; Joe Pulizzi, "2013 B2B Content Marketing Benchmarks, Budgets and Trends," Content Marketing Institute, October 24, 2012, accessed at http://contentmarketinginstitute.com/2012/10/2013-b2b-content-marketing-research/; "What is content marketing?" Content Marketing Institute (n.d.), accessed at http://contentmarketinginstitute.com/what-is-content-marketing/; Sarah Johnson and Laura Sparks, "How to launch a content marketing strategy," *CPA Practice Management Forum* 9 (2013), pp. 5–7.

9. Chima Adiele, "Towards promoting interactivity in a B2B web community,"*Information Systems Frontiers* 13 (2011), pp. 237–249; Umberto Miletti, "B2B Companies Must Keep Pace with the Customer 2.0." *Social Media B2B*, June 7, 2010, accessed at http://socialmediab2b.com/2010/06/b2b-company-customer; "2013 content marketing awards," *B to B* 98 (2013), p. 38; "About" (n.d.), HealthBiz Decoded, accessed at http://healthbizdecoded.com/about/; Kate Maddox, "BMA conference focuses on content, innovation," *B to B*, June 13, 2011; and "2013 Content Marketing Awards," *B to B*, September 30, 2013, accessed at www.btobonline.com/article/20130930/CONTENTMARKETING01/309269992/xerox-corp?template=CMAprofile.

10. This listing and portions of the following discussion are based on F. Robert Dwyer and John F. Tanner, Jr., *Business Marketing*, 2nd ed. (Burr Ridge, IL: McGraw-Hill/Irwin, 2002); and Edward G. Brierty, Robert W. Eckles, and Robert R. Reeder, *Business Marketing*, 3rd ed. (Upper Saddle River, NJ: Prentice Hall, 1998); and Dominic F. Wilson, "Why divide consumer and organizational buyer behaviour?" *European Journal of Marketing* 34 (2000), pp. 780–796.

11. "TTC and Bombardier sign contract to build 204 new street cars," Toronto Transit Commission, news release, June 30, 2009, accessed at www.ttc.ca/News/2009/June/TTC_and_Bombardier_sign_contract_to_build_204_new_streetcars.jsp; J. T. Connelly, "Bombardier: 186 Subway Cars Ordered for Toronto Transit," *Business Review Canada*, May 13, 2010, accessed at www.businessreviewcanada.ca/news/transportation/bombardier-186-subway-cars-ordered-toronto-transit; Tess Kalinowski, " TTC unveils Toronto's new streetcars," *Toronto Star*, November 15, 2012, accessed at www.thestar.com/news/city_hall/2012/11/15/ttc_unveils_torontos_new_streetcars.html.

12. "The Changing B2B Buyer" (n.d.), Marketo, accessed September 2014 at www.marketo.com/cheat-sheets/the-changing-b2b-buyer/; "What makes business-to-business marketing different" (n.d.), Proteus Marketing, accessed September 2014 at www.proteusb2b.com/b2b-marketing/difference.php; R. B. Ferguson, "The uh-oh factor: Fundamental shifts in social business and what to do about it," *MIT Sloan Management Review* 54 (2012), pp. 1–4.

13. J. Castaldo, "Brands we trust: Those emotional Canadians," *Canadian Business*, April 7, 2011, accessed at www.canadianbusiness.com/business-strategy/brands-we-trust-those-emotional-canadians/; J. Buckland, "Top 10 places to work in Canada," *MSN Money*, April 13, 2010, accessed at http://money.ca.msn.com/savings-debt/gallery/gallery.aspx?cp-documentid=23864240.

14. O. El Akkad, "BlackBerry's last stand: A big bet on corporate buyers," *Globe and Mail*, September 22, 2013, accessed at www.theglobeandmail.com/report-on-business/blackberry-to-give-up-on-consumer-market-in-face-of-dismal-sales/article14455492/; J. Buckland, "Relax, Blackberry users: RIM not ditching its signature keypad," *MSN Money*, May 3, 2012, accessed at www.everydaymoney.ca/2012/05/relax-blackberry-users-rim-not-ditching-its-signature-keypad.html.

15. S. Andersson and P. Servais, "Combining industrial buyer and seller strategies for international supply and marketing management," *European Business Review* 22 (2010), pp. 64–81, doi:http://dx.doi.org/10.1108/09555341011009016; J. H. Bantham, "An exploratory study of satisfaction in buyer-seller partnerships," *Journal of Consumer Satisfaction, Dissatisfaction and Complaining Behavior* 23 (2010), p. 130; definitions adapted from F. E. Webster and Y. Wind, *Organizational Buying Behavior* (Englewood Cliffs, NJ: Prentice Hall, 1972).

16. T. V. Bonoma, "Major Sales: Who Really Does the Buying?" *Harvard Business Review*, July 2006, accessed at http://hbr.org/2006/07/major-sales-who-really-does-the-buying/ar/1.

17. Ibid.

18. Ibid.

19. Webster and Wind, *Organizational Buying Behavior*; F.E. Webster Jr. and Y. Wind, "A General Model for Understanding Organizational Buying Behavior," *Journal of Marketing* 36 (1972), pp. 12–19.

20. "Contract awarded for St. Lawrence project bridge," *Purchasing B2B*, October 21, 2013, accessed at www.canadianmanufacturing.com/purchasing-and-procurement/news/contract-awarded-for-st-lawrence-project-bridge-120780; "Government of Canada awards contract for engineering and coordination services for the new bridge for the St. Lawrence project," Transport Canada, press release, October 18, 2013, accessed at www.tc.gc.ca/eng/mediaroom/releases-2013-h139e-7388.html.

21. Representative studies on the buy-class framework that document its usefulness include E. Anderson, W., Chu, and B. Weitz, "Industrial purchasing: An empirical exploration of the buy-class framework," *Journal of Marketing* 51 (1987), pp. 71–86; M. Ghingold, "Testing the 'buy-grid' buying process model," *Journal of Purchasing and Materials Management* 22 (1986), pp. 30–36; P. Matthyssens and W. Faes, "OEM buying process for new components: Purchasing and marketing implications," *Industrial Marketing Management* 14 (1985), pp. 147–157; and T.W. Leight and A.J. Ethans, "A script-theoretic analysis of industrial purchasing behavior," *Journal of Marketing* 48 (1984), pp. 22–32. Studies not supporting the buy-class framework include J.A. Bellizi and P. McVey, "How valid is the buy-grid model?" *Industrial Marketing Management* 12 (1983), pp. 57–62; and D.W. Jackson, J.E. Keith, and R.K. Burdick, "Purchasing agents' perceptions of industrial buying center influences: A situational approach," *Journal of Marketing* 48 (1984), pp. 75–83.

22. N. Weinberg, "Evolution, Not Revolution," *Forbes*, May 21, 2001, accessed at www.forbes.com/best/2001/0521/038.html; "Business connections: The wired way we work," *Newsweek*, April 30, 2001; V. Vijayasri, "Arriving at a systems paradigm: Measuring and managing the complexity of organizations and consumers online," Order No. 3019131, Syracuse University, ProQuest Dissertations and Theses (2001).

23. This discussion is based on M. Roberti, "General Electric's Spin Machine," *The Industry Standard* (2001), pp. 74–83; "Grainger lightens its 'digital load,'" *Industrial Distribution* 90 (2001), pp. 21–24; and K. Kuryllowicz, "The future of the net: We called up the smartest internet users we know to ask where the net is headed next," *Profit*, May 1, 2001.

24. "Surprise upturn for online trading," *Supply Management* 6 (2001), p. 9; T. Gignac, "E-barter exchanges play matchmaker: Businesses are using online trading networks to swap services, save money and discover new customers," *Calgary Herald*, (May 28, 2001); J.O. Soo and S.W. Kim, "The effect of B2B e-marketplace type on buyer-supplier relational advantages of e-marketplace and firm performance," *Asian Journal on Quality* 12 (2011), pp. 189–203, doi:http://dx.doi.org/10.1108/15982681111158742

25. "Etiquette guide to japan; know the rules that make the difference," rev. ed., *Reference and Research Book News* 24 (2009); L. Laroche and S. Morey, "Minding your manners: Business etiquette and gift-giving are part and parcel of conducting business abroad," *CMA Management* 74 (2000), pp. 38–41; B. Bradley, "Best behaviour: Business etiquette in Japan," *Report on Business Magazine*, March 2001; G. Cotton, "Do this, not that when doing business overseas," CNBC, April 6, 2013, accessed at www.cnbc.com/id/100588894.

26. "Nike Tattoo Leggings Pulled After Deemed Exploitative Of Samoan Culture," *Huffington Post*, August 15, 2013, accessed at www.huffingtonpost.com/2013/08/15/nike-tattoo-leggings_n_3763591.html; V. Tapaleao, "Nike commits cultural faux pas," *New Zealand Herald*, August 14, 2013, accessed at www.nzherald.co.nz/business/news/article.cfm?c_id=3&objectid=10912088; "Nike debuts athletic ware, offends all of Samoa, pulls athletic wear," MSN, August 14, 2013, accessed at http://now.msn.com/nike-apologizes-for-using-samoan-tattoo-as-inspiration-for-running-tights.

27. "Our Story" (n.d.), Ariba website, accessed at www.ariba.com/ourstory.

28. Christian McIntosh, "Online auctions push E-commerce," *PC World Online*, April 29, 1999; R. Bray, "Reverse auctions going full speed ahead," *Summit* 6 (2003); Olivia Korostelina, "Online reverse auctions: a cost-saving inspiration for businesses," *Dartmouth Business Journal*, March 17, 2012, accessed at http://dartmouthbusinessjournal.com/2012/03/online-reverse-auctions-a-cost-saving-inspiration-for-businesses/.

29. Mary Kwak, "Potential pitfalls of e-auctions: smart ideas on reverse auctions," *Working Knowledge for Business Leaders*, Harvard Business School, September 9, 2002, accessed at http://hbswk.hbs.edu/archive/3086.html; Bob Tedeschi, "GE has a bright idea," *Smart Business*, September 25, 2001.

30. Sandy Jap, "Going, Going, Gone," *Harvard Business Review*, November 2000, accessed at http://hbr.org/2000/11/going-going-gone/ar/1; L. Wichmann, "Avoiding the pitfalls of e-procurement: Seminar lays down the pros and cons of internet commerce," *Plant* 59 (2000), p. 16; G. Cameron, "Reverse auctions remain high on OGCA hit list," *Daily Commercial News and Construction Record* 76 (2003), p. 5.

Chapter 6

1. Personal interview with Rob Morash, general manager, HEAD Canada, May 2013.

2. Adapted from the American Marketing Association's resource library, at www.marketingpower.com/_layouts/dictionary.aspx?dLetter=N.

3. Kashi website, accessed September 2013 at http://kashi.ca/en/AboutUs/.

4. Mashable website, accessed September 2013 at http://mashable.com/about/.

5. Maison Le Grand website, accessed September 2013 at http://maisonlegrand.com/en/; Jennifer Bain, "Green bean salad with lemon sauce," *Toronto Star*, April 12, 2012, accessed at www.thestar.com/life/food_wine/recipes/2010/04/12/green_bean_salad_with_lemon_sauce.html; "Canadian Company Capabilities: La Maison Le Grand- Company information," Industry Canada, September 20, 2012, accessed at www.ic.gc.ca/app/ccc/srch/nvgt.do?lang=eng&prtl=1&sbPrtl=&estblmntNo=234

567128003&profile=cmpltPrfl&profileId=501&app=sold; "Introduc-ing Maison Le Grand," press release, October 7, 2009, accessed at www.prlog.org/10367664-introducing-maison-le-grand.html; Heather Tyree, "Best of the 2008 Summer Fancy Food Show," *Epicurious,* July 1, 2008, accessed at www.epicurious.com/articlesguides/blogs/editor/2008/07/best-of-the-200.html.

6. Hershey website, accessed September 2013 at www.hersheys.com/kisses/experience/send-a-kiss.aspx.

7. "From City to City: car2go Now Offers Multi-City Access,"CNW, press release, June 5, 2012, accessed at www.newswire.ca/en/story/1004085/from-city-to-city-car2go-now-offers-multi-city-access; Car2go website, accessed September 2013 at www.car2go.com; Jeremy Cato, "A green future for Smart?" *Globe and Mail,* August 14, 2012, accessed at www.theglobeandmail.com/globe-drive/new-cars/auto-news/a-green-future-for-smart/article4480809/; Marco Chown Oved, "With car sharing gaining in popularity, a comparison of Toronto's services," *Toronto Star,* January 6, 2013, accessed at www.thestar.com/business/2013/01/06/with_car_sharing_gaining_in_popularity_a_comparison_of_torontos_services.html.

8. "Maclean's Media Kit 2013,"accessed September 2013 at www.rogersconnect.com/files/Macleans_MediaKit.pdf.

9. Euromonitor website, accessed September 2013 at www.euromonitor.com/canada.

10. Environics Analytics Prism C2, accessed September 2013 at www.environicsanalytics.ca/environics-analytics/data/consumer-segmentation/prizmc2.

11. Pitney Bowes Software Psyte HD, accessed September 2013 at www.utahbluemedia.com/pbbi/psyte/psyteCanada.html.

12. SuperDemographics, accessed September 2013 at www.superdemographics.com.

13. "Aimia Study Makes Case for Segmentation-Driven Social Media Strategy Based on Six Social Media Personas," Aimia, news release, May 31, 2012, accessed at www.aimia.com/English/Media-Center/News-Releases/News-Release-Details/2012/Aimia-Study-Makes-Case-for-Segmentation-Driven-Social-Media-Strategy-Based-on-Six-Social-Media-Personas/default.aspx; "New Aimia study reveals six social media personas," Examiner.com, June 12, 2012, accessed at www.examiner.com/article/new-aimia-study-reveals-six-social-media-personas; Mona Askalani, "Staring at the Sun. Identifying, Understanding, and Influencing Social Media Users. Research Brief, The Leading Edge of Consumer Insight," Aimia, June 4, 2012, accessed at www.aimia.com/files/doc_downloads/Aimia_SocialMedia_Whitepaper.pdf; Pam Dyer, "The 6 Types Of Social Media Users," *Social Media Today,* June 25, 2012, accessed at http://socialmediatoday.com/pamdyer/564409/6-types-social-media-users.

14. Canadian Press, "McDonald's earmarks $1-billion for Canadian renovations," *Globe and Mail,* September 7, 2011, accessed at www.theglobeandmail.com/globe-investor/mcdonalds-earmarks-1-billion-for-canadian-renovations/article593454/; "McDonald's Canada invests $1 billion in brand transformation," Marketwire, press release, September 7, 2011, accessed at www.marketwire.com/press-release/mcdonaldsr-canada-invests-1-billion-in-brand-transformation-1557901.htm; "McDonald's® Canada enters nation's fastest-growing beverage category with national launch of McCafé® Real Fruit Smoothies®," McDonald's Canada, press release, March 28, 2012, accessed at www.mcdonalds.ca/ca/en/our_story/corporate_info/press_room/articles/PR_Smoothies.html; Francine Kopun, "McDonald's new veggie wrap: Delicious but high in fat, calories," *Toronto Star,* August 28, 2013, accessed at www.thestar.com/business/2013/08/28/mcdonalds_new_veggie_wrap_delicious_but_high_in_fat_calories.html; "Canadian Households 'Perk Up' with McCafé® Premium Roast Take Home Coffee," PR Newswire, press release, November 8, 2012, accessed at www.prnewswire.com/news-releases/canadian-households-perk-up-with-mccafe-premium-roast-take-home-coffee-177869021.html; "McDonald's outlets getting comfy look," *Toronto Star,* September 13, 2007, accessed at www.thestar.com/Business/article/256023.

15. Burberry corporate website, accessed September 2013 at www.burberryplc.com/; Burberry brand website, accessed September 2013 at http://ca.burberry.com/store/; Angela Ahrendts, "Burberry's CEO on Turning an Aging British Icon into a Global Luxury Brand," *Harvard Business Review,* January–February 2013, accessed at http://hbr.org/2013/01/burberrys-ceo-on-turning-an-aging-british-icon-into-a-global-luxury-brand/ar/3; "Digital vital to Burberry's growth," WARC, January 2, 2013, accessed at www.warc.com/LatestNews/News/EmailNews.news?ID=30825&Origin=WARCNewsEmail#ZPRYdg7ggYDBKhmt.99; "Brand "purification" boosts Burberry," WARC, July 14, 2010, accessed at www.warc.com/LatestNews/News/ArchiveNews.news?ID=26965; Rachel Lamb, "Burberry unleashes tech expertise, heritage with most-advanced brand flagship," *Luxury Daily,* September 13, 2012, accessed at www.luxurydaily.com/burberry-unleashes-tech-savvy-heritage-with-new-flagship-launch/; Mark J. Miller, "Burberry Turns Global Flagship Into Living Website Ahead of London Fashion Week," *BrandChannel,* September 14, 2012, accessed at www.brandchannel.com/home/post/2012/09/14/Burberry-London-Regent-Street-091412.aspx; Diane O'Brien, "Burberry square," *BrandChannel,* June 16, 2003, accessed at www.brandchannel.com/features_profile.asp?pr_id=130; Ashirvad Tomar, "Retail-led Strategy by Burberry to Target High Net Worth Individuals in Asia Pacific," *MarketLine,* February 27, 2013, accessed at www.marketline.com/blog/retail-led-strategy-by-burberry-to-target-high-net-worth-individuals-in-asia-pacific/; John Kotter, "Burberry's Secrets to Successful Brand Reinvention, *Forbes,* February 26, 2013, accessed at www.forbes.com/sites/johnkotter/2013/02/26/burberrys-secrets-to-successful-brand-reinvention/; Karen Dacre and Rosamund Urwin, "Magic mirrors, 25 staircases and a giant 22ft screen—Burberry flagship store lands in Regent Street," *London Evening Standard,* September 13, 2012, accessed at www.standard.co.uk/news/london/magic-mirrors-25-staircases-and-a-giant-22ft-screen-burberry-flagship-store-lands-in-regent-street-8134688.html.

Chapter 7

1. Interview with Ian Gordon, May 2013; "Loblaw launches the President's Choice® black label line of fine food products, sourced the world over," press release, October 13, 2011, accessed at www.newswire.ca/en/story/857809/loblaw-launches-the-president-s-choice-black-label-line-of-fine-food-products-sourced-the-world-over; "President's Choice ® black label collection of fine foods features new delights just in time for the holiday season," press release, December 5, 2012, accessed at www.loblaw.ca/English/Media-Centre/news-releases/news-release-details/2012/Presidents-Choice--black-label-collection-of-fine-foods-features-new-delights-just-in-time-for-the-holiday-season1132203/default.aspx; Rob Gerlsbeck, "Loblaw's PC Black Label," *Canadian Grocer,* January 10, 2012, accessed at www.canadiangrocer.com/top-stories/loblaws-pc-black-label-11045; Dana Flavelle, "Loblaws gambles on luxury food line," *Toronto Star,* September 13, 2011, accessed at www.thestar.com/business/personal_finance/spending_saving/2011/09/13/loblaws_gambles_on_luxury_food_line.html.

2. "Gross Domestic Product (GDP) by Industry Sector: 2001-2009," Canadian Industry Statistics, Statistics Canada, accessed January 2011 from Industry Canada at www.ic.gc.ca/eic/site/cis-sic.nsf/eng/h_00016.html#gdp2c.

3. "Consumerology: Customer service has the power to make or break a brand," Bensymon Byrne, press release, September 6, 2012, accessed at http://bensimonbyrne.com/press_room/2012#/press-release/consumerology-customer-service-has-the-power-to-make-or-break-a-brand; Bensymon Byrne, "The Bensimon Byrne Consumerology Report: Consumerology 17: Customer service," August 2012, accessed at http://bensimonbyrne.com/wp-content/uploads/2012/09/Customer-Service-August-2012_RevisedSEPT5.pdf.

4. Christina Clements, "Gap Logo Redesign—A Look Back," *Mktg-Cliks* blog, December 12, 2010, accessed January 2011 at http://mktgcliks.blogspot.com/2010/12/gap-logo-redesign-look-back.html (adapted with permission); Juli Weiner, "New Gap Logo, Despised Symbol of Corporate Banality, Dead at One Week," *Vanity Fair*, October 12, 2010, accessed January 2011 at www.vanityfair.com/online/daily/2010/10/new-gap-logo-despised-symbol-of-corporate-banality-dead-at-one-week.html; Armin, "Don't Mind the Gap, or the Square," *Brand New* blog, October 6, 2010, accessed January 2011 from www.underconsideration.com/brandnew/archives/dont_mind_the_gap_or_the_square.php; Jennifer Van Grove, "Gap Asks Facebook Fans for Alternative Designs to Derided New Logo," *Mashable* blog, October 7, 2010, accessed January 2011 at http://mashable.com/2010/10/07/gap-logo-redesign; Marka Hansen, "The Gap's New Logo," *Huffington Post*, October 7, 2010, accessed January 20111 at www.huffingtonpost.com/marka-hansen/the-gaps-new-logo_b_754981.html; Melissa Bell, "After Internet hazing, Gap logo goes away," *Washington Post*, October 12, 2010, accessed January 2011 at http://voices.washingtonpost.com/blog-post/2010/10/gap_logo_gets_internet_hazed_a.html; "Gap Listens to Customers and will Keep Classic Blue Box Logo," Gap, press release, October 11, 2010, accessed January 2011 at www.gapinc.com/public/Media/Press_Releases/med_pr_GapLogoStatement10112010.shtml.

5. Kristin Laird, "Hudson's Bay Taps into Heritage for Modern Day Adventure," *Marketing*, June 26, 2013, accessed at www.marketingmag.ca/News/Marketer-News/Hudson%E2%80%99s-Bay-Taps-Into-Heritage-For-Modern-Day-Adventure-82445; Canadian Press, "Hudson's Bay Aims to Become 'House Of Brands' With New Renovations," *Marketing*, April 11, 2013, accessed at www.marketingmag.ca/News/Marketer-News/Hudsons-Bay-Aims-To-Become-House-Of-Brands-With-New-Renovations-76340; Canadian Press, "Retailer The Bay unveils rebranding," CBCNews, March 6, 2013, accessed at www.cbc.ca/news/business/retailer-the-bay-unveils-rebranding-1.1394847; Susan Krashinsky,"New logo, old name: The Bay returns to its roots," *Globe and Mail*, March 6, 2013, accessed at www.theglobeandmail.com/report-on-business/industry-news/marketing/new-logo-old-name-the-bay-returns-to-its-roots/article9356220/; "Hudson's Bay Celebrates its Past, Present and Future with Modern New Logo," press release, March 6, 2013, accessed at www3.hbc.com/press-release-container/hudsons-bay-celebrates-its-past-present-and-future-with-modern-new-logo/; Reneé Alexander, "Canada's The Bay Rebrands in Light of Target Launch," *BrandChannel*, March 11, 2013, accessed at www.brandchannel.com/home/post/2013/03/11/The-Bay-Rebrands-031113.aspx; Ross Marowits, "HBC planning Saks stores in Asia and Europe," Canadian Press and CTV News, September 23, 2013, accessed at www.ctvnews.ca/business/hbc-planning-saks-stores-in-asia-and-europe-1.1467711.

6. "Point of View. The Most Influential Brands in Canada 2013," Ipsos Reid, 2013, accessed at www.ipsos.ca/common/dl/pdf/IpsosReid_Marketing_Influential_Brands.pdf and www.ipsos.ca/en/products-tools/marketing/consumer-trends-product/the-ipsos-influence-index.aspx.

7. "What is a Patent?" Canadian Intellectual Property Office, accessed October 2013 at www.cipo.ic.gc.ca/eic/site/cipointernet-internetopic.nsf/eng/h_wr00001.html.

8. "What is a Trade-mark?" Canadian Intellectual Property Office, accessed October 2013 at www.cipo.ic.gc.ca/eic/site/cipointernet-internetopic.nsf/eng/h_wr00002.html.

9. Facebook application "Wordscraper," accessed January 2011 at www.facebook.com/apps/application.php?id=2521910901; Facebook application "Scrabble," accessed January 2011 at www.facebook.com/Theofficialscrabble; Facebook group "Save Scrabulous," accessed January 2011 at www.facebook.com/group.php?gid=4772916593; Nick Parrish, "Hasbro Moves Beyond Uproar to Create a New Web 'Monopoly,'" *Advertising Age*,

February 22, 2010, accessed at http://adage.com/digitalalist10/article?article_id=142172; "Scrabble loses copyright claim but wins trademark," KNS Partners website, accessed January 2011 at www.knspartners.com/files/Scrabble_loses_copyright_claim_but.pdf; "Facebook asked to pull Scrabulous game," CBC News, January 16, 2008, accessed at www.cbc.ca/technology/story/2008/01/16/tech-scrabulous.html; Mathew Ingram, "Viral marketing or trademark theft?" *Globe and Mail*, January 16, 2008, accessed, at www.theglobeandmail.com/servlet/story/RTGAM.20080116.WBmingram20080116132835/WBstory/WBmingram/?page=rss&; Matt Semansky, "How Do You Spell 'D-I-L-E-M-M-A'?" *Marketing* magazine, April 14, 2008, accessed at www.marketingmag.ca/english/news/marketer/article.jsp?content=20080414_71238_71238; Chris Sorensen, "Scrabble makers want Scrabulous scrapped," *Toronto Star*, January 16, 2008, accessed at www.thestar.com/Business/article/294676; "Scrabble knockoff returns," Associated Press, July 31, 2008, accessed at www.theglobeandmail.com/servlet/story/RTGAM.20080731.wgtscrabulous0731/BNstory/Technology/home.

10. Suzanne Vranica and Amir Efrati, "Apple Tablet Draws Jeers, Legal Rumblings Over iPad Name," *Wall Street Journal*, March 30, 2010, accessed at http://online.wsj.com/article/SB10001424052748704194504575031532455016738.html; Hiroko Tabuchi, "IPad? That's So 2002, Fujitsu Says," *New York Times*, January 28, 2010, accessed at www.nytimes.com/2010/01/29/technology/companies/29name.html?_r=0; Tim Worstall, "Apple Loses The iPad Mini Trademark," *Forbes*, March 31, 2013, accessed at www.forbes.com/sites/timworstall/2013/03/31/apple-loses-the-ipad-mini-trademark/; Lance Whitney, "U.S. Patent Office withdraws refusal of iPad Mini trademark," CNET, April 8 , 2013, accessed at http://news.cnet.com/8301-13579_3-57578449-37/u.s-patent-office-withdraws-refusal-of-ipad-mini-trademark/; Jack Purcher, "USPTO Oddly Refuses Apple's 'iPad mini' Trademark Filing," *Patently Apple*, March 30, 2013, accessed at www.patentlyapple.com/patently-apple/2013/03/uspto-oddly-refuses-apples-ipad-mini-trademark-filing.html; Melanie Lee and Samuel Shen, "Apple pays $60-million to settle China iPad trademark dispute," *Globe and Mail*, July 2, 2012, accessed at www.theglobeandmail.com/report-on-business/apple-pays-60-million-to-settle-china-ipad-trademark-dispute/article4384925/; "Apple 'settles China iPad trademark dispute for $60m,'" BBC, July 2, 2012, accessed at www.bbc.co.uk/news/business-18669394; Christina Warren, "Apple Acquires the iPad Trademark," *Mashable*, March 2010, accessed at http://mashable.com/2010/03/26/ipad-trademark-settled/.

11. "Best Global Brands 2013," Interbrand, accessed October 2013, at www.interbrand.com/en/best-global-brands/2013/top-100-list-view.aspx.

12. "Branding, Advertising, and Marketing Dictionary," Brandchannel.com, accessed October 2013 from www.brandchannel.com/education_glossary.asp#B.

13. Rob Osler, "The Name Game: Tips on How to Get It Right," *Marketing News*, September 14, 1998, p. 50; and Keller, *Strategic Brand Management*. See also Pamela W. Henderson and Joseph A. Cote, "Guidelines for Selecting or Modifying Logos," *Journal of Marketing*, April 1998, pp. 14–30; and Chiranjeev Kohli and Douglas W. LaBahn, "Creating Effective Brand Names: A Study of the Naming Process," *Journal of Advertising Research*, January–February 1997, pp. 67–75.

14. "A Survey of Multinationals," *The Economist*, June 24, 1995, p. 8.

15. Rachel Hanley, "From Googol to Google," *Stanford Daily*, February 12, 2003, accessed January 2011 at www.stanforddaily.com/2003/02/12/from-googol-to-google.

16. Paul Thurrott, "The Fun Never Stops: Microsoft vs. MikeRoweSoft," *Windows IT Pro*, January 20, 2004, accessed at www.winnetmag.com/Article/ArticleID/41510/41510.html.

17. "Canadian private label; The value alternative 2011," The Nielsen Company, 2011, accessed at www.nielsen.com/us/en/reports/2012/private-label-outlook--us-and-canada.html

and www.nielsen.com/content/dam/corporate/us/en/reports-downloads/2012-Reports/Canadian-Private-Label-White-Paper.pdf.

18. "Canadian Company Receives Final Tender Approval from Rwanda for Vital AIDS Drug," Apotex, press release, May 7, 2008, accessed at www.apotex.com/PressReleases/20080507-01.asp?flash=Yes; "Second Shipment Of Life-Saving Aids Drug Leaving for Africa," Apotex, press release, September 18, 2009, accessed at www.apotex.com/global/about/press/20090918.asp.

Chapter 8

1. Personal interview with Morgan Mathews, October 2013.
2. Ethan Bloch, "A Year of Twitter," *Flowtown* blog, December 13, 2010, accessed at www.flowtown.com/blog/a-year-of-twitter; Larry Popelka,"What We Learned From Twitter's IPO: The Value of Innovation Is at an All-Time High," *Bloomberg Businessweek*, November 18, 2013, accessed at www.businessweek.com/articles/2013-11-18/what-we-learned-from-twitter-s-ipo-the-value-of-innovation-is-at-an-all-time-high; Victor Luckerson "Twitter IPO Leads to Sky-High $24 Billion Valuation," *Time Business and Money*, November 7, 2013, accessed at http://business.time.com/2013/11/07/twitter-ipo-leads-to-sky-high-24-billion-valuation/#ixzz2nYVmnDUA; "From TWTTR to $TWTR: The Moments That Made It Happen," *Simply Measured Analytics* blog, November 8, 2013, accessed at http://simplymeasured.com/blog/2013/11/08/from-twttr-to-twtr-the-moments-that-made-it-happen.
3. C. Phocas, *The management of innovations with specific reference to the compact disc.* M.B.A. Dissertation, University of Bradford Management Centre, 1983.
4. Sony website, accessed November 2013 at www.sonymobile.com/ca-en/.
5. "Book Club Gadgets," *Chatelaine*, December 2010, p. 178; Amazon.com Kindle Store, accessed January 2011 at www.amazon.com/dp/B002Y27P3M/?tag=gocous-20&hvadid=5729120357&ref=pd_sl_cazfqv6ny_b; "Introducing the All-New Kindle Family: Four New Kindles, Four Amazing Price Points," Amazon.com, press release, September 28, 2011, accessed at http://phx.corporate-ir.net/phoenix.zhtml?ID=1610968&p=irol-newsArticle&c=176060; Kindle 3rd generation product information accessed from the Amazon.com Kindle Store, January 2011, at www.amazon.com/dp/B002Y27P3M/?tag=gocous-20&hvadid=5729120357&ref=pd_sl_cazfqv6ny_b; Kindle 4th generation product information accessed from Amazon.com, October 2011, at www.amazon.com/gp/product/B0051QVESA.
6. Gabriel Madway, "Jobs Blast Rivals as iPad Sales Disappoint," Reuters, October 19, 2010, accessed at www.reuters.com/article/idUSTRE69H4UX20101019; Ben Patterson, "iPad Sales Cross Million Mark Twice as Fast as Original iPhone," Yahoo News, May 3, 2010, accessed at http://news.yahoo.com/s/ytech_gadg/20100503/tc_ytech_gadg/ytech_gadg_tc1901.
7. Patterson, "iPad Sales Cross Million Mark Twice as Fast as Original iPhone."
8. Barry Silverstein, "UGG Australia the Good, the Bad, and the UGGly," *BrandChannel*, December 10, 2007, accessed at www.brandchannel.com/features_profile.asp?pr_id=365; Barry Silverstein, "New Counterfeit Gambit; Knock off Cheaper brands," *BrandChannel*, August 3, 2010; accessed at www.brandchannel.com/home/post/2010/08/03/New-Counterfeit-Gambit-Knock-Off-Cheaper-Brands.aspx#continue.
9. Marina Strauss, "Can Tim Hortons fight off McDonald's attack?" *Globe and Mail*, February 23, 2013, accessed at www.theglobeandmail.com/globe-investor/can-tim-hortons-fight-off-mcdonalds-attack/article8993325/?page=all; "Tim Hortons Pilots New Dark Roast Coffee," *Globe and Mail*, October 28, 2013, accessed at www.theglobeandmail.com/globe-investor/news-sources/?mid=cnw.20131028.C7552; Hollie Shaw, "Tim Hortons to offer new dark roast coffee blend in two test markets," StarPhoenix, October 29, 2013, accessed at www.thestarphoenix.com/life/Hortons+offer+dark+roast+coffee+blend+test+markets/9095316/story.html; Hollie Shaw, "Tim Hortons to offer new dark roast coffee blend in two test markets," *Financial Post*, October 28, 2013, accessed at http://business.financialpost.com/2013/10/28/tim-hortons-dark-roast-coffee/; Tim Hortons website, www.timhortons.com/ca/en/menu/merchandise-tassimo.html; Hollie Shaw, "New blonde in town," *Financial Post*, March 2, 2013, accessed at http://business.financialpost.com/2012/02/03/new-blonde-in-town/; "Coffee remains dominant," *Canadian Vending and Office Coffee Service* magazine, October 28, 2013, accessed at www.canadianvending.com/content/view/3423/57/.
10. "Canada's Top Brands 2013; Canadian Brand Top 40," *Canadian Business* special report, accessed November 2013 at www.canadianbusiness.com/canadian-brand-top-40-ranking/; "Tim Hortons ranks number one in The Reputation Institute's survey of Canada's top brands in 2013," CNW, news release, April 30, 2013, accessed at www.newswire.ca/en/story/1155265/tim-hortons-ranks-number-one-in-the-reputation-institute-s-survey-of-canada-s-top-brands-in-2013.
11. Robert Levy, "2013 BrandSpark Canadian Shopper Study: Critical Insights for Engaging Shoppers," BrandSpark International, May 2, 2013, accessed at www.brandspark.ca/pdf/Robert_Levy_BrandSpark_Canadian_Shopper_Study_Engaging_Shoppers.pdf
12. "10th Annual Best New Product Award Winners," Metronews.ca, accessed November 2012 at http://metronews.ca/bnpa-test/; "The 2013 Best New Product Award Winners announced: More than 93,000 Canadians choose the best new products in Canada's largest consumer study," press release, January 7, 2013, accessed at www.bestnewproductawards.biz/canada/pdf/2013_BNPA_Winners_Jan07_2013.pdf.
13. Trefis Team, "How Instagram's Monetization Can Help Facebook," *Forbes*, October 21, 2013, accessed at www.forbes.com/sites/greatspeculations/2013/10/21/how-instagrams-monetization-can-help-facebook/; Julie Kuehl, "Apple Picks Instagram, Snapseed for App of the Year," *Mac Observer*, December 9, 2011, accessed at www.macobserver.com/tmo/article/app_store_picks_2011_apps_of_the_year; Robert Hof, "So Much for Facebook Ruining Instagram—It Just Hit 150 Million Monthly Active Users," *Forbes*, October 8, 2013, accessed at www.forbes.com/sites/roberthof/2013/09/08/so-much-for-facebook-ruining-instagram-it-just-hit-150-million-monthly-active-users/; Steven Bertoni,"Instagram's Kevin Systrom: The Stanford Billionaire Machine Strikes Again," *Forbes*, August 1, 2012, accessed at www.forbes.com/sites/stevenbertoni/2012/08/01/instagrams-kevin-systrom-the-stanford-millionaire-machine-strikes-again/4/; Stephanie Mlot, "First Instagram Ad Showcases Designer Michael Kors," *PC Magazine*, November 1, 2013, accessed at www.pcmag.com/article2/0,2817,2426690,00.asp.
14. Kevin J. Clancy, Peter C. Krieg, and Marianne McGarry Wolf, *Market New Products Successfully: Using Simulated Test Market Technology*, Lexington Books, page 5, The Rowan and Littlefield Publishing Company, 2006.
15. Lisa C. Troy, Tanawat Hirunyawipada, and Audhesh K. Paswan, "Cross-functional I and New Product Success: An Empirical Investigation of the Findings," *Journal of Marketing*, November 2011; Calvin Hodock, "Winning the New Products Game; Know What Kills and Innovation Ahead of Time and Dodge Failures," *Advertising Age*, November 12, 2007, accessed at http://adage.com/print?article_id=121912; Clancy, et al, *Market New Products Successfully: Using Simulated Test Market Technology*; Copernicus Market Consulting, "10 Reasons Why New Products and Services Fail," Copernicum University, accessed at www.copernicusmarketing.com/univers/reasons_for_product_failure.shtml; Eugene Sivadas and F. Robert Dwyer, "An Examination of Organizational Factors Influencing New Product Success in Internal and Alliance-Based Processes," *The Journal of Marketing*, Vol. 64, No. 1 (Jan., 2000), pp. 31-49, American

Marketing Association, accessed at www.jstor.org/pss/3203389; J.C. Narver, S.F. Slater, and D. L MacLachlan, "Responsive and Proactive Market Orientation and New-Product Success," *Journal of Product Innovation Management*, Vol. 21, pp. 334–347, September 2004; Lane Anderson, "Ten Keys to New Consumer Products," *Prospecta Marketing*, accessed January 2011 at www.prospectamarketing.com/ArticlesAndCaseStudies/tenkeys.htm; R. G. Cooper and E. J. Kleinschmidt, "New Products—What Separates Winners from Losers?" *Journal of Product Innovation Management*, September 1987, pp. 169–84; Robert G. Cooper, *Winning at New Products*, 2nd ed. (Reading, MA: Addison-Wesley, 1993), pp. 49–66; and Thomas D. Kuczmarski, "Measuring Your Return on Innovation," *Marketing Management*, Spring 2000, pp. 25–32.

16. Chris Sorensen, "Bright Idea: Drama for 3-D TVs," *Maclean's*, January 31, 2011, p. 45.

17. "Coca-Cola Blak Enters Canada," Canwest News Service, August 31, 2006, accessed at www.canada.com/topics/finance/story.html?id=9b4cd2d7-344b-4095-ba60-31b1bbf2166d&k=4816.

18. "Mixed Reviews for 'Lord of the Rings' Musical," CBC News, March 25, 2006, accessed at www.cbc.ca/arts/story/2006/03/24/lordoftherings-reviews.html; Jordan Timm, "With This Ring, They Thee Mock. A New Production Sends up Toronto's Disastrous 'Lord of the Rings: The Musical,'" *Macleans*, accessed at www.macleans.ca/article.jsp?content=20070709_107127_107127.

19. John Gilbert, "To Sell Cars in Japan, U.S. Needs to Offer More Right-Drive Models," *Star Tribune*, May 27, 1995, p. M1.

20. "Sonic Sinker," *The Economist*, November 23, 2002, p. 58.

21. Kevin J. Clancy and Peter C. Krieg, "Surviving Innovation: Common Testing Mistakes Can Derail a Promising New product Launch," *Marketing Management*, March/April 2003, pp.14–20.

22. Robert Berner, "Why P&G's Smile Is So Bright," *Business Week*, August 12, 2002, pp. 58–60.

Chapter 9

1. Personal interview with Hilary Zaharko, director of marketing, H&R Block Canada, October 2013.

2. Aaron Robinson, "2011 Bugatti Veyron 16.4 Super Sport—First Drive Review," *Car and Driver*, October 2010, accessed September 26, 2011, at www.caranddriver.com/reviews/car/10q4/2011_bugatti_veyron_16.4_super_sport-first_drive_review.

3. Adapted from Kent B. Monroe, *Pricing: Making Profitable Decisions*, 3rd ed. (New York: McGraw-Hill, 2003); and K. Davey, P. Markowitz, and N. Jonnalagadda, "The pricing opportunity: Discovering what customers actually value," *Strategy & Leadership* 34 (2006), pp. 23–30. doi:http://dx.doi.org/10.1108/10878570610660573

4. Roger A. Kerin and Robert A. Peterson, "Throckmorten Furniture (A)," *Strategic Marketing Problems: Cases and Comments*, 9th ed. (Englewood Cliffs, NJ: Prentice Hall, 1998), pp. 235–245; J.K. Kalita, S. Jagpal, and D.R. Lehmann, "Do high prices signal high quality? A theoretical model and empirical results," *Journal of Product and Brand Management* 13 (2004), pp. 279–288.

5. For the classic description of skimming and penetration pricing, see Joel Dean, "Pricing Policies for New Products," *Harvard Business Review*, November–December 1976, pp. 141–53. See also, Reed K. Holden and Thomas T. Nagle, "Kamikaze Pricing," *Marketing Management*, Summer 1998, pp. 31–39.

6. Jean-Noel Kapferer, "Managing Luxury Brands," *Journal of Brand Management*, July 1997, pp. 251–60.

7. "Why That Deal Is Only $9.99," *Business Week*, January 10, 2000, p. 36. For further reading on odd-even pricing, see Robert M. Schindler and Thomas M. Kilbarian, "Increased Consumer Sales Response through Use of 99-Ending Prices," *Journal of Retailing*, Summer 1996, pp. 187–99; Mark Stiving and Russell S. Winer, "An Empirical Analysis of Price Endings with Scanner Data," *Journal of Consumer Research*, June 1997, pp. 57–67; and Robert M. Schindler, "Patterns of Rightmost Digits Used in Advertised Prices: Implications for Nine-Ending Effects," *Journal of Consumer Research*, September 1997, pp. 192–201.

8. Thomas T. Nagle and Reed K. Holden, *The Strategy and Tactics of Pricing*, 3rd ed. (Englewood Cliffs, NJ: Prentice Hall, 2002), pp. 243–49.

9. Ibid., pp. 237–39.

10. Dana Flavelle, "Credit card fee battle in the cards?" *Toronto Star*, November 29, 2008, accessed at www.thestar.com/article/545726; "What Are These Fees?" accessed at http://stopstickingittous.com/about/; Dana Flavelle, "Complaint against Visa, Mastercard dismissed by Competition Tribunal," *Toronto Star*, July 24, 2013, accessed at www.thestar.com/business/personal_finance/2013/07/23/complaint_against_visa_mastercard_dismissed_by_competition_tribunal.html.

11. Peter M. Noble and Thomas S. Gruca, "Industrial Pricing: Theory and Managerial Practice," *Marketing Science* 18, no. 3 (1999), pp. 435–54.

12. George E. Belch and Michael A. Belch, *Introduction to Advertising and Promotion*, 5th ed. (New York: Irwin/McGraw-Hill, 2001), p. 93.

13. Tyler Hamilton, "Sharing the Road," *Toronto Star*, February 20, 2010, accessed at www.thestar.com/business/article/768531; "Taking Car-sharing to the Max," *Toronto Star*, February 20, 2010, accessed at www.thestar.com/business/article/768533.

14. S. Makridakis, "Forecasting: Issues challenges for marketing management," *Journal of Marketing* 41 (1977), p. 24.

15. S. Doyle, "Business application of forecasting with a campaign management content," *Journal of Database Marketing & Customer Strategy Management* 12 (2004), pp. 87–93.

16. M. Man and L. Gadau, "The profit and loss account in different approaches: Advantages and disadvantages," *Annales Universitatis Apulensis : Series Oeconomica* 12 (2010), pp. 152–160.

17. D. Peppers and M. Rogers, "Return on customer: A new metric of value creation—return on investment by itself is not good enough," *Journal of Direct, Data and Digital Marketing Practice* 7 (2006), pp. 318–331.

18. Frank Bruni, "Price of Newsweek? It Depends," *Dallas Times Herald*, August 14, 1986, pp. S1, S20.

19. Elizabeth Weise and Roger Yu, "'Newsweek' sold to 'International Business Times,'" *USA Today*, August 5, 2013, accessed at www.usatoday.com/story/money/business/2013/08/03/newsweek-sold-to-international-business-times/2615727/.

20. "Despite a strong preference for paper books, older readers actually have an easier time reading electronic tablets." *Review of Optometry*, March 2013.

21. "Henderson jersey coming back to Canada: Buyer," CBC News, June 23, 2010, accessed at www.cbc.ca/canada/story/2010/06/23/henderson-hockey-canada.html.

22. "Will Tablets Close the Book on e-Readers?" *Knowledge @ Wharton*, July 7, 2010, accessed at http://knowledge.wharton.upenn.edu/printer_friendly.cfm?articleid=2539.

23. Brent Jang, "Airlines fined $1.1-billion over price-fixing," *Globe and Mail*, November 9, 2010, accessed at www.theglobeandmail.com/globe-investor/air-canada-others-fined-for-price-fixing/article1791755.

24. Marina Strauss, "Grafton-Fraser fined for misleading sale prices," *Globe and Mail*, July 28, 2006, p. B8.

25. Hollie Shaw, "Hershey Canada pleads guilty to chocolate price-fixing," *Financial Post*, June 21, 2013, accessed at http://business.financialpost.com/2013/06/21/hershey-canada-pleads-guilty-to-chocolate-price-fixing/; Canadian Press, "Canadian chocolate makers to pay $23.2-million in price-fixing lawsuit," *Globe and Mail*, September 16, 2013, accessed at www.theglobeandmail.com/report-on-business/canadian-chocolate-makers-to-pay-232-million-in-price-fixing-lawsuit/article14361922/.

26. "Stores Told to Lift Prices in Germany," *Wall Street Journal*, September 11, 2000, pp. A27.

27. "Rotten Apples," *Dallas Morning News*, April 7, 1998, p. 14A.

28. "When Grey Is Good," *The Economist*, August 22, 1998, p. 17; Neil Belmore, "Parallel Imports and Grey Market Issues," The Canadian Institute, December 5–6, 2001.

29. "How Dell Fine-Tunes Its PC Pricing to Gain Edge in a Slow Market," *Wall Street Journal*, June 8, 2001, pp. A1, A8.

30. For an extensive discussion on discounts, see Kent B. Monroe, *Pricing: Making Profitable Decisions*, 2nd ed. (New York: McGraw Hill, 1990), chaps. 14 and 15.

Chapter 10

1. Personal interviews with Lenny Malley and Paul Paquette, partners of AMJ Campbell, August 2013.

2. G. Collins, "A Coke Coup in Venezuela Leaves Pepsi High and Dry," *New York Times*, August 17, 1996, accessed at www.nytimes.com/1996/08/17/business/a-coke-coup-in-venezuela-leaves-pepsi-high-and-dry.html; E. Fuhrman, "Bottler of the year: Pepsi bottling ventures," *Beverage Industry* 100 (2009), pp. 24–26, 28, 30, 34.

3. This discussion is based on Rosenbloom, B. (1999). *Marketing Channels: A Management View*, 6th edition. (Fort Worth: Dryden Press).

4. J.K. Johansson, "International alliances: Why now?" *Journal of the Academy of Marketing Science* (1995). pp. 301–304.

5. Allan J. Magrath, "Channel Vision: Getting Your Channels Right," *Ivey Business Journal*, November/December 2002, accessed at www.iveybusinessjournal.com/topics/innovation/channel-vision-getting-your-channels-right#.Uh6XMxbvzR1; Adrienne Mand, "Eddie Bauer's banner time of year," *Advertising Age*, October 1, 2001, accessed at http://adage.com/article/focus-design/databank-retail-eddie-bauer-s-banner-time-year/53693/; D.L. Duffy, "Case study: Multi-channel marketing in the retail environment," *Journal of Consumer Marketing* 21 (2004), pp. 356–359.

6. E. Wexler, "Best Buy Canada's bold plan to stay #1," *Strategy*, August 28, 2012, accessed at http://strategyonline.ca/2012/08/28/best-buy-canadas-bold-plan-to-stay-1; N. Klosek, "Creating the omni-channel," *Dealerscope* 54 (2012), pp. 28–32; "About us," Best Buy website, accessed at www.bestbuy.ca/en-CA/about-best-buy-canada.aspx?path=9825360f7559258208ae2438cb28c580en99.

7. E. Brynjolfsson, Y.J. Hu, and M.S. Rahman, "Competing in the age of omnichannel retailing," *MIT Sloan Management Review* 54 (2013), pp. 23–29.

8. M. Krantz, "Click Till You Drop," *Time*, July 20, 1998, pp. 34–39; Gap Inc., "Gap Inc. Creates Global Brand Management Structure to Drive the Company's Long-Term Growth," press release, October 16, 2012, accessed at www.gapinc.com/content/gapinc/html/media/pressrelease/2012/med_pr_GPS_Global_Brand_Management_Structure101612.html.

9. D. Rigby and M. O'Sullivan, *Fighting Fire with Water—From Channel Conflict to Confluence* (Cambridge, MA: Bain & Company); D. Peppers and M. Rogers, "'Tis the season for E-retailing," *Sales and Marketing Management* 151 (1999), pp. 30–32

10. For an overview of vertical marketing systems, see L. Pelton, D. Strutton, and J.R. Lumpkin, *Marketing Channels*, 2nd ed. (Burr Ridge, IL: McGraw-Hill/Irwin, 2003); and Peter R.J. Trim and L. Yang-Im, "Vertically integrated organisational marketing systems: A partnership approach for retailing organisations," *Journal of Business & Industrial Marketing* 21 (2006), p. 151.

11. M.R. Portmann, "Franchising the concept of the future," *World Trade* 13 (2000), pp. 46–50; L. Patton, "McDonald's Franchisees Rebel as Chain Raises Stores Fees," *Bloomberg*, August 6, 2013, accessed at www.bloomberg.com/news/2013-08-06/mcdonald-s-franchisees-go-rogue-with-meetings.html; and "FAQs," McDonald's Canada website, accessed at www.mcdonalds.ca/ca/en/contact_us/faq.html.

12. "Apple to Open 25 Retail Stores in 2001," Apple Computer, press release, May 15, 2001, accessed at www.apple.com/pr/library/2001/05/15Apple-to-Open-25-Retail-Stores-in-2001.html; K. Anderson, "Apple unveils its offline strategy," BBC News-Online, May 19, 2001, accessed at http://news.bbc.co.uk/2/hi/business/1339150.stm; D. Sellers, "Apple 'manifesto': 5 down, 95 to go," *Macworld*, May 15, 2001, accessed at www.macworld.com/article/1017497/manifesto.html.

13. For an extensive discussion on channel conflict, see A.T. Coughlan, E. Anderson, L.W. Stern, and A.I. El-Ansary, *Marketing Channels*, 6th ed. (Upper Saddle River, NJ: Prentice Hall, 2001); and K.L. Webb and J.E. Hogan, "Hybrid channel conflict: Causes and effects on channel performance," *Journal of Business & Industrial Marketing* 17 (2002), pp. 338–356.

14. S. Zucker, "Coke Returns to Costco with its Dignity Intact," *BrandChannel*, December 11, 2009, accessed at www.brandchannel.com/home/post/2009/12/11/Coke-Returns-To-Costco-With-Its-Dignity-Intact.aspx; M. Geller, "Costco to resume stocking Coca-Cola drinks," Reuters, December 10, 2009, accessed at www.reuters.com/article/2009/12/10/cocacola-costco-idUSN1020190520091210.

15. For an extensive discussion on power and influence in marketing channels, see A.T. Coughlan, et al., *Marketing Channels*.

16. *What's It All About?* (Oakbrook, IL: Council of Logistics Management, 1993); S.M. Rutner and C.J. Langley, "Logistics value: Definition, process and measurement," *International Journal of Logistics Management* 11 (2000), pp. 73–82.

17. This example is described in D. Sinchi-Levi, P. Kaminsky, and E. Sinchi-Levi, *Designing and Managing the Supply Chain* (Burr Ridge, IL: McGraw-Hill/Irwin, 2000).

18. This discussion is based on R. Meredity, "Harder than the Hype," Forbes, April 16, 2001, pp. 188–194; R.M. Monczka and J. Morgan, "Supply Chain Management Strategies," *Purchasing*, January 15, 1998, pp. 78–85; R.B. Handfield and E.Z. Nichols, *Introduction to Supply Chain Management* (Upper Saddle River, NJ: Prentice Hall, 1998); and P. Charan, "Supply chain performance issues in an automobile company: A SAP-LAP analysis," *Measuring Business Excellence* 16 (2012), pp. 67–86.

19. Major portions of this discussion are based on S. Chopra and P. Meindl, *Supply Chain Management: Strategy, Planning, and Operations* (Upper Saddle River, NJ: Prentice Hall, 2001); M.L. Fisher, "What Is the Right Supply Chain for Your Product?" *Harvard Business Review*, March 1997, pp. 105–117; and P.M. Madhani, "Value creation through integration of supply chain management and marketing strategy," *IUP Journal of Business Strategy* 9 (2012), pp. 7–26.

20. R. Walberg, "Never Lose Inventory Again," *Financial Post*, July 6, 2010, accessed at www.financialpost.com/Never+lose+inventory+again/3239772/story.html; M. Bustillo, "Wal-Mart Radio Tags to Track Clothing," *Business Technology*, July 23, 2010, accessed at http://bx.businessweek.com/rfid/view?url=http%3A%2F%2Fonline.wsj.com%2Farticle%2FSB10001424052748704421304575383213061198090.html.

21. "SmartWay Comes to Canada," Supply Chain & Logistics Association of Canada, accessed September 2014 at www.scmanational.ca/en/tools-a-resources/smartway; "SmartWay in Canada," Natural Resources Canada, June 19, 2012, accessed at www.nrcan.gc.ca/energy/efficiency/transportation/commercial-vehicles/smartway/7615/.

Chapter 11

1. Personal interview with Aaron Surkis, manager, in-store communications, TELUS, September 2013.

2. K. Cline, "The devil in the details," *Banking Strategies* 24 (1997); R. Trap, "Design your own jeans," *The Independent*, October 18, 1998, p. 22; H. Cho and S.S. Fiorito, "Self-service technology in retailing: The case of retail kiosks," *Symphonya* 1 (2010), pp. 42–54.

3. "Retail trade, operating statistics, by province," Statistics Canada, March 7, 2013, accessed at www.statcan.gc.ca/tables-tableaux/sum-som/l01/cst01/trad38a-eng.htm.

4. *Global Powers of Retailing 2013: Retail Beyond*, Deloitte, accessed at www.deloitte.com/view/en_GX/global/industries/consumer-business/a336253eda30c310VgnVCM2000003356f70aRCRD.htm#.UlAkDhbvz-Y.

5. Marina Strauss and Jacquie McNish, "With Target, Canada's retail landscape set for massive makeover," *Globe and Mail*, January 13, 2011, accessed at www.theglobeandmail.com/

globe-investor/with-target-canadas-retail-landscape-set-for-massive-makeover/article1868308; D. Hood, "Target won't kill Canadian retail: It will save it," *Canadian Business*, October 15, 2012, p. 4.

6. "Retail Trade-Establishments, Employees, and Payroll," *Statistical Abstract of the United States*, 120th ed. (Washington, DC: U.S. Department of Commerce, Bureau of the Census, 2000); G. Koretz, "Those Plucky Corner Stores," *Bloomberg Businessweek*, December 5, 1994, accessed at www.businessweek.com/stories/1994-12-04/those-plucky-corner-stores; J. Fraser, "Mapping out the treasure hunt," *Canadian Grocer* 122 (2008), p. 73.

7. J. Cowan, "Retail: The genius of Dollarama," *Canadian Business*, April 7, 2011, accessed at www.canadianbusiness.com/business-strategy/retail-the-genius-of-dollarama/; J. Daly, "How Dollarama turns pocket change into billions," *Globe and Mail*, March 29, 2012, accessed at www.theglobeandmail.com/report-on-business/rob-magazine/how-dollarama-turns-pocket-change-into-billions/article4097813/; J. McElgunn and K. Shiffman, "Canada's entrepreneurs of the decade," *Profit*, December 2010, pp. 44–53.

8. "Foundations of Franchising," International Franchise Association (n.d.), accessed at www.franchise.org/code.aspx; S. Shane and C. Spell, "Factors for New Franchise Success," *MIT Sloan Management Review*, April 15, 1998, accessed at http://sloanreview.mit.edu/article/factors-for-new-franchise-success/; R. Branson, "Richard Branson on Building a Strong Reputation," *Entrepreneur*, April 8, 2013, accessed at www.entrepreneur.com/article/226296.

9. A. Lopez-Pacheco, "Customers expect quality even in recession," *National Post*, January 27, 2008, p. FP7; C. Stephenson, "Thriving in turbulent times," *Ivey Business Journal* (2009), accessed at http://iveybusinessjournal.com/departments/from-the-editor/thriving-in-turbulent-times#.UlSo_BbvzR0; H. Shaw, "Online sales complement brick-and-mortar retail, Harry Rosen CEO says," *Financial Post*, August 1, 2013, accessed at http://business.financialpost.com/2013/08/01/online-sales-complement-brick-and-mortar-retail-harry-rosen-ceo-says/.

10. T. Manners, "Shopper Marketing," *Fast Company*, June 14, 2008, accessed at www.fastcompany.com/blog/tim-manners/shop-talk/shopper-marketing; "With U.S. consumers watching their wallets more than ever, tuning into shoppers' mindsets key to warding off brand switching," Nielsen, press release, October 16, 2008, accessed at www.nielsen.com/content/dam/corporate/us/en/newswire/uploads/2008/10/press_release18.pdf; "Shopper marketing," *Marketing*, 116 (2011), p. 29.

11. M. Strauss, "Holt's Opens Doors a Little More Widely," *Globe and Mail*, September 1, 2010, accessed at www.theglobeandmail.com/report-on-business/holts-opens-doors-a-little-more-widely/article1693204/?cmpid=tgc; H. Shaw, "Holt Renfrew wants to make you feel welcome," *National Post*, September 2, 2010; S. Kelsey, "Holt Renfrew celebrates 175 years: Luxury retailer announces major expansion plans," *Huffington Post Canada*, September 7, 2012, accessed at www.huffingtonpost.ca/2012/09/07/holt-renfrew-celebrates-1_n_1864421.html.

12. R. Eagan, "The green capitalist," *Library Journal* 134 (2009); "Defining the Green Economy," ECO Canada, 2010, accessed at www.eco.ca/pdf/Defining-the-Green-Economy-2010.pdf; J.G. Hae, "Are fashion-conscious consumers more likely to adopt eco-friendly clothing?" *Journal of Fashion Marketing and Management* 15 (2011), pp. 178–193. doi:http://dx.doi.org/10.1108/13612021111132627; D. Gong, "10 Best Canadian Eco-Shops," *Flare*, March 28, 2013, accessed at www.flare.com/fashion/10-best-canadian-eco-shops/; "Corporate Social Responsibility," Foreign Affairs, Trade and Development Canada, October 22, 2013, accessed at www.international.gc.ca/trade-agreements-accords-commerciaux/topics-domaines/other-autre/csr-rse.aspx?lang=eng; "The Greening of Roots," Roots (n.d.), accessed at http://about.roots.com/on/demandware.store/Sites-RootsCorporate-Site/default/Link-Page?cid=THE_ENVIRONMENT_OurCommitment.

13. V. Pallandino, "Apple Store receives trademark for 'distinctive design and layout,'" *Wired*, January 30, 2013, accessed at www.wired.com/design/2013/01/apple-store-trademark/; "Canadian Trade-Mark Data," Canadian Intellectual Property Office, October 22, 2013, accessed at www.cipo.ic.gc.ca/app/opic-cipo/trdmrks/srch/vwTrdmrk.do;jsessionid=0001aVzIlRWXB-TRtDf81OHAa5I:3UAPV7CT3?lang=eng&status=OK&fileNumber=1503650&extension=0&startingDocumentIndexOnPage=1.

14. F.J. Mulhern and R.P. Leon, "Implicit Price Bundling of Retail Products: A Multiproduct Approach to Maximizing Store Profitability," *Journal of Marketing* 55 (1991), pp. 63–76; S. Hamilton, "U.K. retail sales increase as discounts spur consumer demand," *Bloomberg*, July 18, 2013, accessed at www.bloomberg.com/news/2013-07-18/u-k-retail-sales-increase-as-discounts-spur-consumer-demand-1-.html.

15. F.S. By, "The 'sale' is fading as a retailing tactic—in pricing shift, 'everyday lows' replace specials," *Wall Street Journal*, March 1, 1989; G.K. Ortmeyer, J.A. Quelch, and W.J. Salmon, "Restoring Credibility to Retail Pricing," *MIT Sloan Management Review* 33 (1991), pp. 55–66; T. Busillo, "Bed, bath & more: A Canada first," *Home Textiles Today* 19 (1998), pp. 8, 23; and A. Cheng, "Wal-Mart pitches 'everyday low prices' overseas," *MarketWatch*, June 1, 2011, accessed at www.marketwatch.com/story/wal-mart-pitches-everyday-low-prices-overseas-2011-06-01.

16. W.B. Dodds, "In Search of Value: How Price and Store Name Information Influence Buyers' Product Perceptions," *Journal of Services Marketing* 5 (1991), pp. 27–36; D. Grewal, R. Krishnan, J. Baker, and N. Borin, "The effect of store name, brand name and price discounts on consumers' evaluations and purchase intentions," *Journal of Retailing* 74 (1998), pp. 331–352; N. Williams, "Profile: GM shifting gears from price to brand image," *Strategy* (2005), p. 53.

17. B. Brown, "Edmonton Makes Size Pay Off in Down Market," *Advertising Age*, January 27, 1992, pp. 4–5; "Facts," West Edmonton Mall website (n.d.), accessed at www.wem.ca/about-wem/facts; R. Warnica, R. (2011, Oct 03). "Taking West Edmonton Mall to New Jersey," *Maclean's*, October 3, 2011, p. 41.

18. N. Ramage, "Edo Japan leaves the malls behind," *Marketing* 108 (2003), p. 2; A.G. Hallsworth, K. G. Jones, and R. Muncaster, "The planning implications of new retail format introductions in Canada and Britain," *Service Industries Journal* 15 (1995), p. 148; B.J. Lorch, "Big Boxes, Power Centres and the Evolving Retail Landscape of Winnipeg: A Geographical Perspective," Institute for Urban Studies, University of Winnipeg, 2004.

19. K. Buscemi, "Vending gets smarter," *Appliance Manufacturer* 52 (2004), pp. 25–26; "Vending embraces growth and technology," *Beverage Industry* 102 (2011), pp. 118–119.

20. D. Demerjian, "Fast Talk," *Fast Company*, November 2008, pp. 29–30,32,34,36,38; "Adapting to the changed consumer," *Chain Store Age* 87 (2011), pp. 2–9; E. Glazer, "Retail shopping is taking off at the airport," *Wall Street Journal*, July 1, 2012; "Best Buy expands kiosks into Halifax Stanfield International Airport," Best Buy Canada, press release, January 29, 2013, accessed at www.newswire.ca/en/story/1105791/best-buy-expands-automated-kiosks-into-halifax-stanfield-international-airport; "Best Buy Prices. Kiosk Convenience," Best Buy website (n.d.), accessed at www.bestbuy.com/site/Global-Promotions/regularCat%3Apcmcat259500050000/pcmcat259500050000.c?id=pcmcat259500050000; Associated Press, "Best Buy stores to feature Samsung kiosks," Global News, April 4, 2013, accessed at http://globalnews.ca/news/455339/best-buy-stores-to-feature-samsung-kiosks/.

21. Christopher Brown-Humes, "Ikea creates a challenge for postmen of the world: The store catalogue is published in 36 countries and is free, writes Christopher Brown-Humes," *Financial Times*, August 14, 2003; "IKEA appoints McCann New York as global agency of record to re-invent the IKEA catalogue," *Marketing Weekly News*, news release August 2, 2011; "2014 IKEA Catalogue Comes to Life with Augmented Reality," IKEA Canada, press release. August 12, 2013, accessed at www.newswire.ca/en/story/1209085/2014-ikea-catalogue-comes-to-life-with-augmented-reality.

22. "Knockout strategies of the 90s: Telemarketing and direct marketing," *Canadian Business*, advertising supplement, March 1993, pp. 45–54; "Canada's Do Not Call Registry," *The Gazette*, December 29, 2007.

23. N. Byrnes, "Avon's new calling," *Bloomberg Businessweek*, September 18, 2000, accessed at www.businessweek.com/2000/00_38/b3699001.htm; D.B. Van, "Avon calling on global ad effort to change its image,"*Marketing* 105 (2000), p. 6; "About Avon," Avon website (n.d.), accessed at www.avoncompany.com/aboutavon/avonmarkets.html.

24. M. Schifrin, "Okay, big mouth," *Forbes*, October 9, 1995, p. 47; V. Byrd and W. Zellner, "The Avon Lady of the Amazon," *Business Week*, October 23, 1994, accessed at www.businessweek.com/stories/1994-10-23/the-avon-lady-of-the-amazon; D.L. Duffy, "Direct selling as the next channel," *Journal of Consumer Marketing* 22 (2005), pp. 43–45; C. Rawlins and P.R. Johnson, "Let's party: The remarkable growth in direct sales," Allied Academies International Conference, Academy of Organizational Culture, Communications and Conflict.Proceedings 10 (2005), pp. 47–50.

25. T. Grant, "More Canadians Shopping on Net," *Globe and Mail*, September 28, 2010, accessed at www.theglobeandmail.com/report-on-business/more-canadians-shopping-on-net/article1727434; Canadian Press, "Canadian retailers running out of time on in e-commerce, report says," CBC News, May 6, 2013, accessed at www.cbc.ca/news/business/canadian-retailers-running-out-of-time-in-e-commerce-report-says-1.1410261; H. Shaw, "Online retail sales to hit $34-billion in Canada by 2018," *Financial Post*, July 23, 2013, accessed at http://business.financialpost.com/2013/07/23/online-retail-sales-to-hit-40-billion-in-canada-by-2018/.

26. B. Hameed, "Facebook, Twitter Influences up to 28% of Online Buying Decisions," Startup Meme blog, December 14, 2009, accessed at http://startupmeme.com/facebook-twitter-influences-upto-28-of-online-buying-decisions; L.P. Forbes, "Does social media influence consumer buying behavior? An investigation of recommendations and purchases," *Journal of Business & Economics Research* 11 (2013), p. 107; Lara O'Reilly, "Women make friends with 'liked' brands on Facebook," *Marketing Week*, August 9, 2012, p. 6.

27. S. Casimiro, "Shop Till You Crash: Just in time for Christmas, online retailing is getting bigger, smarter, faster, and easier. You'll notice we're not calling it flawless. Yet," *Fortune*, December 21, 1998, accessed at http://money.cnn.com/magazines/fortune/fortune_archive/1998/12/21/252661/index.htm; D.A. Pitta, "Internet currency," *Journal of Consumer Marketing* 19 (2002), pp. 539–540; "Lands' end improves online profitability via my virtual model technology," *Direct Marketing* 64 (2001), p. 11.

28. Wen-Jang Jih, "Effects of consumer-perceived convenience on shopping intention in mobile commerce: An empirical study," *International Journal of E-Business Research* 3 (2007), pp. 33–40, 43–48; J. Ramaprasad, "Online social influence and consumer choice: Evidence from the music industry," (Order No. 3364967, University of California, Irvine). ProQuest Dissertations and Theses (2009); "Consumers and Changing Retail Markets," Office of Consumer Affairs, Industry Canada, July 27, 2012, accessed at www.ic.gc.ca/eic/site/oca-bc.nsf/eng/ca02096.html#a21; "5 Canadian consumer trends to shape the future of retail," CBC News, October 21, 2013, accessed at www.cbc.ca/news/business/5-canadian-consumer-trends-to-shape-the-future-of-retail-1.2129072.

29. B. Tuttle, "Why Monday is e-retailers' favorite day of the week," *Time*, January 9, 2012, accessed at http://business.time.com/2012/01/09/why-monday-is-e-retailers-favorite-day-of-the-week/; S. Silcoff, "What keeps online retail in Canada from clicking?" *Globe and Mail*, May 12, 2012, accessed at www.theglobeandmail.com/report-on-business/what-keeps-online-retail-in-canada-from-clicking/article4178807/?page=all; A. Infantry, "Not all Canadians love to shop online: study," *Toronto Star*, August 21, 2013, accessed at www.thestar.com/business/tech_news/2013/08/21/not_all_canadians_love_to_shop_online_study.html; "2014

Canada Digital Future in Focus," comScore, April 2014, accessed at www.comscore.com/Insights/Presentations_and_Whitepapers/2014/2014_Canada_Digital_Future_in_Focus.

30. A. Lopez-Pacheco, "Welcome the New Consumer," *Financial Post*, October 5, 2010, accessed at www.canada.com/business/fp/money/Welcome+consumer/3551652/story.html

31. N. Kumar, "Social Media Recommendations May Increase Online Purchases," PSFK.com. July 1, 2010, accessed at www.psfk.com/2010/07/social-media-recommendations-may-increase-online-purchases.html.

32. "Global Advertising: Consumers Trust Real Friends and Virtual Strangers the Most," Nielsen, press release, July 7, 2009, accessed at www.nielsen.com/us/en/newswire/2009/global-advertising-consumers-trust-real-friends-and-virtual-strangers-the-most.html.

33. J. Weidauer, "QR codes: Building a mobile loyalty program beyond key tags," Retail Customer Experience.com, April 20, 2010, accessed at www.retailcustomerexperience.com/article/21622/QR-codes-Building-a-mobile-loyalty-program-beyond-key-tags; C. Sherburne, "Are QR codes for real?" *Printing Impressions* 52 (2010), p. 36; M. Partee, "Everyone's going crazy for QR codes!" *Credit Union Management* 34 (2011), pp. 32–33.

34. "Retail's Mobility Imperative: A Measured Approach to the Emerging Channel," *Forbes Insight* (2010), accessed at www.forbes.com/forbesinsights/retailmobility/.

35. J. Boyd, "The web goes wireless—popular site operators set their sights on mobile users," *InternetWeek* 828 (2000), pp. 20–27; R. Shields, "Digital strategy: Are you making the most from mobile?" *Marketing Week*, November 2010, pp. 69–71; J. Wisniewski, "Mobile websites with minimum effort," *Online* 34 (2010), pp. 54–57; C. Murphy, "Mistakes," *InformationWeek* 1345 (2012), pp. 32–35.

Chapter 12

1. Interview with Rosanne Caron, president, Out-of-Home Marketing Association of Canada, May 2013; "Innovative Western Union Canada Ad Campaign Recognized With Award," *Western Union News*, February 12, 2013, accessed at http://westernunioncanada.ca/news/content/innovative-western-union-canada-ad-campaign-recognized-with-award; "Western Union 5 for 50," Cassies.ca, accessed at http://cassies.ca/entry/viewcase/7261; "CASSIES Bronze: Western Union taps holiday traditions," *Strategy*, January 28, 2013, accessed at http://strategyonline.ca/2013/01/28/cassies-bronze-western-union-taps-holiday-traditions/.

2. Arianna Huffington, "The Brave New World of the 'New Media,'" *Advertising Week 2010*, January 26, 2010.

3. "Consumerology Report: Technology and the Consumer," Bensimon Byrne, January 2010, accessed at www.consumerology.ca.

4. "The Mobile Marketing Roadmap: How Mobile is Transforming Marketing for Targeting Next Generation Consumers," Mobile Marketing Association, accessed December 2013 at www.mmaglobal.com.

5. "2012 Cell Phone Consumer Attitudes Study," Le groupe Conseil/Quorus Consulting Group, April 23, 2012, accessed at http://cwta.ca/facts-figures/.

6. "Mobile Future in Focus 2013," comScore, February 2013, accessed at www.comscore.com.

7. "2014 Canada Digital Future in Focus," comScore, April 2014, accessed at www.comscore.com/Insights/Presentations_and_Whitepapers/2014/2014_Canada_Digital_Future_in_Focus.

8. "Media Metrix Data for Canada," comScore, August 2013, accessed at www.comscore.com.

9. "Cross Media Reach and Time Spent 2013, RTS data," TVB Canada, November 2013, accessed at www.tvb.ca/pages/RTS.

10. "AOL Agrees to Acquire The Huffington Post," AOL and The Huffington Post, press release, February 7, 2011, accessed at www.huffingtonpost.com/2011/02/07/aol-huffington-post_n_819375.html.

11. Steve Ladurantaye, "The Globe to roll out metered paywall as industry shifts to digital revenue," *Globe and Mail*, October 15,

2012, accessed at www.theglobeandmail.com/report-on-business/the-globe-to-roll-out-metered-paywall-as-industry-shifts-to-digital-revenue/article4612259/; Rachel McAthy, "Globe and Mail to launch metered paywall next week," Journalism.co.uk, October 15, 2012, accessed at www.journalism.co.uk/news/canada-globe-and-mail-to-launch-metered-paywall/s2/a550783/.

12. Chris Powell, "Globe's Stackhouse on Editorial Incentives and Driving Subscriptions," *Marketing*, October 9, 2013, accessed at www.marketingmag.ca/news/media-news/globes-stackhouse-on-editorial-incentives-and-driving-subscriptions-90724; Sarah Marshall, "Why the Globe and Mail is 'incentivising' newsroom staff," Journalism.co.uk, October 8, 2013, accessed at www.journalism.co.uk/news/-wpe13-why-the-globe-and-mail-is-incentivising-newsroom-staff-/s2/a554375/; Sarah Marshall, "#editors13: Paywall lessons from Canada's Globe and Mail," Journalism.co.uk, June 3, 2013, accessed at www.journalism.co.uk/news/-editors13-paywall-lessons-from-canada-s-globe-and-mail/s2/a553140/.

13. Anne Austin, Jonathan Barnard, and Nicola Hutcheon, "Advertising Expenditure Forecasts—September 2013," ZenithOptimedia.

14. "Real-Time Marketing Is Madison Avenues's Next Big Challenge," *The Economist Group*, March 21, 2013, accessed at www.economistgroup.com/leanback/social-media/real-time-marketing-is-madison-avenues-next-big-challenge/; Steve Hall, "7 Steps to Becoming a World-Class Real-Time Marketer," *HubSpot* blog, March 26, 2013, accessed at http://blog.hubspot.com/how-to-be-a-world-class-real-time-marketer; Rebecca Lieb, "7 Inspiring Examples of Real-Time Marketing in Action," *HubSpot* blog, October 12, 2012, accessed at http://blog.hubspot.com/blog/tabid/6307/bid/33696/7-Inspiring-Examples-of-Real-Time-Marketing-in-Action.aspx.

15. Jennifer Rooney, "Behind the Scenes of Oreo's Real-Time Super Bowl Slam Dunk," *Forbes,* February 4, 2013, accessed at www.forbes.com/sites/jenniferrooney/2013/02/04/behind-the-scenes-of-oreos-real-time-super-bowl-slam-dunk/; Ryan Caligiuri, "Four ways to build on Oreo's winning Super Bowl marketing play," *Globe and Mail*, February 15, 2013, accessed at www.theglobeandmail.com/report-on-business/small-business/sb-marketing/advertising/four-ways-to-build-on-oreos-winning-super-bowl-marketing-play/article8616201/; Gian LaVecchia, "Oreo's 'Dunk in the Dark' Strategy and the Future of Real-Time Marketing," *Fast Company*, April 18, 2013, accessed at www.fastcompany.com/3008486/oreos-dunk-dark-strategy-and-future-real-time-marketing.

16. "What is Content Marketing?" Content Marketing Institute, accessed at http://contentmarketinginstitute.com/what-is-content-marketing/; "Content Marketing: Harnessing the Power of Content to Fuel your Brand," American Marketing Association, events, April 2013, brochure accessed at www.marketingpower.com/Calendar/Documents/FY13%20Training%20Series/Q4/ContentMarketing_Apr_Brochure.pdf.

17. Joe Pulizzi, "Build a Brand Content Empire: What You Can Learn From LEGO," Content Marketing Institute, June 22, 2013, accessed at http://contentmarketinginstitute.com/2013/06/build-brand-content-empire-learn-from-lego/; Christopher Ratcliff, "The LEGO Movie's solid social marketing strategy," *Econsultancy* blog, November 6, 2013, accessed at http://econsultancy.com/ca/blog/63745-the-lego-movie-s-solid-social-marketing-strategy; Svend Hollensen, "LEGO Global Marketing," *Global CMO*, September 2013, accessed at www.theglobalcmo.com/lego-global-marketing/; "The Lego Empire," CBC Saskatchewan, June 12, 2013, accessed at www.cbc.ca/morningedition/episode/2013/06/12/the-lego-empire/.

18. comScore data, December 2013, accessed March 2014 from http://mymetrix.comscore.com.

19. "MMA Updates Definition of Mobile Marketing," accessed December 2013 at www.mmaglobal.com/node/11102.

20. "Murphy's When It Rains It Pours Case Study," Publicis Dublin, May 2013, accessed at http://vimeo.com/64886847; "When It Rains It Pours," accessed January 2014 at www.murphys.com/whenitrainsitpours/; "The Cannes Mobile Lions winners 2013: The award-winning mobile campaigns with case studies and videos," MobiThinking, accessed January 2014 at http://mobithinking.com/mobile-awards/Cannes; "Publicis Dublin Scores at Cannes with Murphy's App," *AdWorld News*, accessed January 2014 at www.adworld.ie/news/read/?id=8f9b58ea-d287-491e-8d0e-f8c20c9fafa4.

21. "SickKids' iPhone app, Pain Squad, helps children with cancer report their pain," *Toronto Star*, May 7, 2012, accessed at www.thestar.com/business/2012/05/07/sickkids_iphone_app_pain_squad_helps_children_with_cancer_report_their_pain.html; Cundari, "Case Study: Pain Squad Mobile App—Helping Young Cancer Patients Track Pain," AIGA, March 8, 2013, accessed at www.aiga.org/case-study-pain-squad-app/; Christine Wong, "A checkup on Pain Squad, the Canadian app that gamified health care," CommerceLab, October 10, 2013, accessed at www.commercelab.ca/a-checkup-on-pain-squad-the-canadian-app-that-gamified-health-care/; "Pain Squad," Cassies Winners 2013, accessed January 2014 at http://cassies.ca/entry/viewcase/7099.

22. Google, "Real Beauty Shines Through: Dove Wins Titanium Grand Prix, 163 Million Views on YouTube," Google Think Insights, June 2013, accessed at www.google.ca/think/case-studies/dove-real-beauty-sketches.html; News release, "Dove recreates Real Beauty Sketches for Canadian moms," PR Newswire, May 12, 2013, accessed at www.prnewswire.com/news-releases/dove-recreates-real-beauty-sketches-for-canadian-moms-207121581.html; "Six in 10 girls quit activities they love because of how they feel about their looks," CNW, news release, April 9, 2013, accessed at www.newswire.ca/en/story/1143231/six-in-10-girls-quit-activities-they-love-because-of-how-they-feel-about-their-looks; Dove Canada's YouTube channel, www.youtube.com/user/DoveCanada; Dove website, www.unilever.ca/brands/personalcarebrands/dove.aspx.

23. Nina Bahadur, "Dove 'Real Beauty' Campaign Turns 10: How A Brand Tried To Change The Conversation About Female Beauty," *Huffington Post*, January 21, 2014, accessed at www.huffingtonpost.com/2014/01/21/dove-real-beauty-campaign-turns-10_n_4575940.html; Maryam Siddiqi, "A Cultured Life: Dove's latest 'Real Beauty' ads are about selling soap, but they raise debate over body image, too," *National Post*, April 23, 2013, accessed at http://life.nationalpost.com/2013/04/23/a-cultured-life-doves-latest-real-beauty-ads-are-about-selling-soap-sure-but-they-raise-debate-over-body-image-too/; Google, "Real Beauty Shines Through: Dove Wins Titanium Grand Prix, 163 Million Views on YouTube," Google Think Insights, June 2013, accessed at www.google.ca/think/case-studies/dove-real-beauty-sketches.html; Dove Canada's YouTube channel, www.youtube.com/user/DoveCanada; Dove website, www.unilever.ca/brands/personalcarebrands/dove.aspx.

24. Next Generation Day event, Toronto, January 29, 2014 at 2014 Advertising and Marketing Week.

25. "Competition Bureau Secures Over $9 Million and Money Back to Victims for Business Scam," Competition Bureau, March 2, 2012, accessed at www.competitionbureau.gc.ca/eic/site/cb-bc.nsf/eng/03439.html; Ashley Weber, "Canadian court comes down hard on misleading business directory scam," Stikeman Elliott, March 15, 2012, accessed at www.thecompetitor.ca/2012/03/articles/competition/competition-bureau/canadian-court-comes-down-hard-on-misleading-business-directory-scam/#more; "Competition Bureau Sues to Shut Down Business Directory Scam," Competition Bureau, July 28, 2011, accessed at www.competitionbureau.gc.ca/eic/site/cb-bc.nsf/eng/03394.html.

26. Personal interview with Livia Grulich, co-founder and managing director On-Q Communications, and Gene Swinton, national marketing manager Baskin-Robbins.

27. *Maclean's* 2014 advertising rates, accessed at www.rogersmedia.com/brands/macleans/.

28. Carly Lewis, "RBC goes back to school in new web series," *Marketing*, July 16, 2013, accessed at www.marketingmag.ca/

news/marketer-news/rbc-goes-back-to-school-in-new-web-series-83654; Stephanie Startz, "Webisodes Offer Brands Like Ikea, Sara Lee and Maybelline a New Outlet," *BrandChannel*, November 25, 2009, accessed at www.brandchannel.com/home/post/2009/11/25/Webisodes-Offer-Brands-Like-Ikea-Sara-Lee-And-Maybelline-A-New-Outlet.aspx.

29. Canadian Media Directors' Council, "Media Digest 2013/2014," *Marketing* magazine, 2013.

30. Ibid.

31. "PMB 2013 Fall Topline Report," Print Measurement Bureau, accessed at www.pmb.ca.

32. Canadian Media Directors' Council, "Media Digest 2013/2014."

33. "Leo Burnett and Raising the Roof see great potential in homeless youth," Leo Burnett, press release, February 24, 2011, accessed at www.raisingtheroof.org/RaisingTheRoof/media/RaisingTheRoofMedia/Documents/Releases/Ad-Campaign-Media-Release.pdf; Raising the Roof website, accessed at www.raisingtheroof.org/; "On Toque Tuesday, buy a toque (or socks!) and help Canada's 200,000 homeless," Raising the Roof, media release, February 3, 1014, accessed at www.raisingtheroof.org/RaisingTheRoof/media/RaisingTheRoofMedia/Documents/Releases/Media-Release-2014-FINAL.pdf; Leo Burnett Worldwide, "Raising the Roof—Repackaging help," YouTube video, May 14, 2013, accessed at www.youtube.com/watch?v=Ior8bhBroo8&list=PL3IbgymsTKo68VHl1NR-eJeaw-fOrXiEd.

34. Adapted from American Marketing Association Marketing Power Resource Library Dictionary, February 19, 2010, accessed at www.marketingpower.com/_layouts/Dictionary.aspx?dLetter=P.

35. Sarah Schmidt, "CFIA allows non-accredited labs to do some listeria work," *National Post*, April 29, 2009, accessed at www.nationalpost.com/CFIA+allows+accredited+labs+some+listeria+work/1547167/story.html; "Maple Leaf Foods Media Statement," CNW Group, news release, March 4, 2009, accessed at www.newswire.ca/en/releases/archive/March2009/04/c5969.html; "Maple Leaf Listeriosis Settlement Headed to Courts for Approval," CNW Group, news release, February 2, 2009, accessed at www.newswire.ca/en/releases/archive/March2009/04/c5969.html; "CFIA still moving on Listeria recommendations," CBC News, October 24, 2010, accessed at www.cbc.ca/health/story/2010/10/22/con-listeria-report.html; "Maple Leaf settles class action listeriosis lawsuits for $27M," CBC News, December 18, 2008, accessed at www.cbc.ca/canada/story/2008/12/18/listeriosis-settlement.html#ixzz1EQB5fskP.

36. David Biello, "How Did the BP Oil Spill Affect Gulf Coast Wildlife?" *Scientific American*, April 20, 2011, accessed at www.scientificamerican.com/article/how-did-bp-oil-spill-affect-gulf-of-mexico-wildlife-and-ecosystems/; Mark Schleifstein, "National Wildlife Federation says environmental effects of BP spill far from over," *Times-Picayune*, April 2, 2013, accessed at www.nola.com/news/gulf-oil-spill/index.ssf/2013/04/national_wildlife_federation_s_1.html.

37. "Made in Bangladesh," The Fifth Estate, CBC, October 11, 2013, accessed at www.cbc.ca/fifth/episodes/2013-2014/made-in-bangladesh; "Bangladesh garment workers to get compensation from Loblaw," CBC News, October 24, 2013, accessed at www.cbc.ca/news/business/bangladesh-garment-workers-to-get-compensation-from-loblaw-1.2223499; "Q&A: Loblaw," The Fifth Estate, CBC, October 11, 2013, accessed at www.cbc.ca/fifth/blog/qa-loblaws; "Loblaw official statement," The Fifth Estate, CBC, October 11, 2013, accessed at www.cbc.ca/fifth/blog/loblaw-official-statement; Marina Strauss and Bertrand Marotte, "Loblaw outlines Bangladesh compensation plan," *Globe and Mail*, October 24, 2013, accessed at www.theglobeandmail.com/report-on-business/international-business/loblaw-to-compensate-victims-of-bangladesh-factory-collapse/article15041964/.

38. Google, "Real Beauty Shines Through: Dove Wins Titanium Grand Prix, 163 Million Views on YouTube," Google Think Insights, June 2013, accessed at www.google.ca/think/case-studies/dove-real-beauty-sketches.html.

39. "ROLL UP THE RIM TO WIN®CONTEST—2013," Tim Hortons website, accessed at www.rolluptherimtowin.com/en/in-restaurant-rules-and-redemption.php; Chris Powell, "The Roll Up The Rim Marketing Phenomenon," *Marketing*, February 25, 2011, accessed at www.marketingmag.ca/news/marketer-news/the-roll-up-the-rim-marketing-phenomenon-23355.

40. Rogers Cup website, accessed at www.rogerscup.com/men/english/sponsors.php.

41. Adapted from the Word of Mouth Marketing Association, "WOM—COMM 101," accessed at http://womma.org/wom101.

42. "Groupon Dresses Up to Celebrate Five Years with New Website, Mobile Apps," Groupon, news release, November 1, 2013, accessed at http://investor.groupon.com/releasedetail.cfm?ReleaseID=803467; Groupon website, accessed January 23, 2014, at www.groupon.com; Reuters, "Online advertising business Groupon's IPO expected to sell at US$31.59 a share," *National Post*, January 3, 2011, accessed at www.nationalpost.com/todays-paper/Online+advertising+business+Groupon+expected+sell+share/4051382/story.html; NBC Today Show, aired December 4, 2009, accessed at www.youtube.com/watch?v=54WKCfjLinU; Michael Hickins "The Groupon Frodo Memo," *Wall Street Journal* blog, February 25, 2011, accessed at http://blogs.wsj.com/digits/2011/02/25/the-groupon-frodo-memo.

Chapter 13

1. Personal interview with Jake Rich, president and founder, Rich Media.

2. "AdReaction 2012—Global Report: Marketing in the Mobile World," Millward Brown, December 2012, accessed at www.warc.com.

3. "The Mobile Marketing Roadmap: How Mobile is Transforming Marketing for Targeting Next Generation Consumers," Mobile Marketing Association, accessed December 2013 at www.mmaglobal.com.

4. "MMA Updates Definition of Mobile Marketing," accessed December 2013 at www.mmaglobal.com/node/11102.

5. "The Mobile Marketing Roadmap," Mobile Marketing Association; PCmag.com Encyclopedia, accessed December 2013 at www.pcmag.com/encyclopedia/term/62894/feature-phone.

6. "2014 Canada Digital Future in Focus," comScore, April 2014, accessed at www.comscore.com/Insights/Presentations_and_Whitepapers/2014/2014_Canada_Digital_Future_in_Focus.

7. "The Mobile Marketing Roadmap," Mobile Marketing Association; "2012 Cell Phone Consumer Attitudes Study," Le groupe Conseil/Quorus Consulting Group, April 23, 2012, accessed at http://cwta.ca/facts-figures/; "2014 Canada Digital Future in Focus," comScore.

8. "2013 Canada Digital Future in Focus," comScore, March 2013, accessed at www.comscore.com/Insights/Presentations_and_Whitepapers/2013/2013_Canada_Digital_Future_in_Focus.

9. Gregor Smith, "The Impact of Connected Devices on Consumer Behaviour, "comScore, Mobile World Congress presentation, February 2013, accessed at www.comscore.com/Insights/Presentations_and_Whitepapers/2013/The_Impact_of_Connected_Devices_on_Consumer_Behavior.

10. "Our Mobile Planet: Canada Understanding the Mobile Consumer," Ipsos MediaCT, May 2013, accessed at www.thinkwithgoogle.com/mobileplanet/en/.

11. "2012 Cell Phone Consumer Attitudes Study," Quorus Consulting group.

12. "AdReaction 2012," Millward Brown.

13. "Mobile app marketing quick start guide, 2010-2011" Canadian Marketing Association, CMA Mobile Marketing Taskforce, accessed at www.the-cma.org; Nathan Ingraham, "Apple announces 1 million apps in the App Store, more than 1 billion songs played on iTunes radio," *The Verge*, October 22, 2013, accessed at www.theverge.com/2013/10/22/4866302/apple-announces-1-million-apps-in-the-app-store; Chris Welch, "Google: Android app downloads have crossed 50 billion, over 1M apps in Play," *The Verge*, July 24, 2013, accessed at www.theverge.com/2013/7/24/4553010/google-50-billion-android-app-downloads-1m-apps-available.

14. Michelle Maisto, "Apps, Marketing and the Cloud: Gartner Predictions for 2013," *eWeek*, October 12, 2012, accessed at www.eweek.com/mobile/apps-marketing-and-the-cloud-gartner-predictions-for-2013.

15. "Our Mobile Planet: Canada Understanding the Mobile Consumer," Ipsos MediaCT.

16. "2012 Cell Phone Consumer Attitudes Study," Quorus Consulting group.

17. "AdReaction 2012," Millward Brown.

18. Raluca Budiu, "Mobile: Native Apps, Web Apps, and Hybrid Apps," Nielsen Norman Group, September 14, 2013, accessed at www.nngroup.com/articles/mobile-native-apps/.

19. Ernst & Young, "2013 Actual + 2014 Estimated Canadian Internet Advertising Revenue Survey," IAB Canada, September 17, 2014, accessed at http://iabcanada.com/files/Canadian-Internet-AdRev-Survey_2013-14.pdf; "Mobiles to drive faster global advertising growth: Publicis unit," Reuters, December 8, 2013, accessed at www.reuters.com/article/2013/12/09/us-advertising-spend-idUSBRE9B800420131209; Brent Bernie, "Brave New Digital World—What media measurement business must address," comScore, IAB Canada Mixx presentation, March 21, 2013; "Annual Online Advertising Revenue Reports," IAB Canada, accessed at http://iabcanada.com/research/revenue-reports/.

20. "AdReaction 2012," Millward Brown.

21. "Salesforce.com Introduces Salesforce1," Salesforce, news release, November 19, 2013, accessed at www.salesforce.com/company/news-press/press-releases/2013/11/131119.jsp; Salesforce1 for Android, accessed December 2013 at https://play.google.com/store/apps/details?id=com.salesforce.chatter&hl=en; "Introducing the Salesforce1 mobile app," Salesforce website, accessed December 2013 at www.salesforce.com/mobile/service/; "Service Cloud Product Overview," Salesforce website, accessed at www.salesforce.com/ca/service-cloud/features/?d=70130000000tGOz&internal=true; discussion with Salesforce, January 2014.

22. Text messaging stats accessed December 2013 at the Canadian Wireless Telecommunications Association website for administering CSC messaging at http://txt.ca/english/consumer/press.html.

23. "Competition Bureau Sues Bell, Rogers and Telus for Misleading Consumers: Bureau Seeks Customer Refunds and $31 Million In Penalties," Competition Bureau, September 14, 2012, accessed at www.competitionbureau.gc.ca/eic/site/cb-bc.nsf/eng/03498.html; Laura Payton, "Text message costs prompt suit against Bell, Rogers, Telus," CBC.ca. September 14, 2012, accessed at www.cbc.ca/news/politics/text-message-costs-prompt-suit-against-bell-rogers-telus-1.1144226; Canadian Press, "Competition Bureau sues Canada's three wireless giants over texting advertising," *Maclean's*, September 14, 2012, accessed at www2.macleans.ca/2012/09/14/competition-bureau-sues-canadas-three-wireless-giants-over-texting-advertising/.

24. Geoff Linton, "Infographic: Email Opens on Mobile Devices SPIKE again in 2013," Canadian Marketing Association, June 12, 2013, accessed at www.the-cma.org/about/blog/infographic-email-opens-on-mobile-devices-spike-again-in-2013.

25. "Mattel and Walmart Canada Offer Holiday Shoppers Toys on the Go," PR Newswire, press release, November 4, 2013, accessed at www.prnewswire.com/news-releases/mattel-and-walmart-canada-offer-holiday-shoppers-toys-on-the-go-230475721.html; Vanessa Milne, "Mattel and Walmart Partner Again To Expand Virtual Store Concept," *Marketing*, November 4, 2013, accessed at www.marketingmag.ca/news/marketer-news/mattel-and-walmart-partner-again-to-expand-virtual-store-concept-92868; Chantal Tode, "Walmart, Mattel boost QR code-driven toy sales with more locations," *Mobile Commerce Daily*, November 6, 2013, accessed at www.mobilecommercedaily.com/walmart-mattel-boost-qr-code-driven-toy-sales-with-more-locations.

26. "The CRTC Wireless Code," Canadian Radio-television and Tele-communications Association, accessed December 2013 at www.crtc.gc.ca/eng/info_sht/t13.htm; "CRTC wireless code comes into force: Canadians can cancel their contracts without penalty after two years," Canadian Radio-television and Telecommunications Association, news release, December 2, 2013, accessed at www.crtc.gc.ca/eng/com100/2013/r131202.htm#.UqMX0MRDuSo.

27. Jason Kerr, "Text Messaging in Canada," Canadian Wireless Telecommunications Association; "Canada standard rate short code pricing," Clickatell, November 18, 2010, accessed at www.clickatell.com/downloads/Clickatell_Canadian_Shortcode_pricing_revenue_share.pdf; "Canadian Common Short Code Application Guidelines Version 2.2," Canadian Wireless Telecommunications Association, August 9, 2012, accessed at www.txt.ca/english/business/doc/Canadian%20Common%20Short%20Code%20Application%20Guidelines.pdf.

28. "Global Code of Conduct," Mobile Marketing Association, July 15, 2008, accessed at www.mmaglobal.com/bestpractice.

29. "The Mobile Marketing Roadmap," Mobile Marketing Association.

30. Louise Julig, "3 Ways Sharpie Is Engaging Teens with Social Media," *Social Media Examiner*, January 31, 2013, accessed at www.socialmediaexaminer.com/connect-with-teens-on-social-media-sharpie-case-study/; Jennifer Boshan, "A Creative Social Media Marketing Mini Case Study: Sharpie," Rooftop Agency, April 2012, accessed at, http://rooftopagency.com/2012/04/a-creative-social-media-marketing-mini-case-study-sharpie/; Kelly Jennex, "Social Media Outreach: Examples From Molson, Sharpie & Ford," InNetwork, April 10, 2013, accessed at http://innetwork.net/2013/04/social-media-outreach-examples/.

31. Greenpeace Kit Kat Killer website, accessed at www.greenpeace.org/international/en/campaigns/climate-change/kitkat/.

32. "Sweet success for Kit Kat campaign: you asked, Nestlé has answered," Greenpeace, news release, May 17, 2010, accessed at www.greenpeace.org/international/en/news/features/Sweet-success-for-Kit-Kat-campaign/; Simon Houpt,"Kit Kat spat goes viral despite Nestlé's efforts," *Globe and Mail*, May 17, 2010, accessed at www.theglobeandmail.com/report-on-business/kit-kat-spat-goes-viral-despite-nestles-efforts/article4313965/; Robin Shreeves, "Greenpeace and Nestle in a Kat Fight," *Forbes*, March 19, 2010, accessed at www.forbes.com/2010/03/18/kitkat-greenpeace-palm-oil-technology-ecotech-nestle.html; Greenpeace Kit Kat Killer website, accessed at www.greenpeace.org/international/en/campaigns/climate-change/kitkat/; " Greenpeace vs. Nestle," CNN, May 23, 2010, accessed at www.cnn.com/video/?/video/world/2010/05/23/int.eco.naidoo.nestle.cnn.

33. comScore data, August 2014, accessed at http://mymetrix.comscore.com.

34. Timothy Stenovec "Myspace History: A Timeline of the Social Network's Biggest Moments," *Huffington Post*, June 29, 2011, accessed at www.huffingtonpost.com/2011/06/29/myspace-history-timeline_n_887059.html#s299496title=August_2003_Myspace; Felix Gillette, "The Rise and Inglorious Fall of Myspace," *Bloomberg Businessweek*, June 22, 2011, accessed at www.businessweek.com/magazine/content/11_27/b4235053917570.htm; Nicholas Jackson, "As MySpace Sells for $35 Million, a History of the Network's Valuation," *The Atlantic*, June 29, 2011, accessed at www.theatlantic.com/technology/archive/2011/06/as-myspace-sells-for-35-million-a-history-of-the-networks-valuation/241224/; Michele Catalano, "MySpace Attempts to Rise from the Ashes," *Forbes*, January 17, 2013, accessed at www.forbes.com/sites/michelecatalano/2013/01/17/myspace-attempts-to-rise-from-the-ashes/; Molly McHugh, "Myspace now boasts 36M users and a 340 percent increase in artists using the network," *Digital Trends*, October 1, 2013, accessed at www.digitaltrends.com/social-media/myspace-releases-new-user-numbers/#!zxkwj.

35. Facebook Newsroom, March 2014, accessed at https://newsroom.fb.com/Key-Facts.

36. "Top Brands on Facebook: Content, Tactics & Engagement. A Study of the Interbrand Top 100 Brands on Facebook," *Simply Measured* blog, July 2013, accessed at http://cdn.simplymeasured.com/wp-content/uploads/2013/08/SimplyMeasured-Facebook-Study-July-2013.pdf .

37. David Griner, "Oreo Surprises 26 Million Facebook Fans with Gay Pride Post; Photo goes viral but also sparks backlash,"*Adweek,* July 25, 2012, accessed at www.adweek.com/adfreak/oreo-surprises-26-million-facebook-fans-gay-pride-post-141440.

38. YouTube statistics accessed March 2014 at www.youtube.com/yt/press/statistics.html; Facebook 2013 awards accessed at www.facebook-studio.com/gallery/submission/oreo-daily-twist.

39. "Psy—Gangnam Style (강남스타일) M/V," YouTube, July 15, 2012, accessed at www.youtube.com/watch?v=9bZkp7q19f0; Laura Edwards, "How Did Gangnam Style Go Viral?" *Social Media Today,* November 7, 2012, accessed at http://socialmediatoday.com/laurahelen/980476/how-did-gangnam-style-go-viral; Andy Yeti-Barr, "How Did Gangnam Style Go Viral? The Gangnam Viral Marketing Style Playbook," *10YETIS* blog, accessed at www.10yetis.co.uk/how-gangnam-style-went-viral.html.

40. Craig Smith, "(February 2014) By the Numbers: 21 Amazing Google+ Statistics," DMR Digital Marketing Ramblings, February 2, 2014, accessed at http://expandedramblings.com/?p=16715; Matt McGee, "Google+ Hits 300 Million Active Monthly "In-Stream" Users, 540 Million Across Google," *Marketingland,* October 29, 2013, accessed at http://marketingland.com/google-hits-300-million-active-monthly-in-stream-users-540-million-across-google-63354.

41. Twitter website accessed at https://about.twitter.com/company; Craig Smith, "How many use 415 of the top social media, apps, & tools (March 2014)," DMR Digital Marketing Ramblings, March 9, 2014, accessed at http://expandedramblings.com/index.php/resource-how-many-people-use-the-top-social-media/4/#.UybwifldWSo.

42. Jade Furubayashi, "[INFOGRAPHIC] How Top Brands Are Using Twitter," *Simply Measured* blog, January 30, 2014, accessed at http://simplymeasured.com/blog/2014/01/30/infographic-how-top-brands-are-using-twitter/; Taylor Soper, "Social media study: Here's how the world's top brands effectively use Twitter," *GeekWire,* January 21 2014, accessed at www.geekwire.com/2014/social-media-study-top-brands-twitter/ .

43. Christopher Heine, "Arby's Dishes on Awesome Pharrell Williams Tweet. It took 'just a few seconds' to write," *AdWeek,* March 7, 2014, accessed at www.adweek.com/news/technology/arbys-dishes-awesome-pharrell-williams-tweets-156149; Adam Schoenfeld, "Measuring The Impact of One Perfect Tweet: Arby's Case Study," *Simply Measured* blog, March 4, 2014, accessed at http://simplymeasured.com/blog/2014/03/05/measuring-the-impact-of-one-perfect-tweet-arbys-case-study/.

44. LinkedIn website accessed at www.LinkedIn.com; Nate Smitha, "10 Top Brands Driving Engagement on LinkedIn," *Simply Measured* blog, July 12, 2013, accessed at http://simplymeasured.com/blog/2013/07/12/10-top-brands-driving-engagement-on-linkedin/.

45. "As Instagram Rolls Out Ad Platform, Brands Are Seeing Record Engagement," Business Wire, news release, October 29, 2013 accessed at www.businesswire.com/news/home/20131029005603/en/Instagram-Rolls-Ad-Platform-Brands-Record-Engagement#.Uybs7PldWSo.

46. Kevin Shively, "Why Tumblr is Worth $1.1 Billion To Yahoo," *Simply Measured* blog, May 20, 2513, accessed at http://simplymeasured.com/blog/2013/05/20/why-tumblr-is-worth-1-1-billion-to-yahoo/; Nate Smitha, "Should Tumblr Be A Part of Your Social Strategy?' *Simply Measured* blog, August 29, 2013, accessed at http://simplymeasured.com/blog/2013/08/29/should-tumblr-be-a-part-of-your-social-strategy/; Nate Smitha, "5 Tips To Succeed With Tumblr," *Simply Measured* blog, September 5, 2013, accessed at http://simplymeasured.com/blog/2013/09/05/5-tips-to-succeed-with-tumblr/.

47. Craig Smith, "(March 2014) By the Numbers: 59 Amazing Pinterest Stats," DMR Digital Marketing Ramblings, March 4, 2014, accessed at http://expandedramblings.com/index.php/pinterest-stats/; Josh Horwitz, "Semiocast: Pinterest now has 70 million users and is steadily gaining momentum outside the US," *The Next Web,* July 10, 2013, accessed at http://thenextweb.com/socialmedia/2013/07/10/semiocast-pinterest-now-has-70-million-users-and-is-steadily-gaining-momentum-outside-the-us/#!z9xUF; "Study: Instagram Proves More Effective than Pinterest for Top Brands," Business Wire, news release, May 9, 2013, accessed at www.businesswire.com/news/home/20130509005427/en/STUDY-Instagram-Proves-Effective-Pinterest-Top-Brands#.UyXjkfldWSo.

48. "Social Media Marketing Quick Start Guide," Canadian Marketing Association, CMA's Digital Marketing Council, 2013.

49. "Socialogue: Old Friends? Check. Long-lost Relatives? Sure. Brands? You Bet," Ipsos, January 22, 2013, accessed at www.ipsos-na.com/news-polls/pressrelease.aspx?id=5963.

Chapter 14

1. Personal interview with Marci Maddox, senior director, customer experience marketing, OpenText, October 2013.

2. M. Cunningham, *Customer Relationship Management: Marketing,* 1st ed. (Oxford: Capstone Publishing, 2002); M.R. Ciraulo and K.S. Auman, "Insurers can unlock value via CRM," *National Underwriter* 106 (2002), pp. 27:29; Philip Kotler et al., *Principles of Marketing,* 7th Canadian edition (Toronto: Pearson, 2008).

3. A. Reid and D. O'Brien, "Creating a single view of the customer for CRM strategy." *Interactive Marketing* 6 (2005), pp. 357–365.

4. D. Grewal, M. Levy, and V. Kumar, "Customer experience management in retailing: An organizing framework," *Journal of Retailing* 85 (2009), pp. 1–14. doi:http://dx.doi.org/10.1016/j.jretai.2009.01.001

5. M. Hinshaw, "Customer Satisfaction is Not Enough—Why High Satisfaction Scores May Actually Spell Danger for Your Brand," *Brandchannel,* November 19, 2010, accessed at www.brandchannel.com/brand_speak.asp?bs_id=259&utm_source=feedburner&utm_medium=feed&utm_campaign=Feed%3A+Brandchannel+%28brandchannel.com%29; J. Ozimek, "The disloyalty ladder—two rungs further down," *Journal of Direct, Data and Digital Marketing Practice* 11 (2010), pp. 207–218. doi:http://dx.doi.org/10.1057/dddmp.2009.45; L. Kimbell, "Designing for service as one way of designing services," *International Journal of Design* 5 (2011).

6. "Why Some Companies Succeed at CRM (and Many Fail)," *Knowledge@Wharton,* January 15, 2003, accessed at http://knowledge.wharton.upenn.edu/article.cfm?articleid=699.

7. S.E. Robinson, "Customer satisfaction: The Xerox Canada story," *Managing Service Quality* 7 (1997), pp. 12–15.

8. B. McKenzie, "Customer relationship management and customer recovery and retention: The case of the 407 express toll route," *Knowledge Management Research & Practice* 6 (2008), pp. 155–163. doi:http://dx.doi.org/10.1057/kmrp.2008.5

9. B. Talbot, "The Power of Personal Service," The Centre for Hospitality Research, Cornell University, 2006, pp. 6–14; "The Story of the Four Seasons," Four Seasons Hotels and Resorts, August 7, 2013, accessed at http://press.fourseasons.com/trending-now/corporate/the-story-of-four-seasons/.

10. K.W. Li, "The critical success factors of customer relationship management (CRM) technological initiatives," (Order No. MQ68423, Concordia University (Canada)). ProQuest Dissertations and Theses (2002); B.L. Soumaya and J. Perrien, "The impact of E-CRM on organisational and individual behavior: The effect of the remuneration and reward system," *International Journal of E-Business Research* 3 (2007), pp. 13–16,18,20–23.

11. D. Rigby, F. Reicheld, and C. Dawson, "Winning customer loyalty is the key to a winning CRM strategy," *Ivey Business Journal,* 2003, accessed at http://iveybusinessjournal.com/topics/social-responsibility/winning-customer-loyalty-is-the-key-to-a-winning-crm-strategy#.Ujj8fhbvzR0.

12. M. Johne, "Brand building after the merge," *CMA Management* 77 (2003), p. 32; E. Beauchesne, "Customers Want Friendly Service Most," *Star Phoenix,* June 20, 2008.

13. A. Darling, "Social media & CRM: Conversation starter,"*New Media Age,* 2010, pp. 20–21; R. King, "How Companies Use

Twitter to Bolster Their Brands," *Bloomberg Businessweek*, September 6, 2008, accessed at www.businessweek.com/technology/content/sep2008/tc2008095_320491.htm.

14. C. Campbell, "Tuning into Twitter," *Maclean's*, October 7. 2010, accessed at www2.macleans.ca/2010/10/07/tuning-in-to-twitter/.

15. L. Carmi, "Airlines use Twitter, other social tools to revolutionize customer service," *Toronto Star*, October 10, 2010, accessed at www.thestar.com/business/companies/porter/article/871979--airlines-use-twitter-other-social-tools-to-revolutionize-customer-service; N. Sreenivasan, C. Lee, and D. Goh, "Tweeting the friendly skies: Investigating information exchange among Twitter users about airlines," *Program: Electronic Library & Information Systems* 46 (2012), pp. 21–42. doi:10.1108/00330331211204548

16. R. Sawhney, "Broken Guitar Has United Playing the Blues to the Tune of $180 Million," *Fast Company*, July 28, 2009, accessed at www.fastcompany.com/blog/ravi-sawhney/design-reach/youtube-serves-180-million-heartbreak; M. Unnikrishnan and R. Wall, "All That Twitters," *Aviation Week & Space Technology* 172 (2010), pp. 42–44.

17. K. Barry, "Ford Bets the Fiesta on Social Networking," *Wired*, April 17, 2009, accessed at www.wired.com/autopia/2009/04/how-the-fiesta/all/1; "Power to the People! Fiesta Movement: A Social Remix Gives Control of New Ford Fiesta Ad Campaign to the People," Ford, press release, February 19, 2013, accessed at http://corporate.ford.com/news-center/press-releases-detail/pr-power-to-the-people-fiesta-37706; S. Edelstein, "Ford relaunches Fiesta movement Social Media marketing campaign," *Digital Trends*, February 20, 2013, accessed at www.digitaltrends.com/social-media/2014-ford-fiesta-goes-viral-with-fiesta-movement-social-media-campaign/.

18. R. Buchanan and C. Gillies, "Value Managed Relationship: The Key to Customer Retention and Profitability," *European Management Journal* 8 (1990); V. Spencer, "Customer relationship management: Who is your customer?" *Canadian Underwriter* 68 (2001), pp. 12–16; V. Kumar, R. Venkatesan, and B. Rajan, "Implementing profitability through a customer lifetime value management framework." *GfK Marketing Intelligence Review* 1 (2009), pp. 32–43,64.

19. C. Papadatos, "The art of storytelling: How loyalty marketers can build emotional connections to their brands," *Journal of Consumer Marketing* 23 (2006), pp. 382–384. doi:http://dx.doi.org/10.1108/07363760610712902

20. D. Friend, "Canadian companies aim for balance as customers expect more for loyalty," *Globe and Mail*, July 21, 2013, accessed at www.theglobeandmail.com/report-on-business/canadian-companies-aim-for-balance-as-customers-expect-more-for-loyalty/article13332480.

21. "About Us," Starwood Hotels and Resorts website (n.d.), Moments, accessed at http://auction.starwoodhotels.com/cgi-bin/ncommerce3/ExecMacro/static/aboutus.d2w/report?wl=67280009; S. Trelevaven, "Loyalty is a virtue and it's rewarded when you travel," *National Post*, March 22, 2013, accessed at http://life.nationalpost.com/2013/03/24/loyalty-is-a-virtue-and-its-rewarding-when-you-travel/.

22. "HMV Rewards Top Cool Category," *Globe and Mail*, November 24, 2010, p. RR3; HMV (n.d.), puremusic signed merchandise, purehmv, accessed at www.purehmv.ca/Search.aspx?d1=1&d2=1&d3=0&d4=0.

23. "A Guide for Individuals Protecting Your Privacy," Office of the Privacy Commission of Canada, 2014, accessed at www.priv.gc.ca/information/pub/guide_ind_e.asp.; Canada's Anti-Spam Legislation website, 2014, accessed at http://fightspam.gc.ca/eic/site/030.nsf/eng/home

24. "Target Canada Last In Forum Research Customer Satisfaction Survey," *Huffington Post Canada*, August 19, 2013, accessed at www.huffingtonpost.ca/2013/08/19/target-canada-customer-satisfaction_n_3779175.html#slide=2815273; M. Strauss, "Target's Canadian effort receives a poor grade from shoppers," *Globe and Mail*, August 18, 2013, accessed at www.theglobeandmail.com/report-on-business/targets-canadian-effort-receives-a-poor-grade-from-shoppers/article13832051/; M. Strauss, "Talking Target: A bullseye for a reader response," *Globe and Mail*, August 23, 2013, accessed at www.theglobeandmail.com/commentary/a-bullseye-for-reader-response/article13950239/; "About Target: Our Passion and Commitments," Target website, 2013, accessed at https://corporate.target.com/about/.

25. J. Łodziana-Grabowska," Significance of database marketing in the process of target segments identification and service," *Problems of Management in the 21st Century* (2013), pp. 640–647; I. Gregurec, T. Ević, and D. Dobrinić, "The importance of database marketing in social network advertising," *International Journal of Management Cases* 13 (2011), pp. 165–172.

26. T.J. Siragusa, "Implementing data mining for better CRM," *Customer Inter@ction Solutions* 19 (2001), pp. 38–41; J. Ranjan and V. Bhatnagar, "Role of knowledge management and analytical CRM in business: Data mining based framework," *The Learning Organization* 18 (2011), pp. 131–148. doi:http://dx.doi.org/10.1108/09696471111103731; Vikas Saraf, MBA,PhD., P. Thakur, and L. Yadav, "CRM with data mining & warehouse: 'Optimizes customer insight,'" *International Journal of Marketing and Technology* 3 (2013), pp. 177–187.

27. N. Sutton, "RBC creates e-marketing council to assess client data," *Computing Canada*, June 20, 2003, p. 6; L. Ang and F. Buttle, "CRM software applications and business performance," *Journal of Database Marketing & Customer Strategy Management* 14 (2006), pp. 4–16.

28. N. Ciarelli, "How Visa Predicts Divorce," *The Daily Beast*, April 6, 2010, accessed at www.thedailybeast.com/articles/2010/04/06/how-mastercard-predicts-divorce.html.

29. Peter Hadekel, "Loyalty Programs Start to Pay Off for Grocer Metro," *The Gazette*, November 24, 2010, accessed at www.montrealgazette.com/columnists/Loyalty+program+starts+grocer+Metro/3875329/story.html.

30. Carl Sewell and Paul Brown, *Customers for Life*, Doubleday Publishing, 2002.

31. T. Kildaze, "TD, CIBC battle for Aeroplan loyalty," *Globe and Mail*, June 27, 2013, accessed at www.theglobeandmail.com/report-on-business/td-to-take-over-as-aeroplan-provider-as-parent-to-split-with-cibc/article12852318/; R. Marowits, "TD Bank wins battle for Aeroplan," *Metro*, August 12, 2013, accessed at http://metronews.ca/news/canada/763882/td-bank-wins-battle-for-aeroplan/; "About Aeroplan," Aimia website, 2013, accessed at www.aimia.com/English/About/Our-Businesses/Aeroplan/default.aspx; Canadian Press, "TD, CIBC reach deal on Aeroplan credit card migration," CBC News, September 16, 2013, accessed at www.cbc.ca/news/business/td-cibc-reach-deal-on-aeroplan-credit-card-migration-1.1855664.

32. T. Duncan, *Principles of Advertising + IMC*, 2nd Edition (New York: McGraw-Hill/Irwin, 2005) ; M. Tokman, L.M. Davis, and K.N. Lemon, "The WOW factor: Creating value through win-back offers to reacquire lost customers," *Journal of Retailing* 83 (2007), pp. 47–64. doi:http://dx.doi.org/10.1016/j.jretai.2006.10.005

33. Reuters, "Sprint hangs up on high-maintenance customers," FoxNews.com, July 9, 2007, accessed at www.foxnews.com/story/2007/07/09/sprint-hangs-up-on-high-maintenance-customers/; "Why firing your worst customers isn't such a great idea," Knowledge @Wharton, December 12, 2007, accessed at http://knowledge.wharton.upenn.edu/article.cfm?articleid=1870.

Chapter 15

1. John A. Pearce, II, "The company mission as a strategic tool," *Sloan Management Review* 23 (1982), p. 15.

2. http://espncareers.com/about-us/mission-values.aspx.

3. G.H. Watson, "Design and execution of a collaborative business strategy," *Journal for Quality and Participation* 28 (2005), pp. 4–9.

4. Personal interview with Mike Jackson, Vice President, Strategy, webTactics, October 2014.

5. Roger A. Kerin, Vijay Mahajan, and P. Rajan Varadarajan, *Contemporary Perspectives on Strategic Marketing Planning* (Boston: Allyn & Bacon, 1990), chap. 1; and Orville C. Walker, Jr., Harper W. Boyd, Jr., and Jean-Claude Larreche, *Marketing Strategy* (Burr Ridge, IL: Richard D. Irwin, 1992), chaps. 1 and 2.

6. "Ben & Jerry's," Unilever website (n.d.), accessed at www.unilever.com/brands-in-action/detail/ben-and-jerrys/291995/?WT.contenttype=view%20brands.

7. The definition of *strategy* reflects thoughts appearing in Michael E. Porter, "What Is Strategy," *Harvard Business Review*, November 1, 1996, pp. 4,8.

8. "Why do you need a business plan," Canada Business Network, 2014, accessed at www.canadabusiness.ca/eng/page/3426/; "Developing a marketing plan," Canada Business Network, 2014, accessed at www.canadabusiness.ca/eng/page/2690/.

9. Theodore Levitt, "Marketing Myopia," *Harvard Business Review*, July–August 1960, pp. 45–56.

10. "CMOs And CFOs Are Misaligned," *Investor's Business Daily*, June 9, 2014, p. A07.

11. "Things That Matter," MEC website, 2013, accessed at www.mec.ca/AST/ContentPrimary/Sustainability/AccountabilityReport.jsp.

12. Alex Ballingall, "How corporate social responsibility improved these companies' bottom lines," *Maclean's*, June 14, 2012, accessed at www2.macleans.ca/2012/06/14/how-corporate-social-responsibility-improved-these-companies-bottom-lines/.

13. "Writing your business plan," Canada Business Network, 2014, accessed at www.canadabusiness.ca/eng/page/2753/#toc-_financial_forecasts_and_other_information.

14. C. Moorman, "From Marketing Spend to Marketing Accountability," *Marketing News* 48 (2014), pp. 24–25.

15. "Budgeting and forecasting," Canada Business Network, 2014, accessed at www.canadabusiness.ca/eng/page/2642/.

16. Tilley Endurables website, accessed at www.tilley.com/home.asp.

17. George Stalk, Phillip Evans, and Lawrence E. Shulman, "Competing on Capabilities. The New Rules of Corporate Strategy," *Harvard Business Review*, March–April 1992, pp. 57–69.

18. Tilley Endurables website, accessed at www.tilley.com/home.asp.

19. Adapted from "The Experience Curve Reviewed, IV. The Growth Share Matrix of the Product Portfolio" (Boston: The Boston Consulting Group, 1973).

20. Kerin, Mahajan, and Vardarajan, *Contemporary Perspectives*, p. 52.

Credits

Chapter 1

p. 3: Used by permission of Mucho Burrito
p. 7: Used by permission of hotels.com
p. 8: Used by permission of Mucho Burrito
p. 9: SMARTIES® is a registered trademark of Société des Produits Nestlé S.A., Vevey, Switzerland.
p. 10: AFTER EIGHT® is a registered trademark of Société des Produits Nestlé S.A., Vevey, Switzerland.
p. 12 (Infographic): Used by permission of Bell Canada
p. 13: Used by permission of Bell Canada
p. 16: © Anatolii Babii/Alamy
p. 17 (top): Google and the Google logo are registered trademarks of Google Inc., used with permission.
p. 17 (middle): Tim Hortons, the Tim Hortons logo, Timbits, and Camp Day are trademarks of Tim Hortons. Used with permission.
p. 18: Photo taken for McGraw-Hill Ryerson.
p. 19: © 3dm1983/Dreamstime.com/GetStock.com
p. 20: DIGIORNO® is a registered trademark of Société des Produits Nestlé S.A., Vevey, Switzerland.
p. 21: © Arrow/Dreamstime.com/GetStock.com
p. 23: Used by permission of Leo Burnett Worldwide
p. 24: © Copyright Salesforce.com, Inc. Used with permission.
p. 25 (top): Used by permission of Cineplex Entertainment
p. 25 (bottom): © Deshacam/Dreamstime.com/GetStock.com
p. 26: Used by permission of Canadian Marketing Association
p. 28: Courtesy of *Marketing* magazine
p. 29: Used by permission of I Love Dust Ltd.

Chapter 2

p. 33: Used with permission from GrapeTrail
p. 35: Used with permission from GrapeTrail
p. 36 (bottom left): © Dragonimages/Dreamstime.com/GetStock.com
p. 36 (Infographic): Statistics Canada, accessed at www12.statcan.gc.ca/census-recensement/index-eng.cfm
p. 40: © Lucie Lang/Alamy
p. 41: © Jose Luis Pelaez Inc/Getty Images
p. 42 (top): Used with permission of Rogers Broadcasting Limited. All Rights Reserved.
p. 42 (bottom): © Copyright Salesforce.com, Inc. Used with permission.
p. 43: No credit
p. 44: Used by permission of Withings
p. 45: ECOLOGO® is a trademark of UL LLC.
p. 47 (Infographic): Scott Deveau, "'Year of the truck' pushes Canadian auto sales to record in 2013," *National Post*, January 4, 2014
p. 49: © Oleksiy Maksymenko Photography/Alamy
p. 50: © Photosoup/Dreamstime.com/GetStock.com
p. 51 (bottom): © Floydsphoto/Dreamstime.com/GetStock.com

p. 53: Fraud Prevention Month poster, 2014, Industry Canada. Reproduced with the permission of the Minister of Industry, 2014.
p. 54 (middle): © Reprinted with permission from Advertising Standards Canada
p. 54 (bottom): © Reprinted with permission from Advertising Standards Canada
p. 57: © Tony Cardoza/Getty Images
p. 58: No credit
p. 61: Used with permission from GrapeTrail

Chapter 3

p. 65: The WALKING FINGERS & DESIGN trade-mark is a trade-mark of the Yellow Pages Group Corp. used under license.
p. 68 (Infographic): Google/Ipsos/Sterling, 2012
p. 68 (bottom): Used by permission of Core Online Marketing
p. 69 (top): © Marian Stanca/Alamy
p. 69 (bottom): © Darrenbaker/Dreamstime.com/GetStock.com
p. 70: © Cineplex Entertainment, Inc.
p. 71 (top): © Radub85/Dreamstime.com/GetStock.com
p. 71 (middle): Courtesy IBM Corporation
p. 71 (bottom): © 2010-2012 McDonald's, All Rights Reserved
p. 72: © Iofoto/Dreamstime.com/GetStock.com
p. 74: © John Hasyn/Getty Images
p. 75: Used by permission of Unilever Canada Inc.
p. 76 (top): © Aaron Harris/The Canadian Press
p. 76 (bottom): © Drive Images/Alamy
p. 77: Photo courtesy of Loblaw Companies Limited
p. 80 (left and right): Courtesy Tag Heuer SA
p. 81 (left): © Aflo Foto Agency/Alamy
p. 81 (right): © The Canadian Press/Paul Sakuma, File/AP Photo
p. 82: Courtesy of Haggar Clothing Co.
p. 83: Used by permission of WOMMA
p. 85: © Richard Lam/The Canadian Press
p. 86: © Pepsi via Getty Images
p. 87 (left): © Wam1975/Dreamstime.com/GetStock.com
p. 87 (right): © Bcbounders/Dreamstime.com/GetStock.com
p. 88 (middle): Used with permission from PepsiCo Beverages Canada
p. 88 (bottom): Courtesy of Nestlé
p. 89: Courtesy Colgate-Palmolive Company

Chapter 4

p. 93: © Anatolii Babii / Alamy
p. 97: © Copyright Salesforce.com, Inc. Used with permission
p. 99: © Thomaspajot/Dreamstime.com/GetStock.com
p. 100: © Copyright Salesforce.com, Inc. Used with permission
p. 101: © Ml12nan/Dreamstime.com/GetStock.com
p. 102: © Burke/Triolo Productions/Getty Images
p. 106 (left): © Tracy Leonard

p. 106 (right): © Maigi/Dreamstime.com/GetStock.com
p. 108 (top): © Tim MacPherson/Getty Images
p. 108 (middle): © Burke/Triolo/Getty Images
p. 109 (Infographic): Kathy Sheenan, "The Consumer Journey to 2020: Five Trends Driving the Future of Brands," GFK Roper Webinar for CMA, July 30, 2013
p. 110: Used with permission from AC Nielsen Company of Canada
p. 112: Used with permission of Communispace
p. 113: © Katie Quinn Davies/Getty Images
p. 115: © Andreypopov/Dreamstime.com/GetStock.com

Chapter 5

p. 121 (top): Used by permission of Rovi
p. 121 (bottom): © Graham Hughes / Alamy
p. 123: © Auremar/Dreamstime.com/GetStock.com
p. 124: © Bill Pugliano/Stringer/Getty Images
p. 126: The Twitter name, logo, Twitter T, Tweet, and Twitter blue bird are trademarks of Twitter, Inc.
p. 127 (Infographic): Used by permission of Staples
p. 128: Royalty-Free/CORBIS
p. 129 (left): © Photo by Peter Power/The Globe and Mail/The Canadian Press.
p. 129 (right): Used with permission of Bombardier/TTC
p. 130: © Tetra Images/Alamy
p. 131: Copyright © 2014 BlackBerry. All rights reserved.
p. 132: © PhotoAlto sas/Alamy
p. 138: © Phillip Jarrell/Getty Images

Chapter 6

p. 143: Used by permission of HEAD Canada
p. 144: Used by permission of HEAD Canada
p. 147: © Paolo_frangiolli/Dreamstime.com/GetStock.com
p. 148: No credit
p. 149: Used by permission of Maison le Grand
p. 150 (top): Used with permission from Stitt Feld Handy Group
p. 150 (bottom): © Kristin Lee/Alamy
p. 151: © Howesjwe/Dreamstime.com/GetStock.com
p. 153 (top): © Stockbyte
p. 153 (bottom): © Michael Neelon(misc)/Alamy
p. 155 (top): © Auremar/Dreamstime.com/GetStock.com
p. 155 (bottom): © Photosdl/Dreamstime.com/GetStock.com
p. 156 (Infographic): Used by permission of Pitney Bowes Software
p. 157: © Robert Kneschke/Alamy
p. 158: Used by permission of Pitney Bowes Software
p. 159 (middle): © Jackbluee/Dreamstime.com/GetStock.com
p. 159 (bottom left [Happy Meal]): © Michael Neelon(misc)/Alamy
p. 159 (bottom right [McCafé]): No credit

p. 160: © MARKOS DOLOPIKOS/Alamy

p. 161 (bottom left): Used with permission from Harmony Organic Milk

p. 161 (bottom middle): Used with permission from Organic Meadow

p. 161 (bottom right): Used with permission from Organic Valley

pp. 162–163: © 2008 David Young-Wolff All Rights Reserved

p. 165: Used by permission of HEAD Canada

Chapter 7

p. 169: Courtesy of Loblaw

p. 173 (Infographic): Press Release, "Consumer-ology: Customer service has the power to make or break a brand," Bensymon Byrne, September 6, 2012, accessed at http://bensimonbyrne.com/press_room/2012#/press-release/consumerology-customer-service-has-the-power-to-make-or-break-a-brand; Bensimon Byrne, "The Bensimon Byrne Consumerology Report: Consumerology 17: Customer Service," August 2012, accessed at http://bensimonbyrne.com/wp-content/uploads/2012/09/Customer-Service-August-2012_RevisedSEPT5.pdf

p. 173 (right): With permission of the British Museum and the Royal Ontario Museum

p. 175: © whiteboxmedia limited/Alamy

p. 176 (top): Used with permission from GAP

p. 176 (bottom left): Used by permission of LivingLou.com

p. 176 (bottom right): Used by permission of LivingLou.com

p. 177: Used with permission from PepsiCo Beverages Canada

p. 178 (left): HBC Corporate Collection. With thanks for the co-operation and contribution of Hudson's Bay Company.

p. 178 (right): HBC Corporate Collection. With thanks for the co-operation and contribution of Hudson's Bay Company.

p. 179: No credit

p. 181 (top): © Rex Features [2005] all rights reserved/The Canadian Press

p. 181 (bottom inset): Used with permission from The Cupcake Shoppe

p. 181 (bottom): © Alenkasm/Dreamstime.com/GetStock.com

p. 184: Courtesy of Procter & Gamble

p. 185: © The McGraw-Hill Companies, Inc./Jill Braaten, photographer

p. 186: © BMO Financial Group

p. 187: © Michalrojek/Dreamstime.com/GetStock.com

p. 189: © 2008 Shoppers Drug Mart Inc. Shoppers Drug Mart and Life Brand are trade-marks of 911979 Alberta Ltd., used under license.

Chapter 8

p. 195: Used by permission of Tackla

p. 198: © Amazon.com

p. 202: © AP Photo/Jon Super/The Canadian Press

p. 204: No credit

p. 205: Tim Hortons, the Tim Hortons logo, Timbits, and Camp Day are trademarks of Tim Hortons. Used with permission.

p. 206 (Infographic): Hollie Shaw "Tim Hortons to offer new dark roast coffee blend in two test markets," *Financial Post*, October 28, 2013, accessed at http://business.financialpost.com/2013/10/28/tim-hortons-dark-roast-coffee/ "Coffee remains dominant," *Canadian Vending and Office Coffee Service*

magazine, October 28, 2013, accessed at www.canadianvending.com/content/view/3423/57/

p. 206 (right): Used by permission of Unilever Canada Inc.

p. 207 (left): © T. Harris

p. 207 (middle): No credit

p. 207 (right): © T. Harris

p. 209: © Vampy1/Dreamstime.com/GetStock.com

p. 210: © webpics/Alamy

p. 211: Photo courtesy of Wikipedia.org

p. 213: Courtesy of Hewlett-Packard Company

p. 216: Tim Hortons, the Tim Hortons logo, Timbits, and Camp Day are trademarks of Tim Hortons. Used with permission.

Chapter 9

p. 221: Used by permission of H&R Block

p. 223 (Infographic): Used by permission of Accenture Corporate

p. 224: © culture-images GmbH/Alamy

p. 225: © Steve Stock/Alamy

p. 226: © The McGraw-Hill Companies, Inc./Jill Braaten, photographer

p. 227 (top): © AFP/Getty Images

p. 227 (bottom): © Reuters 2001

p. 228: © Flynt/Dreamstime.com/GetStock.com

p. 230: © Chuck Savage/CORBIS

p. 231: © Ulana Switucha/Alamy

p. 232: © Lertsnim/Dreamstime.com/GetStock.com

p. 233: © Kristoffer Tripplaar/Alamy

p. 239: © Francis Vachon/The Canadian Press

p. 240: © Nathan Denette/The Canadian Press

p. 242: © Kristoffer Tripplaar/Alamy

p. 243: © Tracy Leonard

p. 244: Courtesy of The Toro Company

p. 247: Used by permission of H&R Block

Chapter 10

p. 251: © Blend Images/Alamy

p. 255: © Toronto Star/GetStock.com

p. 258: © Bradcalkins/Dreamstime.com

p. 259: © Lucadp/Dreamstime.com/GetStock.com

p. 260: © McGraw-Hill Ryerson

p. 261 (left): © Allstar Picture Library/Alamy

p. 261 (right): Used by permission of H&R Block

p. 262 (Infographic): Used by permission of Restaurants Canada.

p. 263: © Michael Neelon(misc)/Alamy

p. 264 (top right): © Gergely/Dreamstime.com/GetStock.com

p. 264 (bottom right): © eye35.pix/Alamy

p. 266: © Tracy Leonard

p. 267: © John Lee/Aurora Photos/getstock.com

p. 270: © The McGraw-Hill Companies, Inc./Jill Braaten, photographer

p. 271: No credit

p. 272: U.S. Fish and Wildlife Service

p. 273: © Cultura Creative (RF)/Alamy

Chapter 11

p. 277 (both): © Moe Doiron/The Globe and Mail/The Canadian Press

p. 283: Dollarama/Matthew Plexman Photography Ltd.

p. 284: © David Cooper/GetStock.com

p. 285: Used by permission of Harry Rosen

p. 287: Used by permission of Roots Canada

p. 288: Used with permission from Indigo

p. 289: © Piero Cruciatti/Alamy

p. 290: © Steve Leonard

p. 292: Used by permission of Best Buy Canada

p. 293: © Inter IKEA Systems B.V. 2014.

p. 294 (left): Used by permission of Wal-Mart Stores, Inc.

p. 294 (right): Used by permission of eBay Inc.

p. 295 (Infographic): Used by permission of Tech Vibes

p. 296: © Alex Segre/Alamy/getstock.com

p. 298: © Jeffrey Blackler/Alamy

p. 299: © Digital Vision/Punchstock

p. 301: Courtesy PepsiCo, Inc./Frito-Lay, Inc.

Chapter 12

p. 305: Used by permission of Western Union

p. 308 (Facebook, Twitter, LinkedIn): © dolphfyn/Alamy

p. 309: Courtesy of The Globe and Mail Inc.

p. 311 (top): © Tribune Content Agency LLC/Alamy

p. 311 (bottom): © Brownstock/Alamy

p. 313 (top): Reproduced with kind permission of Unilever Canada Inc.

p. 313 (bottom): Reproduced with kind permission of Unilever Canada Inc.

p. 314 (top): Reproduced with kind permission of Unilever Canada Inc.

p. 314 (bottom): Reproduced with kind permission of Unilever Canada Inc.

p. 316: Used by permission of ICA Canada

p. 317 (top): Reprinted with permission from Advertising Standards Canada

p. 317 (bottom): © Alisonh29/Dreamstime.com/GetStock.com

p. 319 (top left): Used with permission of Baskin Robbins

p. 319 (top right): Used with permission of Baskin Robbins

p. 321: Used by permission of Rogers Media

p. 323: No credit

p. 324 (Infographic): Used by permission of *Ski Canada Magazine.*

p. 325: © Oleksiy Maksymenko/Alamy

p. 326: Used by permission of Leo Burnett Worldwide

p. 329: Tim Hortons, the Tim Hortons logo, Timbits, and Camp Day are trademarks of Tim Hortons. Used with permission.

p. 330: © Darren Hick

p. 331: © Tracy Leonard

p. 332: © Rob Melnychuk/Getty Images

p. 333: Courtesy Groupon, Inc.

Chapter 13

p. 341: Used by permission of Rich Media

p. 344: © Monkeybusinessimages/Dreamstime.com/GetStock.com

p. 345 (top right): © Scanrail/Dreamstime.com/GetStock.com

p. 346: © Steve Leonard

p. 347 (Infographic): "Our Mobile Planet: Canada Understanding the Mobile Consumer," Ipsos MediaCT, May 2013, and data charts accessed at www.thinkwithgoogle.com/mobileplanet/en

p. 350 (top right): © Barry Diomede/Alamy

p. 350 (middle): © Copyright Salesforce.com, Inc. Used with permission.

p. 351 (top): Used by permission of Destination British Columbia.

p. 351 (bottom): Used by permission of Pelmorex Media Inc.

p. 352: Canadian Wireless Telecommunications Association

p. 353: © CNW Group/Mattel Canada, Inc.

p. 354: © Artur Marciniec/Alamy

p. 355 (top): CRTC's Wireless Code Know Your Rights, www.crtc.gc.ca/eng/info_sht/t16.htm. Used by permission of Canadian Radio-television and Telecommunications Commission.

Name Index

Company/Product Index

Subject Index